Sociological Theory

Classical Statements

FIFTH EDITION

David Ashley
University of Wyoming

David Michael Orenstein
Wright State University

Allyn and Bacon
Boston   London   Sydney   Toronto   Tokyo   Singapore

Series Editor: Sarah L. Kelbaugh
Editor-in-Chief, Social Sciences: Karen Hanson
Editorial Assistant: Lori Flickinger
Composition: Linda Cox
Manufacturing Buyer: Julie McNeill
Cover Administrator: Jenny Hart
Production Administrator: Deborah Brown
Editorial-Production Service: P.M. Gordon Associates, Inc.
Electronic Composition: Omegatype Typography, Inc.

Library of Congress Cataloging-in-Publication Data

Ashley, David, 1950–
    Sociological theory : classical statements / David Ashley, David Michael Orenstein.—
5th ed.
        p. cm.
    Includes bibliographical references and index.
    ISBN 0-205-31940-8
    1. Sociology—Methodology—History. 2. Sociologists—Biography. I. Orenstein, David
Michael, 1951– II. Title.
HM511 .A85 2000
301'.01—dc21

                                                                    99-086825

Printed in the United States of America
10 9 8 7 6 5 4 3 2   05 04 03 02 01 00

To our mothers
Jill Clarke
and Edith Orenstein

CONTENTS

PREFACE

This book tries to make social theory come alive by showing that it is the product of individuals who were creatures of their era and of their place and who were responding to issues and concerns that became significant in the context of their time. We have not tried to organize our text around various themes (e.g., "class," "religion," "crime," etc.), or types of theory (e.g., "functionalism," "conflict theory," "symbolic interactionism," etc.). Instead, we have elected to introduce the eleven individuals (Comte, Durkheim, Spencer, Hegel, Marx, Weber, Simmel, Freud, Pareto, Veblen, and Mead) who seem to have played the most influential intellectual role in the institutionalization of contemporary sociology. We have also included one social philosopher (Nietzsche) who doubted the value of modern social science from its very inception and who seems to have foreseen its decline.

The approach we have chosen to follow does not try to suggest that the history of sociological theory reflects increasing convergence and closure along lines of scientific discovery. But we might as well make it clear from the very start that the twelve theorists described in this book never believed they were engaged in a unified or common project of intellectual closure. All of them were capable of great insight, and, directly or indirectly, they all helped shape the course of modern sociology. Yet their work as a whole is not only disparate but also—and quite often—contradictory.

This theory text includes the following:

1. Two introductory chapters—Chapter 1, which sets the context (historical, ideological, national, etc.) of classical sociological theory, and Chapter 2, which discusses the nature and types of theoretical orientation in social theory.
2. A concluding chapter (Chapter 15) that discusses the heritage of classical sociological theory, taken as a whole. This chapter emphasizes that the "classical" theorists were all responding to, and trying to steer, *modernity* (something that will become apparent as readers work through this text).
3. A description of the background affecting each of the twelve people discussed in this book, and an analysis and description of their most important ideas (Chapters 3–14). Each of these particular chapters is organized in a consistent format to facilitate comparison. The divisions and subdivisions of each chapter deal with (1) biography; (2) social environment; (3) intellectual influences; (4) view of society; (5) view of the individual in society; (6) methodology; (7) other themes and foci of attention, where warranted; and (8) the significance of each theorist's work, as perceived by subsequent generations.
4. Text that is readable but not simplistic. Although major theoretical terms are defined in the text where they first appear, glossaries are also provided for each chapter. In addition, annotated bibliographies of primary and secondary works in English have been supplied. We have tried to include the most useful and informative books that are most readily available.

5. Theorists from all of the major national schools of classical theory (French, British, German, Italian, and American), who are introduced chronologically within each national grouping. The exception is Nietzsche, who, more than any other person discussed in this book, can be placed in a group of his own.
6. A brief guide to classical theorists on the World Wide Web, which should aid students in locating primary classical theory works written both by authors discussed in this book and by others of their era. Such sources can serve as supplemental readings and provide useful material for inclusion in student term papers.

Readers familiar with previous editions of *Sociological Theory: Classical Statements* will note numerous changes in the fifth edition. Several minor corrections, improvements, and updates have been included. In addition, we have moved the "postmodernity" section from Chapter 1 to Chapter 15, where we believe it more properly belongs. Also, in response to comments from readers, we have completely redrafted Chapters 1 and 2. The foci of these chapters remain primarily the same, but through organizational and stylistic changes, we have attempted to make their content more easily apprehensible and to clarify links to arguments in later chapters. Also, a number of chapter conclusions have been rewritten (e.g., those in Chapters 3, 5, and 13) to reflect recent scholarship.

David Ashley had primary responsibility for Chapter 2 and for the chapters on Hegel, Marx, Weber, Freud, Pareto, and Nietzsche. David Orenstein had primary responsibility for the chapters on Comte, Durkheim, Spencer, Veblen, and Mead. The chapter on Simmel was written jointly by David Ashley and Barbara Renchkovsky. The introductory and concluding chapters (Chapter 1 and Chapter 15) were written jointly by Ashley and Orenstein.

We wish to acknowledge the colleagues, students, friends, and dozens of reviewers who aided us in the production of this and previous editions. In particular, we would like to thank Glena Buchholtz and Kristine Zamora. We owe special thanks to Julie E. Orenstein and Yarong Jiang Ashley, and to our editor, Sarah L. Kelbaugh, at Allyn and Bacon.

1

Ideology, History, and Classical Sociological Theory

THE RISE OF SOCIOLOGY

How best to define "classical sociological theory"? Is it whatever the specialists or experts in sociology say it is? Or, can we use sociological insights themselves to help explain why certain theoretical insights have become foundational?

We suggest that certain sociological statements are "classical" first because they have an ideological significance, and second because they have been instrumental in helping to build sociology as an autonomous discipline and as an institutionalized profession. These two characteristics are not mutually exclusive. To some extent, classical sociological theory was always ideologically interested in its own legitimation.

The theoretical statements discussed in this book were written largely between the time of the great French Revolution of 1789–1799 and World War I, which officially ended in 1919. During this period, both European and North American societies were transformed. At the end of the eighteenth century, most Europeans were rural, conservative, uneducated, isolated, lacking in organizational affiliation, and—unless they were criminal—largely ignored by the state. By the beginning of the twentieth century, Europeans tended to be relatively liberal and relatively well educated; were quite likely to be members of a union, a professional association, or some other kind of organization; and were relatively closely supervised by governmental and non-governmental bureaucracies. In other words, these latter individuals lived in a modern, bureaucratic nation-state. The most dramatic change that occurred in the nineteenth century involved a transformation in the way subjects viewed the social world and their place in it. For instance, feudal conceptions of a natural distinction between commoner and aristocrat were replaced by the popular ideals of democracy and equality of rights. Sociology itself was both a part of and a response to this shift in human self-conception.

By the 1920s, most of the salient characteristics of our present (or modern) age had been established. For instance, by 1920, the typical American had become urban rather than rural. (This same threshold was crossed a little earlier in Britain, Germany, and France.) During the 1920s, people's life-styles were dramatically altered by modern industrial technology, widespread bureaucratization, and a massive increase in governmental intervention in their lives. Weapons of mass destruction were invented and used in the Great War of 1914–1918, and people were forced to adapt to the onset of total war. Also, by the 1920s, the competing social and political ideals of capitalism and socialism had displaced the eighteenth-century clash between monarchic and republican forms of government. During this decade, women's rights became a significant political issue, mass unions tried to consolidate their position in economic life, and distinctions between suburban white-collar and urban blue-collar life-styles took shape. At the same time, a popular youth culture involving pop music, an ideological rejection of traditional sexual and aesthetic mores, and drug experimentation came to the fore. The flappers of the 1920s were the antecedents of the zoot-suiters of the 1930s and 1940s, the beat generation of the 1950s, the hippies and flower children of the 1960s and 1970s, the punks of the 1980s, and the "grunge" adherents of the 1990s.

It would, of course, be misleading to suggest that growing up in the United States or England in the year 2000 is like growing up in these countries in the 1920s or 1930s. Still, the most salient characteristics of modernity either were institutionalized or had become readily observable by the 1920s. Thus, for the contemporary individual, a Western society in the 1920s would be familiar and understandable, though backward in many respects. On the other hand, the gulf between the experiences of twentieth-century individuals and the life-style and orientations of a French peasant living during the reign of King Louis XVI (1774–1792) is so enormous that it would seem to us that the latter individuals were inhabitants of a distant planet.

In brief, we suggest that the modern world came into existence between the end of the eighteenth and the beginning of the twentieth century. The thirteen decades between 1790 and 1920 mark the definitive watershed that separates our modern world from the totally unfamiliar traditional and feudal system that existed prior to the French Revolution. In part, classical sociological theory was an attempt to come to terms with the problems and issues of the emerging modern era. Among other things, these included social atomization, alienation, and loneliness (Hegel, Marx, Durkheim); social disorganization (Comte, Durkheim); secularization and the decline of traditional religious belief (Weber, Comte, Durkheim); a growing pessimism about individuals' capacity to take rational control of their destiny (Freud, Pareto); and widening class division and class conflict, together with many other types of social fracture and social dissension (Simmel, Pareto, and others). Although classical sociology attempted to come to grips with what were seen as typically modern problems, sociology itself is a product of the modern era. Indeed, we believe that the development of a sociological way of looking at the world is one of the most definitive characteristics of the modern age.

Sociological theory is often said to have attained its maturity between 1880 and 1920. During this period, sociology was established in its own right both in the United States and in many Western European societies. In this book, however, we have included not just those major theorists who wrote during the decades when sociological theory reached its maturity (Durkheim, Weber, Simmel, Pareto, and Mead), but also earlier sociological theorists such as Comte and Spencer who developed ideas about emerging modern societies that are likely to strike the contemporary reader as curiously naive and optimistic.

We have also included five theorists who did not call themselves sociologists: Hegel, Marx, Veblen, Nietzsche, and Freud. Hegel, a professor of philosophy, lived at the very beginning of the modern era, before the idea of "sociology" was invented. We hope to show that much of his work is definitively sociological in orientation nevertheless. Marx was an intellectual giant who never attained an academic position but whose influence on contemporary sociological modes of thought has been greater than that of any other theorist. Veblen, one of the founders of modern social economics, died shortly before the economic collapse of 1929. His work has proved to be seminal for the understanding of contemporary forms of social and economic behavior. Nietzsche developed an antimodern critique that has become increasingly influential in the United States over the last decade. Finally, Freud, a medical doctor who founded the discipline of psychoanalysis and who lived until the end of the 1930s, would have rejected the label "sociologist." Nevertheless, like the other four theorists mentioned here, he made crucially important contributions to our understanding of ourselves as creatures whose experiences are shaped and fashioned by that which is recognized as socially variable or contextual. This essentially *sociological* viewpoint is shared by all the theorists discussed in this book.

SOCIOLOGY AS SCIENCE AND AS VALUE-ORIENTING CRITIQUE

Social theory is often condemned by its critics because it sometimes seems to have a not-so-hidden ideological agenda. Marxist theory, for instance, was often dismissed because it made no secret of the fact that it sought to portray history from the vantage point of an exploited and insurgent working class. By the same token, Weberian sociology has, at times, adopted a specific, if less transparent, *anti*-Marxist agenda.

We believe, however, that the undeniable intersection between ideological commitment and focus on the one hand and sociological theory on the other has not necessarily impeded the growth of sociological knowledge. Ideological commitment often is a spur for the development of new modes of knowing. Moreover, ideology itself should be acknowledged as something more than just a biased or distorted view of reality. Ideology ensues when groups try to organize conceptions of authority and shared commitments in order to deal with social, economic, and political problems that have become salient for them. This is the *creative* side of ideology—the attempt to make political society meaningful and legitimate. Ideology also has a *restrictive* side, however: It places limits on what can be thought. Although ideology is not constrained by the need to reach only those conclusions that have received experimental verification, it nonetheless loses much of its effectiveness when it becomes implausible or obviously false in its assertions. For ideology to be effective, it must, of course, appear to have at least some grasp on what is going on in the world.

Ideology is largely a modern invention because it is modernity that was responsible for the breakdown of the dogma and uncertainties associated with traditional societies. Ideology, in short, represents a refusal to accept that present conditions reflect the best of all possible worlds. To put the best possible gloss on ideology, we could say it is a striving toward truth at a time during which blind adherence to custom, tradition, and habit is loosening its grip on the human mind.

Ideology, of course, should not be confused with experimentally corroborated scientific knowledge. Not surprisingly, some social theorists (e.g., Spencer and Pareto) believed that sociology is most powerful when it is most scientific and least ideological. On a superficial level, it would seem difficult to dispute this point of view. However, we should keep the following in mind: Humans need bearings in life. Even if we cannot be certain that a particular theoretical orientation is absolutely objective, it certainly does not follow that it would be rational to jettison it. It might be most reasonable sometimes to try to develop explanations that receive the highest possible amount of empirical corroboration, that are theoretically powerful, and that provide guidelines for action. In actuality, social theory has often attempted to steer human practices and has tried to help humans choose among competing values and different social options. It would be foolish to pretend otherwise. But, nonetheless, as Hegel and Marx would insist, perhaps even value-orienting explanations can be subject to critical analysis if not experimental confirmation.

Among the theorists studied in this text, some "positivists," such as Comte, Spencer, and Pareto, believed strongly that sociology should base its mode of inquiry on the methodology of the already established natural sciences. By contrast, critical theorists such as Hegel and Marx saw their social philosophies as negative in their effects—that is, as striving to critique and to supercede all those customs, habits, and ideologies that constrain the human spiritual quest for freedom. Both for Hegel and for Marx, it is not reason's purpose to pursue what is, in any case, an entirely illusory "objective" mode of knowing. Rather, reason endeavors to make human practices as transparent as possible. Hence, reason must acknowledge that theoretical insight is, in part, an expression of human will and purpose. From this perspective, the goal of anti-positivistic critical theory is to enhance human freedom and to enable the emergence of human subjects who are optimally free by virtue of the fact that they have become optimally self-reflective, hence maximally self-producing.

Not all classical sociological theorists, though, focused so intently on the question of whether sociology should be value-orienting or "value-free." Unlike Hegel and Marx, Simmel and Mead, for instance, made seminal contributions to sociology that treat broader ideological issues as tangential. Nevertheless, the era of classical sociological theorizing is bounded at one end by the gradual awareness of modernizing trends that brought chaos, disruption, and dislocation. Although this was most obvious in the area of political authority, it was observable in all areas of social life. Thus Hegel, Nietzsche, Weber, and Simmel addressed the problem of the bureaucratization of life in the emerging modern nation-state. Durkheim, Comte, and Spencer examined the difficulties of social relationships in a world increasingly characterized by functionally specialized roles and diverse modes of consciousness. Unlike Pareto, who believed social inequality was a fixity in *all* societies, Veblen showed how it might be overcome one day. The optimist Marx and the pessimist Freud both studied the way in which modern societies mandate a "distorted" or "false" consciousness in order to function effectively. All these concerns reflect an ideological interest in restructuring modes of consciousness and social commitments for the purpose of dealing with salient social problems. It is archetypically sociological to believe that organized *social action* can make a difference in addressing problems such as these.

THE INSTITUTIONALIZATION OF SOCIOLOGY

Few of the scholars discussed in this book taught in sociology departments. Nevertheless, most of them helped to institutionalize sociology as an acceptable academic discipline. Whereas Comte and Spencer were academic outsiders, Durkheim broke ground in being the first professor of sociology in France. Weber and Simmel were instrumental in organizing the first sociological association in Germany, whereas Durkheim helped create the first sociological research institute in France.

Although teaching, founding journals, and training a younger generation of researchers are of obvious importance in the development of a field, such institution building also requires a legitimization of the practices of a college of experts or members of a profession. This was clearly understood both by Durkheim and by Weber. Whereas Durkheim had ambitious ideas about the professional sociologist's role in the social and political hierarchy of the nation, Weber was careful to place certain limitations on what society could reasonably expect from the sociologist. Weber emphasized that sociologists had special skills that could help resolve some issues but that these skills did not enable them to make authoritative judgments about all human concerns. By emphasizing the *limitations* of sociological knowledge, Weber believed he would strengthen the impact of professional sociology by not permitting it to make promises it could not fulfill.

The arguments for sociology as a legitimate and independent discipline are most forcefully presented in the writings of Comte, Durkheim, Spencer, Pareto, and Simmel. With the exception of Simmel, these men all favored positivism. As we have seen, positivists maintain that scientific method can ensure that scientific explanations, *per se*, are value-free. According to Durkheim, Comte, and Spencer, sociology is an instrumental science, capable of providing knowledge about cause-effect relations that is useful in understanding and adapting to a social system that is external and coercive for individuals. In Comte's and Durkheim's work, sociological knowledge is presented as capable of restructuring social relationships and organizations on lines perceived by their authors to be both moral and harmonious. Thus both Comte and Durkheim wanted to believe that ideological disputes could be settled by the scientific method. In Spencer's writings, "scientific" social knowledge is treated as useful in isolating areas of life in which governmental intervention and regulation would disturb the "natural" balance. Although they all argued for a science of society along positivistic lines, Comte and Durkheim thus favored interventionistic reform, whereas Spencer preferred anti-interventionistic, antigovernmental *laissez-faire.*

During the twentieth century, sociology was able to establish itself with least difficulty in the United States. Although sociology developed from European intellectual roots, the earliest departments of sociology in the world were founded at such places as the University of Chicago, the University of Wisconsin, the University of Kansas, and Ohio State University. Americans in these departments were interested in the instrumental use of sociology in social reform; thus they tended to emphasize the scientific or positivistic nature of the discipline. Mead, for example, emphasized the utility of social science in providing a basis for scientifically grounded reformism. In the 1920s, the famous "Chicago School" provided detailed studies on slum life, race relations, immigration, and urbanization, and, to this extent, Mead (like Marx, perhaps) was most successful in combining—but *not* melding—critical and positivistic approaches.

From World War I until the Vietnam era U.S. sociologists exhibited relatively little understanding of sociology's ideological roots, and they tended to emphasize their discipline's promise as a legitimately scientific discipline. At the middle of the twentieth century, many American practitioners looked forward to the day when sociology would seem as authoritative as more established fields such as physics or chemistry. By the end of World War II, sociology in the United States had developed a preoccupation—some would say an obsession—with methodological issues and the development of statistical measurements and scales that, while limited in their scope and explanatory bite, would be demonstrably scientific and provide reliable data for instrumental manipulation and control.

In the 1950s, social scientists were most interested in second-level concerns (e.g., how people could be helped to adjust to paramount social reality), and they focused largely on how existing social relations could be strengthened and reformed, rather than transformed. Nonetheless, ideas abstracted or adapted from classical theorists still did form a basis for the development of much contemporary theory (see Chapter 15). For example, critical theorists (mostly French and German until the 1960s) drew heavily on Hegel, Marx, and Freud; functionalists on Spencer and Durkheim; action theorists on Weber and Pareto, conflict theorists on Marx and Simmel; symbolic interactionists on Mead, and so on.[1] But in this country and in Britain it was not until the mid-1960s that intellectuals were ready once again to pay some attention to large-scale issues of power and domination and ask if there was something fundamentally wrong with the structure of modern societies. Not surprisingly, Marx was rediscovered (perhaps reinvented) during this period by U.S. sociologists eager to take a more critical stance towards what was happening to their own nation state.

Compared with their Anglo-American counterparts, continental (i.e., French and German) theorists were always more interested in broad theoretical and philosophical issues. They also were more ready to acknowledge that the institutionalization of sociology depended on the new discipline's ability to demonstrate that it could help fulfill national or political goals. Whereas U.S. sociologists were often naive and unreflective about how social-scientific knowledge would be used by a power elite, French and German social theorists were more likely to recognize that the authorized development of any kind of knowledge—*including* scientific knowledge—is something that can come about only as a result of wider social and political backing. Recognizing this, Durkheim at the end of the nineteenth century allied sociology in France with the liberal and reform-oriented wing of the French political establishment.[2] In Germany, Weber had to deal with a long-standing intellectual tradition that emphasized the uniqueness of human existence *vis-à-vis* the world of nonhuman things. Moreover, Weber attained his maturity as a scholar at a time when Germany was struggling to establish a sense of national identity.[3] It is not surprising, then, that Weber showed particular sensitivity to the question of how a sociologist might mediate between the competing goals of value-relevance and "the plain duty of intellectual integrity."

In sum, classical sociology was both part and product of changes in social existence that led to the contemporary social world. We can readily understand the concerns of the classical theorists because, for the most part, they were writing about a world we still inhabit. In many instances, classical theory was instrumental in helping to persuade governmental and educational bureaucracies that sociology was a useful and legitimate academic subject. Although all sociologists attempted to account for social change and the structure and processes of modern society, some borrowed heavily from the methodology of the natural sciences, whereas others were more self-conscious about sociology's value-relevance and the discipline's unique status as a mode of human inquiry. In the United States, where positivism held greatest sway, the institutionalization of sociology as an academic discipline was most successful. The price of this success was a turning away from larger questions to a narrower emphasis on statistical practice and toward studies aimed at the limited production of effective instrumental knowledge.

Two important intellectual developments that particularly influenced classical sociology were the "Enlightenment" and the idea of social evolutionism. In the following two sections, we present a brief discussion of their influence upon sociology.

ENLIGHTENMENT PHILOSOPHY AND CLASSICAL SOCIOLOGICAL THEORY

The "Enlightenment" of the seventeenth and eighteenth centuries had its beginnings in the European Renaissance of the fifteenth and sixteenth centuries, but it was given force and direction by the development of modern, natural science during the 1600s.

Broadly speaking, the Enlightenment was a critical reaction against traditional authority. Enlightenment philosophers argued that neither knowledge of nature nor self-knowledge could derive from obedience to authority and tradition. Neither could they result from practical, everyday experience.

Although they were not, themselves, social theorists, the two greatest progenitors of Enlightenment thought were, perhaps, René Descartes (1596–1650) and Isaac Newton (1642–1727). The Frenchman Descartes demonstrated that rationalistic control over phenomena could be obtained through a rigorous use of the mathematical method. Descartes believed that careful observation and clarity of expression served the pursuit of knowledge more faithfully than did blind obedience to the dogma of the Roman Catholic Church. Characteristically, in 1663, the church's reaction to Descartes was to place his writings on the *Index* of forbidden books, which the faithful were enjoined from studying.

The Puritan scientist Newton was a devoutly religious man who believed that there was no contradiction between his Protestant faith and his use of reason and observation to understand the universal and necessary laws of nature. For Newton, scientific investigation was a form of worship. After all, science upheld the dignity of man—God's most sublime creation on earth—and enabled the individual to wonder at the grandeur and subtlety of the magnificent universe that the Deity himself had set in motion.

For those who followed Descartes and Newton, it was but a short step to subjecting historical and social phenomena to the same kind of rational analysis that had proven so successful for physics, optics, and mechanics. The French *philosophes* Voltaire (1694–1778), Jean-Jacques Rousseau (1712–1778), and Denis Diderot (1713–1784) all believed that both the physical and social worlds could be understood by means of reason. In other words, the universe was held to follow natural laws that could be revealed by rational inquiry and scientific investigation. Thus the philosophy of the Enlightenment emphasized the possibility of social progress and the "perfectibility" of humankind. The *philosophes* extended notions of reason and natural law to all areas of existence—including the social. Their acceptance of natural laws, reason, and social analysis, and their belief in progress through rational self-understanding, provided an intellectual foundation for much of classical sociological theory.

Diderot, the editor of the great French *Encyclopédie*, held that religious dogmatism was truth's worst enemy. Like the other *philosophes*, Diderot was deist in orientation, though he ended his life as an atheist and materialist. According to Diderot, no person has a natural right to govern another. This theme was taken up by Rousseau and analyzed at length in his *Social Contract* (1762). In this famous and influential work, Rousseau inquired after the basis of all *legitimate* authority. Agreeing with Diderot that no person has natural authority over another, and dismissing the possibility that force gives rise to any right, Rousseau concluded that civil liberties derive their legitimacy from a social contract to which individuals must consent freely. For Rousseau, the social contract is the sole foundation of the political community. By virtue of this social contract, individuals lose their natural liberties (limited merely by their ability to exercise force over one another). However, man's natural liberty promoted unlimited acquisitiveness and avarice and thus encouraged individuals to destroy the freedom of others weaker than they. By submitting to a law vested in a so-cial contract—a mandate that can be withdrawn at any time—individuals find in the laws to which they consent a pure expression of their being as civilized human enti-ties. Rousseau's social philosophy had a major impact, especially on Hegel and Marx. For instance, Marx's assertion that capitalism destroys the individual's human social essence is informed by Rousseau's understanding that human freedom and human potential are not realized individualistically. Rather, they are obtained by means of an ensemble of social relations that has been exposed to reasoned and rational modes of critical self-reflection.

Perhaps the greatest Enlightenment theorist was the German philosopher Immanuel Kant (1724–1804). If Rousseau was the most radical of Enlightenment thinkers, Kant's philosophy was representative of the more conservative and cautious modes of thought that developed later in the eighteenth century. Nevertheless, Kant's answer to the question *"Was ist Aufkläring?"* (What is Enlightenment?) is de-servedly famous:

> Enlightenment is man's leaving his self-caused immaturity. . . . Such immaturity is self-caused if it is not caused by lack of intelligence, but by lack of determination and courage to use one's intelligence without being guided by another. *Sapere Audere!* Have the courage to use your own intelligence! is therefore the motto of the Enlightenment. . . . All that is required for this enlightenment is *freedom*; and particularly the least harmful of all that may be called freedom, namely, the freedom for man to make *public* use of his reason in all matters.[4]

In this statement we see the main features of Enlightenment thought: the appeal to reason over authority and tradition; the claim that the individual can take control by means of the critical faculty of the intellect; and the powerful idea that freedom and truth are complementary, mutually reinforcing principles in life. Perhaps of greatest significance is this latter belief that there need be no contradiction among truth, free-dom, individual development, and the social good.

Rousseau had suggested that the individual not only was a product of the social mi-lieu, but also was responsible for creating those institutions that would permit hu-manity to attain its full potential. Kant, who admired Rousseau greatly, but who countered some of his more radical ideas, argued that the free individual was innately capable of moral self-direction. As *objects* of investigation, the properties or behaviors of individuals could be investigated according to the same scientific methodologies that would be appropriate for any natural object. As *moral subjects*, however, individ-uals are not part of the natural world, for God has given the individual free choice to act in either a moral or an immoral fashion. A civilized society is one that encourages individuals to act morally. But society cannot deterministically generate morality be-cause moral action is always, in part, an outcome of free will.

As a result of the Enlightenment—specifically as a result of Rousseau's philoso-phy—the humanity and perfectibility of the individual were seen as contingent upon the level of social development. This particular aspect of Enlightenment thought became absolutely fundamental for Marx. The Kantian emphasis on the dualism of the individual—the view of man as both natural object and moral subject—strongly influenced Simmel and Weber. Both of these latter theorists were Kantian in their belief that, in the final analysis, the moral decisions of individuals never could be judged good or bad from a sociological point of view. For Simmel and Weber, sociology, unlike biology or chemistry, had to come to terms with the fact that, to some extent, the individual was not, and could not be, constrained by determinate laws. Kant's greatest impact on modern thought then was perhaps the idea that as a rational, independent, moral entity, the individual is free from at least some extrinsic, causal determinants of behavior. This particular point has been used against Marx and by Marxists. Thus Enlightenment philosophies have been used effectively on both sides of the major schism within social theory of the twentieth century: both by Marxists and by anti-Marxists.

Some classical theorists (e.g., Comte and Pareto) were influenced not by Enlightenment ideals but by *counter*-Enlightenment arguments about the need for traditional social institutions; others (e.g., Pareto and Freud) were highly skeptical about the Enlightenment claim that individuals were potentially rational and perfectible beings. Like Nietzsche, Weber believed that nihilistic tendencies in late modernism—trends that encouraged individuals to believe that they had complete freedom to create meaning in the universe—paradoxically would lead to the destruction of meaning. Humans need custom and tradition; if everything extrinsic to the individual can be objectively mastered and controlled, humankind finds itself in a rationalized universe that is devoid of mystery or subjective commitment. Even the Kantian moral law would not be of any help in a fully rationalized universe, because, although Kantian philosophy proscribes certain actions as immoral, it fails to give positive guidelines about how people *should* behave. Even though Weber did not equate twentieth-century nihilism with eighteenth-century Enlightenment, he was pessimistic about the long-term consequences of eating from the "tree of knowledge," an act of arrogance that was portrayed as wholly good by eighteenth-century rationalists.

According to Comte, the Enlightenment writings of Voltaire and Rousseau were partially responsible for the French Revolution and for its excesses. Although we need not accept such an idealistic and simplistic explanation of the origins of antiaristocratic revolutions, the *philosophes* clearly were influential both with the Jacobins of the French Revolution and with the founding fathers of the American republic. The victory of the entrepreneurial capitalist class—the bourgeoisie—whose interests were strongly antagonistic to those of traditional aristocracies, was ideologically justified in terms of appeals to universalism, progress, and rational self-interest. As Marx pointed out, the bourgeoisie initiated a class revolution against entrenched traditionalists and aristocracy. Although bourgeois rebellion (e.g., in France in 1789 and America in 1775) largely furthered the interests of a small minority of the population, the rhetoric of these revolutions demagogically appealed to ideologies of political emancipation that never could have existed without the development of Enlightenment philosophies. By the end of the eighteenth century, the bourgeoisie were in control of the state in Britain, France, and the United States. Thus, two hundred years ago, dominant classes in at least three nation-states had a vested interest in the reproduction of social philosophies that had been buttressed, if not generated, by Enlightenment ideologues.

SOCIAL EVOLUTIONISM AND CLASSICAL SOCIOLOGICAL THEORY

For the most part, the theorists discussed in this book did not treat the study of "social change" and "social order" as discrete or separable problems. During the 1950s and early 1960s many U.S. sociologists tended to approach the topic of "social change" as if it were a specialized, rather exotic, area of investigation. The conservative theorists of four or five decades ago failed to grasp the *historicity* of society; that is, they did not appreciate the immense variety and contingency of all social forms. Furthermore, they were inclined to believe that U.S. society after World War II best represented what a well-integrated, well-ordered social system should look like.

Even today, U.S. sociologists have a tendency to treat studies of social change as somehow detached from theories of social order. Yet many classical sociological theorists (e.g., Marx, Weber, Durkheim, or Spencer) would have argued that this dualistic approach is awkward and fragmented. Marx and Weber, for instance, would have pointed out that no social formation or civilization can be understood without grasping how it reflects a history. To understand the present, the social theorist must show how extant institutions continuously reproduce and revivify the effects of past defeats, victories, or developments in social understanding. For Spencer or Hegel, the whole point of social analysis was to develop a unified field theory of different types of order both in and through change. For these theorists, to suggest that theories of social change and social order should be separated would make about as much sense as arguing that Newton should have developed one theory explaining the motion of objects and another accounting for their nonmovement.

Most classical social theorists believed that societies followed a series of sequential stages, each with its own form of social organization. Facts culled from ethnographic and historical studies were seen as indicative of the stage of development obtained by a particular society. Many classical theorists believed that all societies were fundamentally similar in that they all go through the same sequence of stages, albeit at different rates of change. Thus, when classical theorists described existing societies, their typologies did not represent a mere static array of social possibilities but a hierarchy of developmental stages. Many of the classical theorists tended to rank their own societies (and European societies in general) very high, and they placed contemporary non-European societies lower on the sequence of development. As we shall see, Spencer found no difficulty in ascribing low levels of development to particular non-Western societies and in presenting these societies as equivalent to those that had existed in earlier periods of European history. Similarly, Durkheim's *The Elementary Forms of the Religious Life* assumed that Arunta society in Australia represented a simple "undifferentiated" social form, an analysis of which can reveal the basic features of social organization that exist in a more advanced state in European societies. We can refer to this view of societal development as "classical social evolutionism."

In essence, classical social evolutionism viewed social change as a more or less universally applicable set of stages and explained social order with reference to these stages. This is not to say, of course, that this model was unequivocally defended by all classical sociological theorists. Clearly, some were more accepting of it (like Comte and Spencer), and others were more critical of certain of its implications (like Weber and Pareto). Nonetheless, at least some of the elements of classical evolutionism found their way into the work of virtually all of the theorists discussed in this book.

We can trace the roots of social evolutionism to Saint Augustine's (354–430) "Christian evolutionism" and to the "universal histories" written by Bishop Bossuet (1627–1704), Baron Turgot (1727–1781), Marie Condorcet (1743–1794), and others. Whereas the ancient Greeks had conceptualized change as part of a repetitive, cyclical pattern of advance, maturity, decline, and advance, the Christian evolutionists saw time as linear. The Christian narrative was, of course, strongly influenced by the Old Testament story of the Jews as God's chosen people. Furthermore, Christ's supposed sacrifice made no sense in terms of a cyclical model of history. What meaning could crucifixion and ascension have if they were fated to be repeated eternally? As far as Christians were concerned, life on earth had not only a definitive beginning but also an end that would be followed by the final reckoning.

As classical social evolutionism developed, it posited the following about change: (1) it is inevitable; (2) it is directional and teleological; (3) it is analogous to organic stages of growth; and (4) it generally is progressive in nature. Classical evolutionism sought to explain the development of types of individuals as well as of societies, civilizations, and even humanity taken as a whole. Frequently, similar processes of development were assumed to apply to both individuals and society.

For the classical social theorists, change was integral to society. Thus Marx acknowledged that the features he assigned to "feudal society" were not fixed in time but underwent a dynamic development that would lead to the decline of feudalism and the rise of capitalism. Similarly, when Durkheim presented a functionalist methodology in the *Rules of Sociological Method,* he insisted that sociological explanations could be valid only if they were accompanied by an analysis of how the objects of study developed. For social evolutionists, the absence of perceivable change generally was ascribed to a misperception of reality, a pathological state, or a "survival" of something that is destined to disappear. For instance, Spencer argued that in very simple societies change is so slow (he believed it accelerated as societies advanced) that all but the most careful researcher might fail to detect it. Both he and Veblen liked to use the concept of "survival" to account for an apparent lack of change. A "survival" was a feature from an earlier social form, which, while it persisted, was not integrated and so was displaced. Both Spencer and Veblen looked at military aggressiveness as a survival in an industrial age and thus anticipated its demise.

Classical evolutionism also viewed change as directional: It is like the water in a stream, flowing in a particular direction. Many classical theorists placed the various societies reported by eighteenth- and nineteenth-century travelers and explorers along a sequence of social development from simple to complex, as if such a sequence described transformations within a single society. In these terms, non-Western societies were typically portrayed as throwbacks to earlier, simpler social forms that European societies had long since surpassed. Social evolutionists typically posited both a first and a final stage in evolution. For Comte, society went from a theological to a positive stage; for Marx, society developed from primitive to advanced communism; and for Veblen, societies evolved from savagery to civilization. Classical evolutionists did not believe that, once a final stage was achieved, history came to an end; rather, they thought that, once the final stage arrived, change would involve a continued elaboration and development of this final form.

The idea that society has a natural direction along which it must develop implied the notion of *teleology*, a belief that there is an innate drive (*telos*) toward an end state. In Hegel's writings, history *is* a teleological movement that strives to overcome "alienation" and realize itself in a universal form. Mead, who was quite critical of some aspects of traditional evolutionism, was, nonetheless, much influenced by Hegel. He explicitly defended the notion of teleology in social scientific analysis and offered his own conception of a universal society toward which, he believed, humanity was heading. The teleological component of classical social evolutionism separated it quite clearly from the evolutionary logic of Charles Darwin's theory of natural selection. Darwin (1809–1882) explicitly rejected teleological reasoning and viewed biological entities as (1) determined in form by environmental factors of selection and not by their innate nature; and (2) always subject to further change in form, and therefore, not having any final form. Classical social evolutionism antedated Darwinian evolution. The major ideas of Comte, Hegel, and Spencer were developed before the publication of Darwin's *Origin of Species* in 1859, and it is important to note that the logic of classical social evolutionism is quite different from that of Darwinian theory.

Classical social evolutionists tended to view the teleological movement from the earliest state of social existence to its final form as analogous to the growth of a living individual organism from infancy to maturity. In so doing, they confused processes involved with the *evolution* of the members of a species with the *development* of an organism. No contemporary Darwinist would make such a mistake. Whereas the development of an organism *is* predetermined (a normal mouse embryo will develop four legs; a human, two), evolution is open-ended. In other words, it is not predetermined, and it is not teleological. For the classical model of evolutionism, though, evolution was like development. Just as an organism does not jump from birth to maturity but goes through successive stages of development, so do societies as they "evolve." For Comte, society went from the theological to the metaphysical to the positive stage; for Marx, it went from primitive communism to ancient slave society, feudalism, capitalism, socialism, and, ultimately, advanced communism; for Spencer, the movement was from simple society to doubly compound society to trebly compound society; and, for Veblen, who developed stages described by the anthropologist Lewis Henry Morgan, society moved from savagery to barbarianism to civilization. Within each stage, there were usually substages that had to be traversed in strict order, with one substage preparing the way for the next. For example, Comte's theological stage involved the substage sequence of fetishism, polytheism, and monotheism.

The social evolutionists tended to reject the idea that some stages can be skipped (not surprisingly, given that they had conflated evolution with development). Generally, they argued that society must go through *all* the stages and substages in proper order. Exceptions from the usual developmental path, when allowed, were usually explained in terms of the peculiar circumstance of a particular society. Marx, for example, conceded that Asian societies, such as China, could develop into Oriental despotism and not into ancient slave societies. He also suggested that Russia could skip the capitalist stage and go directly from feudalism to socialism.

Just as the names of stages, the number of stages, and the features ascribed to particular stages varied from theorist to theorist, there also was disagreement among classical theorists about the content of evolutionary change (i.e., social development). Comte explained social evolution as an outcome of the evolution of human mental states; Hegel looked at it in terms of a dialectical movement based on the alienation of spirit; Marx presented a dialectical and materialist view of change; Spencer believed social evolutionism was subject to a universal law that stated that all matter went from a state of incoherent homogeneity to a state of coherent heterogeneity; and Veblen offered both a materialist and cultural causal analysis of why social evolution occurred.

Classical evolutionary theories generally (but not always) tended to be combined with theories of social progress. Social evolution refers to change in the size, complexity of organization, and institutional features of a society; social progress implies that change is for the better. Comte, Veblen, Hegel, Marx, and Spencer all incorporated some ideas of progress in their theories of development. This is not to say that, for them, each successive stage was necessarily better than the one before it; but that, taken as a whole, the final stage of development is superior to all earlier stages. Thus Marx and Hegel could see alienation as actually increasing before finally being eradicated.

Although a number of social evolutionists incorporated an element of "progress" in their theorizing, they differed widely in their ideas about how humans should act toward the attainment of that progress. As we have seen, Spencer argued that progress was inherent in social development and could best be achieved if people and governments let things alone. On the other hand, Marx believed progressive change came about through the organized actions of people acting in consort with general social evolutionary developments. He advocated, and took part in, revolutionary movements designed to bring about the termination of capitalism, and he tentatively outlined the actions revolutionary governments would take in the development of socialism and during the movement from socialism to communism.

Not all social evolutionists, however, believed in the idea of progress. Durkheim, who in many regards was a classical evolutionist, subscribed to a type of moral relativism. He argued that society did not develop toward an ultimate morality or an ultimate conception of the good but, rather, that there was a morality that was most appropriate and best suited for each stage of social evolutionary development. Durkheim rejected the *laissez-faire* philosophy of Spencer and the revolutionary position of Marx and, instead, advocated a series of reforms that would, he believed, achieve appropriate moral rules for his own society, given its particular stage of development.

Of all the sociological theorists discussed in this book, Weber and Pareto (both of whom rejected most of the general tenets of traditional social evolutionism) were most critical of the idea of progress. Pareto saw social activity as greatly influenced by a set of unvarying human instinctual inclinations that did not change with social evolution. Ideas of progress were merely that—ideas—and did not impinge upon people's desires for power and control. Weber did not see modernization as particularly progressive. He viewed the triumph of legal-rational authority over earlier traditional authority as producing a demystified and bureaucratized social life.

A final and perhaps most significant feature of the classical social evolutionary approach was the extent to which it represented a comprehensive explanatory device. The institutions of a society, features of group life, class divisions, attitudes and values of individuals, and all other collective phenomena could be explained as manifestations of a particular stage of development or as a result of disruptions that occurred in periods of transition. For example, one of the earliest and still most famous empirical studies in sociology is Durkheim's classic *Suicide.* In that work, what Durkheim views as pathologically high rates of "anomic" and "egoistic" suicide are explained as a manifestation of a transition from one stage of social change to the next. Durkheim argues that such high suicide rates resulted from the decline of social rules governing the earlier stage of society and the failure of rules appropriate to the next stage to develop fully. He concluded by discussing what those new rules should be like and how, once the evolutionary change had been completed, the pathologically high rates of suicide would decline.

With its assumptions about the naturalness of change, directionality, and teleology (and usually progress), classical social evolutionism greatly influenced a number of classical social theorists. Even those theorists who were quite critical of evolutionary ideas (particularly Weber and Pareto, and, to some extent, Mead) developed their own approaches with reference to social evolutionism and in dialogue with those who accepted this orientation.

SOCIOLOGY AND PROBLEMS OF MODERNITY

Classical sociological theory is very much a product of *Western* social experience, and, as citizens of eighteenth- and nineteenth-century West European and North American societies, the theorists on whom we focus in this book were, to a great extent, confronted with similar circumstances and social problems. For instance, all Western societies in the nineteenth century had to deal in one way or another with the promise and problem of capitalism.

In general terms, besides the Enlightenment, the explorations, discoveries, and imperialistic expansion of the sixteenth, seventeenth, and eighteenth centuries; the spread of antiaristocratic revolution in the eighteenth and nineteenth centuries; and the industrial revolution of the nineteenth century were all critically important for the development of Western modernity.

Social theory requires that people think comparatively, and, in this regard, the exploration of the Americas, Africa, and Asia forced intellectuals to acknowledge that the world was far more diversified than Europeans had previously accepted. Before the sixteenth century, travel was highly limited, and medieval Europe formed a relatively closed society whose contact with non-Western cultural traditions was sporadic.[5] The publication of the accounts of Western explorers, however, which had become popular reading in the nineteenth century, provided scholars with many examples of alien societies, unusual social customs, and exotic traditions and activities. As exploration gave way to imperialistic expansion in the eighteenth century, information about so-called primitive societies continued to grow. Such information proved to be invaluable to most classical theorists, and, as we have seen, faraway societies often were cited as hypothetical way stations in theories of social evolution.

The spread of revolutionary movements at the end of the eighteenth century was significant in a number of ways for the emergence of sociology. Most directly, there were some theorists whose sociologies were directly grounded in the ideological assumptions of the emergent capitalist class. Spencer, who was an apologist for the status quo and for the market economy, ranks foremost among these; Mead also was sympathetic to some degree to the capitalist system. On the other hand, in the works of Hegel, Marx, and Veblen, one finds a critical and negative reaction to the world order implied by the ideology of the middle classes. In Marx's and Veblen's works, there are arguments in favor of further revolution that would extend human rights beyond the limits of property ownership. For Marx and for Veblen, the control of the state apparatus by the bourgeoisie was seen as a passing stage in historical development. Not all theorists, however, were ideologically either in harmony with or in opposition to bourgeois ideology; some of them tried to distance themselves from what they considered to be bourgeois political theory. For instance, Durkheim's and Comte's sociologies contain unacknowledged ideological arguments that are both in favor of, and antithetical to, the achievements of republicanism. Although both Durkheim and Comte accepted the principles of equality before the law, private property rights, and the abolition of aristocratic privilege, they also insisted on the need to develop social institutions that would restrain and control precisely those acquisitive desires that flourish in modern capitalist societies. The influence of the bourgeois revolutionary movement, as well as that of the more conservative, counterrevolutionary opposition, can be seen in the reaction of classical sociology to the problems that resulted from the conflict and uncertainty that followed the decline of traditional authority. This conflict and this uncertainty were particularly pronounced in France, Germany, and Italy.

The bourgeois class itself was the prime mover behind the rapid industrialization of the late eighteenth and nineteenth centuries—what the historian Arnold Toynbee referred to as "the industrial revolution."[6] This revolution displaced older forms of cottage and craft-guild production with factory production. As a result, the major class divisions within Western society changed dramatically. In some ways, the new class of factory workers (the proletariat) was worse off than the peasants had been earlier. The proletariat did not enjoy the protection of a powerful lord; they did not have the right to reside in a certain village; and they lost their access to small plots of land that could be used to grow food. Consequently, they were forced to sell their labor to those who owned the factories, the cotton mills, and the coal mines. Low wages, unsafe working conditions, and long hours led to the rise of workers' movements and to conflicts between owners and workers. Class conflict, of course, was central in Marx's work; it was also discussed at length, however, in the works of Durkheim, Comte, Pareto, Weber, Veblen, and others. The classical theorists were also centrally interested in the urbanization, bureaucratization, and nationalism that accompanied industrialization.

Although Weber was most concerned with the spread of bureaucracy, this was also studied by Durkheim, Spencer, and others. An analysis of urbanization and the rise of urban life-styles runs throughout classical theory and was considered by all classical theorists to be basic to an understanding of modern society.

Most classical theorists gave a clear ideological response to the problems and the promise of industrial society. Spencer was the most forthright advocate for, and defender of, unrestricted industrialization. Blind to most of its negative attributes, he saw industrial society as unqualifiedly superior to the "militant societies" that had preceded it. This is not true of Durkheim, Marx, or Veblen, each of whom believed that the advantages of industrialization must be set against the miseries and social disruption that it had caused ordinary people. For Durkheim and Comte, industrialization was chaotic or "anomic"; but they also believed that a future harmonious relationship between owners and workers was possible. For Marx and Veblen, industrialization meant the rise of a new form of class society that would pave the way for its own negation and for a better and more just form of life. Marx believed that the overthrow of capitalism would come about as a result of class revolution, whereas Veblen believed the coming revolution would be a revolt of managers and engineers. Both Marx and Veblen concluded that industrialization was necessary for social progress. Unlike other classical theorists, Weber (who feared the bureaucratization of everything) and Nietzsche placed quite a bit of emphasis on the dark side of modern existence.

Modernity provided a common reference point for all of the individuals discussed in this text. However, as noted above, all these men responded to the particular circumstances of their own nation-states. The twelve theorists in this book were from France (Comte, Durkheim); Germany (Hegel, Marx, Weber, Simmel, Nietzsche); Italy (Pareto); England (Spencer); and the United States (Veblen, Mead). Freud spent most of his life in Austria-Hungary but thought of himself as a German Jew. The particular problems and circumstances of what by the end of the nineteenth century had become five distinct nation-states will be considered briefly in the following sections.

FRANCE: REVOLUTION AND COLLECTIVISM

France emerged in the seventeenth century as the most powerful nation-state in Europe. Over the previous two hundred years, various principalities, independent fiefdoms, and dukedoms had been absorbed by the French monarchy as it consolidated its power. The starting point for French unification was a long war fought with the ruling dynasty in England in the fourteenth and fifteenth centuries, which led ultimately to a unified nation and a centralized government. Long before other European nations, the French had centralized political authority, an effective system of national taxation and accounting, and a standing army made up largely of professionals and conscripts who served only the state and not a multitude of private employers.

Unified, wealthy, and the center of style and aristocratic culture, France by the seventeenth century was also a center of learning and social philosophy. In the eighteenth century, "salon society" encouraged social speculation, and men like Voltaire and Rousseau were patronized by the leisured classes. As we have seen, the *philosophes* not only endeared themselves to those members of the aristocracy who liked to think of themselves as enlightened, cultivated, and in touch with the latest intellectual fashions, they also found an audience with the rising entrepreneurial and professional classes. Barred from political power and denied the rights and privileges of the aristocracy, the emerging middle classes were receptive to the ideas of social change.

The debts of an extravagant monarchy led King Louis XVI to summon the Estates-General in 1789. This feudal parliament comprised the three medieval estates: the aristocracy, the clergy, and the commoners. It was supposed to represent the interests of the French people and to aid the king in raising revenue for his family and for the state. In 1789, rather than approving the king's request for money, the representatives of the so-called third estate (the commoners) refused to disperse when ordered and helped to initiate an insurrection in the streets of Paris. The great revolution of 1789 ultimately led to the execution of King Louis XVI and some thirty thousand other people. Many of the revolutionaries, or Jacobins, were themselves liquidated by their more radical brethren. For the next hundred years France vacillated between republicanism and dictatorship. For a short time the monarchy was reestablished. Under Napoleon, French republican ideals, which were used by Bonaparte to legitimate his usurpation of power, were spread throughout Western Europe by military conquest.

Whereas the revolutionaries of 1789 were primarily bourgeois in orientation, in the course of the 1800s, the workers of France—and especially of Paris—increasingly saw their interests as divergent from those of the ruling middle classes and therefore turned to socialism. The socialist movements that sprang up ranged from utopian experimentation to the advocation of violent revolution. Sporadic worker revolts occurred throughout the nineteenth century and culminated in the Paris Commune of 1871, a worker-controlled socialist government. Ultimately, the Commune was destroyed by government troops, and about twenty thousand working-class citizens lost their lives.

Throughout the classical period (1789–1919), the French tended to favor forms of social collectivism rather than individualism. Collectivist theories view individuals as naturally part of, dependent on, and—to some extent—subservient to the social whole. Socialism is a politically radical form of collectivism; French Catholic conservative philosophy represented its traditional—and usually reactionary—form. Whereas socialists wanted an egalitarian and industrial collective, French conservatives tended to look backward and paint a romantic picture of medieval, feudal institutions. Conservatives viewed feudal life as a stable and organic whole that permitted each person to fulfill some necessary role that would be in harmonious relation with every other role in society.

The young Marx, who lived in exile in Paris during the 1840s, was influenced by French socialist theory. Both Comte's and Durkheim's writings reveal the influence of the radical and conservative variants of French collectivism, although the conservative influence is definitely more pronounced in Comte. Both Comte and Durkheim combine the conservative emphasis on an organic view of the collective good with a radical conception of progress and equality of opportunity. Whereas Durkheim favored indirect representative democracy, Comte was antidemocratic and supported the idea of political control by an intellectual elite. Both men were fundamentally concerned about political and social disorganization, and both were interested in some form of collectivist restructuring for France.

GERMANY: DISUNITY AND IDEALISM

As a nation-state, Germany is a product of the late 1800s. In the eighteenth century and throughout most of the nineteenth, the German-speaking *Reich* contained many small, independent principalities and two larger states: Prussia and Austria.

Prior to national unification, the territory of the Germans was marked by diverging custom and divided by political boundaries and religious differences (Prussia was officially Lutheran, and Austria, Catholic). Throughout most of the nineteenth century, "Germany" was not a nation-state but an idea. The feudal German "nation" had been held together by a common language, a common religion, common customs, and an elected "Emperor of the Holy Roman Empire of the German Nations." This so-called empire, however, was already archaic and falling apart when Napoleon forced the last Emperor to give up his crown in 1807.

The absence of national unification became particularly troublesome to many Germans during the nineteenth century. With the decline of traditional political institutions, Germans lacked the means to give political expression to their feelings of cultural unity. Furthermore, it was increasingly apparent that Germany lagged behind the more modern nations of France and England in terms of social and economic development. Nearly all middle-class Germans believed that rapid modernization could not take place without rational, centralized political authority. In 1871, the Prussian aristocrat Count Otto von Bismarck persuaded the Rhenish and southern German states to unite with Prussia as one modern German nation under the supposedly constitutional authority of the Prussian king.

Although they were exposed to radical, republican ideals when their western territories were seized by France at the beginning of the nineteenth century, throughout the 1800s most Germans lived under the authority of princes or, after 1871, under the authority of the German Emperor or Kaiser. Whereas in other Western European countries, the middle classes had achieved political control, in Germany, control of the state—even after 1871—was largely in the hands of Prussian landowners and aristocrats (the *Junkers*). Compared with their English and French counterparts—not to mention the North Americans—the German bourgeoisie were conservative and docile. Nevertheless, Bismarck was able to fashion a remarkable political compromise between the German bourgeoisie and the traditional landed German ruling classes. By the end of the nineteenth century, many German factories had begun to outproduce their competitors in Britain and France.

The academic establishment in Germany was closely monitored by political authorities and, particularly after the failed revolution of 1848, was dominated by philosophical idealism. Briefly put, philosophical idealism (which is discussed more fully in the chapters on Hegel and Marx) emphasizes the significance of mind, ideas, or "spirit" as the prime movers and shapers of society. German intellectuals liked to believe that they were the guardians of all that was most cultured and most highly developed in the life of the mind. As Johann Schiller, a contemporary of Hegel's, wrote: "Each people has its day in history, but the day of the German is the harvest of time as a whole."[7] Yet, as the historian Fritz Ringer has pointed out, German academics' emphasis on idealism was an escape from actual political weakness and disunity.[8] Idealism was a wholly intellectual response to a political situation in which all important decisions were made by a shrewd but deeply conservative ruling class.

Despite radically different conceptions of the merits of philosophical idealism, both Hegel and Marx were strongly influenced by the German interest in community and national unity. In particular, both theorists were absorbed by the problem of what "community" and "unity" could mean in the modern era. Hegel, Marx, Weber, and Simmel were all interested in the problem of how individuals could satisfy their own needs as subjects while at the same time playing a meaningful role as part of some social or collective aggregate. Like Hegel and Marx, Weber was also centrally concerned with the problem of political authority—specifically, the problem of *legitimate* authority. Weber, an academic and a frustrated politician, was deeply interested in the idea of a political solution to Germany's problems. Above all, he wanted to understand the political options available to practical men in modern capitalist societies. Throughout most of his life, Weber believed that the German government was backward, unimaginative, and unnecessarily authoritarian. An ardent patriot, he wanted Germany to compete effectively with other capitalist and imperialist powers, and he wished to help his country adjust to the demands of industrialism, bureaucracy, and modernization in general.

ITALY: CITY-STATES AND MACHIAVELLIANISM

Whereas most of northern Europe developed a feudal order after the fall of the Roman Empire, much of northern Italy split up into city-states that competed with each other for political, military, and commercial supremacy. In the midst of such competition, Florence, Genoa, and Venice in the thirteenth and fourteenth centuries came to dominate Mediterranean trade, and Italian banking houses became the financiers of Europe. It was not unusual for both sides in a European war during the Middle Ages to arm themselves using the credit of the same Italian banking house. In an era of limited mobility, Italian banks had branch offices in many northern cities. Wealth did not lead to unity, however. The city-states constantly conspired against each other, forming shifting allegiances that often changed in the middle of a campaign. These wars gave rise to mercenary groups, whose leaders were known to Italians in the fourteenth and fifteenth centuries as *condottiere*—men happy to offer their services to whomever paid the highest price. Occasionally, these mercenaries extorted protection money from towns; at other times they set themselves up as local tyrants or as petty monarchs.

Italian political life was thus one of shifting alliances, self-serving deals, secret agreements, regular bribings, organized poisonings, and planned assassinations. Even for the Middle Ages, Italian politics were notoriously self-serving and hypocritical. In Italian political life, quick-wittedness rather than servility was the key to political survival. Bishops conspired against cardinals, and it was commonplace for Catholic rulers to declare war on the pope, who had both spiritual and temporal control over much of central Italy.

It was in this social and political context that Niccolò Machiavelli (1469–1527) wrote his masterpiece, *The Prince,* in 1513. Modeled partly on the life of the *condottiere* Cesare Borgia (1476–1507), *The Prince* described the actions a ruler should take in order to maximize his chances of maintaining control over the state. Machiavelli discusses candidly how political control is best secured through the use of deceit, threat, and violence. As political theory, *The Prince* can be seen as a superb piece of work—once it is put in its social and historical context. (Unlike sixteenth-century Italian princes, most modern rulers understand that political hegemony is most effectively achieved by ideological manipulation rather than by the constant use of violence.) Although the need to attain technical control over the vehicle of political authority remains the same from era to era, the means to this end may vary considerably.

In the case of Italy, however, it is no exaggeration to say that *The Prince* was probably as relevant a piece of political theory during the classical sociological period as it was during the Middle Ages. Like their counterparts in Germany, the northern Italian bourgeoisie, who were relatively few in number, were unable to take political control of the Italian state, which was not unified until late in the nineteenth century. Unlike Germany, Italy was never able to become a great industrial and military power; compared with Britain and France at the end of the nineteenth century, Italy was economically, socially, and politically backward. Thus in many respects Italy was only tangentially affected by modern trends during the classical period. It is not surprising, then, that the Italian theorist Pareto was more influenced by the medieval scholar Machiavelli than by the *philosophes* or by any of his near contemporaries like Comte or Marx. As an Italian theorist, Pareto was fundamentally concerned with the problem of how sociopolitical control is maintained and how political elites gain and lose power. Like Weber—though to a far lesser extent—Pareto tended to see the problem of political control as a technical one. Unlike Hegel, Durkheim, or Marx, Pareto believed it was a mistake to confuse political with moral authority.

BRITAIN: INDUSTRIALIZATION AND UTILITARIANISM

England was the first country to experience the effects of the industrial revolution and, during the first half of our classical period, was politically and economically in advance of all other European societies. In England, industrialization came about without widespread governmental assistance. The relatively large and powerful bourgeois class in England was able to achieve political and ideological hegemony slowly and peaceably, without having to think of themselves as a revolutionary class who had violently seized control of the state. English politics tended to be a remarkably amiable affair throughout much of the nineteenth century. The two major parties—the Whigs and the Tories (later Liberals and Conservatives)—had divergent policies in some respects, but they agreed on fundamentals. The Conservative party was the party of the landowners, and the Liberal party putatively was the party of the entrepreneurial and middle classes. It was typical of British politics during this period, however, that the Jewish leader of the Conservatives, Benjamin Disraeli, was generally considered to be more radical, and a better friend of the lower-middle classes, than the leader of the Liberals, William Ewart Gladstone. The policies of Gladstone, in fact, were preferred by many upper-class Englishmen.

During the nineteenth century, the upper-middle classes in England were comfortable and secure. Drawing on the work of the Scottish economists and moral philosophers Adam Smith (1723–1790) and Adam Ferguson (1723–1816), the English bourgeoisie took for granted the fact that their highly successful economy was in a state of "natural" balance. Consequently, it was generally believed that governmental interference and regulation were not only unnecessary but also harmful. Because they had attained political power gradually, and because there was a policy of compromise and assimilation between the English aristocracy and the English bourgeoisie, the middle classes were able to persuade themselves that their outlook on life was pragmatic and sensible, rather than "ideological" or "theoretical." (To some extent this self-satisfied and complacent attitude still exists in present-day England.) The British middle classes, therefore, had little time for the abstruse philosophical or ideological peregrinations of men like Hegel, Durkheim, or Marx. It is hardly surprising that, compared with France and Germany, England has produced few sociological theorists.

In opposition to the collectivist and interventionist ideas held by many French theorists, English conceptions of the natural balance of the market economy and English belief in the general utility of enlightened self-interest led to the conclusion that there was no contradiction between action that is taken for the social or collective good and action that is taken for reasons of self-interest. Deregulation, decentralization, and personal freedom (at least among the bourgeoisie) were important value orientations in England during the 1800s. These values were expressed ideologically and were used against the privileges of the landed aristocracy by the commercial and business classes.

Although theories about the natural rights of "free-born Englishmen" can be traced back to common-law customs of the Middle Ages, it was rapid industrialization in England that effectively fostered the belief that the world could—and should—be improved by the rational actions of self-interested individuals. Unlike France, where equality came to be thought of as equality of outcome, in England equality predominantly meant equality to compete (and therefore, inequality of outcome). As Durkheim argued, it was English competitive individualism that made the philosophical school of utilitarianism possible and meaningful.

Utilitarianism, as defined by Jeremy Bentham (1748–1832) and John Stuart Mill (1806–1873), cannot be summarized easily. One of its main tenets, however, is an analysis of the utility of various actions in terms of the overall increase in general happiness or in terms of improvement in the general welfare. From the vantage point of bourgeois political economy—which was largely British—utilitarianism was linked to ideals of open opportunity, equality of rights before the law, and a minimal amount of governmental regulation. As we shall see, these ideals, together with a general acceptance of utilitarianism, were central to the sociological theories of the Englishman Herbert Spencer.

THE UNITED STATES: EXPANSION AND VOLUNTARISM

Unlike Europe, where bourgeois ideals competed with older notions of feudal and aristocratic privilege, the United States had no indigenous aristocracy and no conservative counterbalance to the new ideas of individualism, progress, and opportunity. In the United States, the bourgeois ideal of a democratic-egalitarian society for white, male, middle-aged property owners was largely realized. Throughout the nineteenth century, business interests, unhampered (indeed, often helped) by the federal government, were able to realize a dramatic return on money invested in coal, steel, railroads, and industrial concerns of all descriptions. Economic growth, which tended to be consistently impressive, accelerated during the industrial and railroad boom following the Civil War. By the beginning of the twentieth century, the United States was an industrial giant with a level of production that in many respects had surpassed those of Britain, France, and Germany.

The ideology of democratic equality, coupled with the obvious inequality of opportunity between the wealthy and the poor, was something that many American intellectuals struggled to understand and to justify. During the era of the capitalist "robber barons" at the end of the 1900s, the paradox of U.S. "democracy" became more extreme. On one hand, millions of industrial workers toiled for wages of sometimes less than a dollar a day. On the other, a few thousand men controlled the Democratic and the Republican parties and derived much of their wealth from unearned income.

A critique of mass democracy, as well as a fear of plutocratic control, runs throughout much of Veblen's writings. Veblen was strongly critical of the wealthy, "predatory" businessmen whom he perceived as members of a class whose days were numbered. In contrast to Veblen's radicalism, Mead saw U.S. society as evolving peacefully toward egalitarianism, despite its obvious internal contradictions. In their different ways, both these theorists tried to come to grips with the obvious discrepancy between the promise and the reality of American democracy.

Another facet of American thought, which was connected to the idea of individualism, was an emphasis on *voluntarism:* the belief that social action involves the ability to choose between alternative forms of behavior. This conception of action as dependent on choice as well as reason was widely held by U.S. theorists. Although they did not all accept the tenets of voluntarism, American theorists all reacted to it in one form or another. Veblen espoused it cautiously, whereas Mead made voluntaristic progress the very cornerstone of his theoretical system.

THE INFLUENCE OF CLASS, RACE, AND GENDER ON CLASSICAL SOCIOLOGICAL THOUGHT

There will always be disagreement about which theorists should be selected for a volume such as this. As reviews of earlier editions of this text revealed, the "favorite" classical theorists of one person may well be viewed as largely irrelevant by another. But our purpose in writing this book was never to canonize our own favorite "masters of sociological thought" toward whom we expected students to show a worshipful attitude. Rather, we aimed to write a balanced history of the institutionalization of sociology and the emergence of general sociology. As was mentioned earlier, sociology was developed, in part, as a response to the problem of modernity, and, in this sense, classical sociology is a creature of its time. From this perspective, Comte's *A General View of Positivism*, Spencer's *The Study of Sociology*, or even Durkheim's *The Rules of Sociological Method* should not be read by contemporary students as exemplars of sociological inquiry. Rather, it is our position that students should become familiar with the ideas and works that shaped our discipline in its formative period and established its underlying goals, assumptions, foci, and biases. It is, of course, apparent that the theorists given their own chapter in this book have certain characteristics and outlooks in common. But this is not because *we* are prejudiced. Rather, it is because sociology was developed at a time when certain voices were privileged and relatively easily authorized, while others were typically ignored. To claim otherwise would be gross intellectual dishonesty.

The criteria we used for selecting our classical sociological theorists were: (1) that they developed their ideas and published them during the period from 1789 to 1919; (2) that they developed a general sociological theory; and (3) that their writings helped to institutionalize the discipline. By "general sociological theory," we mean theory that gives an account of social forces; that tackles, and suggests solutions to, social problems; that describes the causes and processes of social and historical change; that helps explain the formation of the social individual; and that describes the methodological or epistemological rules that generate adequate explanation. As was suggested in the first section of this chapter, the "institutionalization" of a discipline occurs when a college of experts or professionals is socially authorized to be the guardians of a particular branch of knowledge. Almost invariably, this means that the discipline in question is established as a university subject.

Applying the criteria just specified, we excluded many social theorists who wrote during our classical era but did not produce general sociological theory, or play a significant role in helping to make sociology a discipline that would come to be taught in virtually every college or university. Additionally—due largely to considerations of length—when the work of theorists overlapped significantly, we included only the one we believe made the greatest contribution to the field. Thus, for instance, we include Mead, but not Charles H. Cooley; Pareto, but not Gaetano Mosca.

It should come as no great surprise that the twelve theorists featured in this text are all white, bourgeois, European or U.S. men. The closest we came in our research to an African-American general classical theorist was W. E. B. DuBois (1868–1963). Although DuBois was born only four years after Max Weber, he developed his most important general theoretical work after the classical period, and in partial response to the ideas of people who wrote during the classical period. With one exception—Pareto, who was a minor member of the Italian nobility[9]—all the men we have selected for inclusion here were bourgeois, or middle-class, not working-class or aristocratic. Most aristocrats during the early-modern period showed disdain for the vulgarities of the modern era, and working-class individuals, of course, had few opportunities for extensive study and entry into the intellectual elite. Finally, during our classical period, women were typically excluded form having a chance to make a major contribution to social theory. This came about because of the difficulties that they experienced when they tried to have serious work published; their greater focus on applied topics, as opposed to abstract general theoretical works; discrimination in the area of university employment; and the prevailing belief among most males at the time that a woman was simply incapable of making much of an academic or intellectual contribution.

It was, perhaps, no coincidence that a few women who managed to publish well-received social essays during the classical period—such as Germaine de Staël (1766–1817), Mary Wollstonecraft (1759–1797), Harriet Martineau (1802–1876), Charlotte Perkins Gilman (1860–1935), and Marian Evans (1819–1880)—had first established themselves as writers of fiction. In addition, Wollstonecraft and Martineau, together with Jane Addams (1860–1935) and Marian Schnitger Weber (1870–1954), tended to focus on pressing social problems and injustices, rather than more abstract, theoretical issues. Jane Addams (the only one of these women to gain a university appointment) was ultimately forced out of her position in the Sociology Department at the University of Chicago and placed in the less prestigious Social Work Department, where—so it was believed—a woman would be more at home.[10] Both Martineau and Gilman wrote works of some distinction, but never received the credit they deserved. The arguments in Martineau's *How to Observe Morals and Manners* (1837) parallel, and are as sophisticated as, those advanced by Spencer in *The Study of Sociology* (1871). But, the former work was largely ignored, and the latter was highly influential and was frequently cited over the years following its publication. In a similar fashion, whereas the arguments made by Durkheim in *The Division of Labor in Society* (1893) had an immediate and continued impact on the development of sociology, Gilman's work on the significance of the division of labor in modern society, which was developed in her writing, *Women and Economics* (1898), was largely ignored by sociologists, even though it was well received by the public at large.

Quite obviously, the historical exclusion of racial minorities, working-class individuals, and woman from sociology's institutionalization had a significant impact on the discipline's foci of attention. Even though some of the theorists discussed later in this text had a certain amount of sympathy toward women's rights, working-class emancipation, and so on, many of our classical theorists clearly regarded women, minorities, and workers as inferior to a greater or lesser extent. We do not plan to conceal such blemishes but, rather, we shall explore how they were incorporated into classical social theory, and examine their influence on the development of sociology. Again, we do not seek to canonize our "classical theorists," nor do we wish to promote ancestor worship. Instead, our goal is to give an accurate and realistic account of sociology's beginnings. Sociology is—and must be recognized as—a human product: It is a reflection of the social circumstances that produced it, as well as a reflection *on* those circumstances.

Before turning to the following chapters, we should briefly justify our inclusion of Friedrich Nietzsche in this book. Nietzsche, who is best described as *anti*-sociological, became of increasing relevance to us in earlier versions of this text as we began to focus on the rise of "postmodernity," and as we started to think about how it might be possible to contextualize the era for which classical theory was written. Toward the end of our classical period, Nietzsche was a major influence on Freud and Weber and was a philosopher of considerable influence. Nietzsche is a figure of major and growing importance for us because, more than any other writer, he anticipated how the more ambitious goals of classical theory would themselves be undercut by the very modernizing forces that sociology had initially set out to explain and—so it was once hoped—would one day humanize.

NOTES

1. This change in sociology after 1920 is especially obvious in the United States. Before 1920, U.S. sociology was dominated by general theory that was evolutionary and comparative. After 1920, a movement toward the refining of instrumental and methodological techniques (such as the "Chapin living-room scale") can be observed.

   For critical theory, see, for instance, Herbert Marcuse, *One-dimensional man* (Boston: Beacon Press, 1964). Note the uneasy fusion of Marxian and Freudian concepts in Marcuse's work.

   For functionalism, see A. R. Radcliffe-Brown, *Structure and function in primitive society* (Glencoe, IL: Free Press, 1952).

   For action theory, see Talcott Parsons, *The structure of social action* (New York: Free Press, 1968). Originally published in 1937, this highly influential book draws on the work of Weber, Durkheim, Pareto, and the economist Alfred Marshall.

   For conflict theory, see Lewis Coser, *The functions of social conflict* (New York: Free Press, 1956), and Ralf Dahrendorf, *Class and class conflict* (Stanford, CA: Stanford University Press, 1959).

   For symbolic interactionism, see Herbert Blumer, *Symbolic interactionism* (Englewood Cliffs, NJ: Prentice-Hall, 1969).

2. For a discussion of Durkheim's political career, see Steven Lukes, *Emile Durkheim, his life and works* (London: Penguin Books, 1973), especially Chapter 17.

3. A good analysis of the role of German intellectuals in this era is Fritz Ringer, *The decline of the German mandarins* (Cambridge, MA: Harvard University Press, 1969).

4. Immanuel Kant, "What is Enlightenment?" pp. 132–134, in Carl J. Friedrich (Ed.), *The philosophy of Kant: Immanuel Kant's moral and political writings* (New York: Modern Library, 1977).

5. For a discussion of geographical mobility in the late Middle Ages, see Barbara Tuchman, *A distant mirror: The calamitous fourteenth century* (New York: Knopf, 1978), especially pp. 51–58.

6. Arnold Toynbee, *The industrial revolution* (first published in 1884.).

7. Johann Schiller, *Die Horen.* Quoted by Geoffrey Hawthorn, *Enlightenment and despair: A history of sociology* (Cambridge: Cambridge University Press, 1976), p. 41.

8. See Ringer, *The decline of the German mandarins.* (Cambridge, MA: Harvard University Press, 1969).

9. Pareto's grandfather was ennobled by Napoleon Bonaparte.

10. See Mary Jo Deegan, *Jane Addams and the men of the Chicago School, 1892–1918* (New Brunswick, NJ: Transaction Books, 1988).

GLOSSARY

Action theory: A theoretical orientation that focuses on how individuals construct *value-oriented* modes of behavior, taking into consideration a number of environmental (i.e., externally defined) constraints on such behavior.

Bourgeoisie: The class of merchants, bankers, and businessmen.

Chicago School: School of theorists who taught or were trained at the University of Chicago in the 1920s and the 1930s and who emphasized models of social interaction and shared meaning.

Condottiere: Italian mercenary leaders.

Critical theory: Theory based on the reflective critique of language and oriented toward human emancipation (see Chapter 2).

The Enlightenment: Eighteenth-century intellectual movement that stressed the applicability of reason and science to the improvement of society and humankind in general.

Feudalism: Political system that prevailed in Europe from the ninth to the fifteenth century and that gave powerful noblemen who controlled vast estates the right to govern those required to live on that land.

Functionalism: A theoretical orientation that treats society as if it were composed of mutually dependent and determinant parts working together to maintain and preserve the social whole.

Ideology: The attempt to organize conceptions of authority and shared social commitments in order to deal with social, economic, and political problems. The justification of a political order.

Laissez-faire **economics:** Economics given a free hand by political authorities.

Nihilism: A philosophy that acknowledges that humans have infinite capacities to create a universe of meaning. The acknowledgment that, as God is dead, humans should have the courage to learn how to live without values.

Philosophes: French *Enlightenment* philosophers.

Positivism: Inquiry based on the methodology of the natural sciences that is produced by a technical-cognitive interest and that seeks to predict and control changes in human environments (see Chapter 2).

Proletariat: The class of workers who earn their living selling their labor to the *bourgeoisie*.

Secularization: The decline of religious institutions, beliefs, and practices.

Symbolic interactionism: A theoretical orientation focusing on how society is a product of shared communications and understandings among self-conscious individuals engaged in cooperative undertakings.

Utilitarianism: Philosophical position derived from British moral philosophy. Claims to morality are based on calculations that assess how the greatest good for the greatest number is to be attained.

Value freedom: Entailed by the belief that science can be indifferent to, and neutral about, competing *value orientations.*

Value orientations: Goals that express values and embody human choice and commitment.

Voluntarism: Belief that human social action involves the ability to choose among alternative and competing modes of behavior.

2

The Nature and Types of Sociological Theory

THEORY AND SOCIAL LIFE

"Theory" (as in "social theory") often seems remote, abstruse, abstract, and irrelevant, not to mention pretentious, confusing, and self-contradictory. In this book, however, we start from the premise that "theory" of all kinds—but especially social theory—is grounded in human interests and in commonplace experience. We hope to demonstrate that theory is not as remote or as abstruse as is often believed.

Social theory can be particularly confusing for the student because it often appears that sociologists or social theorists have developed multivarious—often incommensurable—kinds of thought. As we have seen, one major divide between social theorists is that some believe sociology should model itself after the natural sciences, and others argue that sociology should be classified as part of the "humanities." Some social theorists have used mathematics to model social processes; others have suggested that a competent sociologist is like a good investigative journalist. Some have argued that sociology should steer clear of ideological issues (as should be evident by now, we are inclined to believe this is impossible). By way of contrast, other theorists (e.g., Marx) have insisted that the whole point of theory is to promote critical self-understanding and to change the world. Although the range of human theorizing seems endlessly varied, we believe—and try to show in this section—that all theoretical orientations can be classified in one of three categories: *positivist, interpretive,* or *critical.* Positivist explanation, on the one hand, and interpretive and critical thought, on the other, emerged from two distinct learning processes. These can be described as follows.

First, organisms have to learn how to adapt to, and process information about, their environments; in the process they acquire behavior that maximizes the possibilities of instrumental control over them. Environments are always experienced as objectively given and can be natural (e.g., the weather) or social (e.g., tradition and custom). (For the civilized human being, *social* environments often become much more constraining and objectlike than natural ones.) Birds construct nests; humans learn how to build skyscrapers. Caribou are "hard-wired" to make the right decisions to survive in a harsh natural environment. Yet, a human from a rural, isolated area might have great difficulty when learning how to take the necessary steps to survive in a large city. This is because humans deal with changing or varying environments (that they themselves often construct) not by using built-in programs but by means of symbolic blueprints that are creatively and imaginatively put together.

Second, all organisms have to learn to communicate with others of their species. Again, communication among nonhuman animals is mostly—although not entirely—hard-wired. In contrast to this, human communication is arbitrary, reflective, and intersubjective. For instance, humans cannot participate in meaningful speech patterns unless they learn a culturally bound language that requires them to think about how their speech practices are interpreted by the target audience. As Mead emphasized, human symbolic interaction requires subjects to "take the role of the other" in order to participate meaningfully in cultural practices that often are quite creative, dynamic, and open-ended.

The type of adaptive learning that is driven by the *technical* interest in optimizing instrumentalist control over an environment yields positivistic explanations in a modern context. In other words, modern scientific explanation is the highest expression of the need to master objectively defined or given environments. Positivism is *nomothetic,* that is, it seeks generalizable, universally applicable laws. As positivistically inclined sociologists, both Comte and Pareto believed that social scientists should try to grasp the laws that determine human behavior so that they can plan for a better society. Hence, they were interested in technical knowledge. As Comte put it: "From Science comes Prevision, from Prevision comes the ability to control." From this perspective, if the sociologist were able to discover those laws that were to explain the causes, say, of crime or suicide, humans could have greater technical mastery over the ways in which their social environments affect them. For instance, Durkheim's attempt to discover the social causes of suicide were, in part, driven by an interest in controlling and reducing "pathological" rates of this phenomenon.

Unlike the social sciences (sociology, anthropology, political science, etc.), the natural sciences (physics, chemistry, biology, etc.) are driven almost exclusively by an interest in technical theorizing. In other words, the most fundamental interest of the natural sciences is an interest in prediction and control. Thus, for a physicist or chemist, the corroboration of a theory *is* that it predicts successfully. Of course, the individual motivations of scientists are not necessarily technical in orientation. Many natural scientists would emphatically deny that they turned to their studies in order to enhance modes of instrumental control. Nevertheless, we maintain that the logic of explanation in the natural sciences is predicated on the ability of theory to predict or objectively master environments.

As was noted earlier, human communicative interaction requires the use of reflective, *interpretive* practices. This becomes most obvious when we contrast communication among humans with communication among other type of social actors—honeybees, for example. Within the setting of the hive, honeybees use the "waggle dance" to transmit information about the direction and proximity of nectar. This system of signification is literally implanted in the insect; hence, it is unnecessary for each honeybee to learn requisite communicative skills. By contrast, human signification systems (e.g., the cross, which might represent the hope of "salvation") are both arbitrary and learned. Insects cannot mentally distance themselves from their communicative practices. Indeed, as successful forms of life, they are, in essence, little other than an outward expression of the communicative practices that are coded by their genes. Humans, though, can reflect on the supposedly extrinsic realities that are expressed by their communicative modes. An historian, for instance, could ask how the people of Salem, Massachusetts, managed to define their world in such a way that they believed "witches" were real. When compared with human, insects seem simple creatures. Nontheless, unlike us, at least they do conduct their affairs without recourse to fantastical projections. Perhaps insects are better centered than we are. The moth *Bombyx mori*, for example, can detect a female of the species on the basis of a single molecule of bombykol located half a mile away. He thus "performs as little more than a sexual guided missile, programmed to home on an increasing gradient of bombykol centered on the tip of the female's abdomen—the principal goal of [his] adult life."[1] Are we this elegant, or nearly as focused?

Interpretive, or more hermeneutical, theorists, such as Weber, understand the limitations of the positivistic method because they recognize the significance of cultural or historical context in understanding the meaning of human behavior. Human societies, Weber acknowledged, differ greatly by virtue of the fact that they institutionalize quite different modes of communicative interaction. Such symbolic modes have to be understood from "within" a cultural or civilizational complex, not from "without." In other words, the investigator has to understand how action becomes meaningful for the particular subjects under investigation. As a consequence, explanation does not rely on general scientific laws, but is *ideographic* (i.e., it explains something that might be unique and unrepeatable). An event of some significance in one historical context may have quite a different relevance in another. For instance, the invention of the mechanical clock meant little to the rulers of Song dynasty China (907–1276). But this "new" technology was a development that held great importance in the West because in a modern—as opposed to a traditional—setting, time came to be seen quite differently. In a modern, capitalist society, the precise measurement of time is absolutely indispensable for the articulation of social relations.

Apart from positivism and interpretive theory, there is a third kind of theory, which, we suggest, is characteristically modern. Although it had its roots in classical Greece, this third mode of explanation—*critical theory*—did not become a major part of human understanding until after the Enlightenment. As we have noted, human subjects do not respond to their environments in a direct, unmediated fashion, but participate in constituting them by an act of interpretation. All subjects have the ability to reflect on how they themselves are the product, as well as the creators, of modes of communicative interaction.

For instance, relations of authority among people are implied and reinforced by our use of language. Thus in caste societies, the description of people who are born into a group that has a low status is very often synonymous with the description of dirt or filth. Not surprisingly, people from low-status groups are often thought of as unclean. Similarly, as Marx pointed out, we are inclined to view employers who lay off workers when they can no longer profit from their labor as rational, not immoral or inhuman. The authority of "hard-headed" businesspeople derives from a common belief that their policies represent everyone's interests in the long run. So long as these policies are viewed as "rational" and not "immoral," the employer's authority is secure. In capitalist countries, newspapers reporting layoffs do not usually describe the actions of businesspeople as immoral. Nevertheless, any presentation of social reality always reinforces authority relations that are possibly unjust and that could be questioned. The use of a particular communicative style might enable us to understand the presence of authority, but it does not always enable us to grasp the underlying relations of dominance and submission implied by nearly all forms of communicative interaction.

Critical theory is the analysis of how domination is institutionalized within modes of communicative interaction. Whereas a positivist might use scientific methods to study how factory laborers can be made to work harder and more profitably, a critical theorist would be more likely to ask, for instance, whether it is just for young women in the Third World to be turned into cheaply purchased, animate tools destined to turn out low-cost commodities for Western consumers. In methodological terms, critical theory is a rigorous form of self-reflection. Why do we treat others this way? Is it because we are encouraged not to recognize these others as subjects such as we? Do our social institutions require such lack of recognition? How are we a product of, and diminished by, such arrangements? Is our own freedom and humanity jeopardized as a result?

As was noted earlier, critical theory is a classically modern orientation. Humans within primitive or traditional societies are not particularly self-reflective or self-critical. This is because the social context that produced such humans does not require, or even permit, much reflectivity. By contrast, modernity is a reflective project, and it is for this reason that sociology, itself, is part and product of the modern era.

Having introduced three distinct types of theory—positivism, interpretive theory, and critical theory—we shall examine these distinct orientations in greater detail in the following sections.

POSITIVISM

Positivism requires a commitment to (1) *determinism*, and (2) *empiricism*.

A commitment to determinism compels the scientist to look for postulated mechanisms in the world. For instance, the explanation that astronomers can give of the motion of the planets within the solar system is ideal from this perspective, because the solar system can be viewed as a giant mechanism, understandable in terms of quantifiable laws describing fixed relations among the various parts of this complicated machinery. It is the commitment to determinism that encourages the scientist to define cause-effect relations that are as inclusive as possible. The causal relationships de-

TABLE 2.1   Deductive-Nomological Explanation

Explanans	Laws:	$L_1 \ldots L_2$
	Conditions:	$C_i \ldots C_n$
Explanandum	Statement describing what is predictable	

scribed in scientific theorizing fit into the logic of scientific explanation according to the following model. This kind of explanation is described as *deductive-nomological explanation,* or *nomothetic* science. Most scientists consider this type of explanation to be the ideal for which scientific investigators should strive (see Table 2.1).[2]

Deductive-nomological explanation consists of the production of certain scientific laws ($L_i \ldots L_n$), which are described in terms of some abstract theoretical language. In addition, such an explanation lists a set of conditions ($C_i \ldots C_n$) that describe the circumstances under which the laws apply. The *explanandum* (that which is explained and predictable) is deduced from the *explanans* (that which does the explaining). In other words, given that the laws described are true and that the conditions listed really do apply in a particular instance, what is described by the explanandum must come to pass. Thus, if the law "if iron is heated then it expands" is true, and if a particular piece of iron is heated, we can conclude with complete certainty that this iron must expand.

In order to test scientific laws, it is necessary to set up an experiment carefully so that precisely the circumstances described under $C_i \ldots C_n$ come into effect. Unless experimentation occurs in a laboratory setting, it is usually impossible for sociologists to create an experimental design that would provide grounds for the corroboration or refutation of any sociological law. Often, corroboration is ethically impossible: Social scientists, for instance, might learn a great deal from being able to raise children under precisely controlled circumstances. However, it is not currently possible to engage in testing of this kind.

As we noted earlier, nomothetic science strives for generalizable explanation. In other words, nomothetic science seeks scientific laws that enable individuals to predict what will happen under certain circumstances at *any* time and in *any* place. Scientific laws of the type described earlier are not merely supposed to explain what happened at one time and in one place, but also they should give us knowledge about what will always occur under circumstances $C_i \ldots C_n$, whenever and wherever such conditions occur. Nomothetic explanation is the kind of explanation in which physicists, chemists, and engineers have always been most interested.

Much of the time, social scientists have accepted that they are not going to come up with the perfect nomothetic type of explanation that we have described. In other words, few social scientists have looked for laws using the same methodology that is applied by physicists or biochemists. Natural scientists have been relatively successful in applying and using the deductive-nomological model of explanation (although it would be more accurate to say that the deductive-nomological model has accurately reflected the type of explanation for which natural scientists strive).

With the exception of Comte and Spencer, sociologists who have expressed an interest in positivistic inquiry generally have not looked for invariable cause-effect relations but have searched for statistical correlations. When contemporary social scientists become interested in "crime," "suicide," "prejudice," or "likelihood of participating in a riot," they generally look to see what *tends* to be associated with this activity or particular piece of behavior. Knowledge about such correlations might, indeed, help the investigator to predict when, say, "criminal activity" or "suicidal activity" tends to occur.

Social scientists who exhibit a willingness to look for statistical correlations from which cause-effect relations can be inferred clearly maintain an interest in the enhanced technical control made possible by knowledge about statistical probabilities. It is noteworthy that this interest takes precedence over a commitment to the inherent advantages of the deductive-nomological model of explanation. Deductive logic guarantees human *certainty* about the validity of particular conclusions. As we have seen, with deductive-nomological explanation, conclusions (stated by the explanandum) are always valid and must be true—provided that the premises (contained in the explanans) are true. In terms of human certainty about future events, statistical explanation, of course, is immeasurably inferior to deductive-nomological explanation. Thus, although they maintain a positivistic interest in technical control, social scientists who reduce sociology to a search for statistical correlations generally make enormous concessions with respect to the reliability of their conclusions.

Besides a commitment to determinism, the other commitment that positivism requires of an investigator is *empiricism.* Empiricism compels the scientist to accept that empirical knowledge about the external world is ultimately grounded in what we can learn from our sense impressions. My sense impressions are almost invariably the same as yours, provided we are exposed to the same stimuli. Thus, if we agree to treat sense impressions *as if* they carry with them information about external reality (or if we are naive enough to believe that sense impressions actually describe external reality), we can agree that we are both in touch with the same universe. This agreement has important consequences, for, as Comte pointed out, unless an investigator can describe and classify phenomena in such a way that people can orient themselves to what they take to be the same reality, knowledge of deterministic relationships is impossible.

Empiricism, then, is a doctrine that assumes, for example, that when we receive information about something external to us by being able to touch it, we gain knowledge about external reality—that is, about the way the world really is, independently of our knowing it. In short, positivism treats raw data as if they consist of what can be seen, heard, smelled, touched, or tasted—and empiricism assumes that what we can see, hear, smell, touch, or taste gives us pure information about the world. Nevertheless, of course, the meaning of such information still has to be interpreted.

Positivistic theorizing cannot involve the simple description of sense data, for this would not permit us to meaningfully organize our experiences. Without organization, our sense of reality would be scrambled so radically that the external world would appear to be nothing more than a confusing kaleidoscope of color, shape, sound, and motion. Therefore, positivistic analysis invariably contains several levels of description, including these:

1. Abstract theory, which specifies particular relationships among concepts.
2. Particular concepts, defined by the language that scientists use.

3. Operational definitions, which relate concepts to empirically observable conditions.
4. A description of sense impressions (seeing, touching, etc.).

It should be noted that the actual concepts that a positivist uses are several levels removed from the raw description of impressions received through the senses. Thus when physicists are checking the results of a sophisticated experiment by observing a whole array of dials and instruments, raw data come to them in the form of observations about changes in these instruments. Scientists describe the experiment in question in terms of higher-level (more abstract) concepts, which describe what they believe these changes mean. Analysis requires an interpretation of what actually happened during the experiment in terms of concepts that other scientists will find meaningful. Thus scientists do not report the result of an experiment by saying that the needle of a dial moved several times; rather, they report what this motion *meant* in a particular experimental setting. Such reporting requires them to interpret the meaning of data by reference to concepts that they accept because of authoritative social networks of communication, not because these concepts are mandated by empirical data. Positivism and interpretive theory can be separated analytically, but all positivists are hermeneutists too—at least in the sense that they all have to learn how to participate within a community of scientists. Science is a social, not a solitary, pursuit. To become a successful scientist who can generate communicable knowledge, you have to learn how to interact effectively with your peers. In positivistic explanation, what is defined at a higher level serves to organize conceptually what exists at a lower—that is, more concrete—level. The scientist's assumption that what is perceived at the lowest level of analysis (level 4) is related in any way whatsoever to what is talked about at higher levels is highly tentative. Although definitions, concepts, and theories help the physicist to organize the way in which physical reality is experienced, such organization is always functionally related to particular scientific—and specialized—language that the scientist learns.

As scientific language becomes more specialized and more abstract, it often becomes more *reductionist*. Reductionism occurs when phenomena are described in terms of elementary units of analysis. For example, to try to explain human beings in terms of their molecular structure would be strongly reductionist. The advantage of reductionism is that the scientist is likely to exercise greater control over specific phenomena. Its disadvantage is that the scientist fails to grasp how analytically defined parts tend to be influenced by more comprehensive properties.

If humans wish to decide on the most effective way to achieve fixed goals, then positivistic theorizing is entirely rational. For instance, if the goal of theory is to control a disease, to discover a way in which space travel can become possible, or to explore the way in which people's behavior can be altered by drugs, then a positivistic approach is necessary. Behind positivism is always an interest in selecting the most efficient means for achieving fixed ends. The interest that positivism exhibits is in methodical, calculating control; and this interest in instrumentalism can be applied to both natural and social environments. Theories of crop management seek to increase the yield of an agricultural product; from a positivistic point of view, theories about the cause of crime should enable agencies of social control to reduce the crime rate.

It must be remembered, however, that the use of both positivistic and hermeneutical theories compels investigators to make certain kinds of human commitments. The choice of a positivistic orientation, for instance, commits the scientist to the belief that "there is no other way that [scientific] knowledge can be useful in making practical decisions except in an instrumentalist manner."[3] Unfortunately, many people, who mistakenly view positivistic science as a neutral way of looking at the world, conclude, wrongly, that it gives us a straightforward, simple description of reality. Although most of us are aware that science and the technology to which it gives rise have radically changed the world as we know it, few of us reflect on the way in which the institutionalization and blind acceptance of the positivistic method create a certain kind of human being who will experience—and be shaped by—a particular kind of reality. As we have seen, for instance, positivists apply only those operations that enable them to measure sense impressions and experience a world over which there is some theoretical chance of instrumental control.

To simplify somewhat: To live in the modern age means to live in a society that has displaced tradition with technology. Until a few centuries ago, the most prestigious form of learning was always purely hermeneutical. Until quite recently, universities trained an elite to see the world in a particular, "cultured" way. Medieval universities, for instance, were not centrally interested in dispensing technical knowledge, which was looked on as an inferior mode of knowing until the eighteenth, or perhaps even the nineteenth, century. Today, however, we live in an age that places relatively few checks on positivism. This has disadvantages as well as advantages for us. For instance, a commitment to empiricism encourages us to believe *falsely* that an objective, external reality is accessible to us without hermeneutical interpretation and without the implementation of human interests. Empiricism encourages us to believe in the *fiction* that scientific evidence really does arrive without human interference; that, at their roots, scientific models of reality represent the neutral model of a universe that is the same for all of us. But what enables scientists within a particular research tradition to experience the same reality is the theoretical language that they share. This language permits scientists to interpret the meaning of raw data in the same way. Positivism mandates a hermeneutic interest in interpreting the meaning of information, but it does not require that scientific practitioners be reflective about this process.

Because positivists believe that all knowledge is generated in the same manner, through the same process of discovery, they place great emphasis on collating and systematizing what is known. As we shall see, for instance, this was an important part of Comte's and Spencer's work. Furthermore, positivists are committed to the belief that there is a knowable world "out there" that has a structure and form that can be grasped by the competent investigator who is value-neutral—and committed to nothing but the search for truth. Whereas Comte believed in "natural social laws" that determined the mechanism of social life, Spencer took it for granted that there was a "natural" (that is, objective, external, and impersonal) balance to orderly social existence, which could be discovered by the sociologist. And, whereas positivism always takes it for granted that what is known or discovered is never constituted by the knowing subject, it is axiomatic for hermeneutics and critical theory that both the scope and the content of knowledge reflect the value orientations of historical actors.

If sociology is to be modeled after the natural sciences (that is, if it is to adopt a *positivistic* point of view), it follows that it should strive for the same standards of objectivity as the natural sciences. In other words, if sociology is to be positivistic in orientation, it should explain how investigators can best control human behavior. A positivistic sociology could investigate how the influence of the group could be used to break the resistance of political prisoners—or it could study the way in which certain social situations cause domestic violence or child abuse.

Although positivism is not *overtly* ideological, its lack of interest in critical self-reflection often results in a situation where adherence to scientific knowledge—and an insistence that positivism is the *only* correct mode of theorizing for human subjects—provides simultaneous support for goals that have been selected by particular groups and that cannot even be questioned by means-oriented scientists. As we have seen, positivistic inquiry does not give us a straightforward, simple description of reality but interprets reality in a manner consistent with instrumentalism—that is, technical control over some environment. Many sociologists and philosophers of science have pointed out that positivism is not itself ideological, but "value-free." The truth of this claim, however, conceals the obvious fact that science (rational, instrumental control) can exist as a *social institution* only when society sets the particular goals and ends of scientific activity. For instance, much of U.S. science in the last five decades has been a dispassionate, rational inquiry into how the destructive military capacity of the state can be maximized; it has not, say, been a dispassionate and rational inquiry into how to provide adequate nutrition for all Americans. We would not suggest that the hundreds of thousands of scientists and technicians who have worked for the so-called defense establishment over the last fifty years have produced anything other than objective knowledge. We would like to point out, however, two traps into which naive observers of institutionalized science are likely to fall. The first would be to equate actual scientific research with pure rational inquiry in the service of objective, value-free goals. As we have seen, the goals of institutionalized science are *always* political. The second trap that nearly everyone falls into is to assume that the *type* of inquiry favored, for instance, by the "Defense" Department (that is, positivism), is the only kind of rational inquiry possible. This is nothing other than ideological support for technocratic institutions. Although positivism is *not* itself ideology, an uncritical acceptance of the way in which science is institutionalized leads individuals to defend and accept noncritically the political status quo.

INTERPRETIVE THEORY

During the 1950s and 1960s, the American sociologist C. Wright Mills forced many of his colleagues to begin to look more carefully at what had always been an important issue for classical sociology—namely, what should be involved in the production of sociological theory. In questioning the suitability of determinism and empiricism (that is, positivism) for *sociological* theorizing, Mills argued that "there is, I believe, no [law] stated by any social scientist that is transhistorical, that must not be understood as having to do with the specific structure of some period."[4]

Language is created by the exigencies of human practice and in the service of human interests. The range of possible activities that humans find meaningful is always dependent on value orientation and social context. As humans organize and consolidate the range of these activities through time, they create a history. The hermeneutist, or interpretive theorist, sees individuals as agents or components of a living history or tradition and thus assumes that history does not belong to us, but that we belong to it.[5] Accordingly, historical research is not only research about tradition—it is the *transmission* of tradition. Language, then, is the medium by which history is transmitted. From this perspective, we learn about other people who are separated from us in time or by physical space by understanding the rules that made meaningful the culture or the language of the people we are studying. From a hermeneutical point of view, sociological research is basically comparative, and it involves a process of translation: The rules that define how action becomes meaningful in one context must be translated by the investigator into rules that can be seen as meaningful by members of a larger audience—the audience for whom the explanation is intended. Often, it is a simple matter to understand the actions of people who were raised in the same tradition or who come from the same community as the observer; but to understand people who have internalized the rules implicit in what seems, from the observer's perspective, to be an alien culture is often extremely difficult. Occasionally, it must be acknowledged that the rules that make action meaningful within one particular cultural context cannot find expression in the language used in another context. Thus we find the actions of people within some "alien" cultures to be hopelessly bizarre, disgusting, or—worst of all—meaningless.

Just as positivism mandates a particular kind of measuring operation, interpretive theory requires a commitment to what can pass for explanation before any kind of knowledge can be generated. From a sociological point of view, one difficulty with positivism is that sociological research does not seem to get very far if empiricist investigators ignore the issue of how the subjects being studied view the meaning of their behavior. Some sociologists have argued that the sociological theorist must engage in a *double* hermeneutic. As we have seen, any kind of theorizing requires an investigator to learn a theoretical or highly specialized language that creates the conditions under which the meaning of data can be interpreted. The sociologist, however, also has to understand the mode of communication used by subjects to create the world in which these subjects live. Hermeneutists try to achieve reciprocal understanding with subjects based on symbolic interaction *with* them, not on an empiricist observation *of* them. If we interact with individuals from a different culture, we speculate about the meaning of their actions for us and the meaning of our actions for them. We believe we comprehend the actions of such individuals when it becomes apparent that we are beginning to understand them in the same way that they understand themselves and that the individuals we are communicating with are understanding *us* in the same way that we understand the meaning of our own actions. Consequently, we can never understand a historical subject—an individual who is deceased—unless we share a common tradition or language with that subject.

In short, whereas positivism strives for technical control over phenomena, interpretive theory seeks reciprocal intersubjective understanding with subjects. Whereas, for positivism, prediction is identified with an interest in technical control, for interpretive theory an interest in prediction is subordinated to the need to grasp how actions become reciprocally meaningful. For instance, we cannot communicate with another person unless we comprehend how that person will respond to a message that we intend to send. In order for us to reach that person, we have to know what he or she will make of certain symbols that we use to communicate with others and that have a particular meaning for us. A positivist can predict the behavior of objects without having to engage in symbolic interaction with them, without having to see things from their point of view. *A hermeneutist cannot communicate with human subjects without being able to see things from their perspectives.*

For an interpretive theorist, there is no possible neutral standpoint, for hermeneutics cannot escape the language presuppositions and background assumptions involved in any human act of explication. The most fundamental presupposition made by the hermeneutical disciplines is that there are no standards of objectivity that can be recognized independently of the attainment of intersubjective agreement among people engaged in dialogue. If sociologists choose a positivistic mode of theorizing, they commit themselves to trying to explain the behavior of humans in terms of the organization of sense impressions that give the investigator information about this behavior. For many sociological positivists, including Durkheim, this has turned out to be an impossible task; in the interests of *empirical* understanding, they have had to abandon empiricism. This is also what happened to Freud, who began as a strict positivist and moved slowly and inexorably toward hermeneutical inquiry.

For hermeneutists, then, raw data consist of the description of activity. As we have seen, an interest in technical control and an interest in understanding communicative interaction are not incompatible. Many sociologists who express an interest in technical control over subjects as *objects* of analysis are compelled to take into consideration how these objects of analysis respond to what *they* have decided is meaningful—in other words, how these "objects" respond to what the sociologist believes is a significant cause of their behavior. Modern sociologists—unlike many of the men described in this book—tend to emphasize the positivistic side of their analysis and often downplay the significance of hermeneutical interpretation. One reason for this is the greater prestige of the natural sciences and the positivistic method in contemporary societies. Another reason is that most of the state-affiliated associations in modern societies that tend to organize and finance social scientific research are more interested in controlling subjects than in understanding them. In contemporary societies, when a hermeneutical interest is deemed desirable, it is often seen merely as a means of supplementing positivism.

In summary, the major presuppositions of interpretive theory are as follows:

1. There is no such thing as a sociological law—that is, a relationship among variables that remains constant through time and across different societies. Sociological variables are brought into existence and defined by means of human language.

2. The institutionalization of a language or a symbolic medium of interaction by which people communicate means that human action becomes meaningful in terms of social rules. People are not always aware of the existence of these rules (just as they are not always aware of the existence of muscles as they make a physical movement).

Nevertheless, these rules constitute the possibility of an act's being seen as meaningful—or of its being said to occur at all.

3. To test the accuracy of an interpretive theory, it is necessary to refer to human practice. Interpretive theory fails to receive corroboration when there is a disappointment of expectation within a context of communicative interaction. For instance, one's knowledge of a foreign language can be tested by seeing whether it is possible to give orders successfully in that language and to have such orders obeyed by performance of the actions one intended to produce through speech.

CRITICAL THEORY

There is no intrinsic antagonism between positivism and hermeneutical inquiry. An interest in technical control and a hermeneutic interest are not mutually exclusive. In fact, as we have seen, positivists have to be hermeneutically oriented to some degree in order to interpret the meaning of scientific data. There is, however, one very basic reason critical theory and positivism have to be mutually antagonistic. As we have seen, positivism leads the scientist to treat objective knowledge as if it were unconnected with any value orientation other than a dispassionate interest in "objective knowledge." But critical theory questions the ability of any style of theorizing to erect standards of proof or objectivity that can, themselves, be severed from human interests, human practice, or human agreement about what "proof" or "objectivity" could mean. Nonetheless, although positivistic investigation and critical theory are methodologically incommensurable (i.e., it would be a mistake to try to pursue the ends of both kinds of theory simultaneously), there is nothing in principle that would prevent sociologists from combining *results* extracted from positivistic explanation with a critical agenda. Marx, for example, definitely sought to identify the "laws" that explained revolutionary social rupture. But he also was interested in using theory as a means of showing how social environment might more fully be humanized.

As was noted earlier, critical theory draws our attention to methods of communicative interaction in order to discover how and why we organize our experience in a particular way. Critical theory goes beyond hermeneutics in expressing an interest in emancipation. First, it tries to make our use of language as transparent and as clear as possible, so that it becomes fully understandable to us; second, and *concomitantly*, it works to undermine the legitimacy of those social institutions that help to organize the means of exploitation or injustice. Although we can never directly understand physical reality, we can, potentially, understand language completely, for the structure of language is wholly produced by us and by our modes of interaction. Our understanding of self and other is, of course, contingent on our use of language. From this perspective, what creates artificial barriers among human beings, and what works to sustain the legitimacy of relations of authority that are intrinsically unjust, is not the inevitability of class, caste, or racial distinctions, but the opaqueness of language itself.[6]

As a particular type of orientation, positivism is morally indifferent. By this claim, we do not mean that science cannot help us to produce a better world: It can. Science, however, cannot help people to secure the *ends* of action, that is, tell them how to live. Moreover, as the sociologist Ernest Gellner has pointed out: "The price of genuine, powerful, technologically enriching science is that its style of explanation ruthlessly destroys those very notions in terms of which we identify ourselves."[7] By contrast, critical theory seeks to explain the ends of action, not the appropriate means to attain fixed ends. As we have seen, critical theory is value-orienting; it tries to tell us how we should live. Hence it competes not so much with science as with the dead hand of custom, habit, and tradition, which, as Marx once said, can weigh "like a nightmare on the brains of the living."[8]

Of course, the rise of positivism in the West has also done a great deal to undermine and destroy the traditions by which people used to live. For the most part, it would be difficult not to see this transformation as beneficial. Whereas people once used spells and incantations to ward off sickness, they now draw on the more effective resources of modern medical science. Whereas over 90 percent of the population once struggled to produce enough food for everyone, now, in the most technologically advanced part of the world, only a small part of the labor force has to work in agriculture. In more general terms, whereas people once took for granted abstractions and conceptualizations that served only to promote the interests of the church or of a tiny ruling elite, today (even though class divisions still persist) people can learn and apply abstractions and conceptualizations that serve to increase humankind's control over natural and social environments. Nevertheless, the rise of modern science occurred simultaneously with the decline of those all-encompassing feudal traditions that served to organize the experience of all individuals within a common or shared framework or tradition.

In modern societies, our experiences tend to be highly specialized, differentiated, and fragmented to an unprecedented extent. We have lost a sense of continuity with the past, and we have also lost the sense of community that characterized premodern societies and enabled traditional individuals to understand and take as unassailable their places in the social order. Whereas positivism encourages reductionism and a division of labor in intellectual work, critical theory encourages us to reflect on the way in which human actions and institutions are produced collaboratively by people who share a history. Thus critical theory is *holistic*, not reductionistic—that is, it relates parts to a whole or totality, rather than viewing such parts in isolation. Positivism encourages us to exercise control over particular aspects of our environment; it does not, however, permit us to reflect on the way in which our actions and social institutions are themselves produced by human activity, sometimes in ways that are not immediately obvious to us. As we have seen, positivism is not interested in reflecting on the relationship between human interests and styles of theorizing. Thus, from the perspective of critical theory, positivism is incapable of relating the type of society it produces to the style of theorizing it engenders.

Critical theory begins with an interest in interpreting the meaning of action in order to increase communicative interaction and to reproduce social life. It goes beyond hermeneutics, however, in the following way:

1. Critical theory assumes that it is possible to reflect on the use of language and thereby to come to a more complete understanding of the way in which reality is socially constructed.

2. In its examination of rules of interaction, critical theory assumes that people are not always aware of the rules by which they live and by which they organize their experience of the world. Thus such rules might have unintended consequences.

3. Critical theory is always a critique of the way in which people are constrained to act and to identify themselves in terms of particular social institutions. It analyzes the extent to which particular ideas help to sustain authority relations that are inherently unjust or repressive.

SOCIOLOGY AND THE CAUSALITY OF FATE

As can be seen from the preceding discussion, the social philosophical goal of critical theory is to sweep the process of knowing into the domain of what is known. Some critical theorists (such as Hegel) have come dangerously close to regarding the world as we know it as little other than a reflection of mind. But, although it must, of course, be reflective, critical theory does *not* have to resort to such rampant idealism.

For positivists, phenomenal reality is perceived by means of objectively verifiable data. For critical theorists, phenomenal reality is made up of what Peter Berger and Thomas Luckmann have called "the social construction of reality."9 "Reality," in other words, is already constituted by human practice, purpose, and will, but the processes that produced it are not necessarily known to the subjects it constrains. For critical and interpretive theorists, the dynamic opposition (or reciprocal interdependence) between conscious subjects and their objects of apprehension is the stuff from which reality emerges. With regard to such an opposition, we can say that:

1. Objects of attention are not merely the extension of subjective consciousness (the idealist fallacy). If they were, subjects could *think* the world into existence.

2. Subjects are not themselves wholly shaped by objective processes (the determinist fallacy). If they were, there would be no free will.

3. Subjects, nonetheless, do not have complete freedom to express themselves as they will (the romantic fallacy). If they did, there would be no constraints on human action.

Any theoretical orientation that is narrowly or one-sidedly idealist, determinist, or romanticist is partial and incomplete. Nonetheless, we must still acknowledge (1) that society is a human product in that it is we (collectively, historically and symbolically) who have made it; (2) that we human subjects are indeed constrained by socially produced objectifications (such as "classical literature," occupational categories, and formal law); and (3) that, in principle at least, we have the freedom to make the world other than it is. In this context, the purpose of critical theory is to defeat reification—in Berger's and Luckmann's terms, the paradox that "man is capable of producing a world that he then experiences as something other than a human product."10 Positivism, as we have seen, is predicated on a technical interest in prediction, manipulation, and control. But critical theory is based on a goal of changing the world—of making it other than it is. For critical theory, causality is not the causality of nature, which we experience as we search for deterministic relations among external (or objectified) variables that allow us to exercise control over what we take to be a separate reality. Rather, *causality* in critical theory refers to what Hegel called "the causality of fate"—something that we subject ourselves to as we respond to a world that was humanly created but that we experience as alien and impersonal. Freud, for instance, believed that neurotically disturbed individuals could be helped by giving them insight into the manner in which they have forced themselves to display rigid and compulsive "objectively necessary" modes of behavior for which they were unable to take responsibility. Marx, for his part, claimed that a just form of society could come into existence only when the working class freed itself from the reification of a dominant ideology that worked against its interests. The "causality of fate," therefore, can be overcome by the power of reflection and by the change in direction that insight can make possible. By contrast, the "causality of nature" is set in concrete by our interest in technical control.

CONCLUDING REMARKS

Sociology has always struggled to pass itself off as a science capable of generating objective knowledge, and it would be a distortion to discuss the history of sociology without making any reference to the promise or achievements of positivistic sociology. Nevertheless, it would be equally misleading to treat classical sociological theory as if it could be understood as something apart from the search for a fair and just society. To varying degrees, most of the men discussed in this book saw sociology as a humanistic discipline as well as a science. Above all, each of these figures tried to transcend, or go beyond, the categories of reality construction that were familiar in the societies from which they came.

A fundamental assumption that we make in this text is that a society produces its own category of functioning or means of social formation. In other words, our experience of ourselves, and our experience of the meaning of the actions of fellow human beings, emerge from our participation in social life. Yet, as we suggested earlier, the decline of tradition and the rise of modern science compel us to reflect on this process. Stripped of many of our illusions, and assured only of our grip on instrumentalism, today we have no choice but to participate self-consciously—and with critical self-insight—in the social construction of reality.

This conclusion certainly does not mean that interpretive or positivistic sociology is worthless or of secondary importance compared with critical theory. Positivism, for instance, will exist as long as humans value instrumental activity and wish to exercise a technical control over their natural and social environments. Interpretive theory, as we have seen, is constitutive of the very existence of social life. What should be emphasized, however, is that theorizing, in itself, can never be understood as a *human* activity unless we examine the relationship between knowledge and human interest, theory, and practice. The sociologist should not lose sight of the relationship between selecting a style of theorizing and choosing a way of life. If we fail to reflect on this relationship, the fate of sociology will be merely to mirror what it *now* must help to produce.

NOTES

1. Edward O. Wilson, *Sociobiology: The abridged version* (Cambridge, MA: The Belknap Press of Harvard University, 1980), p. 93.
2. See Carl G. Hempel & Paul Oppenheim, "Studies in the logic of explanation," *Philosophy of Science, 15* (April 1948), 135–175.
3. Brian Fay, *Social theory and political practice* (London: Allen & Unwin, 1975, paper), p. 39.
4. C. Wright Mills, *The sociological imagination* (New York Oxford University Press, 1959), p. 150.
5. See Hans-Georg Gadamer, *Truth and method* (Garrett Barden & John Cumming, trans.) (New York: Seabury, 1975).
6. All civilizations have had some understanding of this: "For now we see through a glass, darkly, but then face to face: now I know in part, but then shall I know even as also I am known." 1 Corinthians 13:12.
7. Ernest Gellner, *Legitimation of belief* (Cambridge: Cambridge University Press, 1974), p. 101.
8. Karl Marx, *The Eighteenth Brumaire of Louis Bonaparte.* Quoted in Robert C. Tucker (Ed.), *The Marx Engels reader* (New York: W. W. Norton, 1978), p. 595.
9. Peter L. Berger & Thomas Luckmann, *The social construction of reality: A treatise in the sociology of knowledge* (New York: Doubleday, 1966).
10. Ibid., p. 61.

GLOSSARY

Authority: Power that is *institutionalized* and seen as legitimate by the members of a collectivity.

Causality of fate: The causality affecting life chances that humans experience when they subject themselves to *institutions* that are humanly produced but that are perceived to be impersonal, unyielding, and inevitable in their effects.

Causality of nature: The causality among external, impersonal variables that is experienced by humans as they strive to exercise control over their *environments.*

Critical theory: Theory based on the reflective critique of language and oriented toward human emancipation.

Culture: All the assumptions and premises *internalized* by humans that organize the way in which reality is experienced.

Deduction: Logical process involving a claim to knowledge based on a series of propositions derived from a basic set of axioms or assumptions.

Deductive-nomological explanation: Explanation in which scientific laws act as premises in deductive reasoning.

Determinism: Metaphysical position that relates every event to preexisting events and that denies the possibility of human choice and free will.

Empirical inquiry: Inquiry that acknowledges the presence of an obdurate reality that is experienced as external to the human mind, with a structure and form that await discovery by a competent investigator.

Empiricism: Process involving a claim to knowledge based on some systematic form of sense observation (e.g., seeing, hearing, touching, etc.).

Environment: Natural or social phenomena that are seen as external to an observer.

Epistemology: A theory of the process by which humans can possess knowledge.

Externalization: The process by which humans create external institutional arrangements to which they must then adapt.

Hermeneutics: Interpretive theory that attempts to develop reciprocal understanding among humans in a process of *symbolic interaction.*

Holism: The idea that specific phenomena can be understood only in terms of some overarching totality or whole.

Idealism: Doctrine that states that reality consists of mental elements alone—for example, ideas, beliefs, mind, spirit, and so forth.

Ideographic explanation: The kind of understanding that treats elements of social reality as unique and as qualitatively different from other aspects of reality.

Ideology: The attempt to organize conceptions of authority and shared social commitments in order to deal with social, economic, and political problems.

Institution: A pattern of interaction among humans that is regularized and seen as meaningful.

Instrumentalism: An orientation that seeks to find the most effective means to achieve what are perceived to be fixed goals.

Internalization: The process by which humans learn the rules that define the institutional arrangements of a society.

Natural history: The development or evolution of species in their natural *environment.*

Natural selection: A natural process whereby organisms best fitted to survive in a given *envi-ronment* have a marginal advantage in passing on their genetic structures over those organisms relatively less fitted to survive.

Nomothetic explanation: Explanation that tries to explain orderly relationships in the world by reference to general laws.

Objectification: The process by which *institutions* that are humanly produced come to be seen as part of a fixed, external *environment.*

Positivism: Inquiry based on the methodology of the natural sciences that is produced by a technical interest and that seeks to predict and control changes in human environments.

Reductionism: The belief that phenomena should be described and explained in terms of more elementary units of analysis.

Reflection: The human ability to analyze the structure of communication.

Reification: The process by which *institutions* that were humanly produced are experienced involuntarily as objects of attention to which humans must adapt.

Sense impression: Information that comes to us via our senses—that is, through seeing, touching, hearing, smelling, or tasting.

Social construction of reality: The process by which human experience is organized within a context of social interaction.

Symbolic interaction: Interaction among humans who use symbols to evaluate the meaning of their speech and actions for others.

Tradition: "Naturelike" culture that is taken for granted and is not critically evaluated by the members of a society.

Value-free inquiry: The view that certain aspects of explanation do not rely on changing human values for their support.

B_y the review of the former social states of mankind, and the sketch of the future organization of society which I have now completed, I trust I have fully redeemed my promises, as offered both at the beginning of this work, and at the outset of the sociological portion. At a time when moral and political convictions are fluctuating for want of a sufficient intellectual basis, I have laid the logical foundation of firm convictions, able to withstand discordant passions, public and private. At a time when practical considerations are excessively preponderant, I have restored the dignity of philosophy, and established the social reality of sound theoretical speculations by instituting a systematic subordination of the one to the other, such as is essential to social stability and greatness. At a time when human reason is liable to be frittered away under an empirical system of dispersive specialty, I have announced, and even introduced the reign of the spirit of generality, under which alone a universal sentiment of duty can prevail.

These three objects have been attained by the institution of a new science, the last and most important of all, which is as positive and logical as any of the other sciences I have treated of, and without which the system of true philosophy can have neither unity or substance. The future progress of Sociology can never offer so many difficulties as this original formation of it; for it furnishes both the method by which the details of the past may serve as indications of the future, and the general conclusions which afford universal guidance in special researches. This scientific foundation completes the elementary system of natural philosophy prepared by Aristotle, announced by the scholastics of the Middle Ages, and directly proposed, in regard to its general spirit, by Bacon and Descartes. All that remains for me to do is to coordinate the elements which I have passed under review, in the form of six fundamental sciences, under the heads of Method, Doctrine, and the general unity of the positive philosophy.

—Auguste Comte,
The Positive Philosophy

3

(Isidore) Auguste Marie François- Xavier Comte

(1798–1857)

Life

Isidore Auguste Marie François-Xavier Comte was born in Montpellier, France, during an era of revolutionary upheaval so intense that a new calendar had been put into use. The date of his birth was accordingly recorded not as January 19, 1798, but as the thirtieth day of Nivôse in year VI of the French Republic. Many French citizens applauded the decline of the old order and the new promise of liberty, equality, and brotherhood for all, but Comte's parents were not among them. As staunch monarchists and conservative Roman Catholics, Felicité-Rosalie and Louis Auguste Comte were distraught over the fact that, because all the churches in Montpellier had been closed since 1793, they could not baptize their first child.

Yet, despite the turmoil around them, Comte's family continued to live in relative comfort. As a minor official working in a regional tax office, the cold and aloof Louis Auguste earned enough to provide adequately for his wife and his children Isidore, Alix (born in 1800), and Adolphe (born in 1802). Seven years older than her husband, Felicité-Rosalie had a deep concern for her children that served to offset the indifference of a father who spent most of his time tending his garden when he was not at his desk. But Isidore, who came to show a disdain for his father, soon became a source of distress to his mother. By the age of thirteen, he openly rejected his parents' deepest beliefs and declared himself to be a republican and a freethinker.

Comte's early education was with an elderly tutor who recognized his desire for learning of all kinds. Young Isidore "knocked at the tutor's door so early in the morning that he had to wait until the good man got out of bed to admit the small enthusiast."[1] At age nine, Comte was enrolled in a local residential military school, the *Lycée de Montpellier*. Mischievous but brilliant, he impressed his teachers with his ability to repeat long pages of text from memory. He was by far the best student at the school.

Having mastered all the courses taught at his school, Comte took the entrance exam for the *Ecole Polytechnique* in Paris. This school was, at the time, the most prestigious scientific institution in the world, whose curriculum later served as a model for the Massachusetts Institute of Technology. Although he passed the exam with the fourth highest score in all of France, Comte, at fifteen, was a year too young to be allowed to begin his studies there. So, before entering the school, he spent a year taking advanced courses in mathematics at a local university and teaching mathematics at the *Lycée de Montpellier*. Small in stature, the fifteen-year-old instructor had to stand on a box as he lectured on geometry, algebra, and calculus.

Once he entered the *Ecole Polytechnique*, which had been reorganized under Napoleon on a military basis, Comte spent his two years there wearing a uniform, undergoing military drills, living in barracks, and, at times, suffering strict (and occasionally arbitrary) discipline. The rigors of surviving the school's free education were rewarded on graduation with the guarantee of a good government job in the military or in some other public agency. Although he was respected by students and teachers alike for his superior academic performance, Comte repeatedly got in trouble for questioning authority and breaking curfew regulations. At one point in 1815, he was imprisoned by the school for two weeks for talking back to a school official. But, in 1816, a much more serious incident occurred that ended Comte's formal education along with his chance of pursuing a career in government.

An ardent republican who kept a copy of the Constitution of the United States in his desk, Comte took a central role in the informal political discussions that occurred among students after classes. His wit and humor made him a natural leader. This leadership role was apparent in a student protest against a dictatorial mathematics professor. The protest was pointed but peaceful, and later reports of a destructive student riot were untrue. Nevertheless, because of his participation in this demonstration, Comte was dismissed from the school on April 13, 1816. He was sent home, accompanied by police officers who told him and his parents that the young man was not to return to Paris. Mary Pickering, who has examined the available records of the whole affair, concluded that the incident was used as a pretense by pro-Royalist faculty to get rid of republican members of the student body.[2]

In Montpellier, a restless Comte took a biology course at the *Ecole de Médecine*, but he found life back home in the provinces with his conservative family intolerable. He grew to hate his sister, who espoused his parents' outlook and values. Ignoring the ban that had been placed on him, he returned to Paris in July 1816. However, when the newly independent young man was informed that he and his classmates could petition for readmission to the *Ecole Polytechnique* if they made a pledge of good conduct, Comte showed no interest in this offer. He did take money from his parents, though, and he let them assume that he was using these funds to get back into school. Failing to secure the engineering jobs that he applied for, Comte lived precariously for over a year as an intermittently employed private tutor. He spent much of his time attending the public scientific lectures and discussions that made the Paris of the day a center of scientific debate. Despite his extremely limited income, Comte's parsimony enabled him to attend the theater (an activity of which his parents would have disapproved) and also to enjoy the services of prostitutes (another activity his parents would not have found acceptable). He stopped buying sex after an affair with a married woman produced a daughter.

In 1817, Comte met Henri de Saint-Simon (1760–1825). Almost forty years Comte's senior, Saint-Simon had led an interesting life. Born to a French family of minor nobility, he had run away from the home of an authoritarian father at the age of nineteen, arrived in the United States during the American Revolution, and ended up as an officer and aide to General George Washington. After fighting in the final battle at Yorktown, Saint-Simon returned to France, and made and lost a number of fortunes before he devoted the rest of his life to philosophical pursuits. His goal was to develop an applied reformist philosophy suited to the industrial nature of modern society. Disorganized and contradictory in parts, Saint-Simon's philosophy looked to scientists to fulfill the role of society's new "spiritual leaders" who would help bring in an era of progress and social stability.

Lacking any formal education in science, Saint-Simon recognized in Comte a young energetic individual with the intellectual passion and scientific knowledge that made him capable of assisting him in his intellectual work. From 1817 to 1824, Comte worked as Saint-Simon's secretary and general assistant, editing, rewriting, and even producing first drafts of articles for him. In turn, the older philosopher provided Comte with a place to live, introduced him to leading members of society, and paid him a salary (when he was able). It was when Comte began his employment with Saint-Simon that, for unknown reasons, he dropped the use of his first name, and, henceforth, presented himself to the world as Auguste Comte.

In 1824, Comte and Saint-Simon had a falling out that led to a permanent rift between them. From the numerous recriminations traded by the two thinkers and their respective followers, it is impossible to be sure about the precise causes of this split. Among the explanations put forth are the young Comte's rejection of the religious elements that Saint-Simon began to incorporate into his work, his jealousy of the senior philosopher's fame, and his anger at Saint-Simon for publishing under his own name essays that Comte had written. Comte's disagreement with Saint-Simon over the need to systematically reorganize the sciences before meaningful social reforms were possible may have also contributed to the break. For Comte, such a systematizing was a necessity; for Saint-Simon, it represented useless delay. After leaving Saint-Simon, Comte worked again as a private tutor, and, occasionally, until 1851, as an entrance examiner for the *Ecole Polytechnique*. He also began to write a series of public lectures that would provide the basis of his first major work, *The Positive Philosophy* (1830–1842).

On May 3, 1821, Comte—who had begun to visit prostitutes again—met a Parisian streetwalker, Caroline Massine. According to Comte's account, Massine was born on July 2, 1802, the illegitimate daughter of two theatrical performers. After being raised by a loving maternal grandmother, Caroline was sent back to her mother in 1813 when her grandfather's death left her grandmother destitute. Recognizing an opportunity to make some money, Caroline's mother sold her daughter to a wealthy young lawyer. The lawyer left her when she was sixteen, the same year that her grandmother died. Seeing no alternative, Caroline became a prostitute in order to survive, and registered as such with the Paris police.

For six months, Comte visited Caroline regularly, but she then ended both their relationship and her career as a prostitute. She and Comte met again in 1823. They had a platonic friendship for a year before becoming lovers again. As Comte tells the story, he married her in 1824 to prevent her from returning to prostitution. Their civil ceremony was not accepted as legitimate by Comte's mother, who treated her daughter-in-law coldly on the couple's few visits to Montpellier.

Some marriages are made in heaven, but not this one. Comte expected his wife to show him gratitude for having saved her, and he expected her to defer to his beliefs. However, Caroline insisted on thinking for herself. Although she had had little formal education, she had read widely and had her own opinions on the issues of the day. Comte was infuriated when his wife disagreed with his dogmatic declarations. (Indeed, as he got older, he had less and less toleration for *anyone* who rejected his views and social agenda.) Their marriage, moreover, was complicated by constant money problems, as Comte failed to get any of the teaching positions for which he applied. Additionally, Caroline had to deal with his mother's intense dislike of her. Before long, Comte's intense bouts of jealousy and the periods of deep depression that had started before they met began to worsen. Clearly, their life together did not typify the ideal form of marriage that Comte portrayed in his writings, and, ultimately, after a number of separations, the partners agreed to a final parting in 1841.

In the spring of 1826, Comte began to develop a series of public lectures intended to systematize all scientific knowledge. These lectures were to provide the foundation for *The Positive Philosophy*. The first two lectures were but a partial success. Although a number of leading intellectuals were present, overall attendance was sparse. While feverishly preparing the third lecture, Comte suffered a mental breakdown. The stress of the lectures, combined with worry over his meager income and marital difficulties, contributed to his collapse. (Caroline had recently left Comte after he had flown into a rage at her suggestion that she could supplement their income by allowing private visits from a wealthy lawyer.) Comte was institutionalized for months, and Caroline was forced to care for him both during this period and later when her husband was released as "uncured."

Upon release, Comte continued to suffer from a depression that left him unable to work. He bitterly denounced the Catholic Church, signed his name "Brutus Napoleon Comte," and twice attempted suicide. After the second suicide attempt, when he was saved from drowning in the River Seine by a passing guard, Comte recovered sufficiently to begin to write again. Volumes of *The Positive Philosophy* were published in 1830, 1835, 1838, 1839, 1841, and 1842. Although Comte had previously used the term "sociology" (*sociologie*) in private correspondence, it was in *The Positive Philosophy* that this name for his proposed science of society first appeared in print.

In 1844, at the age of forty-six, Comte became enraptured with Clotilde de Vaux, a thirty-year-old minor novelist who was descended from an aristocratic family. At the age of twenty, she had married to escape a tyrannical father. Her husband, a minor government official, was discovered to have embezzled 15,000 francs, and disappeared when Clotilde was twenty-five. Thus, when Comte and de Vaux met, both were already married to other individuals.

Comte knew Clotilde for only two years before she died. Yet in Comte's final works, he credits de Vaux with showing him the significance of "love" in the maintenance of social harmony and social evolutionary progress. In the introduction to the *System of Positive Polity* (1851–1854), Comte credits her with having given him a "new birth." He refers to her as "my saint Clotilde" and writes, "I place her above all women that I have read of in the past, have seen in the present or can conceive [of] in the future."[3]

After de Vaux's death, Comte concentrated on the formulation of his ideas into a "religion of humanity." He erected an altar to Clotilde's memory and visited her grave every Wednesday. As Comte turned from social science to the creation of his own religion, he became increasingly hostile to all criticism of his thought. Obsessed by his mission, he assigned to himself the title "Great Priest of Humanity." Surrounded by a few totally dedicated followers, he lived an austere existence, and gave up all tobacco, coffee, and wine.

On September 5, 1857, directly after examining with a smile some shriveled flowers given him years earlier by his "Saint Clotilde," Auguste Comte died. He had left instructions to his devout followers that his rooms be preserved as he left them. Whether he can be credited with being the "founder" of sociology is debatable; that he was one of the first persons to envision the possibility of a science of society is uncontested.

Social Environment

Auguste Comte insisted that the goal of sociology was neither the development of idle speculation nor the production of solutions to abstract questions; rather, sociology involved the discovery of knowledge that would be of instrumental utility in the progressive improvement of society. Comte characterized his own society as in dire need of such improvement; throughout his work, he used France and the problems it confronted as a model for all of modern society and its problems. For Comte, his contemporary society lacked political order and spiritual unity, and was overrun with bureaucratic and governmental corruption, violent ideological disagreements, nonscientific dogma, and what Comte termed, in general, "intellectual chaos" and "moral anarchy."

Born only nine years after the great revolution of 1789, Comte grew up under a series of governments, each of which was incapable of successfully resolving chronic international conflicts and internal domestic crises. The government changed from the more or less democratic assemblies of the revolution (1789–1795), to the oligarchic control of the "Directories" (the antidemocratic and antimonarchical middle-class governments of 1795–1799), to the military expansionistic dictatorship of Napoleon (1799–1814), and finally to the restoration of the Bourbon monarchy (1814–1830). In the midst of these governmental changes, France suffered from rampant inflation and other economic difficulties, and was enmeshed in a series of foreign military and diplomatic entanglements. Even more than in other European nations, widespread economic and political problems in France generated serious religious turmoil.

Unlike most other Western and northern European nations, France had survived the Reformation era with the Roman Catholic Church as the sole recognized religious authority in the country. Protestants had generally been killed off or had fled to Germany, Britain, or Switzerland, with relatively few remaining in France; the Jews of eastern France were also a small minority who lacked many political and civil rights. Thus, despite various minor squabbles over power and authority between the church and the monarchy, prior to the revolution, the place of the Roman Catholic Church in France was secure. This security had been achieved with the aid of the French government, but at the price of accommodation to the monarchy. Upper-level positions in the church hierarchy in France were generally appointed only with the approval of the king; accordingly, they were filled from the ranks of the wealthy and powerful aristocrats. By the time of the 1789 revolution, the church hierarchy replicated, to a great extent, the class divisions of the country as a whole; its top positions were drawn from the nobility, the parish priests from the middle and lower levels of society.

Its accommodations with the old order and its control by the aristocracy marked the church as an enemy to many of the revolutionaries. Not surprisingly, in the course of the revolution, the powers of the church were restricted, its role in education was terminated, much of its land was confiscated, and many of the churches themselves were closed for a period of time. In the aftermath of the revolutionary upheavals of Comte's youth and adulthood, religious belief remained inseparable from political doctrine. Conservative Catholic monarchists and liberal democrats consistently opposed one another on all the issues of the day. Both groups were in turn the target of the nascent but growing socialist movements, whose spokespersons saw the revolution as having aided the bourgeois entrepreneurs, while accomplishing little to improve the lot of the working class.

For Comte, the goal of sociology was *to re-create a unified spiritual order that would help to institutionalize a new era of political and social stability.* Sociology was the science that would replace the anarchy of postrevolutionary political, religious, ideological, and class disputes by the discovery of natural laws of social order and change. Comte believed that sociology would also replace what he viewed as the failed doctrines of the Roman Catholic Church, without falling prey to the chaos of the ideological disputes then current in France. In sum, sociology was expected to end what Comte saw as the dissolution of the intellectual, political, and social harmony that had started in the late Middle Ages and culminated in the revolution and its resultant discord. Sociology was envisioned as the discipline that would scientifically diagnose the sociomoral ills of society and provide a blueprint for rebuilding France.

Intellectual Roots

One of the most important early influences on Comte's thought was the American philosopher, publisher, scientist, moralist, and diplomat Benjamin Franklin (1706–1790). After his return to Paris in 1816, the young Comte spent six months immersing himself in the study of English, and seriously considered emigration to the United States. Although he never did make the move, Comte was impressed with the possibilities of the new nation (and sent copies of his early work to both James Monroe and Thomas Jefferson). According to Pickering:

> What particularly inspired Comte was Franklin's code of secular . . . morality, which was grounded in scientific deductions from human nature and was supposed to lead to "moral perfection." . . . Comte considered Franklin the "modern Socrates" because he aimed to create a terrestrial morality, emphasizing virtuous simplicity and moderation. This morality would unite humanity by transcending divisive dogma.[4]

For the young Comte, Franklin provided the model of a man who had combined a skeptical scientific outlook with faith in progress and freedom, the acceptance of Enlightenment ideals, and a belief that one could discover rules for moral conduct that were not polluted by traditional religious dogma.

To show that these elements could be the foundation of a science of society required Comte to describe how such a science would look. In general terms, Comte's image of science is built on Francis Bacon's (1561–1626) conception that all scientific principles had to be grounded in empirical observation, on René Descartes's (1596–1650) views that all science, regardless of subject matter, exhibited a unity of method, and on Sir Isaac Newton's theory of gravity that focused on the study of relationships between objects without reference to either initial causes or ultimate goals.

Comte found the idea of a social science reflected in the works of numerous thinkers, foremost among whom was the French philosopher and legal theorist the Baron de Montesquieu (1689–1755). "Montesquieu taught Comte a scientific approach to social reality by stressing an empirical search for laws of both social variation and social development; such laws were to be based on concrete facts culled from all areas of the globe and all periods."[5] It was Montesquieu who laid the foundation for the comparative approach and for the classification of different types of societies that were central to Comte's methodological approach. He also was responsible for Comte's emphasis that society should always be viewed as an integrated entity whose parts could be studied and comprehended only in relationship to its totality.

Comte found additional ideas to support the development of a social science in the thought of the French theologian Jacques Bénigne Bossuet (1627–1704), the English philosopher Thomas Hobbes (1588–1679), the Italian political thinker Niccolò Machiavelli (1469–1527), and the French literary theorist and writer Germaine de Staël (1766–1817). Bossuet had argued that human society could be viewed as a natural phenomenon that developed according to logical rules; Hobbes had emphasized the existence of discoverable rules of social organization and political order; Machiavelli had shown the possibility of developing a dispassionate, technical analysis of the organization of government and its relationship to the rest of society; and de Staël provided the logical arguments for creating a "positive" social science that would share a scientific approach with the physical sciences, while simultaneously showing how to integrate a modern "spirituality" into an industrial society.

By 1824, Comte had come to appreciate the ideas of a set of Scottish thinkers whose formulations became increasingly important to him. These "common sense" moral philosophers included Adam Ferguson (1723–1816), William Robertson (1721–1793), Adam Smith (1723–1790), and David Hume (1711–1776). Comte approved of their attempts to establish moral principles on an empirical and secular foundation; he also liked their emphases on cumulative social progress, their belief in laws of social change, their view that it was the division of labor that made much social and industrial progress possible, their acceptance of the "natural" sociability of humans, and their image of science as something that focused on observable relationships (as opposed to the search for "metaphysical" or "first" causes of things).

Comte, himself, believed that three individuals had been particularly important in the development of his thought: Franz Joseph Gall (1758–1828), the Marquis de Condorcet (1743–1794), and Joseph de Maistre (1753–1821). Gall was a German physiologist whose course Comte took. Although Comte was not particularly influenced by his ideas, he did see Gall as a role model. He also believed Gall had moved physiology from a "metaphysical" to a "positive" scientific field of study—an achievement that Comte intended to match in sociology.

Comte's claim that he was strongly influenced both by Condorcet and by de Maistre has puzzled many observers, but it does point to Comte's ability to borrow from and synthesize seemingly contradictory viewpoints. Condorcet was a participant in the French Revolution of 1789. He detested the institutions of the Middle Ages, and his optimistic work stressed the importance of individual freedom, science, and the inevitability of progress by means of changes in human understanding, perception, and action. By contrast, de Maistre opposed virtually everything that Condorcet advocated. He was an antirevolutionary, conservative, Catholic thinker who was sympathetic to the communal structures and institutionalized traditional authority of the Middle Ages and who valued the rituals and spiritual authority of the church as a source of social order. Comte took from Condorcet a view of social evolution as something that passed through various stages in its movement toward a rational scientific society. He developed Condorcet's methodological approach of focusing on diverse historical and ethnographic data *as if* such data represented the development of a single society, and merged this model with de Maistre's concept of society as a living, integrated, organic entity, together with de Maistre's anti-Enlightenment argument that a stress on individual rights and freedom generated antisocial egoism.

Unsurprisingly, Comte's work exhibits persistent tension regarding the aforementioned positions of Condorcet and de Maistre. The scientific optimism of Comte's "dynamic" sociology exists side by side with his organic, "static" sociology that stresses the need to constrain individuals in order to keep them from antisocial self-aggrandizement. Comte's belief in scientific rationality and individual freedom is joined by an emphasis on the need for public rituals and the creation of a new "spiritual" authority. And Comte's presentation of himself as the greatest living scientist ultimately merges with his declaration that he is, in addition, the "high priest of humanity."

Finally, when we look at Comte's intellectual roots, we must also consider the influence of his estranged mentor, Saint-Simon. There is considerable debate concerning this issue. Some have argued that Comte was directly building on Saint-Simon's ideas; others have insisted that Saint-Simon was only a limited and temporary influence on Comte and that Comte's own mature work owed nothing to the older philosopher. The evidence does tend to support the latter view. On the other hand, Comte's belief that society developed from a state of militant warfare to an industrially based organization does clearly parallel the position taken by Saint-Simon. On this point, at least, the influence of Saint-Simon is evident.

IDEAS

Society

Comte's sociology rests on an assumption of social realism—a position that can be traced (through de Maistre and others) back to medieval French Catholic philosophy. For Comte, as for others in this tradition, society exhibits a "real" existence in which it manifests properties other than and separate from those manifested by particular individuals or mere aggregations of individuals. For Comte, society was a "real being"—an entity with its own "organic" structure, systematic properties, determinant patterns of change, and definite and predictable variations and influences.

Comte's social realism was so extreme that he insisted that, whereas society is real, the individual exists only as an "abstraction." The denial of individual life as having an independent existence from social reality is clearly demonstrated in Comte's hierarchical classification of the sciences. Comte presented sociology as directly following biology in reference to the complexity of the "reality" on which each science focuses. With his denial of an individual reality, Comte excluded psychology (or any equivalent field) from an intermediate position between the science of living organisms (biology) and the science of society (sociology). What most theorists would view as individual psychological phenomena (thoughts, feelings, wishes, etc.), Comte ascribed to either biological or social reality.

Comte viewed society as real in both a spatial and a temporal sense. For him, society existed as a "continuous whole." At any one point in time, a society's parts are related to one another in specifiable and scientifically lawful relationships; across time, society links one era to another in specific and predictable actions. Thus *the social organism parallels a biological entity as a coordinated system of parts, each of which is engaged in different but mutually supportive activities.*

Comte argued that, structurally, the most fundamental unit of society, upon which its organization is dependent, is the family:

> As every system must be composed of elements of the same nature with itself, the scientific spirit forbids us to regard society as composed of individuals. The true social unit is certainly the family—reduced, if necessary, to the elementary couple which forms its basis. This consideration implies more than the physiological truth that families become tribes, and tribes become nations: so that the whole human race might be conceived of as the gradual development of a single family, if local diversities did not forbid such a supposition. There is a political point of view from which also we must consider this elementary idea, inasmuch as the family presents the true germ of the various characteristics of the social organism. Such a conception is intermediate between the idea of the individual and that of the species, or society. There would be as many scientific inconveniences in passing it over in a speculative sense as there are dangers in practice in pretending to treat of social life without the inevitable preparation of the domestic life. Whichever way we look at it, this necessary transition always presents itself, whether in regard to elementary notions of fundamental harmony, or for the spontaneous rise of social sentiment. It is by this avenue that Man comes forth from his mere personality, and learns to live in another, while obeying his most powerful instincts.[6]

Comte argued that it is families that produce individuals, and not individuals that produce families. As social entities, families are "real"; individuals removed from families, however, exist only as "abstract entities." Comte held that families combine to form cities and cities combine to form societies. Within cities, families serve as functional parts in accomplishing tasks necessary for the city as a whole; as virtually complete functioning entities in themselves, cities are held together by the actions of political or governmental forces to form the greater organism of a society. Comte believed that, ultimately, all the societies on earth would combine as the functional parts of an even greater entity—the "great being" of humanity. The evolution of society (considered as a single entity) toward this "great being" forms the basics of Comte's "social dynamics."

Central to Comte's dynamic formulation of society is the belief that all social organisms go through a process of innately generated, gradual, cumulative, determinable change from a state of "social infancy" to one of maturity. This belief underlies Comte's famous "law of three stages." In terms of the law of three stages and on the basis of his studies of the history of science and other social institutions, Comte maintained that *all societies develop at a gradual rate from what he termed a "theological stage" to a "positive stage," passing through an intermediate, transitional, and chaotic "metaphysical stage."*

Comte presented his three stages of social development mentalistically—that is, in terms of changes in how the world is usually, generally, and collectively understood and thus acted toward. The theocratic stage involves the explanation of events in terms of the will or actions of humanlike gods, spirits, demons, ghosts, or other supernatural beings. In the metaphysical stage, events of the external world are understood in terms of innate essences, original causes, underlying natures, and inherent teleological tendencies. As opposed to the preceding two stages, in the final and mature "positive" social stage, phenomena are explained solely in terms of observable scientific relationships, without regard for supposed inherent propensities, original causes, or actions of supernatural agencies. Thus, for Comte, the evolution of society is characterized by a long-run transition from a social organization based on a supernatural understanding to one based on objective scientific understanding.

Comte drew on ethnographic and Western (particularly French) historical data to illustrate the predominant characteristics of the "theological" stage of society. He divided this stage into three substages or periods—"fetishistic," "polytheistic," and "monotheistic." These periods appear in a determinable order, and—just as the first two major stages prepare the way for the third, "positive" stage—each substage produces the development of social elements that prepare the way for the emergence of succeeding progressive social change. Comte's analogy between societal change and the cumulative growth of a single biological organism led him to deny the possibility that sociocultural diffusion could lead to any major departure from this particular sequence.

Fetishism formed the earliest period of human mental and social activity. Simply put, *fetishism* involves the view that every object in existence is alive and exhibits humanlike spiritual, motivational, and affective qualities. Supernaturalism thus permeates all spheres of social activity. Rocks, trees, rivers, tools, cooking pots, weapons, and all other artifacts encountered daily are seen as having the ability to undertake willful acts that can help, hinder, or be irrelevant to human social activities. Comte reasoned that little abstract or reflective thought would develop during a period in which any event could be explained by ascribing it to the will or desire of some object. (For example, the death of an individual by drowning would not inspire reflection on the ultimate meaning of life and death but would be seen merely as the actions of some malevolent river spirit.) Comte further reasoned that the absence of analytical thought and the existence of daily encounters with supernatural agencies in the course of one's practical affairs would remove the possibility of fetishistic society ever producing any hierarchical priestly organization with power over the rest of society. The lack of abstract thought precluded the development of complex theological explanations, and the daily encounter with supernatural forces did not create a felt need for a professional religious group to interpret and intercede with spiritual forces for the benefit of the rest of the society.

Comte maintained that the social bonds that united fetishistic society would be weak in comparison with those that later evolutionary progress would produce. The perceived existence of both beneficial and dangerous personal, familial, and local spirits would do little to develop either broadly shared collective values and ideas or a sense of overall collective social unity. Yet Comte did see the fetishistic period as giving rise to the domestication of animals, agriculture, military organization, commerce, and the production and use of currency. Accordingly, Comte held that the greatest significance of the fetishistic period of society was the origin of social activities and social organization upon which later social progress would be elaborated and built.

Comte theorized that the "highest" form of fetishism—star worship—served as a transitional phase to the polytheistic period of the theological stage. With star worshipers arose soothsayers and conjurers, from whom, eventually, the first priests arose. A conception of the stars' (and other heavenly bodies') impact on people's lives (what Comte termed "astrolatry") provided a foundation for a conception of anthropomorphic deities who concerned themselves with human affairs. With the development of polytheism, the objects of the world were no longer perceived as having their own spirits, but instead were viewed as lifeless, inert substances, capable of being manipulated by the arbitrary will of a collection of deities. At first, each specific deity ruled over a particular related set of objects and events. Comte claimed that contemplation of the relationship between the actions of the supposed deities on this-worldly events led to the origin of focused observation of, and abstract reflection upon, reality. According to Comte, such observation and reflection formed the germ from which scientific analysis would develop in later social evolution.

Comte presented the polytheistic era as the longest period of social evolution. It was characterized by the rise of combined priest-kings, an organized priestly group, aggressive expansionist warfare, the emergence of slavery, and the development of the arts and aesthetic appreciation. Despite his criticism of aggressive warfare and slavery in more advanced societies, Comte argued that in the polytheistic period, both institutions served the purpose of expanding the size and cohesion of society and helped make possible the accomplishment of larger collective enterprises of greater endurance than those that had been previously undertaken. Meanwhile, the priestly group, removed from mundane activities (despite its use of most of its time to contemplate supposed deities and their actions) did spend time and effort in developing nascent "scientific" research, technological innovation, and the aesthetic and the practical arts (such as medicine). Comte also believed that the aggressive warfare of this period led to an infusion of militaristic moral ideas throughout the whole of polytheistic society. (Indeed, in that polytheism is the longest period of the theological stage, Comte often referred to the whole stage as one of aggressive warfare, while associating the "metaphysical stage" with "defensive warfare" and the "positive stage" with industrialism.)

Comte subdivided the polytheistic period of theological society into three consecutive phases—the Egyptian, the Greek, and the Roman. Despite their names, Comte presented these as general evolutionary developments, not merely as manifestations of particular societies. Egyptian polytheism was characterized by a strict caste division between an upper priestly caste and a lower caste in a position of "collective servitude." Greek polytheism represented the breakdown of the previously highly stable caste division and the rise of intellectual investigations, especially the development of mathematics and philosophical speculation. Roman polytheism was oriented toward warfare and represented increased organization of social development achieved in the Egyptian and Greek phases. With its emphasis on a hierarchy of gods subjected to the control of a single most powerful god, Roman polytheism served as a transitional phase for the development of monotheism.

For Comte, the monotheistic period constituted the final period of the theological stage of society. He believed that once a society reached a period wherein phenomena were explained predominantly in reference to a single deity in the form of an all-powerful god, theological thinking would have exhausted its explanatory utility and evolutionary development. Comte explicitly based his analysis of monotheism on its Roman Catholic form as it was manifested in central and western Europe. A monotheistic society was organized in terms of the separation of religiomoral authority (represented by the church) and secular political authority (held by governments). Under monotheism, the moral authority of the church was international and constrained the actions of local and national secular authorities. Comte believed that the openness of the church hierarchy to entrants from all levels of society broke up the upper-caste dominance of theological speculation. Socially, the monotheistic society manifested a feudal organization; the slavery that characterized polytheistic society was replaced by serfdom, and relations of power were replaced by those of feudal mutual obligation and duty. Comte held that the origin and spread of the feudal institution of chivalry significantly improved the lot of women by respecting what he argued were the inherently different capacities of the two sexes. Overall, he argued that within the monotheistic period, there was both less interest in warfare and a rise in collective feelings and expressions of universal brotherhood. This period also produced advances in music, art, and industry (for example, water- and windmills), and the formulation of proto-social-evolutionary theories in the form of "universal histories" (such as the writings of Bossuet), which began to lay the foundation that Comte claimed would lead eventually to his own sociological formulations. Additionally, and most importantly, monotheism developed forms of metaphysical speculation that would lead to a rejection of theological explanations of reality by intellectuals, and hence would lead to the end of the theological stage of social development and its replacement by the brief but tumultuous "metaphysical stage."

To appreciate fully his criticisms of his own society and his belief in the necessity of creating a sociologically guided reformation of the social order, one must understand that Comte insisted that the metaphysical stage of social evolution could be understood only as a *transitional* era between the theological and positive stages. It was an essentially "critical" or "negative" state—a stage in which the intellectual foundation and feudal institutional structure of monotheistic society were destroyed in the absence of any permanent forms of social organization to replace them. Accordingly, it was a stage of disharmony, conflict, and chaos. For Comte, the metaphysical stage was thus only an "irresistible necessity" in the sense that the destruction of old social forms cleared the way for the later emergence of positive society.

In *The Positive Philosophy*, at the outset of his discussion of the metaphysical stage, Comte wrote:

> Turning now to the Metaphysical polity, we must first observe and carefully remember that its doctrine, though exclusively critical, and therefore revolutionary, has still always had the virtue of being progressive, having, in fact, superintended the chief political progress accomplished during the last three centuries, which must be, in the first instance, essentially negative. What this doctrine had to do was to break up a system which, having directed the early growth of the human mind and society, tended to protract that infantile period: and thus, the political triumph of the metaphysical school was a necessary preparation for the advent of the positive school, for which the task is exclusively reserved of terminating the revolutionary period by the formation of a system uniting Order with progress. Though the metaphysical system, considered by itself, presents a character of direct anarchy, an historical view of it, such as we shall take hereafter, shows that, considered in its origin, and in its antagonism to the old system, it constitutes a necessary provisional state, and must be dangerously active till the new political organization which is to succeed it is ready to put an end to its agitations.[7]

Comte used western European history from the Reformation to the end of the French Revolution to illustrate the metaphysical stage, which he subdivided into two periods: the "Protestant" and the "deistic."

For Comte, the first period of the metaphysical stage, Protestantism, created a negative philosophy that undermined the doctrine and organization of the Catholic Church. Even in nominally Catholic nations, national churches replaced the international moral authority of the Catholic Church, thereby freeing secular political thought and actions from the constraints of a larger religiomoral social authority and organization. The decentralized feudal system, which had depended on the church organization for support, in turn disintegrated. It was replaced by the rise of the nation-state under the control of a single monarch, who was supported by centralized ministries and a powerful standing army. The Protestant period also saw the subordination of the clergy to secular authorities, which in turn opened up the possibility of the critical or metaphysical doctrines that would be developed in the deistic period of the metaphysical stage.

The deistic period represented the full development of the metaphysical stage. It was characterized by a rational critique of theistic doctrines, assertions of the right to free intellectual inquiry and criticism, and attempts to account for and reorganize social order in terms of supposed inherent natural rights. Comte asserted that the naturalistic philosophies of this period were de facto of a dogmatically atheistic nature—replacing "God" with "nature" as their focal point. Comte noted that, in Europe, the ideas of the critical deistic philosophers were popularized by Voltaire (1694–1778) and turned toward political criticism by Jean-Jacques Rousseau (1712–1778). The outbreak of the French Revolution was, for Comte, the ultimate outcome of their individualistic—and therefore antisocial—doctrines. The failure of the revolutionary governments to establish a permanent social harmony based on the "natural rights" of liberty, equality, and brotherhood demonstrated to Comte the inability of metaphysical thinking to create a new social order; it thus revealed to him that the metaphysical stage was to be a passing "negative" era to be replaced by a "positive" era of social reconstruction. Yet Comte judged metaphysical society as progressive in its creation of centralized authority, increased industrial development, the abolition of serfdom, and increased scientific inquiry.

Comte's dynamic view of society culminates with his formulation of "positive society." *In the positive stages of society the world was explained in terms of neither supernatural agencies nor innate natural rights or propensities, but instead in terms of scientific observation of the relationships of events.* Comte held that the scientific view had been long in its development and was completed only with his own formulation of "sociology." Comte thus maintained that positive society was coming into existence only with the publication of his own works. He believed that with a creation of a science of society, sociological laws could be developed that would show how to organize modern industrial society into a harmonious order—an order that would have all the benefits of the stable medieval society without the faults inherent in a theological world view. In his later years, Comte began to describe in great detail what he perceived to be the emerging structure of positive society. His image of the future (which will be discussed later in this chapter) was sufficiently unusual to alienate a number of Comte's early followers and to raise questions by later generations of sociologists about the value of examining Comte's sociological thought. Simply put, Comte envisioned positive society as a hierarchical social order under the control of "sociological priests," with a high priest located in Paris. These priests, through the control of education, would disseminate scientifically correct views throughout society, which in turn would lead to a scientifically based harmony among the various parts of society. Comte saw positivistic society as eventually spreading to encompass first all the countries of Europe and then the entire world. He thus concluded that his dynamic conception of society could be seen as the growth of a single social organism from infancy to maturity into a single harmonious world order (see Table 3.1).

Comte thus conceptualized society *statically,* as a *social organism of interrelated parts,* and *dynamically,* in terms of *mentalistically based evolutionary stages and substages.* In other words, Comte viewed society as manifesting both a physiological system of related organs at any one point in time and a growth toward mental maturity

TABLE 3.1 Comte's Stages of Social Evolution

STAGE	PERIOD	PHASE
I. Theological (understanding based on ascription of events to wills of supernatural agencies)	Fetishistic	Pre–star worship Star worship
	Polytheistic	Egyptian Greek Roman
	Monotheistic	
II. Metaphysical (understanding based on assumption of essences, first causes, and teleological predisposition)	Protestant Deistic	(None given)
III. Positive (understanding based on observation of relationships between events)	(None given)	(None given)

across time. Unfortunately, to most present-day sociologists who read his multivolume works, Comte's formulation of society presents some conceptual difficulties. His organic view of social statics is extremely abstract and lacking in the precise examples to be found in later works (such as those of Herbert Spencer). This weakness is especially notable in Comte's failure to specify the particular ways in which the "social organism" structurally *differs* from a biological organism. Also problematic are attempts to understand what Comte meant by his declarations that society is "real" and individuals only "abstractions." Comte seemed to go beyond a statement that social reality is constituted by its own organizational attributes and developmental patterns (as Durkheim later argued), without explicitly clarifying what he was asserting. Comte's denial of individual reality creates even more problems when he expresses social dynamic evolution in mentalistic terms. If individuals have only an abstract reality, where is this mental evolution taking place? It is certainly not purely biologically determined; Comte explicitly rejected a biological reductionist explanation of social reality.

Comte's general dynamical view of society is made difficult to understand by his use of specifically European (and especially French) historical details to illustrate his position. Despite his insistence that he was discussing general and universal patterns of change, Comte used very specific European historical illustrations, and even labeled eras of development "Greek," "Roman," and "Protestant." To what extent he believed, for example, that other, non-European societies would go through processes parallel to the Protestant Reformation, the French Revolution, the reign of terror, the rise of Napoleon, and so forth remains entirely unspecified.

Finally, Comte's "law of three stages" relegates teleological reasoning to the transitional era he referred to as the "metaphysical state" of society and asserts that such reasoning will be supplanted in positive society by scientific formulations based on the observation of relationships. Yet, Comte's overall social evolutionary formulation (his "dynamic" theory) is, itself, fundamentally a teleological argument that presupposes that society has an innate tendency to develop in one particular direction. In other words, Comte's own central arguments that he claimed would serve as a foundation for a new scientific order do not meet the most basic criterion that he himself establishes for valid scientific knowledge.

The Individual in Society

Rather than viewing individuals as rational components of a society, Comte saw them as beings whose affective or emotional instincts tended to dominate their rational intellectual abilities and whose self-centered emotions would, without adequate social control, dominate altruistic or socially oriented feelings. Comte asserted that individuals so constructed were incapable of self-control; in order to live together harmoniously, they needed to be under the influence of socially generated restraint and control.

In terms of their affective makeup, Comte maintained that individuals had evolved biologically with three fundamental types of instincts—"egoistic instincts," "intermediate instincts," and "social instincts." Egoistic instincts were defined by Comte as biologically innate propensities from which behaviors aimed purely at self-gratification emerge. He subdivided egoistic instincts into "instincts of preservation" and "instincts of improvement." Instincts of preservation, in turn, involved three separate instinctual drives—a "nutritive" instinctual drive (including a drive for food and shelter), a "sexual" instinctual drive, and a maternal instinctual drive. Instincts of improvement were divided by Comte into "destructive" (or "military") and "constructive" instincts. The former involved a drive to improve one's circumstances through combative behavior; the latter would accomplish the same end through productive activity.

Intermediate instincts are those that Comte claimed existed between egoistic and social instincts. These are personal in nature but social in the object of their action. Comte pointed out two such instincts—the "instinct of pride" (or the "love of power"), which creates leadership abilities and aids the achievement of collective ends, and the "instinct of vanity" (or the "love of approbation"), which inspires actions that, to a degree, are of social benefit.

Last, but most important, social instincts are those innate propensities that allow one to exist in society by subordinating oneself to the demands and concerns of the greater social organism. The three social instincts in Comte's work are those of "attachment," "veneration," and "universal love" (or "goodness"). The instinct of attachment bonds the individual to one other person. Under its influence, one is willing to sacrifice oneself for the benefit of the other. The instinct of veneration is broader in scope. Under the sway of this instinct, the individual is capable of self-sacrifice that benefits a social group or community, ranging in size from the family to the nation. The most developed social instinct is that of "universal love," which underlies those actions and individual sacrifices that are aimed at benefiting humanity as a whole.

Comte maintained that the "lower" the instinct, the greater its "energy." Thus without socially generated constraints (through education and other moral forces), the individual would be more likely to engage in actions based on the lower egoistic instincts than on the higher intermediate instincts or the highest social instincts. Similarly, within the social instincts, without external social constraint, instincts of attachment and veneration would predominate over the highest instinct: universal love.

Comte followed his discussion of instincts with an analysis of human intellectual capacities, which he divided into "faculties of conception" and "faculties of expression." The former has two distinct functions—"contemplation" and "meditation." Contemplation involves the "passive" reception of ideas; meditation implies the "active" construction of thoughts based on those received ideas. Comte further divided contemplation into "synthetic contemplation," which is concerned with concrete objects, and "analytical contemplation," which deals with events. Meditation is likewise divided into "inductive meditation" and "deductive meditation." The former involves the production of comparisons that lead to static generalizations about reality; the latter involves the coordination of generalizations and the production of dynamic systematic generalizations. "Faculties of expression" refer essentially to language abilities. Comte wrote that this intellectual function combines all other intellectual elements and allows social continuity from one generation to the next.

A third and final component of the individual's makeup was termed by Comte the "active functions" of the individual. Comte presented three active functions: "courage in undertaking," "prudence in execution," and "firmness in accomplishment." Just as all individuals possess more or less the same fundamental affective and intellectual makeup, so they also possess some degree of courage, prudence, and firmness (see Table 3.2).

TABLE 3.2 Comte's Typologization of Human Attributes

TYPE OF ATTRIBUTE

Affective (Emotional)	*General Instincts*	*Subtype of Instinct*	*Specific Instinct*
	Egoistic	Preservation	Nutritive
			Sexual
			Maternal
		Improvement	Destructive
			Constructive
	Intermediate	Pride	
		Vanity	
	Social	Attachment	
		Veneration	
		Universal love	
Cognitive (Rational)	*Faculties*	*Function*	*Subfunction*
	Conception	Contemplation	Synthetic contemplation
			Analytical contemplation
		Meditation	Inductive meditation
			Deductive meditation
	Expression		
Active Functions	*Type*		
	Courage		
	Prudence		
	Firmness		

According to Comte, contemporary individuals, in the course of maturation, develop their own intellectual abilities in a manner parallel to the way society as a whole develops. That is, in the course of intellectual growth a child goes through stages of reasoning similar to the theological, metaphysical, and finally positive forms of thought. But Comte maintained that intellectual ability is not equally distributed in all individuals. In fact, Comte claimed that intellectual variations in the human species were greater than the obvious variations in physical abilities. Comte believed that only a small minority would ever reach the highest level of intellect and understand the world, in all its manifestations, in a positivistic scientific manner.

Although Comte rejected ethnic and racial accounts of variations in intellectual ability, he did assert that the two genders were intellectually unequal. Comte incorporated into his sociology a belief in the intellectual superiority of men over women. This is somewhat perplexing when one considers Comte's acquaintance with a number of women of high intellectual ability, such as his English translator, Harriet Martineau

(1802–1876), and his long friendship with John Stuart Mill (1773–1836), who openly disagreed with Comte's position on women's intellectual and occupational abilities. Although he called for equality in basic education, Comte held that only males had the intellectual ability to become sociologists and to understand a scientific examination of social reality. Yet despite the argued intellectual superiority of men, Comte maintained that women were more important, overall, in the maintenance of social order. He insisted that, if men had superior intellect, women were superior in the affective development of social instincts. Comte pointed out that, whereas only a small percentage of a society's population would even be involved in advanced scientific undertakings, all women serve social order by encouraging and providing children and men with examples of socially oriented, altruistic actions. Thus he believed that women's influences control the actions of men and children and thereby make social harmony possible. Accordingly, Comte argued that if society is to be made more harmonious, it must increase the influence that women have over men:

> All classes, therefore, must be brought under women's influence, for all require to be reminded constantly of the great truth that Reason and Activity are subordinate to Feeling. Of their influence upon philosophers I have spoken. These, if they are men worthy of their mission, will be conscious of the tendency which their life has to harden them and lead them into useless speculation; and they will feel the need of renewing the ardour of their social sympathy at its native source. Feeling, when it is pure and deep, corrects its own errors, because they clash with the good to which it is ever tending. But erroneous use of the intellectual or practical faculties cannot be even recognized, much less corrected, without the aid of Affection, which is the only part of our nature that suffers directly from such errors. Therefore whenever either the philosopher or the people deviate from duty, it will be the part of women to remonstrate with them gently, and recall them to the true social principles which are entrusted to their special charge.[8]

Methodology

Starting with Comte's earliest writings, one finds a persistent attempt to delineate precisely what the methods of research ought to involve. For Comte, the sociologist as a scientist is to be concerned with positivistic "observation." The goal of the observer is to link observed facts with more general statements and to reduce the number of general statements to a system of the fewest number of statements sufficient to account for the phenomena with which one is concerned. As an observational science, sociology is to exclude "metaphysical" concern with "essential natures" and the "first causes" of things. It is, instead, to focus on static and dynamic relationships. The result of the sociological enterprise is thus to be *the enumeration of the fixed and invariable laws of social statics and dynamics.* Comte's assumption of the discoverability of "invariable laws" was based on a strict deterministic view of social reality and a rejection of the possibility of an individual or group having the capability to choose to act contrary to the laws of social existence.

Despite Comte's emphasis on the observation of relationships, he also held to a belief in the necessity of the development of systematic theory *prior* to research. For Comte, one must start by deducing what to observe from a general systematic theory. Without the guidelines offered by such a general theoretical orientation, Comte argued, the sociologist would be lost when confronting the vast complexities and multiple occurrences of social life. The sociologist, accordingly, would produce poor results and be incapable of producing an overall explanation of social relationships. Although Comte took the position that theoretical deductions should guide research, he also argued that conclusions induced from sociological observations should be used to modify and expand the scope of the original theoretical conceptions. Comte thus claimed that his own assertions about social reality had been proved or verified, not in terms of modern tests of validity but by having amassed a great number of observed relationships that had modified and that fitted the contours of his original theoretical assertions.

Comte's approaches to the study of static and dynamic social relationships rest on an important assumption. In terms of social statics, he assumed that the parts of society formed an integrated whole and manifested a tendency toward order and harmony. Thus *the parts of society always had to be studied in relationship to the totality, and observed disharmonies were assumed to be temporary.* In the study of social dynamics, Comte assumed that one could take observations from many societies and, with the aid of a theory of social evolution, assume that these observations could be viewed *as if* they had come from a single society over a long period of development.

Two assumptions made by later sociologists that Comte rejected involved the use of mathematical procedures and materialistic forms of explanation. Mathematically expressed theories in general were rejected as lacking utility in the study of the organic relationships of statics and the evolutionary relationships of dynamics. Comte saw them as requiring a precision of measurement useful only in the simpler physical and chemical sciences, and thus as being incapable of dealing with the complex relationships of the biological and social sciences. Probability mathematics was held to be especially useless in sociological research; Comte maintained (mistakenly) that the notion of probability assumed an idea of chance and thus was incompatible with the assumption of determinism necessary to all scientific endeavors. Materialistic explanations, like mathematical theories, Comte held to be useful only in the simpler and less complex sciences; thus their use in sociology would represent a lack of appreciation for the unique lawful relationships to be found in social reality.

Comte presented direct observation, experimentation, and comparison as the specific observational methods that he believed a sociologist could use. He cautioned direct observers to apply a specific theoretical viewpoint, lest their results be "vague and incoherent." As for the types of phenomena to be observed, Comte suggested that the researcher might focus on such occurrences as social customs, forms of languages, and collectively erected monuments and other collective symbols. Although direct observation was seen as easily accomplished, direct (or manipulative) experimentation was presented as not possible in sociological research. Instead, Comte suggested the use of "indirect experimentation," by which he actually meant the analysis of two similar or parallel instances of the same social relationship. Finally, by comparison, Comte was in fact presenting three distinct approaches: the comparison of human to nonhuman societies (such as insect societies), the comparison of societies at the same level of development, and the comparison of societies at different levels of development. The first two forms of comparison were held to be most useful in social static research; the third form, which Comte often referred to as the "historical method," served as the foundation for Comte's dynamic sociology. Of course his actual use of this "historical method" was never meant to question his overall dynamic theory of social evolution, but only to seek evidence that would appear to support it.

Comte insisted that the "historical method" was the most characteristic of, and useful in, sociological analysis. It segregated sociology from biology and from traditional (and noncomparative) history, and it allowed one to see across time the relationship of parts of society to the whole in terms of progressive social development:

> The historical comparison of the consecutive state of humanity is not only the chief scientific device of sociology in a logical as well as a scientific sense. By the creation of this new department of the comparative method, sociology confers a benefit on the whole of natural philosophy; because the positive method is thus completed and perfected, in a manner which, for scientific importance, is almost beyond our estimate. What we can now comprehend is that the historical method verifies and applies, in the largest way, that chief quality of sociological science—its proceeding from the whole to the parts. Without this permanent condition of social study, all historical labor would degenerate into being a mere compilation of provisional materials. As it is in their development, especially, that the various social elements are interconnected and inseparable, it is clear that any partial filiation must be essentially untrue. Where, for instance, is the use of any exclusive history of any one science or art, unless meaning is given to it by first connecting it with the study of the new political philosophy. Its rational development constitutes the substratum of the science, in whatever is essential to it. It is this which distinguishes it thoroughly from biological science, as we shall presently see. The positive principle of this separation results from the necessary influence of human generations upon the generations that follow, accumulating continuously till it constitutes the preponderating consideration in the direct study of social development. . . . The prevailing tendency to speciality in study would reduce history to a mere accumulation of unconnected delineations, in which all ideas of the true filiation of events would be lost amid the mass of confused descriptions. If the historical comparisons of the different periods of civilization are to have any scientific character, they must be referred to the general social evolution: and it is only thus that we can obtain the guiding ideas by which the special studies themselves must be directed.[9]

Other Themes and Foci: Positivism and the Hierarchy of the Sciences

Comte's formulation of sociology was part of a larger theoretical system—his "positive philosophy." This overall system was concerned with the delineation of the scope of the sciences, the analysis of each particular science, the establishment of relationships among the sciences, and the systematic reorganization of the sciences. Comte used the term "positivism" to refer to his total system of thought—a system in which he held the science of sociology to be his most significant innovation and contribution to knowledge. In the presentation of conclusions about society, Comte often used such phrases as "sociological conclusions" and "positivistic conclusions" interchangeably. This interchangeability of terminology makes it necessary to caution the contemporary student not to read into Comte's work implications he did not intend. The contemporary use of the word "positivistic" (Chapter 2) has a number of important differences from, as well as similarities with, Comte's use of the term. The most obvious differences result from Comte's rejection of the use of mathematics and probability theories in his positivistic system. The most important similarities are Comte's acceptance of the instrumentalist use of knowledge (that is, for control); his belief in strict scientific determinism; and his emphasis on external observation over subjective (or interpretive) understanding. Also, like later positivists, Comte insisted that the logic of inquiry of the physical and social sciences are fundamentally the same.

The central thesis of Comte's system of positive philosophy is that the *"law of three stages" is applicable to the development of each particular science:*

> From the study of the development of human intelligence, in all directions, and through all times, the discovery arises of a great fundamental law, to which it is necessarily subject, and which has a solid foundation of proof, both in the facts of our organization and in our historical experience. The law is this:—that each of our leading conceptions—each branch of our knowledge—passes successively through three different theoretical conditions: the Theological, or fictitious; the Metaphysical, or abstract; and the Scientific, or positive. In other words, the human mind, by its nature, employs in its progress three methods of philosophizing, the character of which is essentially different, and even radically opposed: viz., the theological method, the metaphysical, and the positive.[10]

In other words, in the course of its historical evolution, each science develops from a *theological* stage (wherein phenomena are explained with references to supernatural agencies), through a *metaphysical* stage (wherein phenomena are accounted for in terms of innate propensities), to a *positive* stage (wherein phenomena are explained via observed relationships). Comte believed that the particular sciences move through the stages at different times; thus some sciences reach the positive stage before others. The differential rate of advancement to the positive stage formed the basis of what Comte presented as the "hierarchy of the sciences."

Comte argued that the less complex a science, and the more removed it is from the common individual's daily activity and reflections, the sooner it will reach the final or positive stage of development. He held that observable relationships are easier to apprehend in simpler phenomena, whereas the abstract reasoning necessary for positivistic understanding is more easily achieved the farther the object of contemplation is analytically removed from everyday contemplation. Comte maintained that social phenomena emerge from biological phenomena, which are built out of chemical phenomena. Chemical phenomena, in turn, are built on physical phenomena. Thus he claimed that physical phenomena are "more removed" from the individual than are his or her biological makeup and social life. Comte concluded that therefore the order in which the sciences reach the positive stage should be as follows: physics, chemistry, biology, and finally social physics. Comte divided physics into the basic sciences—astronomical physics and earthly (geological) physics—and argued that, because heavenly bodies are more removed from human action, astronomy was the first science to reach the positive stage, followed by earthly physics, chemistry, biology, and social physics. He further subdivided particular scientific fields in terms of when each subfield would achieve positivistic understanding.

Midway through the production of *The Positive Philosophy* (1830–1842), when Comte learned that the Belgian statistician Adolphe Quetelet (1796–1874) had used "social physics" as the name for his statistical analyses of social behavior, Comte began to call his own scientific analysis of society "sociology." He further modified his hierarchy in his later work, the *System of Positive Polity* (1851–1854), by the addition of the sciences of mathematics and morals. Although, in his earlier works, Comte claimed that mathematics contained no subject matter, was purely abstract, and thus was not a science, he evidently changed his mind and later argued that its complete abstract nature made mathematics the first and most basic science. In his later work, he also discussed the possible development of a science of morals that would be more complex and rank higher than sociology in his hierarchy. Comte's most developed hierarchy of the sciences (starting with the least complex, the most removed from human activity, and the earliest to become a positive science) was thus: mathematics, astronomy, physics, chemistry, biology, sociology, and the science of morals.

Comte maintained that each level of reality, to which each science corresponds, builds most directly from the level directly preceding it. Thus he justified the sociological use of borrowed organic logic and the static and dynamic dichotomy from biology. He insisted that the sciences of life (biology and sociology) have a greater affinity for each other than they would for the sciences of inert matter, or what Comte called the "concrete sciences" (astronomy, physics, and chemistry).

Comte also maintained that once sociology had achieved the positive stage, it would be possible to organize all the sciences into one systematic presentation of knowledge—which is precisely what he claimed to have done in *The Positive Philosophy*. Furthermore, once the sciences had been abstractly coordinated, Comte maintained that it would be possible to develop an applied (as opposed to a purely theoretical) sociology. Comte claimed that the applied science of sociology would allow the reorganization of society on a scientific basis and thus usher in the positivistic stage of social evolution.

SIGNIFICANCE

Vision of the Future

Comte believed that the purpose of sociology was to study objective relationships of both structure and change in order to predict future events. Predictive abilities, based on a positivistic deterministic view of social reality, would in turn allow the development of an applied sociology—a sociological analysis concerned with an instrumentalist reconstruction of society on scientific notions of order and progress. Comte wrote at the outset of *A General View of Positivism*:

> The object of our philosophy is to direct the spiritual reorganization of the civilized world. It is with a view to this object that all attempts at fresh discovery or at improved arrangement should be conducted. Moral and political requirements will lead us to investigate new relations; but the search should not be carried farther than is necessary for their application. Sufficient for our purpose, if this incipient classification of our mental products so far worked out that the synthesis of Affection and of Action may be at once attempted; that is, that we may begin at once to construct that system of morality under which the final regeneration of Humanity will proceed. Those who have read my *Positive Philosophy* will, I think, be convinced that the time for this attempt has arrived. How urgently it is needed will appear in every part of the present work.[11]

Comte believed his delineation of the organization of the forthcoming positive society to be the crowning achievement of his positive philosophy and his sociology; other sociologists, since Comte, have seen it as a fantastic monstrosity constructed on ideas, wishes, and fears extrinsic to sociology.

Although Comte's early works reveal a concern with the future of society, specific statements about what the future will entail are most developed in his last works. These statements were developed at a time when Comte had come to detest thoroughly the Enlightenment ideals of Voltaire and Rousseau (which he associated with the chaos of metaphysical society) and to admire the orderly and spiritually oriented image of the Middle Ages portrayed by de Maistre and other Catholic conservatives. Much of Comte's conception of the positive reorganization of society thus involved a rejection of Enlightenment ideals and their offshoot ideologies (specifically, liberal democracy and socialism). Comte replaced such ideals with a glorifying reconceptualization of the institutions of medieval Europe.

For Comte, the Enlightenment notions of natural rights and individual freedom of thought and action were metaphysical ideas ungrounded in scientific analysis; moreover, they were socially dangerous. According to Comte, the danger lay in the impossibility of ever establishing a social order based on reasoned self-interest and free mutual association. As noted earlier, he believed that individuals were swayed more by emotions than by reason, and any attempt to organize society on the basis of the idea of free expression and individual choice was doomed to failure. Comte thus rejected liberal democracy as an unworkable system, wherein those of little intellect, with unrestrained passions, would be allowed to dictate the organization of society, while capitalist entrepreneurs would be free to exploit the population for their own greedy ends. Liberal democracy would lack an overall unifying (or "spiritual") moral force capable of the production of a harmonious progressive social order. Comte thus saw British parliamentary democracy as a doomed historical aberration and the nascent North American democracy of the United States as another inevitable failure in the attempt to base a society on the "negative" and "metaphysical" concepts of natural rights.

Comte's rejection of liberal democracy is coupled with a rejection of the other ideological child of the Enlightenment—socialism. Although Comte admired the socialist emphasis on sacrifice for the good of society, he believed that the socialists lacked an appreciation of innate human inequalities and the need for subordination and control of the population by a moral (or "spiritual") force in order to achieve collective harmony. Furthermore, Comte opposed the elimination of the inheritance of concentrated private wealth. Comte maintained that wealth, though in fact a public trust, was used most efficiently as capital when it remained in the hands of private individuals who were born members of a moneyed class. Comte held that if society were sociologically reorganized, private wealth could exist without capitalist exploitation. For Comte, the evil was not private wealth but the failure of a sociomoral force conducive to the direction of that wealth for social benefit and progress.

Neither liberal democracy nor socialism, but what might be termed "medievalism," formed the locus of Comte's positive stage. Comte sought the re-creation of the distinction between spiritual and temporal authority that he believed existed in medieval society (that is, the monotheistic period of the theological stage). He envisioned an international spiritual authority that would oversee and control all political authority. His model of such an international spiritual authority was the medieval Roman Catholic Church. The failure of that church to maintain social order and the deterioration of its moral and spiritual authority in the recent metaphysical stage were attributed not to the goals or organization of the church, but to its reliance on a false and outdated theological world view. Comte believed what was needed, and what would emerge in the positive stage of society, was an international spiritual body organized along positivistic thought. He called this new spiritual body the "positivistic church" and termed the doctrine that it would propagate "the religion of humanity." Comte's reputation as a sociologist in later generations might have fared better had he simply been content to prophesy the new spiritual order of the positivistic stage. Comte, however, was not a Moses, willing to lead his people to the approach of the promised land but not to enter it; instead, in his final years, Comte energetically set about establishing the "positivistic church" and "the religion of humanity."

Comte declared that the center of his church was in Paris, that he was its first high priest, and that it involved the worship of the "great being of humanity." Comte delineated in some detail the robes the priests would wear, the course priestly training would take, the missionary work the church would undertake, the public rituals that would be followed, the prayers to humanity that would be said, the holy days that would be respected, and other religious activities modeled after those of the Roman Catholic Church. He also stipulated how the positivistic church would govern the education of children (down to a detailed statement of elementary school curricula), regulate relationships between the genders (by reintroducing a chivalric code), exercise moral control over the actions of businessmen, and morally and spiritually guide the secular governments of the world. He developed a plan for the reorganization of world governments into a single centralized body composed of sixty persons drawn from various specified regions of the globe. Comte even presented a new calendar conducive to the aims of the positivistic church and the worship of the "great being of humanity," and he dated his letters in accordance with his new system of months and days.

The optimistic Comte expected to amass a large following quickly. He particularly expected first to attract women (who he believed would be "emotionally" drawn to the positivistic church) and workingmen (whose minds would not have been filled with "metaphysical doctrines" and who would soon turn from the "false" doctrine of socialism) to his church, which would then spread to the rest of Europe and the world. Needless to say, history has shown Comte's expectations to be quite wrong; Comte's religious adherents were few in number, and many of those attracted to Comte's sociological ideas made a point of differentiating themselves from the adherents of his positivist church.

One can conclude that in an abhorrence for the perceived evils of the modern age, Comte retreated into a medievalism that involved a highly romanticized image of a historical period that preceded his own. In so doing, Comte increasingly cast off his scientific skepticism for a secure belief in a harmonious and peaceful world order to come—a world spiritually led by sociologist-priests and a church that replaced God with humanity. Yet even in his final works, where Comte is totally enthralled with his new religion, there remains some detailed analysis of the relationship of societal parts and the nature of social change—analysis that belongs more properly to a sociological undertaking than to the declarations of the self-anointed high priest of humanity.

Contemporary Relevance

Comte's goal was the creation of what a contemporary theoretical physicist like Brian Greene would call a "T.O.E."—a "theory of everything." A theory of everything is " . . . a theory that underlies all others, one that does not require or even allow for a deeper explanatory base."[12] Comte was certain that he had already established a T.O.E. and all that remained for later thinkers was to investigate its details and apply its conclusions to all facets of our existence. In order to understand later reaction to Comte's overall thought (of which his sociology was only a part, albeit an essential one), we must briefly examine the construction of his T.O.E. and the fundamental contradiction it contained. This contradiction was between Newtonian deterministic mechanistic assumptions and the assumptions of a paradigm that included a social evolutionary emerging and discoverable obligatory moral order.

Following an extension of the logic of Newton's theory of gravity (as Comte understood it), Comte argued that: (1) scientific analysis could be extended to all things in the heavens and on the Earth; (2) such things could be scientifically explained only by deterministic "laws" firmly grounded in "observed relationships"; and (3) no scientifically valid knowledge could be obtained of original states and ultimate goals. (Indeed, any claims to such knowledge were presented as unsound, pre-scientific "metaphysical" thinking.) Simultaneously, and in contradiction to such assertions, Comte, building on the assumptions of progressive evolution, argued that: (1) an underlying developing moral order existed in the universe; (2) this moral order had a natural and necessary developmental direction; and (3) the contours of this moral order could be scientifically deduced. Accordingly, the role of the sociologist extended beyond the mere statement of lawful relationships to engaging in the implementation of programs to bring society into conformity with the objective moral order. Comte thus both rejected and espoused the "metaphysical" thinking of underlying causes and ultimate goals as he presented the role of scientists as both objective observers and the new leaders of society who had clear and "positive" knowledge of how everyone in every societal role ought to act. Not only did Comte fail to resolve contradictions between his assertions, the increasingly dogmatic self-proclaimed founder of sociology and eventual "high priest of humanity" refused even to acknowledge their existence. He insisted that his followers accept *all* of his teachings. And while there were those who did submit to the totality of his views (and joined his "positivistic church"), others took a decidedly more critical view toward his works.

Comte's one-time English follower, John Stuart Mill, asserted that, although Comte had envisioned the possibility of a science of society, Comte should not be considered a scientist or the founder of sociology. Comte's work contained too many non-scientific dogmatic and metaphysical proclamations for Comte to be considered either.[13] Mill's countryman, Herbert Spencer, also published "reasons for dissenting from the philosophy of M. Comte."[14] Aside from his stated reasons, Spencer, the foremost popularizer of sociology in the English-speaking world, had his own competing "theory of everything" built on a very non-Comtean moral theory.

Wilhelm Dilthey (1833–1911), the influential German philosopher of history, was even more hostile to Comtean formulations than was either Mill or Spencer. Dilthey rejected both the positivistic application of the logic of Newtonian science *and* the assumptions of Comte's unilinear progressive evolutionism. Comte's Newtonian determinism violated Dilthey's belief that humans made choices that researchers could come to understand.[15] And Comte's unilinear evolutionism obscured the influence of *unique* cultural and historical settings on such choices. Dilthey's criticism of Comte led to a wide-ranging late-nineteenth-century German academic debate on the proper methodological approach for social and cultural studies that, in turn, created the intellectual environment in which Max Weber would develop his socio-logical contributions.

Less critical of Comte than were the German academicians, was Emile Durkheim—the major institutionalizer of academic sociology in France. Durkheim credited Comte with being the founder of sociology and his own immediate predecessor. Durkheim disavowed some aspects of Comte's thought (e.g., Comte's "religion of humanity"), and made methodological and conceptual contributions beyond anything found in Comte's works. In other areas, however, Durkheim's writings differ from Comte's more by de-gree and style of presentation than in overall outlook. Durkheim's justification for so-ciology as a distinct discipline builds directly on Comte's hierarchy of sciences, as Durkheim maintains that each level of reality needs a corresponding science to dis-cover its properties and regularities. Durkheim's notion of society as a "*sui generis* re-ality"[16] clearly is in a Comtean "realist" tradition, but is less extreme, allowing for the existence of psychology as an independent discipline. Durkheim's arguments that ob-jective scientific analysis can discover the appropriate moral rules for a society have a definite Comtean ring. And Durkheim's rejection of both Marxism and liberal capi-talism in preference for a highly regulated economy that allows private ownership of the means of production resembles key elements of Comte's political and economic positions.

Like Durkheim, the American sociologist Jane Addams (1850–1935) also sought to link social scientific investigation with the discovery of appropriate moral rules for modern society. On a trip to England as a young woman, she was influenced by the ideas of a number of British neo-Comteans. The research she sponsored at Hull House in Chicago, her focus on an emerging peaceful world order, and her belief in science as an aid to moral development are reflective of Comtean themes. Although Addams has been less influential and less cited in American sociology than have other Chicago so-ciologists of her era, she is generally recognized as the foremost founder of profes-sional social work in the United States. Thus, an investigation into the roots of social work ideology might focus on the persistence of Comtean ideas (via Addams) about sci-ence and social reform, the role of experts, and the role of government in regulating people's lives in a capitalist society.

As was previously noted, Comte never achieved a large following, even though he expected one. His dual rejection of socialism and liberal capitalism put him outside the main political movements of the modern era. Similarly, his views do not fit well with the prevailing social and political views of contemporary American sociologists. Yet, there are a few features of the field that, unknown to most of its current practitioners, remain Comtean. Two such features involve the mainstream sociology distinctions between the study of "social change" and the study of "social order," and that between "pure" research and "applied" research.

Comte argued that, although social reality should be understood as a structured set of relationships undergoing *continuous* progressive development, it is epistemologically justifiable to *analytically* separate the processes that produce differences (i.e., change) from the study of the persistence of relationships among societal parts (i.e., order). (In-deed, such an "analytical" distinction allowed him to keep ideas derived from Condorcet partially separated from those derived from deMaistre, thereby avoiding having to deal with the previously mentioned contradictions between the two.) Via Durkheim and others, the distinction has been passed on to later sociologists and has engendered such bizarre debates as the 1960s dispute as to whether change or order is more fundamental to society. The distinction continues to be reflected in university course offerings (with "social change" listed in sociology course offerings as a distinct subject) and in mainstream sociology introductory text books (in which chapters on "social organization" usually come early, and a chapter or two on "social change" come near the end). Yet, despite its seeming ubiquity, the change/order distinction, central to Comtean positivism (and descended and related approaches), does not make sense from a critical perspective (such as Hegel's) or an interpretive perspective (such as Weber's). From these other perspectives, historically and dialectically emergent social forms and culturally based motivations are not meaningfully separable into those underlying the persistence of order and those conducive to change only.

The distinction between "pure" and "applied" research that separates study of the features of an "objective" social reality from an engineeringlike study of how to utilize such knowledge is also a Comtean legacy that has widespread acceptance in American sociology. This distinction is grounded in two underlying positivistic assumptions—that the social world can be broken down into component elements that can be studied in a "value-free" manner independent of human interests, and that knowledge obtained from such study can (and should) be instrumentally put to use by trained experts. Again, critical and interpretive theorists would reject this distinction. They could argue, for example, that research questions about society are never "pure," in that such questions can never be totally extricated from the social and historical circumstances that give rise to them, nor from the need to gain interest-based support necessary to carry out research and to "apply" its findings.

Comte declared himself to be a sociologist, created a systematic and deductive model of theorizing imitated by later sociologists, formally stated distinctions that are still part of sociology, and followed a set of assumptions, some of which still are reflected in mainstream sociological research and text books. Yet, at the same time, Comte is today generally relegated to the role of a nonsociologist philosopher and disparaged even by those who accept a number of his fundamental assumptions. Perhaps it is telling of the ideological commitments of contemporary sociology that Comte tends to be taken seriously only by critical theorists who wish to distinguish their approach from that of positivistic practitioners. Positivistic sociologists, on the other hand, who assert beliefs in value-neutrality, objectivity, and a social science whose problems are independent of sociocultural-historical settings, find him to be a historical embarrassment who is best not discussed or cited. It is easier to dismiss Comte as the founder of the "religion of humanity" than to explore the persistent influence he has had on the field of sociology.

NOTES

1. F. J. Gould, *The life story of Auguste Comte*, p. 2.
2. See Mary Pickering, *Auguste Comte: An intellectual biography*, Vol. 1.
3. *System of positive polity*, Vol. 1, p. xvi.
4. Pickering, *Auguste Comte*, p. 44.
5. Ibid., p. 47.
6. *The positive philosophy*, p. 502.
7. Ibid., p. 406.
8. *System of positive polity*, Vol. 1, p. 25.
9. *The positive philosophy*, pp. 481–482.

10. Ibid., p. 25.
11. *A general view of positivism*, p. 49.
12. Brian Greene, *The elegant universe: Super-strings, hidden dimensions,* and *the quest for the ultimate theory* (New York: Norton, 1999), p. 16.
13. See John Stuart Mill, *Auguste Comte and positivism.*

14. See Herbert Spencer, *Reasons for dissenting from the philosophy of M. Comte* (Berkeley, CA: Glendesary Press, 1968 [1871]).
15. Dilthey's notion of understanding (or *verstehen*) would be modified by Max Weber and became a central feature of Weber's sociological approach.
16. See discussion in the next chapter.

GLOSSARY

Active functions: Abilities in the individual other than those arising out of instinct or intellect. For Comte, these included courage, prudence, and firmness.

Antirationalism: Rejection of rationalist philosophies of the Enlightenment, usually in favor of a position that truth is revealed through either faith or intuition, or a combination of both.

Common-sense philosophy: School of thought developed out of the skepticism of David Hume (and others), which claims that everyday understanding is the basis of philosophical speculation.

Deduction: As used by Comte, a philosophical position whereby claims to knowledge are based on principles or statements derived from a larger, systematic, and abstract body of thought.

Deistic period (deism): As used by Comte, refers to the second and final period of the *metaphysical stage* of society. Characterized by emphasis on "natural rights."

Determinism: Intellectual position that denies either choice or "free will" and maintains that the occurrence of social events is absolutely controlled by natural laws.

Egoistic instincts: For Comte, biologically innate propensities of preservation and improvement.

Egyptian polytheism: Earlier phase of the polytheistic period of the *theological stage* of society; characterized by strict caste division between the upper priestly group and the rest of society.

Fetishism: First period of the *theological stage* of social evolution. Phenomena are generally understood to possess and act on humanlike motivations and desires.

Greek polytheism: Middle phase of the polytheistic period of the *theological stage* of society. Characterized by development of mathematical and philosophical intellectual abilities.

Hierarchy of sciences: Comte's arrangement of "basic" sciences in terms of complexity, "distance" from human activity, and rate at which they reach the positive level of development.

Historical method: As used by Comte, this term refers not to historical analysis *per se* but to the comparisons of societies at different levels of development.

Indirect experimentation: As used by Comte, refers to the analysis of two parallel situations in cases where controlled manipulation of variables is not possible.

Induction: As used by Comte, the philosophical position where knowledge of a higher order is produced by a combination or linking of facts.

Intellectual function: As used by Comte, non-instinctually controlled contemplative and expressive abilities.

Intermediate instincts: Biologically innate propensities or drives that engender egoistic advantage but that, to a degree, benefit society. For Comte, these included drives toward power, pride, and vanity.

Law of three stages: Central thesis of Comte's philosophical and social analysis. The "law" maintains that society as a whole and each particular science develop through three mentalistically conceived stages: the *theological stage*, the *metaphysical stage*, and the *positive stage*.

Materialism: Philosophical position whereby social phenomena are explained in terms of underlying material phenomena. As used specifically by Comte, the term also often was applied to the explanation of phenomena in terms of particles of matter in motion.

Medievalism: The use of the social structure of Europe in the Middle Ages as a model or an ideal in social speculation and planning.

Mentalism: Position that society can be analyzed in terms of the ways in which phenomena are intellectually understood.

Metaphysical stage: Middle era of development in Comte's *"law of three stages."* In this era, phenomena are understood in terms of supposed innate essences or *a priori* dispositions. Applied to the development of society as a whole and to the development of each particular science.

Monotheism: As used by Comte, the final period of the *theological stage* of social development. Phenomena are generally understood as subject to the actions of a single all-powerful god.

Moral forces: As used by Comte, predominant, socially generated commands and obedience to such commands that are conducive to the functioning, persistence, and development of society.

Organicism: Position that, to some extent, the structure and functioning of a society can be analogized to the structure and functioning of a living biological entity.

Phrenology: Archaic science developed by Joseph Gall. Central to its practice was the belief that the configurations of the skull were directly correlated with specific personality traits.

Polytheism: Middle and longest period of the *theological stage* of social evolution. Phenomena are generally understood as subject to the actions of a group of humanlike deities.

Positive (or positivistic) stage: Final era of development in Comte's *"law of three stages."* In this era, phenomena are explained in terms of observed relationships of order and change. Applied to the development of society as a

whole and to the development of each particular science.

Positivism: As used by Comte, the term referred to (1) the totality of Comte's philosophical speculation inclusive of his sociology; (2) the scientific analysis of phenomena; (3) the most advanced stage of society (see *Positive stage*); and (4) Comte's conception of a future society that involves a "religion of humanity."

Positivistic church: Organization promoted by Comte in his later years to propagate the "religion of humanity." Structurally modeled, to an extent, after the Roman Catholic Church.

Protestantism: As used by Comte, the first period of the *metaphysical stage* of society. Characterized by the breakdown of international spiritual authority and the decline of the feudal system.

Rationalism: Philosophical position whereby claims to truth are based on reason and logic, as opposed to, for example, faith, intuition, or empirical data.

Religion of humanity: Unifying the "spiritual" belief that Comte believed would develop in the *positive stage* of society. Involves the worship of humanity as a single "great being."

Roman polytheism: Final phase of the polytheistic period of the *theological stage* of society. Emphasis on a single god with power over all the other gods. Serves as a transitional era to *monotheism*.

Social dynamics: Relationships or the study of relationships of elements of society across time and in terms of change, evolution, or progress.

Social forces: Elements or relationships conducive to the functioning, persistence, and development of a group or larger social entity. Analogized by Comte to the functioning of tissues in a biological organism.

Social instincts: Biologically innate propensities to subordinate oneself to the demands and goals of society. For Comte, these included instincts of "attachment," "veneration," and "universal love."

Social realism: Position that society constitutes or manifests an existence in and of itself that is nonreducible to or explainable in terms of any other form of existence.

Social statics: Relationships or the study of relationships of elements of society at one point in time. Emphasis is on functional and systematic relationships.

Star worship: Transitional era from the fetishistic to the polytheistic period of the *theological stage* of society. Phenomena are understood in terms of being under the influence of heavenly bodies.

Theological stage: First era of development in Comte's *"law of three stages."* In this era, phenomena are understood in terms of the actions of supernatural agencies such as spirits, demons, or gods. Applied to the development of society as a whole and to the development of each particular science.

ANNOTATED BIBLIOGRAPHY

Primary Sources

Auguste Comte and positivism (Gertrud Lenzer, Ed.). New York: Harper & Row, 1975 (paper).

A selection from Comte's work, emphasizing his later writings. Contains a good bibliographical listing of Comte's work.

Auguste Comte: The foundation of sociology (Kenneth Thompson, Ed.). New York: Wiley, 1975.

A selection of Comte's writings from *The Positive Philosophy* and the *System of Positive Polity*; divided into sections on philosophy and science, methods and scope of sociology, social statics, social dynamics, and views on socialism and communism. Also includes selections from Comte's and Mill's correspondence.

The crisis of industrial civilization: The early essays of Auguste Comte (Ronald Fletcher, Ed.). London: Heinemann, 1974.

An excellent selection of Comte's early writings, starting with those from his Saint-Simon period. Emphasis is on the nature of science and its relationship to social change. Contains a highly informative seventy-page introductory essay by Fletcher.

A general view of positivism (J. H. Bridges, Trans.). New York: Robert Speller and Sons, 1957 [1849].

Comte's first attempt to delineate fully the role of sociology in the production of the positive reorganization of society and the rise of the religion of humanity. Includes long discussions of the social positions of workers, women, and intellectuals.

The positive philosophy (Harriet Martineau, Ed. and Trans.). New York: AMS Press, 1974 [1830–1842].

Condensed from six volumes by Martineau, this version of Comte's first major work won praise from Comte himself. In essence, the work attempts a synthesis of all the sciences; the law of three stages is developed, the distinction between statics and dynamics is discussed, the hierarchy of sciences is presented, and the word *sociology* is publicly used herein for the first time.

System of positive polity (4 vols.; John Henry Bridges, Trans.). New York: Burt Franklin, 1976 [1851–1854].

Comte's final major work. Although it emphasizes the development of the religion of humanity, this work (often ignored by sociologists in lieu of Comte's earlier writings) contains elaborations of Comte's conception of social statics and dynamics, an analysis of the individual in society, a discussion of affect and social order, and a modification of Comte's hierarchy of the science.

Secondary Sources

Aron, Raymond. *Main currents of social thought* (Vol. 1) (R. Howard & H. Weaver, Trans.). New York: Doubleday, 1965 (paper).

Contains a clear, concise treatment of Comte's ideas in a chapter organized around Comte's law of three stages.

de Coppens, Peter Roche. *Ideal man in classical sociology.* University Park: Pennsylvania State University Press, 1976.

A good analysis of the image of the individual portrayed in Comte's sociological writings.

Gould, F. J. *The life story of Auguste Comte.* Austin, TX: American Atheist Press, 1984 [original n.d.].

This short work presents many of the details of Comte's life.

Manuel, Frank E. *The prophets of Paris.* New York: Harper & Row, 1965 [1962] (paper).

Contains a highly readable analysis of Comte's thought in the light of his social environment and biographical experiences. The student of Comte will also be interested in chapters on the life and thought of Turgot, Condorcet, and Saint-Simon.

Marcuse, Herbert. *Reason and revolution.* Boston: Beacon Press, 1968 [1941] (paper).

A classic work that includes a comparison of Comte's "positive" thought with Hegelian and Marxian "negative" dialectics.

Mill, John Stuart. *Auguste Comte and positivism.* Ann Arbor: University of Michigan Press, 1968 [1865].

Despite its age, this short, well-reasoned critique of Comte by a former admirer and popularizer of his thought remains worthwhile in its analysis of key problematic aspects of Comte's thought.

Pickering, Mary. *Auguste Comte: An intellectual biography* (Vol. 1). Cambridge: Cambridge University Press, 1993.

The best biography of Comte in English. Pickering gives us a detailed account of Comte's life and of the influences on him from the time of his birth to the writing of *The Positive Philosophy.* She corrects many errors in previous views of Comte, and her own positions are consistently well argued and well documented. Her narrative style is clear.

Simon, E. M. *European positivism in the nineteenth century.* Ithaca, NY: Cornell University Press, 1963.

This book deals primarily with Comte's religion of humanity, its critics, and its followers after Comte's death.

Sokoloff, Boris. *The "mad" philosopher Auguste Comte.* Westport, CT: Greenwood Press, 1975 [1961].

Despite this work's pejorative title, it presents one of the most detailed accounts of Comte's life to be found in the English language.

Standley, Arline Reilein. *Auguste Comte.* Boston: Twayne, 1981.

A highly readable work that presents an overview of Comte's life and major works. Written by a professor of English and linguistics, it has an interesting chapter on Comte's aesthetic theories.

M oral facts exist as phenomena like other phenomena. They consist of rules of action that have certain distinctive characteristics. It must then be possible to observe them, describe them, classify them; and to seek out laws which explain them. This is what we intend to do for some moral facts. One might object to this in terms of free choice, but such an objection would militate against all determinant laws and be an insurmountable obstacle, not only for psychological and social sciences, but for all the sciences. Because human choices are always tied to external movement, an emphasis on freedom would make determinism unintelligible outside as well as inside of us. However, no one will contend the reality of the physical and natural sciences. We claim the same right for social science.

Thus understood, our science is not in opposition with any sort of philosophy, because it is premised on entirely different grounds. It is possible that morals may have some transcendental end beyond the reach of experience—this is a question for metaphysicians to occupy themselves with. But it is also true that morals develop historically, in terms of historical causes, and that they serve some functions in our temporal life. Whatever morals are (or are at any given point in time) the conditions in which people live do not permit them to be otherwise and the proof of this is that they change when conditions change. Today it is no longer possible to maintain that moral evolution consists of the development of a single idea, which, confused and uncertain in primitive man, makes itself clear and precise little by little with the spontaneous progress of knowledge. If the ancient Romans did not have the wide conception of humanity that we have today, it was not the result of an error due to the narrowness of their intellect, but because ideas identical to our own would have been incompatible with the nature of Roman civilization. Our cosmopolitanism would not have been able to appear there, any more than a plant can germinate in soil incapable of nourishing it. Moved to Rome from somewhere else, modern cosmopolitan ideas would have been unable to survive. Since our modern attitudes have not made their appearance due to philosophical discoveries, they did not arise because our minds have opened to truths that the ancients ignored. It is changes in the structure of society which have produced changes in our mores. Morals are then formed, transformed and maintained due to experiential reasons; these are the only reasons which a science of morality attempts to determine.

—Emile Durkheim, Preface to
The Division of Labor in Society

4

(David) Emile Durkheim

(1858–1917)

BACKGROUND

Life

On April 15, 1858, in the Jewish section of the town of Epinal, David Emile Durkheim was born to Melanie and Moise Durkheim. Epinal is situated in the French eastern-border province of Lorraine. Along with the neighboring province of Alsace, Lorraine had been the home of Durkheim's ancestors since the Middle Ages. Moise was a chief rabbi of the Vosges and Haute-Marne regions and was the last member of an unbroken line of eight generations of father-son rabbis. Despite being the fourth child of the family and the second son, David Emile was destined early to be the next rabbi in the Durkheim family. Throughout his youth, he was given a thorough religious training but also attended local secular schools. His father encouraged this dual education. He would have himself completed philosophical and scientific studies in Paris had it not been for financial limitations. At both types of schools, David Emile showed himself to be an excellent student.

With the exception of the occupation of Epinal by German troops in the Franco-Prussian War, the circumstances of David Emile's upbringing were relatively pleasant. Although the family was not wealthy, it was highly respected, happy, and close-knit. In his youth, while studying with a local teacher, David Emile came under the influence of a mystical form of Catholicism. Although his commitment to Catholicism was brief (he was an agnostic for most of his life), David Emile turned away from a rabbinical career and set his future goals on a more secular vocation. Upon his graduation from the local secondary school, Emile Durkheim (who at this point dropped his Hebrew first name of David) left for further study in Paris. His goal was to attend the prestigious *Ecole Normale Supérieure*. Admittance there, which involved competing with the best students in France, was difficult to attain. After three years of studying and two failed attempts at entrance, Durkheim was accepted. He was thus on his way to becoming a member of the French intellectual elite. Trained in philosophy and history, and reading texts on sociology by Comte and Spencer in his spare time, Durkheim went on to earn a doctorate at the University of Paris and began a promising academic career.

After teaching briefly at a secondary school, in 1887 Durkheim received a faculty appointment at the University of Bordeaux. At that time, there were not yet any sociology courses taught in French universities. Instead, his primary responsibilities were in presenting education courses to prospective secondary school teachers. Durkheim did, though, introduce a sociology course at Bordeaux and held the Chair of Social Science there from 1896 until 1902, when he was invited to become a faculty member at the prestigious Sorbonne in Paris. At first, he was given the Chair of the Science of Education. In 1913, his appointment was changed to the Chair of the Science of Education and Sociology, thus finally giving official recognition to the discipline with which he most identified.

Both of Durkheim's university appointments were obtained with the aid of sympathetic officials in the French government who saw the compatibility between Durkheim's liberal prorepublican views and their own political agenda. They also recognized that Durkheim would be a formidable ally against the conservative and reactionary political parties. In Paris, Durkheim was seen by political friends and foes alike as highly influential in shaping the political and moral attitudes of a whole generation of French students. Robert Alun Jones has written:

> His [Durkheim's] lecture courses were the only courses required at the Sorbonne, obligatory for all students seeking degrees in philosophy, history, literature and language; in addition he was responsible for the education of French school teachers, in whom he instilled all the fervour of his secular, rational morality.[1]

Yet if Durkheim rose in academic rank with the aid of powerful political allies, he also tended to avoid taking any part in overt political activity. The one major exception to his disdain for public political activity was Durkheim's passionate involvement in the "Dreyfus Affair" that polarized French politics and public opinion.

In 1894, Captain Alfred Dreyfus, an officer on the French General Staff and a Jew, was railroaded and falsely convicted of treason by reactionary anti-Semitic elements in the French military and sentenced to life in prison on Devil's Island. The right-wing political parties gleefully participated in the railroading to protect a Major Ferdinand Walsin Esterhazy; the liberal and socialist parties recognized that Dreyfus was the innocent victim of right-wing reactionary forces. Durkheim publicly sided with the pro-Dreyfus forces (the "Dreyfusards") and took an active role in the support movement *Ligue pour la Défense des Droits de l'Homme* (League for the Defense of Human Rights). As a member of the *Ligue,* Durkheim gave "fiery" public speeches that brought support to the Dreyfusards, and he convinced his old friend and former schoolmate Jean Jaurès, the leader of the Socialist Party in France, to throw the full weight of the socialist movement behind the cause of freeing Dreyfus and investigating the military.

Durkheim's famous essay "Individualism and the Intellectuals" can be interpreted as a defense of the Dreyfusards against charges that their opposition to conservative elements in the military was indicative of a lack of patriotism. Ultimately, Dreyfus's sentence was reduced to ten years in prison, and in 1906 the French Supreme Court completely exonerated him and reinstated his military rank. By then, the affair had been used by the liberal and republican forces to reduce military influence in France, and, in opposition to right-wing elements, establish a total separation of church and state.

Up until World War I, the Dreyfus Affair was the only event that took energy away from Durkheim's goal of establishing sociology as a respected academic discipline. British sociologist Frank Parkin has asserted that Durkheim pursued this goal with "the nerve and passion of a holy crusader," and he refers to Durkheim's student Georges Davey's assertion that hearing Durkheim lecture was like hearing "a prophet of a nascent religion."[2] In the course of pursuing his goal, Durkheim published more than five hundred articles, books, and reviews; trained a large number of graduate students; founded the first sociology research institute in the world; and organized and edited a major journal of sociology (*L'Année sociologique*). Among Durkheim's studies and writings were investigations into the nature of social order, social change, suicide, sociological methodology, the sociology of education, the sociology of knowledge, the sociology of morality, and the sociology of religion. These studies contained many ideas, concepts, methods, and arguments that later sociologists have explored and developed.

Durkheim was married during his early years of teaching. It was essentially a traditional marriage, with Louise looking after household affairs and the children (Marie and André). When he grew older, André Durkheim developed into one of his father's best students and co-workers. Indeed, Emile Durkheim surrounded himself with a number of highly competent young students (including a number of his nephews) who later diffused Durkheim's sociological formulations into many areas of French academics. Thus Durkheim's conceptions penetrated French historical writings, linguistics, philosophy, anthropology, and educational thought.

At the outbreak of World War I, many of Durkheim's students enlisted in the military. Durkheim himself went to work for the government, writing and coordinating the publication of pro-French pamphlets. Some of these were designed to convince the United States to enter the war against Germany. Early in the conflict, many of Durkheim's students were killed or lost in battle. Among those missing in action was André, who was later found to have died of combat wounds. Stricken with grief, Durkheim found it impossible to discuss the death of his son. He found it increasingly difficult to work on his sociological studies. Depressed, having lost his son and many of his finest students, Durkheim died on November 15, 1917. In his fifty-nine years, he had, perhaps more than anyone else, helped institutionalize sociology and make it a respected discipline in its own right.

Social Environment

Durkheim dedicated his adult life to developing the discipline of sociology. He maintained that sociology would be beneficial to society as a whole and referred to his dedication to the field as a "moral calling." Durkheim believed that sociology was absolutely necessary for improving society and for solving major social problems that confronted France in particular and all modern societies in general. For Durkheim, modern society was in a state of "moral anarchy," "disunity," "disorganization," and "decadence." Sociology was to serve as a tool for diagnosing and analyzing social problems or "pathologies" and for finding their solutions or "cures." By using positivistic scientific methods of defining, observing, comparing, and formulating laws, Durkheim argued, sociology could show how to develop a better society. Durkheim believed that only by developing and using positivistic scientific principles of analysis could society be improved and moral disunity ended. In the preface to his first major book, Durkheim wrote:

> Although we set out primarily to study reality, it does not follow that we do not wish to improve it; we should judge our researches to have no worth at all if they were to have only a speculative interest. If we separate carefully the theoretical from the practical problems, it is not to the neglect of the latter; but, on the contrary, to be in better position to solve them.[3]

In answering the question of why Durkheim saw modern society as being in a state of "crisis" and as needing a sociological cure, one can point to three phenomena in the French society of Durkheim's youth: the defeat of France in the Franco-Prussian War, repeated political crises, and persistent economic and industrial conflicts and problems.

In the summer of 1870, France entered into a disastrous war against Prussia and its allied German states. The war culminated in a French defeat, with humiliating terms of surrender. Early in the war, Durkheim's hometown of Epinal was captured and occupied by German troops. The experience of defeat and occupation had a profound effect on the lives of the members of the Jewish community of that town. Up until that time, the Jews of eastern France had been treated with almost complete toleration. With the occupation of Epinal, however, outbreaks of anti-Semitic violence and accusations occurred. The Jews were accused of being responsible for the French defeat and its accompanying problems of economic and political instability. Durkheim—who personally witnessed these outbreaks and who, with the other members of his family, was a loyal citizen of France—must have been puzzled over this scapegoating. By his late teens, he interpreted the attacks on the Jewish community as resulting from a widespread lack of moral unity and purpose. Furthermore, he perceived this lack of moral purpose as being exemplified in the economic and political events of the day.

The industrialization of France had occurred rapidly. By the time of Durkheim's youth, there were large populations of factory workers in Paris and other large cities. Competition between industrial enterprises, as described by Durkheim, was vicious; relationships between employers and employees were antagonistic and, on occasion, violent. The most extreme violence of this kind occurred toward the end of the Franco-Prussian War, when a large number of workers seized Paris and established a separate egalitarian republic known as the Paris Commune. The French government ruthlessly crushed the Commune and killed some twenty thousand working-class inhabitants. After these events, Durkheim saw relationships between owners and employees as crisis-ridden. He believed owners were disregarding the workers' basic needs; consequently, the workers became increasingly attracted to violent revolutionary movements and ideologies.

Military defeat and economic oppositions were combined with political instability in the France of Durkheim's youth. The great French Revolution of 1789, which swept away the monarchy of Louis XVI, ended with a series of factional political disputes, the rise of the dictatorship of Napoleon, and the restoration of the Bourbon monarchy after Napoleon's final military defeat. The Bourbon monarchy was overthrown in a revolution in 1830, which established the monarchy of Louis Philippe. This monarchy ended in a revolution in 1848 that established the Second Republic. Short-lived, the Second Republic was taken over by Emperor Napoleon III, who lost his throne with the French defeat in the Franco-Prussian War. Durkheim grew up in the Third Republic, established after the war.

The Third Republic was built on a history of political change and disorder. There were sharp divisions in the country among the adherents of capitalist democracy, monarchy, and socialism. Political disputes and disagreements were used by those wishing to place blame for the French defeat, economic conflict, and inflation. This state of affairs indicated to Durkheim that France had lost the feeling of a common purpose and an underlying moral unity. In search of a doctrine that could provide such a common purpose and unity, nineteen-year-old Emile Durkheim left Epinal to continue his education in Paris.

Durkheim's first days in Paris heightened his awareness of the disunity that pervaded France. He saw Paris as a city lacking any sense of community; Parisians were in competition with each other and were devoid of any concerns about others or about anything other than self-interest. In order to understand and ultimately to overcome this moral disunity, which he saw pervading modern societies in general, Durkheim turned toward sociology and a scientific analysis of society.

Intellectual Roots

At the *Ecole Normale*, no sociology courses were taught, nor did any individuals on the faculty identify themselves as sociologists. Instead of sociology, Durkheim's training was in the traditional academic subjects of history and philosophy. Although he admired and was influenced by a number of his instructors, such as the historians Gabriel Monad and Fustel de Coulanges (1830–1889) and the philosopher Emile Boutroux (1845–1921), Durkheim chose to follow a different intellectual path: that of sociology. He did so because he believed that the traditional humanities were incapable of developing solutions to the moral crises and disunity that he saw as pervading modern forms of life. Traditional history, he felt, was too concerned with particular events; it was not aimed at discovering general social scientific laws. Yet such positivistic laws were necessary, Durkheim believed, if one wanted to develop programs to solve the major social problems confronting France. Durkheim rejected traditional philosophy for similar reasons. He saw the "methods" of philosophy as incapable of developing valid positive laws. Philosophy, Durkheim pointed out, does not use scientific techniques of observation and an empirical investigation of social phenomena. Instead, it relies exclusively on logical proofs and deductions. Durkheim believed that, in order to discover solutions that would work in the real day-to-day social world, one could not rely on deduction alone; instead, one needed evidence based on valid scientific procedures. Thus, although Durkheim borrowed insights and ideas from traditional philosophy and history, he believed that to improve society one first needed to investigate it from a positive scientific, empirical perspective. The field of study to which he turned was, of course, sociology.

By his third year at the *Ecole Normale*, Durkheim had decided that sociology would be his future field of study. The writings that most influenced him at that time were those of Immanuel Kant (1724–1804), Henri de Saint-Simon (1760–1825), Auguste Comte, Herbert Spencer, Wilhelm Wundt (1832–1920), and Charles Renouvier (1815–1903).

Kant had been one of the great German moral philosophers. His interests in demonstrating what actions were necessary for a moral social existence were in harmony with Durkheim's own. (Indeed, in his later years, Durkheim would attempt to give a "sociological" explanation of some of Kant's ideas.) Saint-Simon, a Frenchman, was, like Kant, also a philosopher. Whereas Kant was concerned with age-old problems of morality in society, Saint-Simon saw modern society as different from all previous societies. Saint-Simon emphasized that what was unique about modern society was that it was an industrial society. He argued that industrial organization, employment, and relationships increasingly affect the whole of people's lives. Durkheim accepted this argument and believed that sociology must study social and moral phenomena in terms of the essentially industrial nature of society. For Durkheim, the goal of sociology was to develop social laws that would allow the creation of a morally unified industrial social order.

Durkheim was also influenced by the sociological ideas of Comte and Spencer. Although Durkheim disagreed with aspects of both men's sociological writings, he nonetheless built on insights from each. Durkheim believed that Comte's "religion of humanity" and his focus on "sociological priests" were nonscientific and unacceptable. Yet Durkheim did borrow from Comte's ideas about social and moral order, his focus on both social structure and social change, his arguments for the existence of a science of society, and his insistence that sociology must be of practical utility in the reformulation of society if it is to be of any worth.

Similarly, Durkheim borrowed selectively from Spencer's thought. He was impressed by Spencer's conceptions of social evolutionary "societal types" based on increasing size, level of complexity, differentiation, and integration. Durkheim formulated his own conceptions of "societal types" or "species" in reference to those of Spencer's. On the other hand, Durkheim found Spencer's emphasis on utilitarian action unacceptable. Durkheim felt that utilitarianism was an amoral doctrine that ignored the necessity (for social harmony) of placing societal needs above one's own. Durkheim also argued that utilitarianism was scientifically unsound because it failed to acknowledge the great degree to which individual goals and desires are shaped by society.

Additional influences on Durkheim included the writings of Wundt and Renouvier. Wundt was a German psychologist whose importance for Durkheim lay in the fact that his work presented an example of how one could apply scientific experimental techniques to the study of human life. (Durkheim was so impressed with German experimental psychology that as a student he took a one-year study trip to Germany.) Renouvier, unlike Wundt, was not a practicing scientist. What Durkheim borrowed from him was the argument that the social collective reality was a phenomenon that was just as real as individual psychological reality. Durkheim claimed that the experimental approach that Wundt showed could be used at the individual level of existence, could also be used at the social level. Durkheim was also influenced by Renouvier's critique of utilitarian philosophers. These stressed that what constituted the "good" or the "moral" was that which benefited the interests of the largest number of members of a society. For Durkheim morality and justice could never be reduced to individual utility. They had to be understood in terms of the overall collective values around which social life was structured.

So far, Durkheim's intellectual roots have been examined by focusing on specific intellectuals. One can also think of Durkheim as synthesizing elements derived from two opposed schools or traditions of social thought. These two traditions were that of the French Enlightenment and that created by the conservative anti-Enlightenment reaction (the latter in spite of the fact that Durkheim's political sympathies were with the prorepublican liberals of his own day). From the former (which includes the *philosophes* Jean-Jacques Rousseau [1712–1778], Voltaire [1694–1778], and Denis Diderot [1713–1784]), Durkheim incorporated ideas of individualism, individual liberties, specialization, democracy, scientific rationality, and secular social examination. From the anti-Enlightenment reaction, Durkheim derived a view of society in terms of an organismic analogy and a focus on social institutions, the individual's need for social support and control, and the superior moral influence of society in shaping the nature of the individual.

Finally, a major influence on Durkheim's thought, but one whose impact is difficult to assess, is that of his early Jewish religious training. Durkheim scholars have asserted that Durkheim "always remained the product of a close-knit, orthodox Jewish family"[4] and that "despite his early abandonment of the Jewish faith, the influence of his early life and family origins cannot be lightly dismissed."[5] In his own day, opponents of Durkheim, to some extent, saw his sociology as an emanation of his Judaic background when they referred to it as "Talmudic sociology." According to Durkheim's nephew Henri, Durkheim once answered a question about the content of his thought by remarking, "It is necessary not to forget that I am the son of a rabbi."[6] Clearly, there is an element of truth in Steve Fenton's contention that the unified Jewish community of Epinal served as a model for Durkheim of what a morally integrated community should be and was contrasted by Durkheim to the discordant egoism and "anomie" that he saw rampant in broader French society. Also Durkheim's persistent focus on religion as a subject of sociological study emanates to a degree from his early religious training. Durkheim defines religion in terms of the social institution that distinguishes the "sacred" from the "profane" (see discussion below under the sub-heading "Social Institutions"). It is more than coincidental that one of the traditional Jewish prayers at the end of the Sabbath refers to God as separating the "sacred" from the "profane." Last, it can be noted that a number of attributes a traditional Jew would ascribe to God were ascribed by Durkheim to society. Durkheim held society to be the ultimate origin and object of all moral action, the ultimate revealer of knowledge and understanding, beneficient and all-knowing, with a consciousness superior to that of mere individuals, and the ultimate object of our devotion and study. Rabbi Moise Durkheim would have had no difficulty surmising how his nominally agnostic son developed these ideas.[7]

IDEAS

Society

In his writings, Durkheim used the term "society" (*société*) in a number of different ways. At times, the term merely refers to group or collective life or to the group's influence on the individual. At other times, it appears to be the sum total of all social activities. Occasionally, it signifies the goal, purpose, or motivating force behind individual and group actions. Elsewhere, "society" refers to what are today considered to be properties of "culture" and involves shared beliefs, values, sentiments, and ways of thinking and understanding. In some places, Durkheim used "society" to refer to a "social organism" composed of a number of social parts or social organs. These parts work or function together to maintain the existence of the whole organism or society. Despite the multitude of ways in which Durkheim used the term "society," however, there are some central conceptions of what a society entails that run throughout Durkheim's writings. Essential to Durkheim's overall conception of a society is the definition of it as a distinct form of reality. In other words, society forms a reality in and of itself. Durkheim often used a Latin phrase to express this last point when he referred to society as a *sui generis* reality—one that cannot be reduced to, or explained in terms used to describe, other realities. Thus the properties of society, or social reality, cannot be reduced to mere expressions of other realities like biological or psychological realities. Society or social reality emerges from and depends on the existence of other nonsocial realities, but it is different from and more complex than any of them.

For Durkheim, the universe manifested a number of levels of reality: the physical, the chemical, the biological, the psychological, and the social. Each level (except the physical, which is the simplest) emerges from a simpler level. Emergence occurs from the interrelationship of elements of a simpler or less complex reality. The outcome of this interrelationship is a phenomenon at the level of a more complex reality that manifests new characteristics. For example, Durkheim pointed out that water emerges from the interrelationship of the physical elements hydrogen and oxygen, in proper proportions and under proper conditions. The chemical properties of water (its liquid state at room temperature and its utility in putting out fires, for example) emerge from this interrelationship; these properties cannot be found in the highly volatile gases oxygen and hydrogen from which the water emerged. Similarly, the phenomena of biological reality emerge from the interrelationship of simpler physical and chemical phenomena. Though composed of inorganic matter, the emergent biological entity has the unique property of life. Thus living things form a unique reality that cannot be understood merely in terms of physical and chemical properties. Mental or psychological reality, in turn, emerges from biological reality. Mind or psychological processes, of course, depend on the existence of the brain. Yet the existence of mind also involves new emergent properties such as consciousness, thought, reflection, and understanding. It is from the interrelationship of minded beings (individuals capable of symbolic communication and reflection) that society or social reality emerges. As with the other realities, social reality has its own *sui generis* properties that cannot be reduced to or understood in terms of any other, simpler reality. According to Durkheim:

> Society is not the mere sum of individuals, but the system formed by their association represents a specific reality which has its own characteristics. Undoubtedly no collective entity can be produced if there are no individual consciousnesses: this is a necessary but not a sufficient condition. In addition, these consciousnesses must be associated and combined, but combined in a certain way. It is from this combination that social life arises and consequently it is this combination which explains it. By aggregating together, by interpenetrating, by fusing together, individuals give birth to a being, psychical if you will, but one which constitutes a psychical individuality of a new kind. Thus it is in the nature of that individuality and not in that of its component elements that we must search for the proximate and determining causes of the facts produced in it. The group thinks, feels and acts entirely differently from the way its members would if they were isolated. If therefore we begin by studying these members separately, we will understand nothing about what is taking place in the group. In a word, there is between psychology and sociology the same break in continuity as there is between biology and the physical and chemical sciences. Consequently every time a social phenomenon is directly explained by a psychological phenomenon, we may rest assured that the explanation is false.[8]

When people interact to form a society, collectively shared beliefs, values, and norms develop or emerge. These socially shared conceptions are referred to as *collective representations* (as opposed to the less important, nonshared conceptions that Durkheim called *individual representations*). Every society or social group is characterized by a particular set of collective representations that are shared by most, if not all, of its members. Together, these representations can be said to form a united collective set of social rules and ways of understanding the world—in Durkheim's terms, a "collective consciousness" or "collective conscience." Thus, although the collective consciousness depends on the existence of individuals sharing beliefs, values, and norms, it has emergent properties that represent a social level of reality. As an aspect of society, collective consciousness has three unique and important properties. It preexists and outlives particular persons, it is felt by persons to be a general external power or force, and it is capable of both shaping and constraining action.

The individual, Durkheim asserted, is born into an ongoing social world. We are educated or socialized into the shared consciousness of our group or society. Thus social reality, even though it emerges from interrelationships, antedates each one of us and is a force that determines how we will come to interpret the world and to interpret social activity. Furthermore, once a generation is socialized, it matures and brings into the world another new generation of individuals, who are, in their own turn, socialized into shared values, beliefs, and norms. Thus, as a distinct reality, the social consciousness is passed from generation to generation and outlasts any particular person or persons.

Not only does society exist as a reality both before and after each of us, but we also tend to be aware of society as a general external real force that affects each one of us. Thus, according to Durkheim, we can refer to society as approving or disapproving of this or that behavior or activity. We can talk about the difficulties one encounters when one goes against the "wishes" or "desires" of society. Indeed, we can actually feel pressured to conform to the "dictates" or "commands" of society when they go against our own personal inclinations or desires. In other words, there is an emergent social reality, and we are aware of it as a force in considering our own actions. Just as we might take pleasure in helping society or in conforming to the social goals, we can also feel or be aware of the reality of social forces when our intentions run counter to those of society.

In that we are aware of society as a force when we consider our actions, we can say that society *constrains* our activity. We feel it as a force pushing us toward some activities and away from others. We are especially aware of its constraint through our knowledge of the punishments that occur should we violate social rules. Thus Durkheim asserted that society represents a unique level of reality characterized by special properties such as externality, generality, and constraint.

Durkheim conceived of society not as a static organization of human activity but as an organization that is constantly in a natural process of development through a series of sequential evolutionary types or stages. Durkheim's earliest works depict social change in terms of a movement from mechanical to organic forms of social organization; in later works, however, Durkheim tended to develop and to emphasize a more complex set of evolutionary societal types. Accompanying social organizational change are changes in human nature. Additionally, although social change is normal and natural to a society, particular dynamic or transitional periods can be accompanied by social problems (or pathologies). Furthermore, it should be noted that, although he emphasized change, Durkheim argued that much social change is a process of differentiation of parts and specialization of activities. Consequently, the basic elements that underlie the makeup of all social life are not fundamentally altered.

Durkheim's earliest evolutionary distinction is between simple mechanical and complex organic solidarity. In the former, individuals live in small societies where they share all the collective representations. Individualism is hardly developed, and there is a unity based on likeness of world view, similarity of activity, and near-total identification with the society. Through a process involving increases in population density, interaction, and occupational competition, *mechanically* organized society is replaced by *organically* organized society. Organic social organization is a much more specialized society where individuals pursue different occupations, develop separate identities, and have a degree of difference in their world views. In this society, individuals are bound together not just by similarities (which are much fewer than in mechanical society) but also by the functional dependence of individuals and groups on one another that results from occupational specialization.

A difference in human nature that occurs in the course of social change can be illustrated in terms of types of suicide that tend to be more prevalent in mechanical than organic society. Because of a lack of individualism, what Durkheim terms "altruistic" suicide tends to be the most prevalent type in mechanical societies; in organic societies, where individualism is more developed, "egoistic" and "anomic" forms of suicide tend to be more frequent. Altruistic suicide, such as ritualistic suicide, involves an extreme identification with the society's collective conscience whereby the individual sacrifices himself or herself because of an overconformity to social rules. Egoistic and anomic suicide, on the other hand, tend to occur because of a *lack* of identification with the social whole. Egoistic suicide is likely to occur following the frustration of individual desires and where the individual part of the self is not tempered by a more socially developed orientation; anomic suicide occurs when social rules are insufficient to create the impression for individuals that they are a significant part of a larger social group.

Durkheim turned from the simple dichotomy of mechanical-organic to a more complex conception of social types based on size and complexity of organization. These types are (from the simplest to the most complex) the horde, simple polysegmental society, polysegmental simple compound society, and polysegmental doubly compound society (although an even more complex listing of societies is implied by Durkheim's work). More complex societies are characterized by a higher degree of differentiation or, in other words, by more developed and integrated specialized groups and institutions.

All societies, according to Durkheim, will typically progress through the sequence of types in a natural, normal, slow, step-by-step, and internally generated series of evolutionary changes. Periods in which a society is between one social type and another are thus possible; Durkheim terms these "transitional periods," "stages," or "social forms." Durkheim maintained that such transitional periods are likely to be characterized by a high degree of social disorganization and widespread social problems. This state of disorganization occurs because the sociomoral rules held over from the earlier evolutionary stage are no longer applicable to events in the evolving, more differentiated, complex stage. Furthermore, although social rules suitable to the new social stage are still in a process of creation and thus are not developed to an extent great enough to order social life properly, Durkheim maintained that such transitional problems and disorganization will terminate as the society evolves fully into the higher social stage or type.

Despite his overall dynamic conception of society, and despite the fact that he saw social change as a natural elaboration and differentiation of society, Durkheim believed that all societal types share certain underlying similarities. Earlier social forms are viewed by Durkheim not just as being simpler than later ones, but as presenting a persistent basis or fundamental frame or structure on which more complex societal types are structured. In his last major work, *Elementary Forms of the Religious Life* (1912), Durkheim turned to an empirical investigation of a simple societal type in order to understand the fundamental nature of his own complex industrial society.

The Individual in Society

Durkheim's conception of the individual or of human nature was referred to by him as "dualistic." A dualistic view of human nature means that a person's self or personality is viewed as composed of two basic parts. These parts can be referred to as a *social* part and an *individual* part, respectively. The social part is developed in the course of socialization and sustained throughout life by interactions with others and by participation in collectively oriented activities. The individual part is inborn and organic. Paralleling the different origins of these two parts are their different objects of orientation. The social part is altruistic and motivated toward fulfilling collective goals and following social rules. The individual part is self-centered and concerned with the individual's egoistic desires and interests. Durkheim wrote:

> It is not without reason, therefore, that man feels himself to be double: he actually is double. There are in him two classes of states of consciousness that differ from each other in origin and nature, and in the ends toward which they aim. One class merely expresses our organisms and the objects to which they are most directly related. Strictly individual, the states of consciousness of this class connect us only with ourselves, and we can no more detach them from us than we can detach ourselves from our bodies. The states of consciousness of the other class, on the contrary, come to us from society; they transfer society into us and connect us with something that surpasses us. Being collective, they are impersonal; they turn toward us ends that we hold in common with other men; it is through them and them alone that we can communicate with others.[9]

Durkheim argued that in simple societies the social part completely dominates the individual part, whereas in modern society this is not the case. Yet, Durkheim insisted, if harmonious relationships among people are to be maintained and if the individual is to be happy and well adjusted, the social part must be well developed and sustained even within persons dwelling in modern society.

If the social part of the individual is not well developed, both society as a whole and its individual members suffer. Society suffers because people who are governed only by their own desires and interests and who do not take those of others into account will inevitably encounter a clash of interests and enter into conflict. Such conflict will involve the ignoring or circumvention of social rules and might engender such violent oppositions that society itself is endangered. Meanwhile, the individual who lacks a completely developed social part also suffers. Durkheim claimed that if one's appetite for things is not limited by an internalized social constraint, one's desires would become insatiable. No matter how much wealth or luxury was amassed, the individual composed of, or dominated by, untempered egoism would never be satisfied. No matter how much one had, one would feel frustrated and unhappy at not having more. One's desires, argued Durkheim, would be like a bottomless abyss that could never be filled. Durkheim called this the "malady of infiniteness."

Thus Durkheim argues that the individual needs a part that can be developed only in society. Only by interacting with others, and by taking part in collective activities, can individuals develop their social part and become complete beings. It follows that only when society itself is organized, stable, and harmonious can the individual complete him- or herself by developing fully his or her social part. Thus, if society is not well organized, problems will follow for the individual. Durkheim referred to the state of disorganization where social norms and rules exist in a weakened state, or do not exist at all, as "anomie."

Durkheim considered much of modern society as being in anomie, and as lacking sufficient organization and the rules necessary to provide both social and individual harmony. Accordingly, modern society manifests all sorts of conflicts between self-seeking individuals. For example, Durkheim argues that employers try to gain as much profit for themselves as possible and have no concern for the well-being of workers, who organize into groups in order to attack owners. In general, the anomic state of modern society has led to a relatively unrestrained citizenry, wherein people primarily look out for their own interests and have a disregard for those of others. However, Durkheim was not a Machiavelli or Hobbes who believed that the state of self-centered concern is the basis of human nature. The individual's social part, Durkheim insisted, is just as natural to humans as their individual part. The problems of modern society are due not to a basically antisocial human nature but to the structure of contemporary society, which does not adequately nurture, develop, and sustain the individual's socially oriented part. Durkheim argued that sociology, by studying society in an objective and scientific manner, could develop programs for the creation of a nonanomic society—a society in which the individual could fully develop a social nature and live a happy, harmonious, socially productive life.

Methodology

Durkheim maintained that there is an underlying positivistic unity of science. In other words, all the sciences—physical, chemical, biological, psychological, and social—share certain basic methodological principles and procedures. As the physicist studies relationships between physical facts in order to discover physical laws, and the biologist studies relationships among biological facts in order to discover biological laws, according to Durkheim, the sociologist studies relationships among objective "social facts" in order to formulate determinant social laws.

Social facts are characteristics of the *sui generis* society. As properties of society, they cannot be reduced to or redefined as individual or psychological facts. For instance, the degree of social integration, the amount of division of labor, or the rate of change in a society cannot be reduced to mere statements about particular persons. In Durkheim's terms, "social facts" are characterized by "generality." They are diffuse, or spread throughout society, and thus are not exclusively the property of any single individual.

A basic rule in the study of social facts, for Durkheim, involved the positivistic approach of "treating social facts as if they are things." In so doing, Durkheim focused on *external, objective, demonstrable, measurable* relationships among social facts—just as the physicist objectively measures and records the relationships among physical things as the facts or data of study. Although social facts might not be tangible like a piece of metal in a physicist's experiment, they do have certain thinglike qualities. Social facts (along with generality) are characterized by *externality* and *constraint*. Social facts, according to Durkheim, have a thinglike "external" existence that does not depend on the mere will or wishes of individuals. Furthermore, as aspects of a *sui generis* society, social facts influence, inhibit, or constrain human activity. Thus, according to Durkheim, social facts present a measurable constraint on human action, analogous to the constraint that such a physical thing as a wall, for example, can have on one's behaviors.

Although social facts can be treated as having thinglike qualities, they differ from physical things in not being easily observable. Thus, in order for sociologists to proceed with their studies, they must use indirect means of observing social facts. This involves the use of social indicators. Just as an observable change in the color or texture of a compound might indicate an underlying chemical reaction or relationship for a chemist, so the sociologist can observe changes in social indicators in order to examine relationships among social facts. Social indicators were thus the means by which Durkheim's positivistic approach linked his abstract theoretical statements with operational definitions usable in empirical analysis. The three types of social indicators that Durkheim used in his studies were statistical comparisons, historical comparisons, and ethnographic comparisons. Although Durkheim tended to combine the use of all three in his various sociological studies, some of his works reveal a greater emphasis on one kind of indicator than on the other two. Durkheim's *Suicide* (1897) emphasizes statistical indicators; *The Division of Labor in Society* (1893) relies on historical indicators; and *Elementary Forms of the Religious Life* (1912) involves a focus on ethnographic indicators.

In *Suicide*, among other concerns, Durkheim investigated the extent to which modern society is a harmonious, socially integrated society that is developing a strong social aspect and feeling of social unity and purpose in the individual. Durkheim assumed that in modern societies suicide rates are a good indicator of the extent to which a society is integrated. A high suicide rate shows a society characterized by low levels of integration, and containing people who (on the average) have a poorly developed social aspect and a weak sense of social unity and collective purpose.

A pioneer in the positivistic use of statistics, Durkheim in his study of suicide used government records containing suicide rate statistics for various societies, ethnic groups, religious groups, time periods, and social strata; and according to gender and marital status. Durkheim attempted to demonstrate in a series of comparisons (for example, between Protestants and Catholics, males and females, periods of war and peace, periods of economic stability and change) that suicide rates are a good measure of social integration and that the greater the integration of a group or society, the lower the suicide rate. In general, he concluded that modern society is insufficiently integrated to provide the supports necessary for both social harmony and individual well-being.

In *The Division of Labor in Society*, Durkheim relied heavily on historical records in developing indicators to study social facts. The social facts with which Durkheim was concerned involve the extent to which a particular society was characterized by "mechanical" as opposed to "organic" solidarity. A *mechanically* organized society is one in which social integration is based on a high level of shared beliefs, values, customs, and ritual interactions. All persons in such a society are very similar in their conceptions of reality, their social behavior, and their reactions to the behavior of others. People thus have little sense of individuality and share a unity based on common activity and feelings of likeness. An *organically* organized society, on the other hand, involves individuals and groups that are engaged in highly different activities. Such individuals and groups have a well-developed sense of individual differences and uniqueness. Social unity, rather than depending on likeness, is built on an interdependence of individuals and groups in the accomplishment of specialized tasks necessary for society's functioning and continued survival.

One of Durkheim's main contentions in *The Division of Labor* is that in the course of societal evolution, societies generally move from mechanical to organic forms of solidarity. The historical data Durkheim used to indicate the extent of one type of solidarity versus the other were written in legal codes. Rather than viewing historical data in a hermeneutical interpretive approach, Durkheim used them in a positivistic quantitative manner. Durkheim argued that the greater the amount of "repressive" law in a society, the greater the indication of mechanical solidarity; and the greater the extent of "restitutive" laws, the greater the extent of organic solidarity. Repressive law involves violent sanctions and aims to punish or destroy the rule violator. Restitutive law, on the other hand, involves a judgment in terms of damages done by the rule violator and a fine that "restores" the loss of the innocent victim. By the use of such historical indicators, Durkheim argued that he had quasi-quantitative evidence that demonstrated a long-run social change from mechanical to organic types of society.

Unlike the previously discussed studies, Durkheim's *Elementary Forms of the Religious Life* depends primarily on ethnographic (or cultural-anthropological) indicators. Durkheim's concern in this study involved examining that which is basic and fundamental in the nature and formation of social, moral, and religious rules. In order to comprehend what is most basic in all societies, Durkheim analyzed observational data from a simple, preliterate Australian tribe. He argued that whereas complex societies are too large and complicated to be observed as a whole, a small, simple society could serve as a good indicator, revealing social facts that exist in modern society but are obscured from the sociologist's view. At the beginning of *Elementary Forms of the Religious Life*, Durkheim wrote:

> In this book we propose to study the most primitive and simple religion which is actually known, to make an analysis of it, and to attempt an explanation of it. A religious system may be said to be the most primitive which we can observe when it fulfills the two following conditions: in the first place, when it is found in a society whose organization is surpassed by no others in simplicity; and secondly, when it is possible to explain it without making use of any element borrowed from a previous religion.
>
> We shall set ourselves to describe the organization of this system with all the exactness and fidelity that an ethnographer or an historian could give it. But our task will not be limited to that: sociology raises other problems than history or ethnography. It does not seek to know the passed forms of civilization with the sole end of knowing them and reconstructing them. But rather, like every positive science, it has as its object the explanation of some actual reality which is near to us, and which consequently is capable of affecting our ideas of today, for there is nothing which we are more interested in knowing. Then we are not going to study a very archaic religion simply for the pleasure of telling its peculiarities and its singularities. If we have taken it as the subject of our research, it is because it has seemed to us better adapted than any other to lead to an understanding of the religious nature of man, that is to say, to show us an essential and permanent aspect of humanity.[10]

For Durkheim, the study of social facts through indicators was not an end in itself; instead, it was to lead to the formulation of determinant sociological laws that would allow sociologists to predict the effects of various types of social facts on one another, as well as to predict the direction of future social change. The knowledge of social laws would also allow the sociologist to develop scientifically based programs for the solution of major social problems. Such solutions, Durkheim believed, would lead to a control and elimination of the major problems confronting modern society. Thus, as the end result of his methodological approach to the study of society, Durkheim envisioned deterministic positive social laws that would allow instrumental social control in the production of a better future.

Other Major Themes and Foci

Alongside those mentioned, a number of other topics or themes run throughout Durkheim's work. Among these are concerns about justifying the existence of sociology as a discipline in its own right, the nature of social institutions, the sociology of knowledge, and the sociology of morality.

Justification of the Field of Sociology

A significant portion of Durkheim's writings involves an attempt to justify the existence of sociology as an independent field and proper academic subject. Durkheim's argument for sociology's right to exist involved the presentation of sociology as a discipline that focuses on a unique subject matter, the need to develop a sociological method, the role of sociology in unifying more specialized subdisciplines, the need for sociology to promote change and solve social problems, and the failure of traditional humanistic and philosophical approaches to adequately understand the nature of the social world.

Basing his arguments on the *sui generis* nature of social reality, Durkheim asserted that sociology has a right to exist as a separate discipline because it focuses on a unique subject matter. Durkheim claimed that in order to fully understand a separate level of reality that manifests unique properties, there must be a specialized field to study that reality and its properties. Just as specialized fields had been developed in the past to study other levels of reality (physics for physical reality, chemistry for chemical reality, biology for biological reality, and psychology for psychological reality), so sociology must be developed to study social reality. A science can be established only when it has for its subject matter facts *sui generis*, facts that are different from those of the other sciences. If society did not produce phenomena that are different from those observable in the other realms of nature, sociology would be without a field of its own. Its existence can be justified only if there are realities that deserve to be called social and that are not simply aspects of another order of things.

For Durkheim, the development of sociology was especially important because of the extreme complexity of emergent social reality and the resultant necessity of specialized attention in order to comprehend its basic principles. Although the study of society shares certain basic positivistic assumptions and approaches with all the other sciences, Durkheim asserted that the uniqueness of its subject matter requires differences in methods of investigation and analysis. Because of the uniqueness of the subject matter, the study of social reality demands a field that is specifically concerned with the creation of specialized accurate techniques of study, including the creation of methodological indicators. Once sociology formulated a methodology, Durkheim claimed that it would be able to develop positive social laws that in turn would facilitate the prediction of social events and the creation of scientifically based cures for social problems. Furthermore, Durkheim insisted that sociology is necessary because these ends cannot be achieved by other, more specialized social sciences.

As a general social science, sociology would not just develop general techniques and methods of study but would also allow the integration of specific findings into general knowledge about the social world. Durkheim argued that, whereas studies of criminology, demography, family, education, politics, economics, and so on look at particular aspects of social reality, sociology as a unified discipline could organize and relate these various particularistic findings. Sociology could thereby produce an organized general body of social scientific propositions. Durkheim insisted that the various specialized disciplines are too concerned with the parts of social reality to comprehend the totality, but that such comprehension is necessary for the creation and implementation of adequate social reforms. Only with the *instrumental* knowledge of a full-fledged science of society would it be possible to predict and change social development in such a way as to create a harmonious social order.

Finally, sociology was necessary, according to Durkheim, because of the failures of the existing field of traditional philosophy to adequately grasp the nature of social reality. Traditional philosophy, Durkheim maintained, proceeded by a method of conjecture and deduction. It further assumed that principles of social and moral order are universal or the same in all societies. Durkheim thus concluded that knowledge derived by traditional philosophers is of little use in creating a better social world. Accordingly, crises and problems of modern society demand an independent field focused on a scientific study of social phenomena. That field is, of course, sociology.

Social Institutions

Durkheim's sociology emphasized an analysis of social institutions as basic developmental and functional components of society (or the "social organism"). Among the various institutional areas about which Durkheim wrote are the religious, educational, familial, economic, and political. His focus on institutional areas usually involved a concern with social origins, functions, and change. In terms of origins, religion is for Durkheim the most fundamental social institution. It is both the earliest institution to develop and the foundation on which the other institutions are based. Its most basic function is to integrate individuals into society and produce sentiments of unity, belonging, and common purpose.

Religion is defined by Durkheim as essentially that which focuses on the distinction between the sacred and the profane and on the properties, beliefs, feelings, and social rituals related to the sacred. Durkheim pointed out that, although religions exist that lack sacred writings, conceptions of a god or gods, and priesthoods or a clergy, all religions make a fundamental distinction between the sacred and profane. The *sacred* involves that which is collectively held in awe and which is apart from everyday use. Violations of sacredness by individuals always result in severe punishment. The *profane* is that which is used in an everyday utilitarian manner. Durkheim maintained that the sacred is an emanation from society; in other words, something is sacred because it is collectively held to be so. Furthermore, Durkheim believed that sacred phenomena and rituals are a mythologized representation of society itself. In one of Durkheim's most central and controversial assertions, he claimed that all religion is socially oriented, and that the later conception of God represents the society on whose existence the individual's life is dependent. Thus, if the source of all other institutions and conceptions lies in religion, it is because religion itself is a manifestation of the total society. As society develops, religious beliefs, ideas, and sentiments (what Durkheim would call "collective representations") develop and separate into the various specialized fields of philosophy and the sciences, while other social activities increasingly take on a secular (nonsacred) character.

Whereas in the past, education had been dominated by religious orders, Durkheim noted that it increasingly came under the control of the secular state. For Durkheim, education and the school system were at least as important for social and moral function as for the teaching of technical skills and knowledge. It is in the school, Durkheim wrote, that the child first learns to take part in collective activities outside the family. It is the function of the school not just to transmit knowledge, but to inculcate in the child a spirit of teamwork and collective purpose, a desire to develop specialized skills in terms of the needs of others, and a tendency to subordinate his or her own interests to those of the group. For Durkheim, the teacher was a representation of society as a whole; the teacher's authority directly derives from that of the society over the individual. Durkheim argued that in order for the social and moral functions of education to be maintained, the teacher must be seen as an authority figure who controls the classroom in a fair and just manner. He maintained that although the need for basic moral and social education will continue to exist, more advanced education will continue to develop into increasingly specialized subfields as specialization in society continues to occur.

As specialization becomes the hallmark of education, it serves to undermine the traditional strengths and functions of the family. With specialization in production, the individual spends increasingly larger amounts of time in occupational training and in following pursuits away from familial socialization, constraint, and moral influence. As family members spend less time with one another, they begin to develop different conceptions, interests, outlooks, and goals in life. Accordingly, family bonds weaken, and the family's ability to integrate the individual into social life declines. Socialization, once almost exclusively the province of the family, increasingly takes place outside the home. Durkheim predicted that this trend would continue. He argued that modern society must develop institutional forms capable of handling the functions of socialization and integration in a complex, differentiated society.

If Durkheim's concern with familial and educational institutions involved an interest in the socialization of individual life, his concern with the economic institution of society was premised on a belief that it is within this institution that much of one's adult life will take place. The economic institution, according to Durkheim, is primarily concerned with the productive activities through which the adult individual contributes to the social whole. In the past, economic forms were to a significant degree an extension of family-centered activity, but this is not the case in modern society. Durkheim saw modern industrial society as being characterized by economic activity based on specialized knowledge and training and as taking place in locales removed from family supervision. This separation from traditional supervision, though necessary for industrial development, has, according to Durkheim, produced many of the problems found in the economic sphere. Durkheim maintained that as the new industrial economic entities developed rapidly outside the traditional family, religious, and political institutions, they developed without the benefit of a set of widely shared sociomoral rules. Lacking such rules, economic egoism produces continuous and relatively unmitigated employer-employer and employer-employee conflicts. (The former included vicious competition in which manufacturers tried to destroy one another's businesses; the latter included violent strikes and lockouts.) Accordingly, the modern economic sphere is one of both social crises and sudden changes. These crises were all the more significant for Durkheim because he believed they had a general tendency to spread beyond the economic institution to infect all the other social institutions.

According to Durkheim, the contemporary political institution does indeed bear the mark of unhealthy crisis. In a healthy state, Durkheim believed, the political institution should function as a "social brain" or as the central consciousness-coordinating aspect of society. Durkheim did not see the political institution in France as being in a healthy state, however. Instead, Durkheim perceived that his society's present political institution manifested an archaic system of geographically structured political districts and ideological disunity, and that in general it was conducive to the representation of special, not general, social interests.

In sum, then, Durkheim saw the various modern social institutions (religious, familial, educational, economic, and political) as being in a state of drastic change and as suffering from disunity and social pathology. Accordingly, much of Durkheim's other sociological work focused on attempts to understand the process of change engulfing modern social institutions in order to enable the instrumental development of cures for their persistent problems.

The Sociology of Knowledge

With the development of his thought, Durkheim's writings show an increasing concern with the sociology of knowledge. The sociology of knowledge examines the social influences that affect how people perceive, understand, and formulate concepts and ideas about the world. Durkheim argued that the very categories by which we think are not biologically innate but, rather, develop through the impact of social forces. This position emerges from Durkheim's sociological reinterpretation of ideas developed by the German philosopher Immanuel Kant.

Kant argued that we never perceive the world as it actually exists. Instead, all our perceptions are filtered through the structures and processes of our mind. Events or occurrences that are external to us are not directly apprehended but are conceptualized as a result of such structures and processes. Thus, for Kant, our minds are prepared to organize perceptions and cognitions according to certain mental categories. Kant's philosophical writings entail a statement of what these categories are, and contain the assumption that these *a priori* categories are basic to human beings—and thus are transcendental, or universally shared.

In reinterpreting Kant, Durkheim argued that basic categories of perception and understanding should not be conceived of as innate. Instead, they should be seen as a product of social life and development. According to Durkheim, the structure of early or primitive social relationships gave rise to the mental categories by which humans developed their perceptions and cognitions. These categories involve the interpretation of the world in terms of time sequences, cause and effect, hierarchies, logical relationships, and wholes and parts. Durkheim believed that all these mental categories developed out of early social life. He argued, for instance, that conceptions of time derive from the periodic repetition of social encounters and rituals; conceptions of cause and effect result from the influence of society on its members; conceptions of hierarchical relationships derive from hierarchies in social statuses; logical relationships (in general) are modeled after social relationships among individuals and groups; and conceptions of wholes and parts develop from an understanding of the society and its subgroups by its members. Thus, according to Durkheim, our knowledge of the world is a direct outcome of social life. Furthermore, Durkheim pointed out that as society changes and develops, forms of understanding develop and become more complex. Nonetheless, despite later developments, the basic mental categories formed in primitive social existence persist as the foundation of human perception and understanding.

To some extent, Durkheim's ideas about the sociology of knowledge constituted a break from his general positivistic and instrumentalist view of the study of social life. Rather than asserting the thinglike nature of social facts, as in his earlier works, in his sociology of knowledge Durkheim emphasized the extent to which understanding is mediated by socially created constructs. Yet one should be wary of making too much of this development in Durkheim's thoughts; for, despite his later emphasis on knowledge as a socially relative construct, he never abandoned his positivistic emphasis on the unity of science and the instrumental uses to which sociological knowledge would be put. The end result of sociology was to be positive laws permitting the determinant control and restructuring of social life.

The Sociology of Morality

Pervasive throughout Durkheim's thought is a concern with the nature of moral action and the utility of sociology in achieving moral ends. Indeed, at the time of his death, Durkheim was preparing to write a final major work that was to focus on morality. Durkheim's principal thesis about moral action is that, despite variations in what is considered moral in different societies, the ends to which moral action is oriented always involve the benefit of the collective social whole. In other words, moral action is always aimed at achieving social or societal ends and is never focused on purely individual wishes, goals, or desires. An orientation to collective ends, which is the hallmark of moral action, is developed through socialization and the creation of the social (or moral) part of the individual's dualistic nature. Furthermore, the "healthiness" of a society is directly dependent on the degree to which moral, socially oriented action is developed in the average or typical individual. Thus, in a society that has an anomic lack of social (and moral) rules, and that includes many individuals who have not been adequately socialized or supported in morally oriented actions, social problems based on individual and group competition and antagonism will be endemic.

Durkheim asserted that the moral individual is affected both by feelings of obligation and desirability, although the degree to which either of these feelings is dominant can vary. According to Durkheim, not only does an individual feel socially constrained to perform actions, but additionally, the normal individual (who should feel himself or herself a part of society) has a desire to perform acts that are oriented toward the benefit of the social whole. This statement is true of individuals in all types of society, although precisely what actions are considered moral will vary with the social type. Durkheim asserted that

> the notion of duty does not exhaust the concept of morality. It is impossible for us to carry out an act simply because we are ordered to do so and without consideration of its content. For us to become the agents of an act it must interest our sensibility to a certain extent and appear to us as, in some way, *desirable*. Obligation or duty only expresses an aspect abstracted from morality. A certain degree of desirability is another characteristic no less important than the first.
>
> Something of the nature of duty is found in the desirability of morality. If it is true that the content of the act appeals to us, nevertheless its nature is such that it cannot be accomplished without effort and self-constraint. The *élan*, even the enthusiasm, with which we perform a moral act takes us outside ourselves and above our nature, and this is not achieved without difficulty and inner conflict. It is this *sui generis* desirability which is commonly called *good*.[11]

Durkheim argued that one of the failings of traditional philosophy has been its attempt to discover or formulate a universal definition of what is moral. Durkheim maintained that, because what is moral is tied to what is beneficial to the society, as the nature or type of society changes, so too will the nature of what is moral. In other words, that which is moral is not universal in its particulars but varies with social type. Each social type, according to Durkheim, will be characterized by a particular conception of morality and moral action.

The way to discover the appropriate form of morality of a particular society, Durkheim thus asserted, is not by logical deduction but rather by empirical investigation of the types of moral activity that are related to and found in various types of society. Such investigation, he claimed, will show that the forms of moral action that are appropriate in one society or at one historical stage of social development are not necessarily the appropriate ones in another society or at another stage of development. Durkheim thus maintained that sociology, with its emphasis on empirical analysis, is ideally suited to analyze the forms of morality and moral action appropriate for modern industrial society and to aid in developing reforms necessary for the creation of a harmonious society characterized by morally oriented individuals.

SIGNIFICANCE

Vision of the Future

According to the philosopher Mark Cladis:

> Social theory . . . , in Durkheim's view, is a normative discipline. Its task is to help us understand who we are by analyzing past and present institutions so that we can better understand where we are to go in the future.[12]

A large portion of Durkheim's work is dedicated to detailing those features of modern society that he viewed as in need of reform, while simultaneously pointing to the institutional areas whose socially necessary activities needed to be preserved. As we have seen, Durkheim considered his society to be an anomic one, characterized both by a lack of adequate moral regulation of individuals and by insufficient coordination and harmony among groups. For Durkheim, modern society is marked by conflicts in the industrial world that spread disharmony and misery throughout society. Such disharmony and misery can be seen in the high anomic and egoistic suicide rates of modern societies and in the meaninglessness and purposelessness that characterize the lives of many individuals. Durkheim claimed that these problems persisted because the family, traditional religion, and the state all lack the strength to confront them adequately. Durkheim wrote:

> We are living precisely in one of those critical, revolutionary periods when authority is usually weakened through the loss of traditional discipline—a time that may easily give rise to a spirit of anarchy. This is the source of the anarchic aspirations that, whether consciously or not, are emerging today, not only in the particular sects bearing the name, but in the very different doctrines that, although opposed on other points, join in a common aversion to anything smacking of regulation.[13]

Despite this negative evaluation of modern society, Durkheim's view of the future was optimistic. The problems that seemed so massive, he believed, would in the future be open to solution. Durkheim's optimism was based on the belief that modern society was in a transitional period, facing many problems that were due to rapid social changes that had occurred recently. Durkheim believed that rapid change in the way people organize their lives and in the organization of society had swept away old moral rules and regulations. He argued that the social rules tied to a preindustrial feudal society ceased to be effective as society rapidly became industrial and democratic. These changes made the social moral rules that had developed in the older feudal society meaningless for modern day-to-day life. Social problems thus existed because the old rules had declined without any new ones taking their place. Given time, Durkheim argued, new rules should naturally develop from the interaction of people and groups in industrial society. He maintained that as new rules for individual life and social organization emerged, society would move from a disharmonious transitional form to a harmonious mature form.

According to Durkheim, this movement to a harmonious mature modern industrial societal type would be advanced by the development of sociology as a positive science. As sociologists expanded their studies and increased their knowledge of social laws, they would be able to offer instrumental advice to decision makers on how society might be modified for the better. Thus, for Durkheim, a science of society would not only make us aware of the social problems inherent in society but would also provide the best means for overcoming those problems.

In envisioning the form that a mature modern industrial society would exhibit, Durkheim rejected both liberal *laissez-faire* capitalism (such as espoused by Spencer) and socialism (as presented by Marx) because he viewed both as presenting fundamentally flawed images of society as basically an economic system. For Durkheim, society was essentially a *sui generis* moral entity, and any successful reformation of it had to recognize it as such and involve the creation of a moral unity suited to industrial society. Such a unity would necessarily respect and reflect the individualism of modern society, but would keep that individualism from degenerating into a divisive and self-destructive egoism. In a number of works, Durkheim attempted to envision what such a mature industrial society would entail. Essentially he presented a society organized in terms of industry-specific communal entities that would perform many basic social functions. He termed these entities "corporations." Thus his conception of a sociologically reformed society of the future can be termed "corporatism."

In order to overcome industrial conflict and promote understanding and solidarity, all members of a particular occupation in a region would belong to the same association or "corporation." The corporation would be made up of both employees and employers. It would be administered by a council, some of whose members would represent the employers and others the workers in particular occupational fields. This council in turn would send representatives to a group governing the occupation on a national level (or a national corporate body). Each national corporation, which together would represent all the members of a particular occupational area in society, would send representatives to a parliament governing the nation. Thus the national governing body would represent the interests of everyone, as well as having all the varied expertise and knowledge of its diverse membership to call on in the formulation of national policy.

The function of the national parliament, once it was established, would be to set general national policy and to settle any disputes that might arise between various national corporations. Each national corporation would be in charge of interpreting general national policy and of applying it to the particular occupation it represented. The national corporation would also judge any disputes that might arise between various local corporations representing members of the same occupation. The local corporation would have a duty to interpret national corporate policy in terms of local circumstances and environment. It would also set wages and fair working conditions, and would regulate competition; thus it would prevent conflicts between employees and employers and between one owner and another. Additionally, the local corporation would be in charge of education, social welfare, and recreational facilities. Durkheim believed it would create harmonious feelings among individuals in industrial society and would bring an end to the unregulated anomie of Durkheim's day:

> The occupational group has the three-fold advantage over all others that it is omnipresent, ubiquitous and that its control extends to the greatest part of life. Its influence on

individuals is not intermittent, like that of political society, but it is always in contact with them by the constant exercise of the function of which it is the organ and in which they collaborate. It follows the workers wherever they go; which the family cannot do. Wherever they are, they find it enveloping them, recalling them to their duties, supporting them at need. Finally, since occupational life is almost the whole of life, corporative action makes itself felt in every detail of our occupations, which are thus given a collective orientation. Thus the corporation has everything needed to give the individual a setting, to draw him out of his state of moral isolation; and faced by the actual inadequacy of the other groups, it alone can fulfill this indispensable office.[14]

In sum, Durkheim envisioned a future in which equality of opportunity and democracy would be perpetuated in a society organized in terms of industrial occupational categories. Such a society, he believed, was not only possible: It would develop out of the current transitional societal state and from the application of sociological knowledge.

Contemporary Relevance

Durkheim's intellectual influence has been widespread, in terms of both a variety of disciplines that reflect his ideas and the number of countries whose intellectual traditions have incorporated elements of his thought. In France, Durkheim not only, almost single-handedly, institutionalized sociology; his ideas were also highly influential in later developments in anthropology, linguistics, and history. (Prominent historians, such as Marc Bloch, Lucien Febvre, and Fernand Braudel admit to having been greatly influenced by his works.[15]) In the United States, the significance of Durkheim's thought for contemporary sociology is considerable. Indeed, Durkheim's influence is of such scope that it cannot be appreciated fully in this brief sketch. Yet despite his present importance, Durkheim's sociological ideas were not widely accepted by his American contemporaries, such as William Sumner (1840–1910), Charles Cooley (1864–1929), Lester Ward (1841–1913), and Franklin Giddings (1855–1931). It has been suggested that Durkheim's emphasis on a *sui generis* society (and all it entailed) conflicted with his American contemporaries' emphasis on voluntarism and individualism. With changes in U.S. society and American sociology, however, Durkheim's sociological influence grew considerably by the later 1930s.[16] In 1937, Talcott Parsons published his influential interpretation of Durkheim in English,[17] and in 1939, Harry Alpert's book, emphasizing Durkheim's similarity to U.S. thought, was published.[18] From this point, Durkheim's reputation and influence continued to grow. By the 1940s and 1950s, he was widely considered to be one of the founders of modern sociological thought and research.

This view still prevails today, and the degree of acquaintance of the practicing American sociologist with Durkheim's thought has continued to expand. All of Durkheim's major works and many of his minor ones are currently in publication in English, most of them in readily available paperback editions. *Suicide* is probably the most widely read by sociologists and in sociology graduate courses. *The Division of Labor in Society, Elementary Forms of the Religious Life,* and *The Rules of Sociological Method* are also widely read. (On the other hand, some works, such as *Professional Ethics and Civic Morals, The Evolution of Educational Thought,* and *Sociology and Philosophy* receive considerably less attention.) Another sign of interest in Durkheim's thought is the continuous English-language publication of works on the French sociologist. Additionally, articles interpreting, commenting on, applying, testing, or developing Durkheim's thought frequently appear in American sociological journals.

Various aspects of American sociology reveal a marked Durkheimian influence. These include conceptions of the field, methodological and stylistic approaches, the study of social change, the study of social order or integration, the theoretical orientation of functionalism, and the study of values and beliefs. Additionally, Durkheim's influence is particularly significant in the subareas of the sociology of deviance, the sociology of religion, the sociology of knowledge and science, the sociology of education, and the sociological study of suicide.

Durkheim asserted that sociology is a unique form of study, and most contemporary sociologists would agree with this assertion. The study of society, Durkheim maintained, could not be reduced merely to the study of psychology, nor could society be explained in terms of geographic or racial characteristics. Durkheim's claim that, when people come together to form groups, phenomena or forces emerge from their interaction that are the property of the group (not merely the psychological property of particular persons), is widely accepted today as a sociological truism. Following Durkheim, most contemporary sociologists (though with some notable exceptions) think of sociology as the study of roles, norms, institutions, social patterns, and characteristics of group life in general. After Durkheim, sociologists have tended to assume that such group characteristics shape, affect, influence, or determine the activities of subgroups or individuals. Thus, in accepting a Durkheimian conception of the field, sociologists explain activity in terms of such societal characteristics as demographic patterns, family structure, religious rituals and collectively shared beliefs, socialization, norms and practices, and the like.

Along with accepting a Durkheimian conception of the discipline, many, though by no means all, sociologists follow techniques and styles of study he pioneered. Of especial influence in shaping modern methodological approaches has been Durkheim's study *Suicide.* This volume has been judged by a number of eminent sociologists to be one of the first works to demonstrate how propositions grounded in sociological theory can be satisfactorily examined and tested.[19]

The style and presentation of research in contemporary sociological journals show a marked Durkheimian influence. As with Durkheim's classic study of suicide, the standard form of presentation involves the statement of theoretical position, the derivation of testable propositions, the use of statistics and correlational measures to test the propositions, a reexamination of the propositions in terms of statistical evidence, and an examination of the implication of these tested propositions.

More substantively, Durkheim's conception of society as moving toward increasing complexity, functional differentiation, and integration has informed and influenced many conceptions of social change or evolution. For example, Durkheim's influence can be seen in Parsons's and Gerhard Lenski's respective theories of general social evolution,[20] Robert Bellah's work on religious evolutionism,[21] Samuel

Eisenstadt's conceptions of political evolution,[22] and Marion Levy's writings on "modernization."[23]

Durkheim's writings have also influenced studies of social order or integration. Academics concerned with social order have been particularly influenced by Durkheim's conception of society as an organic whole characterized by functionally specialized parts. Building on these Durkheimian conceptions of order, A. R. Radcliffe-Brown (in anthropology) and Talcott Parsons (in sociology) developed the orientation of *functionalism*.[24] Functionalism emphasizes the study of social phenomena in terms of their (functional) contributions to other social phenomena within the context of a social whole. As a theoretical orientation, it dominated sociology in the 1950s and is still presented as a major orientation in contemporary sociology. (For instance, many introductory texts simplistically, but revealingly, categorize contemporary sociological approaches as either "conflict" or functionalist oriented.)

Although functionalists tend to proudly present themselves as direct intellectual heirs of Durkheim, questions have been raised about the extent to which functionalists not only borrowed Durkheim's ideas, but also systematically distorted them. As the reader will recall, Durkheim developed his own ideas out of the organic (functionalist) reasoning of the conservative anti-Enlightenment *and* the individualistic arguments arising out of the French Enlightenment. Durkheim's essay "Individualism and the Intellectuals" (1898), for instance, attempts a balanced presentation on the need for social order *and* the need to protect individual rights and opportunities within the context of a modern industrial society. Durkheim looked at society as a sociomoral system concerned not just with functionally maintaining itself, but also with dispensing justice for its members. His orientation sought to confront the pathologies of his contemporary society in order to aid in the development of a new sociomoral order that would no longer be characterized by the conflicts and injustices of the "transitional" period that he saw reflected in French society. According to Mike Gane, Durkheim's sociology has an integral "radical" element—an element of social criticism—peculiarly missing from functionalist writings that claim to be derived from Durkheim's thought. In the introduction to a collection of writings entitled *The Radical Sociology of Durkheim and Mauss*, Gane asserts:

> In its mainly American form, Durkheim's theory has been transformed into a functionalist celebration of American society . . . purged of its critical analysis of modern social pathology.[25]

Gane's comment is fundamentally correct. For example, Durkheim's concept of anomie, used by him in *Suicide* and *The Division of Labor in Society* to diagnose society and to reveal social problems necessitating sociologically guided reforms, was redefined by Robert Merton, one of the founders of American functionalism, as an inevitable outcome of social structure. Thus for Merton, and unlike Durkheim, anomie does not necessitate either social criticism or social reform.[26] Similarly, Durkheim's attempts to understand inequality and develop the outlines of a sociomoral system that would be neither capitalist nor socialist are replaced in American functionalist thinking with arguments that justify the current structure of inequality on the grounds of functional necessity. Both Kingsley Davis's and Wilbert Moore's well-known article on social stratification[27] and Parsons's essay on inequality[28] lack any critical element whatsoever and instead legitimize contemporary inequality.

Not all, or perhaps even most, later sociologists who have borrowed from Durkheim have done so using a prevailingly functionalist logic. Many later sociologists have been more interested in Durkheim's "cultural" focus on the emergence and social significance of shared meanings and collective values. Such concerns have made Durkheim a major influence in the sociology of religion and the study of religious and quasi-religious activities. Jeffrey Alexander claims that Durkheim's ideas have "significantly influenced the developments in cultural studies that are invigorating the world today"[29] and has published a volume of such studies that build directly on concepts developed by Durkheim in his *Elementary Forms of the Religious Life* and other later works. The relevance of Durkheim is revealed in such articles as Edward A. Tyiryakin's "From Durkheim to Managua: Revolutions as Religious Revivals," Eric W. Rothenbuhler's "The Liminal Fight: Mass Strikes as Ritual and Interpretation," Danial Dayan and Elihu Katz's "Articulating Consensus: The Ritual and Rhetoric of Media Events," and Jeffrey Alexander's "Culture and Political Crisis: 'Watergate' and Durkheimian Sociology."[30]

Durkheim's influence on functionalism, symbolic/cultural studies of religion and religious-like phenomena, and various subareas of sociology (such as the sociology of deviance, knowledge, law, and education) has long been recognized. However, an argument has been made that Durkheim has been a major influence on a sociological orientation not typically connected with him. In *The Classical Roots of Ethnomethodology: Durkheim, Weber, and Garfinkel*, Richard A. Hilbert argues that Durkheim had a profound, though indirect, influence on the development of ethnomethodology by Harold Garfinkel. According to Hilbert, Garfinkel restored to sociological analysis a number of elements that his teacher Talcott Parsons had discarded from Durkheim. In other words, Garfinkel recognized gaps in sociological thinking left by Parsons's effort to subordinate Durkheim's view to his own theoretical system. Garfinkel created ethnomethodology by reintegrating what Hilbert says were "neglected" and "suppressed" Durkheimian elements back into sociological discourse. Accordingly, ethnomethodology reflects a number of fundamental Durkheimian principles. Hilbert says these elements include an emphasis on viewing society as a *sui generis* order produced by the actions of individuals, as opposed to Parsons's view whereby human action is looked at in the context of some presupposed "rule-governed model."[31] Hilbert asserts that both Durkheim and Garfinkel view the very categories and terms by which we understand society as emerging from society itself.

Hilbert's ethnomethodological reading of Durkheim emphasizes his emphasis on emergent properties. Unfortunately, this reading, too, distorts Durkheim. It ignores Durkheim's emphasis on society forming an objective reality understandable through positivistic scientific methods. It also ignores the larger social evolutionary context of Durkheim's thought. For instance, Hilbert's ethnomethodological reading of Durkheim's concept of anomie does not take into account that for Durkheim anomie existed as an objective, discoverable, and measurable social fact and that the level of anomie served as a diagnostic tool in measuring the degree of social pathology in the transition from one social evolutionary type to another. Additionally, the arguments made by Gane toward functionalists like Parsons might equally be applied to Parsons's student Garfinkel. The ethnomethodologist no more attends to the social critical and reformist elements central to Durkheim's view of sociology than does the functionalist.

Perhaps, when one assesses the overall influence of Durkheim on contemporary sociology, the most salient feature is that sociologists from a wide variety of orientations and subareas in the discipline find it fruitful to selectively borrow Durkheimian images and ideas. As the British sociologist Frank Parkin has asserted, sociologists "continue to wrestle with the questions he [Durkheim] raised and to plunder the Aladdin's cave of concepts he bequeathed."[32]

NOTES

1. Robert Alun Jones, *Emile Durkheim*, p. 20.

2. Frank Parkin, *Durkheim*, p. 6.

3. *The division of labor in society*, 1964, p. 33.

4. Jones, *Emile Durkheim*, p. 15.

5. Steve Fenton, *Durkheim and modern sociology*, p. 15.

6. See W. S. F. Pickering, *Durkheim's sociology of religion: Themes and theories*.

7. For an opposing view, see Stjepan G. Meštrovic, *Emile Durkheim and the reformation of sociology*, and Ivan Strenski, *Emile Durkheim and the Jews of France*.

8. *The rules of sociological method and selected texts on sociology and its method*, 1982, p. 129.

9. "The dualism of human nature," in *Essays on sociology and philosophy*, p. 337.

10. *Elementary forms of the religious life*, 1965, p. 13.

11. *Sociology and philosophy*, 1974, p. 36.

12. Mark S. Cladis, *A communitarian defense of liberalism: Emile Durkheim and contemporary sociological theory*, p. 28.

13. *Moral education*, 1973, p. 54.

14. *Suicide*, 1964, p. 379.

15. Kenneth Thompson, *Emile Durkheim*, p. 17.

16. See Roscoe C. Hinkle, "Durkheim in American sociology," in *Essays on sociology and philosophy*.

17. Talcott Parsons, *The structure of social action*, Vol. 1 (New York: Free Press, 1968 [1937]).

18. Harry Alpert, *Emile Durkheim and his sociology* (New York: Columbia University Press, 1939).

19. Such as Pitrim Sorokin, Robert Merton, and Talcott Parsons.

20. See Talcott Parsons, *The system of modern societies* (Englewood Cliffs, NJ: Prentice-Hall, 1971); Parsons, *Societies, evolutionary and comparative perspectives* (Englewood Cliffs, NJ: Prentice-Hall, 1966); Parsons, "Evolutionary Universals," *American Sociological Review*, 29 (1964), 339–57; and Gerhard Lenski, *Human societies* (4th ed.) (New York: McGraw-Hill, 1980).

21. See Robert Bellah, "Religious evolution," *American Sociological Review*, 29 (1964), 358–74.

22. See Samuel Eisenstadt, *Modernization: Protest and change* (Englewood Cliffs, NJ: Prentice-Hall, 1965); Eisenstadt, "Social change, differentiation, and evolution," *American Sociological Review*, 29 (1964), 375–85; and Eisenstadt, *The political system of empires* (New York: Free Press, 1963).

23. See Marion Levy, *Modernization and the structure of societies* (Princeton, NJ: Princeton University Press, 1966).

24. See A. R. Radcliffe-Brown, *Structure and function in primitive society* (New York: Free Press, 1965), and Talcott Parsons, *The society system* (New York: Free Press, 1951).

25. Mike Gane (Ed.), *The radical sociology of Durkheim and Mauss* (London: Routledge, 1992), p. 5.
26. Robert Merton, "Social structure and anomie," *American Sociological Review, 3* (1938), 672–82.
27. See Kingsley Davis & Wilbert E. Moore, "Some principles of stratification," *American Sociological Review, 10* (1945), 242–49.
28. Talcott Parsons, "Equality and inequality in modern society, or social stratification re-visited," in Parsons, *Social systems and the evolution of action theory* (New York: Free Press, 1977).
29. Alexander, *Durkheimian sociology,* p. 10.
30. All in ibid.
31. Hilbert, *The classical roots of ethnomethodology,* p. 46.
32. Parkin, *Durkheim,* p. 1.

GLOSSARY

Altruistic suicide Form of self-sacrificing behavior that occurs as a result of overconformity with group rules and overidentification with the collective whole. Most prevalent in simpler societies.

Anomic suicide Self-destructive behavior arising in a social setting that lacks sufficient sociomoral rules to constrain actors by integrating them into the collective whole. Most prevalent in period of transition to modern society.

Anomie State of social disorganization brought on by the lack of, or insufficiency of, social and moral rules regulating activity between persons and groups.

A priori Latin term meaning that which is innate or preexisting.

Collective consciousness or conscience (translation of *conscience collective*) An emergent characteristic of a group or society arising from and supporting a unified mental and emotional response to the events of the world.

Collective representations (translation of *representation collective*) Shared beliefs, values, norms, ways of thinking, and ways of feeling that characterize a particular social group or society.

Corporatism Durkheim's plan for the reorganization of modern society, involving the centrality of occupational specializations in reshaping the political and other institutions.

Differentiation Social evolutionary process by which functional institutional areas separate from one another, increasing the complexity of social organization.

Dualism (of human nature) The position that human nature is composed of two basic irreducible parts, elements, or components.

Egoistic suicide Self-destructive behavior occurring when the social part of an individual's nature is insufficiently developed. Most prevalent in the transitional period to modern society.

Emergence Process of interaction of parts by which more complex levels of reality arise from simpler ones.

Empiricism Process involving a claim to knowledge based on some systematic form of sense observation (i.e., seeing, hearing, touching, tasting, smelling).

Ethnographic indicators of data Elements of knowledge derived from cultural anthropological sources, such as the study of preliterate peoples.

Externality: That which is characterized by having an existence independent of the will of a particular person or an aggregate of persons.

Function: Contribution made by the individual or group to maintenance of another group or the social whole.

Generality: That which is characterized by a property that resides in or is derived from a collective whole as opposed to any particular person or aggregate of persons.

Horde: Simplest undifferentiated form of society.

Individual representations: Ways of thinking, feeling, and reacting that are not shared in the society but are the property of particular individuals. (Compare with *Collective representations.*)

Levels of reality: Conception that the universe can be divided into a series of separate, though related, basic forms of existence (that is, forms manifesting different fundamental characteristics) in terms of their degree of complexity. For Durkheim, these realities were, in order from simplest to most complex: physical, chemical, biological, psychological, and social.

Malady of infiniteness: Durkheim's conception of an individual characterized by pathological insatiable desires brought on by an underdeveloped social aspect of his or her nature.

Mechanical solidarity: Form of social organization in simple societies based on similarity or likeness of persons in terms of their conceptualization of reality and orientation toward the collective whole. (Compare with *Organic solidarity.*)

Methodological indicators: Indirect means of empirical analysis used in scientific investigation. Durkheim's work manifests three kinds of methodological indicators: statistical, historical, and ethnographic.

Moral action: According to Durkheim, that activity which is oriented toward the benefit of the social whole and which is characterized by feelings of obligation and desirability.

Organic solidarity: Form of social organization in more complex societies based on occupational specialization and functional differentiation of social parts. (Compare with *Mechanical solidarity.*)

Polysegmental doubly compound society: More differentiated and complex societal type than polysegmental simple compound society.

Profane: The realm of the nonsacred. That which is used or acted on in an everyday, utilitarian manner.

Repressive law: Laws involving punishment or destruction of violator of social rules. (Compare with *Restitutive law.*)

Restitutive law: Laws involving obligation of the violator of social rules to reestablish situation as it was before the violation occurred, in order to compensate the victim of the violation. (Compare with *Repressive law.*)

Sacred: The defining characteristic of religion, according to Durkheim. The sacred emanates in society, is collectively held in awe, and is forbidden in everyday use.

Simple polysegmental society: Next to simplest form of society. Created by the union of two or more hordes.

Social evolution: Process of social change that is usually conceived of as natural, normal, necessary, internal, slow, step-by-step, cumulative, and directional. Proceeds through a series of sequential stages.

Social facts: Attributes, characteristics, or properties of social reality that cannot be reduced to psychological, biological, chemical, or physical attributes or properties.

Social indicators: See *Methodological indicators.*

Social pathologies: Deviations from what is typical, normal, or usual for a particular societal type.

Social types: Durkheim's conception of evolutionary ranked forms of social organization differentiated by size, the number of basic component parts, and the complexity by which those parts are arranged.

Sui generis reality: Latin term expressing a conception that something is a reality in and of itself and cannot be reduced to its subparts or components without loss or destruction of its most central and fundamental characteristics.

Utilitarianism: Philosophical position derived from British moral philosophy, in which claims to morality and truth are based on calculations of what produces the greatest good for the greatest number.

Voluntarism: Opposed to determinism. A position that conceives of individual social activity as being (at least partially) a product of free will or choice.

ANNOTATED BIBLIOGRAPHY

Primary Sources

The division of labor in society (G. Simpson, Trans.). New York: Free Press, 1964 [1893] (paper).

Durkheim's earliest major work. Discussions include many of his central ideas, with detailed treatments of "anomie" and the movement from "mechanical" to "organic" forms of society.

The division of labor in society (W. D. Halls, Trans.). New York: Free Press, 1984 [1893] (paper).

This is a much superior translation of *De la division du travail social* than the earlier English version. Lewis Coser's introductory essay is worthwhile reading.

Durkheim: Essays on morals and education (W.S.F. Pickering, Ed.; H. L. Sutcliffe, Trans.). London: Routledge & Kegan Paul, 1979.

Durkheim held a joint appointment in education (pedagogy) and sociology and wrote extensively on the subject of education—especially in terms of the inculcation of moral values in the student. This volume introduces a number of Durkheim's writings not previously translated into English and is worthwhile reading together with *Education and Sociology* and *Moral Education*.

Durkheim and the law (Steven Lukes & Andrew Scull, Eds.). Oxford, England: Martin Robertson, 1983.

Following a good 27-page introductory essay by the editors summarizing the central themes of Durkheim's sociology of law, a number of excerpts are presented from both Durkheim's major and minor writings. Topics focused upon include law as an index of social solidarity, the movement from repressive to restitutive law, the relationship of crime and punishment, the evolution of punishment, legal prohibitions of suicide, and the origins of law, property rights, and contracts.

Durkheim on politics and the state (Anthony Giddens, Ed.; W. D. Halls, Trans.). Stanford, CA: Stanford University Press, 1986.

A collection of Durkheim's otherwise scattered writings on political themes divided into sections on the state, democracy, socialism, Marxism, political obligation and punishment, the state and education, and patriotism and militarism.

Education and sociology (S. D. Fox, Trans.). Glencoe, IL: Free Press, 1956 [1922].

A collection of four essays expanding on themes presented in *Moral Education*.

Elementary forms of the religious life (J. W. Swain, Trans.). New York: Free Press, 1965 [1912] (paper).

Durkheim's last major work. Involves an analysis of primitive religious belief and ritual in order to understand the basic foundations of all moral and religious rules. Also focuses on the development of society and knowledge in general.

Emile Durkheim on morality and society (R. N. Bellah, Ed.). Chicago: University of Chicago, 1973 (paper).

A collection of long excerpts from a number of Durkheim's major and minor works, focusing on morality and society but covering a large number of topics.

Essays on sociology and philosophy (Kurt Wolff, Ed.). New York: Harper & Row, 1964 (paper).

This work contains a number of essays by Durkheim, as well as essays on Durkheim's thought by others. Includes Durkheim's important essay "The Dualism of Human Nature and Its Social Conditions."

The evolution of educational thought: Lectures on the formation of secondary education in France (P. Collings, Trans.). London: Routledge & Kegan Paul, 1977 [1938].

Durkheim's most ambitious historical study. Concerns the rise of advanced education from the Middle Ages up until his own day.

Montesquieu and Rousseau (R. Manheim, Trans.). Ann Arbor: University of Michigan, 1965 [1953] (paper).

Durkheim's two essays examining the sociological value of the two philosophers in question.

Moral education: A study in the theory and application of the sociology of education (E. K. Wilson & H. Schnurer, Trans.). New York: Free Press, 1973 [1925] (paper).

Durkheim's major analysis of the nature of socialization and education. Concerns the proper role of the teacher in the classroom and the social dynamics of learning.

Pragmatism and sociology (John B. Allcock, Ed.; J. C. Whitehouse, Trans.). Cambridge: Cambridge University Press, 1983.

This translation of Durkheim's famous lectures reveals Durkheim's hostility toward the philosophical school of pragmatism. His arguments are especially interesting owing to the great influence that pragmatic philosophy had on the development of American sociology (via the works of William James, John Dewey, and especially George Herbert Mead). These lectures also give us a deeper understanding of Durkheim's epistemological views concerning the nature of truth, science, and knowledge.

Professional ethics and civic morals (C. Brookfield, Trans.). Glencoe, IL: Free Press, 1958 [1950].

Taken from a series of university lectures, this volume entails Durkheim's longest discussions of politics, the state, and corporatism.

The rules of sociological method (S. A. Solovay & J. H. Mueller, Trans.). New York: Free Press, 1964 [1895] (paper).

Durkheim's attempt to detail the approach used by a sociologist in the course of a study. Includes arguments for sociology as a unique science with methods of its own.

The rules of sociological method and selected texts on sociology and its method (Steven Lukes, Ed.; W. D. Halls, Trans.). New York: Free Press, 1982 [1895] (paper).

A superior translation of *Les Règles de la méthode sociologique.* Lukes's introduction is

excellent. Among the other short writings included are Durkheim's discussions of methodological approaches, Marxian analysis, ethnology, history, political economy, psychology, and philosophy as they compare to those of sociology.

Socialism (C. Stattler, Trans.). New York: Collier, 1962 [1928] (paper).

Durkheim's analysis and critique of a number of major forms of socialist thought and ideology. The main emphasis is on the ideas of Saint-Simon.

Sociology and philosophy (D. F. Pocock, Trans.). New York: Free Press, 1974 [1924] (paper).

A series of essays and answers to questions in which Durkheim attempts to treat traditional philosophical concerns in a sociological manner. Topics include the nature of morality and moral action, questions of duty and authority, the nature of mind, and the creation of knowledge.

Suicide: A study in sociology (J. A. Spaulding & G. Simpson, Trans.). New York: Free Press, 1964 [1897] (paper).

A pioneering study, combining theoretical and statistical analysis. Durkheim defines and develops the major "types" of suicide while using suicide statistics to demonstrate the problems facing modern society and the utility of sociological investigation.

Secondary Sources

Alexander, Jeffrey (Ed.). *Durkheimian sociology: Cultural studies.* Cambridge: Cambridge University Press, 1988.

This book is premised on a supposed distinction between an earlier Durkheim, who wrote through the mid-1890s, and a later Durkheim, who had a more "cultural" approach with an emphasis on "symbolic process." Articles in this book attempt to explicate, expand, and apply the thought of the later Durkheim.

Allen, N. J., W. S. F. Pickering, & W. Watts Miller (Eds.). *On Durkheim's "Elementary forms of religious life."* London: Routledge, 1998.

Of all of Durkheim's work, *Elementary Forms* has generated the most interest in recent years. The articles in this volume focus on a broad variety of topics related to that work and range from explaining Durkheim's conceptual framework to exploring difficulties with his accounts of the origins, development, and significance of religious phenomena.

Besnard, Phillip. *The sociological domain: The Durkheimians and the founding of French sociology.* Cambridge: Cambridge University Press, 1983.

Durkheim was not just a scholar, but also an inspired teacher who produced a number of students whose works developed (and modified) his conception of sociology and related disciplines. The essays in this volume focus mainly on the intellectual directions that his students took.

Cladis, Mark S. *A communitarian defense of liberalism: Emile Durkheim and contemporary sociological theory.* Stanford, CA: Stanford University Press, 1992.

Written by a philosopher, this work emphasizes the lasting influence of the Dreyfus Affair on Durkheim's thought. Durkheim is presented as having developed the conception of "moral individualism" in order to transcend a debate between a radical *laissez-faire* egoistic individualism and a despotic, reactionary anti-individualism.

Clark, Terry. *Prophets and patrons: The French university and the emergence of the social sciences.* Cambridge, MA: Harvard University Press, 1973.

Well-researched analysis of the institutionalization of the social sciences in France, with an emphasis on Durkheim's contributions and the development of *L'Année sociologique*, Durkheim's sociological journal.

Fenton, Steve. *Durkheim and modern sociology.* Cambridge: Cambridge University Press, 1984.

A very good analysis in terms of Durkheim's overall goals, his political orientation, and the impact of his work on later sociological theory

and research. The work postulates a possibly overstated distinction between the works of an early and later Durkheim.

Gane, Mike. *On Durkheim's rules of sociological method.* London: Routledge, 1988.

Gane summarizes the arguments in Durkheim's *The Rules of Sociological Method*, explores the critical reaction to that book from Durkheim's time to the present, and investigates the logic and consistency of Durkheim's own application of his "rules" in the course of his research on a variety of topics.

Giddens, Anthony. *Emile Durkheim.* Harmondsworth, Middlesex, England: Penguin Books, 1978 (paper).

Perhaps the best short (132-page) introduction to Durkheim. A good first book for the student interested in a summary of the scope of Durkheim's thought.

Hamilton, Peter (Ed.). *Emile Durkheim: Critical Assessments.* Vol. I. London: Routledge, 1995.

This book of articles and reviews, mostly by Durkheim's contemporaries, allows one to see the immediate, broad, and international influence of Durkheimian thought. Note that, even when critical of Durkheim's formulations, leading scholars saw in Durkheim a formidable intellect whose ideas needed to be seriously considered.

Hilbert, Richard A. *The classical roots of ethnomethodology: Durkheim, Weber, and Garfinkel.* Chapel Hill: University of North Carolina Press, 1992.

Hilbert forcefully argues that Durkheim exerted a profound, though indirect, historical influence on the emergence of ethnomethodology and that numerous similarities exist between Durkheimian views and those of ethnomethodologists such as Harold Garfinkel. The arguments given are both interesting and overstated.

Jones, Robert Alun. *Emile Durkheim: An introduction to four major works.* Beverly Hills, CA: Sage, 1986 (paper).

The four major works in question are *The Division of Labor in Society*, *The Rules of Sociological Method*, *Suicide*, and *Elementary*

Forms of the Religious Life. Jones addresses each of these works in terms of the questions Durkheim asked, the answers he developed, and brief but interesting critiques of Durkheim's views and procedures. Jones's clear but nonsimplistic approach makes this a good place to begin one's reading on Durkheim.

Lukes, Steven. *Emile Durkheim: His life and works.* London: Penguin, 1975 (paper).

A comprehensive analysis of the chronological development of Durkheim's ideas in the context of biographical, social, and intellectual environments. Perhaps the best work on Durkheim in any language. Contains an extensive list of writings by and about Durkheim.

Meštrovic, Stjepan G. *Emile Durkheim and the reformation of sociology.* Totowa, NJ: Rowman & Littlefield, 1988.

Meštrovic questions the extent to which Durkheim's Judaic background had any lasting or significant influence on Durkheim's sociological theorizing, while maintaining that a strong filiation exists between the work of Durkheim and the thought of the German philosopher Arthur Schopenhauer.

Miller, W. Watts. *Durkheim, morals and modernity.* London: UCL Press, 1996.

Miller views Durkheim as a moralist and reformer who wished to use sociology as a bridge between a knowledge of what "is" and an understanding of what "ought" to be. Durkheim's main concern was to create a modern society that would avoid the polar dangers of an atomized individualism and a totalitarian crushing of the individual. Miller views Durkheim as avoiding the mistakes of a simplistic empiricist view of social reality.

Parkin, Frank. *Durkheim.* Oxford, England: Oxford University Press, 1992.

This short, very readable overview of Durkheim's theorizing maintains that the value of Durkheim's thought lies more in the questions he raised than in the answers

he found. Parkin consistently contrasts Durkheim's positions to those of Marx and Weber.

Pearce, Frank. *The radical Durkheim.* London: Unwin Hyman, 1989.

This book attempts to create a dialogue between "Durkheimism" and Marxism, using each to critique the other. Pearce's ultimate goal is a synthesis of the two.

Pickering, W.S.F. *Durkheim's sociology of religion: Themes and theories.* London: Routledge & Kegan Paul, 1984.

This work forms the most comprehensive analysis of Durkheim's overall views of religion in print. Excellent chapters on the sacred and the profane and on the nature of ritual and effervescence.

Pope, Whitney. *Durkheim's "Suicide," a classic analyzed.* Chicago: University of Chicago Press, 1976 (paper).

A step-by-step analysis and critique of the methods and techniques followed by Durkheim in his classic study on suicide.

Schmaus, Warren. *Durkheim's philosophy of science and the sociology of knowledge: Creating an intellectual niche.* Chicago: University of Chicago Press, 1994.

An interesting book by a philosopher knowledgeable about the historical and intellectual context in which Durkheim wrote. Schmaus argues that Durkheim was remarkably consistent in his methodological approach, that Durkheim was highly tolerant of different views of his research colleagues, and that a review of Durkheim's approach to data would help contemporary sociologists overcome the increasing split between theorists and empirical researchers.

Strenski, Ivan. *Emile Durkeim and the Jews of France.* Chicago: University of Chicago Press, 1997.

Strenski argues that there is no "essential" Jewish core in Durkheim's thought and that, for all intents and purposes, knowledge of Durkheim's Jewish roots does not enlighten

one about the origins or meaning of Durkheim's sociological ideas.

Thompson, Kenneth. *Emile Durkheim*. London:
Tavistock, 1982 (paper).

A highly readable introduction to Durkheim's
thought. Organized in terms of a presentation
of a number of Durkheim's major works in
chronological order.

Walford, Geoffery & W. S. F. Pickering (Eds.).
Durkheim and modern education. London:
Routledge, 1998.

Durkheim, who taught high school and who
was a Professor of Education, is generally
considered the founder of the "sociology of
education." The well-written articles in this
volume focus respectively on an analysis and
contextualization of Durkheim's educational
writings, the application of a "Durkheimian
framework" to "current educational issues,"
and the relationship of Durkheim's thought
to that of other educational theorists.

And here let me point out distinctly, the truth already implied, that studying Sociology scientifically, leads to fairer appreciations of different parties, political, religious, and other. The conception initiated and developed by Social Science, is at the same time Radical and Conservative—Radical to a degree beyond anything which current Radicalism conceives; Conservative to a degree beyond anything conceived by present Conservatism. When there has been adequately seized the truth that societies are products of evolution, assuming, in their various times and places, their various modifications of structure, and function; there follows the conviction that what, relatively to our thoughts and sentiments, were arrangements of extreme badness, had fitnesses to conditions which made better arrangements impracticable; whence comes a tolerant interpretation of past tyrannies at which even the bitterest Tory of our own days would be indignant. On the other hand, after observing how the processes that have brought things to their present stage are still going on, not with a decreasing rapidity indicating approach to cessation, but with an increasing rapidity that implies long continuance and immense transformations; there follows the conviction that the remote future has in store, forms of social life higher than any we have imagined; there comes a faith transcending that of the Radical, whose aim is some re-organization admitting of comparison to organizations which exist. And while this conception of societies as naturally evolved, beginning with small and simple types which have their short existences and disappear, advancing to higher types that are larger, more complex, and longer-lived, coming to still-higher types like our own, great in size, complexity, and duration, and promising types transcending these in times after existing societies have died away—while this conception of societies implies that in the slow course of things changes almost immeasurable in amount are possible, it also implies that but small amounts of such changes are possible within short periods.

—Herbert Spencer, *The Study of Sociology*

5

Herbert
Spencer

(1820–1903)

Life

Herbert Spencer was born in a small brick house on the edge of Derby, England, on April 27, 1820. His mother, Harriet, was a quiet and pious Wesleyan (that is, Methodist). His father, William, was a self-employed teacher, well regarded in the community. Given to philosophical, political, and theological questioning, William had left the Methodism of his youth and attended Quaker meetings for the rest of his life. Practical-minded, disdainful of supernaturalistic explanations, William Spencer appreciated the quiet and freedom from dogma of a Quaker meeting. He preferred it to both the religious intensity of early Methodism and the medieval ritualism of the dominant Anglican Church. On Sunday mornings, Herbert's mother took him to Methodist services, and on Sunday evenings, his father brought him to Quaker meetings. Rather than orienting Spencer toward the spiritual, however, this double dose of religion had the opposite effect. Spencer would later attribute his publicly avowed atheism to the inability of either religious orientation to get a full grasp on him as a result of the counterinfluence of the other. He remarked that what he was told was true on Sunday morning he learned was false that same evening.

In *An Autobiography* (1904), written late in his life, Spencer is full of praise for his father and the practical, naturalistic, independent, and skeptical attitudes he saw him embodying. On the other hand, Spencer, who saw no use for spiritual belief in modern society and who throughout his whole life proved incapable of any sustained close emotional relationship with a woman, scarcely mentions his mother.

Herbert Spencer's youth and education were pleasant, if nontraditional. Derby, which was just about to undergo industrialization, was still a peaceful small town surrounded by rural greenlands. Young Herbert wandered freely through the creeks and fields around the town. Although his days were spent in classrooms dominated by old-fashioned rote learning (an approach Spencer would criticize in his later educational writings), young Spencer was often taken by his father to evening meetings of the Derby Philosophical Society. In his biography of Herbert Spencer, J. D. Y. Peel portrays that society as anything but the small-town parochial gathering of amateur philosophers that one might imagine.[1] Instead, led by such a distinguished figure as Erasmus Darwin (Charles Darwin's grandfather), the society exposed Spencer to well-organized debates and discussions on major scientific discoveries, philosophical theories, and political questions of the day.

At the age of thirteen, Spencer was sent to live with his uncle Thomas Spencer, a reform-oriented minister who ran a small school. Spencer's education stressed the practical—chemistry, mathematics, mechanics, and physics—and virtually ignored the more traditional humanities: history, poetry, literature, and the classics. Indeed, Spencer would never develop much of an interest in any of these latter subjects. His writings, so different from those of other social scholars of his day, are almost devoid of literary and poetical references.

Years later, in the essay "The Philosophy of Style,"[2] Spencer, who always tended to believe that the way he did things was the best possible way, developed a philosophical justification for prose devoid of all poetry and flowery encumbrances. He argued that good writing is marked by clear, concise, straightforward prose that uses short Anglo-Saxon (as opposed to Latin-derived) English words and states clean causal propositions. Using mechanistic and instrumentalist language, he argued:

> Regarding language as an apparatus of symbols for conveying thought, we may see that, as in a mechanical apparatus, the more simple and the better arranged its parts, the greater will be the effect produced. In either case, whatever force is absorbed by the machine is deducted from the result. A reader or listener has at each moment but a limited amount of mental power available. To recognize and interpret symbols presented to him requires part of this power; to arrange and combine the images suggested by them requires a further part; and only that part which remains can be well used for framing the thought expressed. Hence the more time and attention it takes to receive and understand each sentence, the less time and attention can be given to the contained idea, and the less vividly the idea will be conceived.[3]

In *Education: Intellectual, Moral, and Physical* (1861), Spencer would argue that true poetry was to be found not in the wordy glorification of the trivial, but in the scientific observation of the world. For him:

> Those who have never entered upon scientific pursuits know not a tithe of the poetry by which they are surrounded. Whoever has not in youth collected plants and insects, knows

not half the halo of interest which lanes and hedgerows can assume. Whoever has not sought for fossils, has little idea of the poetical associations that surround the places where imbedded treasures were found. . . . Sad, indeed, is to see how men occupy themselves with trivialities, and are indifferent to the grandest phenomena.[4]

Prepared for life with a practical education, at age sixteen Spencer left formal schooling forever to take a job as a civil engineer in the building of the London and Birmingham Railroad. From the vantage point of our own day, with its considerable emphasis on attaining a college education, it is difficult to believe it possible that someone with an education as limited as Spencer's could have been able to follow a scholarly career. Yet Spencer did follow such a career, and with great success. It was an age when the "gentleman amateur" could still be highly respected and accepted in literary and intellectual circles. While working for railroads (up until 1846), Spencer continued his scientific readings, worked on some ideas that would lead to patented inventions (such as a device for holding sheet music in place), wrote and published scientific and political essays, and served as assistant editor of a political and philosophical magazine.

In 1848, Spencer moved to London where he found work as a journal editor. He was soon accepted as a member of London's intellectual circles and exposed to the ideas then current among the British educated elite. Spencer's later writings would draw from and fuse both the ideas he was exposed to as a youth in Derby (stressing individualism and equality of opportunity) and those that were fashionable in London (stressing social change and supposed fundamental inequalities between peoples). The contradiction between his earlier and later intellectual influences would be reflected in his writings (see the following section, "Social Environment").

In 1850, Spencer published *Social Statics*, the first of his many books. His other major works included *Education: Intellectual, Moral, and Physical, The Study of Sociology* (1873), and *The Man versus the State* (1884). Though all of these eventually sold well (especially in the United States) and helped Spencer overcome some initial financial difficulties, Spencer's most ambitious work was his *Synthetic Philosophy*. Aided by unsolicited financial assistance from such notable figures as the biologist Thomas Huxley (1825–1895) and the political philosopher John Stuart Mill (1806–1873), Spencer's production of the volumes of the *Synthetic Philosophy* over a thirty-seven-year period (1860–1897) represented a single-minded determinism and a faith in his own intellectual formulations that were Spencer's dominant personality characteristics.

The goal of the *Synthetic Philosophy* was to present basic principles of development and change and demonstrate how these principles operated in the fields of biology, psychology, sociology, and ethics. It included *First Principles* (1862), which distinguished between the "knowable" and the "unknowable" and laid out what Spencer believed to be universal evolutionary principles, the two volumes of *The Principles of Psychology* (published in one volume before the *Synthetic Philosophy* in 1855, but expanded into two volumes and included therein in 1864 and 1867), the three volumes of *The Principles of Sociology* (1876, 1879–1885, 1897), and the two volumes of *The Principles of Ethics* (1879–1892, 1891–1893).

Three main themes run throughout Spencer's major works: (1) antigovernment individualism, (2) naturalistic evolutionism, and (3) positivistic uniformitarianism. Antigovernment individualism asserts that society functions best (that is, most harmoniously) when governmental regulation and control are reduced to a minimum involving only military defense and the protection of individual rights. Naturalistic evolutionism posits causal sequences of growth and development. Positivistic uniformitarianism maintains that the same processes of evolutionary progress were applicable to all areas of existence: inert, living, psychological, and social. Spencer's lifelong work was the systematization of knowledge in accord with these three principles; his sociology was thus an integral part of a larger philosophical endeavor.

From our contemporary perspective of specialized disciplines, a work with such a broad scope as the *Synthetic Philosophy* would probably be seen not as the work of an expert in a number of fields but as the product of someone lacking expertise in any. Spencer, however, was writing at the end of a time when one could still be respected as being on the cutting edge of a variety of academic disciplines. In fact, simultaneously, *The Principles of Biology* was being used at Oxford University, *The Principles of Psychology* was being used by William James (1842–1910) at Harvard, and *The Study of Sociology* was being used by William Graham Sumner (1840–1910) at Yale. Late in his life, Spencer was honored at a banquet in New York organized by the robber baron Andrew Carnegie. A great admirer of Spencer, Carnegie gathered together many intellectual and industrial leaders in the United States to hail Spencer as the greatest thinker of the time.

The increasing acclaim that Spencer received in his public life was paralleled by increasing loneliness and discontent in his private life. The only close personal relationship that he formed in his adult years was with a woman who, like him, had been born and raised in the English Midlands, where she was exposed to similar intellectual movements. Also like Spencer, she was to a great extent self-educated, worked as an editor for an intellectual journal, and had "won fame among the ranks of the most prolific and ambitious thinkers of their time."[5]

When Spencer met Marian Evans (1819–1880) in 1851, she had yet to achieve the fame as a novelist and intellectual that she would acquire under the pen name of George Eliot. She immediately found enjoyable the company of the philosopher who had already begun to gain some respect as the author of *Social Statics* (which had been published the year prior). He found the broad scope of her scientific learning, her logical mind, and her quick wit equally attractive. Spencer began to visit her often. Together they would take walks, attend gatherings, and engage in long discussions. They could often be seen attending London's theaters and operas in each other's company.

Although Spencer had found the intellectual relationship with Evans enjoyable, he became upset when he was informed that people in their circles were beginning to expect them to announce a marriage date. Spencer quickly informed her that he perceived their relationship to be on purely intellectual terms, that he was not in love with her, and that he was not interested in either marriage or even a more intimate relationship. Evans agreed to remain friends and to keep their relationship on a level of intellectual dialogue. Based on a review of Spencer's autobiography and the letters they wrote at this time, Evans's biographer, Margaret Crompton, has written:

> It seems fairly certain that Spencer did not fall in love with Marian for the very simple reason that he was incapable of falling in love with anybody. His outlook on life was keenly analytical, detached, ultra-critical. Kind-hearted, reliable, truthful though he certainly was, he was also cold-hearted and essentially self-centered.[6]

Although Spencer intellectually decided that marriage was a desirable state, within a year of his telling Evans he would not marry her, he came to the conclusion that he could never marry. After a nervous breakdown in 1856, he reacted to his doctor's advice that he marry with the response that he could not financially afford to do so and that he never found a woman with the right combination of physical beauty and intellectual ability to sufficiently attract him. Yet these remarks seem only to mask a self-perceived feeling on Spencer's part that he was incapable of forming the deep emotional attachments he thought necessary for a successful life together with another person. Again, to quote Crompton:

> That his incapacity for deep feeling was a source of worry to him is proved more than once in his writings. In another letter to a friend he says that he is convinced that bachelorhood is "an unnatural and very injurious state." He longs for his affections to be called out, but having had no brothers or sisters he feels that he has dropped permanently into a state of being only "half alive." His unsettled life, his "unattractive manners towards those in whom I feel no interest," and his habit of arguing were, he felt, factors of difficulty that had helped to bring this about. In later years he confided sadly to Beatrice Webb [1858–1943] . . . that he had never been in love and that he was often disturbed by his lukewarm emotions, even towards old friends and relations.[7]

Despite eventually gaining financial security, Spencer never bought or even rented a house. He moved from one rooming house to another and lived for a long period in lodgings patronized by unmarried retired military officers. As the years went by, Spencer increasingly complained of ill health. The numerous physicians he consulted could find no physical-organic causes for his periods of tiredness, loss of concentration, and lethargy. He became a hypochondriac and turned to a narcotic, morphia, to deal with his persistent sleeplessness.[8] Spencer developed a series of eccentricities in order to deal with his perceived maladies. Stories about his odd behavior, whether true or not, reveal how he began to be viewed by those he knew in later years. These include assertions that he always carried earplugs with him so that he could stop up his ears to avoid unhealthy overexcitement if a discussion became overheated, and that he made his driver stop periodically so he could take his pulse and see if he needed to remove himself to a more calming environment.

Spencer's fear of overstimulation was used as his justification for retreating more and more from social relationships. Withdrawn from life, Spencer became increasingly disillusioned with the world as the turn of the century approached. Although throughout most of his life he expressed an optimistic faith in natural evolution and the emergence of a peaceful industrial order based on a free-market economy, in his last years he came to see this optimism as illusory. He was disgusted by the militant and vicious imperialism of his own nation and the application of the most advanced technology to instruments of war by the nations of Europe. Whereas Great Britain ideologically claimed that its colonies were outposts of civilization, Spencer saw imperialist wars as manifestations of a barbaric militancy that used advanced technology to impede, rather than to facilitate, social progress. Meanwhile, most of his friends had died; of those who remained, most broke with Spencer's romantic idealization of free-market economics and converted to various versions of socialism (for example, Huxley, Evans, and Beatrice Webb). Spencer saw the anathema of collectivism and war on the horizon. Progress, he reasoned, was much slower than he had previously realized and subject to transitory, but terrible, reversals.

Herbert Spencer died on December 8, 1903, and was interred in Highgate Cemetery in London. The headstone of his grave overlooks Marx's tomb, which is situated just to the other side of a path that leads through the graveyard. At the end of his life, Spencer suffered the fate of living to see his predictions proved false by events. The industrialism that he thought would produce order and harmony exacerbated class divisions, centralized tyranny, and produced imperialism and war. Spencer's life's work encapsulated the knowledge and hopes of the nineteenth century; it could not survive the social and political changes wrought by the less optimistic century that was to follow.

Social Environment

From today's perspective, the phrase "middle-class rural radicalism" sounds like a contradiction in terms. "Middle class" has come to imply moderate, if not somewhat conservative, politics, whereas "rural" signifies a truly conservative political outlook. Both appear incompatible with "radicalism," a word that to most contemporary readers means a political philosophy considerably to the left of center, with at least some socialistic ideological elements. Yet in the 1820s and 1830s, middle-class rural radicalism was not a self-contradiction. It signified a coherent political and social ideology and a movement that influenced all of Spencer's philosophical and sociological writings.

In most respects middle-class English radicalism was not so different from the political ideology of the American revolutionary movement of 1776, to which it had a historical affinity. John Locke (1632–1704), Adam Smith (1723–1790), and Thomas Paine (1737–1809) were names that those meeting in both the Philadelphia Continental Congress and the town meetings of Derby would hold in high esteem. Ideologically, middle-class radicalism involved an antiaristocratic egalitarianism, an opposition to centralized regulatory authority, a belief in the absolute separation of church and state, an individualistic assertion of "natural rights," a defense of private property, an antagonism to all forms of socialism or collectivism, a commitment to antimilitarism, and a strong faith in secular progress and human reason.

Middle-class radicalism of the late 1700s and early 1800s was organized around a deep hostility to aristocratic privilege and government. Like the founding fathers of the U.S. Constitution, the English middle-class radicals laid the fault for the majority of social ills at the feet of the nobility. Although it had once been a military class integral to a feudal order, the aristocracy appeared to the small merchants and manufacturers of small English towns to be a useless holdover from an age gone by: a "survival," in Spencer's term. The aristocracy was seen as adding nothing to the well-being of society, while its wealth, protected by governmental privilege, could not contribute to the public good. Imbued with an entrepreneurial spirit, the middle-class radicals perceived the aristocratic class as a lazy, self-indulgent blight on society, whose expenditures, privileges, and misuse of the nation's wealth produced economic misery and inhibited progress.

Dominated by aristocratic interests, the centralized authority of the government, with its mass of regulations, was seen by the radicals as restricting their entrepreneurial and innovative activities. The radicals viewed such regulations as protecting inept, inefficient, monopolistic, and wasteful enterprises and as inhibiting social progress. Spencer's *Social Statics* contains long discussions of governmental regulations and their detrimental long-run consequences. Clearly, middle-class radicals shared Thomas Jefferson's dictum that "the government which governs least governs best." Spencer's assertion that the proper role of government was to provide only military defense and the protection of individual rights was generally accepted in middle-class radical circles. Limited rule by an elected assembly and decentralization of political power represented the most persistent of middle-class radical ideas. Spencer's most extreme endorsement of the radical attack on governmental regulation comes in *The Man versus the State*, in which he wrote:

> Such an interpretation soon brings us to the inference that among men's desires seeking gratifications, those which have prompted their private activities and their spontaneous cooperations, have done much more towards social developments than those which have worked through governmental agencies. That abundant crops now grow where once only wild berries could be gathered, is due to the pursuit of individual satisfactions through many centuries. The progress from wigwams to good houses has resulted from wishes to increase personal welfare; and towns have arisen under the like promptings. Beginning with traffic at gatherings on occasions of religious festivals, the trading organization, now so extensive and complex, has been produced entirely by men's efforts to achieve their private ends. Perpetually, governments have thwarted and deranged the growth, but have in no way furthered it; save by partially discharging their proper function and maintaining social order. So, too, with those advances of knowledge and those improvements of appliances, by which these structural changes and these increasing activities have been made possible. It is not to the State that we owe the multitudinous useful inventions from the spade to the telephone; it was not the State which made the discoveries in physics, chemistry, and the rest, which guide modern manufacturers; it was not the State which devised the machinery for producing fabrics of every kind, and for ministering in a thousand ways to our comforts. The world-wide transactions conducted in merchants' offices, the rush of traffic filling our streets, the retail distributing system which brings everything within easy reach and delivers the necessaries of life daily at our doors, are not of governmental origin. All these are results of the spontaneous activities of citizens, separate or grouped. Nay, to these spontaneous activities governments owe the very means of performing their duties. Divest the political machinery of all those aids which Science and Art have yielded it—leave it with those only which State-officials have invented; and its functions would cease. The very language in which its laws are registered and the orders of its agents daily given, is an instrument not in the remotest degree due to the legislator, but is one which has unawares grown up during men's intercourse while pursuing their personal satisfactions.[9]

For middle-class radicals, a limited government meant an absolute separation of church and state. England did not have such a separation. The Anglican Church was the established Church of England. The monarch served as the head of the church, and taxes were levied on the whole population to support it. Also, the Anglican Church, with its medieval pomp and ritual, appeared to the middle-class radicals as an anachronistic institution dominated by aristocratic interests and ideology. The radicals viewed the

Anglican Church as thus incompatible with their own ideological perception that Christianity was fundamentally egalitarian in nature. Although a majority of England's population belonged to the established church, various dissenting Protestant sects and denominations were represented by the middle-class radicals. Derby was both a center of radicalism and an area strong in Unitarianism and Methodism.

The middle-class radicals believed that distinctions of aristocratic privilege were artificial and that all individuals shared fundamental natural rights. Rights were conceived of *not* in terms of actual standard of living (the right to a certain income, objects, living quarters, and the like), but in terms of opportunity. The rights to work, to own property, to sell one's products, to do with one's property and products as one pleased, to be unrestrained by officials of the state, and to be unhampered in the goal of attaining happiness to the extent that one did not infringe on the rights of others were fundamental to middle-class radical ideology. Equality of rights did not mean equality of outcome, however. The middle-class radicals believed that opportunity should be equal, but that it was perfectly natural that those with greater ability or those who worked with greater diligence should attain more than those with less ability or less diligence. They generally accepted Adam Smith's belief that if those who could attain the most were able to do so, in the long run their prosperity would enhance the prosperity of society as a whole.

In the nineteenth century, the English middle-class radicals saw industrialization as the antithesis of militarism (and, as we shall see, Spencer drew a very sharp distinction between "militant" and "industrial" societies). Militarism was connected to the aggressive spirit, industrial incompetence, and overall stupidity of an aristocratically biased government. Military expeditions were seen as costing a nation more than the wealth that they might produce. The radicals believed that every nation would be better off if militaries were reduced to defensive capacities and free trade between nations allowed. Tariffs and other trade barriers were seen as unjust governmental seizure of property, which inhibited the exercise of one's natural rights to accumulate property and dispose of it as one wished. The radicals, rightly, placed the blame for a number of famines and shortages on governmental trade policies that benefited the few to the detriment of the many.

Despite the negative tone of most of the ideological positions of the middle-class radicals, underlying much of their criticism of the present order was a profound faith in human reason and progress. Unlike such classic conservatives as Thomas Malthus (1766–1834), the founder of modern population studies, and Jonathan Swift (1667–1745), satirist and author of *Gulliver's Travels*, the radicals saw humans as capable of overcoming their baser instincts. They envisioned the formation of a society grounded in human reason and self-restraint. They insisted that humans do not require a strong repressive government to restrain them from destroying one another. Instead, the radicals believed that the traits inculcated through living a productive, industrious life could lead to a social order free of harsh and coercive restraints. They expressed a faith in secular human moral progress that could only have been held in the brief historical period when the idea of progress had been freed from its otherworldly religious connotations and the disillusioning barbarity of two world wars had not yet unleashed advanced technology in unimaginably destructive forms on civilian populations.

The greatest strength of middle-class radicalism as an intellectual and social movement was also its greatest weakness. Its strength lay in taking on a dominant aristocratic class that could rally diverse groups in society in opposition; its weakness was that, as the power of the aristocratic group declined, so did middle-class radicalism as a coherent ideology and movement. Once in power, in order to control or expand markets, industrialists were just as apt to seek governmental protections through regulatory control and just as likely to use the military for the expansion of economic markets as proaristocratic governments had been. Indeed, through joint interest and intermarriage, the wealthier industrialists and the old aristocratic class were merging to form the upper class of contemporary England.

While the new upper class was emerging, so was an industrial working class. This class did not see the old aristocrats as its enemy, but saw the rich, rising middle-class industrialists as its exploiters. An ideological claim to a "right" to dispose of one's property as one chose meant little to a factory worker whose whole family was engaged in unsafe and unsanitary labor fourteen hours a day. Guarantees of decent wages, good housing, safe working conditions, and educational opportunities meant much more to the urban English worker than did abstract freedoms. To achieve these ends, British workers and their sympathizers were drawn to various socialist movements which promised immediate improvements in living conditions.

Although Spencer continued to be committed to the basic tenets of middle-class radicalism throughout his life, the faith in individual rationality and local entrepreneurism that marked the middle-class rural radicalism of England in the 1820s and 1830s was not typical of the intellectual climate in which he found himself during his more mature years in London. Whereas middle-class radicalism emphasized the rationality and shared potential of all humanity and the equality of rights (in a libertarian sense) of all individuals, decidedly different notions were becoming popular among the educated elite in England's capital. Here, Spencer encountered notions that stressed social determinism (as opposed to individual rational choice in shaping human behavior) and notions that stressed inequality and differences between Europeans and non-Europeans (as opposed to those stressing the common humanity and equality of rights of everyone in the world).

These notions of social differences and inequalities between nations were presented in a concrete and easily apprehended way at the first world's fair—the Great Exhibition of Industry of All Nations—which opened its doors in London in 1851. The Great Exhibition was housed in a single building known as the Crystal Palace. The Crystal Palace itself was an amazing piece of architecture that represented recent European breakthroughs in building materials and construction techniques. Built entirely of glass framed in iron, it was six football fields in length and "tall enough to enclose a group of Hyde Park's great elms."[10] In its massive halls, arranged by both nation and level of technological sophistication, one saw technology from throughout the world, including the new great machines of the industrial revolution. The arrangement of the items emphasized both the degree of recent industrial advances made in Europe and the disparity between European and non-European technology. Spencer spent days roaming around the exhibits and made a point of remarking about how he found the experience of doing so extremely educational as well as very enjoyable.

Like other writers of the period in England, Spencer created and used ideas about social evolutionary development to account for differences in technological development between nations and then extended the logic of such an evolutionary view to also account for national differences in customs, traditions, and psychological makeup of individuals. That such ideas were not merely the unique creation of Spencer, but were to a great extent a product of the intellectual climate in London at the time, is evidenced by the fact that the anthropologist E. B. Tylor (1832–1917) independently developed arguments similar enough to Spencer's in numerous crucial points for him to accuse Spencer of plagiarism.

Spencer fused rural middle-class ideas with conceptions of social evolutionary notions of inequalities between societies to form the basic assumptions of his sociological theorizing. This fusion was not always easily achieved and resulted in some tensions or contradictions in his work. For instance, we will see that Spencer's views on gender roles changed as conceptions of equality derived from middle-class radicalism were displaced by a social evolutionary emphasis on disparity and inequality.

Intellectual Roots

Whereas it is relatively easy to analyze the general influence on Spencer of both ideas of societal inequality and middle-class radical ideas, for a number of reasons it is considerably more difficult to point out the specific scholars to whom Spencer owed the greatest intellectual debt. First of all, Spencer freely admitted that he rarely read books from cover to cover because he would lose patience with them when he found their authors advocating positions that he believed to be wrong. In a sense, Spencer did not read books in order to develop new positions, but instead he "mined" them for facts and ideas that he could synthesize into his own preconstructed theoretical system. Additionally, Spencer was prone to both borrow from and criticize scholars whom he had never actually read at all, but whose ideas he was reacting to based on secondary sources or conversations that he had had with various learned individuals in London's intellectual circles. He thus often responded to scholarly ideas only after they had been interpreted, and possibly distorted, by others. Finally, Spencer was much more likely to make specific references to writers he disagreed with (such as Thomas Malthus and Auguste Comte) than to those he used in structuring his own theoretical system.

Despite the foregoing, there are a number of identifiable persons from whom Spencer borrowed insights and ideas. Spencer's ideological notions about individual rights and his belief in the possibility of the "perfectibility" of human nature are in part derived from the ideas of Joseph Priestley (1733–1804), Thomas Paine, and William Godwin (1756–1836). Spencer's ideas concerning economics and his beliefs that government should not interfere with a self-maintaining system of supply and demand are clearly dependent on the prior work of Adam Smith and his followers. Spencer's assumption concerning uniformitarianism (i.e., the belief that the same forces at work over long periods of time account for persistent change) was influenced by ideas developed by the geologist Charles Lyell (1797–1875). And a number of principles central to Spencer's overall theorizing were derived by him from the work of the German naturalist Karl Ernst von Baer (1792–1876).

Von Baer's emphasis on understanding evolution as a process of differentiation, whereby organisms become more structurally complex as each structure (or organ) comes to perform some specific function, was applied by Spencer to both biological organisms and to the "superorganic" entity of society. Similarly, Spencer applied to society von Baer's notion that each organism, in its own development, replicated the evolutionary sequence of developments that the species had gone through. Spencer used this idea both to justify his interpretation of children as representing social-psychological features of members of simple societies and to justify the arguments that existing simple societies can be used to represent stages that more advanced European societies must have gone through in the past.

Despite the great significance of von Baer and others from whom Spencer borrowed the ideas and elements of his theoretical system, the two most important figures in Spencer's intellectual development in terms of their sustained influence on his thought were not the various writers on social and physical science of his day, but his friend the novelist Marian Evans and his schoolteacher father, William. Whereas Spencer encountered the ideas of many others, digested them, incorporated them into his own theoretical system, and went on to look at other ideas, the dialogue he had with Evans lasted over many years, and the influence of his father informed Spencer's thinking for the whole of his intellectual life.

Although the influence of Spencer's ideas on Evans's novels (written, of course, under the pen name George Eliot) has been recognized and studied since their day, because of gender biases the influence of her ideas on his work has only recently come to be more fully appreciated. Their long intellectual relationship, their regular discussions, the fact that she commented on his works in manuscript and proof forms, and his (at times) unreserved publicly stated admiration for her show that over a long period of time Spencer engaged in a dialogue with her that influenced his writings in myriad areas. Two such areas of influence have been documented by Nancy Paxton in *George Eliot and Herbert Spencer: Feminism, Evolutionism, and the Reconstruction of Gender*. These areas are gender relations and the goals (or ends) toward which human social development is heading.

Spencer's early views of feminism were greatly influenced by Evans. Coming from a social background similar to his, she was able to convince him early in his career that his conceptions of equality of opportunity and equality of rights needed to be extended to women, both in sociological theorizing and in the legal system of Great Britain. By 1851, both Evans and Spencer "agreed on the need for reform of marriage and divorce laws, on the value of women's emancipation, and on the right to better educational and vocational opportunities."[11] Spencer incorporated such views into his writings, even including a chapter titled "The Rights of Women" in early editions of *Social Statics*. Eventually, though, under other influences (see the later section "The Individual in Society"), Spencer would reject his early profeminist views. In 1861, so as to retain their friendship and intellectual exchanges on other topics, Spencer and Evans mutually agreed no longer to discuss with each other issues of gender and some related concerns. After Evans's death in 1880, Spencer reedited new editions of his early works to remove the profeminist views he now rejected.

If Evans's views on gender-related matters did not have a lasting influence on Spencer's theorizing, her views on "sentiment," altruism, and the long-run goal of human social development seem to have profoundly and increasingly influenced Spencer's thought. In the course of his career, Spencer went from an early enshrinement of egoistic self-interest as the proper and natural direction that human motivations would take in future social evolution, to a position in his later works (such as *The Philosophy of Ethics*) in which he discussed a "higher altruism" that would involve individuals taking pleasure through helping others. Under Evans's influence, Spencer came to see that unmitigated egoism would ultimately be destructive to a harmonious social order and thus was incompatible with the direction toward a peaceful order that Spencer saw social evolution taking.

Spencer's dialogue with Evans lasted more than three decades, but the influence of his father on his thought lasted his whole career. Spencer's autobiography is full of praise for William Spencer as the wellspring for much of his own thought. Clearly, Spencer's emphasis on "natural causation" as applicable to all areas of existence and his faith in his own ability to rationally think through and explain all aspects of social life are attributes he acquired in Derby from his father.

Overall, in looking at the intellectual influences on his work, Spencer can be presented as either one of the least or one of the most original of sociological thinkers. On the one hand, the specific ideas he espoused were mostly borrowed from others; his writing gave expression to philosophical, political, and scientific ideas available in his milieu without adding anything that could be categorized as profoundly new. On the other hand, Spencer took highly diverse ideas and intellectual currents and formulated them into a seemingly coherent synthesis in which each element was logically supported by all the others. If his ideas themselves were not profoundly original, the synthesis was; and it was his system—his synthetic philosophy—that gave his writings their significance for others of his generation. Spencer's philosophy made the world clear and understandable. The elements of the "knowable universe" were laid out in terms of a single, unified process of development and order. Understanding was given in naturalistic, causal, and evolutionary terms that did not require one to know the abstruse languages of Kantian or Hegelian philosophy. Further, Spencer promised to explain the processes and structures of the physical and social world, as well as future social development and ethical ways of acting. The originality of Spencer's work clearly lay not in its particulars but in its totality. While the forest of his ideas was grown in common maples, oaks, and pines, the contours of the intellectual forest had order, symmetry, and exceptionally well-marked trails.

IDEAS

Society

Spencer often referred to society as a "superorganic" form (or level) of reality. For Spencer, society was a "social organism," with both parallels to, and differences from, the structures and processes of biological organisms. He enumerated these parallels and similarities in both *The Study of Sociology* and *The Principles of Sociology*, and they form the central focus of his 1860 essay "The Social Organism." In that essay, he presented four fundamental parallels between biological (or individual) and social organisms:

1. Both begin as small organisms and, through slow insensible development, increase in size ("mass") up to "ten thousand fold."
2. Both begin as simple structures and, in the course of their growth, become structurally more complex.
3. Both begin with parts that are loosely organized, with a minimum of mutual dependence, and, with increased growth and complexity, become increasingly integrated and mutually dependent.
4. Both biological and social organisms have a life span that is greater than those of their respective units.

Thus, in parallel to a biological entity, a society grows in size, becomes more complex, increases the dependence between the individual and social groups, and lives longer than do the individuals who compose it.

Spencer, who had a penchant for symmetry in his writings, also found four fundamental *differences* between social and biological organisms. Presented in the same essay, these were as follows:

1. Biological entities have a specific and fixed observable external form, whereas societies do not.
2. The units (cells and organs) of a biological entity are physically connected to each other, whereas the members of a society may be spread over great distances without direct physical contact.
3. The parts of a biological organism are more or less fixed and stable in their proximate positions to one another, whereas the individuals who compose a society are not stationary but are capable of physical mobility from one place to another, rearranging their spatial relationships.
4. Consciousness is located in only one part of the biological entity—the brain—whereas each individual in the social organism is capable of independent consciousness of reality.

Spencer found the implications of this last point very significant in justifying the individualistic ethical position that ran through his writings. Whereas most writers who draw an analogy of a society to a biological organism (for example, Comte and Durkheim) tend in some ways to subordinate the individual to the collective whole, Spencer asserted that the existence of a consciousness in each of the members of a society supported his contention that the social whole existed to facilitate the achievements of its members:

> We have here a tolerably decided contrast between bodies-politic and individual bodies; and it is one which we should keep constantly in view. For it reminds us that while, in individual bodies, the welfare of all other parts is rightly subservient to the welfare of the nervous system, whose pleasurable or painful activities make up the good or ill of life; in bodies-politic the same thing does not hold, or holds to but a very slight extent. It is well that the lives of all parts of an animal should be merged into the life of the whole, because the whole has a corporate consciousness capable of happiness or misery. But it is not so with a society; since its living units do not and cannot lose individual consciousness, and since the community as a whole has no corporate consciousness. This is an everlasting reason why the welfares of citizens cannot rightly be sacrificed to some supposed benefit of the State, and why, on the other hand, the State is to be maintained solely for the benefit of the citizens. The corporate life must here be subservient to the lives of the parts, instead of the lives of the parts being subservient to the corporate life.[12]

As a superorganic entity, a society has a functional relationship of parts in an "equilibrium." In addition, it slowly evolves over time. Like a biological entity, a social organism is characterized by a functional organization, and the various parts of the organism are characterized by a degree of functional unity. The various parts of the organism each serve a function or functions that fulfill the needs of the total society and thus maintain its existence. Not all societies, however, are seen as manifesting the same degree of functional unity. In simpler societies, the functional dependence of one group on another is weaker than it is in larger, more complex, and advanced societies. Spencer believed that society is more efficient in maintaining itself to the extent that a single group (or "social organ") in society serves a single function. Thus an advanced society, divided into a large number of educational, political, productive, and distributive organs, each with its own functional tasks, is more efficient than a simple society that is not so divided. The more advanced a society, the more its parts are functionally distinguishable, and the more secure are its continued existence and future development.

As a society increases in functional efficiency (by means of separation of functions among its parts), these parts come to exist in an increased state of mutual dependence. Spencer believed that a simple society, cut in half, might continue to exist in its two halves, with functions of the missing parts being taken over by other groups. On the other hand, an advanced, more efficient society, where groups perform very particular functions and where functions are divided by different regions (for example, mining regions, textile regions, governmental centers, and so on), would, if divided in half, cease to exist as a functioning society. An advanced society characterized by a high degree of functional specialization could no more survive a cutting in half than could an advanced biological organism such as a dog or a cow.

Spencer was not naive enough to believe that simply because a group exists in society, it necessarily serves some useful function. He realized that, once in existence, groups tend to perpetuate themselves and may possibly change functions or lose functions altogether. For example, Spencer perceived the aristocratic groups in England as having gone from serving a predominantly military function, to serving a predominantly political function, to serving no worthwhile function at all. Indeed, although Spencer did not use the term "dysfunction," his arguments included the belief that the aristocratic class, as a result of its privileges, its anti-industrial ideals, and its use of societal resources, was in fact dysfunctional for the maintenance and development of society.

Despite his acceptance of some nonfunctional elements in society, Spencer believed that overall a society existed in a state of functional equilibrium. In Spencer's usage, "equilibrium" does not imply a fixed or static state, but an ongoing process. He wrote in *First Principles:* "Each society taken as a whole, displays the process of equilibration in the continuous adjustments of its population to its means of subsistence."[13] As a functioning entity, a social organism requires its component groups or organs constantly to readjust to meet the demands of existence. Changes in raw material supplies, supply routes, foreign relations, and so on cause some groups in society to change their activities in order to accomplish their functional ends. The process of equilibrium involves the change of the other units in society to be in harmony and coordination with the ones that have changed. Thus equilibrium as a general process implies neither a lack of conflict nor a perfect harmony, but rather a constant state of readjustment.

In the third volume of *The Principles of Sociology*, Spencer divided the functional groups of society into three societal systems. He termed these the sustaining (or internal) system, the regulating (or external) system, and the distributing system. The *sustaining system* includes those groups concerned with the production of goods. The *regulating system* involves groups concerned with maintaining political order and organizing a society's military apparatus. The *distributing system* links the producing and regulating systems. It involves groups concerned with the maintenance of the transportation lines (for example, roads) and channels of communications in a society. At one point, Spencer draws an analogy between the distributing system of a society and the circulatory system of a living body in terms of the functions of bringing sustenance to the various parts of society and allowing the removal of waste products.

If, for Spencer, society was a functional organic entity, it was also an organic entity that grew and developed. An interest in societal change, growth, and evolution dominated Spencer's writings. *All* natural phenomena were seen as following parallel principles of evolutionary growth. Spencer believed that to view a society as a static functioning entity is to abstract an image from an actual process of continuous growth and development. Like other nineteenth-century evolutionists, Spencer saw society as developing by a slow, step-by-step, cumulative, directional, progressive advance—an advance that encompassed all of a society's institutional areas.

The image of social evolution as a slow process of minute, nearly imperceptible steps runs throughout most of Spencer's work. In *Social Statics*, he accepted the position that slowness of change was universal. As he explained:

> One would have thought it sufficiently clear to everybody that the great changes taking place in this world of ours are uniformly slow. Continents are upheaved at the rate of a foot or two in a century. The deposition of a delta is the work of tens of thousands of years. The transformation of a barren rock into life supporting soil takes countless ages. If any think society advances under a different law, let them read.[14]

Spencer goes on to cite the thousands of years it took to abolish slavery and serfdom; the "hundred generations" it required for printing to develop out of picturewriting; and the "tardy pace" of scientific, commercial, and technological change. All in all, Spencer was committed to a metaphysical position of *uniformitarianism*—the belief that reality is the result of the cumulative effect of minute but persistent changes taking place over very long periods of time. This uniformitarianism gives Spencer's work a strong positivistic bent, with the processes of change in the social world mirroring biological and physical processes. Spencer also used his emphasis on uniformitarian social evolution to support his belief in limited governmental regulation. He argued that natural change proceeds as a result of persistent long-run forces; thus attempts to change society rapidly through governmental regulation and intervention are foolish and are likely to cause more harm than good. Whereas for Durkheim, Comte, and Marx, the purpose of social scientific knowledge was to aid in guiding human action to improve society, for Spencer it was to serve as a guide for *restraining action*, with the assumption that in the course of evolution society would naturally improve and progress of its own accord.

Although uniformitarianism continued to pervade Spencer's total thought, in later years he asserted that social change might not be uniformly slow, but instead might start off slowly and then increase exponentially. He referred to the increase in the rate of social evolutionary progress as "compound accumulation." In Volume 3 of *The Principles of Sociology*, he wrote:

> The often-used illustration of rapid growth furnished by a rolling snowball, exemplifies what may be named compound accumulation. The snowball does not gain in size by like increments but by increments of larger and larger amounts. At every roll over, its augmented weight gives it additional power of licking up the snow; and, further, at every roll over, the increase of its bulk increases the surface for the adhesion of more snow.[15]

Thus Spencer came to believe that although social evolution starts slowly, its rate constantly increases. The process of progressive change is still uniform, but uniform in its constant increase. This change to a belief in a constantly increasing rate of evolution, however, did not undermine Spencer's faith in his noninterventionist view of government. The perception that natural evolutionary change was occurring faster only indicated to Spencer that it was more important than ever to let the natural forces work at their own rate.

For Spencer, social change was neither random, open-ended, nor subject to long-run distortions in direction. Instead, overall, it was unidirectional. Societies evolved over time in the direction of greater geographical and population size, greater density of population, differentiation into a larger number of parts, greater functional specialization of groups and regions, and increased integration and communication between parts. Societies over time also exhibited an increased capability to undertake large cooperative enterprises and a greater adaptation to the exigencies of existence. For Spencer, social evolution implied all this; it also implied *progress*. Change was not a neutral phenomenon—neither good nor bad—but a long-run movement toward increased social harmony and human happiness. In the long run, societies would change from small entities wherein life was precarious, to larger coerced cooperative enterprises, and eventually to complex states of voluntaristic cooperation. There is definitely a degree of utopianism in Spencer's work—a utopianism that underlies his sociological faith in the natural perfectibility of humanity.

In terms of directionality, Spencer was not a simple unilinearist; he did not believe that every society that ever existed went through exactly the same developments at exactly the same rate. He was, however, a *prevailing unilinearist* in that he did believe that the general direction and steps of development were pretty much the same everywhere, with some exceptions due to peculiar geographical circumstances, contact with other societies, or other unusual events. In *The Study of Sociology*, he admitted the possibility of slight variations in societal development and asserted that what he was attempting to do in his writings was to present the overall "normal course of social evolution" that a typical society followed.[16] Thus some societies may be smaller and less complex than others when they move from a nomadic life-style to an agricultural mode of existence. Similarly, some societies at the same level of complexity may differ in their degree of military aggressiveness. Yet overall, for Spencer the similarities of development far outweighed the differences.

In most of his writings, Spencer asserted that progressive evolutionary change is uniformly slow or increases at a uniform rate. Yet toward the end of his life, Spencer seemed to abandon the view of constant progressive change in favor of a conception of "rhythmical" change. By *rhythmical* he meant that, although change was usually forward, there might be periods of backsliding between progressive periods of development. Spencer clearly saw the militant imperialism of his native land as an example of such a temporary rhythmical movement in a nonprogressive, backward direction. In a letter written in 1895, he declared that "there is a bad time coming, and civilized mankind will (morally) be uncivilized before civilization can again advance."[17]

For Spencer, both evolutionary and progressive change occurred in a delineated set of stages. In his biological writings, Spencer asserted that the first and simplest multicellular organisms arose from the coming together of single-celled entities in order to enhance the survival of each. Similarly, he maintained that society first emerged as a means of enhancing individual survival. Yet, like a multicellular biological entity, once in existence a society developed like an entity, producing its own internal divisions, and its own patterns of integration and growth. Spencer's work presents the reader with typologies (or sets) of stages of social development. One set of stages is presented in terms of levels of *organizational complexity* (what Spencer termed "degrees of composition"): It categorizes societies in terms of differentiation, integration, and size. The other set of stages is presented in terms of *organizational purpose:* It categorizes societies in terms of whether they are organized primarily for warfare or primarily for industrial production.

In terms of organizational complexity, Spencer presented four evolutionary forms (or types) of societies: simple society, compound society, doubly compound society, and trebly compound society. He pointed out that actual societies at each level of development would vary somewhat in makeup as a result of contact (through trade, slaves, war, and the like) with other societies at different levels. They also vary in terms of whether they are near the beginning, middle, or end of their particular developmental stage.

Spencer vaguely defined a *simple society* as "one which forms a single working whole unsubjected to any other, and of which the parts co-operate with or without a regulating center, for certain public ends."[18] These societies were predominantly small, nomadic, and lacking in stable leadership structure; they had low degrees of differentiation, specialization, and integration. Examples given included the Eskimos, the Fuegians, Guiana tribes, the New Caledonians, and the Pueblo Indians.

Compound societies were presented as having generally come about through either a peaceful or a violent merger of two or more simple societies. They tended to be predominantly settled agricultural societies (although a minority were mainly pastoral) and tended to be characterized by a division of four or five social strata and an organized priestly group. They also were characterized "by industrial structures that show an advancing division of labor, general and local; by buildings of some permanence clustered into places of some size; and by improved appliances of life generally."[19] Examples given included the Teutonic peoples in the fifth century, Homeric Greeks, New Zealanders, Hottentots, Dahomans, and Ashantis.

Doubly compound societies were completely settled; were more integrated; and had a larger and more definite political structure, a religious hierarchy, a more or less rigid caste system, and a more complex division of labor. Furthermore, in such societies, "to a greater or lesser extent, custom has passed into positive law; and religious observances have grown definite, rigid and complex. Towns and roads have become general; and considerable progress in knowledge and the arts has taken place."[20] Examples given included thirteenth-century France, eleventh-century England, the Spartan confederacy, the ancient Peruvians, and the Guatemalans.

Trebly compound societies included "the great civilized nations" such as the Assyrian Empire, and modern Great Britain, France, Germany, Italy, and Russia. Spencer does not outline their traits in detail but points to their increased overall size, complexity, division of labor (differentiation), population density, integration, and general cultural complexity.

The distinction between societies organized for war ("militant societies") and societies organized for productivity ("industrial societies") crosscuts the foregoing division into simple, compound, doubly compound, and trebly compound societies. Simple societies start off as relatively peaceful but develop aggressive military capabilities in the course of compounding and recompounding. Although Spencer referred to some simple societies as nonmilitaristic, he generally used the militant/industrial dichotomy to distinguish between aggressive and warlike states that have existed in the past (such as feudal and caste-based societies) and what he saw as emergent peaceful industrial orders that he perceived through most of his career as contemporaneously developing in the West. Spencer's militant/industrial dichotomy appears, in fact, to be an idealized distinction between a feudal-aristocratic order and a social order based on industrial production and free-market exchange.

Again, in distinguishing militant and industrial societies, Spencer admitted that he was presenting polar forms that have only been approximated in real societies. All empirically existent societies have had both military and industrial components. Yet Spencer did believe that a completely industrial society was in the process of evolutionary development and that militant aggressiveness would one day come to an end.

Spencer presented a *militant society* as one in which the regulating (or external) system dominates the sustaining (or internal) system of the society. In a pure militant society, the military organization dominates the society. The military is the society mobilized. It is a society in which centralized control and the authority necessary for war permeate all areas of social life. The society is divided into a graded series of ranks that replicate military rank, with each level totally subordinated to the ones above it. Private initiative is restrained; all aspects of individual life—food, dress, movement, recreational activities, and so on—fall under state regulation. Governmental censorship is ubiquitous, and private conduct is scrupulously observed by state examiners and spies. Productivity of goods is totally controlled (or regulated) by the state and focused on producing in accordance with the needs of the military. Regimentation, status, and regulation thus pervade all of social life. Political freedom is nonexistent; individuals' lives and possessions are at the total disposal of the state, which is run on a philosophy that individuals exist to serve the purposes of the social whole.

An *industrial society* is one that is dominated by its sustaining system. Such a society is organized to allow free initiative in the development and production of industrial goods. Politically, the elected representative government functions only to protect individual initiative and rights. Government authority and regulative powers are kept minimal. All individuals are equal in rights; castes, slavery, and serfdom do not exist. Freedom of belief, religion, and productive activity is pervasive; and disputes are generally settled through peaceful arbitration. Philanthropic and other private and voluntaristic organizations emerge, which aid both individual and general welfare. Coercive force disappears, and cooperative efforts are based on contractual arrangement, freely entered into. As a decentralized order lacking a strong regulative body, the industrial society is characterized by a high degree of plasticity. It is thus a highly adaptive society, capable of changing rapidly to meet new circumstances and unrestrained by rigid dogma or authority structures. In all, an industrial society is one in which the social whole is viewed as an agency to protect individual freedom, rights, and initiative.

Although Spencer wrote a great deal about society itself, he ultimately believed that the makeup of a society was dependent on the makeup of its members. Society was built on the relationships of individuals. Thus to understand society—its stages, its forms of organization, and its possible future—one must understand the social individual. Ultimately, Spencer believed that the systematic evolution of society resided in the systematic evolution of the individual.

The Individual in Society

Three fundamental ideas dominated Spencer's conception of the individual in society: (1) Lamarckianism, (2) the dominance of emotion (or sentiments) over intellect, and (3) the correlation of individual makeup and societal form. Lamarckianism was a pre-Darwinian view of biological evolution that pervaded virtually all of Spencer's writings. It contends (1) that biological and psychological traits develop through use and decay through disuse, and (2) that traits developed by one generation through exercise or use can be passed on to the next generation by biological transmission. In other words, if an individual works at something and develops a certain skill or temperament, that skill or temperament is biologically transmitted to the individual's offspring, who can further develop it (through practice) or let it decline (by disuse). Thus, if a person accepted Lamarckianism and wanted an unborn offspring to be a pianist, that person would take up the piano and thereby engrain a musical skill in his or her future child.

Spencer viewed the Lamarckian process of use and disuse as the primary means of human biological and social adaptation. It was the means by which individuals evolved and adapted biologically, psychologically, and socially. Human limbs and dexterity advanced through use and disuse; mental facilities involved in perception and cognition advanced through use and disuse; and social sentiments of cooperation, morality, and altruism advanced through the same process of use and disuse. Over many generations, the exercise of the physical body, mental facilities, and social sentiments—in the course of coping with the environment by means of cooperative efforts with others—led to the development and perfection of human attributes. Simultaneously, the same process led to the development of physical attributes, mental capacities, and social sentiments most conducive to well-being in an advanced social state.

Although Spencer saw different psychological and social sentiments existing in different portions of humanity (that is, by society, social stage, and class), he did view all of humanity as in a constant state of adaptation and improvement. Indeed, Spencer envisioned a world in which all human beings would have achieved the highest levels of physical, psychological, and social well-being. Yet he also asserted that not all those who were living would survive to pass on their traits and to have descendants. It was Spencer—not Darwin—who coined the phrase "the survival of the fittest." Spencer maintained that in situations where individuals are not given the chance (by means of use and disuse) to adapt to new circumstances, they or their offspring might well perish. Spencer used such logic to justify a hands-off, *laissez-faire* government. He argued that if government aided an individual (through public education, welfare, and other assistance), it would undermine the aided individual's own ability to develop adaptive traits on his or her own and thus doom both the individual and the individual's offspring. Spencer argued that governmental assistance was thus a disservice both to the taxpayer and the recipient. At times, Spencer's arguments on this point get a bit convoluted, as in the following quote from *Social Statics*:

> The expediency-philosophy, of which this general State-superintendence is a practical expression, embodies the belief that government ought not only to guarantee men the unmolested pursuit of happiness, but should provide the happiness for them. Now no scheme could be more self-defeating. Man . . . consists of a congeries of faculties qualifying him for surrounding conditions. Each of these faculties, if normally developed, yields to him, when exercised, a gratification constituting part of his happiness; while in the act of exercising it, some deed is done subserving the wants of the man as a whole, and affording to the other faculties the opportunities of performing in turn their respective functions, and of producing every one of its peculiar pleasures: so that, when healthily balanced, each subserves all and all subserve each. We cannot live at all unless this mechanism works with some efficiency; and we can live entirely only when the reciprocity between capacities and requirements is perfect. Evidently, then, one who is thus rightly constituted cannot be helped. To do anything for him by some artificial agency, is to supersede certain of his powers—is to leave them unexercised, and therefore to diminish his happiness.[21]

On the basis of his Lamarckian assumptions, Spencer argued in his works on education against the use of corporal punishment and in favor of education by example, aimed at the development of self-sufficiency, hard work, and restraint necessary to live in a socially advanced society.

Spencer's concern with the inculcation of independent and self-sufficient "sentiments" (feelings or emotional predispositions) in his educational writings corresponds to a fundamental tenet of his social-psychological thinking. That tenet held that in terms of shaping the contours of social activity, sentiments or emotional predispositions are more important than intellectual understanding. Although both intellectual cognitive skills and emotional makeup evolve in the human species, Spencer believed that sentiments took precedence over cognitive elements in the actual production of behavior.

Although the dominance of sentiments (or emotions) is implicit in his social, psychological, and educational works, it is made most explicit in his early philosophical works and in his last major work, *The Principles of Ethics*—a work that he saw as the culmination of his writings. Whereas intellectual abilities were seen as the servants of instrumental thinking, Spencer maintained that emotional sentiments prompted the desires, dispositions, and goals toward which instrumental thinking was oriented.

The intellect was fundamentally a tool of the emotions. For Spencer, emotional pre-dispositions necessarily corresponded to the types (or forms) of society. Thus he distinguished the emotional sentiments typical of individuals in militant societies as contrasted with those typical in industrial societies. Spencer also distinguished between the emotional sentiments of individuals in "simple" societies and those characteristics of individuals in more "highly compounded" societies.

A large portion of Volume 2 of *The Principles of Sociology* is given over to the explication of personal traits of the typical members of militant and industrial societies. The sentimental predispositions inculcated and manifest in militant society are presented as those conducive to prowess in physical combat. These include bodily courage; an identification of bravery with virtue; a strong sense of revenge; "delight in a forcible exercise of mastery";[22] little regard for others' claims to life, liberty, and property; a disinclination and contempt for productive labor; strong sentiments of patriotism and identification with a leader; faith in and subordination to authority figures; a fatalistic acceptance of the future; lack of sentiments of private initiative and enterprise; an attribution of events to individual luck or prowess (as opposed to natural causation); and a tendency toward ritualism and supernaturalism.

As opposed to the personality of the typical member of a militant society, the industrial individual lacked knee-jerk tendencies toward subordination to authority and, instead, manifested "a strong sense of individual freedom and a determination to maintain it."[23] Such sentiments of individuality were tied to sentiments of respecting the individuality of others. Thus, whereas the militant personality takes great delight in domination and destruction, the industrial personality is predisposed to respect the life and rights of others. This concern with the rights of others is combined with a resolve to resist unjust authority, a concern with general human welfare (as opposed to divisive patriotic feelings), an absence of sentiments of vengeance and destruction, and a self-reliant entrepreneurial initiative that is conducive to voluntaristic cooperation with others.

Spencer appears to have intended the foregoing dichotomy between the emotional sentiments of militant and industrial personalities to serve as a polar or ideal-typical distinction. Actual societies contain individuals with complex mixtures of sentiments, ranging from predominantly militant to predominantly industrial. In *The Principles of Psychology*, Spencer pointed out that individuals always manifest a combination of egoistic and altruistic sentiments, and in *The Study of Sociology*, he maintained that individuals often have conflicting tendencies. Actual behavior was viewed as caused by complex factors and was ascribed to those sentiments left after the conflicting emotional predispositions had canceled one another out.

In contrasting the militant individual and the industrial individual, Spencer focused on differences in emotional sentiments. In contrasting individuals in simple societies and those in more advanced ("highly compounded") societies, Spencer focused on intellectual capacity. Individuals in simple societies were presented as having very limited intellectual abilities, compared with the scientific cause-and-effect reasoning possible of individuals in advanced societies. Whereas the militant individual was presented as not sentimentally predisposed to thought in terms of a natural sequence of causes, the individual in a simple society was presented as intellectually incapable of such thought. Behavior of members of simple societies was seen as spasmodic and inconsistent, reflecting the lack of an ability to plan and act toward long-run future goals and given to unthinking habitual and ritualistic activity. With social advance, individuals' behavior becomes increasingly coherent, consistent, innovative, and oriented toward the future.

In the course of his many writings, Spencer did not always indicate clearly whether his particular remarks were in reference to the militant/industrial or societally simple/complex dichotomy of individual personal, intellectual, and emotional makeup. He often juxtaposed "primitive" individuals—those who manifested the combined traits of militant and simple-society personality—with modern individuals who manifested the traits corresponding to industrial and socially complex societies.

In *The Principles of Psychology*, Spencer applied the distinction he made between the social-psychological makeup of "primitives" and his European contemporaries to that between contemporary adult men and boys. The logic of this position is derived directly from von Baer's assertion that the development of an individual member of a species follows the stages of evolution that the species itself, as a whole, goes through. For Spencer this was true not just of biological evolution, but of psychological and social evolution as well. (Indeed, Spencer's Lamarckian beliefs tended to confound questions of biological change with those of psychological and social development.) Thus Spencer drew a wholesale equation between the emotional reactions, thought patterns, and social relations of boys and primitive adult men. To see a bunch of boys at play without adult supervision was to see what life was like in an earlier stage of social evolution.

If it was held as true that boys in advanced society began as "savages" but ended up as "civilized" men, was the same true of girls and women? The answer that Spencer gave to this question depended upon when he gave it. If we look at his writings from the early 1850s, we see a decidedly different position taken on the question of gender differences and relations than we find in writings produced later in his career.

Coming from the individualistic assumptions of middle-class radicalism and a belief in equality of opportunity, Spencer's early writings on gender rejected the notion of *a priori* inborn differences between men and women that could be used to justify limiting a woman's individual rights. He wrote in an early edition of *Social Statics*, for instance, that those who would argue based on tradition that a woman should be confined to domestic duties fail to appreciate the wide differences in customs from one society to another in terms of gender roles. Spencer insisted that no one had the knowledge to assert whether the social limits placed on women in English society were justifiable. Accordingly, he argued that women should be given equal rights to achieve for themselves. At this time, Spencer, while not endorsing a nonbiological view of gender difference, raised the possibility that gender differences of aptitude are socially learned and ingrained. In an 1854 article on elocution, Spencer seemed to be moving to a position that a good deal of the intellectual difference between men and women may actually be a product of upbringing and education, and he criticized the general education of girls at the time for focusing on a limited number of subjects and not giving enough attention to science and mathematics.[24] Thus, by 1854, Spencer could be seen as "progressing" toward a view of understanding gender roles in sociocultural terms; but, as Spencer himself came to realize late in life, progressive movements are subject to reversals, and by 1858, Spencer began to develop a view of gender inequality that would attempt to justify the traditional subordinate role of women.

The context of Spencer's change in viewpoint was a London in which intellectually there was an emphasis on differences in human nature among peoples as opposed to an emphasis on equality. One does not need to be steeped in the sociology of knowledge to realize that such an emphasis allowed the educated middle classes to justify both imperialistic expansion and the subordination of an indigenous working class to a new entrepreneurial class arisen out of the industrial revolution. Although Spencer himself rejected imperialism, he accepted ideas, as we have seen, that stressed the moral, intellectual, and emotional inequality between his ilk and members of more "primitive" societies. Moreover, an emphasis on biological differences between men and women was being bolstered by new biological notions that differences in external form had to have profound and all-encompassing consequences for, and reflect, differences in internal makeup. Charles Darwin's publication of *On the Origin of Species* in 1859 would provide the foundation for making biologically based arguments more popular for segments of the educated public, Spencer included. As years went on, Spencer would see gender differences more and more in biological terms that justified traditional roles and less and less in terms of social learning that could bring the rigid division of activity between the sexes into question.

Spencer fitted into his *Synthetic Philosophy* (in *The Principles of Biology* and *The Principles of Psychology* as well as *The Principles of Sociology*) arguments that assumed an intellectual and emotional inferiority of women due, in great part, to "a somewhat earlier arrest of individual evolution in women; necessitated by the reservation of vital power to meet the cost of reproduction."[25] In other words, he claimed that as girls, unlike boys, mature, their available "energy" is not used to develop mentally and emotionally, but to prepare themselves for giving birth and taking on the role of mothers. Spencer presents women as having the intellectual abilities of members of simple societies, combined with the submission to, and admiration of, power and authority characteristic of the "militant" personality. Based on this view, he rejected the feminist agenda he had previously supported. He argued that women were destined by nature to take on a domestic role of motherhood, that it was unnatural for them not to marry, and that their education and opportunities should be limited to learning those things necessary for their biologically ordained social role.

Once a position had been incorporated into his overall system, Spencer, as always, assumed that it was correct and that his duty lay in explaining to his associates their errors. He persisted in his now reactionary gender beliefs despite an awareness of strong arguments in opposition to such views that had been presented by his old benefactor John Stuart Mill, despite his knowledge of materials arising from the Victorian feminist movement, and despite his acknowledgment in the final volumes of the *Synthetic Philosophy* (*The Principles of Ethics*) of the suffering that women had had to endure through the ages because of their subordination to men:

> In the history of humanity as written, the saddest part concerns the treatment of women; and had we before us its unwritten history we should find this part still sadder. I say the saddest part because, though there have been many things more conspicuously dreadful—cannibalism, the torturings of prisoners, the sacrificing of victims to ghosts and gods—these have been but occasional; whereas the brutal treatment of women has been universal and constant. If, looking first at their state of subjection among the semi-civilized, we pass to the uncivilized, and observe the lives of hardship borne by nearly all of them—if we then think what must have gone on among those still ruder peoples who, for so many thousands of years, roamed over the uncultivated earth; we shall infer that the amount of suffering which has been, and is, borne by women, is utterly beyond imagination.[26]

Perhaps the most astounding fact about the antifeminism of Spencer's later years is his persistence in defending a position of female intellectual inferiority despite his personal acquaintance with such thinkers as Harriet Martineau (1802–1876), Beatrice Webb, and, of course, Marian Evans. Spencer, who warned in *The Study of Sociology* that the sociologist needed to be aware of and overcome political, religious, class, and national biases, ignored and fell prey to gender bias in construction of his sociological theory. Moreover, as we shall see in the next section, Spencer's whole methodological approach involved finding data that supported the elements of his theoretical system. Thus once gender biases, as well as other biases, were incorporated into his overall system, he proved incapable of either detecting or eradicating them.

Methodology

Spencer's methodological approach in sociology was dominated by a belief in naturalistic evolutionism. His reasoning was quite simple: All natural phenomena can be explained by reference to the process of evolution. Social occurrences are natural phenomena. Therefore, social occurrences should be explained in terms of evolutionary processes.

In *First Principles*, Spencer distinguished between the "knowable" and the "unknowable" (often referred to as "ultimate reality" or "ultimate ideas"). The unknowable referred to questions of ultimate causes, essences of existence, and ultimate purposes of life. Spencer asserted that, by definition, the unknowable is beyond the grasp of science and philosophy and that speculation concerning it is a worthless intellectual exercise:

> Ultimate Scientific Ideas, then, are all representative of realities that cannot be comprehended. After no matter how great a progress in the colligation of facts and the establishment of generalizations ever wider and wider, after the merging of limited and derivative truths in truths that are larger and deeper has been carried no matter how far, the fundamental truth remains as much beyond reach as ever. The explanation of that which is explicable does but bring into greater clearness the inexplicableness of that which remains behind. Alike in the external and the internal worlds, the man of science sees himself in the midst of perpetual changes, of which he can discover neither the beginning nor the end. If, tracing back the evolution of things, he allows himself to entertain the hypothesis that the Universe once existed in a diffused form, he finds it utterly impossible to conceive how this came to be so; and equally, if he speculates on the future he can assign no limit to the grand succession of phenomena ever unfolding themselves before him. In like manner, if he looks inward, he perceives that both ends of the thread of consciousness are beyond his grasp; nay, even beyond his power to think of as having existed or as existing in time to come. When, again, he turns from the succession of phenomena, external or internal, to their intrinsic nature, he is just as much at fault.[27]

Science and philosophy were to concentrate on explaining the "knowable." Such explanations had to be naturalistic; that is, they had to be based on this-worldly forces and causes and *not* explain phenomena in terms of spirits, gods, or other supernatural agencies.

For Spencer, a naturalistic explanation necessarily entailed explanation in terms of what he saw as the universal process of evolution. To Spencer, an evolutionary explanation included the assumption that phenomena went through the interrelated processes of progressive increase in mass, density, differentiation, specialization, integration, and adaptation.

By increase in mass, Spencer meant an increase in the number of basic units composing a phenomenon. Thus, in terms of social explanation, Spencer *assumed* a natural increase in population. By increase in density, Spencer meant an increase in the amount of mass per given unit of space. Thus Spencer not only assumed a natural population increase in social explanation, but he also *assumed* an increase in crowding in terms of the number of persons in a given geographical area.

The process of differentiation implied a separation into increasingly larger numbers of suborganizations in the organization being studied. Thus a society was assumed to differentiate as it developed, with the formation of more and more groups and subgroups within it. As societal mass and density increase, Spencer *assumed* that individuals formed more and more distinguishable groupings. For Spencer, organizational differentiation was necessarily accompanied by functional specialization.

As the number of groups increases, the tasks (or functions) that groups perform become different from one another. Again, Spencer took it for granted that societal explanation would show how different groups come to take on different functions (that is, produce different types of goods and services) necessary for a society's continuance. Specialized differentiation, in turn, implies increased social integration.

As parts of an organization become functionally specialized, Spencer maintained that the parts must increasingly become more coordinated to the activities of one another. Thus, in sociological explanation, Spencer *assumed* that the different social groups increasingly modified their activities in terms of the functioning of other groups. For example, groups producing raw materials are assumed to coordinate their activities increasingly to the demands of the producers of finished products. These producers coordinate their production to demands of wholesalers. Wholesalers coordinate their purchases to the demands of retailers. Retailers, in turn, coordinate their purchases to the demands of consuming groups.

Spencer summarized the assumption of increases in differentiation, specialization, and integration as a movement from "incoherent homogeneity" (unorganized likeness) to "coherent heterogeneity" (organized unlikeness). Spencer thereby *assumed* that in the course of an explanation, a researcher would find that phenomena increasingly divide into unlike parts and become organized into more and more complex wholes. Spencer insisted that all sociological explanations must take this assumption both as their starting and their end points and must endeavor to show how a coherent social heterogeneity comes about.

Spencer further believed that the integration of functionally specialized units increased overall efficiency in the handling of internal and external problems of maintenance. He thus *assumed* that with societal development came increasing adaptation to internal and external circumstances. Overall sociological explanations were to give an account of increasing social adaptation to the exigencies of existence.

Spencer maintained that sociology is to be accomplished by a process of "deduction" followed by a process of "induction." In actuality, Spencer equated deduction with a derivation of the principles of social development and order from his evolutionary methodological assumptions. Thus, for example, Spencer claimed to have deduced the development of society in terms of the levels of compounding and recompounding by logically applying the general principles of the evolutionary process to societal change.

Unlike most philosophers, Spencer did not view "deduction" as an independent process, but rather insisted that it needed to be supported by a subsequent methodological process of induction. By "induction," Spencer did not mean creating theories on the basis of grouping data together. Rather, he followed a procedure of fitting ethnographic observations and historical facts into the contours of the evolutionary view of society that he had previously deduced from applying his general evolutionary assumptions. In other words, his inductions involved merely placing data on the evolutionary outline that he assumed to be true. Thus, although Spencer handled masses of data, in general his data did not lead to the reshaping of his theories; rather, his theories determined the perceived significance of his data. Spencer thereby assumed *a priori* the fundamental validity of his theory.

Spencer's overall macroevolutionary assumptions about society also served as the guidelines by which social institutions and groups were to be analyzed. In the opening paragraph of *The Principles of Ethics,* Spencer asserted a fundamental methodological rule that governed his sociological analysis: Parts are to be explained with reference to the whole, and wholes are to be explained with reference to the parts:

> The doctrine that correlatives imply one another—that a father cannot be thought of without thinking of a child, and that there can be no consciousness of superior without a consciousness of inferior—has for one of its common examples the necessary connection between the conceptions of whole and part. Beyond the primary truth that no idea of a whole can be framed without a nascent idea of parts constituting it, and that no idea of a part can be framed without a nascent idea of some whole to which it belongs, there is the secondary truth that there can be no correct idea of a part without a correct idea of the correlative whole. There are several ways in which inadequate knowledge of the one involves inadequate knowledge of the other.[28]

Spencer's evolutionary assumptions served as his methodological tool for linking parts with wholes. Institutions, group activities, and individual social-psychological characteristics were explained in terms of the level of societal evolution that they manifested, whereas levels of societal evolution were accounted for in terms of the institutions, group activities, and social-psychological characteristics of its members. Spencer denied that this procedure of explaining parts in terms of wholes and wholes in terms of parts was tautological. Instead, he maintained, such explanations took into account the fact that society and its components mutually influence one another and thus tend to serve as causal factors in each other's progressive development.

Spencer also believed in the interdependence of the study of change and the study of order. Although Spencer was predominantly concerned with evolutionary development, as we have seen, he conceived of such development in terms of progressively more differentiated, specialized, and functionally integrated social entities. Thus change is to be studied in terms of a society's level of progressive development. In *First Principles,* Spencer made clear that this interrelating of order and change was the proper methodological approach—not just for sociology, but for all the sciences.

Spencer maintained that as a naturalistic science, sociology should be concerned with establishing verifiable causal linkages. Events are to be accounted for in terms of sequences of cause and effect. Spencer believed the sociologist was concerned with the impact of "social forces" on individuals to produce societal effects. He cautioned that causality in the social world is rarely simple and that it usually involves multiple forces of different strength and direction having an impact on a sequence of events. For Spencer, such a multiplicity of causes, coupled with the complexity of social life, made the study of sociology a demanding enterprise fraught with the possibility of false causal inference. Spencer warned against drawing causal conclusions about social institutions and processes where one lacked a number of comparable cases drawn from ethnographic and historical data. He believed that the lack of a number of comparable cases would almost certainly lead to false perceptions of causal sequences. He also warned the would-be sociologist of the dangers of inferring causality from the study of simultaneous events. Unlike many positivists of today, who have attempted to produce rules for deriving causal conclusions from correlational data, Spencer maintained that to infer causality where one lacks any records of temporal sequence is an effort conducive to bias and error.

Spencer's emphasis on causality and on comparing events abstracted from their particular societies and historical eras places him squarely in the positivist camp. Together with John Stuart Mill, Spencer served as a major influence on positivistic social-scientific thinking in the English-speaking world, especially in the United States. As is traditional with positivists, Spencer posited a "unity of science." He believed that, in general, the same fundamental causal forms of reasoning and processes of structure and change were common to all fields of scientific inquiry. Yet, the precise extent to which he subscribed to this unity is somewhat unclear. In some writings, he implied that this unity is virtually complete. In *Social Statics*, for example, he asserted that there was an "entire correspondence"[29] in the principles of physical and moral study, and in *First Principles*, he referred to the "several orders of existence as forming one natural whole" with the division of the subject matters of geology, biology, psychology, and sociology having no existence in reality. Instead, the divisions represented by these fields were presented "as mere conventional groupings, made to facilitate the arrangement and acquisition of knowledge."[30] Yet in *The Principles of Ethics*, Spencer asserted that differences of degree between the fields existed in terms of the clarity of data and confidence in the validity of findings. Spencer wrote: "Where the data are few and exact, definite conclusions can be drawn, but where they are numerous and inexact, the conclusions drawn must be proportionately indefinite. Pure mathematics exemplifies the one extreme and sociology the other."[31]

In *The Study of Sociology*, Spencer divided the sciences into two fundamental groups. Together with geology, biology, and psychology, sociology was grouped as an "inexact" science. As opposed to the "exact" sciences (for example, physics, chemistry, and astronomy), which predominantly involve a mathematical, quantitative handling of data, sociology and the other "inexact" sciences use mostly nonmathematical, qualitative data. In sociology, data usually are ethnographic and historical in nature. Because such data are "less precise" than the mathematical measurements of the exact sciences, Spencer maintained that sociological generalizations could not be made in terms of the precise prediction of events. Yet, despite his distinction between exact and inexact sciences, Spencer still maintained that all scientific generalizations are fundamentally of the same nature.

Spencer's emphasis on ethnographic and historical facts in terms of sociological methodology forced him to investigate how different ethnographic and historical data were to be compared and theoretically categorized. Spencer maintained that data were to be grouped in terms of relations (for example, temporal relations of sequence or physical relations of proximity) of likeness and unlikeness. He recognized that at different time periods and in different societies, parallel customs and group activities would not appear exactly alike. Differences would be due either to slightly different levels of development or to peculiar environmental adaptations (such as to climate or geography). In such cases, or in cases where one sees an atypical level of development in a particular trait, Spencer suggested that one "average the evidence." Thus his delineation of levels of societal development involves an interpretation of what is usual or typical (but not mandatory) for that particular level. It is this necessity for judgment and interpretation that led Spencer to categorize sociology as an inexact science. Spencer further accepted the notion of *survivals*—that a cultural trait might persist for a time in a society after that society had progressed to a higher level. Decisions about what features of a society constitute survivals imply the existence of further interpretation, judgment, and inexactness in the production of overall sociological generalizations.

As opposed to abstract methodological principles that could be stated easily, Spencer believed the actual study and formation of sociological generalizations could be achieved only with great personal effort. The greatest difficulties one had to overcome in the practice of sociology involved the social and cultural biases that sociologists were apt to find in themselves. Although Spencer did not use the term, he did argue that sociologists must attempt a cultural relativist position, wherein they look at societal traits in the context of the society being studied. Throughout *The Study of Sociology*, Spencer warned would-be sociologists of the danger of misinterpretation in analyzing cultural traits from the basis of sociologists' own value biases:

> Here, then, is a difficulty to which no other science presents anything analogous. To cut himself off in thought from all his relationships of race, and country, and citizenship—to get rid of all those interests, prejudices, likings, superstitions, generated in him by the life of his own society and his own time—to look on all the changes societies have undergone and are undergoing, without reference to nationality, or creed, or personal welfare is what the average man cannot do at all, and what the exceptional man can do very imperfectly.[32]

Such imperfections are, of course, quite apparent in Spencer's own works, which reflect a commitment to the ideologies of his day. Indeed, as we have pointed out in Chapters 1 and 2, sociological theorists can never fully escape the influence of their own backgrounds and ideological precommitments.

Finally, there is an omission in Spencer's methodological writings that might strike contemporary sociologists as quite peculiar. Spencer never conceived of the possibility of sociologists formulating studies to gather their own data; rather, Spencer's methodological rules are for handling and interpreting the ethnographic and historical data gathered by others. In Spencer's work, the *systemization* of knowledge takes total precedence over the *accumulation* of new knowledge. It was a systemization, moreover, in which Spencer assumed that his own *a priori* evolutionary assumptions were correct.

SIGNIFICANCE

Vision of the Future

Working with past historical and present ethnographic data, Spencer maintained that the prediction of the *exact contours* of future social life was beyond the intellectual grasp of the sociologist. In *The Principles of Sociology*, he referred to the possible eventual emergence of a new form of social existence that was neither militant nor industrial, but qualitatively different from both. In *The Study of Sociology*, he wrote:

> Everywhere sociological thinking is more or less impeded by the difficulty of bearing in mind that the social states toward which our race is being carried, are probably as little conceivable by us as our present social state was conceivable by a Norse pirate and his followers.[33]

Yet, if Spencer did not believe that the future of society was fully knowable, he did believe that the role of science was prevision and that sociology, as a science, could shed considerable light on what might come to pass. Further, Spencer believed that sociology confirmed his general view of evolutionary adaptation and progressive improvement. Barring interference from ill-conceived governmental regulation, he saw human society continuously adapting until it reached a state of near perfection.

For Spencer, continuous adaptation of humans to social existence could produce a state in which evil would be eradicated, harmony would be spontaneous, and all the traditional Christian virtues involved in "loving thy fellow man" would be achieved. In *Social Statics*, he boldly wrote that "all evil results from the non-adaptation of constitution to conditions," that nonadaptation was the "one generic cause of evil," and that "due to the natural process of adaptive evolution . . . evil perpetually tends to disappear."[34] With the adaptation of both society and the individuals who compose it, evil will thus continually be reduced until it approaches nonexistence.

Spencer believed that the process of Lamarckian evolution would lead to an individual who was spontaneously cooperative with others; who eventually would find pleasure in doing the tasks necessary for life (that is, the distinction between desire and obligation would disappear); and who would be free from dogma and open to new ideas and improved technology. Built out of the relationships between such persons, society would become efficiently organized on the basis of spontaneous voluntaristic cooperation, without a need for any central organizing or regulating body. Progressive social differentiation, specialization, harmonious integration, and adaptation would thus go on unhampered and produce a high level of happiness for all.

Spencer, who presented himself as an avowed atheist, in fact was not an atheist at all. If he did not believe in a god *per se*, his sociology was based on a faith in evolutionary progress. *Evolutionary progress was not an outcome of his sociology; it was a fundamental assumption on which his sociology was constructed.* His faith in it was pervasive in his writings and persistent in its influence on his conclusions. What doubts he had about it arose only late in his life, after all his major works had been completed.

If evolution replaces a beneficent god for Spencer, how was Spencer able to account for the persistence of nonadaptive evil in the world? It appears that Spencer had an equivalent of the devil on which he could heap blame. He inherited the devil in his thinking from the middle-class radical movements of his youth. It was a force that would attempt to undo all the good being brought about naturally by evolution and that was working to undermine the natural progression toward a harmonious utopian existence on earth. His devil—the unholy antiprogressive force—was that of governmental social intervention and regulation.

Spencer never stopped detailing in his writings the evils that governmental regulation had wrought in the past and could bring down on humankind in the future. Attacks on such regulation run throughout his writings; they form the central thrust of *The Man versus the State.* Whether guided by good or bad intentions, Spencer maintained that, beyond a bare minimum, all governmental regulations harmed society. By aiding the weak, all welfare measures undermined the forces of adaptation and thus perpetuated evil and misery. Spencer viewed the only proper activity of government in an advanced society as maintenance of a limited military (where it was needed for defense) and protection of the rights of individuals. Anything beyond these he viewed as detrimental to human progress. Spencer went so far as to describe the notion of general public education as evil.

Despite the evil of governmental regulation, throughout most of his career Spencer believed that a much better society was on the horizon. Toward the end of his life, however, he came to doubt that such was the case. His observations in his own society of militant nationalism, imperialism, public rituals, antiscientific attitudes, an increased role of government, and socialist movements among the working class led him to believe that society could change no faster than human nature, and that human nature was a long way from perfection.

Contemporary Relevance

From the publication of his earliest works, through the completion of his massive "synthetic philosophy" in 1897, Spencer amassed a large and loyal following among segments of the British and American business middle and upper classes, as well as their intellectual and academic apologists. This following did not diminish until after World War I. A major part of Spencer's appeal to his fans was that he claimed to be presenting scientific, unbiased, value-neutral images of the individual, society, and social change that, in actuality: (1) incorporated ideological elements that justified the prevailing moral, political, and economic views of the dominant propertied classes; (2) rejected critical theoretical approaches as unscientific and incompatible with society's supposed predetermined necessary internal rate of progressive change; and (3) deflected any meaningful progressive change that would challenge the class structure of society. Spencer told white, male, upper and middle class property owners that they were morally superior beings who were naturally entitled to all the wealth that they possessed, and that their freedom of economic activity and control of the political apparatus of society not only was morally justified, but was absolutely necessary for further social progress. Although in his more utopian passages, Spencer foresaw a society characterized by altruism and universal suffrage, for the immediate future he extolled the egoism characteristic of nineteenth-century competitive capitalism and simultaneously denigrated the intellectual abilities of blue-collar workers, nonwhite populations, and women—whom he argued would undermine morality, property rights, and progress should they obtain equal political and voting rights. Following a principle that philosophers call "equal freedom," Spencer presented a utilitarian justification whereby he defined equal rights only in terms of the right to control property.[35] As Spencer grew older, he reacted to the demands of workers' and women's movements for expanded rights with an increasingly adamant defense of his views and by presenting increasingly conservative positions in his last works and in the revised, reissued editions of his earlier writings.

With their built-in class bias, Spencer's works became the foundation upon which much American sociology was developed in its formative period from 1885 to 1915. As Charles H. Cooley (1864–1929), the first sociologist at the University of Michigan, famously remarked of the first generation of sociologists in American universities: "At first we were all Spencerians."[36] Certainly, the founders of academic American sociology held varied intellectual positions. Each disagreed with Spencer on certain elements of his thought. Yet, as a group, they accepted Spencerian positions concerning the appropriateness of middle-class values, change as evolutionary, a rejection of radical working-class movements, a rejection of critical analysis in favor of a more positivistic sociology, an ahistorical comparative methodology, and a view of sociology as a "value-neutral" science. Even William Graham Sumner (1840–1910), who rejected Spencer's evolutionary view of progress, did so on neo-Spencerian grounds. (Sumner argued that social order and progress in the twentieth century would be undermined by a mass democracy whose incompetent working-class "mass" of voters would fall under the sway of socially destructive demagogues.)

Despite his early influence, direct citations of the works of Herbert Spencer by academic sociologists declined after World War I. By the 1920s, American sociology was coming into the hands of native-trained practitioners who were inspired by their own teachers and did not need the reputation of Spencer to either justify or build their own theoretical arguments. Moreover, the application of positivistic statistics (pioneered at Columbia University) and ethnographic techniques (developed at the University of Chicago) to population and small-scale studies, respectively, left Spencer's macrotheorizing less relevant to the research concerns of a new generation of sociologists. Finally, social evolutionism, with its commitment to the idea of progress, became unfashionable. Belief in a slowly progressing, peaceful industrial society could not be reconciled with the industrialized butchery of the Great War. By the mid-1930s, at the time he was constructing a decidedly non-Spencerian general theory, Parsons could write in his highly influential *The Structure of Social Action:* "Herbert Spencer is dead."[37]

Parsons attributed the "death of Spencer" to the outmodedness of social evolutionary thought, and proceeded, with his Harvard students, to develop a "functionalist" theory that discarded the evolutionist concern with change and progress in favor of the "Hobbesian question" of explaining how social order was possible. Although achieving preeminence in the field in the 1950s, Parsonians, who celebrated the "homeostatic" (or self-maintaining) virtues of post–World War II American society, were increasingly confronted by competing thinkers (e.g., C. Wright Mills) who were raising questions about social injustices, conflict, and change. Parsons' solutions to this challenge was to integrate his functionalist thinking with an evolutionary model that both explained extant injustices as necessary for social development and viewed social change as a process of evolutionary differentiation and reintegration of social components. Parsons now echoed Spencerian thought. Accordingly, Spencer, who had previously been declared "dead," was resurrected. In the introduction to a 1961 reprinting of Spencer's *The Study of Sociology,* Parsons wrote, that though dated in parts, Spencer's book " . . . contains much that is surprisingly modern and relevant to our time,"[38] and that the revival of social evolutionism in sociology " . . . testifies to Spencer's importance."[39] But Parsons' late embrace of Spencerian ideas came at a time when Parsons' own influence was beginning to wane. Most sociologists did not rush to dust off old copies of Spencer's works, and the prevailing view of introductory texts—influenced by an earlier Parsons—was that Durkheim and Weber were the true "founders" of sociology and that Spencer, like Comte, belonged to its prehistory.

In recent decades, those sociologists who have tried to rehabilitate Spencer's reputation in a post-Parsonsian era have tried to disassociate Spencer's moral/political/ideological positions from what they see as his contributions to objective methodological procedures and sound principles of structural sociology. Jonathan Turner has been foremost among such sociologists. Turner wrote:

> I am distressed, even angry, about how contemporary social theorists have treated Herbert Spencer. . . . [W]e spit on the grave of Spencer because he held a moral philosophy repugnant to the political biases of many contemporary theorists. I share these biases, but they should not blind all of us to the simple fact: Spencer's sociology and his moral philosophy are written in separate places and are worlds apart.[40]

Although we have no desire to spit on Spencer's grave, it is important to note here that Turner appears to be wrong on both points: Spencer's sociological ideas and his "moral philosophy" were intermingled in the same writings, and, rather than being "worlds apart," the former were used to justify the latter. As David Weinstein has recently written: "For Spencer, social and moral evolution were roughly complementary if not synonymous phenomena."[41] Moreover, Spencer grounded his political views in his intermingled sociological/moral philosophical formulations. Thus, as Michael Taylor concludes: "Although Spencer presented his thought as a value-neutral account of the nature of social aggregates, he nonetheless readily drew political conclusions from it."[42] Illustrative of this point is Spencer's use of arguments stated in "The Social Organism," *The Principles of Sociology,* and *The Study of Sociology* (a work praised by Turner) to justify his individualistic, anti-state, *laissez-faire* economics and to oppose all political movements that wanted immediate social change, greater access to political processes, and a more widespread distribution of wealth.

Turner notes that there are numerous contemporary sociological researchers whose work is Spencerian in their conceptualization of social structure. Turner laments that such individuals generally do not acknowledge or even recognize the contributions made by Spencer to sociology nor their filiations to Spencer's sociological theorizing. Turner attributes this lack of contemporary recognition to a variety of factors, including Spencer's failure to hold an academic position in which he might have produced students who would have perpetuated an awareness of his contributions. But, let us suggest two alternative reasons why contemporary positivistic researchers in sociology do not cite (and are not likely to cite) Spencer's work. First, the very nature of a positivistic approach (during Spencer's time, and today) involves the assumption that there is a discoverable, scientific, value-neutral methodological approach for sociological investigation and that followers of such an approach, as scientists, have no need to examine historically the roots of their own ideas and their historical linkages to older thinkers. Second, and more importantly, close analysis of Spencer's work by contemporary sociologists may prove too revealing of their ties to Spencerian formulations. Specifically, detailed study of Spencer's works shows how easily conclusions drawn from a supposedly value-neutral assemblage of abstracted facts can incorporate cultural, class, racial, gender, political, moral, and other biases. It is our historical distance from Spencer that enables us to see how the moral and political biases of his ilk and era prejudiced his sociological findings. If, like Parsons, contemporary sociologists were to consider bringing Spencer back into focus, perhaps they would conclude that, this time, it is best to leave Spencer dead and buried.

NOTES

1. See J. D. Y. Peel, *Herbert Spencer, the evolution of a sociologist.*
2. "The philosophy of style," in *Literary style and music.*
3. Ibid., p. 3.
4. *Education: Intellectual, moral, and physical,* p. 69.
5. Nancy L. Paxton, *George Eliot and Herbert Spencer,* p. 5.
6. Margaret Crompton, *George Eliot, the woman* (New York: Thomas Yoseloff, 1960), p. 80.
7. Ibid., p. 81.
8. See *An autobiography,* Vol. 2, p. 203.
9. *The man versus the state,* pp. 100–101.
10. George W. Stocking, Jr., *Victorian anthropology,* p. 1.
11. Paxton, *George Eliot and Herbert Spencer,* p. 15.
12. "The social organism," in *The man versus the state,* p. 397.
13. *First principles,* p. 501.
14. *Social statics,* p. 170.
15. *The principles of sociology,* Vol. 3, p. 327.
16. *The study of sociology,* p. 63.
17. In *Herbert Spencer on social evolution,* p. 260.
18. *The principles of sociology,* p. 63.
19. Ibid., p. 553.
20. Ibid.
21. *Social statics,* p. 125.
22. *The principles of sociology,* Vol. 2, p. 513.
23. Ibid., p. 628.
24. See Paxton, *George Eliot and Herbert Spencer,* p. 30.
25. *The study of sociology,* p. 391.
26. *The principles of ethics,* Vol. 2, p. 353.
27. *First principles,* pp. 78–79.
28. *The principles of ethics,* Vol. 1, p. 37.
29. *Social statics,* p. 168.
30. *First principles,* p. 537.
31. *The principles of ethics,* Vol. 1, p. 497.
32. *The study of sociology,* p. 67.
33. Ibid., p. 109.
34. *Social statics,* p. 28.
35. See the arguments in D. Weinstein's meticulously researched and argued *Equal Freedom and Utility, Herbert Spencer's Liberal Utilitarianism.*
36. Along with Cooley, the other early sociologists in American universities were William Graham Sumner (1840–1910) at Yale University, Albion Small (1854–1926) at the University of Chicago, Franklin Giddings (1855–1931) at Columbia University, Edward

A. Ross (1866–1951) at the University of Wisconsin, and Lester F. Ward (1841–1913) at Brown University.

37. Talcott Parsons, *The structure of social action*, Vol. 1. (New York: Free Press, 1937), p. 3.

38. Talcott Parsons, introduction to *The study of sociology*, p. v.

39. Ibid., p. viii.

40. Jonathan Turner, *Herbert Spencer*, p. 7

41. D. Weinstein, *Equal Freedom and Utility, Herbert Spencer's Liberal Utilitarianism*, p. 31.

42. Michael Taylor, *Herbert Spencer and the Limits of the State*, p. xv.

GLOSSARY

Coherent heterogeneity: For Spencer, direction in which all evolutionary change develops. Involves an integrated system composed of unlike and functionally distinct parts (compare with *Incoherent homogeneity*).

Compound accumulation: Spencer's notion that the rate of social change itself had a natural rate of increase, like a rolling snowball.

Compound society: A society produced by the merger of two or more *simple societies*. First socially stratified social form. Has an organized priestly group.

Deduction: In Spencer's usage, the development of a systematic theory to guide the organization of data.

Differentiation: A process of development in which a system separates into an increasing number of subsystems.

Distributing system: One of the three major parts of society. It is concerned with transportation and communication, and links *regulating* and *sustaining systems*.

Doubly compound society: Completely settled societies with definite political structure, religious hierarchies, codified laws, and a separation of town and country.

Dysfunction: Actions of a part of a system that interfere with the maintenance of the total system.

Equal Freedom: Nineteenth-century moral philosophical position that each individual had the "right" to act toward his/her betterment. Spencer applied this primarily in terms of property rights and viewed other rights (e.g., the right to vote) of secondary importance at best.

Equilibrium: In Spencer's usage, a state in which parts of a system are in constant adaptive readjustment to one another.

External system: See *Regulating system*.

Function: For Spencer, the task a unit of a whole performs in the maintenance of that whole.

Incoherent homogeneity: For Spencer, the starting point of evolutionary change, where a phenomenon is in a state of unintegrated and disorganized likeness of substance (compare with *Coherent heterogeneity*).

Induction: In Spencer's usage, involves the organization of data in terms of an *a priori* theoretical model.

Industrial society: Society organized for the production of goods, where the *sustaining system* dominates the *regulating system* (compare with *Militant society*).

Internal system: See *Sustaining system*.

Lamarckianism: Archaic theory of biological evolution, which is based on the inheritance of traits acquired and lost through use and disuse.

Middle-class rural radicalism: Antiaristocratic social and political movement of the late 1700s and early 1800s in England, which stressed governmental deregulation, separation of church and state, private property, and individual rights.

Militant society: A society organized for warfare where the *regulating system* dominates the *sustaining system* (compare with *Industrial society*).

Naturalism: The belief that events of the world can be accounted for in terms of this-worldly forces and without recourse to gods, spirits, or other supernatural agencies.

Regulating system: One of the three major parts of society. It is concerned with governmental regulation and military organization. Dominant part of society in a *militant society* (compare with *Sustaining system*).

Rhythmical change: Belief that social change proceeds in a general direction, but with occasional reversals.

Sentiments: In Spencer's usage, emotional noncognitive determinants of behavior.

Simple society: Simplest society in terms of organizational complexity. Usually nomadic and lacking stable leadership. Has low degrees of differentiation, specialization, and integration.

Superorganic: Of or relating to the parts of a society or the society as a whole.

Survivals: Elements of a society that have persisted from a prior evolutionary stage that serve no positive functions and are destined to die out.

Sustaining system: One of the three major parts of society. Concerned with the production of goods. Dominant part of society in an *industrial society* (compare with *Regulating system*).

Tautology: Circular reasoning; reasoning in which the conclusions are logically implied in the assumptions.

Trebly compound societies: Highly complex, differentiated, integrated, densely populated civilizations.

Uniformitarianism: Metaphysical belief that phenomena are shaped and developed through the persistent actions of natural forces, as opposed to sudden or cataclysmic causes.

Unilinearity: Belief that all societies develop through a single set of evolutionary stages.

Utilitarianism: Philosophical position in which claims to morality and truth are based on calculations of what course of action would produce the greatest good for the greatest number.

ANNOTATED BIBLIOGRAPHY

Primary Sources

An autobiography (2 vols.). New York: D. Appleton, 1904.

Although these volumes are written in the driest of prose, the perseverant reader can gain a substantial understanding of how Spencer formulated his ideas from reading them. Considerable mention is made of Spencer's monetary troubles.

Education: Intellectual, moral, and physical. Boston: Educational Publishing Company, 1889 [1861].

Spencer's attack on traditional educational techniques and content in favor of a practical hands-on science-based curriculum is expounded. Spencer's disdain for rote learning and the learning of historical "trivia" is forcefully presented.

The evolution of society: Selections from Herbert Spencer's principles of sociology (Robert C. Carneiro, Ed.). Chicago: University of Chicago Press, 1967.

Carneiro has done an excellent job of presenting the core of Spencer's sociological ideas while editing out many of the examples and repetitions that are typical of Spencer's writings.

First principles. New York: P. F. Collier and Son, 1902 [1862].

The first volume of Spencer's *Synthetic Philosophy*, it focuses on the limitations and possibilities of scientific understanding. More important, it presents an overview of Spencer's general principles of evolutionary development in the physical, biological, and social sciences.

Herbert Spencer on social evolution (J. D. Y. Peel, Ed.). Chicago: University of Chicago Press, 1972 (paper).

A good collection of essays and chapter excerpts. Of special import is the inclusion of

Spencer's essay "The Social Organism," in which he lays out the analytical similarities and differences between a society and an individual biological organism.

Literary style and music. Port Washington, NY: Kennikat Press, 1970 [1852–1857].

The four essays contained herein are not the most well-known nor the most significant of Spencer's essays. The first essay, on literary style, though, shows Spencer's preference for short Anglo-Saxon words and clear and concise prose over any semblance of flowery or poetic style.

The man versus the state, with six essays on government, society, and freedom. Indianapolis: Liberty Classics, 1981 [1843–1884].

This recent edition contains Spencer's main individualistic argument plus six essays, among them "The Social Organism."

The principles of ethics (2 vols.). Indianapolis: Liberty Classics, 1978 [1879–1893].

The final volumes of the *Synthetic Philosophy*. This work reiterates many of Spencer's sociological ideas with a greater emphasis on the role of altruism in social development.

The principles of psychology (rev. ed., 2 vols.). New York: D. Appleton, 1895 [1870–1872].

Although Volume 1 of this work focuses on nineteenth-century physiological psychology, which will be of little interest to the typical sociology student, Volume 2 contains many of Spencer's ideas about the social individual's makeup.

The principles of sociology (3rd ed., 3 vols.). New York: D. Appleton, 1898 [1876–1897].

Inundated with details and examples, these works involve the most comprehensive overall presentation of Spencer's sociological thought.

Reasons for dissenting from the philosophy of M. Comte and other essays. Berkeley, CA: Glendessary Press, 1968 [1871].

The student of classical sociology will be interested in the title essay of this collection, involving Spencer's moral, political, and scientific disagreements with Auguste Comte.

Social statics and *The man versus the state* (rev. eds.). New York: D. Appleton, 1897 [1850, 1884].

An interesting volume, containing Spencer's earliest and one of his later works. Reading them together, one sees how persistently middle-class radical ideas permeated Spencer's thought. Whereas the first work is highly optimistic in tone, however, the second reflects the beginning of the pessimism of his last years. In this later edition of *Social Statics*, Spencer's early profeminist views have been edited out.

The study of sociology (Talcott Parsons, Ed.; Introduction by Parsons). Ann Arbor: University of Michigan Press, 1961 [1873] (paper).

If one is going to read only one of Spencer's works, this probably should be it. This work contains a clear discussion of Spencer's basic ideas about society and how it should (and should not) be studied.

Secondary Sources

Abrams, Phillip. *The origins of British sociology, 1834–1914.* Chicago: University of Chicago Press, 1968 (paper).

This work combines a long essay by Abrams with essays by various early British sociologists (including Spencer). Abrams's essay presents a clear analysis of the basic elements of British sociology at the time of Spencer; the other essays present Spencer's contemporaries, offering ideas both in sympathy and in opposition to his.

Burrow, J. W. *Evolution and society, a study in Victorian social theory.* Cambridge: Cambridge University Press, 1966 (paper).

Written by an eminent British historian, this highly readable book looks at the historical context in which Spencer's ideas emerged.

Fletcher, Ronald. *The making of sociology: A study in social theory* (Vol. 1). New York: Scribner's, 1971.

Fletcher's coherent 140-page treatment of Spencer focuses on the contours of Spencer's conception of social evolution. Includes interesting discussions of Spencer's views on marriage, family, religion, and Comte's sociology, as well as a number of criticisms of Spencer's sociology.

Gray, Tim S. *The political philosophy of Herbert Spencer*. Avebury, England: Avebury, 1996.

Gray reviews and attempts to reconcile seemingly contradictory individualistic and organicist positions held by Spencer. He argues that such a review may be helpful in clarifying the debate between contemporary communitarians, who wish to extend state authority, and those who see a more limited role for the state in human affairs.

Kennedy, James G. *Herbert Spencer*. Boston: Twayne, 1973.

Kennedy's book is openly hostile to Spencer's thought. He writes in its preface that today "attention to his [Spencer's] works must be like one's interest in an outmoded encyclopedia. . . . Studying Spencer means recognizing his errors." Coming from a background in literary criticism, Kennedy is most interesting when he comments on Spencer's use of, and views about, language, and Kennedy even includes a chapter on Spencer's prose style.

Paxton, Nancy L. *George Eliot and Herbert Spencer: Feminism, evolutionism, and the reconstruction of gender*. Princeton, NJ: Princeton University Press, 1992.

Chronological discussion of the personal and intellectual relationships between Herbert Spencer and Marian Evans.

Peel, J. D. Y. *Herbert Spencer, the evolution of a sociologist*. New York: Basic Books, 1971.

An excellent work. It clearly analyzes Spencer's intellectual roots, social environment, life, ideas, and intellectual heritage. The exposition of Spencer's relationship to middle-class radicalism is unsurpassed.

Stocking, George W., Jr. *Victorian anthropology*. New York: Free Press, 1987.

An excellent account of the intellectual environment in which Spencer developed his social evolutionary ideas.

Taylor, Michael (Ed.). *Herbert Spencer and the limits of the state, The late nineteenth-century debate between individualism and collectivism*. Bristol, England: Thoemmes Press, 1996.

An informative introductory essay by Taylor is followed by fourteen articles from the 1800s and 1890s that take respective pro or con positions on various aspects of Spencer's individualistic arguments.

Turner, Jonathan H. *Herbert Spencer: A renewed appreciation*. Beverly Hills, CA: Sage, 1985.

Not a historical treatment of the development of Spencer's thought, this book instead focuses mostly on those aspects of Spencer's sociology that Turner believes are still of value for modern sociologists. Turner praises both Spencer's methodological arguments (in *The Study of Sociology*) and Spencer's structural analytical view of society, which, he claims, can be separated from Spencer's ideological commitments.

Weinstein, D. *Equal freedom and utility, Herbert Spencer's liberal utilitarianism*. Cambridge, England: Cambridge University Press, 1998.

An intellectually demanding book by a philosopher that should be read by any serious student of Spencer. Among other concerns is a focus on the linkages between Spencer's sociological views and his positions on moral and political issues. Weinstein also explores the increasing conservatism of Spencer's later years.

Wiltshire, David. *The social and political thought of Herbert Spencer*. Oxford: Oxford University Press, 1978.

This is a well-written but highly critical analysis of Spencer's life and work. Given to occasional bold assertions, Wiltshire concentrates on Spencer as a political actor and thinker. The first half of the text is given over to the development of Spencer's thought; the second half focuses on Spencer's ideas and their sociopolitical implications.

To comprehend what is, this is the task of philosophy, because what is, is reason. The individual is always a child of his time; so philosophy, too, is its own time apprehended in thoughts. It is just as absurd to believe that a philosophy can transcend its contemporary world as it is to fancy that an individual could overleap his own age, could jump over Rhodes. If his theory really goes beyond actually experienced reality and constructs an idealized world, that world does exist, but only in his imagination, a ghostly realm where anything the individual pleases may be imaginatively constructed. . . . What lies between reason as self-consciousness and reason as an actual world before our eyes, what separates the former from the latter and prevents it from finding satisfaction in the latter, is the fetter of some abstraction or other which has not been liberated [and so transformed] into the concept. To recognize reason as the rose in the cross of the present and thereby to enjoy the present, this is the rational insight which reconciles us to that actually experienced, the reconciliation which philosophy affords to those in whom there has once arisen an inner voice bidding them to comprehend, not only to dwell in what is substantive while still retaining subjective freedom, but also to possess subjective freedom while standing not in anything particular and accidental but in what exists absolutely.

—G.W.F. Hegel,
Preface to *The Philosophy of Right*

6

Georg Wilhelm Friedrich Hegel

(1770–1831)

Life

Georg Wilhelm Friedrich Hegel was born in Stuttgart, a middle-sized town in the German state of Württemberg, on August 27, 1770. His father, Ludwig, was councilor to the Duke of Württemberg.

Georg was educated by private tutors and at the Stuttgart *Gymnasium* (high school). He began studying classical subjects at the age of five, and by the time of his graduation at the age of eighteen, he was fluent in both Latin and Greek. His favorite subject, however, was religion; in 1788, he left his parents' home to travel to the Theological Seminary at Tübingen, where he intended to prepare for the Protestant ministry.

At Tübingen, Hegel began to read the social philosophy of his day, in particular the work of Jean-Jacques Rousseau (1712–1778). Hegel was a diligent student, but not a model seminarian; he enjoyed drinking fine German wines, and he spent a great deal of time carousing with his fellow students.

The Theological Seminary at Tübingen was not a large or important school; by an odd coincidence, however, Hegel's cohort of students included two others who became world famous in later years. The first of these was Friedrich von Schelling (1775–1854), who became well known as a philosopher at a very early age. Hegel and Schelling remained friends most of their lives but quarreled in middle age over their diverging philosophical systems. The second contemporary of Hegel's was Friedrich Hölderlin (1770–1843), who became one of Germany's most respected poets.

After successfully defending his theological dissertation, Hegel left Tübingen in 1793. His final certificate is noncommittal about his grasp of theology. It declares Hegel to be "no great orator" but adds that the graduating student "devoted much labor to philosophy."

In his final years at Tübingen, Hegel lost interest in the idea of taking religious orders. From 1793 to 1796, he worked as a private tutor for a wealthy family in Bern, Switzerland, where he took full advantage of his employer's fine library. During his years in Switzerland, Hegel made a careful study of the work of several philosophers, including the British social and political philosophers Thomas Hobbes (1588–1679), David Hume (1711–1776), and John Locke (1632–1704), and the French *philosophes* Voltaire (1694–1778) and the Baron de Montesquieu (1689–1755). Above all, Hegel absorbed the philosophy of the great German idealists J. G. Fichte (1762–1814) and Immanuel Kant (1724–1804).

In 1796, thanks to a recommendation from Hölderlin, Hegel obtained a position as tutor to a family in Frankfurt, Germany. As in Bern, Hegel was able to spend most of his time studying and writing. By now he was almost thirty. He had published nothing, whereas his friend—and rival—Schelling was already famous. Hegel's position in Frankfurt, though pleasant, did not offer any hope of advancement. In 1799, however, a substantial legacy from his father guaranteed him a steady income for several years. Because beginning lecturers at German universities of the day could not expect to earn a regular salary until they had established themselves as reputable figures within their field of knowledge, it was this inheritance that made an academic career possible for Hegel.

In 1800, Hegel swallowed his pride and wrote to Schelling, asking for help in obtaining "a few addresses" where he might stay while trying to obtain a position at the University of Jena in the German state of Saxe-Weimar. Schelling had received a teaching position at Jena in 1798 at the behest of the minister of education, Johann Wolfgang von Goethe (1749–1832). Goethe, who was considered to be Germany's greatest man of letters, was an enormously influential figure. Hegel told his friend that he was looking for "cheap food, a stout beer for my physical well-being and a few acquaintances."[1] Upon receiving his friend's letter, Schelling invited Hegel to stay with him.

Within a year of his arrival, Hegel successfully defended the dissertation that gave him the right to teach at the university. For some time, Jena had been a bastion for the followers of Kant, as well as the academic home of Fichte, who was himself a disciple of Kant. Thus it was appropriate that Hegel's dissertation was entitled "On the Differences between Fichte's and Schelling's Systems of Philosophy." Although he preferred Schelling's system, Hegel was able to point out to his examiners some minor deficiencies in his friend's work.

Shortly after Hegel's arrival in Jena, Hegel and Schelling founded the *Journal of Critical Philosophy*. From 1801 to 1806, Hegel worked assiduously to develop his own system of philosophy and published several articles in the new journal. In 1806, Hegel was forced to leave his home when Napoleon's troops occupied the town after defeating a Prussian army. Although French soldiers ransacked his house, Hegel spoke admiringly of Napoleon and described him as a progressive and enlightened "world-historical figure." Hegel's first major work, *The Phenomenology of Mind*, was finished in haste a few days before he left Jena.

On February 5, 1807, Hegel's landlady in Jena gave birth to her third illegitimate child. Hegel, who was the father of the boy, agreed to provide for his son, who was named Ludwig Georg. Although he later permitted Ludwig to live as a member of his household, Hegel never fully accepted his illegitimate son, who died in obscurity in the Dutch East Indies at the age of twenty-four.

Once Hegel had left Jena, he was in no hurry to return to the university. For one thing, most of the important people at Jena, including Schelling and Fichte, had left for good. In any case, Hegel thought he was now ready for a better position. By this time, his work had come to the attention of Goethe, who tried to find employment for Hegel. For a few months, Hegel edited the *Bamberger Zeitung*, a newspaper in Bamberg, Bavaria. This position had been obtained for him by Friedrich Immanuel Niethammer, an old friend who was a member of the Bavarian civil service. In 1808, Niethammer found Hegel a position as the headmaster of a *Gymnasium* in Nuremberg. In nineteenth-century Germany, the position of headmaster was prestigious; it was considered a post that only a scholar could fill. Furthermore, the *Gymnasium* in Nuremberg was the oldest and most distinguished school of its kind in Germany.

From 1808 to 1816, Hegel performed the duties required of him as the rector of this school. These included a great deal of teaching. Hegel insisted that what was most important for the boys was that, besides receiving a good grounding in classical subjects, they should be taught to think abstractly. A year after he relinquished his post, Hegel published his *Encyclopedia of the Philosophical Sciences*, which was largely a compendium of the lecture notes that he had used in teaching at the *Gymnasium*.

In 1811, Hegel married Marie von Tucher, who was twenty-two years younger than he. The marriage produced two legitimate sons. By this time, Hegel had enough of a reputation as a scholar and as a philosopher to be offered positions at several German universities, and from 1816 to 1818, he taught as a professor at the University of Heidelberg. In December 1817, he received a letter from the Baron von Altenstein, the Prussian minister of religion and education. In the name of King Friedrich Wilhelm III of Prussia, Altenstein asked Hegel to accept the position of full professor on the Philosophical Faculty at the new University of Berlin. Hegel accepted the offer and remained at Berlin for the rest of his life.

In his inaugural lecture at Berlin, Hegel spoke approvingly of the emerging self-awareness of the Prussian state. He wholeheartedly endorsed what he described as the Prussian willingness to "foster and nourish" the "sacred light of philosophical science." At Berlin, Hegel's lectures were attended not only by students but also by army officers, civil servants, and even ministers of state.

In 1821, Hegel published his *Philosophy of Right* (apart from *The Phenomenology* undoubtedly his most important contribution to social theory). In the last decade of his life, he produced articles only. Much of his philosophy was published posthumously. For instance, Hegel's work on aesthetics, the philosophy of history, and the philosophy of religion was published by editors, mainly from a reconstruction of students' notes written in the 1820s.

In the years before his death, Hegel became famous throughout Europe. He came to be admired by men of the stature of Goethe and by the leaders of Prussia, which by this time had become the most powerful state in Germany. At the pinnacle of his career, Hegel suddenly succumbed to cholera on November 14, 1831. Within a decade of his death, the intellectual and political climate in Prussia changed dramatically. A new Prussian king, Friedrich Wilhelm IV, summoned Schelling to Berlin to help the king's counselors stamp out "the dragon seed of Hegelianism." Since his death, Hegel's reputation as a philosopher and social theorist has fluctuated wildly. Nevertheless, the influence of his ideas over the last century and a half has been enormous.

Social Environment

At the end of the eighteenth century, the German Reich was divided into more than three hundred independent and semiautonomous political entities. The German states were supposed to exist as a federation—the Holy Roman Empire of the German nation. In name this empire had lasted for over a thousand years. By the year of Hegel's birth, however, the few remaining imperial institutions, like the Imperial Assembly (*Reichstag*) and the Supreme Court (*Reichskammergericht*), had become ineffective and had little if any authority.

In 1800, the archaic structure of the Holy Roman Empire contained the powerful monarchies of Austria and Prussia; many smaller states like Württenberg, Saxe-Weimar, and Bavaria; and an even greater number of tiny secular and ecclesiastical holdings. Without exception, these states and principalities were economically and politically backward. At the end of the eighteenth century, at a time when England was well on the way to becoming an industrial power with a modern parliamentary form of government, most German states were still feudal.

One of Hegel's earliest surviving manuscripts is entitled "The German Constitution" (1801). In this pamphlet, Hegel laments the willingness of Germany to sink "irresistibly into the abyss of her dissolution." He points out that Germany is no longer a holistic cultural or political entity. In order for Germany to be great, according to Hegel, "a universal sovereign power" had to emerge that could subjugate the self-destructive and particularistic activities of the German nations in the interest of reason. Reason is universalistic because the human interest that it expresses can be generalized—that is, shown to be grounded in the interests of all parties and factions.

In many ways, "The German Constitution" shows a high degree of critical and sociological insight. For instance, Hegel points out that the social order of the old German Reich was grounded in the unconscious acceptance of traditional ways of life. The revolutionary changes in intellectual orientation and political organization at the end of the eighteenth century, however, had undercut the traditional institutions of the Reich. As a result, by the beginning of the nineteenth century, Germany was no longer a living whole; traditional institutions were becoming progressively less relevant for people's lives.

The single most important event in Europe during Hegel's lifetime was the French (Jacobin) Revolution and its aftermath. Events in France led enlightened Germans to hope that what had happened in 1789 would help to trigger social and political change that would transform central Europe. Kant and Fichte, for example, enthusiastically acclaimed the Jacobin ideals of equality and brotherhood, and on July 14, 1790, there were public celebrations throughout Germany to commemorate the first anniversary of the fall of the Bastille.

As a young man in Tübingen, Hegel fully supported the goals of the revolutionaries in France. In the spring of 1791, he and Schelling planted a "freedom tree" in a meadow outside Tübingen to celebrate the momentous events of the previous two years. Although he later came to criticize revolutionary violence, Hegel always commemorated Bastille Day by drinking a toast to the ideals of the great revolution.

The French Revolution was followed by the Directory and by the rise of the republican Napoleon Bonaparte. After crowning himself Emperor of France in 1804, Napoleon began to meddle in the byzantine politics of the Holy Roman Empire. The French initiated a military campaign against Austria, the most powerful state in central Europe, and in 1805 they destroyed the Austrian army at Austerlitz. In the years that followed, Bonaparte's forces defeated Prussian forces at Jena and at Auerstadt. Following these battles, French troops occupied much of Prussia, including Berlin. At the Peace of Tilsit in 1807, Napoleon was able to impose his will on most of central Europe. Prussia was forced to give up its Rhineland territories and pay war indemnities to the French. However, the machinery of Prussian government was left intact by Napoleon, who admitted later that his greatest blunder had been not to destroy Prussia while he had had the chance.

Hegel had no difficulty in siding with Bonaparte against Austria and Prussia. As far as Hegel was concerned, Prussia in 1807 was just one more authoritarian, rigid, backward-looking German nation, whereas Napoleon represented the forces of enlightenment. In "The German Constitution," Hegel had dismissed the possibility that Prussia might have a role to play in the unification of a new Germany. In 1801, Hegel's fear had been that if Prussia were permitted to dominate Germany, it would merely "Prussianize Germany" in its own interests.

After the Peace of Tilsit, the shock of defeat and the desire for recovery compelled the Prussian ruling class to implement reforms that would modernize their state and make it stronger. By 1807, Napoleon's armies had transformed European social and political arrangements. The last emperor of the Holy Roman Empire was required to surrender his imperial crown; and Napoleon forced many western German states to enter into an alliance with republican France, to adopt the *Code Napoléon*, and to carry out drastic internal reforms.

From 1797 to 1840, Prussia was ruled by Friedrich Wilhelm III, a relatively enlightened and liberal monarch. After the war with France from 1805 to 1807, Friedrich appointed extraordinarily talented ministers, who helped him put the Prussian state back on its feet. The most prominent of these counselors was the Baron Heinrich Friedrich Karl von und zum Stein (1757–1831), who encouraged liberal reform as long as it was imposed and controlled from above. The baron, an enlightened authoritarian, had been greatly affected by the ideals of the French Revolution but had learned to fear the "excesses" of republican zeal. Stein had studied the Scottish economists Adam Smith (1723–1790) and Adam Ferguson (1723–1816) and had concluded that Prussia should look to England as the model of a modern, progressive state. He hoped that Prussia might be instrumental in Germany's unification.

Stein was ultimately dismissed for insubordination, but before he left office, he drafted an edict decreeing the emancipation of serfs throughout Prussia. This reform gave the serfs freedom in name only: Stein's edict gave landowners the right to expel peasants from their property, and it enabled an emerging capitalist class to draw on a supply of ready labor when appropriate. Nevertheless, the emancipation of the serfs brought Prussia more into line with the rest of Europe.

The Baron Stein was succeeded by Count Hardenberg, who continued his reforms. Hardenberg lifted more of the restrictions on free trade; granted political and economic rights to Jews; restricted the property rights of the Roman Catholic Church; and set up an assembly wherein the nobility, the peasantry, and the emerging middle class could be represented.

During the reign of Friedrich Wilhelm III, Prussian military might was transformed. The key figure in the reorganization and modernization of the Prussian army was General Karl von Clausewitz, who headed the Prussian War Academy from 1818 to 1830. Clausewitz was far ahead of his time in grasping that warfare had become so complex that rational forms of organization and an ethic of professionalism were vitally important for military success. Consequently, he emphasized the necessity of theory and planning in the conduct of war, which he viewed as "the continuation of politics by other means."

Shortly before Hegel arrived in Berlin, the minister of education, Wilhelm von Humboldt, reformed the curriculum of the Prussian *Gymnasien* and helped to charter the University of Berlin in 1810. Humboldt, Clausewitz, and Hardenberg were all outstanding figures in what had become Prussia's greatest strength: its civil service. Under Friedrich Wilhelm III, Prussian civil servants were given the opportunity to take their country out of the sixteenth and into the nineteenth century within the span of a few decades. Although many German academics and intellectuals—like Hegel and Fichte—who came to Berlin at the invitation of Humboldt believed sincerely that the Prussian state would serve as a catalyst for necessary and progressive change for the whole of the German Reich, in the 1820s and 1830s a virulently nationalistic and conservative faction of disgruntled aristocrats came to the fore. These men objected to what they felt was Hardenberg's willingness to turn their kingdom into a modern "Jew-state." They formed secret societies to protect their interests and sought to synthesize their conservatism with militant authoritarianism, nationalism, and anti-Semitism.

In 1807, the Prussian aristocracy saved their state—and themselves—by implementing reform and by building a new sense of nationhood. By the time of Hegel's death, however, there was no longer any need for liberalization. In 1813, a combined force of Austrians, Prussians, and Russians had defeated Napoleon's army at Leipzig.

In 1815, the British and the Prussians applied the *coup de grâce* to Bonaparte at the battle of Waterloo. After this victory, the Prussians regained the territory they had lost in 1807. When Hegel was invited to Berlin in 1817, Prussia was consolidating and reflecting on its gains. The urgent need for radical reform was over.

Hegel is known as a great philosopher in the tradition of German idealism, but he was also a man deeply interested in contemporary political and economic affairs. He spent many hours every week reading newspapers and periodicals from all parts of Europe, and he was extremely knowledgeable about current events. Above all, Hegel was interested in uniting humankind's interest in reason for its own sake with the will to create a political entity based on reflective self-insight. Because of the relatively progressive and enlightened policies of Prussia during his tenure in Berlin, Hegel felt quite at home in his adopted state.

Intellectual Roots

By the end of the eighteenth century, most German intellectuals had become painfully aware that the archaic framework of a "Holy German Reich" was falling apart. At the turn of the century, German intellectuals had become quite familiar with the new ideas of the French *philosophes*. However, burgeoning radicalism in France during the 1790s and a growing awareness of the disruption and misery that bourgeois modernization was causing in England forced many of these intellectuals to take a more critical stance toward the economic and political transformations that were the corollary of Enlightenment thought.

Striving to develop a new sense of nationhood, men like the hermeneutist Johann Gottfried von Herder (1744–1803) tried to describe how the German people were the bearers of a unique culture and form of consciousness. Herder argued that the ideals of the *philosophes* were not representative of the German *Volk*. Similarly, in his widely read book *The Aesthetic Education of Man*, the philosopher Friedrich von Schiller (1759–1805) declared that the division of labor within society, and too sharp a division between the rights of the "private" individual and the ethical foundations of the state, would lead to unhappiness and conflict. Schiller pointed out that such disruption would lead to dislocation not only within society as a whole but also within the individual. Neither Herder nor Schiller was anti-Enlightenment, but both recognized that the spread of Enlightenment philosophy in central Europe during the Napoleonic Wars had served to accelerate the decline of German tradition.

By 1795, when Hegel read Schiller's book, he was already familiar with the work of Herder. At Tübingen and in Bern, he studied the *philosophes* and read Smith's and Ferguson's works. Although strongly influenced by Enlightenment ideals, Hegel accepted that bourgeois political economy was undermining traditional folk relationships and replacing them with impersonal networks of exchange and contract among increasingly atomized individuals. Hegel referred to that type of sociation enhanced by the rise of the money economy as *civil society*. Civil society is a domain of *universal egoism* in that within this sphere individuals think of themselves as autonomous and as self-centered, treat others as means to their ends, and assume that others too are adopting and universalizing this principle.

There was no doubt in Hegel's mind that many of the changes wrought by En-lightenment political philosophy were here to stay. For instance, he accepted that the modern capitalist economy, the secularization of reason, and the technical rational-ization of the means of administration were all the products of irreversible change. Furthermore, he believed that the political effects of the Enlightenment were positive in many respects. Nevertheless, pointing out they had failed to consider how the dif-ferent aspects of what had become individuals' pluralistic and fragmented being could be reconciled in the modern state, Hegel classified the activity of many eighteenth-century intellectuals as a form of "spiritual disintegration."

Rousseau was particularly important to Hegel because he had tried to show that the gap between the private individual and the *just* polity to which the individual was morally obligated might be closed if the state were to permit free individuals to de-velop a "general will." This general will would result from communicative interaction and from reflective self-insight; it could not be developed by a conglomerate of pri-vate individuals acting alone and in terms of self-interest. In short, Rousseau argued that the will to freedom could be understood only as the expression of a community, not as the expression of detached, self-interested individuals. In opposition to this, Kant had argued that the will of individuals to be free was what bound them to the moral law. If subjects respected their responsibilities as well as their rights, a moral society was possible.

Hegel completely rejected Kant's view of the relationship between the individual and political society, pointing out that Kantianism forces political subjects to treat the free will of the individual and the collective need for political programs of expedience as incongruous. Kant had acknowledged that the well-governed society had to imple-ment policies that were instrumentally effective for the collectivity as well as those that were good in themselves, and had argued that the ideal of just government should be understood *negatively.* Thus he believed governments should not restrict the free will of citizens more than is strictly necessary. (What is "necessary," of course, is open to debate.) In effect, Kant's practical philosophy helped to legitimate utilitarianism, in-strumentalism, and individualism.

As far as Hegel was concerned, Kant had simply failed to resolve the original prob-lem of how to integrate the moral and pragmatic aspects of modern forms of selfhood. For Hegel, it was a sign of failure that Kant's moral philosophy posited moral individ-uals, rather than a moral community. Hegel believed that the problems of practical philosophy could not be solved without turning to what we would recognize as socio-logical issues and problems.

Whatever the value of Kant's moral philosophy, Hegel acknowledged that Kantian epistemology was very successful in explaining how positivistic knowledge was possi-ble. Kant had argued that the objects of reference in a scientific explanation were not simply discovered in the world but were constituted and synthesized, *a priori,* as a nec-essary condition for experience. In other words, the world that we experience as a re-sult of sense impressions is not a simple copy of external reality; it can be experienced by us only in terms of the *a priori* forms and categories of the understanding. The way in which the human mind functions determines the *form* of empirical reality, but not its content. For instance, Kant pointed out that relations of "causality" do not simply describe the relations among "things-in-themselves" (things as they are, without form being imposed on them by human experience). The idea that one thing is causally linked to another is supplied by the mind as a necessary ground of human experience. Our belief in causality cannot be subjected to empirical test, for this would require us to recognize the existence of a different kind of world. Kant thus concluded that the idea of causality is nothing other than a necessary precondition of our conception of a stable and familiar universe.

Although Hegel greatly admired Kant's contributions to epistemology, he criticized Kant's belief that things-in-themselves are, by their very nature, unknowable. He also disagreed with Kant's assertion that the categories of human understanding are fundamentally innate and ahistorical. For Hegel, the workings of the human mind had always to be put into a context of human history and struggle in order to become transparently understandable. Hegel conceived of human reason as the product of a collectivity—and the means by which this grouping achieves an understanding of itself. For Hegel, reason evolves as social individuals come to understand the effects of history and society on human consciousness. Thus reason is cumulative and progressive. As we shall see, Hegel believed that, ultimately, humans could understand the nature of consciousness itself, and that such an understanding would provide the basis for a moral community. According to Hegel, pure reason is wholly self-reflective; it is consciousness that fully comprehends how it has been shaped and fashioned by historical and social contingencies.

Hegel conceded that, to date, historical forms of human reason have always been incomplete and imperfect. In other words, no human collectivity has ever achieved a full and complete understanding of itself. According to Hegel, reason becomes more complete when it understands what we would recognize as the sociological conditions of its own production. For Hegel, the indicator of the "progressiveness" of a human totality is the willingness of social individuals to be open and reflective about how their consciousness of the world and of themselves as social beings has been shaped.

Against Kant, Hegel argued that the categories used to understand the world change as social and political formations are transformed. Hegel believed, moreover, that people could strive self-consciously to change categories of understanding. Above all, he believed that individuals can actively create a just society, for the bounds of human imagination are not fixed but malleable. Thus, before Marx was born, Hegel had concluded that the whole point of philosophy—or of any kind of social theorizing—was to change the world. As far as he was concerned, however, merely to understand the world in new ways and in a new form is *already* to have changed it.

In many ways, Kant was the radical, whereas Hegel took the orthodox philosophical view. Since Parmenides (fifth century B.C.), philosophers had largely accepted that it was sterile and self-defeating to attempt what Kant had authorized: the severance of life as it is lived from the exercise of the human intellect. Hegel's emphasis on reason as the means to self-understanding and the moral integration of a self-consciously, self-determining community was not incompatible with Enlightenment ideology. Hegel, however, attempted to go beyond Enlightenment ideals in synthesizing rational discourse and analysis with the post-Enlightenment concern with the sensual, affective, and passionate side of human nature. Declaring that "nothing worthwhile is achieved without passion," Hegel concluded: "The distinction between thought and will is only that between the theoretical attitude and the practical. These, however, are surely not two faculties; the will is rather a special way of thinking, thinking translating itself into existence, thinking as the urge to give itself existence."[2]

For Hegel, human subjects would actually experience freedom when human consciousness became all it could be, and this end could be achieved only when reason was complete. He referred to the possible reality of this total understanding as the "Idea" or as the condition of "Absolute Spirit." Hegel believed that the Idea was immanent in the universe; it was also a constituent part of every human subject in that the self would always suffer from a lack of freedom and from an incomplete sense of itself if the collective understanding of human reason was less than it could possibly be.

Hegel believed that human consciousness must—and will—strive to be reasonable as it struggles to be free by overcoming its own barriers to self-understanding. He decided that to comprehend this struggle we must turn to an analysis of history that is both critical and—in modern terms—*sociological* in orientation.

IDEAS

Society

Hegel viewed society as the medium by which human subjects experience themselves as social beings. They do this through the categories of mediation that social life provides. Categories of mediation (class identification, educational qualifications, occupational classifications, ethnic identity, and so on) permit the self to reflect on the meaning of its standing within society. For Hegel, society is nothing other than the means by which this standing is determined. He believed that to be human is to use a language to participate in a common culture of discourse and expression: It is to have a sense of oneself as being located in time and space.

Categories of mediation—the means by which we gain selfhood—are constructed by humans collectively—that is, through communicative interaction. Social institutions, therefore, have both a subjective and objective dimension. Hegel referred to the way in which human subjects make themselves meaningful objects both to themselves and for others as the process of "objectification."

Modern subjects experience themselves as individualized and as atomized—that is, as relatively self-contained and autonomous beings. Such individuals, however, are not truly self-determining; their conception of themselves is the product of a form of social mediation that is highly differentiated. When mediative categories are differentiated, the experiences of different people—and of the same people at different points in time—become highly diverse and specialized. Nevertheless, individuals who experience themselves as individualized (for example, the contemporary college student who fashions a life course by choosing among many options) are no less of a social product than those who know themselves to be only the expression of a totality within which they feel at home (such as the peasant who believes he is a small part of a living tradition).

Hegel believed that human society becomes most reasonable and most just when social institutions do not divide and fragment subjects who subsequently must experience themselves as incomplete. As noted earlier, Hegel understood that civil society was destroying the traditional sense of community. He also grasped how the bourgeois transformation of the relations of production was revolutionizing workers' conception of themselves. The factory worker, for example, is compelled to interact with the environment in a mechanical and repetitive fashion. The worker performs a task that is meaningful within the total organization of factory production but is unable to grasp what this totality involves. Factory workers might have total control over some small part of the environment through the use of technology. By objectifying themselves as cogs in an impersonal system of production, however, they lose sight of the ends of human striving. The modern organization of work is often too complex and the involvement of the individual worker too specific for workers to be able to see themselves as expressing the totality of anything *humanly* produced. Thus modern workers are likely to experience themselves as the expression of something that is alien to them.

Hegel believed that before the introduction of modern technology and the modern division of labor, human societies were the embodiment of "natural ethical life." In simple, primitive societies, consumption was a response to natural human need: In hunting-and-gathering societies, people do not labor to produce a surplus, nor do they endeavor to provide for a market. Hegel agreed with Smith that the division of labor in society replaced a simple, natural environment with a social environment that embodied complex and differentiated categories of mediation. In primitive societies, labor is a simple form of interaction between subjects and their natural environment, based on sensual need. In modern industrial societies, however, the organization of labor occurs as a result of highly specific categories of mediation. These differentiate sharply among particular workers and create work environments that are artificial and highly technical.

Unlike the modern, private individual, the primitive human being does not suffer from the sense of being excluded from the totality of possible experience. Hegel believed that primitive societies exhibited an "unreflective universality." This meant that human subjects felt, rather than knew, the totality that had produced them. Because they participated directly in all aspects of communal life, primitive people experienced their place in the community in a direct and often emotional manner. Primitive societies embody natural ethical life, but they are not grounded in political arrangements that are self-consciously self-determining. Thus in a primitive society the subject's experience of being an integral part of a cohesive universality (the sum total of consciousness within a community) is not the product of reason, which can be secured only by its ability to permit subjects to grasp the conditions affecting human experience *per se*. The language of primitive or "natural" man does not place a complex mediative barrier between the subject and his self-conception: Thus he does not experience a fragmented conception of himself. For "natural" man, however, reflection is not at all possible, for he experiences a universality and a totality of experience that is merely taken for granted. Hegel did not romanticize life in its uncivilized form; he declared that the "savage's" lack of rational self-insight, his "brooding stupidity," and his "laziness" distinguish him from the educated and civilized human subject.[3]

During his Jena period, Hegel came to view humankind's recent past as a movement out of unreflective universality toward particularity. In other words, he believed that the increasing complexity of the division of labor in Germany during his lifetime was propelling individuals toward an "ethic" of self-interest that would lead them to understand less, not more, about themselves. Bourgeois civil society represents particularistic society in its classical and most advanced form because it maximizes the division of labor in the name of efficiency.

In his middle years, Hegel gradually came to the conclusion that the embodiment of reason or reflective self-consciousness in the modern world must be the political state. If civil society is the domain of universal egoism, he concluded, then the state was the domain of universal altruism.

Hegel believed that the closest approximation to the ideal state that had ever existed was the ancient Greek city-state or *polis*. These were economically self-sufficient states of about ten thousand citizens. Hegel argued that the origin of the *polis* was the desire for freedom. Within the *polis*, there was little differentiation between the means by which human subjects became conscious of themselves and the means by which they became aware of their moral obligations to the community as a whole. For the individual in such communities, ethical life was self-sustaining and complete in itself; it was not seen as a means toward an end determined by individualized forms of self-interest.

It was clear to Hegel that the modern state could not hope to emulate the direct participatory style of the *polis*. Consequently, he dismissed as fanciful Rousseau's idea that in modern societies the citizen-voter could identify in an immediate and unmediated fashion with the universality of the state. Unlike the *polis*, modern society tends to drive the sense of selfhood and the sense of moral obligation in opposite directions. Within the domain of universal egoism (civil society), individualized subjects experience themselves as autonomous and as self-contained. Within the domain of universal altruism (the state), citizens come to comprehend their duties and responsibilities in universalistic terms—that is, not in terms of self-interest but in terms of what is good for the community. Hegel believed that the central problem for political sociology was to show how to reconcile the needs of the just state—which grounds itself in pure, reflective reason—with the need of human subjects to become free by knowing themselves for what they are and for what they could be. Although this problem preoccupied Hegel as the "official state philosopher" during his tenure in Berlin, he first began to write about this issue in his *System of Ethical Life*, completed in 1803.

Hegel's defense of a strong state was founded on the presupposition that it would be necessary in order to counter the antagonistic and atomized interests of the modern individual. He was wholly opposed to social contract theorists like Thomas Hobbes, John Locke, and Thomas Jefferson (1743–1826), who believed that contemporary political society should be grounded in the desire of individual citizens to cement contractual agreements based on self-interest. Hegel believed that social contract theory approaches the problems of political sociology from the wrong direction altogether, for it is only by participation in political society that individuals come to comprehend what is involved in becoming fully human.

Trying to maximize the participatory role of the citizen in German society, Hegel emphasized the positive functions of traditional class distinctions. He pointed out that the old German estates, like the peasantry and the *Burgher* (merchant) class, had served to integrate the individual subject into a larger political system by giving members of the various estates some right to be represented in the legislature. For Hegel, the main classes in German society were the peasantry or agricultural class, the commercial or business class, and the class of civil servants. Hegel argued that the latter was most closely identified with the state and with the exercise of reason in itself because it did not have its own particular interest as the purpose of its activity. He believed that the civil service would seek knowledge and implement policy in the interests of all. Whereas the agricultural class is conservative and the business class individualistic, state bureaucrats try to act within the domain of universal altruism.

Hegel concluded that the increasingly crucial role that the civil service had to play in modern society was an inevitable corollary of the displacement of old Germany by bourgeois civil society. The more atomized and fragmented society becomes, the more necessary it is to ground political society in an increasingly abstract mode of universal altruism. As we have seen, Hegel believed that the state and its civil servants are the only entities capable of such abstract and universal altruism.

In *The Philosophy of Right,* Hegel suggested that the *self*-interests of those classes and groups that were outside the civil service could best be reconciled with the moral obligations of the citizen in the state by the development of representational "corporations." These corporations (for example, occupational and professional associations) would create spheres of *particular altruism* that would help to reconcile civil society and the state: "Hence, a selfish purpose, directed toward its particular self-interest, apprehends and evinces itself at the same time as universal; and a member of civil society is in virtue of his own particular skill a member of a Corporation, whose universal function is thus wholly concrete."[4]

Thus, besides fulfilling the universalistic function of organizing human labor in the interests of all, corporations particularistically (1) look after the interests of their members; (2) provide education and norms of conduct for workers; and (3) give their members a sense of belonging to an association that replicates the classic example of particular altruism—the family group.

Hegel's discussion of how the social division of labor might actually contribute to a new solution of the problem of moral integration for contemporary societies is remarkably similar to that put forward seventy years later by Durkheim in *Division of Labor.* In *The Philosophy of Right,* Hegel argued that the kinds of corporations that might develop in the modern world (for example, professional associations, trade unions, and workers' educational societies) were an expression of the need to overcome the tension between the orientation of the individual in civil society and the responsibilities of the citizen toward the state. According to Hegel, the "primary purpose" of government in policing society is to "actualize and maintain the universal contained within the particularity of civil society."[5]

Hegel concluded that the modern, liberal state could either attempt to actualize universalistic principles in good faith or use "atomistic" principles of representation, such as the ballot box, to conceal the self-interested policy formation of particularistic ruling groups who would thus gain control of the machinery of government. As far as Hegel was concerned, the rise of the modern state represented a crisis of opportunity and danger. Such states could be progressive and universalistic; but the danger existed—especially in Germany—that the "freemen" who used to be able to participate in political decision making at the local level would now become totally disenfranchised and detached from political society. This would happen if such citizens did not—or could not—have recourse to those institutions that would link them to the collectivity that had constituted them as subjects. Hegel was one of the first modern Germans to understand the horrors that were likely to be visited on the society that produced detached, atomized individuals, while at the same time continuing to build up the machinery of an impersonal and irrational state that would be oblivious to the human needs of such individuals.

The Individual in Society

As we have seen, Hegel believed that the eighteenth-century or modern conception of the self as autonomous and self-contained was highly artificial. According to Hegel, this model of selfhood was the inevitable by-product of the growth in importance and autonomy of civil society. The false sense of oneself as autonomous and as self-contained guarantees servitude and unhappiness because it ensures the existence of an incomplete, and hence not fully reasonable, conception of self. Hegel suggested that this sense of incompleteness is responsible for the "unhappy consciousness" of modern individuals, who cannot bear to acknowledge their estrangement from a society that is humanly produced but not recognized as such. He pointed out that all individuals seek a part in constituting and maintaining the collectivity, for it is social life that makes us recognizably human. Contemporary individuals, however, are compelled to posit a false self that falsely believes itself to be self-determining.

Hegel pointed out that the essence, or nature, of a person's thought lies beyond that particular person; hence the reflective experience of oneself as a particular kind of social object is a product of the social whole, not a product of the individual. Although we all talk of our selves as unique and autonomous entities, there is nothing in my experience of myself that has to be the experience of *my* self, as opposed to the experience of *your* self. Although I might be seen as inferior to you in some respects because I am different to some degree and because these particular differences are interpreted as meaningful within some collectivity, the categories that we use to make our "personal" experiences meaningful in the first place clearly are not developed by ourselves. Such categories derive meaning from their *use* within a system of communicative interaction.

To be recognized—both by others and by oneself—as a complete human being requires subjects to enter into a process of communicative interaction in which the identity of all is *freely* acknowledged. In *The Phenomenology*, Hegel analyzes the master-slave relationship, arguing that the institution of slavery denies the master's liberty as much as it does the slave's. At first sight, it appears that the master can use his power to demonstrate *his* freedom and *his* ability to determine events. Hegel points out, however, that the denial of another's freedom and the application of "unquestionable" authority guarantee that the "superior" person experiences himself as inauthentic. The master receives recognition from the slave, but, upon reflection, is forced to acknowledge that this recognition is not given freely. In his work *The Rebel*, Albert Camus acknowledges this principle and draws our attention to the unhappy fate of the tyrannical master:

The master, to his detriment, is recognized in his autonomy by a consciousness which he himself does not recognize as autonomous. Therefore, he cannot be satisfied and his autonomy is only negative. Mastery is a blind alley. Since, moreover, he cannot renounce mastery and become a slave again, the eternal destiny of masters is to live unsatisfied or to be killed.[6]

According to Hegel, selfhood in bourgeois civil society is very much determined by property ownership. From this, he concluded that it is very important that all citizens in modern society possess some property. Status and identity in capitalist society are reflected by the private property that individual subjects have at their disposal; we know what we are, and we know what others have become, by experiencing ourselves as entities that are reflected by property that appears to have been appropriated individualistically. Once again, however, the appropriation of "private property" is not a personal, private, or individualistic achievement. Shlomo Avineri has summed this point up lucidly:

> Property pertains to the person as recognized by others, it can never be an intrinsic quality of the individual prior to his recognition by others. While possession relates to the individual, property relates to society: since possession becomes property through the others' recognition of it as such, property is a social attribute. Thus not an individualistic but a social premise is at the root of Hegel's concept of property . . . property always remains premissed on social consensus, on consciousness, not on the mere fact of possession.[7]

There are very strong similarities between Hegel's view of the self in *The Phenomenology* and the model of the self put forward by latter-day symbolic interactionists. For Hegel, the self is not a static entity but must be understood as a *process*. As we have seen, Hegel believed that the self develops a sense of itself as mind emerges in the "medium of consciousness." We become conscious of a meaningful universe as we learn how to organize our experiences in terms of categories of mediation that are institutionalized intersubjectively or communicatively. We have no choice but to experience ourselves both as an intending subject and as an *object* of experience; for, as Hegel pointed out, socialization "consists in the process of [mind] becoming an other to itself, i.e., an object for its own self."[8] From this perspective, human understanding and thought—including but not limited to the conception of oneself as object—has "its own otherness within itself." Hegel gives a fine illustration of this process in his analysis of the unhappy fate of the contemporary individual in civil society:

(a) in the course of work I make myself into a thing, to a form which *exists*
(b) I thus externalize this my existence, make it into *something alien* and *maintain* myself in it.[9]

Contemporary symbolic interactionists would not disagree with any of the foregoing. Hegel, however, insisted that "mediating is nothing but self-identity working itself out through an active, self-directed process."[10] He believed that in our world the "medium of consciousness" unfolds according to the ego's need for "immediacy"—that is, according to the subject's yearning for the return to a natural, ethical form of life. The ego strives toward immediacy as it seeks to break down the false separation between the result of reflection (truth) and "the process of arriving at it" (freedom).

According to Hegel, the ultimate truth is that "Freedom is the sole purpose of Spirit" or mind. Contemporary symbolic interactionists do not go so far as to claim that consciousness is teleologically determined; that is, they do not agree that the dynamics of interaction between self and society lead inexorably to a brighter and more progressive future wherein such an ultimate truth is revealed to have been the purpose of human history. Nevertheless, Mead, at least, would have agreed with Hegel that, to arrive at truth, reason has to be reflective—that is, self-consciously self-determining. As Mead put it, "The apparatus of reason would not be complete unless it swept itself into its own analysis of the field of experience."[11]

Hegel believed that human experience in a civilized society always involves the constant, dialectical interplay between what is revealed as universal, or as complete in itself, and what is experienced as particular or as incomplete. As we have noted, in modern society individuals experience themselves as particular and as incomplete. The closer humankind comes to a condition of Absolute Spirit, the more we are able to recognize what is universal in apparently concrete and particular individual selves. In Hegel's perfect society, however, individual self-consciousness would not become defunct; individual subjects would not cease to be self-conscious entities. According to Hegel, "progress" in historical self-development is indicated by the extent to which collective forms of life do not inhibit the recognition that each particular individual embodies, and is part of, a self-conscious, self-determining whole.

Thus for Hegel the story of human history, taken as a whole, is the story of a continuous but arrhythmical unfolding—a mystical return to a condition where Absolute Spirit is the world and the world is Absolute Spirit. Princes, potentates, powers, and "self-contained" individuals all dissolve in this process—not because anything is lost in this unfolding but because the separation of what cannot be seen as particular and as self-determining is reabsorbed in what is acknowledged to be universal and complete in itself.

By "spirit," Hegel did not mean some insubstantial ectoplasm that permeates the universe. On the contrary, he believed that the domain of spirit is humanly produced. One problem with Hegel's system, however, is that by discussing the ideal relationship between individuals and the totality that produced them wholly in spiritual terms, Hegel is forced to talk about human consciousness producing reality. This is a wholly unacceptable foundation for empirical investigation. Another problem associated with Hegel is that the idea of what Absolute Spirit could be is quite incomprehensible. Of course, this is only to be expected, for the idea of the Idea is not the Idea itself. Contemporary and incomplete individuals cannot transcend the totality that produces their incomplete being in order to comprehend fully the nature of human freedom. One way out is to see the domain of Absolute Spirit in divine terms. Unfortunately, this approach puts the possible reality of the integration of the free individual and the just society in the domain of the supernatural and thus beyond mortal grasp.

Without believing in any divinity, it is, of course, possible to have faith in the idea that history has a purpose and to believe that humankind is moving closer to that state where the totality of human consciousness has become all it could be. What makes Hegel's treatment of the relationship between the individual and society so important, however, is his penetrating analysis of the way in which humankind has sentenced itself to struggle against the barriers to self-understanding that *it alone has erected against itself.* While ignoring the imperfect and puzzling picture of the ideal and harmonious totality represented by Absolute Spirit, it is still possible to admire Hegel for this part of his analysis. Any commitment that is made to the possible validity of the positive aspects of Hegel's social philosophy has to be grounded—at least at this point in human development—in reason plus faith, not just in reason alone.

Methodology

Hegel was the first modern theorist to develop an emancipatory interest in a systematic and *critical*, not positivistic, approach to human institutions. He reacted negatively toward positivism largely because of its reliance on empiricism. Empiricism—and hence positivism—forces the investigator to ground human understanding in the ability of the intellect to find sense impressions meaningful. Sense impressions, of course, arrive by means of the nervous system and are the product of sensory organs. Sensory organs, however, are not in and of themselves reflective. For Hegel, then, to accept empiricism is to concede that the conditions under which knowledge is produced cannot, themselves, be known. Empiricism compels us to believe *blindly* that sense impressions really do enable us to grasp the underlying nature of the world. For Hegel, the "fundamental delusion of scientific empiricism" is that it does not know that it accepts this ontology "in a style utterly thoughtless and uncritical."[12]

Hegel also discarded the other strand of positivism: determinism. According to him, determinism searches only for mechanistic relations among objects. Determinism is oblivious to the way in which objects exist merely as a means by which mind can know itself through mediative categories that *it* controls.

According to Hegel, the essence of being is not itself determined by any agency external to it, but is self-positing and self-reflective. Self-reflection occurs as mind reflects on manifestations of itself in *determinate being*: the form that reality takes as a result of the use of mediative categories institutionalized in everyday life. For instance, gender categorizations (e.g., males are tough, rational, and consistent; females are tender, emotional, and inconsistent) enable subjects to "recognize" what it means to be "male" and "female." If these categorizations are accepted uncritically, they remain forms of mediation that determine being in the world. Thus a "tough" female might be regarded (falsely) as going against her own nature. Pure self-reflection requires that we grasp that the world of determinate being is nothing other than the product of arbitrary mediative categories we have implemented within a system of communicative interaction. The categories we use to define each other are *not* immune from self-reflective criticism. The complete freedom of all subjects from being defined by forces over which they have no control would make criticism complete in itself.

For Hegel, then, the only secure forms of understanding were those that were self-determining. As we have seen, Hegel was an idealist: He believed that objective forms of understanding were implemented by mind so that they could be used as mediative categories through which mind could know itself. For Hegel, all thought "must pass through negative mediation to reimmediation" in this manner. Thus he did not regard the universe as made up of physical objects and forces partially unknown by, and totally indifferent to, the efforts of mind to attain a comprehensive understanding of reality. He believed that such objects and such forces are known as a result of the interaction of mind with the forms that it creates and implements, so that within an experiential domain, mind can experience "its own otherness within itself." It is precisely this experience that makes reimmediation—and the exercise of reason—possible.

Reason, therefore, is not merely oriented toward the domain of what *is*; it is most centrally oriented toward what can and *should* be. In other words, reason is centrally concerned with the issue of what would be involved if mind were to attain self-conscious self-determination through negation (the dissolution of mediative categories) and through reimmediation. Mediative categories are "dissolved" when they are understood to be alienating, but humanly produced. Reimmediation is a movement toward pure reason—the production of mediative categories for which mind can take full responsibility. Hegel called the process of negation and reimmediation *the negation of the negation,* thus implying that this process is open-ended and constant.

For Hegel, critical theory is premised on a fundamental distinction between understanding (*Verstand*) and reason (*Vernunft*). "Understanding" involves our ability to make sense of the world through interpretive theorizing—that is, through learning how to use a language competently. "Reasoning," however, involves understanding *plus* the ability to reflect on how language is being used. Whereas human understanding relates to appearance, reason deals with essence—the inner world of being.

Hegel would have insisted that for sociological theory to be as reasonable as it could be, it must be critical and reflective as well as interpretive. He did not foresee or anticipate the enormous importance and prestige that pure positivistic theory would enjoy after his death, and he did not anticipate the impact that modern science would have on the way in which subjects would objectify themselves in modern societies.

Because he never took positivism seriously, Hegel's philosophy of natural science is weak and uninteresting. When he wrote about experimental science, Hegel invariably misunderstood its intentions. As an epistemologist, Hegel's major contribution is that of one who thought deeply and carefully about the nature of *critical* theory.

The Hegelian methodology of reason is often described as the "dialectical method." This compels mind to reflect on how it imperfectly understands itself in forms of determinate being that embody only an alienated sense of selfhood; it tries to break down mind's understanding of its own otherness within itself. This necessitates the deliberate opposition of what is taken for granted (and thus appears to be real) with what is real in terms of potentialities that are not yet actualized. The dialectic forces us to become "aware that everything finite, instead of being stable and ultimate, is, rather, changeable and transient."[13]

According to Hegel, the "soul of the dialectic" is the principle of negation. Negation requires mind to go beyond old forms of consciousness by showing how the image of selfhood that is reflected by archaic forms is less satisfactory than that reflected in new forms. We can transform what we are, but we cannot escape what we have become. Hegel believed that humankind's constantly changing self-image was the expression of a hidden purpose or cunning—"the cunning of reason." What he meant by this was that subjects have often unintentionally exercised reason in history as they willed a reduction in the alien sense of otherness within a world that is humanly created.

Hegel believed that emancipatory reason could become a real possibility only when practice transforms the world of determinate being in the interests of reason. Practice without theory can never deploy itself fully because such practice would be mindless and empty. Thus, for Hegel, (emancipatory) theory and practice always work in tandem: It would be absurd to claim that they could be separated. Many of Hegel's critics have assumed that because Hegel was an idealist, he believed that theoretical progress without social and political change was possible. This is not the case. According to Hegel, the dialectic is likely to *demand* social and political change if humankind's reason is to actualize itself in a more complete form.

In short, the dialectic begins with a particular mode of consciousness or categorization of reality taken to its limits. This requires subjects to reflect on how their mediative categories have created an alien world of determinate being. The "discipline of the unhappy consciousness" requires subjects to have the courage to explore their own sense of alienation and the will to change the means by which this sense of otherness comes about. As Hegel put it: "Love disporting with itself . . . sinks into insipidity if it lacks the seriousness, the suffering, the patience and the labor of the negative."[14]

Hegel believed that the impetus toward rational self-insight was triggered by human suffering. Enormous momentum might be required to overcome the inertia represented by humanity's characteristic capacity for self-deception. In the final analysis, however, the historical actor that knows itself to be incomplete must be humankind as such, not merely the isolated human individual. After all, one person can make only a very partial contribution to the transformation of intersubjectively grounded forms of consciousness. Thus the will to change the world is ultimately *collective*, not individualized. The methodology of reason and insight always entails a political program of collective action and is always the response of humanity to a mode of social formation that is unbearably alienating. For Hegel, the root cause of such alienation was always the same: the institutionalization of modes of thought that make it impossible for subjects to recognize themselves as free and as self-consciously self-determining agents.

SIGNIFICANCE

Vision of the Future

According to Hegel, the dialectic is a method of exposition, not a machine for making discoveries or for cranking out predictions about the future. Hegel believed that if—and only if—humankind chooses to be rational, it will subject itself to the immanent logic of self-discovery described by the dialectic. In human history, there are sudden and momentous events of "world-historical" significance, like the birth of the French Republic, when a sudden breakthrough in humankind's ability to engage in rational self-insight occurs. Most generations, however, can expect to complete their span of years without having to live through such "interesting times."

Hegel believed that genuine historical breakthroughs are irreversible in their effects because they enable subjects to discover truths of which they had previously been unaware. As long as humans remain conscious of such truths, they cannot fail to be continuously bound by them. For instance, Hegel believed that what made the French Revolution a genuinely revolutionary transformation was not that one ruling clique was replaced by another, but that the revolution of 1789 replaced the principle of "ancient" right with that of "abstract" right. Whereas ancient right permits a ruling class to govern as custom dictates, abstract right compels a governing elite to try, at least, to legitimate its rule by demonstrating that it governs in the interests of all. Modern liberal democracies make validity claims for which it is understood they will be held accountable. According to Hegel, such "accountability" does not depend merely on the support of an atomized electorate; it rests—albeit imperfectly—on the ability of representatives to make claims that are legitimate because they are reasonable. There was no doubt in Hegel's mind that politics in the modern era would come increasingly to be about practical truth and would be grounded in self-understanding and in rational self-insight.

Many of his critics have found Hegel's assertion that history has a final aim that is not always intelligible to the people who are carrying out this purpose to be absurd and dangerous. Hegel conceded that history was a "slaughter bench" but insisted that we need to ask "for whom, for what final aim these monstrous sacrifices have been made."[15] In *The Philosophy of Right,* Hegel concludes that violence and organized aggression can hardly be justified as ends in themselves but could truly be rational in the long term—for instance, in helping to bring about victory in a just war. Hegel did suggest that war could have a cleansing effect for a powerful state; he also argued that particular nations have the right to implement their will forcibly in certain "world-historical" circumstances. Unfortunately, he did not foresee how the enormous growth in nationalistic self-pride in the nineteenth and twentieth centuries would be a divisive force in world politics; and he never anticipated the way in which modern nations would use nationalistic, particularistic policies not as a means to a higher, more universalistic world political entity, but as ends in themselves. Hegel's justification of state policy could have been used in the nineteenth century by the men who implemented the reforms of Napoleon's empire. Similarly, in the twentieth century, the Communist Party of the Soviet Union constantly referred to the leadership role that it assumed among "progressive" forces throughout the world to justify a policy that gave the Soviet state a very special place in world history. The following, for instance, might easily have been used by the Communist Party as a justification for official Soviet policy under Stalin:

> The nation to which is ascribed a moment of the Idea is entrusted with giving complete effect to it in the advance of the self-developing self-consciousness of the world mind. This nation is dominant in world history during this one epoch. . . . In contrast with this its

absolute right of being the vehicle of this present stage in the world mind's development, the minds of the other nations are without rights, and they, along with those whose hour has struck already, count no longer in world history.[16]

Napoleon might well have been carrying out history's purpose at the end of the eighteenth century. Similarly, it might be true that the world spirit was once embodied in the Soviet Union. As Hegel himself would have conceded, however, whether or not the *will* to carry out unpleasant policies of social and political transformation actually brings about just ends can be determined only retrospectively. Furthermore, even granting that aggressive and murderous policies can bring about just results, one can never prove, even retrospectively, that this was the only way in which these ends could have been achieved. Although "world history is not the verdict of mere might" but the development "of the self-consciousness and freedom of mind," the philosopher is likely to be quite useless in helping the statesman to develop and implement a particular policy for the future. According to Hegel, because "social philosophy is merely its own time apprehended in thoughts," theory can no more "transcend its own contemporary world" than can an individual "overleap his own age."[17]

It follows from Hegel's political philosophy that a revolution or war, no matter how bloody, might have positive effects merely because it causes a *rupture* in the old order of things. Hegel would have argued that we should not necessarily fear the consequences of the attempt to make such a break with the past: A revolution enables the detritus of an epoch to be flushed away. It is necessary, however, to have faith in humankind's will and capacity for reason in order to believe that the old order will be replaced by something better. Whether or not this faith is justifiable is a contemporary—perhaps a universal—dilemma.

Hegel did believe that the atomistic individualism and social differentiation fostered and accelerated by the Reformation, the Enlightenment, and the French Revolution would lead to a new ethical form of social organization. It would be difficult to conclude that this new ethical form has yet emerged. Most Western social formations produce individuals who are privatized and individualistically oriented. Not surprisingly, "democracy" in these societies tends to be atomistic, formalistic, and utterly trivial in nature. In the West, the state's role has largely been to promote and defend the capitalist mode of production, not to foster or encourage collective or discursive will formation. In the socialist bloc countries, the state dominated and subjugated what Hegel saw as the anarchy of civil society. This domination, however, was achieved largely as the result of a unanimity of will imposed by the party organization and backed up when necessary by organized terror.

Both capitalist and socialist countries have failed to resolve the issue addressed by Hegel in *The Philosophy of Right*: how to ground genuinely democratic forms of collective decision making in thoughtful self-reflection. In both the United States and what used to be the Soviet Union, the organization of a state apparatus of violence stemmed from policies far more expedient and far less emancipatory than anything Hegel would have anticipated. State power has increased dramatically in the twentieth century. Both capitalist and socialist bloc nations, however, failed to integrate their claims to abstract universalism with the particularities of civil society or with the particularities of private, domestic, ethnic, regional, or even—for a large abstraction like the Soviet Union—national identification.

Contemporary Relevance

Hegel's ideas have had an enormous impact on many sociologists, social psychologists, historians, and political scientists. Since his death, Hegel's system has been used by conservatives interested in reconciling Hegel's social philosophy with Christianity and with the political establishment, and by radicals who have seen Hegelianism as a revolutionary creed. In the decade immediately following Hegel's death, the former group was referred to as the Old Hegelians and the latter group, which came to include Marx, was known as the Young Hegelians.

At the end of the nineteenth century, Hegelianism was a powerful intellectual movement in the United States, although here it tended to be more of a conservative than a radical force. The first professional periodical of philosophy in the United States, *The Journal of Speculative Philosophy*, was founded in St. Louis in 1867 by the Hegelian W. T. Harris, who later became the U.S. Commissioner of Education. After the failure of the 1848 revolutions, a group of radical German Hegelians came to the United States and founded the *Cincinnati Republikaner* in Ohio. The first review of Marx's *Critique of Political Economy* appeared in this newspaper in 1859.

In the United States, Hegel's ideas had a strong impact on the work of the American "pragmatists" John Dewey (1859–1952) and Charles Sanders Peirce (1839–1914) and on the intellectual development of the psychologist William James (1842–1910) and the sociologist and social psychologist George Herbert Mead. In Germany, many cultural sociologists have found Hegel's social epistemology to be invaluable. According to the hermeneutist Wilhelm Dilthey (1833–1911), Hegel successfully analyzed what Dilthey believed was at the root of interpretive theory: "the circle of interpretation" that enables the hermeneutist to reflect on the subjective grounds that make interpretation possible in the first place.

During his lifetime, Hegel was one of a small number of post-Enlightenment social philosophers who rejected the radical eighteenth-century assumption that the natural *and social* worlds were mechanistic systems that could be inspected, stripped down, and rebuilt like a machine. On the contrary, they emphasized the ways in which the experiences of the individual are shaped and determined by cultural and historical forces that are, themselves, the embodiment not of impersonal forces but of *human* purpose and will. Hegel's quarrel with the Enlightenment stemmed from his rejection of the idea that reason in history was a positive and impersonal force that would somehow show itself to be a "natural" part of humanity once traditional regimes were abolished. As we have seen, reason, for Hegel, is based on negation. Consequently, he did not share the *philosophes'* belief that the simple exercise of reason could determine correct social policy. Rather, he believed that reason for reason's sake could be applied only retrospectively, to clarify what had already occurred.

Contemporary Hegelians or neo-Hegelians have been prominent among those who have strongly criticized contemporary forms of social engineering based on positivistic social science. Hegelians have pointed out that positivistic social science can posit cause-effect relations among parts of a social whole. Thus positivistic sociology can provide useful knowledge under certain circumstances. As Hegel pointed out, however, positivistic social engineering will always fail to grasp the conditions under which various types of theorizing become meaningful. Positivism, for instance, cannot reflect on the conditions under which the knowledge it produced became meaningful. Hence positivism will always fail to comprehend its own possible use as a tool of political domination.

Most sociologists have ignored the more radical implications of Hegel's critique of positivism. For the most part, however, they have been far more willing to accept the value of other corrections that Hegel made to eighteenth-century thought. For instance, although he agreed with the eighteenth-century radicals that religious belief and dogma are not the acknowledgment of revealed truths handed down by God, Hegel did not believe that religion could be dismissed merely as the product of erroneous thinking. It was Hegel's position that human orientations must be understood as the product of a people who institutionalize particular categories of reality construction as they sustain a particular form of life. He believed that both reason and unreason were the product of a totality of vision secured intersubjectively.

Thus Hegel would have categorically rejected the claim made by twentieth-century analytical philosophy that anything that can be said meaningfully must be said according to the canons and propositions of positivistic science. On the contrary, religious orientations, for instance, become fully understandable not as the belief systems of people who are stupid and confused, but as the product of a collective form of life that unites people who are striving to express and to understand themselves in particular circumstances, not always in the most complete way. Thus one-sided religious and ideological orientations are a source of truth as well as of error and confusion.

Hegel insisted that to try to "explain" nonscientific modes of belief by dismissing them as garbled and as erroneous is to turn one's back on the possibility of explanation. Most contemporary sociologists of knowledge would agree wholeheartedly with this position. For instance, they would acknowledge that sociology is most insightful and most accurate when "ideological" or religious orientations are seen as the product of particular forms of life. This means that the modern sociologist will not just dismiss religious belief as a form of meaningless and wrong thinking for which the "scientific" outlook would be the cure. Most sociologists now accept that nonscientific cultural orientations are certainly meaningful and can be quite rational within a particular social context.

Few modern sociologists, however, have accepted Hegel's argument that positivistic theorizing is just as "partial" or as "relativistic" as other types of orientation. Contemporary sociology has not tried very seriously to give an adequate account of the production of modern scientific knowledge. Of course, a *sociological* account of scientific truth might not be possible, for the simple reason that scientific truth cannot be shown to be contingent on social variables. Many modern sociologists, however, manage to get themselves in a tangle that Hegel always avoided. On the one hand, they accept positivism as the correct methodology for corroborating statements *they* wish to make about their subjects of analysis. On the other, they accept the validity of nonpositivistic methodologies when it comes to describing the validity of the ways in which these subjects attempt to corroborate their beliefs.

Why is positivism acceptable in one context but not in another? An obvious answer is that social scientists have higher standards when it comes to checking the veracity of statements. If this claim is true, however, the sociologist should feel bound to study others with the intention of pointing out the causes of their error. As mentioned earlier, most sociologists have accepted that this intent is not consistent with the practice of good sociology. Contemporary social scientists tend to see the radical eighteenth-century curt dismissal of nonscientific belief systems as inappropriate for their discipline. Thus modern sociology sentences itself to an ambivalence and contradiction that Hegel would have seen as avoidable if it had the nerve to subject positivism itself to a thoroughgoing critique.

The resurgence of interest in Hegel in the 1960s and 1970s was in part a result of the rediscovery of Marx. Marx was strongly influenced by Hegel; he wrote his early "Economic and Philosophical Manuscripts" (1844) after making a careful study of *The Phenomenology*, and he also produced an important critique of, and commentary on, *The Philosophy of Right*. During the 1960s, many student activists became interested in Hegel and the more Hegelian works of Marx by reading Herbert Marcuse (1898–1979), Georg Lukács (1885–1971), Theodor Adorno (1903–1969), and Antonio Gramsci (1891–1937). All these twentieth-century Marxists believed that Marx's sociology could not be comprehended fully without an appreciation of its Hegelian roots. Most students of Hegel in the twentieth century have turned to him in order to understand Marx more completely. Lenin, for instance, declared that *Das Kapital* could not be read profitably without some comprehension of the Hegelian dialectical methodology.

The most important Hegelians in this century have been Lukács and Marcuse. Lukács tried to show that Marxism-Leninism is the embodiment of Hegelian *praxis* in the modern world. Although the proletariat were not a potent force for change in the early nineteenth century, Lukács identified the working class (not the class of civil servants) as the "universal class" in contemporary capitalist societies. According to Lukács, the "standpoint of the proletariat" is the only viewpoint from which the totality of modern society can be grasped. The class interests of all other classes but the proletariat are partial and one-sided, for the proletariat is the only class that does not depend on the exploitation of others for its existence. Only of the working class can it be said that the conditions for its emancipation are the conditions for the emancipation of all.

Although he was subjected to party discipline in the 1920s for theoretical "deviation," Lukács, believing he could be most useful in the East, chose to spend much of his life in the socialist bloc countries. Together with Karl Korsch (1886–1961), who was expelled from the German Communist Party for his views, Lukács struggled to undermine the Second International view of Marxism as a positivistic science. Drawing on Hegel's view of history, Lukács rejected passive or mechanical Marxism and declared the Marxist mode of inquiry to be not so much "materialist" as dialectical. According to Lukács, history is to be understood in terms of "the dialectical relation between subject and object": "It is not the primacy of economic motives in historical explanation that constitutes the decisive difference between Marxism and bourgeois thought, but the point of view of totality."[18]

All the twentieth-century Marxists have questioned Hegel's positive, if incoherent, conception of Absolute Spirit. For instance, Adorno in his *Negative Dialectics* (1966) rejected Hegel's arguments for a possible unity of subject and object and asserted that Hegel's major contribution to human understanding was his conception of negation as the model of rational inquiry. According to Adorno, human reason can express itself only in the negation of the negation—not, as the positivists would have it, by reference to some fixed model of cognitive rationality. Adorno, a member of the Frankfurt School of critical theorists, agreed with Lukács that the primary task of sociology is to analyze the dialectical relationship between human subjects and a world that has been humanly produced but is not fully recognized as such.

In France, there recently has been a resurgence of interest in Hegel. Both the philosopher Gilles Deleuze (1925–1995) and the psychoanalyst Jacques Lacan (1901–1981) appropriated Hegelian themes in their analyses of subjects' appropriation and recognition of desire. The historian and sociologist Michel Foucault (1926–1984) strongly challenged Hegel's belief in holistic reason and in the ultimate unity of dialectical relations. It has been suggested that Foucault and other members of the new French school of "poststructuralists" have engaged in a project that involves the final "overcoming" of Hegel. Whether this claim is true or not, in France at least, Hegelian theories of the subject have received a great deal of attention in the last couple of decades.

In the 1960s and 1970s, a contemporary German sociologist, Jürgen Habermas, published a series of influential books analyzing modern Western societies from the point of view of a Hegelian-Marxist. Though critical of Hegel in some respects, Habermas accepts Hegel's argument that there is an immanent logic to human development—what Habermas calls "the logic of normative development." Habermas has also criticized the willingness of most contemporary social scientists to claim value neutrality for their disciplines. As Habermas points out, a Hegelian epistemology undermines the credibility of such beliefs. All human knowledge is the outcome of the exercise of *human* reason and *human* interests.

All Hegelian-Marxists point out the following: Humans are the only creatures who self-reflectively produce their means of subsistence. Capitalism enhances this process by progressively upgrading the technology of production in the interests of a dominant class that depends on the constant expansion of markets. This class, therefore, encourages the growth of forces of production for its own particularistic purposes. This unprecedented growth in human technology, however, helps solve the basic problem of human life: how to provide the material necessities of life for *all*. When this problem is solved, the idea of a society that strives to fulfill spiritual needs becomes a real possibility, not just a pipe dream. If the mediative—and exploitative—categories that are definitive of capitalist social formations are not brought into question, capitalism will appear to be a natural and unchanging system. Under these conditions, the possibility of human freedom cannot even be acknowledged, let alone realized in practice. The logjam of reification can be broken only by the political struggle to transform the mediative categories by which humans experience themselves as particular kinds of social beings. This is the Marxist line, but the form of argumentation is one with which Hegel would have felt quite at home.

NOTES

1. Quoted by Franz Wiedmann, *Hegel: An illustrated biography*, p. 32.
2. *The philosophy of right*, p. 226.
3. Ibid., p. 270.
4. Ibid., para. 251.
5. Ibid.
6. Albert Camus, *The rebel* (London: Peregrine, 1962), p. 110.
7. Shlomo Avineri, *Hegel's theory of the modern state*, pp. 88–89.
8. *The phenomenology of mind*, p. 96.
9. *Realphilosophie*, Vol. 2, p. 217, quoted in Georg Lukács, *The young Hegel: Studies in the relations between dialectics and economics*, p. 334.
10. *The phenomenology of mind*, p. 96.
11. George Herbert Mead, *Mind, self, and society* (Chicago: University of Chicago Press, 1934), p. 136.
12. *Hegel's logic*, para. 38.
13. Ibid., para. 81.
14. *The phenomenology of mind*, p. 81. Compare this with Freud's statement that "cruel though it may sound, we must see to it that the patient's suffering, to a degree that is in some way or other effective, does not come to an end prematurely." Quoted by Jürgen Habermas in *Knowledge and human interests* (Boston: Beacon Press, 1971), p. 234.
15. *Reason in history*, p. 79.
16. *The philosophy of right*, para. 347.
17. Ibid., p. 11.
18. Georg Lukács, *History and class consciousness: Studies in Marxist dialectics* (Rodney Livingstone, Trans.) (Cambridge, MA: MIT Press, 1971), p. 27.

GLOSSARY

Absolute Spirit The expression of a human totality that permits human experience to be all it can be.

Alienation For Hegel, the experience of part of oneself as separate and alien. Most pronounced in societies with a complex division of labor and with a high degree of structural differentiation.

Civil society The real social and economic relations among subjects. Especially pronounced in liberal, bourgeois society. The rights of egoistic, atomized individuals are held to be absolute.

Corporations Associations that help to link particular subjects with the larger society (for example, occupational associations).

Cunning of reason The process whereby subjects inadvertently create the underlying conditions for a more rational society by transforming political and social institutions.

Determinate being Being that is qualified by certain determinable and particular characteristics. The external world that we experience as a result of *mediative categories*.

The dialectic Probably no other term is used with more imprecision by sociologists. For Hegel, the dialectic was, above all, the process by which humans strive to become more reasonable. This involves an emancipatory interest in critical theory.

Discipline of the unhappy consciousness The impetus to be reasonable that stems from a deep sense of *alienation*.

Domain of particular altruism The domain of activity within which people express the interests of a particular group (for example, a family or a *corporation*).

Domain of universal altruism The domain of activity within which people express the interests of a whole community.

Domain of universal egoism The domain of activity within which the atomistic self expresses egoistic interests.

Essence The inner world of being. For Hegel, pure *spirit*.

General will The will of a community and the expression of generalizable interests.

Idea See *Absolute Spirit*.

Mechanical Marxism Marxism that emphasizes the way in which human consciousness is determined by objective economic factors and that downplays the significance of human *praxis*.

Mediation That which makes *objectification* possible. The means by which subjects can reflect on themselves and come to identify themselves as particular kinds of beings. For Hegel, the most important medium is labor.

Mediative categories Intersubjectively defined categories of reality construction that serve to organize human experience.

Mind The only agency in the universe that can ground itself—that is, be self-positing and self-determining. That which enables the human subject to be reflective.

Natural ethical life The ethical system of a society with little or no division of labor. Ethical life is based on human need rather than on the abstract requirements of a "free-market" system of production and exchange.

Negation The dissolution of *mediative categories* that are alienating.

Negation of the negation *Negation* plus *reimmediation*. The movement from an older, less reasonable mode of consciousness to a newer, more reasonable, more complete form of understanding.

Objectification The process by which humans make themselves objects both to themselves and for others. Unlike Marx, Hegel does not distinguish carefully between objectification and *alienation*.

Particularism Exclusive or special devotion to something particular.

Passive Marxism See *Mechanical Marxism*.

Reason For Hegel, human consciousness is reasonable to the extent that it understands why and how such consciousness is produced. Pure reason is purely self-reflective.

Reflection For Hegel, the mind's image of itself by means of the mirror provided by *mediative categories*.

Reification An abstraction or idea that is treated as if it is a concrete thing.

Reimmediation The capacity of subjects to "liberate abstractions" by recognizing them as being humanly produced. The dissolution of forms of *reification*.

Spirit See *Mind*.

The state For Hegel, the vehicle for reason in the modern world. The actualization of a *domain of universal altruism*.

Transcendence In dialectical synthesis, the emergence of a qualitatively new form subsuming, and yet advancing beyond, old forms.

Understanding The superficial apprehension of the world as it appears to be. A mode of consciousness that is entirely noncritical.

The unhappy consciousness Felt by the alienated self as it experiences its own sense of being incomplete and of being divided against itself.

Universalism The point of view that best expresses the *general will* of all within a community or totality.

Unreflective universality A totalitarian orientation found in simple societies without complex forms of *mediation*.

The *Volk* German term meaning a people with a shared sense of their own history and with a traditional life-style.

Will The mental faculty that enables us to choose and decide.

World-historical figure An individual who expresses the will of a human totality to create for itself a more rational form of life. A great leader who will change the course of history.

ANNOTATED BIBLIOGRAPHY

Primary Sources

The difference between Fichte's and Schelling's system of philosophy (H. S. Harris & Walter Cerf, Trans. & Eds.). Albany: State University of New York Press, 1977 [1801].

The dissertation that Hegel wrote at the age of thirty, enabling him to take up a teaching position at Jena. His first published work in philosophy.

Early theological writings (T. M. Knox, Trans.; introduction by Richard Kroner). Chicago: University of Chicago Press, 1948 [1907].

Contains Hegel's writings on the history and "fate" of Christianity. Written by Hegel in his mid-twenties while he was living in Bern.

Faith and knowledge (Walter Cerf & H. S. Harris, Trans.). Albany: State University of New York Press, 1977 [1802].

A recent translation of *Glauben und Wissen*, first published in the *Journal of Critical Philosophy* by Hegel and Schelling in Jena. Contains a critique of Kant.

Hegel on tragedy (Anne & Henry Paolucci, Trans.). New York: Harper Torchbooks, 1962 (paper).

A collection of Hegel's scattered writings on tragedy that shows how much Hegel had to say about this topic. Illustrates that Hegel's interests were literary and sociological, as well as philosophical.

Hegel's introduction to aesthetics (T. M. Knox, Trans.; interpretive essay by Charles Karelis). Oxford: Oxford University Press, 1979 (paper).

A collection of lectures that Hegel gave in Berlin in the 1820s. Like much of Hegel's published work, put together from students' notes.

Hegel's logic: Being part one of the encyclopedia of the philosophical sciences (William Wallace, Trans.). Oxford: Clarendon Press, 1975 [1817].

Contains Hegel's "Science of Logic." Includes Hegel's criticism of empiricism and his discussion of how secure knowledge is attained.

Hegel's philosophy of mind: Being part three of the encyclopedia of the philosophical sciences (William Wallace, Trans.). Oxford: Clarendon Press, 1975 [1817] (paper).

Contains a discussion of the various modes of subjective mind and of the mind's movement toward Absolute Spirit.

Hegel's political writings (T. M. Knox, Trans.; introduction by Z. A. Pelczynski). Chicago: University of Chicago Press, 1964.

Contains "The German Constitution" (1801) and Hegel's discussion of the English Reform Bill (1831).

The Hegel Reader (Stephen Houlgate, Ed.). London: Blackwell, 1998 (paper).

The best collection of Hegel's writings currently available in English.

Lectures on the history of philosophy (3 vols.; E. S. Haldane & F. H. Simson, Trans.). New York: Humanities Press, 1974 [1896].

A translation of a collection of lectures prepared by Karl Ludwig Michelet, one of Hegel's students. The three volumes include lectures prepared by Hegel and lectures reconstituted from students' notes. An interesting overview of how Hegel the university lecturer viewed his subject matter.

On art, religion, philosophy: Introductory lectures to the realm of Absolute Spirit (J. Glenn Gray, Ed.). New York: Harper Torchbooks, 1970 (paper).

These lecture notes were originally compiled shortly after Hegel's death. They provide an introduction to what Hegel viewed as the three most important activities of the human spirit. The introductory lecture on art comes from *The Introduction to Hegel's Philosophy of Fine Art* (London: Routledge & Kegan Paul, 1905), pp. 37–211; those on religion come from *Lectures on the Philosophy of Religion* (London: Routledge & Kegan Paul, 1895), pp. 1–85; those on philosophy from *Lectures on the History of Philosophy* (London: Routledge & Kegan Paul, 1892), pp. 1–116.

A good book to turn to when first reading Hegel.

The phenomenology of mind (J. B. Baillie, Trans.). New York: Harper Colophon Books, 1967 [1807] (paper).

Probably Hegel's most influential work. Hegel's first attempt to explain his "system" to the world.

The philosophy of right (T. M. Knox, Trans.). Oxford: Clarendon Press, 1967 [1821] (paper).

The thirteen-page preface is the most famous—and probably the most lucid—passage that Hegel ever wrote. It should be read by every student as a summary statement of Hegel's presuppositions about philosophy. The book contains Hegel's mature political sociology.

Reason in history: A general introduction to the philosophy of history (Robert S. Hartman, Trans.). Indianapolis: Bobbs-Merrill, 1953 [1927–1930].

From Hegel's *Lectures on the Philosophy of History* (J. Sibtree, Trans.) (New York: Dover, 1956).

System of ethical life and first philosophy of spirit (H. S. Harris & T. M. Knox, Trans. & Eds.). Albany: State University of New York Press, 1979 [1803], [1804].

The "System of Ethical Life" is Hegel's early political sociology, developed in Jena. The "First Philosophy of Spirit" is an earlier version of *The Philosophy of Mind*.

Secondary Sources

Adorno, Theodor W. *Negative dialectics* (E. B. Ashton, Trans.). New York: Seabury Press, 1973 [1966].

A critical theorist applies the Hegelian methodology of negation to the contemporary world. Pages 300–361 contain a discussion of the relevance of Hegelian ideas today.

Avineri, Shlomo. *Hegel's theory of the modern state.* Cambridge: Cambridge University Press, 1972 (paper).

Probably the best introduction to Hegel's political sociology. Avineri is sympathetic toward Hegel.

Beiser, Frederick C. (Ed.). *The Cambridge Companion to Hegel.* Cambridge: Cambridge University Press, 1993 (paper).

This volume covers Hegel's epistemology, logic, ethics, political philosophy, aesthetics, philosophy of history, and philosophy of religion. Other topics covered include Hegel's relationship with Marx and the development of Hegelianism in the West.

Butler, Judith P. *Subjects of desire: Hegelian reflections in twentieth-century France.* New York: Columbia University Press, 1987.

This book contains an interesting section on Hegel's influence on contemporary French theorists like Jacques Lacan, Gilles Deleuze, and Michel Foucault.

Dallymr, Fred R. *G. W. Hegel: Modernity and politics.* London: Sage, 1993.

Dallymr argues that Hegel is more relevant today than he ever was. According to Dallymr, Hegel was the preeminent philosopher of modernity and of the "modern polis."

Findlay, J. N. *Hegel: A re-examination.* New York: Collier Books, 1962 (paper).

Probably the best general introduction to Hegel's philosophy. Findlay has been one of the leading commentators on Hegel in the twentieth century. The book is written by a professional philosopher for students of philosophy.

Fukuyama, Francis. *The end of history and the last man.* New York: Avon, 1993 (paper).

Not a book on Hegel as such, but one that draws on Hegelian ideas to argue that Western liberal democracies represent the "end point of mankind's ideological evolution" and hence the "final form of human government." Fukuyama is not suggesting that there is anything intrinsically superior about modern (or postmodern) liberal democracies such as those that prevail in North America and Western Europe, but he is suggesting that there may be something to Hegel's philosophical idea of a Universal History with a clear direction and purpose. Rather than take us in a Leninist direction, this History, Fukuyama argues, leads us to the type of banal but stable civilization that stresses not struggle or ideology but the pursuit of security, material well-being, and personal liberty.

Gellner, Ernest. "The Absolute in braces." In *Spectacles and predicaments* (pp. 13–40). Cambridge: Cambridge University Press, 1979.

Gellner was a British sociologist who was unsympathetic toward Hegel and never viewed Hegel as an important theorist. Nevertheless, this short article is a brilliant, witty account of what the reader should be wary of in Hegel's work.

Habermas, Jürgen. *Theory and practice* (John Viertel, Trans.). Boston: Beacon Press, 1973 [1971] (paper).

Difficult. Pages 121–194 discuss Hegel's critique of the French Revolution and his political writings.

Harris, H. S. *Hegel's development: Toward the sunlight, 1770–1801*. Oxford: Clarendon Press, 1972.

A comprehensive account of Hegel's development up to the Jena period. The book gives much useful information about the social and intellectual climate at the end of the eighteenth century.

Hyppolite, Jean. *Studies on Marx and Hegel* (John O'Neill, Trans.). New York: Basic Books, 1969 [1955].

A classic. Particularly important for tracing the connections between Hegel's social philosophy and the development of Marxism as an intellectual and social movement.

Kaufmann, Walter. *Hegel: Reinterpretation, texts and commentary*. New York: Doubleday, 1965.

A comprehensive exposition of Hegel's life's work.

Lukács, Georg. *The young Hegel: Studies in the relations between dialectics and economics* (Rodney Livingstone, Trans.). Cambridge, MA: MIT Press, 1976 [1954].

Written by the preeminent Hegelian-Marxist of this century. Lukács views Hegelian-Marxism as the culmination of German classical philosophy.

Marcuse, Herbert. *Reason and revolution: Hegel and the rise of social theory*. Boston: Beacon Press, 1969 [1941] (paper).

Required reading for the serious student of Hegel. A discussion of the importance of Hegel's views for the development of critical theory. In the 1960s, this book played an important role in the student movement.

Pinkard, Terry P. *Hegel: A Biography*. Cambridge: Cambridge University Press, 2000.

Not yet published when this edition of *Sociological Theory* went to press, but probably worth inspection.

Plamenatz, John. *Man and society: Political and social theory: Bentham through Marx* (Vol. 2). New York: McGraw-Hill, 1963.

Like Gellner, Plamenatz has been schooled in the British tradition of learning to distrust Hegel. Nevertheless, pages 169–268 of this book contain a useful discussion of what Plamenatz believes is important and insightful in Hegel's social and political theory.

Popper, Karl. *The open society and its enemies* (Vol. 2). London: Routledge & Kegan Paul, 1945.

The work of a rabid Hegel-hater. According to Popper, Hegel's sole purpose in life was "to fight against the open society [that is, modern pluralistic democracies] and thus to serve his employer, Frederick William of Prussia." Professor Sir Karl Popper's book is worth looking at because it has been highly influential in shaping people's attitude toward Hegel (and Marx) in Britain and—to a lesser extent—in the United States. According to Popper, Hegel was a very wicked man.

Rose, Gillian. *Hegel contra sociology*. Atlantic Highlands, New Jersey: Athlone Press, 1995 (paper).

Rose argues that most sociology is founded on neo-Kantian principles and that Hegel's philosophy both anticipated and overcame the limitations of this paradigm for the social sciences.

Smith, Tony. *Dialectical social theory and its critics: From Hegel to analytical Marxism and post-*

modernism. Albany: State University of New York Press, 1993.

An examination of the dialectical method used by Hegel, Marx, and more contemporary theorists.

Strathern, Paul. *Hegel in 90 minutes.* Chicago: Ivan R. Dee, 1997 (paper).

No mean achievement.

Taylor, Charles. *Hegel and modern society.* Cambridge: Cambridge University Press, 1979 (paper).

Written by an Oxford professor who has managed to sidestep traditional British anti-Hegelianism. Best of all, Taylor recognizes that Hegel is an important social theorist. Dry in parts, but recommended. This is an abridged version.

Toews, John Edward. *Hegelianism: The path toward dialectical humanism, 1805–1841.* Cambridge: Cambridge University Press, 1980.

An excellent discussion of the importance of Hegelianism as an important intellectual movement in contemporary thought.

Westphal, Merold. *Hegel, freedom, and modernity.* Albany: State University of New York Press, 1992.

A study of Hegel's *Philosophy of Right.* According to Westphal, "Hegel is above all else a philosopher of freedom in the modern world." Like Dallymr, Westphal points out that Hegel has regained his importance at a time "in which modernity has become increasingly problematic to us."

Wiedmann, Franz. *Hegel: An illustrated biography* (Joachim Neugroschel, Trans.). New York: Pegasus Books, 1968 (paper).

Probably the best of the few modern biographies of Hegel.

The subject of our discussion is first of all material production. Individuals producing in society, thus the socially determined production of individuals, naturally constitutes the starting point. The individual and isolated hunter or fisher who forms the starting point with Smith and Ricardo belongs to the insipid illusions of the eighteenth century. These are adventure stories which do not, by any means, represent, as students of history imagine, a reaction against civilized life and a return to a forgotten natural life. They are no more based on such a naturalism than is Rousseau's social contract, which brings naturally independent individuals into contact and develops contractual relations. They are the fiction and only the aesthetic fiction of small and great adventure stories. They are, indeed, the anticipation of that "civil society," which had been developing since the sixteenth century and which made gigantic strides toward maturity in the eighteenth. In this society of free competition the individual appears free from the bonds of nature, etc., which in former periods of history made him part of a definite, limited human conglomeration. To the prophets of the eighteenth century, on whose shoulders Smith and Ricardo still stand, this eighteenth-century individual, constituting the joint product of the dissolution of the feudal form of society and of the new forces of production which had developed since the sixteenth century, appears as an ideal whose existence belongs to the past; not as a result of history, but as its starting point. Since the individual appeared to be in conformity with nature and corresponded to their conception of human nature, he was regarded as a product not of history but of that nature. This illusion has been characteristic of every new epoch in the past.

—Karl Marx, *Grundrisse*

7

Karl Marx

(1818–1883)

Life

Karl Marx was born on May 5, 1818, in Trier, a small German town in the western Rhenish province of Prussia. His father, Hirschl Marx-Levy, was a lawyer who struggled hard to make a living until he converted to Protestantism two years before Karl's birth. The immediate cause of this conversion was the Prussian repossession of territories lost to France during the Napoleonic wars. When the Prussians expelled the French, they made it illegal for Jews to hold public office. As a result of the reforms instituted by King Friedrich Wilhelm III, this prohibition did not apply to Jews baptized as Christian. After his conversion, Hirschl rose to be head of the Trier bar association.

Karl's mother, Henriette, was Dutch. Her family was prosperous, and Henriette brought a sizable dowry with her when she married Hirschl.

Karl was educated at the local *Gymnasium*, where he obtained high grades in Latin and in German composition only. At the age of seventeen, Marx traveled to the University of Bonn to study jurisprudence. At Bonn, Karl earned his parents' disapproval by running up debts, by drinking too much, by failing to write home often enough, by fighting a duel (in which he was wounded), and by being arrested for carrying a deadly weapon. Hirschl Marx worried that Karl was proving to be a spendthrift and a "slovenly barbarian," and he decided his son should transfer to the University of Berlin. Some of the most famous professors in Europe were associated with Berlin; the most illustrious, Hegel, had died five years before Marx's arrival.

Before leaving home once more, Karl secretly became engaged to his childhood sweetheart, Jenny von Westphalen, who lived next door. Jenny was four years older than Karl and had to wait eight years to marry him. She was the daughter of the Baron von Westphalen, a Prussian official who had been ennobled for his services as private secretary to the duke of Brunswick. Ludwig von Westphalen was a liberal and a follower of Henri de Saint-Simon (1760–1825). Fortunately, he was fond of Marx, for his liberality was put to the test by the betrothal of his only daughter to the penniless but opinionated son of a converted Jew. Nevertheless, the marriage between Karl and Jenny was a success. Years later, Marx's son-in-law Paul Lafargue noted in his memoirs that although Jenny Marx was the daughter of a nobleman, and although her brother was a minister to the king of Prussia, not one of the working men and women who were entertained at the Marxes' home in London would ever have suspected it. Jenny was without airs, and for much of her life she was devoted to Karl.

At the University of Berlin, Marx studied philosophy. After his father's death he submitted a doctoral thesis on Greek philosophies of nature, with the hope of winning a university lectureship. When he learned that he had been blacklisted by the Ministry of Education in Berlin for his known radical tendencies, Marx turned to journalism. In 1842, he became editor of the *Rheinische Zeitung* (Rhenish Gazette). This paper was shut down in January 1843, after its editors unwisely published an attack on one of Prussia's allies, the Russian tsar. Marx published several articles in the *Rheinische Zeitung* critical of the Prussian government's treatment of dispossessed German peasants. It was through his association with this journal that Marx met Friedrich Engels (1820–1895) in 1842.

Engels was the son of a wealthy German manufacturer who owned textile factories in Barmen, Germany, and Manchester, England. He had little interest in business or commerce and had experienced for himself the brutal exploitation and degradation of textile workers in his father's mills. Nevertheless, in 1850, Engels agreed to manage his father's company in Manchester. One reason for this decision was that Marx, with whom he had formed a close friendship, had become financially dependent on him. By this time, the two men were collaborating, and Engels had become aware of the world-shattering importance of his friend's work. For many years thereafter, the Marx household received steady handouts from Engels. In 1869, Engels had made enough from what had by then become his business to sell out for a large sum. From the profits that he had netted, Engels paid his friend's many debts and settled an annuity on Marx of 350 pounds a year—about four times the annual income made by the workers in his mills.

In 1844, Marx was in Paris helping to found a new and radical, but short-lived, journal: the *Deutsch-Französische Jahrbücher* (German-French Annals). He also began working on the "Economic and Philosophic Manuscripts" (sometimes referred to as the "Paris manuscripts" or the "1844 manuscripts"). His journalism had come to the attention of the Prussian censors; and on April 16, 1844, the Prussian government issued an order for Marx's arrest on the charge of "high treason." Marx was expelled from Paris and moved with Jenny to Brussels, where they lived in exile for three years.

By 1847, Marx and Engels were both actively involved in the communist movement, and they traveled to London to attend the Second Congress of the Communist League. The members of the league authorized Marx and Engels to draft a manifesto for them, which appeared in print in 1848. That was the year in which revolutions broke out all over Europe. Prophetically, the Communist Manifesto opened with the line: "A specter is haunting Europe—the specter of communism."

In April 1848, Marx and Engels hurried to Cologne to participate in the German revolution. Protest in Germany was sporadic and disorganized. As a preventive measure, Cologne, which was part of the Prussian state, was placed under martial law. For a few months, Marx edited a new paper, the *Neue Rheinische Zeitung*. This publication was openly communist in orientation, and the authorities moved quickly to close it down. Marx was belligerent and recalcitrant. The last issue of the *Neue Rheinische Zeitung*, on May 19, 1849, was printed entirely in red ink and described the Prussian royal family as "dishonorable" and as "royal terrorists."

In the meantime, Marx had been put on trial in Cologne for insulting the authorities and for inciting rebellion. Marx was acquitted by a jury but found himself entirely bankrupt as a result of debts incurred as editor in chief of the *Neue Rheinische Zeitung*. In Brussels, he had spent all his savings from his share of his father's estate to buy arms for an abortive workers' revolution. Marx was now unwelcome in Germany, France, and Belgium. Finally, in 1849, he took refuge in London, where he and his family remained for the rest of his life.

The 1850s were hard years for Karl and Jenny Marx. At first they rented rooms in Soho, a poor district in central London full of immigrants and refugees. They were evicted by bailiffs for nonpayment of rent on at least one occasion, and the family often went hungry. Because of disease and poverty, the Marxes lost three children in infancy. Three daughters survived. At times, Jenny seemed close to despair; once she left Karl and returned to Germany for a short time. Marx, however, never let poverty interfere with his work. He would often write for days at a stretch, stopping only for naps and for irregular meals.

In 1851, Marx's only surviving son was born illegitimately to Helen Demuth, a servant who helped run the Marx household for more than thirty years. Marx persuaded Engels to accept responsibility for the child, who was adopted by a working-class family in London. Jenny Marx never knew about little Frederick's true paternity; if she had found out, she probably would have returned to Germany for good. Frederick had almost no contact with the Marx family, and his sisters found out about his true relationship to them only much later. It is not known what happened to him or to his children.

In 1851, Marx became the London correspondent of the *New-York Daily Tribune*. This newspaper, founded by Horace Greeley, had the largest circulation in the United States. Many of Marx's submissions and commentaries were actually written by Engels. Marx often claimed that he was too busy to meet the *Tribune*'s deadlines and handed assignments over to Engels, pointing out that the latter's grasp of English was better than his own.

During the London years, Marx made a close study of political economy. He spent countless hours in the reading room of the British museum, absorbing the official reports of government statisticians and factory inspectors. These reports, which were published as government "Blue Books," described in horrifying detail the dehumanizing conditions of employment of hundreds of thousands in the capitalist homeland. Although they were distributed free to members of Parliament (MPs), almost no one read them. Many MPs sold them by the pound; others used them as shooting targets, judging the velocity of their bullets by the number of pages pierced.[1]

In London, Marx remained active as a revolutionist. From 1864 to 1872, he was heavily involved in the International Working Men's Association, later referred to as the First International. He put together the rules and statutes of the organization and attended meetings of the General Council in London nearly every week. The International was not as radical as the Communist League had been. It supported workers' rights but did not advocate communism or violent revolution. Nevertheless, the association was genuinely international. It was able to organize links among working-class leaders in England, France, Germany, and Poland.

Marx was often visited by European radicals in exile, and through his participation in the International—which he saw very much as *his* organization—he came to know many English trade unionists. Marx carried out bitter feuds with rivals in France and Germany and often distributed diatribes against those who attacked him or who disagreed with his diagnosis of correct working-class revolutionary strategy. At meetings and conferences, Marx often intimidated his audience with the force of his intellect. He had no qualms about dismissing opinions and assessments that did not square with his own.

On September 14, 1867, Volume 1 of *Capital* was published in Germany. The first translation appeared in Russia in 1872; an English translation did not appear until 1887. (Interestingly enough, the book aroused far more interest in backward Russia than it did in England or Germany, and sales in St. Petersburg were brisk.) Marx had been working on *Capital* for nearly twenty years, but he was unable to finish the book. Engels brought out the second volume in 1885; Volume 3 appeared in 1894, a year before Engels's death. Engels put together these last two volumes from notes and manuscripts that Marx left as part of his meager estate.

Marx died sitting in his study at home on March 14, 1883. He had been ill for some time and had recently lost his wife and his favorite daughter. At his friend's grave in Highgate Cemetery, Engels described Marx as "the discoverer of the fundamental law that determines the course and development of human history." Before Marx died, Engels concluded, he "saw his economic theories becoming the indisputable basis of socialism throughout the whole world."[2]

It is indisputable that both Marx and Engels had a greater impact on social and political theory than did any other figures of their time. Their relationship was symbiotic; together they were more than the sum of their parts. Marx's prodigious intellect was countered by Engels's experience and good common sense. Together, Marx and Engels could read more than forty languages. Between them, they knew almost as much as anyone alive about the living conditions of the laboring poor; about Aristotle, Democritus, and Aeschylus; about political economy, French and Spanish prose, German politics, Goethe, and Shakespeare; and about the latest kinds of machine technology. In some ways they were an odd couple: Engels dressed well and liked to go fox hunting with the local gentry. Marx was totally without bourgeois—let alone aristocratic—pretensions. Although it was important to him that he be thought of as a scholar, he was relatively indifferent to the squalor that often surrounded him at home.

Marx, however, was always the dominant member of the partnership. There was no doubt in Engels's mind that his friend was the greatest intellectual figure of the era. Toward the end of his life, Marx achieved some recognition for his accomplishments. Not surprisingly, however, a dominant class, whom Marx professed to despise, deemed him unfit for a university lectureship. If it had not been for the anonymous laborers in Engels's textile mills, Marx and his family would have starved.

Social Environment

In the preface to the first edition of his book *The Condition of the Working-Class in England* (1844), Engels comments, "The condition of the working-class is the real basis and point of departure of all social movements of the present because it is the highest and most unconcealed pinnacle of the social misery existing in our day."[3] In his study of the English proletariat, Engels documents the brutalizing effects of factory employment on men, women, and young children. He describes the savage competition among rootless laborers for starvation wages and the earliest attempts of workers to organize in their own interests. In this book, Engels notes that "proletarian conditions exist in their *classical form*, in their perfection, only on the British Empire, particularly in England proper."[4]

By the 1840s, Britain was the leading industrial society in the world and facing the very real possibility of political mobilization based on the perception and experience of class oppression. In the 1820s, France had seemed to be at the center of socialist ideology. In 1830, however, King Louis Philippe (the "king of the bourgeoisie") had been placed on the throne by the upper middle classes, who anticipated and required a regime that would govern in their interests. Strikes in Paris and Lyons were effectively put down by the National Guard, and labor legislation remained extremely repressive; workers, for example, were supposed to present the *livret* (a certificate of good conduct) to employers before they could be hired. Thus, although there was much talk of "socialism" in France, the working classes in that country were poorly organized and were not an effective political force. Social reformers like Saint-Simon and Charles Fourier (1772–1837) were more interested in contemplating ideal futures than in organizing for any real change in the scheme of things.

In England, it was different. Throughout the 1820s and 1830s, there was a growing awareness within the English proletariat of their position as members of a class of wage earners who had been robbed of their heritage as "free-born Englishmen." Between 1824 and 1834, the first trade unions appeared in England, and in the 1830s, there was a movement toward union federation that met with limited success.

The great political movement of the 1830s and 1840s in England was the Chartist movement, which was initially organized by a group of radical workers in London. It was a reformist, not a revolutionary, movement: The Chartists wanted the working classes to participate in the electoral process. (Universal manhood suffrage was granted in 1832, but would-be voters had to meet certain property requirements.) Nevertheless, the Chartists—who at one time threatened to organize a national strike—demonstrated that the proletariat in England was capable of effective political mobilization. By the 1830s, it was clear that a certain segment of the English working-class was capable of organizing effectively along class lines.

The absolute deprivation of the industrial working-class in England reached its limits in the 1830s and the 1840s. Wages were kept at starvation level. In the 1830s, it was perfectly legal to work nine-year-old children sixteen hours a day in satanic factories and textile mills. Many factories had no safety regulations whatsoever; children commonly lost fingers and hands in industrial machinery that was kept running most of the night. By the 1860s, however, a series of laws were passed that regulated the hours and conditions of work for all kinds of laborers. Middle-class reformers were responsible for much of this legislation, but there was also a great deal of effective working-class agitation for a shorter working day.

By the 1870s, trade unions were an established political force in Britain. By and large, however, working-class organizations were not radical organizations. The collapse of the International Working Men's Association in 1872 bore testimony to the fact that radical organizations of working people, which cut across occupational, religious, and national boundaries, met with little or no success before World War I. Nevertheless, as the living conditions of workers slowly improved during Marx's and Engels's lifetimes, class politics became increasingly more salient. Marx and Engels were correct in viewing the increasingly self-conscious proletariat as a class with an enormous potential for forcing social and political change.

The revolutions of 1848 terrified the ruling classes throughout Europe. In Paris, working-class demonstrators remained in the streets until they had brought down the French government. In the Hapsburg capital, rebellious workers forced the Austrian royal family to flee from Vienna. In south Germany, rulers of many small states were forced to adopt liberal policies for a short time; and in Berlin, King Friedrich Wilhelm IV felt compelled to recall the United Diet, the German parliament, and to promise a new constitution for Prussia.

The cause of all this unrest was an economic depression triggered by the bad harvests of 1846 and 1848. Unemployment in Europe rose rapidly; and the conservative and hidebound administrations in France, Prussia, and the rest of Europe proved incapable of responding to these new troubles. The paralysis of the central administration in France ultimately led to a short-lived civil war. Although universal manhood suffrage was granted, a conservative administration, headed by Louis Napoleon Bonaparte (Napoleon III), Napoleon's nephew, came to power. The far left in France, however, had considerable support among the masses. In Prussia the extension of suffrage to workers with a permanent residence did much to calm the situation. Throughout Germany, despite the best hopes of Marx and Engels, civil disturbances (like the one that Marx was involved with in Cologne) were a reaction to the increasing chaos of the marketplace rather than the result of burgeoning class consciousness. German artisans tended to be strongly nationalistic. To some extent they welcomed a strong administration in Berlin—provided that it led to a united Germany.

The second great revolution that occurred during Marx's lifetime took place after Napoleon III undertook a disastrous war against Germany in 1870. Revolutionary segments of the working-class, anticlericals, and radical members of the lower bourgeoisie took advantage of the disorder caused by the German victories over the French to mount an insurrection in Paris in the spring of 1871. The revolutionaries set up a commune in working-class neighborhoods in Paris. Government troops had to retake the city by force. To defeat the Communards militarily, they had to massacre at least 20,000 working-class Parisians, and they almost leveled the 20th *Arrondissement*, the area of the city from which the revolt had been organized.

Although Engels referred to the Commune as "the child of the International," the International Working Men's Association gave only moral support to the rebellion. Marx was pessimistic about its outcome. He had believed, quite correctly, that the composition of the Communards was too heterogeneous and the policies of the leadership too vague for the revolution to have any lasting and positive benefits. Marx analyzed the events in Paris in *The Civil War in France* (1871). This pamphlet, issued in the name of the General Council of the International, was a popular success.

Marx pointed out that the civil war in France had increased class polarization. Characteristically he concluded by saying:

> The battle must break out again and again and in ever-growing dimensions, and there can be no doubt as to who will be the victor in the end. . . . Wherever, in whatever shape, and under whatever conditions the class struggle obtains any consistency it is but natural that members of our Association should stay in the foreground. The soil out of which it grows is modern society itself. It cannot be stamped out by any amount of carnage. To stamp it out the governments would have to stamp out the despotism of capital over labor—the condition of their own parasitical existence.[5]

By the year of Engels's death (1895), socialist candidates had won seats in the British parliament. In Germany, the moderately reformist *Sozialdemokratische Partei Deutschlands* (SPD) had become a major force in German politics. The SPD was nominally socialist, but its leaders had been effectively coopted by ruling groups. In the summer of 1893, Engels traveled to Switzerland to address a congress of the Second International, which had been founded by SPD leaders in 1889. The delegates—socialists from all over Europe—gave him a standing ovation, which Engels modestly attributed to his past association with Marx.

The Second International was dissolved at the outbreak of World War I. In 1914, nationalism proved to be a stronger force than working-class solidarity. In 1870, the German section of the First International sided with the German government in the war against the French. Similarly, in 1914, the SPD supported requisitions for a war that would lead to the deaths of millions of British, French, and German workers.

Intellectual Roots

Within a year of his arrival at the University of Berlin, Marx wrote to his father that he was studying the Hegelian system closely. Hegel's influence on Marx would remain strong. In *The Economic and Philosophic Manuscripts of 1844*, Marx notes that Hegel's *Phenomenology of Mind* was "the true birthplace and secret of my philosophy."

In 1837, Marx was admitted to a *Doktorklub* in Berlin, which served as a discussion forum for a group of "Young Hegelians"—students and university lecturers who applied a radical interpretation of the meaning of Hegelianism to the study of religion. The most prominent members of the group were David Strauss (1808–1874) and Bruno Bauer (1809–1882). These men published books that treated the accounts of Jesus' life and the Gospel stories as products of human attempts at self-understanding. Bauer, for instance, argued that religion was not something apart from humanity; it enhanced nothing other than humankind's attempt to understand *itself*.

The Prussian establishment had an understandably negative reaction to the work of the Young Hegelians, who were held to be undermining Christian morality. Files were maintained in Berlin on most of the members of Marx's *Doktorklub*, and Marx was compelled to submit his doctoral dissertation to Jena rather than Berlin because of his association with this unsavory group. Marx's position in society was not advanced by his announcement that he planned to found a militant review entitled *Atheistic Archives.*

Marx ultimately broke with the Young Hegelians because he came to believe that they were incapable of going beyond "metaphysical speculation." By 1844, he had come to the conclusion that philosophy without practical consequences was empty. Marx believed that German intellectuals specialized in abstract theorizing divorced from the technical and practical-moral problems of everyday life. In *The German Ideology* (1845–1846), Marx and Engels draw a telling analogy between German philosophers and a "certain person who once took it into his head that people drown in water because they are obsessed by the notion of weight." Just as this hypothetical person managed to convince himself that "right thinking" would save him from drowning, so, Marx and Engels believed, did German philosophical idealists believe that social and political ills could be cured by philosophy.

In time, Marx and Engels concluded that the divorce that German intellectuals made between theoretical ideas and real practical activity was a reflection of the almost feudal condition of German society. According to Marx, both Kant and Hegel had been inspired enough by the French Revolution to grasp the significance of freedom and self-determination from an abstract and intellectual point of view. In early nineteenth-century Germany, however, it was dangerous for academics to criticize the dominant classes. The Prussian establishment, for instance, took their position in society to be a natural right and expected deference. Not surprisingly, most German academics preferred to talk about human emancipation as if this involved the development of a pure intellectual orientation that was either indifferent to the real world (Kantianism) or that held everyday life to derive from higher spiritual activity (Hegelianism). In either case, it followed that a practical critique of social and political arrangements was moot. Throughout his life, Marx was constantly on his guard against the perils of disembodied thought. Abstract philosophy, he once suggested, has the same relationship to the actual study of the world as masturbation does to sexual love.

Marx greatly preferred Hegel to Kant because of Hegel's emancipatory interest in knowledge and because of his insistence that theory and practice should be united. Marx believed that Hegel was correct in arguing that humankind was the product of the history that it had made for itself. Marx believed, however, that this history was made as the result of practical human activity—specifically, the result of the human need to exercise technical control over a variable natural environment. Marx conceded that Hegel had overcome the dualism between "spirit" and matter. But he had done so by treating material reality as if it were the embodiment of spirit. Marx pointed out that Hegel had described history as if historical subjects lived on a bloodless and ghostly plane where cultural emanations sought to displace one another within the domain of human consciousness. By 1845, Marx had come to the realization that human history was the story of a constant struggle among differentially advantaged groups for the possession and control of scarce material resources. Human aspirations are a reflection of this struggle. As Marx put it:

> In direct contrast to German Philosophy, which descends from heaven to earth, here we ascend from earth to heaven. That is to say, we do not set out from what men say, imagine, conceive, nor from men as narrated, thought of, imagined, conceived in order to arrive at men in the flesh. We set out from real, active men, and on the basis of their real life-process we demonstrate the development of the ideological reflexes and echoes of this life-process.[6]

Marx and Engels completely rejected what they described as "utopian socialism." In *The German Ideology*, Marx pointed out that many German socialists took it for granted that individuals were naturally moral and intrinsically humane, and liked to moralize about the supposedly humanitarian core of human individuals. Marx reacted strongly against this "preaching." (In fact, he often developed his own position toward a specific issue by attacking the views of those with whom he disagreed.) According to Marx, this kind of socialism was a "petty bourgeois" social movement—a movement that is "concerned no longer with real human beings . . . [but] proclaims instead the universal love of mankind."[7]

Although Marx discarded philosophical idealism, he strongly rejected the idea that human consciousness was nothing more than the simple reflection of a material and environmental aspect of social existence over which humans had no control. In *The German Ideology*, Marx and Engels criticize the influential critic of Hegel, Ludwig Feuerbach (1804–1872), who had turned Hegel completely on his head by asserting that human consciousness is merely what we know in relation to some preexisting and determining material reality. Marx and Engels argued that there is indeed an external world, which we apprehend through our senses; this world, however, is shaped and determined by the decisions we make about the actions we wish to take toward our environments. As our practical intentions and practical activity change, so our comprehension of this external world is transformed.

Marx viewed Hegel's distinction between the idealist political state and down-to-earth civil society as an inevitable outcome of Hegel's unwillingness to close the gap between the domains of "spiritualism" and "materialism." According to Marx, effective political reform cannot result from the idealization of the abstract state—that is, merely from the argument that it is possible to *imagine* a state that would be completely just. Marx conceded that modern states guarantee the citizen certain "rights." These rights are one-sided, however. For instance, in the bourgeois state one such "right" is the right to profit from the labor of others. Marx pointed out that this is not a *human* right for the laborer, whose only social significance is to be used as a means to the wealth of others.

In 1843, Marx began to make a study of classical, or bourgeois, political economy. He was highly complimentary about many of the characteristics of the capitalist mode of production, which had "accomplished wonders far surpassing Egyptian pyramids, Roman aqueducts and Gothic Cathedrals."[8]

From the British economists Adam Smith (1723–1790) and David Ricardo (1772–1823), Marx took the labor theory of value. According to Smith and Ricardo, a *commodity,* or any object that is produced through the social organization of work, can have value only insofar as human labor power has been used. Marx agreed with Smith and Ricardo that capitalism was instrumentally rational: It encouraged economic growth for growth's sake, and it rapidly added to the wealth of a society. Marx argued, however, that capitalism was inherently exploitative in that it extracted from the laboring masses part of the wealth that they themselves had created. Furthermore, although historically the bourgeoisie were a revolutionary class bent on destroying traditional society, they were also eager to displace relations of personal dependence with relations based on nothing but cash payment. Marx believed that capitalism promoted atomized, individualized, and alienated human subjects largely because it encouraged relations of mutual indifference. In capitalist society, individuals are not indifferent to the money-making potential of relationships with others, but they are indifferent toward the personal qualities of others if these qualities have no bearing on the universal struggle to maximize one's income.

Smith and Ricardo regarded the time spent on work as a cost to be deducted from the ideal human state: leisure. For Marx, this false dichotomization of work and leisure demonstrated more than anything else that bourgeois political economy was the theoretical expression of what had become the alienated human state. This concept would be evident if civilization were not founded on exploitative class relations that compel some people to slave for others. According to Marx, it is not work that is alienating, but the organization of work in class society.

Marx and Engels: The Relationship

Marx and Engels often are discussed in tandem as if they coauthored everything they wrote or as if they agreed on every topic. Engels's "Outlines of a Critique of Political Economy," submitted to the *Deutsch-Französische* in November 1843, and his *The Condition of the Working-Class in England,* completed in 1844, both had a significant impact on Marx, who drew upon the former work in preparing his own *Economic and Philosophic Manuscripts of 1844.* Engels's "Outlines of a Critique" also provided much of the theoretical background for the jointly written *Communist Manifesto* (1848). However, as Terrell Carver has pointed out in a recent study of Marx and Engels, "Engels seems to have surrendered political economy wholly to Marx after 1844 and never to have expressed regret or further independent interest."[9]

From 1850 to 1869, Engels lived in Manchester managing his father's factories. During this time, he did little theoretical work. Most of his writings during this period were in the form of journalistic articles, reports, and correspondence. After his retirement from business, Engels's major works during Marx's lifetime were *Anti-Dühring,* published in 1877, and the *Dialectics of Nature,* started in 1873, but not published until after Engels's death in 1895. Dühring was a professor at the University of Berlin, a Hegelian and political economist who Marx and Engels believed was exercising an unhealthy influence on the newly formed *Sozialdemokratische Partei Deutschlands.* In *Anti-Dühring,* Engels developed the idea that dialectical laws of motion objectively existed *in* nature and, thus, were as applicable to natural as to social domains of existence. In essence, Marx was skeptical about this claim, but he seems to have avoided confrontation with Engels on this issue. Engels's metaphysical claims were not well thought out, and are not obviously reconcilable with Marx's own system. Nevertheless, "dialectical materialism," a term coined by Engels but never used by Marx, came to represent a metaphysic or logic of being, which, in later years, was ascribed to Marxism *per se.*[10]

After Marx's death, Engels played a major role in introducing Marx's work to an ever-widening audience. After 1883, Engels wrote numerous prefaces for new editions and translations of *The Communist Manifesto* and added an additional seventeen prefaces to other works by Marx that were being reprinted or translated. He also edited and published the second and third volumes of *Capital.* Engels thus was in a position to integrate his later work with his interpretation of Marxist theory taken as a whole. As Carver puts it:

> The Marx-Engels intellectual relationship, as it has come down to us—a story of complete agreement expressed in interchangeable or supplementary works, the division of labour within a perfect partnership—was largely a creation of this period. It emerged from what Engels did, what he said, and what was implied in both.[11]

IDEAS

Society

Marx agreed with Hegel that social life is the process whereby mediative categories emerge that enable historical subjects to comprehend themselves. Society, then, is not just an alien and impersonal system set apart from everyday life; it is an expression of human subjectivity. Marx believed that humankind makes its own history; and, like Hegel, he acknowledged that subjects do not always have a complete understanding of how this process occurs. Unlike Hegel, Marx believed that historical forms of self-awareness are ultimately determined by the relationship of subjects to a natural environment containing both material objects and forces to which the human mind must adapt. The medium of interaction between subjects and this material or natural domain is human labor. By 1844, Marx had come to the conclusion that "the whole of world history is nothing but the creation of man *by human labor.*"

Marx specified that the organization of human labor has undergone several dramatic changes in the course of human history. He described the following stages, which, with the exception of so-called Asiatic societies, follow one another sequentially:

1. *Preclass systems:* These are characterized by a minimal division of labor and by the communal ownership of property. The earliest clans or tribes, which generally follow a migratory existence, have this kind of social organization.
2. *Asiatic societies:* These can exist in the same time frame as preclass systems and ancient societies. They have powerful, despotic leaders. Marx suggested that the need for a centralized system of irrigation, as in China, might create the need for "oriental despotism." In such societies, however, local communities tend to be economically self-sufficient. This is the earliest kind of class society.

3. *Ancient societies:* These develop around large cities, such as Athens and Rome. Land becomes private property, and a slave population comes into existence to create wealth for a few. Marx argued that such societies were destroyed by over-population and by their inability to find enough land for the ruling class. In such societies, there is an enormous gap between the rich and the poor, between the haves and the have-nots.
4. *Feudal societies:* These developed in Europe after the collapse of the Roman Empire. The class of serfs work the land for a small aristocracy. According to Marx, the end of feudalism comes about with the rise of cities dedicated to trade and commerce—for example, Venice and Genoa in the thirteenth century.
5. *Capitalist societies:* These contain two major classes: the *bourgeoisie* (property owners) and the *proletariat* (those who are compelled to sell their labor power for wages).

According to Marx, in all types of societies the social regulation of labor is the foundation and basis of the organization of human experience. Trying to compress his model of society, Marx suggested the following in the preface to *A Contribution to the Critique of Political Economy* (1859):

> In the social production of their existence, men inevitably enter into definite relations, which are independent of their will, namely relations of production appropriate to a given stage in the development of their material forces of production. The totality of these relations of production constitutes the economic structure of society, the real foundation, on which arises a legal and political superstructure and to which correspond definite forms of social consciousness. The mode of production of material life conditions the general process of social, political and intellectual life.[12]

According to Marx, the mode of production, or economic base of a society, is made up of productive forces and the social relations of production. Productive forces permit subjects to act on, and to transform, the material world. They are subdivided into (1) labor power, "the mental and physical capabilities" of the human subject to perform useful work; (2) the means of production—for example, tools, machines, water power, steam power, and nuclear power; and (3) the raw materials of production—for example, coal, iron ore, and uranium. The social relations of production are the relations among individuals with respect to the ownership of productive forces. In their legal form, relations of production are *property* relations.

The organization of work in any civilized society (capitalist and precapitalist) involves relations of production that make the labor power of some individuals the property of others. For Marx this relationship is the essence of class exploitation. In slave societies, for instance, the slave owner has exclusive and total ownership of the slave's labor power. In capitalist societies the employer has ownership of the employee's labor power during the hours of employment. Production in general is always a social enterprise; Marx pointed out that individual workers never work in isolation but always as part of an economic system of production and consumption.

It should also be noted that the "economic base" and the "superstructure" of consciousness are only analytically separable. In real life they are interpenetrable. Descriptions of the economic base always involve the description of elements of the superstructure. For instance, the organization of work in society cannot take place without some customs, values, or rules. Marx did not suggest that the economic base had a causal influence on the consciousness of an epoch. He merely wished to imply that in the final analysis, it is the economic base that gives meaning and form to human experience.

A class exists when a grouping of individuals have in common a specific relationship to productive forces. For instance, the bourgeoisie are characterized by their ownership of private property that is used as a means of production. In capitalist society, which is characterized by the private ownership of the means of production and by production for private gain, membership in the dominant class is determined at root not by personal income, not by prestige, not by the power that a person can exercise, but by the fact that an individual has ownership or part ownership of a business out of which private profit can be extracted.

Marx conceded that other classes existed in early capitalist society—for example, the peasantry, the *petite bourgeoisie* (the class of small business owners), and the *Lumpenproletariat* (the class of people without a steady job who lead marginal and often criminal lives "living on the crumbs of society"). Marx insisted, however, that as capitalism matured, the two main and antagonistic classes in society (the bourgeoisie and the proletariat) would increase in size and would displace more traditional and subsidiary classes.

Marx further concluded that what made humans unique was the ability of subjects to "*produce* their means of subsistence" in self-reflective activity. Marx's materialism resulted from his pathbreaking discovery that humans' "species-being" compels them to take responsibility for the way in which subjects objectify themselves—not just in a childlike and imaginary way but in everyday, practical activity. Only humans have the capacity to take responsibility for what they produce, for only humans have the ability to determine creatively the means by which they use their labor to interact with the natural world. Thus in *Capital*, Marx places man at the center of his economics, declaring human labor to be the "manifestation" of a person's power to be "a living conscious thing."

Unlike Hegel, then, Marx did not believe that pure freedom resulted from "mind reflecting upon mind." Furthermore, we are not ghosts in a machine; the human mind can attain freedom and a full understanding of itself only by comprehending its dependence on a real, objective, and constraining natural universe. Marx's materialist philosophy did not assert that there is an indifferent and objective universe "out there" that humans must acknowledge as determining. Rather, Marx turned toward materialism and away from idealism because he believed that human subjects would inevitably reach a false and incomplete understanding of themselves if they believed their consciousness truly to be *self*-determining. Idealism might appear to be a valid epistemology to the privileged few who specialized in speculation and whose material needs were met by others. As Marx pointed out, however, apart from this tiny intellectual elite, the consciousness of the vast majority of human beings is constrained by interaction with a natural world that is not merely an extension of mind.

Marx believed that the development of productive forces was at the root of social progress. He also believed that such development compelled subjects to objectify themselves in radically new forms by transforming their modes of self-understanding. Marx's social ontology (his economic base–superstructure model) is also an epistemology that answers the following questions: Under what conditions will new types of social formation occur? How do radically new modes of self-understanding emerge? Idealism views language as a medium of self-understanding constrained only by the limitations that the human mind or intellect places on *itself*. Marx argued, therefore, that the idealist position posits no impetus for any material change in the world; human beings can simply replace one fanciful interpretation with another. He insisted that an explanation of human progress and the growth of knowledge should point to the central importance of transformations in the forces of production. Humans attain knowledge about the real forces that determine their reflected being not by retreating into themselves, but by overcoming and mastering these forces.

According to Marx, the possibility of human freedom is enhanced by the development of technology. Although such progress makes it possible to meet subsistence needs more easily, the real significance of technology for Marx is that it can increase human self-determination. In a subsistence economy, if humans were to attain a full understanding of their position in the world, they would have no option but to acknowledge the inescapable and miserable conditions of their existence. In societies with sophisticated technology, however, subjects have a real chance to humanize the world. According to Marx, an individual should—and *can*—be the measure of all things:

> If man draws all his knowledge, sensation, etc. from the world of the senses and the experience gained in it, the empirical world must be arranged so that in it man experiences and gets used to what is really human and that he becomes aware of himself as man. If correctly understood interest is the principle of all morals, man's private interest must be made to coincide with the interest of humanity . . . . If man is shaped by his surroundings, his surroundings must be made human.[13]

In a mature capitalist society, productive forces are sophisticated enough for individuals to satisfy material needs and to escape the drudgery and dehumanizing effects of alienated labor. According to Marx, capitalist societies are dehumanizing despite the sophistication of productive forces because the social relations of production prohibit subjects from achieving the freedom and self-determination that the advance in such productive forces has made possible. What freezes the social relations of production in this regressive manner is the persistence of class domination and class exploitation.

In contemporary capitalist society, members of the working-class are compelled to sell their labor power to the employer class in order to attain for themselves the means to their own subsistence. Marx believed that the private ownership of forces of production always entails alienation because it guarantees that workers will lose control over that which makes them fully human: their ability to determine their own freedom by becoming an object for themselves through labor. For Marx, labor should be an end in itself. Work that is done as a means to some other end (for example, an employer's profit) is always alienating.

According to Marx, class domination is secured, above all, by *ideology*. After all, a ruling class, which always includes only a minority of the population, cannot impose its will on a majority unless class domination is seen as natural and proper—or, even better, is not seen at all. In *Capital,* Marx describes how contemporary ideology is structured and fashioned by objectifications that are part and parcel of capitalist social formations. In such societies people tend to see the capitalist economy as natural and as inevitable. They do not see the capitalist regulation of production as a historically limited mode of self-production.

Marx believed that the working-class was the only force capable of bringing about progressive social change in capitalist society. The bourgeoisie had been a revolutionary class in the eighteenth century: By displacing the class of landed gentry, they had fostered and encouraged rapid economic growth. Furthermore, as Marx pointed out, the bourgeoisie as a class had a vested interest in business efficiency and were constantly seeking to improve the utility of their private property—the commercial and industrial forces of production. Marx concluded, however, that by the end of the nineteenth century, the class of businessmen and property owners had outlived their usefulness. To protect themselves, the bourgeoisie were compelled to undermine the efforts of the proletariat to attain a reflective understanding of their revolutionary role. Marx, in fact, believed that the single biggest obstacle placed in the way of progressive social change was the ability of the dominant classes to prevent the proletariat from attaining true "class consciousness."

The "false consciousness" of the majority in capitalist society ensures their willingness to accept and embrace the ideological justification of an unnecessary and outmoded system. This is not to say that capitalist ideology does not *accurately* reflect the real conditions of life in a capitalist society. For instance, people in such societies commonly believe that it is "inevitable" that some people should be laborers and others bosses, or that it is "human nature" for people to make the possession of expensive commodities the prime purpose of their lives. Marx pointed out that what is significant about such beliefs is not so much that they are demonstrably false but that they accurately mirror the real conditions of the economic structure of capitalist production and exchange. To change false ideas, we need to alter the conditions that give rise to them.

Marx held that many of the ideological beliefs that helped support the capitalist system were the distorted expression of the very real sufferings of workers. For instance, religion is "an *expression* of real suffering and a *protest* of real suffering." However, Marx believed that:

> The abolition of religion as the *illusory* happiness of men is a demand for their *real* happiness. The call to abandon their illusions about their condition is a *call to abandon a condition which requires illusions* . . . . Religion is only the illusory sun about which man revolves so long as he does not revolve about himself.[14]

For Marx, as for Hegel, there is an imminent logic to social development. Human subjects will always strive to attain social relations of production that—given the potential of productive forces—permit the maximum amount of freedom and self-determination. Marx believed that because of the liberating potential of the productive forces that capitalism has created, humankind now has the capacity to create a civilized mode of life without class divisions and, hence, without class exploitation. Socialism, or the public ownership of the means of production, is a step toward this goal.

Moreover, according to Marx, communism is but the final stage of humankind's journey toward communal self-determination and real freedom.

The Individual in Society

Marx viewed the human individual as a creative agent striving toward self-fulfillment. He believed that it was not the individual but society that was responsible for unnecessary suffering and for human unhappiness. Society could damage the individual by warping and distorting human aspirations. On the other hand, only society can enable individuals to comprehend the limits and potential of their own humanity. For Marx, "freedom" and "self-determination" could be realized only within the confines of particular and historically variable types of social formation. To be free and to be self-determined is not to separate oneself from human society but to understand how the limits to one's creative life are set by the limits of one's participation in a collective endeavor. Society did not create the individual's need for self-fulfillment. Marx believed that self-fulfillment was a natural human need; but he conceded that society alone determines the possible limits—and defines the content—of human satisfaction.

Marx agreed with Hegel that, directly or indirectly, the self was shaped and fashioned by everything that a society comprised. He also agreed that the idea of the autonomous, self-determining individual is an absurdity. Nevertheless, he held the individual to be less of a derivative category than did Hegel. For instance, Marx viewed communist society as a society of free *individuals*; unlike Hegel, he did not believe the ideal type of social formation to be a form of communal life that perfectly expresses merely the *idea* of freedom. Nevertheless, Marx did treat selfhood as a form of self-consciousness that comes into existence as a result of specific social and economic relationships. According to Marx, "the human essence is no abstraction inherent in each single individual. In its reality it is the ensemble of the social relations."[15]

Marx believed that "human essence," or "species-being," was something that *unites* individuals, not something that resides in each isolated person. To this extent, Marx's assertion in *The Communist Manifesto* that communist society provides associations "in which the free development of each is the condition for the free development of all" is not merely a rhetorical flourish. For Marx, communism is the ideal state for humankind precisely because it abolishes the wholly artificial distinction between societal needs and the needs of the individual. Only a society that gave humankind a distorted picture of its own potential would ever maintain that such a distinction was real, necessary, or desirable.

Marx viewed human history not so much as the result of the impact of "society" on "individuals," but as a continuous struggle for dominance among groups of specific and concrete individuals. Although he believed that human productivity and creativity were necessary for self-actualization, Marx pointed out that "all production is appropriation of nature by the individual within and through a definite form of society."[16] Thus, at the heart of Marx's analysis is a conception of the individual as a being who strives to attain a self-determination and self-understanding that can result only from the participation of all individuals within a particular kind of society: communist society. Such self-determination and self-understanding result from the means of self-expression involved in the mastery of nature. Productive forces should be utilized to satisfy subsistence needs and to provide the creative outlet for human self-expression. When this development occurs, humankind will achieve a full understanding of its own species-being or potential.

Marx did not believe that in contemporary capitalist societies it was possible to understand the real life chances of individuals without referring to highly abstract and objective relations of interdependence. These were often invisible to the individuals whose fate they determined. Marx agreed with Hegel that the rise of bourgeois civil society and the increasing importance of a money economy had encouraged individuals to think of themselves as autonomous and as self-determining. In capitalist society, what unites people is the pervasiveness of market relationships. Ironically, the reliance on an objective and impersonal market system ensures that individuals in modern society will lose *personal* control over their own destiny.

The primary means of social formation for capitalist society is commodity production and exchange. This means that goods and services are produced for sale by means of an open market. Both at the point of production and at the point of consumption, commodities are evaluated in terms of their significance for this market. For instance, if one looks at a particular commodity—say, a bottle of tranquilizers— it would be possible to trace the social relations among people that are brought about by the production and sale of this drug. The worker who is engaged in the mass production of tranquilizers has an association with his boss, with his fellow employees, and with the people to whom tranquilizers are sold. None of these associations, however, derives from a concern or interest in the satisfaction of human need. It might be the case that Mr. X (along with his co-workers) makes tranquilizers for Mrs. Y and that they make her feel better. As Marx pointed out, however, the capitalist system of production and exchange is oblivious to human subjective need *unless such a need can be recast as a commodity need*—that is, as a need that can be satisfied by production and exchange that proves profitable. The mass of social relations that emerge from commodity production and exchange responds only to the market. Thus although commodity production and exchange follow the dictates of an objective and impersonal market system, this system organizes relations among people based on *indifference* to personal qualities. In the preceding example, Mr. X has an association or social relationship with Mrs. Y, but he does not even know of Mrs. Y's existence. Hence it is not surprising that her personal qualities or subjective needs are of no interest to him.

Very little changes when the market brings people face to face. A used car salesman sees a customer as the means to a commission. Unless this salesman goes against the rationale of the market, he will prefer a larger commission to a smaller one. Again, the salesman will consider the subjective need of the customer only if such need can be recast in a commodity form. Thus he might well steer a customer away from a cheaper model and toward a more expensive car loaded with options. Although these options might benefit the consumer, it is the profit motive—not the well-being of the customer—that prompts the salesman to suggest them. What we can learn from this example is that commodities are not produced in the interest of fulfilling subjective need; rather, subjective need—indeed, subjectivity itself—is manipulated to accommodate the requirements of commodity production and profit.

Marx pointed out that the rise of capitalism had destroyed personal relations and replaced ties of personal dependence with relations of mutual indifference. The fact that these relations are abstract and often invisible does not mean that they are unimportant. Workers who lose their jobs because shifting market conditions make their continued employment unprofitable can bear testimony to this fact.

Marx believed that the transformation of social relations in the modern era was greatly accelerated by the all-important function of money in capitalist economic structures. Money has helped to destroy traditional hierarchies of dependence among human subjects. In precapitalist societies, subjects are more inclined to respond to the perceived personal qualities of other subjects, not to the impersonal needs of a system that takes on a life of its own. Of course, these "personal qualities" are implemented and sustained by a system of social relations among individuals. Nevertheless, in precapitalist societies, individuals respond to each other as particular beings with subjective needs, responsibilities, capabilities, and rights. In capitalist society, subjects are encouraged to be indifferent toward each other *as persons* because, as Marx puts it, "personal relations flow purely out of relations of production and exchange." A system of commodity production and exchange encourages people to see each other merely as means to the satisfaction of market needs. Individuals do not even have to recognize each other as human.

According to Marx, the historical emergence of the capitalist mode of production increased people's false perception of themselves as autonomous and as self-determining precisely because it encouraged relations of mutual indifference. Modern individuals correctly view themselves as relatively free from ties of personal dependence, but they falsely believe themselves to be free from abstract and impersonal bonds. Such individuals fail to understand how their life chances are structured by a pattern of social relationships that is predetermined by the needs of the market. Instead, they fall victim to the ideology of bourgeois individualism. Marx pointed out that the logic of consumption in capitalist societies is predicated on the existence of atomized, incomplete individuals who strive to accumulate private property in what they believe to be their own best interests. The personal independence of modern individuals hinges on their ability to own things—including, of course, the right of all individuals to own their "labor power." Hence the real chances of maintaining any kind of control over one's identity in capitalist society depends more than anything else on one's chances of property ownership.

Methodology

Marx fully agreed with Hegel that human reason (*Vernunft*) had to go beyond a description of taken-for-granted reality and grasp how thought itself is produced. His methodology was fundamentally Hegelian, but with one important difference: He believed that the moving force of social change was the struggle for human control over the material world. Marx agreed that men make their own history but pointed out that "they do not make it just as they please." For Marx, history will be made just as men please when technological resources enable individuals to exercise species-being in real, practical activity. When this occurs, individuals will be truly self-determining because they will exercise control over the real world, not just an imaginary one.

Marx's methodology is often referred to as "historical materialism" or "dialectical materialism" (although as we have seen, this terminology was introduced by Engels, not by Marx). Marxism thus is historical as well as materialistic. For instance, Marx believed that modern society could never be comprehended unless the historical forces that produced it were grasped. As the economist Robert L. Heilbroner has noted, the basis of the Marxian critique of the contemporary world is the insight "that the concealed essence of capitalism is its own forgotten past, its long-disappeared history, preserved in disguise within its existing institutions and beliefs."[17]

Marx strongly disagreed with positivism's assumption that the purpose of scientific explanation is to broaden the expanse of human knowledge by constantly making additions and revisions to what is already known. Marx believed that the purpose of analysis was not merely the accumulation of "facts," but was also the elimination of illusion and self-contradiction. Analysis thus is *negative* in that it attempts to kick away the props to self-delusion that support all human ideologies and all forms of false consciousness. Marx often pointed out that rational inquiry would be superfluous if the essence of things coincided directly with appearances. Empiricism takes it for granted that data that come to us in the form of sense impressions reveal the essential ontology of the natural world. Marx rejected this view. He believed that what was most revealing about *all* human explanation was not so much what was said about the world, but what was revealed about those engaged in such human endeavor.

Marx's methodology is fully Hegelian in its view of facts not as isolated and external data points, but as integral parts of some totality. Marx believed that parts of this totality—for example, the subjective world view of particular individuals, particular relations of production between one individual and another, and the like—could not be understood without reference to the whole that gives meaning to them. According to Marx, "the subject, society, must always be envisaged . . . as the pre-condition of analysis." He believed that effective socioanalysis showed how individuals' dependence on abstract mental categories like "value," "property," and "exchange" was related to the concrete activity of such individuals.

Marx claimed that the purpose of thinking is to "assimilate the concrete"—that is, to reproduce real practical activity as an abstract and mental category. Analysis is therefore a constant process of shuttling between very concrete descriptions of what people do and the highly abstract description of some totality in terms of which mundane and individualistic behavior becomes meaningful and is shown to have a fate. This is the general approach that Marx takes in his most analytical work: *Capital.* In the first volume of this work, Marx describes capitalism in its pure and abstract form: as the organization of the relationship between capital and labor. In succeeding volumes, Marx moves away from the description of the "pure essence" of capitalism and toward a more down-to-earth description of the real-life activities of people in modern society, but he never loses sight of the way in which everyday activity becomes meaningful in terms of the abstract and essential properties of the capitalist mode of production. The underlying purpose of Marx's analysis, of course, is not just to link abstract thought to concrete activity; it is to put analysis to work in the interests of critical and emancipatory theory.

Marx completely rejected "methodological individualism," which assumes that the experiences of individuals provide the basic data from which an understanding of abstractions like "society" can be gleaned. Modern survey research, for instance, commonly takes the reported experiences of *individuals* as the fundamental support for sociological conjectures about the world. The problem with this approach is that it often is concrete without ever becoming abstract. Individuals might accurately report that they have had certain experiences, but these individuals have no control over the way in which these experiences become meaningful. For example, Marx pointed out that social life in modern society is structured in its abstract form by the essential characteristics of the commodity relationship. This abstract commodity relationship, however, is not typically part of the reported experiences of contemporary individuals.

Marx believed that the world of human experience is in a continuous state of transformation. He agreed with Hegel that human progress is triggered by the human will to overcome barriers to self-understanding that subjects have erected against themselves. Unlike Hegel, Marx believed that such barriers were set in concrete by the reification of social relations of production made obsolete by the development of new productive forces. Self-conceptions that are the product of outmoded practices can be sustained only by consciousness that gives humankind a false picture of the meaning of what humanity could possibly entail.

It was axiomatic for Marx that human practice is a real application of humankind's theoretical self-understanding. He pointed out that the distinction that so-called practical people like to make between theory and practice is unwarranted. Practical people, who like to make invidious comparisons between "practical" activity and "theoretical" speculation, are generally content to carry out plans and projects not of their own making. Their inability to take responsibility for their actions makes their action appear necessary and, hence, "practical" because they merely adapt to circumstances that they view as given. In reality, such people have lost sight of the unity of practical and theoretical modes of human endeavor; they have relinquished their abilities to analyze and envision human potentiality.

Marx was very clear about the purpose of intellectual activity: It is to abolish theory for theory's sake. He believed that both crude idealism and crude materialism are wrong in presuming that either mind or objective reality could somehow mirror the other in some simple and mechanical fashion. Mind and objective reality determine each other reciprocally. It was Marx's conclusion that, as far as humankind was concerned, it is intellectual and practical activity that permits us to create a world that we can then experience as constraining. In other words, it is this world that brings home to us the truth of what we are.

Other Major Themes and Foci: The Crisis of Capitalism

Marx was convinced that the capitalist mode of production would ultimately self-destruct. In reaching this conclusion, he took into consideration the interrelationship of economic, social, and political phenomena. It is important to note that Marx did not make a prediction about the demise of capitalism merely by extrapolating from economic data. He believed that economic crises were crises of opportunity and danger both for the bourgeoisie and for the proletariat. No one could predict on the basis of some objective calculations exactly how and when capitalism would collapse. In the long term, however, collapse it would.

Marx claimed that as capitalism matures, it becomes more and more unstable. Perhaps the best way of showing this instability is to compare a typical factory of 1900 with one of 2000. In the following examples (which are to be taken as illustrative only), C refers to *constant capital*—that is, money that has to be put into business in order to replace machinery, pay for the upkeep of the physical plant, buy necessary raw materials, pay for utilities, and so on; V refers to *variable capital*—that is, money that goes to meet the company payroll; and S refers to *surplus value*—that is, what bosses extract from workers. In the following examples, we shall assume that the factories have no trouble in selling everything they make.

Factory in 1900
(Labor-intensive)
Costs per annum per worker:
$C = \$150$
$V = \$250$
$S = \$100$
$C + V + S = \$500$

This example assumes that the factory owner has to put $150 a year into the business to cover the production costs for every worker employed, that each worker earns $250 per annum, and that after paying all the costs, the boss is left with gross profits of $100 per worker. If we assume that our factories sell everything they put on the market, and if we know that gross profits = $100, we can calculate sales per annum for each member of the work force in the preceding example as $C + V + S$, which equals $500. In effect, we are saying that each worker, in collaboration with others, pays the costs associated with his or her being able to work, pays his or her own wages, and hands over $100 to the boss at the end of the working year. Money flowing into the business = money flowing out.

Factory in 2000
(Capital-intensive)
Costs per annum per worker:
$C = \$100,000$
$V = \$20,000$
$S = \$10,000$
$C + V + S = \$130,000$

At first sight, the modern factory seems to be doing a lot better than the factory of a hundred years ago. Although wages and constant capital costs have increased dramatically (even when inflation is taken into consideration), absolute profits have increased from $100 per annum per worker to $10,000 per annum per worker.

As Marx pointed out, however, what is crucial for the factory owner (or for the shareholders of a company) is not *absolute* profit but the *rate* of profit. The rate of profit determines the rate on the dollar invested in a business enterprise. Marx defined the rate of profit as p, where $p = S/(C + V)$. Using this formula, we can make the following calculations:

Factory in 1900: $p = \$100/(\$150 + \$250) = \frac{1}{4}$
Factory in 2000: $p = \$10,000/(\$100,000 + \$20,000) = \frac{1}{12}$

What these results mean is that for every $4 invested in our factory of one hundred years ago, $1 would be returned on this principal at the end of the year. For the modern factory, it would take an investment of $12 to return $1 (before taxes). The rate of return for the earlier factory is 25 percent, and the rate of return for the modern factory is 8 ⅓ percent. Clearly, the factory of one hundred years ago provides the better investment opportunity.

Marx predicted, quite accurately, that as capitalism matured, the "organic composition" of capital would change. What he meant was that the costs of constant capital would progressively become more expensive in proportion to the costs of variable capital. As technology becomes more sophisticated, it also becomes more costly. The cost of paying for expensive machine technology increases far more rapidly than do the costs of maintaining workers. Individual factory owners gain by using expensive and sophisticated technology. Although their profit margin will be slimmer than that of their competitors, they can outsell them many times over by cutting prices. This brings down the rate of profit but increases sales. Thus they can more than recoup their losses. What is good for *individual* capitalists, however, is not necessarily good for capitalists taken as a whole. Before long, everyone is forced to buy state-of-the-art technology merely to stay in business. Furthermore, a desperate struggle for customers and for markets gets under way. As prices are cut, and as businesses become more efficient, many unprofitable factories and businesses go under.

In time, however, the capitalist class will act to protect its interests. According to Marx, there are two obvious ways in which it can do this. First, capitalists can avoid destructive competition among themselves through the development of oligopolies and monopolies. When a few capitalists have a monopoly over a commodity, they can engage in price fixing. In this fashion they can pass on the increased costs of doing business to the customer. As long as markets are growing, however, prices can remain steady because what is lost through lower profits can be recovered by increased sales volume.

The second step that the capitalist class can take is to increase the rate of exploitation of their workers. This is achieved through the simple expedient of either cutting wages or raising the cost of living. Marx believed that class exploitation in capitalist society involved the extraction of surplus value. If wages fall *relative to the cost of living*, class exploitation is intensified.

Because Marx accepted the labor theory of value, he assumed that what created value was the labor power of the workers. In assessing the rate of exploitation of the workers, Marx did not take the cost of constant capital into consideration at all. For Marx, the rate of exploitation of the work force was measured by $S/(V+S)$: the amount of value that bosses held back for themselves in proportion to the amount of value produced by the workers' labor power. Marx had no objection to owners taking money from a business to pay constant capital costs. This, of course, is not exploitative in any way.

Marx believed that as capitalism matured and as individual capitalists were compelled to look for new ways to revolutionize productive forces, certain predictable effects would occur. First, there would be a tendency toward the concentration and centralization of capital. Marx was correct in pointing out that the greatest threat to the so-called free-market system was the capitalist class itself and its oligopolistic tendencies. Second, there would be increasing pressure on the capitalist class to increase the rate of exploitation in order to maintain an acceptable rate of profit. What would really accelerate this latter tendency, however, would be *overproduction*. This occurs when capitalists who have put their money into businesses cannot get a reasonable rate of return on it because factories and businesses cannot sell all that they produce. With a lower turnover, slimmer profits become less acceptable. Worst of all, prices have to be cut to dump goods, and the rate of profit slumps.

For Marx, the fundamental contradiction of capitalism was dislocation between productive forces and the social relations of production. Capitalists upgrade productive forces in their own selfish interests. As we have seen, however, this process changes the organic composition of capital and leads to reduced profits. This development triggers organization among capitalists (that is, oligopoly) and a tendency to hold down wages. An increase in the rate of exploitation, however, increases the likelihood of class consciousness among the proletariat—especially when the working-class realizes the contradiction between the improvement of productive forces and the relative decline in their share of socially produced wealth. As capitalists saturate markets with their goods, overproduction occurs. This increases the need to reduce the living standards of wage earners by reducing wages. The conditions for a vicious circle are created. Seventy or 80 percent of the population is working-class; if they buy less, the business class will be in an even worse position. If the disposable income of workers is reduced, it becomes even more difficult for capitalists to move what their factories and businesses produce.

According to Marx, business recessions are caused by cycles of overproduction that can be corrected only by heightened class oppression. What Marx did not foresee was the massive involvement of the bourgeois state in the capitalist economy. For the last half-century, most capitalist societies have artificially manipulated the demand for goods and services by using public money to buy commodities when a severe recession or a depression threatens. In the United States, since the New Deal policies of the 1930s, the involvement of the government in artificially stimulating demand and in regulating production has been enormous. To a large extent, the state has been successful in masking the effects of class oppression. Although real wages have risen in capitalist societies over the last one hundred years, the *rate* of exploitation—as Marx would have defined it—has not declined. Many advanced capitalist societies successfully have exported expropriation by owning and controlling labor in foreign countries. Capitalism in 2000 is obviously quite different from the capitalism of the 1900s. If one accepts Marx's model of class exploitation under capitalism, however, it is difficult not to conclude that the contradictions and crises of mature capitalism are every bit as extreme and as dangerous as those that Marx documented.

One final point should be made. Although it is integral to the Marxist model of exploitation, the labor theory of value is only tangentially related to the Marxist explanation of economic crisis. The crisis of capitalism is created *objectively* by the change in the ratio of constant to variable capital: the organic composition of capital. A subjective understanding of the exploitative nature of productive relations under capitalism will lead to heightened class consciousness on the part of the proletariat. This *subjective* movement toward the overthrow of the capitalist system, however, is likely to occur only when the objective features of the system have become contradictory and untenable.

SIGNIFICANCE

Vision of the Future

Marx was convinced that the inherent contradictions of the capitalist mode of production would be manifested in a series of worsening crises. Capitalist society would be replaced by socialism, which would pave the way for communism. Answers to the following questions, then, are crucial in determining Marx's view of the future: (1) Under what conditions does the transition from capitalism to socialism occur? (2) What exactly is communist society, and what are the conditions for its emergence?

In *The Communist Manifesto* of 1848, Marx suggests that the demise of capitalism is imminent. Again, in 1871, Marx was prepared to believe that the initial success of the Paris Commune would trigger a revolutionary movement that would engulf all Europe. Marx, of course, believed that the development of the forces of production was the most important objective factor in the development of a revolutionary consciousness among workers. Consequently, he expected revolutionary movements to occur first of all in the most advanced capitalist countries—England, the United States, Germany, and France. Toward the end of his life, however, Marx came to realize that revolutions could not easily be predicted by reference to a few simple and objective factors. He even conceded that a revolution in economically backward Russia might occur before a communist revolution in his own country, Germany.

Marx did acknowledge that the dominant classes in advanced capitalist society could stave off class revolutions almost indefinitely. The economic and political resources of such societies could be used to this end as part of the necessary overhead of doing business. Thus the capitalist class could buy time by raising wages if possible and by offering some kickbacks from the system to privileged elements among the working-class.

Before his death, Marx was fully aware that capitalism had become an international system of exploitation. If class oppression in one country was economically desirable but politically dangerous, it could be exported. Today, for instance, Western societies displace poverty and misery by using their capital to pay subsistence wages not to their own citizens but to foreign "guest workers" or to workers overseas. In foreign-owned factories and businesses in Asia and Latin America, working conditions can be found that are as bad as anything Victorian society had to offer.

Marx did concede that in some advanced societies communism could come about through peaceful means, not as the result of a bloody and protracted revolution. In his address to the International in 1872, Marx suggested that working-class representatives had *some* chance of attaining political power in those societies that permitted parliamentary democracy. Marx cited Britain, Holland, and the United States as examples.

After Marx's death, there were sharp disagreements among Marxists with diverging ideas about the relative importance and appropriateness of revolutionary violence. Under the leadership of Karl Kautsky (1854–1938), who had been Engels's private secretary, the German SPD was pledged to parliamentary democracy. On the other hand, the Bolsheviks in Russia, under V. I. Lenin (1870–1924), were committed to the use of revolutionary violence as the means to destroy the old order and to protect and safeguard the gains of any successful revolution.

Marx did not believe that socialism would bring an end to inequality or to the existence of necessary toil. As we have seen, socialism eliminates the *private* appropriation of socially produced wealth. In a socialist society, the means of production are owned collectively: Production is for general use, not for private profit. Marx believed that socialism would ensure that *surplus labor* (labor over and above what is required for the mere satisfaction of the material necessities of physical subsistence) would be used for the public good rather than for private gain. One consequence of this is the elimination of unnecessary commodities; another is the enhanced utilization of labor power for the satisfaction of human need. A socialist society will treat obvious human necessities like health, education, food, and housing accommodation as human, not commodity, needs.

At the end of the twentieth century, capitalist societies have made many concessions to the socialist ideal of production and consumption. In several Western societies, reformist socialist governments have successfully implemented many socialist programs. For instance, in Britain, as a result of socialist policy, health care is available on the basis of need. Hence the relationship between doctor and patient is not a *commodity* relationship.

Marx was correct in arguing that industrial societies would move toward socialism as they developed economically. In most Western societies, however, this movement has been a slow drift rather than a process of sudden change. In the United States and in Europe today, some attempt is being made to reverse this trend and to reinforce and to widen *market* relations. Whether this effort will heighten class conflict and class consciousness (as Marxists would predict) or will show the continuing vitality of the capitalist system remains to be seen.

Marx's conception of *communism* and of the transition from socialism to communism is more complex and more uncertainly put forward than his view of the transition from capitalism to socialism. Marx suggested that communism is only possible as the act of the dominant people all at once and simultaneously. In Marx's mature work—specifically, in *Capital*—there is a very convincing argument that the revolutionary transformation of the forces of production under capitalism will lead, inevitably, to socialism. However, as we have noted previously, Marx's faith that humankind will prefer communism to socialism is based not on an extrapolation from economic trends but on his belief that people will come to choose a society based on distributive justice.[18]

Whatever else it might be, communism is most certainly the dissolution of an *organized* division of labor. According to Marx, in communist society "nobody has one exclusive sphere of activity." Nevertheless, "society regulates the social production." The work force in a communist society will move from one supervisory position to another, no socially regulated task in communist society will require specialized knowledge or specialized labor, and no occupational task will be the province of any one person. It is important to note that communist society will not eliminate the need for the social regulation of production. What makes communist society a real possibility is *technology*. Communism cannot exist until the forces of production are advanced enough that an organized division of labor is no longer necessary. According to Marx, in the future the working week will be no longer than, say, one day of socially regulated labor in the week.

Under communism, the general regulation of social production would involve moral rather than technical decision making. Ultimately, communism rests on the will to realize justice, not on the inexorability of a specific form of social development. Thus, as the Yugoslavian communist Gajo Petrović claimed, communism is "not simply a new socioeconomic formation, it is the abolishment of the primacy of the economic criteria in distinguishing human communities."[19] This is not a denial of the paradigm of historical materialism. Petrović suggested that a type of social formation might possibly exist in which the "economic base" permits moral forms of argumentation to regulate freely and transparently the participation of humans in socially necessary production. As Herbert Marcuse pointed out, what Marxism indicates is that "the truth of the materialist thesis is thus to be fulfilled in its negation."[20]

"Communism," therefore, must be sharply distinguished from "socialism" as well as from capitalism. Both capitalist and socialist societies make the social regulation of production the basis for a reproduction of real life. In a communist society, people would engage in highly individualized forms of self-expression, and "economic criteria" would be displaced by the real ability of subjects to put moral argumentation above claims to technical expedience.

Contemporary Relevance

The contemporary relevance of Marxism is well known. In the twentieth century, countless revolutionaries, workers, and intellectuals have concurred with Jean-Paul Sartre's assessment that Marxism is the necessary philosophy of our time. Both as a political philosophy and as a theory of revolutionary change, Marxist theory sought to change the world.

Marx expected his ideas to have both an intellectual and a political impact. Only a few years ago, nearly half of the population of the globe lived in societies that at least claimed to be "Marxist" in some fashion. Like Christianity in the fourth century, Marxism was able to establish itself as a political system both by claiming that it was universalistic and by adapting itself to different traditions and cultures. But the "Marxism" of Stalin was not the same as that of Tito, the leader of what used to be the federal republic of Yugoslavia. Similarly, the leftists of the British Labour Party did not see the world in exactly the same way as did Red Guards in Beijing.

The extent to which "Marxist" regimes, like the Soviet Union or the People's Republic of China, subverted Marx's social philosophy and concealed politics as usual behind a rhetoric of emancipation is a much-written-about and an extremely important topic. However, it always was dangerous to think of the old "Soviet-bloc" countries as the product of Marxist theory, while believing that Marxism was not influential in North America or Western Europe. In many ways, tradition was always more significant in "socialist" countries like Russia and China than it ever was in capitalist societies like the United States. It would not be hard to argue that Marxism was a much more potent intellectual force in Western Europe than it was in Eastern Europe during the twentieth century.

It would be a serious error to conclude that Marx's importance as a social theorist ended with the demise of the Soviet Union and with the abandonment of the socialist model in the People's Republic of China. In fact, the total collapse of the Communist Party of the Soviet Union (CPSU) in 1989, together with affiliated regimes in Eastern Europe, could well lead to a revitalization of applied Marxism. Many Marxists always believed that they had some kind of obligation to defend Lenin's revolution, in spite of the obvious defects of Stalin's and Brezhnev's regimes. Now, Marxists are relieved of this obligation. Rather than having to defend "the first workers' state," they can study what happens as this state is made a peripheral part of the world system of capitalism.

Of course, Marx's complicity in the political failure of the Leninists merits examination. Through his association with the Communist League and with the International, Marx was integrally involved with working-class organizations for much of his life. After the counterrevolutions of 1848 and 1849, Marx and Engels drafted a "Letter of the Central Committee to the Communist League" in March 1850. This communication was sent to the remnants of the league's membership in Germany. The letter endorsed the following revolutionary strategy:

1. The members of the league should subject themselves to strict and centralized control.
2. They should agitate against parliamentary regimes and should seek to embarrass such regimes.
3. They should anticipate an aggressive response from ruling groups, which would, however, provide an opportunity for the party organization to help mobilize working-class resistance.
4. They should seize control of the state and rule by force until the victory of the proletariat was secure.

The Bolshevik Party used this strategy in 1917, and Lenin used Marx's document of 1850 to justify a nondemocratic "dictatorship of the proletariat" in the years following the October Revolution. Thus, it would be difficult to argue that the strategy adopted by Lenin in the 1917 insurrection would have met with Marx's disapproval. However, it would be just as difficult to argue that all of the policies implemented by the CPSU could have been justified in terms of Marx's own writings.

Marx believed that a communist party organization should lead and guide the working-classes. When the party is an underground organization, it cannot, of course, be fully democratic. Similarly, in the short term, when socialism itself is under attack, the party organization might have to make policy decisions without consulting the people whose interests it represents. Nevertheless, Marx believed that in the long run, the party organization must be the means of political expression for all workers in a socialist state. Socialism itself must be seen as a morally superior form of social and economic organization. If this view is not accepted, the failure is a clear indictment of the policies of a self-proclaimed socialist regime. Above all else, Marx believed that real socialism would be established on the basis of economic development only, not on the basis of political coercion.

Marx was unable to give his followers a timetable that would specify the amount of time that could reasonably be expected to pass before a communist party organization could do away with the need for revolutionary violence and the need to liquidate dissident elements within the state. This is only to be expected, for the strength of counterrevolutionary opposition cannot be predicted in advance. Marx was very ambivalent about the role of terror during and after a political revolution. He realized that violence was often necessary in order to bring about change (and, more often, in order to protect workers against the violence directed against them). In 1871, Marx blamed the Paris Communards for not being willing to start a civil war and for not pushing home their insurrection more aggressively. On the other hand, Marx was never in favor of revolutionary terror for terror's sake; he believed this was a sign of political immaturity and of impotence.

In 1844, Marx suggested that the need for a political state that was forced to implement policy over the heads of ordinary individuals would quickly be eliminated after the success of a socialist revolution. In his 1875 critique of the Gotha Program of the German SPD, Marx conceded that only in the "higher phase" of communist society would the organization of a division of labor and the need for state control disappear. Marx saw the socialist state as a political means of organization that would prepare the way for communism. He never believed that the political state was anything other than an instrument of violence that inevitably would serve the interests of the dominant class. Hence the state would have no role to play in a communist society. In a communist society, the needs of the *individual* would be paramount.

At the end of the nineteenth century, Marx was generally believed to be the most important revolutionary theorist of his day. In the decades following his death, his work was cited, discussed, and criticized as much as—if not more than—any other social theorist's. Marx's reputation (as well as his notoriety) has grown in the second half of the twentieth century. Some of Marx's early work was not published until the 1930s; other manuscripts of his were not translated into English until the 1970s. These writings have given us new insights into Marx's world view. Many scholars have concluded that the analytical work of Marx's mature years cannot properly be understood unless this work is seen as the fruition and culmination of a project that Marx described in largely philosophical terms during the 1840s.

Perhaps the most important and vital school of neo-Marxism in this century has been the so-called Frankfurt School of critical theorists, named because of their association with the *Institut für Sozialforschung* (Institute for Social Research) in Frankfurt in the 1920s and 1930s. The institute was shut down during World War II but was reorganized in 1949. The most prominent members of the institute were Max Horkheimer (1895–1973), Theodor Adorno (1903–1969), Erich Fromm (1900–1980), Franz Neumann (1900–1954), and Herbert Marcuse (1898–1979). In one way or another, these theorists all investigated the cultural contradictions of capitalism. Horkheimer wrote a scathing critique of the role of positivism in the contemporary world; among other subjects, Adorno analyzed authoritarianism in bourgeois society; Fromm investigated the fate of the individual in capitalist societies; Neumann wrote a neo-Marxist critique of German fascism; and Marcuse produced highly influential works on Hegel and Freud. Today, a second generation of theorists associated with the Institut für Sozialforschung is active in Germany and in the United States. The most visible is probably Jürgen Habermas (b. 1929).[21]

Since the early 1960s, more than five hundred serious, well-researched books have been published on Marxist theory in the United States. Before the 1960s, Marx was treated in a cursory fashion by most U.S. sociologists. Until a few years ago, for instance, it was quite common for Americans with doctorates in sociology, economics, and political science to be almost completely ignorant of Marx. All this now has changed. In the 1950s, few U.S. sociologists believed that much could be learned about society from the study of Marx. As Marx would have expected, this attitude was laid to rest not so much as the result of a change of heart among intellectuals, but because of events in the world that could no longer be ignored or wished away.

Unfortunately, there is still a great deal of confusion in the West about what Marx actually said. For instance, Marx is often seen as someone who advocated revolution as the means to a "totalitarian" society that would absorb individuals and deny them any rights or freedoms. As we have seen, this is almost a complete reversal of the truth. Again, it is often claimed that Marx unfairly denigrated the "free-market system." In fact, Marx had the greatest respect for what capitalism had achieved. He was one of the few modern theorists to understand how progressive and how advantageous the capitalist mode of production had been in the eighteenth and nineteenth centuries.

Today, of course, the world is a lot different than it was during Marx's and Engels's lifetimes. But, in many ways, the power of capital is more globalized and less restrained than ever. As the twenty-first century begins, what used to be the Union of Soviet Socialist Republics is carved up among warring tribal chieftains, Russian Mafiosi, and Western corporate interests. Meanwhile, the People's Republic of China celebrates its fiftieth anniversary by urging its laborers to strive even harder to generate export earnings that, by the end of 1999, equaled about $3 billion a month (U.S. currency) from the United States alone. Still, during that year, the 1.25 billion people in China had a collective income that was less than that of the combined income of the richest 400 people in America.

At the dawn of a new millennium, capitalism is still revolutionizing the forces of production, still ripping up and renewing the social relations of production. Those outside the global capitalist system (much of the population of the Third World) comprise the new, surplus, and increasingly desperate work force. Those at the cutting edge of change (e.g., ex-peasants drafted in to man the New Economic Zones developed by foreign capitalists and Communist Party officials in China) find that their environment has changed in ways they never could have imagined. Meanwhile, the gap between the rich and the poor in the United States and in the world as a whole increases. One and a quarter billion people today survive on less than $30 a month. None of this would have surprised Marx.

NOTES

1. Noted by Paul Lafargue, "Reminiscences of Marx," in Friedrich Engels et al., *Marx and Engels through the eyes of their contemporaries*, p. 32.

2. "The burial of Karl Marx," *Der Sozialdemokrat*, March 22, 1883.

3. Friedrich Engels, *The condition of the working-class in England*, p. 13.

4. Ibid.

5. *Marx and Engels: Basic writings on politics and philosophy*, pp. 389, 390.

6. *The German ideology*, p. 47.

7. Ibid., p. 120.

8. *The Communist Manifesto*, p. 62.

9. Terrell Carver, *Marx and Engels: The intellectual relationship*, p. 48.

10. The three major laws of Engels's theory of dialectics are as follows:

(1) *The law of the transformation of quantity into quality and vice versa.*

According to this principle, in nature and in society quantitative changes (e.g., the rising temperature of water) will ultimately give rise to sudden qualitative changes (e.g., water turning into steam).

(2) *The law of the unity and struggle of opposites.*

This law states that the relation between apparent opposites is always, in fact, interpenetrative. There is always a "unity of opposites" which is manifested through struggle. For instance, capitalists cannot exist without workers, and workers cannot exist without capitalists. The existence of each defines the other.

(3) *The law of the negation of the negation.*

This idea is developed from Hegelianism and describes how change occurs. A movement from a lower to a higher stage always involves the integration of and surpassing in the new stage of what was applicable or valid during the old state of affairs. For example, socialism does not destroy the progressive aspects of capitalism, like enhanced productivity. All that is worth preserving in capitalism is carried forward into the new stage: socialism.

11. Carver, *Marx and Engels*, p. 145.

12. *A contribution to the critique of political economy*, pp. 20–21.

13. *The holy family*, quoted in David McLellan, *The thought of Karl Marx: An introduction*, p. 127.

14. *Contribution to the critique of Hegel's philosophy of right*, in *Karl Marx: Early writings*, p. 44.

15. *The German ideology*, p. 122.

16. *Grundrisse: Foundations of the critique of political economy*, p. 21.

17. Robert L. Heilbroner, *Marxism: For and against*, p. 61.

18. For a good discussion on this topic, see Stanley Moore, *Marx on the choice between socialism and communism.*

19. Gajo Petrović, "Philosophy and politics in socialism," in Gerson S. Sher (Ed. & Trans.), *Marxist humanism and praxis*, p. 14.

20. Herbert Marcuse, *Reason and revolution* (Boston: Beacon Press, 1969), p. 273.

21. Books by members of the Frankfurt School include the following: Max Horkheimer, *Critique of instrumental reason* (New York: Seabury Press, 1974); *Eclipse of reason* (New York: Seabury Press, 1974); Theodor Adorno, *Negative dialectics* (New York: Seabury Press, 1973); *The authoritarian personality* (New York: Norton, 1969); *Philosophie der neuen Musik* (Frankfurt: Suhrkamp, 1973); Erich Fromm, *Escape from freedom* (New York: Holt, Rinehart and Winston, 1941); Franz Neumann, *Behometh: The structure and practice of National Socialism* (New York: Oxford University Press, 1944); Herbert Marcuse, *Reason and revolution; Eros and civilization: A philosophical inquiry into Freud* (Boston: Beacon Press, 1974); *Soviet Marxism: A critical analysis* (New York: Columbia University Press, 1958). Jürgen Habermas's books include *Knowledge and human interests* (Boston: Beacon Press, 1971); *Theory and practice* (Boston: Beacon Press, 1973); and *Legitimation crisis* (Boston: Beacon Press, 1975).

GLOSSARY

Alienation: The experience of part of oneself as alien. For Marx, the experience of oneself as alien and mechanical in the process of labor.

Bourgeoisie: The *class* of merchants, bankers, and businessmen.

Bourgeois individualism: The illusion commonplace in societies where *commodity* production and exchange prevail that the individual can be a self-contained, self-directing entity.

Civil society: The real social and economic relations among subjects. Especially pronounced in liberal, bourgeois society. The rights of egoistic, atomized individuals are held to be absolute.

Class: A group of people who have in common a specific relation to the *means of production.*

Class consciousness: The sense of common identification of members of a *class.*

Commodity: Something with exchange value—that is, something that can be bought and sold.

Communism: A world order that requires high-level technology, production for human use only, and the elimination of all forms of class exploitation.

Concentration and centralization of capital: The development of *monopolies* and *oligopolies* and the centralization of credit facilities in a few large banks.

Constant capital costs: The production costs of a business—that is, money spent on machinery, the physical plant, and so on.

Dialectical materialism: See *Historical materialism.*

Dictatorship of the proletariat: The period immediately following a socialist revolution when the *proletariat* consolidate and maintain their hold on power by force.

Economic base: See *Mode of production.*

False consciousness: The inability to see clearly where one's class interests lie; hence, the inability to experience *class consciousness.*

Historical materialism: An epistemology that explains social change and human consciousness in terms of underlying changes in the *mode of production.*

Idealism: Doctrine that states that reality consists of mental elements alone—for example, ideas, beliefs, mind, spirit, and so forth.

Ideology: Conservative ideology, by accurately reflecting conditions in the real world, serves to legitimate the status quo. Revolutionary ideology anticipates a different, but possible, world.

Labor power: The ability of workers to use muscle and brain to transform their environments.

Labor theory of value: A theoretical treatment of "value" that treats the amount of value a *commodity* has as equivalent to the average amount of labor time necessary for its production.

Lumpenproletariat: Class of people without steady employment—for example, petty criminals and the permanently unemployed.

Materialist philosophy: View of humankind's relationship with the universe that stresses the primacy of the material world in shaping and giving substance to human thought and consciousness.

Means of production: A subcategory of *productive forces*—for example, the tools and machines associated with production.

Methodological individualism: A mode of inquiry that tries to explain social life by concentrating on the experiences and activities of individuals.

Mode of production: *Productive forces* plus the *relations of production.*

Monopoly: The production and distribution of one or several commodities by just one company or business.

Objectification: The process whereby humans make themselves an object to themselves and for others.

Oligopoly: The production and distribution of one or several commodities by just a few companies or businesses.

Organic composition of capital: The ratio of *constant capital costs* to *variable capital costs.*

Petite bourgeoisie: Class of small business peo-ple—for example, shop owners.

Productive forces: These enable humans to act on the material world in order to transform it. They comprise (1) *labor power*; (2) the *means of production*; and (3) the raw materials of produc-tion.

Proletariat: The class of workers who earn their living by exchanging their *labor power* for a wage.

Relations of production: Property relations. Relations among individuals with respect to their ownership of *productive forces*.

Socialism: The public ownership and control of the *means of production*.

Species-being: Our human essence. For Marx, our ability to put ourselves into our work.

Superstructure: The structure of human con-sciousness.

Surplus value: Value created for the boss by workers during the working day after they have produced enough for sale on the market to cover their own wages and the *constant capital costs* as-sociated with their being able to work.

Utopian socialism: Socialism that exists in the minds of political idealists but could not exist in reality.

Variable capital costs: The costs of paying the wages of the work force.

ANNOTATED BIBLIOGRAPHY

Primary Sources

Capital (3 vols.; S. Moore & E. Aveling, Trans.). New York: International Publishers, 1967 [1867, 1885, & 1894].

Marx's most important work. Contains his analysis of the nature and fate of the capital-ist mode of production.

The civil war in France. In *Karl Marx and Frederick Engels: Selected works* (Vol. 2; pp. 202–244). Moscow: Progress Publishers, 1969 [1871].

Marx's address to the General Council of the International Working Men's Association on the failure of the Paris Commune. Marx ar-gues that the proletariat should destroy the bourgeois state, not try to take it over.

The communist manifesto. New York: Washington Square Press, 1964 [1848] (paper). (With Engels.)

Better known than anything else Marx ever wrote. A call to revolution: "The proletarians have nothing to lose but their chains. They have a world to win."

A contribution to the critique of political economy (S. W. Ryazanskaya, Trans.; Maurice Dobb, Ed.). Moscow: Progress Publishers, 1970 [1859].

The preface contains Marx's best summary of the general principles of his sociology.

Critique of the Gotha program. Moscow: Progress Publishers, 1971 [1875] (paper).

Marx's criticism of the program of the Ger-man Social Democrats. The strategy of socialist revolution is discussed. Marx distin-guishes for the first time between a "lower" and a "higher" stage of communist society.

Critique of Hegel's philosophy of right (J. O'Malley, Trans.). Cambridge: Cambridge University Press, 1970 [1843] (paper).

Marx's earliest attempts to develop an ap-proach to society based on the methodology of historical materialism. Illustrates how much Marx was influenced by Hegel in his early years.

The economic and philosophic manuscripts of 1844 (Martin Milligan, Trans.; Dirk J. Struik, Ed.). New York: International Publishers, 1977 [1844–1845] (paper).

Not published until 1932. These early pieces of Marx's are strongly Hegelian in style. The manuscripts show the earliest development of Marxian economics.

The German ideology (C. J. Arthur, Ed.). New York: International Publishers, 1972 [1845–1846] (paper). (With Engels.)

Contains Marx's famous "Theses on Feuer-bach," in which he criticizes Feuerbach's passive materialism. Also contains his attacks on fellow radicals.

Grundrisse: Foundations of the critique of political economy (M. Nicolaus, Trans.). New York: Vintage Books, 1973 [1857–1858].

This manuscript was not translated into English until 1971. Shows Marx's early development of his economic theories.

Karl Marx: Early writings (Tom Bottomore, Trans. & Ed.). New York: McGraw-Hill, 1964 (paper).

A short anthology of Marx's earliest works.

Karl Marx and Frederick Engels: Selected works in three volumes. Prepared by the Institute of Marxism-Leninism under the Central Committee of the CPSU. Moscow: Progress Publishers, 1969.

Contains some of Marx's most important work. The authoritative collection of Marx's and Engels's work is generally held to be *Marx-Engels Werke*, also prepared by the Institute of Marxism-Leninism in Moscow.

Marx and Engels: Basic writings on politics and philosophy (Lewis S. Feuer, Ed.). New York: Anchor Books, 1959 (paper).

One of the best of several paperback anthologies available.

Marx and Engels on economics, politics and society: Essential reading with editorial commentary (John E. Elliott, Ed.). Santa Monica, CA: Goodyear, 1981 (paper).

An excellent anthology. Marx's most important statements are organized by topic. A good reference book.

Marx, Engels: On literature and art. Moscow: Progress Publishers, 1978.

Marx had a great interest in literature. He often used examples from classical works to illustrate his arguments.

Marx, Engels, Lenin: On communist society. Moscow: Progress Publishers, 1975 (paper).

A collection of pieces by these three men that illustrate their views on communism.

Marx, Engels, Lenin: On dialectical materialism. Moscow: Progress Publishers, 1977.

Useful anthology of writings on the methodological approach of Marxist inquiry.

The poverty of philosophy. Moscow: Progress Publishers, 1973.

Marx's attack on the French radical and economist Pierre Joseph Proudhon.

The portable Karl Marx (Viking Portable Library) (Eugene Kamenka, (Ed.). New York: Viking Press, 1983.

A handy and inexpensive collection of some of Marx's more important writings.

Secondary Sources

Anderson, Perry. *In the tracks of historical materialism.* London: Verso, 1983 (paper).

Anderson discusses Marxism's rise in influence in Anglo-American societies since the mid-1970s and its decline in France and Italy during this same period. The priorities for Marxism at the end of the twentieth century are reviewed.

Aronson, Ronald. *After Marxism.* New York: The Guilford Press, 1995 (paper).

A work of "mourning," written by an Old Leftist. According to Aronson, "the Left" fell into "a profound state of denial" after the fall of the Soviet Union and the breaching of the Berlin wall. "The great world-historical project of struggle and transformation identified with the name of Karl Marx seems to have ended. And, as the postmodernists know, an entire world view has crashed along with Marxism."

Avineri, Shlomo. *The social and political thought of Karl Marx.* Cambridge: Cambridge University Press, 1976 [1968] (paper).

Avineri stresses the significance of Hegel's influence on Marx.

Berman, Marshall. *Adventures in Marxism.* London: Verso, 1999 (paper).

Acknowledging the 150-year anniversary of *The Communist Manifesto*, this book emphasizes that Marx still has a great deal to say about the global economy today. Berman, a scholar with a lifelong interest in Marxist theory, cites from sources as unexpected as *The New York Times* and *The New Yorker* to show

how contemporary Marx can be. Highly recommended.

Blumenberg, Werner, Douglas Scott (Trans.) & Gareth Stedman Jones. *Karl Marx: An illustrated biography.* London: Verso, 1998.

Translated from the German. Werner Blumenberg was a leading Marxist scholar in Germany who died in 1964. This biography more than rivals Padover's.

Carver, Terrell. *Marx and Engels: The intellectual relationship.* Bloomington: Indiana University Press, 1983.

Carver shows how Engels's later works, *Anti-Dühring* and the *Dialectics of Nature,* depart radically from Marx's own position. This book carefully differentiates between Marx's and Engels's contribution to Marxism. Carver concludes that Engels contributed little to Marxist theory after 1844.

Carver, Terrell. *A Marx dictionary.* Totowa, NJ: Barnes & Noble, 1987.

A useful book for the student, Marx's most important concepts and terms are defined in context.

Carver, Terrell. *The postmodern Marx.* State College, Pennsylvania: Pennsylvania State University Press, 1999 (paper).

Carver tries to reevaluate Marx in a post-Soviet era and show how Marx is one theorist, at least, who can help us understand our postmodern world.

Eagleton, Terry. *Marx (The Great Philosopher Series).* London: Verso, 1998. London, Routledge, 1999 (paper).

A short (64 pp.) introduction to Marx, written by one of the foremost Marx scholars in Britain.

Elster, Jon. *An introduction to Karl Marx.* Cambridge: University of Cambridge Press, 1986 (paper).

This is a much shorter version of Elster's lengthy *Making Sense of Marx* (Cambridge University Press, 1985). Elster tries to sort out what is dead and what is still alive in Marxism. Still vital, according to Elster, are the dialectical method, the theory of alienation, class struggle, and exploitation. Scientific socialism, the falling rate of profit, the unity of theory, and practice in a revolutionary struggle are rejected as moribund.

Engels, Friedrich. *The condition of the working-class in England.* Moscow: Progress Publishers, 1973 [1844].

This book influenced Marx greatly.

Fischer, Ernst, Franz Marek, Anna Bostock, & John Bellamy Foster. *How to Read Karl Marx.* New York: Monthly Review Press, 1997 (paper).

Includes a chronology of Marx's life, selections from some of Marx's more important works, and "Marx's Method," an introductory essay by Paul M. Sweezy, one of the most influential neo-Marxist economists in the United States.

Graham, Keith. *Karl Marx: Our contemporary social theory for a post-Leninist world.* Toronto: University of Toronto Press, 1992.

Graham presents an interpretation of Marx that is far removed from the endorsement of a Leninist position. He concludes, "The failure of Eastern Europe can be read as a vindication of Marx's argument just as easily as a refutation." (Read the book to find out why.)

Heilbroner, Robert L. *Marxism: For and against.* New York: W. W. Norton, 1980 (paper).

An excellent introduction to Marx's thought. Deals lucidly with central theoretical issues.

Howard, Dick. *The Marxian legacy* (2nd ed.). Minneapolis: University of Minnesota Press, 1988 (paper).

This is a difficult book for the undergraduate. However, it contains a particularly strong discussion of a neo-Marxian phenomenological school consisting of Maurice Merleau-Ponty, Claude Lefort, and Cornelius Castoriadis.

Jordan, Z. A. *The evolution of dialectical materialism: A philosophical and sociological analysis.* New York: St. Martin's Press, 1977.

A comprehensive study of the philosophy of dialectical materialism. Jordan argues that dialectical materialism has never been a single, continuous, or uniform doctrine. He suggests that Marxism is not a coherent body of thought but "a wide and vaguely circumscribed collection of views, often incompatible with each other."

Kolakowski, Leszek. *Main currents of Marxism: Its rise, growth, and dissolution* (3 vols.; P. S. Falla, Trans.). Oxford: Clarendon Press, 1978 (paper).

A history of Marxism tracing its development from its roots in the ancient world to its place in Eastern Europe after World War II. Kolakowski believes Marxism was "the greatest fantasy of our century . . . a dream offering the prospect of a society of perfect unity in which all human aspirations would be fulfilled and all values reconciled."

Lefebvre, Henri. *The sociology of Marx.* New York: Vintage, 1969 [1966] (paper).

This book has become a classical introduction to Marxist sociology. Written by one of the most eminent social scientists in France, it shows that Marx's ideas were receiving a sympathetic reading on the European continent while they were still largely ignored by U.S. sociologists.

McLellan, David. *Karl Marx: His life and thought.* New York: Harper Books, 1977 (paper).

An excellent description of Marx's life and times.

McLellan, David. *The thought of Karl Marx: An introduction.* New York: Harper Torchbooks, 1971 (paper).

A commentary on some of the most important topics addressed by Marx (alienation, class, revolution). Contains extracts from Marx's own writings. A good book to read first.

McLellan, David (Ed.). *Marxism after Marx.* Boston: Houghton Mifflin, 1979 (paper).

A compendium of essays on the fate of Marxism after Marx's death. McLellan discusses the writings of SPD theorists, Leninism, Trotskyism, the works of the Italian communist Antonio Gramsci, the Frankfurt School, Marxism in the United States, and Maoism, among other topics.

Moore, Stanley. *Marx versus markets.* University Park: Pennsylvania State University Press, 1993.

Moore examines Marx's claim that classless societies with markets are inferior to communist societies. He concludes that Marx's ideal of a communist economy is incompatible with his materialist approach to history.

Nelson, Cary, & Grossberg, Lawrence (Eds.). *Marxism and the interpretation of culture.* Urbana: University of Illinois Press, 1988.

An excellent compendium of papers discussing Marx's analysis of culture. This book shows that Marxist theory is not restricted to economics and politics.

Padover, Saul K. *Karl Marx: An intimate biography.* New York: Mentor Books, 1980 (paper).

The best biography of Marx in English. This is an abridged version.

Reiss, Edward. *Marx: A clear guide.* London: Pluto Press, 1997 (paper).

An excellent short introduction to Marx. Lively and well written.

Wolff, Robert Paul. *Understanding Marx: A reconstruction and critique of "Capital."* Princeton, NJ: Princeton University Press, 1984.

Wolff argues, "In the past quarter century . . . Marx has been rescued from the waxworks of Victorian curiosities, and has emerged at last as one of the most original, powerful, and relevant economists since Adam Smith." Although this book is somewhat specialized in orientation, it is worth reading because it shows the applicability of Marxist economics for the world today.

To the person who cannot bear his fate in a manly fashion, one has to say: may he return to us silently and in a plain fashion, without the usual ceremony given to renegades. The arms of the old religions are opened widely and compassionately for him. After all, they do not make it hard for him. One way or another he will sacrifice his intellect, that seems inevitable. If he must really do it, we shall not rebuke him. For such an intellectual sacrifice in favor of absolute religious devotion is ethically quite different from the simple denial of the plain duty of intellectual integrity, which sets in if one lacks the courage to clarify one's own ultimate position and facilitates this by feeble relative judgments. In my view a return to religion stands higher than academic soothsaying, which does not clearly realize that in the lecture-rooms of the university no other virtue holds but simple intellectual integrity. Integrity, however, compels us to state that for the many who long for new prophets and saviors, the situation is the same as that described in the beautiful Edomite watchman's song of the period of exile described in Isaiah's oracles:

> He calleth to me out of Seir, watchman, what of the night?
> The watchman said, The morning cometh, and also the night:
> if ye will enquire, enquire ye: return, come.

The people to whom this was said has inquired and lingered for more than two millennia, and we are shaken when we realize its fate. From this we want to draw the lesson that nothing is gained by yearning and tarrying alone, and we shall act differently. We shall set to work and meet the "demands of the day" in human relations as well as in our vocation. This, however, is plain and simple: each must find and obey the demon who has hold of the very fibers of his existence.

—Max Weber, "Wissenchaft als Beruf." (Translation: "Science as Vocation") in From Max Weber, pp. 77–158.

8

Max Weber

(1864–1920)

Life

Max Weber was born on April 24, 1864, in Erfurt, Saxony. Both Weber's mother, Helene, and his father (also named Max) came from prosperous upper-middle-class families. Weber's paternal grandfather was co-founder of Weber, Laer & Niemann, a highly profitable linen firm in Bielefeld. Helene's father, Georg Friedrich Fallenstein, was a high-ranking Prussian civil servant who had inherited a substantial income from his parents. Fallenstein retired from public life in his mid-fifties and moved into a large house that he had built for his family on the banks of the River Neckar in Heidelberg, Baden. Weber, who lived in Heidelberg for most of his adult life, inherited this house in 1910.

His parents exercised a great influence on the development of Weber's character. Helene Weber was a devout Protestant whose life was governed by a strict ethical code. Weber's wife, Marianne, notes in her biography of Weber that, although "loving service and self-sacrifice" were "second nature" to Helene, "every day she plunged into the depths and was anchored in the supernatural."[1] Weber's father, on the other hand, was a good-hearted but extremely authoritarian and brusque patriarch.

After moving to Berlin in 1869, Max, Sr., sat in both the Prussian House of Deputies and the Reichstag (Imperial Parliament) as a member of the National Liberal Party. This middle-of-the-road party paid lip service to the ideals of constitutional democracy but deferred to the self-proclaimed "iron rule" of the German chancellor, the Prince Otto Eduard Leopold von Bismarck-Schönhausen.

Max Weber, Jr., had mixed feelings about his father's unwillingness to oppose Bismarck's aristocratic disdain for the principles of constitutional rule. The father's attitude of compromise and pragmatism differed markedly from Helene Weber's moral absolutism. As an adolescent, Weber was more in sympathy with his mother's ideals than with his father's attitude of compromise. Because of his father's unassailable position as head of the household, however, Weber was never able to criticize him openly.

Max Weber, Sr., was acquainted with some of the leading politicians and academics in Berlin. Frequent visitors to his house included the historian Theodor Mommsen (1817–1903), the philosopher and historian Wilhelm Dilthey (1833–1911), and the politician Heinrich Rickert, whose son Heinrich Rickert the philosopher (1863–1936) became a colleague of the younger Weber in later years.

In 1882, Weber left his father's house to study jurisprudence at the University of Heidelberg. He joined a dueling fraternity and spent much of his time drinking and brawling. During his first undergraduate year, Weber gained a great deal of weight and acquired the obligatory dueling scar across his cheek. When he returned home for the first time, his mother was horrified to see how much her eldest son's physical appearance had changed.

The following year, Weber moved to Strasbourg to give a year of service to the army. By now he was so corpulent that it proved almost impossible to issue him a uniform. Forced to exercise and to follow meaningless orders, Weber found the Prussian army not to his liking. Nevertheless, his ardent nationalism was not seriously impaired. Marianne Weber notes in her memoirs that, although he was a failure at gymnastics, Weber "pleased even higher superior officers with the impeccable elegance of his goose step."[2]

In accordance with his parents' wishes, the following year Weber returned to Berlin to complete his university education. Until 1894, Weber lived in his father's house and, during this time, followed a demanding regimen made possible by extraordinary self-discipline. The young Max hated to waste his evenings by going to social engagements such as dances organized for the young. At such functions, he complained, people do nothing but "trample, chat, and sweat."

On his return to Berlin, Weber became a member of the highly renowned *Verein für Sozialpolitik* (Association for Social Policy). He remained a member of this association until his death. The members of the *Verein* favored a rational and enlightened system of state support for German industry. Weber fully agreed that political economy should be "nationalistic." In 1895, when he gave his inaugural lecture as a young professor at Freiburg, he selected as his topic "The Nation-State and Economic Policy." In this speech, Weber argued that economic systems could not be evaluated according to an ideal of social justice or an ideal of technical perfection:

> The standards of value of German economic policy can only be *German* standards. . . . The *power* interests of the nation are, wherever they are in question, the ultimate decisive interests that must be served by the nation's economic policy.[3]

Weber's first research in political economy—an investigation of the condition of agrarian workers in East Prussia—was suggested by members of the Verein. The association's leaders, including professors Adolf Wagner, Gustav von Schmoller, and Lujo Brentano—mockingly called *Kathedersozialisten* (literally, "socialists of the lectern") by the political left—helped Weber to establish an academic reputation in Germany.

For some time, Weber could not decide whether he had an academic vocation or whether he should follow a more practical career as a lawyer or civil servant. The success that Weber enjoyed as a student at the University of Berlin, where he was highly praised by his professors, helped him make up his mind. Academic success came very quickly to him. At the age of thirty, Weber became professor of economics at Freiburg, and two years later he was given the chair in political science at the University of Heidelberg. This traditional center of German learning remained Weber's home base for the rest of his career.

In 1893, before moving to Freiburg, Weber married Marianne Schnitger, the daughter of a cousin. In all probability, this marriage was never consummated. In 1911, however, Weber had a love affair with a young woman whose identity has been protected by those who have had access to his private papers.

In 1897, Weber was struck down by a neurotic disorder that was to incapacitate him for the next five years and from which he never fully recovered. The immediate cause of this breakdown was a scene between Weber and his father, who was accused of mistreating Weber's mother and of being a tyrant. The argument ended when the old man was ordered to leave his son's house. Weber's father returned to Berlin and died suddenly seven weeks later. For a time, Weber behaved normally, but within a few weeks he had a complete emotional collapse. He was unable to teach; then, to his horror, he found that he could not find the will to write or even to read. For weeks at a time, Weber did nothing but sit at a window, idly picking at the ends of his fingers. In her memoirs, Marianne Weber recounts how, with therapeutic intent, she bought her husband a set of building blocks and some clay to model. Weber's first creation as a sculptor was a replica of a well-known statue, the *Dying Lion of Lucerne.* Exhausted by his efforts, Weber sent this "paperweight" as a gift to his mother in Berlin.

For several years, the Webers went on extensive rest cures in European resorts. Several temporary recoveries were followed by setbacks. In 1903, Weber felt compelled to resign from his position at Heidelberg, but the university reappointed him as an honorary professor. Slowly, Weber learned how to cope with his affliction, but it was not until two years before his death that he was able to teach again on a regular basis.

In 1903, with the economist Edgar Jaffe and with his close friend Werner Sombart (1863–1941), Weber took over the scholarly journal *Archiv für Sozial-wissenschaften und Sozialpolitik* (Archives for Social Science and Social Policy). In the first issue of the new series, Weber noted that the journal would devote itself to "the historical and theoretical recognition of the general cultural significance of capitalist development." Weber stated that the *Archiv* would include work in political science, the philosophy of law, social ethics, social psychology, "and the research usually grouped together as sociology."

The following year, the Webers traveled to the United States, where Max had been invited to speak at the Universal Exposition in St. Louis. By this time, Weber had resumed his scholarly work and had begun to compose *The Protestant Ethic and the Spirit of Capitalism* (1904–1905). A firsthand observation of the world that unfettered capitalism was creating in the United States undoubtedly helped Weber to substantiate the thesis of this book. He believed that the "spirit of capitalism" existed in "ideal-type purity in turn-of-the-century America." In his recollections of the United States, Weber wrote, "With almost lightning speed everything that stands in the way of capitalistic culture is being crushed."[4]

In 1910, with Simmel, Werner Sombart, Ferdinand Tönnies (1855–1936), and Robert Michels (1876–1936), Weber helped organize the first meetings of the German Sociological Society. Although he had originally been skeptical of sociology's claims to be an autonomous discipline, in the years following his breakdown, Weber became more interested in problems of sociological theory. During this period (1903–1911), he worked on methodological problems and on the problem of general categories for sociological analysis. Part of this work was later published in his major opus, *Wirtschaft und Gesellschaft* (Economy and Society [1925]). After 1911, Weber became centrally interested in the sociology of religion, particularly in the relationship between religious belief and economic development.

At the outset of World War I in 1914, Weber, an officer in the Reserve Corps of the German army, was put in charge of military hospitals in the Heidelberg region. Initially, he was enthusiastic about Germany's and Austria's chances against the allied nations of England, France, and Russia; but as the war dragged on, he became more pessimistic. After 1914, Weber became even more interested in questions of national policy. During this period, he sent countless reports, memoranda, and entreaties to politicians in Berlin. He also published several articles critical of the government in the *Frankfurter Zeitung* (Frankfurt Gazette).

Like most of his countrymen, Weber believed that Germany was fighting a defensive war against Russia. With remarkable prescience, he claimed that the Great War was Germany's last chance to achieve imperial greatness and prevent "the swamping of the entire world" by the decrees of Russian officials on the one hand and the conventions of Anglo-Saxon "society" on the other. According to Weber, the Germans were fighting the war "for *honor,* not for changes in the map and economic gain."[5]

When the United States entered the war on the side of the Allies, Weber knew that his country was finished. After the armistice, and during the short-lived German revolutions of 1918–1919, Weber became even more active in politics. He joined the new German Democratic Party and was nominated for election to the Reichstag. His name was even put forward as a possible candidate for Reich Chancellor. Weber was no longer as conservative or as nationalistic as he had been during his early years. However, he still considered it vitally important that the "crazy" left-wing revolutionary element of the Marxist Social Democratic Party (the so-called Spartacists) be "put down quickly" and prevented from making their *Putsch.*

In 1919, Weber was appointed as a delegate to the meetings at Versailles, France, between the Allies and the Central Powers. To his dismay, he found that Germany was expected to make what he considered to be impossible concessions. Although Weber, along with a few other German representatives, refused to accept the humiliating terms of the Versailles Treaty, they were soon ratified by the new government of Germany. Weber was also appointed a member of the committee that helped draft a new constitution for his country. Although he had always favored a constitutional monarchy for Germany, Weber now backed the formation of what came to be known as the Weimar Republic.

In the same year, Weber accepted a teaching position at the University of Munich. In 1919, a "soviet republic" was twice proclaimed in the Free State of Bavaria, of which Munich was the capital. When Ernst Toller, one of the leaders of this socialist revolution, was arrested for high treason, Weber spoke at his trial, describing Toller—who had visited him in Heidelberg—as a misguided and immature idealist. Weber characterized Toller as a *Gesinnungsethiker*—a man guided by an ethic of ultimate ends. During this period, Weber despaired of what was happening to his country: "To restore Germany to her old glory, I would surely ally myself with any power on earth, even with the devil incarnate, but not with the force of stupidity. So long as madmen carry on in politics from the right to the left, I shall stay away from it."[6]

Weber died suddenly on June 14, 1920, a victim of the influenza epidemic that killed millions in the years following the Great War. The first part of *Wirtschaft und Gesellschaft* had just gone to press; the major part of this work was published posthumously.

Weber's death came just as he seemed to be recovering his intellectual powers and his physical vigor. Although he worked as a sociologist for less than twenty years, his output was enormous. Several commentators have pointed to the intriguing connections between Weber's tormented inner life and his academic work. For instance, it has been suggested that Weber's attack on the political hegemony of the *Junkers* (the Prussian aristocracy) in his earliest work, while he was still living in his father's house, was an indirect attack on the class to which his father had yielded. Similarly, Weber's analysis of the neurotic and compulsive psychosocial mechanisms entailed by the "Protestant ethic" was triggered by his own puritanical belief in the "work ethic"—the belief that work is good in itself. Above all, the emphasis on ascetic "worldly" commitment and mystical "otherworldly" detachment in much of Weber's sociology duplicates the two modes of escape from paramount reality that Weber thought were possible for himself.

Weber once remarked that he was a sociologist because he wanted to see how much he could stand: to test whether he could bear to acknowledge the inevitable antinomies and contradictions of human existence. He believed that modern societies had split faith and reason asunder. This fact had been acknowledged by romantics like Hegel, but such men had refused to accept the irreparability of such a fissure. According to Weber, the only course left open to the modern individual is to learn how to live with the competing and *incommensurable* demands of reasoned analysis and ethical commitment.

Social Environment

In 1870, while he was staying at his grandfather's house in Heidelberg, the six-year-old Weber learned about Prussia's impending war with France. Between then and 1919—when, following Germany's defeat in World War I, he studied drafts for a new German constitution—Weber lived through some of the most important events in the history of modern Germany.

The dominant political figure in Germany from 1862 to 1890 was Count Otto von Bismarck. In 1862, King Wilhelm I of Prussia had asked Bismarck to head his government. At the time, Prussia and Austria were vying for control of central Europe. To accelerate the hegemony of Prussia over German-speaking states, Bismarck engineered a short war with Austria in 1866. Following this successful campaign, he annexed several northern Protestant states and developed a constitution that guaranteed Prussian control over the smaller German states. After the defeat of France in 1871, Bismarck persuaded the mad king of Bavaria, Ludwig II, to lead the southern German states into the North German Confederation. These states, which were heavily Catholic, included Württemberg and Baden. Bismarck persuaded Wilhelm I to take the title of German Emperor (kaiser), and Prussia attained complete control over most of German-speaking Europe.

Bismarck was a Prussian Junker, described as a "master Machiavellian" and a brilliant practitioner of *Realpolitik*, or practical power politics. He was a modern politician in that, although his values were traditional and aristocratic, he understood that the Prussian state could not afford to ignore the rich bourgeoisie and the increasingly self-conscious, if nationalistic, proletariat. Consequently, in the political arena, he shrewdly set all sides against the middle. In the Reichstag, he ensured that his policies of expedience—and not the more constitutional policies of the National Liberal Party— were the only viable alternative to the "extreme" policies of left and right factions. Bismarck used the press to manipulate public opinion, and he favored universal manhood suffrage—not as a way of giving the growing numbers of urban workers control of the Reichstag, but as a means of effectively coopting working-class organizations.

Bismarck's power base was the Prussian House of Deputies, the members of which were appointed and not elected by popular franchise. Consequently, it was dominated by Junkers and the rich bourgeoisie. In the Reichstag, Bismarck was able to cement an alliance between the eastern landowners and the Rhenish industrialists. He also controlled the civil service, which was beyond the reach of the legislature. Thanks to Bismarck's tight control, the Reichstag passed large military budgets without question.

Bismarck's success in balancing the interests of the Junkers (who provided the backbone of the Prussian bureaucracy) and the industrialists of western Germany was no mean achievement. The Junkers were Prussian nationalists who controlled the large agricultural estates of East Prussia. They had played an important role in suppressing the movement for liberal reform in Prussia's western territories in 1848, and their allegiance was not to the idea of a Greater Germany but to the Prussian king and to their aristocratic and largely outmoded values. Thus the Junkers had little interest in the *embourgeoisement* of Germany, for this would mean the disappearance of their way of life.

Weber's study of the Junker estates showed that it was becoming more difficult for Prussian landowners to compete with the price of grain imported from Russia and from the United States. According to Weber, the Junker influence in German politics was wholly negative, for these eastern landowners constantly thwarted the National Liberal Party policy of free trade and the removal of tariffs on imported grain. Weber was seriously alarmed by the Junkers' policy of replacing German peasants with itinerant Polish farm laborers. Many German workers preferred industrial work in cities to field work for the Junkers. In the long run, Weber believed, this westward migration by German peasants would undermine German control of East Prussia.

The policy implications of Weber's study of east German agriculture suggested an enhanced imperialistic role for Greater Germany. Weber believed that, for reasons of national interest, the government would have to provide incentives for German labor in East Prussia. Although it would have been cheaper to use migrant Polish workers, Weber put the national interests of the German people above pure economic models of rational behavior. In order to compensate for the loss of cheaply produced grain, German manufacturing would have to generate greater profits. Weber pointed out that for this aim to be achieved, Germany would need its share of overseas markets. Thus Germany would have to become a world power in order to compete with England and France. One of the young Weber's greatest fears was that the unification of Germany had occurred too late for his country to attain the status of a great imperial power.

In the 1870s and 1880s, the main threat to Bismarck's control of the Prussian state apparatus came from the *Sozialdemokratische Partei Deutschlands* (SPD)—the new German Social Democratic Party. The SPD was nominally a socialist party that appealed to urban artisans and to the lower bourgeoisie. It had come into existence in 1875 at the Gotha Conference, when August Bebel's Social Democrats had united with Ferdinand Lassalle's General Association of German Workers. (Marx wrote a famous critique of what he considered to be the too-tepid program developed by the leaders of this new party.) An assassination attempt on Wilhelm I in 1878 gave Bismarck the excuse to force antisocialist legislation through the Reichstag. This legislation, which remained in effect until Bismarck left office in 1890, permitted police and state censors to suppress working-class organizations whenever necessary.

After Bismarck's retirement, the SPD continued to follow mildly reformist but conciliatory policies. Although by the 1890s the SPD had adopted a manifesto that was officially Marxist, it was not a revolutionary party. The party's program did not advocate revolution but asked for wage increases for workers and for an eight-hour working day. In the elections of 1912, the SPD won 4 million votes to become the largest party in Germany. The Reich, however, continued to be administered by monarchists, militarists, and industrialists.

The unification of Germany in 1871 encouraged rapid economic growth. By 1900, the German steel and chemical industries were outproducing their competitors in Britain. Much of Germany's wealth, however, was used for the military, especially for an ambitious program of naval development. The standard of living of the German working classes during the last part of the nineteenth century did not rise as rapidly as did that of the English proletariat. However, Bismarck did implement a program of social legislation, which was strongly backed by the SPD. This gave German workers a state-run system of social insurance or social security.

After World War I, which was supported by most Social Democrats, a left faction emerged within the SPD. Known as the Spartacus League, this splinter group, led by Karl Liebknecht and Rosa Luxemburg, became increasingly militant. In 1918, the Spartacists split from the SPD to become the German Communist Party. In December of that year, Workers' and Soldiers' Councils were set up in Berlin, backed by the Spartacists and by the Independent Socialists (who had refused to support German militarism). After Germany's defeat in the war, the German kaiser abdicated, and Friedrich Ebert, the leader of the Social Democrats, became head of government. When three thousand sailors occupied the kaiser's recently vacated palace in Berlin,

Ebert sent troops against the communist and socialist factions that were now in control of the capital. In January 1919, savage street fighting broke out in Berlin. Liebknecht and Luxemburg were abducted and murdered by the Freikorps, a special corps of war veterans and misfits that was hurriedly put together by Ebert to suppress communist insurrections in the capital and in Bavaria.

In 1919, Weber believed that the Spartacists were a serious threat to the German nation. In a speech he gave at the time, he stated that "Liebknecht belongs in the madhouse and Rosa Luxemburg in the zoological gardens." When the Freikorps were dispatched to Munich in May 1919 to attack the Bavarian soviet, Weber—who was teaching at the University of Munich at the time—declared that this intervention by "government" troops was necessary in order to restore order. However, he did condemn the "atrocities" that were committed by both sides.

In 1902, the historian Theodor Mommsen declared that Bismarck had broken the will of the German people and that without him it was now impossible to govern the mishmash of states and the kaleidoscope of interests that was the German Reich. Mommsen also pointed out that Bismarck had ensured that the German nation was unable to resist the imposition of authority from above. This was a judgment with which Weber largely agreed, pointing out that Bismarck "left behind him a nation *without any political sophistication.* . . . Above all, he left behind him a nation *without any political will of its own.*"[7] In 1919, Weber believed that Germany could turn neither to the socialist left nor to a "mature" and "responsible" center party. According to Weber, the socialist leaders were irresponsible, and the working classes did not possess the "political maturity" to rule the state. As far as he was concerned, leftists, because they put class before nation, could not be serious candidates for office. Weber conceded that the bourgeoisie had been ruined by Bismarck; thus he concluded that the middle classes could do nothing but search ineffectively for a "new Caesar."

After Weber's death, despite the fact that the SPD consistently outpolled the other political parties in the elections of 1920, 1924, 1928, and 1930, socialists and liberals were unable to consolidate their power and block the intrigues of nationalists and right-wing industrialists. Hence the SPD was unable to govern Germany effectively. In 1930, 1932, and 1933 (the year Hitler came to power), socialist and communist representatives won more than two hundred seats in the Reichstag. In the elections of March 5, 1933, however, the SPD and the Communists were swamped by the Nazi Party. Hitler's supporters won 288 seats, which gave them a plurality of the votes cast. Neither the left nor the center was able to prevent Hitler from becoming German chancellor; nor were they able to stop him from tearing up the unpopular constitution that Weber had helped to draft fourteen years earlier.

Intellectual Roots

In 1883, Carl Menger, professor of economics at the University of Vienna, published a book on the methodology of the social sciences in which he sharply criticized the "historical school" of political economists. Gustav von Schmoller (1838–1917), one of Weber's teachers in Berlin and a leading member of the *Verein für Sozialpolitik*, drafted a response to Menger that precipitated a prolonged dispute in German academic circles about the methodological status of the social sciences. Menger was a supporter of classical economic theory and a defender of the British school of positivistic economics. He argued that the social and cultural sciences should seek "exact laws" describing causal relationships between observable phenomena. Menger believed that the methods of the social sciences should be the same as those of the natural sciences.

Members of the historical school, like Wilhelm Roscher (1817–1894) and Karl Knies (1821–1898), Weber's professor at Heidelberg, held that the social or economic life of a nation could not be understood in terms of ahistorical and transcultural abstractions. These "historicists" pointed out that "economic man"—as posited by classical economic theory—was the product of historical circumstance. According to the historicists, the meaning of "rational" economic decision making can be understood by the economist only when specific and unique contingencies affecting human choice are taken into consideration. In short, the historicists believed that an understanding of the consequences of social action could not be severed from the study of a nation's culture and history. In this light, the younger leaders of the *Verein für Sozialpolitik*—von Schmoller, Brentano, and Wagner—saw the purpose of their association as the production of knowledge that would be useful in helping to resolve the *particular* problems of the German nation.

Throughout the nineteenth century, German scientists acknowledged that different types of methodology were appropriate for the natural and the human, or cultural, sciences. The conception of this divergence in epistemology can be traced back to Immanuel Kant (1724–1804). Kant agreed that the methods of the natural sciences give us true knowledge about the external phenomenal world—the world we experience through our senses. He pointed out, however, that the knowledge we have about ourselves as potentially free subjects is qualitatively different from our knowledge of external and impersonal physical objects and forces in the universe. Human subjects have free will: Their action is not determined in the same manner as the motion of objects like atoms and molecules.

Kant believed that an analysis of what he thought of as "the moral law" was necessary for human society because this transcendental and transhistorical law is an integral part of the practical-cognitive interest. Hence, for Kant, moral philosophy was a vitally important task, for such philosophy explored the very basis of humankind's social being. Moral philosophy, however, is not based on the meaning or significance of empirical data; it involves reflection on moral axioms that appear to be innate and that are understandable without reference to human experience.

Weber agreed with Kant that intellectual analysis and moral understanding were two quite different modes of thought or reason. Thus he believed that the human intellect is useless in distinguishing between good and evil. (In fact, he liked to point out that intellectuals were not particularly adept at making moral judgments.) On the other hand, Weber also believed that the Hegelian conflation of facts and values (what is and what ought to be) was indefensible. For Weber, it was axiomatic that sociology could not derive ethical imperatives from the study of cultural values. Sociology can tell us about the consequences of our value commitments, but it cannot tell us whether these effects are good or bad. This latter assessment involves moral reasoning, and Weber agreed with Kant that empirical analysis and moral judgment are incommensurable.

As an epistemologist, Kant showed how (positivistic) scientific knowledge is possible—that is, why it is that subjects can attain secure and reliable knowledge about causal relationships among *physical* (but not cultural or historical) objects in the world. The historicist Dilthey, whom Weber had met in his father's house in Berlin, tried to do for the human sciences, such as history and sociology, what Kant had done for natural science. Dilthey, who was probably the most prominent member of the "historical school," viewed the "historical sciences" as wholly dependent on interpretive, not positivistic, theory. He pointed out that human history is the result of the human freedom to create an infinite number of "cultural objects," including legal systems, political institutions, and aesthetic works of art.

Dilthey explored the logical foundations of cultural history (*Geistesgeschichte*) by investigating how the historian could explain a particular epoch and show how it defined and limited what human subjects find meaningful. He demonstrated that historical explanation rediscovers the way in which actors respond to a meaningful cultural order created by them. According to Dilthey, human subjects are intelligible as unique historical actors, not as objects driven by impersonal forces. Thus the methods of positivism are completely inappropriate for cultural history.

Dilthey's project was taken up and carried further by the neo-Kantian Rickert. Rickert agreed with Dilthey that we know cultural and historical phenomena by understanding the meaning of cultural objects affecting how subjects think, feel, and act. Unlike Dilthey, Rickert did not try to make a sharp division between "science"—by which he meant objectively verifiable knowledge—and "human studies." He insisted, however, that, whereas the natural sciences search for general and nomothetic knowledge, the task of the cultural or historical sciences is to try to attain ideographic understanding—that is, such sciences should try to comprehend hermeneutically the meaning and effect of particular cultural objects within specific historical settings.

Throughout his career as a sociologist, Weber carried out an explicit and implicit dialogue with the neo-Kantians and the historicists. Weber was strongly influenced by Simmel's work on the epistemological foundations of social thought. He agreed with Simmel that meaningful social action is not truly thinglike or extrinsic for subjects but emerges within a social interactional process. However, Weber rejected both Dilthey's and Rickert's claim that *general* categories of analysis did not exist for the human or cultural sciences. Yet, although he denied that the methodology of the human sciences *must* be different from that of the natural sciences, Weber did acknowledge that the primary or fundamental interest of sociology should be interpretive, not positivist.

As a young man, Weber was introduced by his mother to the work of the American Protestant theologian William Ellery Channing (1780–1842), a founder of the American Unitarian Association. Although he was not a believer in Christian dogma, Weber was strongly influenced by Channing's theological writings. Channing, who had been a popular preacher in the United States in the early part of the nineteenth century, argued that intellectual vigor, analysis, and clear thinking are associated with the life of free men. According to Channing, "the life of communities is subject to the same moral law as the life of individuals."

In her biography of Weber, Marianne Weber notes the parallels between Kantianism and Unitarianism. In describing Channing's significance for Weber, she points out that both Kant and Channing believed "that the purpose of political and social institutions is the development of an autonomous [free] personality." According to Marianne Weber, this was a "conviction that remained with Weber all his life."[8]

Weber, however, did acknowledge that there was likely to be a necessary incompatibility between a strict adherence to Christian ethics (as exemplified, for instance, by the Sermon on the Mount) and the needs of the state. Unlike Kant and Hegel, Weber treated political participation as a pragmatic, not a philosophical, problem. Although he believed it was morally defensible to be a pacifist and to deny the authority of temporal authority, Weber concluded it was not possible to live in terms of ethical ideals without withdrawing from the world.

Until the 1960s, most American sociologists liked to think of Weber's sociology as being antithetical to Marx's and often claimed that Weber had refuted Marx's materialist conception of history. In the 1940s, the American sociologist Talcott Parsons informed his readers that "Weber's earlier development took a course which brought him into close contact with the Marxian position. But he soon recoiled from this, becoming convinced of the indispensability of an important role of 'ideas' in the explanation of great historical processes."[9]

Although Weber did give more weight to the role of ideas in historical change than did Marx, and although he did try to show that Marx had overemphasized the overarching usefulness of the concept "mode of production," Parsons's view of Weber's attitude toward the Marxian position can be justified only by trivializing and vulgarizing Marx's sociology. To be fair to Parsons, however, it should be noted that there is a possibility that Weber himself might have had only a superficial understanding of Marx's work. As a young scholar, Weber was exposed to Marxism largely through secondary sources, and at the end of the nineteenth century, many of Marx's German followers treated him as if he were a strict economic determinist.

Irving Zeitlin has suggested that "Weber's analysis is not so much a refutation as it is an adaptation of Marx's theory to twentieth-century conditions."[10] Weber largely accepted Marx's conclusions about the significance of capitalism in the modern world. It was Weber's belief that "it has been the attainment of *economic power* which has always inspired a class to realize its claim to *political leadership*."[11] He even conceded that "the decisive foundation common to the capitalist private enterprise system" is the "separation" of all kinds of workers from "the means of production in the economy."[12]

At the same time, however, Weber's interest in the effects of bureaucratization and rationalization was designed in part to show that alienation in the modern world was not merely the result of the *capitalist* mode of production. Weber understood that sociology had to deal with subjects raised by Marx, for these were the critical issues of the day. Consequently, he made a point of stressing the *Archiv*'s policy of making "a regular practice of presenting critical analyses of the literature concerning and following the great thinker [Marx]."[13] In the final analysis Weber's work complements rather than refutes Marx's.

IDEAS

Society

Weber wrote a great deal on many different subjects: economics, religion, music, urbanization, politics, and so on. He was less interested in developing a theory of human society for its own sake than in investigating and understanding historical change. His major sociological project was to show why Western capitalist societies had taken a divergent and singular line of development in comparison with other types of societies.

Weber's work was always problem-oriented: He was the applied sociologist *nonpareil*. From his earliest studies to the essays he wrote just before he died, Weber never showed much interest in theory that was not applied to the critical issues facing modern societies. Even when he tried to develop general sociological categories in *Economy and Society*, he treated them as a means by which sociology could study historical trends in order to understand latter-day problems.

Unlike Comte, Hegel, or Marx, Weber did not believe that societies followed general laws of development. He wanted to chart the particular history of Western civilization, not search for what he believed were nonexistent laws controlling the fate of humankind. Weber believed that the unit of analysis for the sociologist should be not the abstraction "society" but the action of real flesh-and-blood social individuals. According to Weber, "Action is social in so far as, by virtue of the subjective meaning attached to it by the acting individual (or individuals), it takes account of the behavior of others and is thereby oriented in its course."[14]

Like Pareto, Weber was particularly interested in how social action is often conceptualized by social actors in terms of means-ends chains. For instance, a large bureaucratic organization will organize the activity of social individuals by assigning each worker a particular role in a hierarchy. The responsibilities associated with this role are rules, or norms, that serve as means to the ends served by the bureaucracy. These norms serve to make organized social action possible; that is, they routinize and formalize social interaction among individuals who, for whatever reason, are committed to serving the organization.

Unlike Pareto, Weber believed that the set of ultimate ends for which human actors could strive was potentially infinite. He did not believe that these ends were constrained by human psychology or by "instincts," nor did he believe that these ends were somehow determined by the functional needs of society. Weber believed that the purpose of human culture was to create a finite segment of meaning from the meaningless infinity of the world process. However, he rejected Hegel's view that reason and progress were immanent in "world-historical development." On the contrary, he insisted that all meaningful human experience is the creative product of specific historical actors. The universe itself is a vast and unknowable entity that looks with complete indifference on the human species.

At the heart of Weber's sociology is an investigation of the consequences of types of social action and a study of how these types of action come into conflict and create tensions for specific individuals. Weber pointed out that in many traditional societies individuals live highly routinized lives, wherein everyday ceremonies are generally seen as ends in themselves. This type of action is very different from the action of modern individuals who have to adopt a great many highly specific roles that require them constantly to shift perceptions and allegiances. For the modern individual, the ultimate ends of action are often far removed from the specific rules and norms that guide everyday behavior. In order to clarify the important differences among types of social action and differentiate between rational and nonrational action, Weber developed the following typology:

1. Rationally purposeful (*Zweckrational*) action.
2. Value-rational (*Vertrational*) action.
3. Affective action.
4. Traditional action.

Rationally purposeful action entails a complicated plurality of means and ends. The ends of action (for example, goals, values) either are taken as means to the fulfillment of other ends, or are treated *as if* they are set in concrete. In this way, action becomes purely instrumental. For instance, if we compare two individuals who are trying to maximize their income over the course of a year, we might find that one person uses far more effective means to achieve this goal than the other: He might cheat on his tax return, take a second job, or sell drugs to workmates. We would describe this individual as more purposively rational than one who acquires and keeps less money. Within the domain of *Zweckrational* action, it is possible to compare the degrees of rationality that various individuals exhibit. In the foregoing example, it is assumed that all individuals will want to maximize their income. This goal is fixed, and it is also a means to other goals (for example, a vacation in Europe, a new car, a complete collection of country music recordings).

Classical economic theory treats individuals *as if* they were rationally purposeful. Such theory presumes that individuals will always try to maximize their utility—that is, make utility itself an ultimate end of action. To do so, however, is to value economic efficiency for efficiency's sake and to ignore subjective or personal pleasures. It is quite possible for particular individuals to be instrumentally rational part of the time; it is not possible, however, to be rationally purposeful all of the time. For each person, and for clusters of individuals, *some* subjectively meaningful ends of action have to be taken for granted. As Weber pointed out, as far as real, historical individuals are concerned, action cannot be meaningful unless it is goal-oriented. Classical economic theory puts to one side the study of how the ends or goals of action are culturally and historically defined; but because it studies rationally purposeful action only, this omission does not matter. Sociology, however, does not study just instrumental action; it examines all types of *social* action.

Value-rational action occurs when individuals use rational—that is, effective—means to achieve goals or ends that are defined in terms of subjectively meaningful values. For instance, the rational calculation of the best way to attain a "meaningful" or "glorious" death would be *Vertrational*, according to Weber. When individuals are value-rational, they make commitments to certain subjective goals and adopt means that are effective in attaining these ends. Because value rationality is measured in terms of subjective meaning, it is often impossible to compare one individual with another. The Buddhist monk who defines "salvation" differently than the Protestant cleric does cannot be described as more or less rational than his counterpart.

Affective action fuses means and ends together so that action becomes emotional and impulsive. Such action is the antithesis of rationality because the actor concerned cannot make a calm, dispassionate assessment of the relationship between the ends of action and the means that, supposedly, exist to serve these ends. Rather, the means themselves are emotionally fulfilling, and become ends in themselves. A golfer who smashes her golf clubs because she fails to play well would be engaged in affective action. The golfer's action is social because she is responding to the way in which she has failed to live up to standards of good play. Her action, however, is not effectively linked to the goal of meeting these standards; it is not, in any sense, rational.

Traditional action occurs when the ends and the means of action are fixed by custom and tradition. For example, some so-called primitive societies have very strict rites of succession for group leaders. What is important about traditional action is that the ends of action are taken for granted and appear to be natural to the actors concerned because they are unable to comprehend the possibility of alternative ends.

Weber acknowledged that human practice could be reified; that is, he conceded that the participation of individuals in society could not be described as truly voluntaristic if individuals were unable to see institutionalized or organized social action as optional. Unlike Marx and Simmel, however, Weber ignored individual consciousness because meaningful action was defined by him in terms of individual orientations to shared meaning. According to Weber, shared meaning, which consists of *external* points of value reference, is the subject matter of sociology. Weber readily conceded that modern, reflective individuals are less likely than their traditional or premodern counterparts to share the same value commitments. This statement is true because modern culture is fragmented and contains multiple life worlds. Thus Weber is somewhat limited by his methodological individualism. Perhaps he might have done better if—like Hegel, Marx, and Simmel—he had recognized a dialectical relationship between external and fragmented value commitments and the alienated self-expression of modern individuals.

One of the most important sociological questions for Weber was the issue of how power operates in social life. Weber argued that this was a particularly complicated issue because power cannot be equated with economic domination, nor is it derived merely from the control of governmental or explicitly political institutions. Weber defined "power" as "the probability that one actor within a social relationship will be in a position to carry out his own will despite resistance."[15] He defined "domination" as the probability that a command will be obeyed.

Weber pointed out that *class* and *status* position in society also helps to determine individuals' ability to impose their will on others. According to Weber, classes come into existence when there is a struggle for control of utilities. Weber agreed with Marx that all class divisions are property divisions:

> We may speak of a "class" when (1) a number of people have in common a specific causal component of their life chances, insofar as (2) this component is represented exclusively by economic interests in the possession of goods and opportunities for income, and (3) this component is represented under the conditions of the commodity or labor markets.[16]

Thus, Weber agreed with Marx that class differences determine power differentials in society. However, he favored a pluralistic model of stratification, as opposed to one that overemphasized the significance of economic relations. Defining "status" as the evaluations made of an individual in terms of positive or negative esteem or honor, Weber pointed out that status as well as class affects an individual's ability to exercise power over others. Although class and status often overlap empirically (particularly in the United States, where status is largely derived from property ownership), analytically they are separate dimensions of stratification. In a caste society, for instance, a member of an inferior caste might have more property than a member of a superior caste, who is nevertheless highly esteemed. Because of status differentials, Weber suggested that status groups would emerge with qualitatively different lifestyles. Membership in these groups can be highly significant in determining an individual's position in an overall system of social stratification.

In his general sociology, Weber isolates a third dimension of stratification: that deriving from association with a political party. *Political parties* are voluntary associations that influence state policy but that do not threaten to compete with the legitimate authority of the state. Such parties are exclusively concerned with power for power's sake. High-ranking members of a dominant party organization exercise power that is not in and of itself derived from their class or status positions.

In distinguishing between "class," "status," and "party," Weber did not mean to suggest that a high (or low) position on one of these dimensions would not be matched by a similar position on another. It is commonplace, for instance, to find political parties controlled by a dominant class. What Weber wished to establish was that class, status, and party should be treated as distinct by the sociologist, for this is the only way to ensure that the interrelationships among these dimensions can be studied.

The most obvious manifestation of power is state power. According to Weber, the state secures its privileged position by establishing a "*monopoly* of the *legitimate* use of physical force in the enforcement of its order."[17] He did not believe that the state could impose its will by appealing to reason. Rather, he assumed that all political states increase their effectiveness through the use of force or by the threat of force. The primary purpose of a state is to impose its order within a particular geographical area. Weber pointed out, however, that the most powerful states do not impose their will by the use of physical force (although all states must be ready to use force against their own citizens if all else fails). Powerful states maximize their ability to enforce their will within the domains they control by ensuring that their authority is seen as *legitimate*. According to Weber, states govern legitimately by the use of either rational-legal or traditional authority. A third kind of authority is charismatic authority.

Rational-legal authority, which can be found in most modern corporations and organizations, emphasizes rationally purposeful action. The authority of individuals derives from the fact that they are officials with clearly defined rights and duties who uphold and implement rules and procedures impersonally. Perhaps the best example of rational-legal authority is bureaucratic authority. *Bureaucratic* officials are organized according to a carefully defined hierarchy; they implement written rules and record their decisions; furthermore, their authority stems not from their personal qualities but from their offices.

Traditional authority, on the other hand, is legitimated by individuals' acquiescence in a system of political rule that has become *habitual* or *customary*. Typically, traditional authority is hereditary, although this is not always the case. For instance, at various points in English history, the English crown was the property of particular families. Throughout most of Europe, it was not until the sixteenth or seventeenth century that kin structure was differentiated from the political system of a nation-state.

Weber's interest in charismatic authority has been much discussed by sociologists. Such authority results from an individual's personal appeal. A *charismatic* leader—who is most likely to emerge during a period of crisis—will appear to have supernatural or superhuman power. The mission of such a leader is very often revolutionary. Because charismatic authority stems from the personal qualities of a particular person, however, Weber points out that if the program that this leader has implemented is to be sustained, the leader's charisma will have to be "routinized" in some form. For instance, after Christ's death—and after it became apparent that his return to earth was not imminent—the apostles began to set up the rudiments of a religious organization with priestly offices. Weber believed that a long-term process of "rationalization" in the West was making rational-legal authority increasingly more important. One of the reasons for his interest in charismatic authority seems to have been his belief that, even in the most bureaucratized of societies, there would always be a place—and a need—for charismatic figures.

Toward the end of his life, Weber engaged in a comprehensive comparative and historical study of religious orientations. He did not summarily reject religious belief as outmoded and regressive, as had some earlier sociologists. Instead, he argued that religion had been and—to a lesser extent—continued to be a vitally important component of social action. Weber was particularly interested in how institutionalized religious belief affected the political and economic life of a society. In his broadscale historical and sociological work, he was able to show that religious belief can underlie traditional action—as is the case, for instance, with Confucianism and Talmudic Judaism. On the other hand, the great religions of salvation like Christianity and Hinduism can point people away from worldly concerns and conventional economic and political spheres.

Weber argued that religions of salvation tended to institutionalize either asceticism or mysticism. *Ascetic* religious belief, like that adopted by monks, enables individuals to view themselves as instruments of God. Such an orientation encourages individuals to avoid and perhaps to eradicate the corruption of the world by following a rigorous pattern of righteous self-discipline. Weber used the example of some of the early Protestant sects to discuss the significance of such social action. Religions of *mysticism*, however, which, like the voodoo cults of the Caribbean, emphasize magic and ceremony, encourage individuals to renounce the world so that they can be vessels through which supernatural forces flow. Weber pointed out that it is commonplace for a tension or contradiction to exist between religious demands and humankind's material needs. The particular way in which such tension is resolved can be crucial for a society or for a whole civilization.

As a sociologist, Weber was most interested in how religion creates a cultural order that affects whole aspects of social life. According to Weber, salvation religions deal with what Weber called "the problem of theodicy"—the problem of how to explain human suffering, tragedy, and death. Religions try to impose a cultural order by showing how life can be meaningful. Christianity, for instance, created a systematization of religious practice over the last two thousand years by institutionalizing a church and priesthood that provided "solutions" to the problem of existence. Over the last two millennia, the church has tried to develop an internally consistent theology that will supply believers with goals and values of ultimate significance. Such a theology obviously has had a great social and cultural impact on the development of Western civilization.

In his sociological investigations, Weber showed that religion did not have merely a conservative impact on society. For example, charismatic religious leaders like the prophets of Israel succeeded in pulling down kings whom they accused of ignoring God's plan for the Jewish people. Moreover, according to Weber, the Protestant Reformation of the sixteenth century had a dramatic impact on the development of the West because many Protestant sects imposed an ascetic and methodical life-style on their members. As we shall see later, in some respects this helped make such individuals "modern" in their outlook.

The Individual in Society

Weber believed that what is termed "society" is the network of social relationships created by individuals who believe themselves to be meaningfully oriented. As we have noted, Weber rejected the Hegelian and Marxist view of the conscious self as an entity that yearns to be reintegrated with a form of social life that negates all forms of alienated self-expression. Unlike Marx, Weber could not envision a possible form of life where the individual and society could exist in perfect harmony and equilibrium.

Weber did concede that modern societies contained increasingly reflective individuals, who were becoming more aware of the optionality of human value commitments. As we have seen, however, he did not believe that *rational* choice between values, or ultimate ends, was possible. As far as Weber was concerned, human freedom meant making informed choices among many different types of commitment. As a Kantian, he accepted that the individual could comprehend duty and morality in a purely formal sense. However, although individuals can comprehend abstractly what terms like "decency," "betrayal," and "honor" mean, this cannot help them to decide what gods to serve or what *specific* values to adopt.

Weber believed that the modern individual was caught between an "ethic of success" (pragmatism) and an "ethic of responsibility" (morality). Again, Weber's perception of this dilemma stems from his acceptance of Kant's strict demarcation between individuals' capacity for instrumental manipulation on the one hand and their understanding of ethical principles on the other. To his credit, however, Weber could never entirely accept the dilemma of having to choose between success and responsibility. Weber pointed out that individuals can try to comprehend the effect of their actions. Although this effort does not eliminate the schism between success and responsibility, it does reduce the likelihood of humans doing harm unintentionally. Weber believed that if individuals are informed about the effects of different kinds of action, they will have a greater capacity to make decisions that are value-oriented but implemented instrumentally.

This approach to the dilemma of choice between the ethic of success and the ethic of responsibility, however, is only a pseudosolution: It does not address the original problem formulated by Kant. Weber's image of the ideal individual in modern society is the image of an individual who is thoughtful, reflective, and cautious—and incapable of making any rational choice with respect to decisions of ultimate importance.

On many occasions, Weber pointed out that the specialization of functions created by the modern economy has led to "a parceling out of the soul." He believed that "high capitalism" has not only destroyed many traditional and "aristocratic" values, but has also tended to standardize the experiences of all individuals. According to Weber, the demand that modern individuals make for freedom from ancient forms of domination leads inevitably to increased bureaucratization and to greater forms of impersonality. For instance, if individuals are to be governed by officials who exercise rational-legal authority over them, then state-run or state-dependent universities will have to attain a monopoly of control over the certification of those who have a "right to office." This is fully democratic in the sense that no one is excluded from the right to participate in the competition to become a trained specialist, or a cog in a bureaucratic machine. What is taught in such universities, however, is little other than what is necessary in order to learn how to become a functional part of the machinery. Likewise, modern society creates individuals in the sense that it needs various kinds of specialists who are quite different from one another. However, it also reduces the individual's chance to be self-directing in that it undermines privatized decision making by institutionalizing collectively articulated forms of impersonal policy formation.

Weber himself was an old-fashioned individualist—one of the last of the private scholars with the means and the status to maintain almost complete independence from governmental or organizational affiliations. He was fully aware that men like him were becoming an anomaly in the modern world, and he was certainly conscious of the fact that his model of the informed, cautious, yet committed human being was becoming increasingly less applicable to twentieth-century individuals. It is perhaps unfortunate that Weber came to conclude that the capacity of individuals to distance themselves from institutionalized modes of instrumentally effective behavior enhanced human freedom. For instance, he suggested that it is precisely the irrationalism and emotionalism of a charismatic movement that enable individuals to escape the "steel-hard cage" of modern, bureaucratic instrumentalism.

Weber assumed that, no matter how bureaucratized or impersonal a society becomes, the search by individuals for a meaningful existence is unending. In contemporary societies, this search becomes ever more frenetic as traditional responses to the problem of theodicy are progressively undermined by those trends loosely associated with modernization (for example, positivism, capitalism, and urbanization). Modern life tends to become increasingly instrumental in orientation and hence to exclude possibilities for shared *value* commitments. Thus the need for charismatic leaders is, if anything, increased.

Weber conceded that early capitalism provided individuals with opportunities for escape and initiative that are withheld from contemporary individuals. For instance, the United States once offered opportunities for the "rugged" and relatively *self-directed* individual. Today, however, rugged individualism is wholly inappropriate for what the United States has become at the end of the twentieth century—a society where, for the typical person, personal success is associated with organizational affiliation and with allegiance to some technocratic master plan of collectively articulated action.

Weber's overall view of the relationship between the individual and contemporary society was, therefore, understandably pessimistic. Modern individuals are condemned to lose all sense of autonomy and self-worth, or to search for nonrational ways of escape from the "steel-hard cage" that contains them. It is no mere coincidence that the two major modes of religious experience that Weber describes—*asceticism* and *mysticism*—parallel what might be called transcendental escape routes—ways of escape that are open to all individuals in all societies.

Those individuals who choose asceticism, as Weber himself did, chain themselves to some task or selflessly apply themselves to some mission. Such individuals derive meaning from turning their backs on the pleasures and rewards of the world. They can survive in contemporary society because the mere performance of a task—and the denial of feeling and sensuality—is more important to them than the nature of the task itself.

Those individuals who choose mysticism reject the idea that anything meaningful can be derived from participation in the everyday world. To them, valid experience derives not from self-mastery but from states of consciousness, or states of mind, that are as far removed as possible from humdrum existence. Drugs are probably the most valuable tools available to individuals who strive for this kind of escape. Others pursue traditional modes of escape like meditation and Zen Buddhism. The less adventurous settle for sexual promiscuity, sport, or travel.

Methodology

In his methodological work, Weber wavers uneasily between an interest in general sociology and an overall acceptance of the main principles of neo-Kantianism and historicism. According to Weber, social science adopts a historical and ideographic approach insofar as it attempts to grasp "cultural reality." At the same time, Weber believed that social science must operate on a systematic level; it must use concepts that are applicable to all societies. Weber never believed that the methodology of the natural sciences was appropriate for the human or cultural sciences. It was important to him, however, that sociology be given the status of a *scientific* discipline (although he did not wish to imply by this that the human sciences should be positivistic in orientation). He also stressed that the sociologist should strive for objective theories of society that could be tested or checked by others.

For Weber, a sociological explanation contained two strands: (1) the interpretation of meaning; and (2) the analysis of causal relationships. The sociologist has to engage in a process of understanding (*Verstehen*) because action to which actors attach a subjective meaning is the subject matter of sociology. It is, of course, quite possible to view human behavior in terms of its phenomenal characteristics. For instance, we could observe the motions of people walking in a plaza by charting the movement of their bodies. Thus we could use our senses to observe human subjects, and we could try to develop laws explaining human behavior in exactly the same way that chemists develop laws explaining the behavior of molecules.

As Weber pointed out, however, in order to explain social action we must "take the role of the other" as a first step toward giving a sociologically adequate account of such action; in other words, we have to ask why action is meaningful to our subjects of investigation. This is not to say that we can literally experience what other people are experiencing. All a sociologist can do is try to reconstruct the interpretations that subjects might give of their own actions. In some instances, this understanding is direct. If we see someone engaged in simple addition, for instance, we should experience no difficulty in understanding why she concludes that 2 + 2 = 4. At other times, it is necessary to understand motive in order to make a person's action explicable. A *motive*, in this sense, is not the psychological cause of behavior; it is the social interactional process by which subjects discover and constitute the meaning of their behavior. Thus, if we say that Othello killed Desdemona because he believed she was an adulteress, we imply (1) that this is a reason for Othello's act; *and* (2) that this is the interpretation that the murderer would have made of his action.

In his methodological writings, Weber often cites the work of his friend and colleague Simmel, and he acknowledges that the concept of *Verstehen* was first made an integral part of sociological explanation by Simmel, not by him. Like Simmel, Weber accepted that meaning emerges not from the configuration of objects external to human subjects and not from the subjective thought processes of the autonomous individual. Rather, meaning is constituted within a social interactional process that is a *precondition* for the emergence of both objects and subjects in the first place.

According to Weber, a general sociology must be able to describe highly complex types of action, involving the articulation of many discrete acts. To this end, Weber believed that sociologists must typify meaningful action in terms of hypothetical cultural values, guiding and constituting large-scale social interactional processes. For instance, if sociologists wish to talk about "capitalism," "feudalism," "bureaucracy," or the "university," they must describe what they consider to be the most essential aspects of types of action associated with these labels. Weber called such an abstract typification an "ideal type." An ideal type is not a simple description of reality: It is a description that *highlights* whatever it is about cultural objects that interests an investigator. Thus, according to Weber:

> An ideal type is formed by the one-sided *accentuation* of one or more points of view and by the synthesis of a great many, diffuse, discrete, more or less present and occasionally absent *concrete individual* phenomena, which are arranged according to those one-sidedly emphasized viewpoints into a unified analytical construct. In its conceptual purity, this mental construct cannot be found empirically anywhere in reality.[18]

Weber believed that ideal types were indispensable for the sociologist, for it is ideal typification that makes social reality tractable for the investigator. According to Weber, whether they are aware of it or not, all sociologists are forced to use one-sided ideal typifications when addressing historical complexity. Historians never report everything that occurs in a specific location and time frame. For instance, historians have shown little interest in what General Custer ate at his last meal before he was slaughtered. A description of this meal would almost certainly be irrelevant to any attempt to explain the battle of the Little Bighorn. Weber argued that all historical and sociological reporting is selective: It emphasizes certain actions or certain characteristics of social reality, while disregarding others. According to Weber, sociologists should acknowledge their use of ideal types in explaining social reality. Furthermore, they should make explicit those aspects of that reality they choose to accentuate.

Confusion about Weber's methodology often arises because, although he believed that sociology was primarily interpretive, Weber pointed out that there was nothing to stop the sociologist from adding a second level of explanation to that provided by interpretive theorizing—namely, causal explanation. For Weber, sociology "is a science which attempts the interpretive understanding of social action in order thereby to arrive at a causal explanation of its course and effects."[19] As far as Weber was concerned, however, the ultimate purpose of causal explanation in sociology is the development of a *hermeneutic* understanding capable of explaining the differences in the development of diverging societies or civilizations: "A correct causal interpretation of a concrete course of action is arrived at when the overt action and the motives have both been correctly apprehended and at the same time their relation has become meaningfully comprehensible."[20]

Thus Weber did not share the positivists' interests in using sociology instrumentally to create a new social order. He sought explanations that were adequate both at the level of causality and at the level of meaning because he wanted sociology to be a comparative "science," and he realized that this search entailed analyzing why some societies had followed a different line of development than others.

Ideal typification permits the sociologist to summarize and abstract subjective meaning and then to search for explanation that is causally adequate. In Weber's well-known study of the relationship between the Protestant ethic and the spirit of capitalism, the ideal typifications that Weber made of this "ethic" and this "spirit" enabled him to suggest a causal connection between the two. This causal connection is tested by making comparative analyses of those societies in which the spirit of capitalism is to be found and those in which it is absent. Weber claimed that the Protestant ethic was unique to those societies that embodied the spirit of capitalism. He noted that Western and non-Western societies were alike in some respects. Technological innovation, state bureaucracy, and urbanization, for instance, could be found in both types of civilizations before the development of capitalism in western Europe. Only in western Europe, however, did capitalism develop on a large scale. From all this, Weber concluded that he had demonstrated a probable causal connection between the Protestant ethic and the development of capitalism.

There has been so much confusion about the Weberian conception of causal explanation that it bears repeating that what Weber meant by "causal explanation" is not what a positivist would mean by this term. Positivism looks for cause-effect relationships that are invariant and generalizable. (This, of course, is a consequence of positivism's technical interest.) Weber's "causal relationships," however, are not meant to be ahistorical, invariant, or generalizable. For instance, the spirit of capitalism has flourished in Japan. Clearly, this is not because of the Protestant ethic, although the rapid development of capitalism in Japan might be linked to an orientation that is akin to the Protestant ethic. Thus, as mentioned earlier, Weber's comparative sociology seeks causal explanation without making any claims that the theory involved in such explanation is generalizable or nomothetic.

According to Weber, the most that sociology can achieve when it seeks general and abstract knowledge is the development of broad sociological categories and the isolation of some of the probable causes of specific lines of historical development. Weber never claimed that sociologists could state definitively that variable x had caused something to happen in one particular society. He argued that a complex set of circumstances was responsible for the occurrence of specific events in a given society. For example, he suggested that the emergence of capitalism in the West resulted from a particular class structure, from technological developments, and from other factors in addition to the Protestant ethic.

Weber pointed out that the types of questions theorists ask are determined by the kinds of answers they need to have. For this reason, he rejected the argument that the methodology of the natural sciences (positivism) could not be applied to the study of humanity. Weber conceded that sociology can be positivistic in orientation. Positivism, however, does not generally permit us to ask the kinds of questions we would *want* to ask as sociologists. For Weber, sociology responds to hermeneutic, not instrumental, interests.

Weber's essays on objectivity in the social sciences have been much discussed and generally misunderstood. Weber argued that sociology should strive for objectivity, although this is not the same for the hermeneutical sciences as it is for the natural sciences. Weber admitted that sociologists cannot prevent their values and one-sided accentuations from affecting the conclusions they draw in the course of their studies. Even though theory expresses human interests, however, and even though it may be policy-oriented, explanations can be checked and corroborated by more than one investigator. In his methodological writings, Weber describes how careful attention to "adequacy at the level of meaning" and "adequacy at the level of causality" enables the sociologist to make a "science" out of sociological research. Although sociological research might be committed to certain value orientations, such as the reduction of racial discrimination, this does not mean that research itself cannot be value-free—that is, objective and impartial—when it comes to testing the adequacy of explanation.

Weber's interest in the possibility of an objective social science stems in part from his attempt to come to terms with his own passionate involvement in value-guided research. Although he had many subjective prejudices and preconceptions, he was also a dedicated scholar who wanted to see sociology established in Germany as an autonomous and respected professional discipline.

However, despite his insistence on the importance of value-freedom and objectivity, Weber was capable of dismissing other people's research for the most spurious of reasons. For instance, he rejected an article submitted to his journal by a Freudian because he found the argument of the paper *ethically* unsound. Furthermore, he was sufficiently unsettled by this submission to write a long letter explaining why it was "not necessary to wash these apparently inescapable diapers in our *Archiv.*"[21]

What Weber absolutely condemned was interference from sources outside the academy. He wanted sociologists to be members of an autonomous profession and strongly criticized academics who became mere servants of the state or of private business, arguing that this turned them into entrepreneurs who would sell their skills to whomever was willing to pay for them. According to Weber, this kind of commitment and "vocation" could have nothing but negative consequences for the profession of sociology.

Other Major Themes and Foci: The Protestant Ethic and the Spirit of Capitalism

Weber's thesis on the relationship between the Protestant ethic and the spirit of capitalism was first published as a lengthy article in the *Archiv* shortly after Weber returned to Germany from the United States. Probably no other thesis in sociology has triggered so much interest and so much controversy. Weber wrote this article, in part, as an attempt to refute the claims of some Marxists that ideas were exclusively the product of the mode of production of a society. What Weber demonstrates in *The Protestant Ethic and the Spirit of Capitalism*, however, is the interrelationship and *interdependence* of "ideational" and "material" factors in history.

By analyzing statistics about the relationship between occupation and denominational affiliation, Weber was able to demonstrate that capitalist entrepreneurs in Germany were disproportionately Protestant. Weber was able to document a close relationship—not just in Europe but also in the United States—between membership in Puritan, Mennonite, Baptist, Methodist, and Quaker sects and successful business activity. In order to explain this relationship, he turned to an interpretation of the meaning of the life-style practiced by these sects. His thesis, in short, was that the Protestants he studied were genuinely religious and, in many ways, profoundly unworldly. However, the *unanticipated* consequences of their conception of duty and vocation led them to adopt a life-style that was uniquely suited to the capitalist mode of production in its earliest stages.

The Protestant Reformation of the sixteenth century attacked the authority of church and pope by preaching the doctrine of "the priesthood of all believers." Traditional Catholicism bound the Christian to God through the doctrine and the sacraments of Holy Mother Church. Both Luther and Calvin taught, however, that human institutions could not displace the individual's personal relationship with God. The Catholic Church had always taught that magical rituals (for example, the mass) stood between God and the true believer. Luther and Calvin asked for the removal of these forms of mediation.

The early Protestant reformers were appalled by the corruption of the church in the Middle Ages. They refused to believe that a hierarchy of priests and bishops could act as an intermediary between human beings and their maker. Nothing was more important to these early Protestants than their own salvation in the next world. Yet, having removed the institutions and rituals of Catholicism, they were faced with the quandary of having to decide how to calculate their standing with a God whom they had made inscrutable.

Lacking external direction about the road to everlasting life, the early Protestants were thrown back on their inner resources. Weber pointed out that this necessity introduced a rational element into the Protestant theodicy that was lacking in Catholicism. Catholics knew that they were part of the body of Christ as long as they were faithful to Mother Church. Protestants, however, were placed in a position of uncertainty about their relationship to the Supreme Being. According to Weber, this laid the foundation for a methodical life-style that was monitored and supervised *internally*. Catholics were as eager for God's grace as Protestants, but they could rely on external institutions and rituals that were not available to the members of Protestant sects.

Underlying the belief systems of many Protestant sects—in particular, those that had adopted Calvin's theology—was a belief in predestination. Calvin had taught that some individuals were born to be saved (the elect), and others were born for hellfire and damnation. Individual believers, who stood naked and alone before God, could not be assured of their ultimate destiny. Whether it was deliberate or fortuitous, the psychological consequence of Calvin's teachings was great fear, insecurity, and anxiety in the minds of believers. As Weber pointed out, this had the result of making Christian individuals even more anxious about their standing with God. Calvin insisted, however, that individuals could not know with certainty whether or not they possessed grace. Under these conditions, the significance of small signs of God's grace would be great.

Weber spent some time reading through the writings of such men as Benjamin Franklin (1706–1790) and the English Puritans John Bunyan (1628–1688) and Richard Baxter (1615–1691). He discovered that these men—whom he thought of as representative of the ideal-typical Puritan—stressed the value of asceticism, hard work, thrift, and diligence. He also discovered that the ideal-typical Puritan adopted a methodical life-style of asceticism because this had the greatest amount of meaning for him. Weber suggested that the "Protestant ethic" stressed self-discipline, diligence, and thrift because this provided some release from the anxiety created by Calvin's doctrine of the elect. Calvinists believed that worldly success (good fortune, a profitable business, and a secure place in the community) was a sign that God did not look unfavorably on them.

According to Weber, the rationalization of personal conduct had a number of consequences that were of secondary importance in the minds of believers but were crucial for the development of capitalism in its earliest forms. These included the willingness to account for every minute "spent" during the course of the day, the rejection of worldly pleasure and of consumerism in all its forms, and the practice of compulsory saving and careful investment in business matters. Such investment occurs not because the Calvinist wishes to become richer but because money that is not spent on personal pleasure must be saved or invested. Puritans were hostile to the enjoyment of wealth, but they made the methodical life-style that was necessary for the accumulation of such wealth morally and ethically desirable. The Catholic Church had never ascribed virtue either to avarice or to a "worldly" life-style of thrift and diligence. The Protestant Reformation, however, removed the traditional restraints placed on the development of a life-style dedicated to capitalist accumulation. It produced individuals who were able to find ultimate significance in the most worldly and mundane of activities.

In *The Protestant Ethic*, Weber did *not* try to turn economic determinism on its head. Rather, he wanted to demonstrate the causal significance of religious orientations in the development of the capitalist West. He did not deny the causal significance of economic and material factors in the development of capitalism, but he suggested that the fortuitous intersection and interdependence of these value orientations and norms had had a demonstrable impact on the rapid development of rational economic activity in the West. Weber did not claim that the capitalist mode of production could have come into existence only as the result of a revolution in religious consciousness. An understanding of the interaction between the Reformation settlements of the sixteenth century and a multiplicity of other factors, however, does help us to understand more about the specific line of historical development experienced in the West over the last three centuries.

Weber suggested that the consequences of the Protestant ethic were tragic in the long run. The early Puritan sects were instrumental in creating the rational economic order of today. The institutions of capitalism, however, once created, require a kind of activity that would have been quite alien to the early Puritans. Although modern rationalism might well have had its roots in a revolution in religious consciousness, it is apparent today that the methodical organization of life serves mainly material, not spiritual, goals. Twentieth-century individuals must adapt to the presence of institutions and organizations that serve the goal of capitalist accumulation for its own sake. No pretense is made that there is anything ethically significant or ultimately meaningful about this. As Weber pointed out:

> The Puritan wanted to work in a calling; we are forced to do so. . . . In Baxter's view the care for external goods should only lie on the shoulders of the "saint like a light cloak which can be thrown aside at any moment." But fate decreed that the cloak should become an iron cage.[22]

SIGNIFICANCE

Vision of the Future

Weber's vision of the future is both pessimistic and paradoxical. It is pessimistic because Weber believed that modern bureaucratization and instrumentalism were, in large part, "escape-proof." It is paradoxical because, although he viewed modern Western rationalism as a "steel-hard cage," Weber rejected all evolutionary theories that treated history as the development or unfolding of predetermined and universal stages.

Weber was too much of a historicist to believe that a general theory of social evolution was possible. For Weber, "cultural reality" results from the value orientations of social actors. Because of his belief that there was no foundation for values other than the *spontaneous* and *nonrational* decisions of historical individuals, Weber concluded that history is an open-ended process. It is this tension between Weber's belief in the escape-proof characteristics of bureaucracy and the open-endedness of history that makes his pessimism about the future appear paradoxical. Weber took a particular interest in the rationalization of culture and of everyday life because he believed that an emphasis on "rationalism" was the most characteristic feature of contemporary Western civilization. He did not suggest that such rationalism was only to be found in the modern West, but he did believe that rationalization could be equated with modernization. By *rationalization*, Weber meant the following:

1. Scientific-technological rationalism (positivism).
2. Metaphysical-ethical rationalism.
3. Methodical life-style rationalism.

We shall look at each of these three strands of rationalism in turn.

Scientific-technological rationalism refers to the rise of science and technology. Weber was extremely interested in tracing the causal interrelationships among science, technology, capitalism, and the rise of the modern nation-state. According to Weber, there is an integral interdependence between capitalism and the modern, bureaucratic nation-state. The state applies social engineering techniques to the practice of social administration in order to manipulate and control citizens effectively and plan for capitalist accumulation.

Metaphysical-ethical rationalism refers to the rationalization of culture and the systematization of meaning. Weber argued that this process was helping to shape contemporary art, music, and architecture. The abstract formalism of modern music, for instance, rationalizes music, making it less sensual and more cerebral.

Metaphysical-ethical rationalism permits individuals to take a unified and standardized approach to the cosmos. For instance, Weber pointed out that the Judaic insistence on a *single* omnipotent God led to a systematized world view for the Jewish people. If there is one powerful God, and if everything in the universe is subsidiary to this Being, then individuals are presented with a philosophy that enables them to envision an overarching and unifying force in the cosmos. Clearly, this orientation allows for a more rational and systematic world view than does a belief in many gods, each to be understood in its own unique manner. Polytheism encourages a multiplicity of orientations; monotheism provides a unifying and monistic context for things of "ultimate significance."

Methodical life-style rationalism refers to the way in which the lives of individuals can become routinized and organized. Weber pointed out that the conception of a "calling," a "vocation," or a "career" can all serve to enhance this kind of rationalism. As we have seen, he believed the Reformation had been extremely important in helping to develop methodical life-style rationalism in the West.

Weber conceded that modern forms of rationality are in many ways a profoundly unsatisfactory response to the "problem of meaning." Scientific-technological rationalism, when applied to problems of living, turns the social actor into an interchangeable and standardized unit. Yet Weber pointed out that this process was unavoidably linked to the "democratization" of the modern world. For instance, the "rights" of citizens can be enforced by state bureaucracies only if the rational-legal authority of these bureaucracies is unchallenged by traditional or charismatic forces. Unless a leveling process takes place, and unless traditional aristocratic privileges and distinctions among individuals are removed, the idea of "democracy" is without meaning.

Similarly, Weber pointed out that, although the rationalization—and, ultimately, the secularization—of metaphysical-ethical world views has left the individual with a feeling of mastery over the world, contemporary individuals now contemplate a universe that has become indifferent to humanity and devoid of meaning. Primitive people had viewed the world as an enchanted garden full of spirits and supernatural forces with whom they had personal familiarity. Modern individuals, on the other hand, view the cosmos as a resource to be manipulated and used for instrumental gain.

Weber suggested, therefore, that there is a necessary ambivalence and tension in the modern world. Modern societies have replaced substantive meaning (founded on orientations toward things of ultimate significance) with a form of rationality that is highly formal and empty of any significance other than instrumental effectiveness in the service of goals that can no longer be questioned. We have become technically rational, but we have also lost sight of the ultimate ends of action. Weber believed that this loss of innocence was irreversible. He rejected out of hand the possibility of a *political* solution to the problem of meaninglessness and alienation. In response to Marx, Weber believed that socialism—which, he conceded, was *the* alternative to capitalism—was likely to accelerate rationalization. Socialism, Weber suggested, would place a greater emphasis on technological mastery of people and things than would capitalism; it would create a vast state bureaucracy, undermine all forms of privatism, and regulate and standardize both the production and consumption of goods and services.

Weber pointed out that as the modern nation-state improved and refined technical-cognitive, or bureaucratic, modes of domination, the control of managerial positions in society would become increasingly important. Political dominance in early capitalist society, Weber suggested, might well be dependent on ownership of the means of production. In advanced capitalist societies, however, such dominance was tied more to rational-legal authority than to class position. This is not to say that Weber failed to understand the symbiotic relationship between bureaucratic domination and capitalist accumulation in the modern world. For instance, he claimed that collective or state ownership of the means of production would not reduce worker alienation; on the contrary, it would rationalize the administration of the work force in the interests of productivity to an even greater extent. Weber did insist, however, that the Marxist equation of political domination with property ownership had been falsified by forces of development that were endemic to capitalist culture. He predicted that the twentieth century would see the "dictatorship of the official," not the "dictatorship of the proletariat."

Weber believed, therefore, that the choice between an ossified and bureaucratized socialist or state-capitalist mode of production on the one hand, and a liberal and competitive capitalism on the other, was the only viable choice for contemporary political society. He preferred competitive capitalism and a market economy to a planned economy and socialism because he believed that a liberal capitalist order was most likely to promote mobility, social dynamism, and personal freedom. Weber was undoubtedly correct in pointing out that both "socialist" and "capitalist" states of the future would use the scientific-technological mode of rationalism in the interests of the state and in pursuit of economic goals. He suggested that freedom for the individual would be maximized by resisting this convergence between economic and political goals. To this extent, Weber, unlike Hegel and Marx, actively supported the differentiation of civil society and the state.

Like Marx, however, Weber was centrally concerned about the fate of the modern individual in advanced industrial nations. Once Weber conceded that the Protestant ethic was no longer necessary for the perpetuation of capitalist relations of production, his analysis of the predicament of the modern individual became not dissimilar to Marx's. Unlike Marx, however, Weber did not believe that the inhumane rationalizing trends of the modern world order could be brushed aside by a political movement.

Weber acknowledged that even in the most bureaucratic of states the possibility of the rise of a charismatic leader cannot be discarded. As noted earlier, however, this alternative to the rigidities of the "steel-hard cage" is totally unrelated to a philosophy of enlightenment. Charismatic leaders might develop a rhetoric of emancipation; but charismatic domination itself is spontaneous, nonrational, and based on the affective and emotional power of collectively binding symbols. Nevertheless, as we have seen, Weber *welcomed* the possibility of such spontaneous and nonrational breakthroughs in human consciousness. He pointed out that no civilization can do without a mixture of all three kinds of legitimate authority—traditional, rational-legal, and charismatic— and he believed that it was desirable to counter rational-legal domination in modern societies to the fullest extent possible.

Weber favored "plebiscitarian leader-democracies" for the modern nation state. He thought that a political system that encouraged the emergence of great leaders, while at the same time holding them accountable to the masses, would allow for the right balance between bureaucratic instrumentalism and the need for substantive meaning in political life. For Weber, modern democracies had to choose between "leader democracies," with relatively pronounced forms of charismatic domination, and "leaderless democracies," where political life was so strongly routinized and bureaucratized that political leaders were hardly necessary at all.

Weber believed that all attempts to abolish the domination of a few individuals over the many were "utopian."[23] The purpose of parliamentary democracy, he pointed out, is not to respond to "the people's will" but to provide some opportunity for charismatic leaders to counter the dead weight of bureaucratic officialdom in political life. Weber's critics have pointed out that Weberian sociology cannot distinguish between the charismatic domination of Benito Mussolini or Adolf Hitler on the one hand, and that of "enlightened" leaders like Franklin D. Roosevelt and Mahatma Gandhi on the other. Yet Weber was consistent in refusing to concede that such a distinction was possible. Because he insisted that *all* value orientations were equally nonrational, Weber believed that sociology could not condemn—and certainly could not support— value-oriented political movements.

Weber's conflation of the way in which authority achieves *dominance* and the way in which it becomes *legitimate* has dangerous consequences. As Wolfgang Mommsen has pointed out:

> Although it is quite feasible to accept the concept of "charisma" in a formal sense as a criterion of leadership even in democratic systems, this surely has nothing to do with their legitimacy. Weber's opinion that in "leadership democracies" authority rests only with the leaders and is, in fact, legitimized by their personal charisma although it is formally derived from the consent of the "governed" . . . was open to political abuse. When he argued that it is the charismatic qualification of leaders which matters whereas the democratic institutions are a mere functional machinery in their hands he overstated his own case and came dangerously close to the *"Fuhrerprinzip,"* the Fascist leadership principle.[24]

Contemporary Relevance

In 1964, the Fifteenth German Sociological Congress was held in Heidelberg to commemorate the centenary of Weber's birth. At this conference, papers were presented by two key figures in twentieth-century social theory: Talcott Parsons (1902–1979) and Herbert Marcuse (1898–1979). Both these men had been profoundly influenced by Weber, but they held sharply contrasting views about the legacy of his life's work.

The Harvard sociologist Talcott Parsons had translated *The Protestant Ethic* into English in 1930 and had played a major role in introducing Weberian sociology into the United States. Parsons had become a graduate student at Heidelberg five years after Weber died and had had a close association with Weber's colleagues and students. Upon his return to the United States, Parsons made Weberian "action theory" foundational for his own "voluntaristic" theory of action. When he turned to structural functionalism in the 1940s, Parsons argued that Weber himself would probably have become a functionalist if he had lived a little longer.[25] Although he was critical of Weber in some respects, Parsons believed that Weber deserved his reputation in the United States as the most important of sociology's founders—a reputation that Parsons himself helped to build.

At the Heidelberg conference, Parsons praised Weber for showing how sociology could be committed to human values while at the same time demonstrating how science "need not be bound to the values of any particular historic culture."[26] Parsons suggested that "it is impossible to classify Weber politically as a 'conservative' in the older German tradition, as a 'liberal' in the economic individualist sense, or as a 'socialist.' "[27] He claimed that Weberian sociology managed to rise above the merely ideological disputes of the late nineteenth and early twentieth centuries. According to Parsons, Weberian sociology transcended the limited and partial perspectives of conservatism, liberalism, and socialism. He concluded his address by claiming that Weber, "as one of the very few true founders of sociology," understood that the "science" of sociology was probably destined to play "a major role" in shaping the world of the future.

In his discussion of Weber's significance, Herbert Marcuse, who had been a refugee from Hitler's Germany in the 1930s, reached quite different conclusions. Arguing that early in his career Weber had "recklessly subordinated value-free economics to the demands of imperial power-politics," Marcuse insisted that Weber's theory of "value-freedom" in sociology merely "[frees] science for the acceptance of evaluations imposed from outside."[28] Marcuse's major indictment of Weber was that he refused to countenance the possibility of "a quantitatively *different* historical rationality"—different, that is, from the formal mechanisms of bureaucratic control that Weber acknowledged were integral to late capitalism. Marcuse suggested that Weber actually began to conflate the instrumental rationalism of contemporary capitalist societies with reason itself. He also accused Weber of failing to investigate the relationship between technical-cognitive rationality and the "specific social interests" of certain classes in society in using scientific-technological rationality as a means of social domination over others. As Marcuse put it, "The *concept of technical reason* is perhaps itself *ideology*."[29]

To a large extent, many of the German sociologists in Heidelberg were critical of the political effects of Weber's career, whereas most of the American scholars were positive about Weber's legacy. For instance, Benjamin Nelson (1911–1977) accused Marcuse of doing "great violence to historical tradition and fact."[30] On the other hand, the German critical theorist Jürgen Habermas (b. 1929) wryly congratulated his

American colleagues for coming from a society that had—so it was thought—transcended ideology. Habermas remarked:

> Weber's political sociology has had a different history here. At the time of the First World War [Weber] outlined a sketch of a Caesar-like leader-democracy on the contemporary basis of a national-state imperialism. This militant latter-day liberalism had consequences in the Weimar period which we, and not Weber, must answer for.[31]

The proceedings in Heidelberg generated a great deal of interest in the United States, and letters were exchanged in the *New York Times* by Marcuse and Nelson that attempted to clarify some of the charges and countercharges made at the German congress.[32]

In retrospect, Parsons's claim that Weberian sociology had foreshadowed "the end of ideology" seems risible. Similarly, the wedge that he tried to drive between Weber's political and academic orientations helped to create a distorted view of Weber's life's work. On the other hand, many of Weber's critics, like Marcuse, did not seem to understand how their deep hatred for Western bureaucratic instrumentalism would have been shared by Weber himself.

The mixture of veneration and hostility shown toward Weber in Heidelberg is indicative of the continuing vitality of Weberian ideas for sociologists in the midtwentieth century. Thanks to prominent U.S. sociologists like Parsons and Nelson, Weber has been more of an influential figure in the United States than in Germany over the last few decades. Part of the reason for this is that Parsons's Weber, for instance, was always presented as a cautious but committed supporter of the U.S. system of "democratic pluralism."

Throughout the twentieth century, Weber has been a critically important figure for theorists of all descriptions. He has left his mark on many of the most prominent intellectuals of the twentieth century, both from the political left and from the right. For example, Georg Lukács (1885–1971), who knew Weber well and who often visited him in Heidelberg, frequently debated with him about the desirability of a socialist mode of production for Germany. Weber had a great impact on Lukács when the latter was still a young man. (Lukács, however, would later claim that Weber had helped, intellectually, to pave the way for Hitler.) The American economist and political scientist Joseph Schumpeter (1883–1950) was also strongly influenced by Weber. Unlike Lukács, Schumpeter claimed that "the whole of Max Weber's facts and arguments fits perfectly into Marx's system."[33]

In the eighty years that have elapsed since his death, Weber's sociology has been used and adapted by many different types of theorists. The phenomenologist Alfred Schutz (1899–1959) took Weber's conception of interpretive theory as the starting point for his own work. Schutz agreed with Weber that the study of subjective understanding (*Verstehen*) is crucial for sociological explanation. The members of the Frankfurt School of critical theorists (including Marcuse) used Weber's analysis of rationalization and rational-legal domination as the starting point of their analysis of modes of class oppression in advanced capitalist societies. In the United States, theories of social stratification have generally been based on a pluralistic—and Weberian, rather than Marxist—model of stratification. After eighty years, Weber's comparative sociology of religion is still viewed by many as the most important contribution any one sociological theorist ever made to this subject.

The continuing importance of Weber in the latter part of the twentieth century stems in part from the fact that he was a brilliant and profound apologist for liberal capitalism and for "plebiscitarian leader democracies." At the same time, however, Weber was more aware of the tensions and contradictions inherent in Western "democracies" than were many Marxists. Weber's most important legacy is probably the challenge that his work presents to the Marxist world view. This does not involve disagreement about the nature of contemporary society, in itself; as we have seen, there is broad agreement between Weberians and Marxists about this. To put it simplistically, the Weberian challenge to Marxism involves the question of whether or not there is some immanent meaning to history.

Weber's disagreement with critical theorists of all descriptions centers on his insistence that those living in the modern epoch, "which has eaten of the tree of knowledge," must accept that they can learn nothing about the intrinsic meaning of the world historical process.[34] Weber claimed that it was the fate of modern individuals to discover that they have to make subjective and arbitrary decisions in deciding which of the many competing gods and demons to serve. Weber did not believe that there was anything intrinsically desirable about reason. As far as he was concerned, an emancipatory interest in reason is ill-conceived and self-defeating. Above all, Weber believed it would be extraordinarily naive to welcome the emergence of a world that contains humans who have grasped that they have sole responsibility for creating meaning in the universe.

NOTES

1. Marianne Weber, *Max Weber: A biography,* pp. 62–63.
2. Ibid., p. 72.
3. "Der Nationalstaat und die Volkswirtschaftspolitik," in *Gesammelte politische Schriften* (Munich: Drei-Masken-Verlag, 1920). Quoted by Marianne Weber in Max Weber: A biography, p. 217.
4. Noted by Marianne Weber, in *Max Weber: A biography,* p. 293.
5. Speech reported by Marianne Weber, in ibid., p. 581.
6. From a lecture delivered in Munich on January 19, 1920.
7. *Economy and society,* p. 1392.
8. Marianne Weber, *Max Weber: A biography,* p. 88.
9. Talcott Parsons, introduction to Max Weber, *The theory of social and economic organization,* p. 6.
10. Irving Zeitlin, *Ideology and the development of sociological theory* (Englewood Cliffs, NJ: Prentice-Hall, 1981), p. 163.
11. *Gesammelte politische Schriften* (Tübingen: J.C.B. Mohr, 1956), p. 19.
12. Ibid., p. 309.
13. *The methodology of the social sciences,* p. 103.
14. *The theory of social and economic organization,* p. 88.
15. Ibid., p. 152.
16. *Economy and society,* p. 927.
17. *The theory of social and economic organization,* p. 154.
18. *The methodology of the social sciences,* p. 90.
19. *The theory of social and economic organization,* p. 88.
20. Ibid., p. 99.
21. Letter dated September 13, 1907.
22. *The Protestant ethic and the spirit of capitalism,* p. 181. Talcott Parsons translated "a steel-hard cage" (ein stahlhartes Gehause) as "an iron cage," and the term has stuck.
23. Wolfgang J. Mommsen, *Max Weber und die deutsche Politik, 1890–1920* (Tübingen: J.C.B. Mohr, 1959), p. 392.
24. Wolfgang J. Mommsen, *The age of bureaucracy,* p. 93.
25. See Parsons's introduction to *The theory of social and economic organization.*
26. Talcott Parsons, "Value-freedom and objectivity," in Otto Stammer (Ed.), *Max Weber and sociology today,* p. 33.

27. Ibid., p. 48.

28. Herbert Marcuse, "Industrialization and capitalism," in Stammer (Ed.), *Max Weber and sociology today*, p. 133.

29. Ibid., p. 149.

30. Ibid., p. 166.

31. Ibid., p. 66. After the Second World War, Parsons was instrumental in helping Nazis flee Germany and come to the United States. He even tried to secure positions at Harvard for some leading intellectuals who had worked with the SS. In 1964, Habermas was not aware of the political associations of the man who became such an avid defender of value-free sociology in the 1950s and 1960s.

32. See *New York Times Book Review*, February 28, 1965, pp. 34–36.

33. Joseph A. Schumpeter, *Capitalism, socialism, and democracy* (New York: Harper & Row, 1950), p. 10.

34. *The methodology of the social sciences*, p. 57.

GLOSSARY

Affective action Emotional and impulsive action that is an end in itself.

Asceticism A type of *social action* that is highly disciplined, self-denying, and relatively individualistic in orientation.

Authority The ability of one individual to command another effectively.

Charisma An individual's ability to exercise *domination* on the basis of personal and superhuman or supernatural qualities.

Charismatic authority *Authority* legitimated through *charisma*.

Class position A position in a system of economic stratification and property ownership that helps determine the "life chances" of individuals.

Cultural object Something that is created through social interaction and is external, but meaningful, for individuals—for example, a social institution, a baseball game, an organization, or a symphony concert.

Domination The probability that an order will be obeyed.

Formal rationality Occurs when means are instrumentally effective for given ends and when the rules that determine *social action* are abstract, formal, and generalizable.

Greater Germany Concept important to nationalistic Germans in the nineteenth and twentieth centuries. Generally understood to encompass all territories in which German was the predominant language.

Historicism The doctrine that states that societies and cultures can be understood only as historically unique entities.

Ideal type Methodological approach developed by Wilhelm Dilthey. Involves the development of the usual, typical, or most complete features of a phenomenon in order to facilitate comparison and analysis. Weber stressed that ideal types were "one-sided" and "partial" descriptions of reality.

Ideographic understanding That kind of understanding that treats each element of social reality as unique and as qualitatively different from other aspects of social reality.

Legitimate authority *Authority* that is accepted as right and proper according to certain cultural prescriptions.

Metaphysical-ethical rationalism The systematization of meaning, so that individuals believe that order and meaning in the universe are somehow interrelated and interdependent.

Methodical life-style rationalism The organization of an individual's life so that it is routinized and orderly.

Methodological individualism Assumption that the basic unit of analysis is the social individual.

Motive The interpretation that is made of *social action* in order to make it meaningful. (Not to be confused with the postulated cause of action.)

Mysticism The antithesis of *asceticism* in that it encourages sensuality and abandonment. An orientation that encourages the rejection of technical-cognitive and rational orientations in the world.

Nomothetic explanation Explanation that tries to explain orderly relationships in the world by reference to general laws.

Otherworldly orientations Orientations that point individuals away from things of this world and toward other, supernatural domains.

Phenomenology A discipline that attempts to describe the foundations of human consciousness.

Plebiscitarian leader-democracies Political systems where leaders attain great power over others but can be toppled from power by an electorate.

Power The probability that one actor within a social relationship will be in a position to carry out his or her own will despite resistance.

Problem of theodicy The problem of explaining human suffering, misfortune, and death.

Protestant ethic An *ascetic* orientation that encourages hard work, thrift, and righteous forms of godliness.

Rationalization The increase of rational orientations and activity in social life brought about by *scientific-technical rationalism, metaphysical-ethical rationalism*, and *methodical lifestyle rationalism*.

Rational-legal authority *Authority* legitimated through a strict observance of the rules of office.

Rationally purposeful action *Social action* that is instrumentally oriented. Occurs when the ends of action are seen as means to higher, taken-for-granted ends.

Routinization of charisma The transformation of *charismatic authority* into *traditional authority* or, more usually, *rational-legal authority*.

Scientific-technical rationalism The organization of experience that results from the effective use of science and technology.

Secularization The decline of religious institutions and of religious beliefs and practices.

Social action Action by individuals that is generally seen as meaningful and that takes the actions and responses of others into account.

Spirit of capitalism An orientation that stresses careful planning and investment so that capital will return the maximum profit.

Status The evaluations made of an individual in terms of positive or negative esteem or honor.

Structural functionalism Theoretical orientation that focuses on the functional requisites or structural needs of a social system.

Traditional action Occurs when the ends and means of *social action* are fixed by custom and tradition. Action is so habitual that it is taken for granted.

Traditional authority *Authority* legitimated through individuals' acquiescence in a system of political rule that has become habitual or customary.

Value-freedom According to Weber, the orientation of the kind of sociological interpretation that analyzes human value commitments without making reference to their worthiness.

Value-rational action Occurs when individuals use effective means to achieve goals that are set by their values.

Verstehen German term that means "understanding" in the sense of understanding the meaning of *social action*.

Voluntaristic action Action that (1) is goal-directed; (2) takes means into consideration; and (3) is normatively regulated with respect to the choice of ends and means.

Weimar Republic Germany between 1919 and the rise of Hitler (1933).

ANNOTATED BIBLIOGRAPHY

Primary Sources

The agrarian sociology of ancient civilizations (R. I. Frank, Trans.). London: New Left Books, 1976 [1896, 1906] (paper).

Not translated until 1976. These early essays show that, far from denying their significance, Weber attributed great importance to the role of economic and material factors in history.

Ancient Judaism (Hans H. Gerth & Don Martingdale, Trans. & Eds.). Glencoe, IL: Free Press, 1952 [1917–1919] (paper).

The last part of Weber's sociology of religion, written shortly after *The Religion of China* and *The Religion of India.*

The city (Don Martingdale & Gertrud Neuwirth, Trans. & Eds.). New York: Collier Books, 1962 [1921] (paper).

Weber's theory of the city as a social and economic unit.

Critique of Stammler (Guy Oakes, Trans.; introductory essay by Oakes). New York: Free Press, 1977 [1907].

This extended review of Rudolph Stammler's book *The Historical Materialist Conception of Economy and Law* was first published in the *Archiv.* In this article, Weber discusses the methodological problems associated with interpretative theory.

Economy and society (2 vols.; Ephraim Fischoff, Hans Gerth, et al., Trans.; Guenther Roth & Claus Wittich, Eds.). Berkeley: University of California Press, 1978 [1925].

Weber's major contribution to sociological theory. Contains his definition of basic sociological terms and sociological categories.

From Max Weber: Essays in sociology (H. H. Gerth & C. Wright Mills, Trans. & Eds.; introduction by Gerth & Mills). New York: Oxford University Press, 1974 (paper).

The essays in this compendium, first translated in 1946, introduced some of Weber's most important papers to the U.S. public.

This collection contains two of Weber's most important papers: "Politics as a Vocation" and "Science as a Vocation" (pp. 77–158). In these essays, Weber lucidly discusses his conception of the limitations of the relationship between theory and practice.

Max Weber on capitalism, bureaucracy, and religion (Stanislav Andreski, Trans. & Ed.). New York: Allen & Unwin, 1983 (paper).

This anthology is particularly useful, as Andreski gives us some new translations of that part of Weber's opus dealing with issues that Weber himself treated as central for sociology.

Max Weber on law and society (Edward A. Shils & Max Rheinstein, Trans.; Max Rheinstein, Ed.). New York: Simon & Schuster, 1954 (paper).

Weber's sociology of law. Translated from *Wirtschaft und Gesellschaft* (Economy and Society).

Max Weber on universities: The power of the state and the dignity of the academic calling in imperial Germany (Edward A. Shils, Trans. & Ed.; introductory note by Shils). Chicago: University of Chicago Press, 1974 [1908–1919] (paper).

Essays dealing with academic freedom and the role of the university in modern society.

The methodology of the social sciences (Edward A. Shils & Henry A. Finch, Trans. & Eds.; foreword by Shils). New York: Free Press, 1949 [1903–1917].

Three essays: "The Logic of the Cultural Sciences," "The Meaning of 'Ethical Neutrality' in Sociology and Economics," and " 'Objectivity' in Social Science and Social Policy."

The Protestant ethic and the spirit of capitalism (Talcott Parsons, Trans.). New York: Charles Scribner's Sons, 1958 [1904–1905] (paper).

Weber's most famous work. First published in the *Archiv.*

The religion of China (Hans H. Gerth, Trans. & Ed.). New York: Free Press, 1964 [1916] (paper).

Weber's major objective in writing about this subject was to compare Chinese civilization with the West and show how the absence of an appropriate religious ethic had inhibited the development of a rational system of capitalist production in China.

The religion of India (Hans H. Gerth & Don Martingdale, Trans. & Eds.). New York: Free Press, 1967 [1916–1917] (paper).

Again, Weber was interested in comparing India with the civilization of western Europe. Contains Weber's sociology of Hinduism and Buddhism.

Roscher and Knies: The logical problems of historical economics (Guy Oakes, Trans.; introductory essay by Oakes). New York: Free Press, 1975 [1903, 1905, 1906].

Originally published in three parts. Weber's first methodological work in which he argues against positivism and intuitionism as methodological devices.

The sociology of religion (Ephraim Fischoff, Trans.; introduction by Talcott Parsons). Boston: Beacon Press, 1964 [1922] (paper).

Weber's summary of his *Religionssoziologie*, first published as part of *Wirtschaft und Gesellschaft*.

The theory of social and economic organization (A. M. Henderson & Talcott Parsons, Trans. & Eds.; introduction by Talcott Parsons). New York: Free Press, 1964 (paper).

The first part of *Wirtschaft und Gesellschaft*. Translated into English in 1947.

Secondary Sources

Antonio, Robert J., & Ronald M. Glassman. (Eds.). *A Weber-Marx dialogue.* Lawrence: University of Kansas Press, 1985.

This extremely valuable book is a collection of essays dealing with the relationship between Weber and Marx. Rather than viewing Weber as someone who conducted "a debate with the ghost of Marx," the contributors to this anthology have analyzed issues within Marxist thought against a Weberian backdrop. Antonio and Glassman argue that Marx and Weber have contributed more to classical sociologi-

cal theory and global political thought than any other figures in social thought. This anthology is a fine contribution to critical scholarship about Marx and Weber.

Bendix, Reinhard. *Max Weber: An intellectual portrait.* Berkeley: University of California Press, 1977 (paper).

The classic introduction to Weber as a man and as a sociologist. Contains a good discussion of Weber's contribution to empirical sociological research.

Breiner, Peter. *Max Weber and democratic politics.* Ithaca: Cornell University Press, 1996.

Breiner evaluates Weber's political sociology. Topics covered include democracy, socialism, capitalism, and the nation. As a political theorist, Weber is compared with Rousseau, Machiavelli, the Marxist theory, and Antonio Gramsci.

Brubaker, Rogers. *The limits of rationality: An essay on the social and moral thought of Max Weber.* London: Allen & Unwin, 1984.

This short work contains a useful discussion of the interplay between Weber's empirical work and his moral vision. This is a particularly useful book for the student interested in this topic.

Collins, Randall. *Weberian sociological theory.* Cambridge: Cambridge University Press, 1986.

In this book, one of the leading U.S. sociological theorists sets out to demonstrate that "Weberian sociology [still] is intellectually alive" and that Weberian ideas continue to mark the frontier of sociological knowledge. Topics covered include Weber's theories of technology, imperialism, culture, the family, and sex.

Diggins, John Patrick. *Max Weber: Politics and the spirit of tragedy.* New York: Basic Books, 1999 (paper).

One of the most important works in English written about Max Weber in the last quarter-century. Diggins shows Weber in a new light—as a man very much concerned with the tragedy of modernity and with the difficulty of reconciling an "ethic of responsibility" with an "ethic of principled convictions." Diggins emphasizes Nietzsche's influence on Weber and makes intriguing connections between the political conditions of pre–World War I Germany and the United States today.

Honigsheim, Paul & Alan Sica. (Ed.). *The unknown Max Weber.* New York & Somerset, New Jersey: Transaction Publishers, 1999.

Paul Honigsheim was an associate of Weber in the 1910s. In the late 1940s, he published four essays, "Max Weber as Rural Sociologist," "Max Weber as Applied Anthropologist," "Max Weber as Historian of Agriculture and Rural Life," and "Max Weber: His Religious and Ethical Background and Development." These are presented here in English for the first time.

Löwith, Karl. *Max Weber and Karl Marx.* London: Allen & Unwin, 1982 [1932] (paper).

A translation of an important essay written more than sixty years ago by one of Germany's most influential philosophers. Löwith emphasizes that Weber and Marx were both working on essentially the same project: a critique of "capitalistic culture." This is an extremely important essay that has been neglected by most American sociologists.

Mitzman, Arthur. *The iron cage: An historical interpretation of Max Weber.* New York: Grosset and Dunlap, 1969 (paper).

A psychobiography that also gives a great deal of information about the intellectual and social milieu in which Weber lived. Speculative in parts, but fascinating.

Mommsen, Wolfgang J. *The age of bureaucracy: Perspectives on the political sociology of Max Weber.* New York: Harper Torchbooks, 1974 (paper).

A discussion of the significance of Weber's sociology for modern societies. Mommsen is a most perceptive critic of Weber. Highly recommended.

Mommsen, Wolfgang J., & Jürgen Osterhammel. (Eds.). *Max Weber and his contemporaries.* London: Allen & Unwin, 1987.

This book contains thirty-seven separate essays dealing with contemporaries of Weber and with Weber's relationships with these individuals.

Portis, Edward Bryan. *Max Weber and political commitment: Science, politics, and personality.* Philadelphia: Temple University Press, 1986.

Portis suggests, rather controversially, that Weber was such a great social scientist precisely because he was a political eunuch. An intelligent discussion of the relationship between political commitment and scientific inquiry.

Ringer, Fritz. *The decline of the German mandarins.* Cambridge, MA: Harvard University Press, 1969.

A discussion of the social and intellectual background of German social theory. Ringer describes the role of the academic in German social and political life.

Ringer, Fritz & Jane Bendix. *Max Weber's methodology: The unification of the cultural and social sciences.* Cambridge, MA: Harvard University Press, 1998.

Ringer again relates Weber's work to the German intellectual debates of Weber's time. According to Ringer, Weber managed to bridge the gap between the humanities and the social sciences.

Sayer, Derek. *Capitalism and modernity: An excursus on Marx and Weber.* London: Routledge, 1991 (paper).

In recent years, sociologists have paid increasing attention to Marx's and Weber's analyses of modernity (see also Bryan S. Turner's work). Sayer's volume makes a concise contribution to this ongoing debate.

Scaff, Lawrence A. *Fleeing the iron cage: Culture, politics, and modernity in the thought of Max Weber.* Berkeley: University of California Press, 1989 (paper).

Scaff argues that the range and depth of Weber's ideas are too extensive to be easily encapsulated. His interest is in the "other Weber" that has been missed in the "rush to establish the conceptual boundaries and methodological foundations of the social sciences."

Schluchter, Wolfgang (Neil Solomon, Trans.). *Paradoxes of modernity: Culture and conduct in the theory of Max Weber.* Palo Alto: Stanford University Press, 1996.

Written by one of Germany's leading Weberians, a Professor of Sociology at Heidelberg University. Schluchter focuses on Weber's work on politics, ethics, and modernity.

Sica, Alan. *Weber, irrationality, and social order.* Berkeley: University of California Press, 1988.

In this original study of Weber, Sica argues that Western scholars have tended to overemphasize Weber's interest in rationalism as a predominant Western characteristic. Citing Pareto, Sica argues that sociology cannot afford to ignore the irrational component of life as "an essential invariant element of lived experience."

Stammer, Otto (Ed.). *Max Weber and sociology today.* New York: Harper Torchbooks, 1972 (paper).

A collection of some of the papers given in Heidelberg in 1964. Contains the important papers by Herbert Marcuse and Talcott Parsons discussing Weber's legacy.

Turner, Bryan S. *Max Weber: From history to modernity.* London: Routledge, 1992 (paper).

Beginning with the chapter "Max Weber and the Panic Culture of Postmodernism," this book is an excellent, up-to-date discussion of the relevance of Weber's sociology for contemporary studies in modernity and postmodernity.

Turner, Charles. *Modernity and politics in the work of Max Weber.* London: Routledge, 1992 (paper).

Turner notes that a substantial part "of Weber's 'greatness' lies in the fact that he was always a man to be reckoned with, never to be followed, that he would not have founded a school." Turner concludes that Weber must still be studied by all social scientists because he grappled with the fundamental issues that will always be central to the study of culture.

Turner, Stephen P. (Ed.) *The Cambridge companion to Max Weber.* Cambridge: Cambridge University Press, 2000 (paper).

Includes essays by leading Weber commentators in Germany and the United States, including Jon Elster on rationality, economy, and society; Alan Sica on rationalization and culture; Wolfgang Schluchter on the psychophysics of culture; Lawrence A. Scaff on the cultural situation of the modern age; and Guenther Roth on global capitalism and multiethnicity.

Weber, Marianne. *Max Weber: A biography* (Harry Zohn, Trans.). New York: Wiley, 1975 [1926].

Written by Weber's wife. Contains a great deal of useful background information about the personal details of Weber's career.

The conflict between society and the individual is continued within the individual himself as the conflict among his component parts. Thus, it seems to me, the basic struggle between society and the individual is integral to the general form of individual life. It does not derive from any single, "antisocial," individualized interest.

Society strives to be a totality, an organic unit of which individuals must be a part. Society expects the individual to utilize all his strength in the service of the particular function that he performs as a social unit; that he shape himself to become the most suitable vehicle for this function. However, the drive toward unity and completeness that is characteristic of the individual is at odds with this expectation. The individual strives to be complete in himself not merely to help make society complete in itself. He strives to develop his full capacities, irrespective of the particular interests that society might have in these different capacities. This conflict between the totality, which imposes a onesidedness upon its elements, and the part, which itself strives to be complete, is insoluble. No house can be built of houses, but only of specially formed stones; no tree can grow from trees, but only from differentiated cells.

—Georg Simmel, *Grundfragen der Soziologie*[1]

9

Georg Simmel

(1858–1918)

Life

Georg Simmel was born on March 1, 1858, the youngest in a family of seven children. His father was a prosperous Jewish businessman, who owned a partnership in a chocolate factory in Berlin. The father, who had converted to Roman Catholicism before Georg was born, died when his youngest son was still an infant. It seems that Georg was never very close to his mother. A family friend, the owner of a successful publishing house, became Georg's guardian, leaving Simmel a considerable legacy when he died.

After graduating from the *Gymnasium* in 1876, Simmel enrolled at the University of Berlin, where he studied history, philosophy, and psychology. At Berlin, Simmel was taught by some of the same professors who were to instruct Max Weber a few years later. These men included the historians Theodor Mommsen and Heinrich von Treitschke. In 1881, Simmel was awarded a doctoral degree for a dissertation on Immanuel Kant's (1724–1804) philosophy of nature. His *Habilitationsschrift* (the dissertation required of those who planned an academic career) was also written about Kant.

In 1885, Simmel became a *Privatdozent* (lecturer) at the University of Berlin. By all accounts, he was a popular and successful teacher. Simmel's early lectures at Berlin concentrated on philosophy and ethics, but before long he began to teach some of the first sociology courses in Germany. Simmel was proud of his renown as a speaker, and he devoted a great deal of time to preparing his lectures for audiences that grew in size every semester. (In all probability, Mead—who studied at Berlin from 1889 until

1891—was among the large number of foreigners who attended Simmel's lectures. In the 1880s, both Simmel and Mead claimed Wilhelm Dilthey [1833–1911] as their mentor.) At the lectern, Simmel impressed and entertained his audience with his ingenuity and his ability to explore subjects in a novel and challenging way.

After making two applications, Simmel was appointed an "extraordinary professor" (*ausserordentlicher Professor*) in 1901. This position, however, was honorary only; it was not remunerative and did not entail the privileges and responsibilities of a regular professorship. Simmel obtained this title largely through Gustav von Schmoller's efforts to elevate him. Schmoller, a close friend of Weber's and a leading member of the *Verein für Sozialpolitik* (Association for Social Policy), was a leading liberal in German academic circles. Together with Weber, he tried to have Simmel appointed as a full professor at a provincial university. Weber hoped that Simmel could be given a professorship at the University of Heidelberg.

When a recommendation on Simmel's behalf was sent to the Ministry of Culture in the state of Baden, the minister of education requested Professor Dietrich Schaefer in Berlin to evaluate Simmel's candidacy. Schaefer reported the candidate to be quite unsuitable for a professorship. He described Simmel as "a dyed-in-the-wool Israelite, in his outward appearance, in his bearing and in his manner of thinking." Though conceding that Simmel's lectures were well attended, he noted they were favored particularly by Jews, foreigners, and ladies. Schaefer reported that Simmel "spices his words with clever sayings" and described the candidate's "academic and literary merits and success" as "very circumscribed and limited." He concluded by pointing out that Simmel's "world view and philosophy of life . . . are only too obviously different from our German Christian-classical education." Schaefer also drew the minister's attention to the fact that in his view "sociology [had] yet to earn its position as a scholarly discipline.[2] As a result of Schaefer's report, Simmel was denied the professorship at Heidelberg. One can only speculate about what the consequences might have been if both Weber and Simmel had served as cochairs of the same department of sociology.

Throughout his career, Simmel suffered from the effects of anti-Semitism, but anti-Semitism alone cannot fully explain why he was always an academic outsider. Simmel was a cultivated man of good family background; and many Jews, both converted and unconverted, were able to overcome the numerous impediments that were placed between them and a full faculty appointment. The major obstacle to Simmel's advancement was that he tended to be seen as a man who did not treat the vocation of a scholar and professor with due deference or with the right kind of seriousness. Even Weber believed that Simmel, though "brilliant," was something of a "dilettante."

In 1910, Leopold von Wiese (1876–1969), who was relatively well disposed toward Simmel, expressed the prevailing view among his colleagues when he wrote:

> As far as I can tell [Simmel's] investigations run the danger of ending in scattered fragments. Surely they contain not only a great many fine observations, but also peaks of the most valuable insight; but they lose themselves in playing with the fullness of forms with the subtlest and nicest of nuances.[3]

Many of his contemporaries were wary of Simmel because he wrote on a great number of nonacademic and nonscholarly subjects. For instance, among other topics,

Simmel published essays on styles of greeting, love, the sociology of smell, secrecy, fashion, and the social significance of chairs. This kind of thing did not endear him to most German intellectuals. Although his *Soziologie* (1908) outlines his general approach to sociological analysis, throughout much of his life Simmel made no attempt to present his own system of thought in an organized fashion to his public. He preferred to publish his material in journals and periodicals that were not devoted exclusively to scholarly work. Furthermore, unlike Weber, Simmel was not good at academic politics. He had little interest in meeting the right people or in joining the right associations for the sake of his career.

Nevertheless, Simmel and Weber, together with Ferdinand Tönnies (1855–1936), were the major figures in the establishment of sociology in the German university system in the first two decades of the twentieth century. Simmel was the first German academic to use the term "sociology" as the title of a book,[4] and he grappled with purely sociological issues and problems long before Weber's and Tönnies's interests were focused on this new subject.

Simmel's earliest interest had been the study of aesthetics, and his first published work was on art. He completed books on the sculptor Rodin, the poet Goethe, and the painter Rembrandt. In 1890, shortly after completing his dissertation, he published a sociological work entitled *Über soziale Differenzierung (On Social Differentiation, 1890)*. This was closely followed in 1892 by *The Problems of the Philosophy of History*, a largely epistemological work. *The Philosophy of Money*, the book that has influenced contemporary sociologists the most, was published in 1900. In all, Simmel published 31 books and monographs and 256 articles during his lifetime.[5]

Although he lived a marginal existence as an academic, Simmel took the professor's role as the upholder and defender of civilized and enlightened ideals seriously. The destruction caused by World War I was a great blow to him. Like Weber, however, he was initially an enthusiastic supporter of Germany's war effort. Germany, Simmel believed, was fighting to uphold what was best and finest about European civilization.

For nearly the whole of his adult life, Simmel remained in Berlin, sharing comfortable apartments with his wife, Gertrud, whom he married in 1890. In 1914, he was finally offered a full professorship at the provincial University of Strasbourg, on the border between Germany and France. Although the university was far from the capital, Simmel was willing to make the move to accept that which had eluded him for so long.

In 1914, however, many students were being called up by the military authorities. A few months after Simmel arrived in Strasbourg, lecture halls were converted into military hospitals and dormitories were turned into barracks. After waiting so long for a regular university appointment, Simmel found that there was now little for him to do.

In 1918, Simmel learned that he had cancer of the liver. For a few months, he retreated into the Black Forest to finish work on his *Lebensanschauung* (philosophy of experience). In this final work, he returned once more to philosophy and to an investigation of how human life—which, he believed, is an unfolding process of growth—shapes and confronts the forms and objects of its experience. Simmel pointed out that there is a dialectical relation, or "eternal tension," between the creative impulse of human existence (life itself) and its static creations—works of art, religious belief, economic systems. These static creations come to exist in their own right and grow to hamper individual creativity and growth. Thus such products, though necessary to human existence, are also capable of producing a profound sense of alienation. Simmel believed that artists and scientists who dedicate their lives to art or science do so at the cost of sacrificing their potential interests and capabilities. They become unidimensional in the process of serving an objectification that was initially created for the sake of *subjective* forms of self-expression.

In many ways, the *Lebensanschauung* is the culmination of Simmel's life's work. The debate about whether Simmel's sociology is fragmentary and capricious, or more serious and systematic than is generally acknowledged, still continues. Nevertheless, there is undoubtedly a unifying conception of human existence in all of Simmel's work. Nicholas Spykman summarized this best when, a few years after Simmel's death, he noted the similarities between Simmel and Hegel. Unlike Hegel, however, Simmel did not have his head in the clouds. As Spykman points out, "While for Hegel the absolute was the self-unfolding Idea, for Simmel the absolute was Life itself."[6]

Social Environment

Simmel was born in the very center of Berlin, the city that was to be his home until four years before his death. Not surprisingly, he was very much a creature of the metropolis, and his sociology reflects his interest in forms of sociation that are cultivated, sophisticated, and urbane. By 1900, Berlin, with a population of four million, had become one of the largest metropolitan areas of Europe. It was the capital of the German Reich and a cultural center for the entire European continent.

Simmel was highly reflective about how the modern, urban individual was compelled to adapt to the mechanical and impersonal forces that were instrumental in shaping the personalities of city dwellers. In his sociological work, he documents how city life helps to produce individuals who are intelligent, calculating, and quick-witted, but also somewhat devious and nervous.

Until the end of the nineteenth century, most German academics had believed that German science and culture formed a homogeneous whole. By the time Simmel and Weber reached adulthood, however, German intellectuals, artists, scientists, and politicians were beginning to lose touch with each other's work. Most academics were willing to accept—and to be a part of—a political establishment that adhered to traditional and aristocratic values. However, a younger generation of artists and intellectuals reacted sharply against the effects of Prussian orthodoxy. It was largely with the members of this official counterculture that Simmel associated during his long tenure in Berlin. In the 1890s, Simmel associated with socialist groups in Berlin. Again, these connections did not help him gain professional advancement.

Simmel was a close friend of the romantic poets Stefan George (1868–1933) and Rainer Maria Rilke (1875–1926). He and Gertrud formed a close association with the circle of people who surrounded these men. Most of Simmel's associates were sharply critical of the stifling effects of authoritarian Prussian control on academic and university life. (Even Weber had complained about this when he taught at the University of Berlin.)

At the same time, the artists and intellectuals with whom Simmel associated were as critical about the rising bourgeoisie in Germany as they were of the old Prussian aristocracy. Like the bourgeoisie, they were resentful about their exclusion from the political establishment in Berlin. Unlike the middle classes, however, they had no desire to play a part in managing the factories and industries that were now becoming the most productive and profitable in the world.

Simmel and his associates were aware of the sharp discontinuity between the political backwardness and inflexibility of the German nation on the one hand, and the creative spirits of many of its artists and intellectuals on the other. In typical idealistic fashion, however, many of them tried to resolve this contradiction or tension by *imagining* a pure world of truth and unmitigated beauty.

This was certainly true of George and Rilke. George was highly enthusiastic about the cultural significance of intellectual elites. Rilke, a genuine bohemian, wrote poetry that expressed his commitment to those sacred and ideal values in which he wanted so desperately to believe. In the process, he became the high priest of a cult of young people who favored mystical detachment from the world of everyday experience and from the coarser aspects of German nationalism.

Both George and Rilke were proponents of cultural modernism. As members of the avant-garde in Berlin, they responded to modernization by seeking to aestheticize life. To a very large extent, George, Rilke, and Simmel were indifferent to the real, and messy, world of political struggle and compromise. In any case, of course, Jews were mostly barred from the most influential social and political organizations. At the turn of the century, anti-Semitism became more pronounced in Berlin. Like Freud, Simmel suffered greatly from the anti-Jewish sentiments that flourished in German-speaking Europe in the years leading up to World War I.

Although, like Freud, he was a part of a counterculture, Simmel was also marginally associated with the academic establishment. Thus he had a foot in two camps. From all accounts, he took his role as a *Privatdozent* seriously. In the eyes of many of his colleagues, his interest in lecturing and in teaching for the sake of teaching indicated low status. Nevertheless, Simmel's view of himself as an independent scholar and outsider who was not afraid to be ingenious, provocative, and "clever" gave him a freedom of sorts that was denied most of his colleagues.

Intellectual Roots

Although he was affected by many individuals and schools of thought, Simmel was clearly a product of German idealism. For a short while, however, he was enthusiastic about Comte and about the possibility of a fully positivistic sociology. (Comte's sociology became popular among some German academics in the 1880s, but it met with vigorous opposition from idealists and historical materialists.) Similarly, in the early stages of his career, Simmel was a supporter of Spencerian ideas about evolutionism. (Among other things, *On Social Differentiation* deals with Spencerian themes.) Simmel was influenced most, however, by Kant, by Hegel, and by Arthur Schopenhauer (1788–1860).

Although Kant opposed metaphysical speculation and supported positivism as a form of knowledge, he restricted positivistic methodology to the study of the phenomenal world (that which can be experienced by means of our senses). Kant pointed out that human observers can never understand phenomena as "things-in-themselves"—that is, as things that exist in their own right, independently of our knowing them. Kantian epistemology was embraced both by positivists like Hermann von Helmholtz (1821–1894), who influenced Freud, and by historicists like Dilthey, who believed that positivism was wholly inappropriate for the human and cultural sciences.

The 1860s witnessed a Kantian revival in Germany. One consequence of this was a renewed interest in epistemology for its own sake. Kant had argued that an answer to the all-important question "How is knowledge of nature possible?" would not be obtained without some comprehension of the mind's innate structure and workings. He had suggested that a transcendental (that is, universal and overarching) frame of reference existed in the mind as a result of *a priori* categories of understanding. These "apriorities," which include the conceptions of "time," "space," and "causality," shape our view of the world; but they are not themselves affected by the content of empirical knowledge.

At the end of the nineteenth century, the so-called Heidelberg neo-Kantians Wilhelm Windelband (1848–1915) and Heinrich Rickert (1863–1936) attempted to develop a theory of the categorization of cultural and historical experience. Like Dilthey, Windelband and Rickert believed that a subject's location within a network of social relationships provided the foundation for human experience. Rickert argued that historiography (the attempt to "understand" history) is a translation of the raw data of historical events into a new language that investigators find meaningful for *their* purposes. For instance, if we want to understand a historical figure like Napoleon, we might want to interpret the meaning of his career using categories that Napoleon himself would not have recognized. Other investigators are likely to use different categories. All these categories transcend specific forms of historical reality; they themselves are not part of the raw data of history.

Simmel was the most sociological of the neo-Kantians. According to Simmel, there are no transcendental and overarching categories in historiography that are not themselves a product of the hermeneutic intent of investigators. Simmel agreed with Dilthey that historiography cannot be thought of as the attempt to make a "photographic reproduction" of past events. Following Kant, Simmel asked: How are "history" and "society" possible? In brief, he suggested that the answer depends on an analysis of the *a priori* presuppositions used to think about, and to create, "history" and "society."

Though he adopted the Kantian mode of analysis, Simmel thus goes beyond Kant by searching for *sociological* apriorities binding on the social individuals who make history or society an object of knowledge. Simmel believed that many of his colleagues had fallen into the trap of "historical realism"; that is, they believed they could literally recapture and understand history "just as it happened." In *The Problems of the Philosophy of History*, Simmel tries to match Kant's critique of empiricism with a critique of historical realism. He points out that the Kantian apriorities are highly abstract: They describe the most general conditions necessary for discovering the order we find in the natural world. Simmel agreed with the historicists, however, that experiencing other individuals was qualitatively different from experiencing nature. Although they are objects in that they are external to the self, other people are also viewed as subjects—that is, as conscious, autonomous entities that are, in this sense, synonymous with the self. This ability to understand the subjective aspect of others means that the *kind* of knowledge that the human sciences produces is qualitatively different from that produced by the natural sciences.

For instance, when we respond to a person as an intelligible object of understanding, we use the concept "personality" in order to acquire knowledge of that other, although we cannot see or touch another's personality, as we can natural or physical objects. Thus "mental facts" (for example, those resulting from the perception of another as having an integrated personality system) are supplied by the observer. In this example, mental facts, which supplement observable facts like the perception of another as "a good athlete," "a tall person," "a person who wears drab clothing," and the like, can be applied, reflectively, to ourselves as well as to others. What Simmel is asking us to consider here is how we "know" that someone has an integrated personality system. Do we see this integrated system in the same way that we observe tallness and drabness of clothing? Or are we always ready to treat random and inherently meaningless acts as understandable in light of our *presuppositions* about the kind of thing we are dealing with? Simmel's major interest as a sociologist was with the presuppositions we *must* make before we can know each other as social individuals. Like Kant, he was interested in such apriorities because he wanted to uncover the way in which knowledge is grounded. Thus Simmel raised the following epistemological questions: What can we know about others? How can we be sure that our knowledge is correct?

For Kant, order in nature results from the *a priori* structure that the knowing subject imposes upon an environment that is recognized as objective and constraining. But as Simmel pointed out, "the unity of society needs no observer" because the elements of society are, themselves, "conscious and synthesizing units." The units of society—individuals and groups—do not exist as isolated things-in-themselves but *relationally.* We can never know another directly or completely, but only through forms of mediation that are intersubjectively meaningful. Sociation thus results from the mutual acts of recognition and response that make society possible. Sociology's most fundamental task, then, is the analysis of the synthetic, *a priori*, constitution of social experience.

Hegel's influence on Simmel is perhaps even stronger than that of Kant. Although Simmel discarded the conception of Absolute Spirit, Hegel's treatment of objectification was important for Simmelian analysis. In particular, Simmel accepted Hegel's conception of the *dialectical* relationship between subject and object. Individuals create cultural, political, and aesthetic objects (among others) that come to have a particular meaning for them *as* they are "socialized" and *as* they learn the meaning of social relationships. These objects of significance, however, are also used and appropriated by individuals as they strive to understand themselves. Simmel agreed with Hegel that there is constant tension and interplay between subjects' conceptions of themselves and the meaning of objects used to categorize experience.

According to Simmel, the tragedy of cultural modernism is that, whereas there are no natural limits to the expansion and differentiation of objective culture, there are intrinsic limits to individuals' ability to organize and appreciate these forms. This difference helps explain the inexorable logic of disintegration, breakage, and dispersal that is found in modernity. Objectified culture compels subjects to become self-reflective because it provides individuals with the opportunity to shuttle backward and forward between an awareness of alienated form (a great work of art, for instance) and unalienated, unmediated subjective expression and feeling.

Simmel's treatment of cultural objectifications, or of objective culture, is identical to Hegel's. He views human institutions and organizations as humanly produced and as an expression of human energy and will. At the same time, he notes that objective culture can develop "a mind of its own." For example, individuals sustain bureaucratic organizations because, as far as subjects are concerned, these organizations have attained an impersonal, inhuman, and apparently independent existence from them. Individuals cannot ignore bureaucracy; but neither can they view it as an expression of their own subjectivity, creativity, or freedom.

Simmel agreed with Hegel that civilization tends to impose categories of mediation, or systems of communicative interaction, that are increasingly complex. In simple societies, the collective articulation of systems of communicative interaction does not involve forms of mediation among individuals that are as highly specialized, as differentiated, or as complex as those in contemporary societies. Therefore, "primitive" people find it far easier to combine an expression of complete subjectivity with an acceptance of the social and collective organization of experience.

Simmel accepted Marx's model of the way in which economic categories of mediation develop in capitalist society according to their own logic. He believed that Marx was correct in arguing that these categories of mediation would remain dominant until the tensions and antagonism between them and the individuals they help produce become so great that the old forms and fetters of existence are burst asunder. Simmel notes, however, that Marx's model of change or development has applications that extend beyond the relations of production. According to Simmel, the conflict between the energies of life and the structures in which they are expressed is inevitable and universal. Thus Simmel did not accept Marx's utopian vision of a communist society.

Simmel did reject Hegel's holistic view of society. Like Weber, he treated the action of the socially oriented individual as the basic unit of sociological analysis.

Besides Kant and Hegel, the other two major influences on Simmel were Nietzsche, and Schopenhauer, whose *The World as Will and Representation* (1819) became influential among German intellectuals in the latter half of the nineteenth century. Schopenhauer had studied under J. G. Fichte (1762–1814) and was a colleague and rival of Hegel in Berlin. Unlike both Hegel and Kant, Schopenhauer developed a deeply pessimistic philosophy of existence. He believed that it was not rationality but the blind, largely unconscious and nonrational will that was the main driving force behind human behavior. The energy of this will, which operates instinctually and impulsively, torments the individual and leads to a restlessness of spirit from which only personal oblivion can offer a permanent solution.

In *Schopenhauer and Nietzsche*—the last of four philosophical works Simmel completed between 1900 and 1907—Simmel contrasts Schopenhauer's view of the individual as something tortured by the frustrated yearning of the will with Nietzsche's more optimistic, life-affirming philosophy. Unlike Schopenhauer, who could detect no ultimate meaning in the endless striving to realize desire and to discharge nonrational life energies, Nietzsche drew on classical themes from ancient Greece to develop the argument that life itself can be made into the goal and purpose of personal existence. From this perspective, the aesthetic, far more than the rational, becomes the most significant human activity.

Perhaps the weakest part of Nietzsche's philosophy was his neo-Darwinian belief that the "exceptional individual" could contribute to a cultural complex that would thereby represent "ascending life." Failing to detect anything admirable about modern society, Nietzsche hoped that the individual would be able to derive meaning from a *personal* quest of becoming that would place the enjoyment of health, vigor, courage, and individual integrity over the doomed human quest for happiness. Discussing the influence of both Schopenhauer and Nietzsche on Simmel, Deena and Michael Weinstein write in the introduction to their recent translation of *Schopenhauer and Nietzsche* that "Schopenhauer concerns [Simmel] the most, because he offered a metaphysics, the form of which was paradigmatic for *Hauptprobleme* [basic inquiries] and the content of which was transposed into the dominant motif of *Lebensanschauung*. Nietzsche is a counterpoint, substituting evolution for metaphysics but providing added dimensions for the later vitalism."[7] Yet, by separating Nietzsche's ethical concerns from his dubious evolutionary individualism, Simmel did largely succeed in avoiding the error of attributing purpose or teleology to evolutionary change.[8] His argument, in brief, is that modern culture provides the conditions under which the subject's alienation from life is likely to be felt most keenly. Yet, at the same time, such culture is most supportive of the subject's efforts to *self-design* a form of existence intended to give life purpose and meaning. For Simmel, personal transcendence did not come in the form of moral universalism or cognitive rationality. Rather, it involved *aesthetics*.

IDEAS

Society

It has often been claimed that, unlike Durkheim and Marx, Simmel did not have a systematic and integrated theory of society. Although he did not have a conventional sociological view of society, Simmel did believe that individuals were compelled to organize their experience in a highly structured and systematic fashion when they make "society" itself an object of knowledge. As a social being, the individual must operate with certain preconceptions and presuppositions in mind. Some of these are highly abstract, others more concrete. Those highly abstract apriorities are likely to be found in all forms of "society" as we would understand the meaning of that term. According to Simmel, social life would not be possible unless individuals made certain assumptions about themselves and others. He cited three apriorities as being fundamental to the existence of a social world. They all express and embody contradictory impulses:

1. Individuals are both inside and outside of society. As Simmel put it, social individuals must recognize that a society is "a structure which consists of beings who stand inside and outside of it at the same time."[9]

2. Individuals are both objects and subjects within a network of communicative interaction.
3. Individuals have an impulse to be self-fulfilling or to be self-completing; that is, they seek an integrated self-concept. Similarly, society itself tends to gravitate toward the means to its own integration. However, the integrity of the individual and the integrity of society are often in opposition.

For Simmel, then, the starting point for the sociologist who wishes to understand society is the careful analysis of how experience is shaped so that social life becomes possible. The study of society requires that the apriorities or forms of sociation should be separated from its content. As noted earlier, Simmel pointed out that there is a fundamental difference between the apriorities that enable us to experience order and system in the natural world and those that permit us to experience an orderly and meaningful social reality. Our interaction with the natural world requires us to synthesize and organize things-in-themselves (things in the natural world whose physical ontology does not depend on mental constructs). The ontology of social reality, however (that is, the forms and styles of interaction that tie us to other human beings), is brought into existence by us. According to Simmel, the sociological apriorities are constitutive of social experience; they are realized as individuals interact with one another.

Thus Simmel rejected the Durkheimian view that society is a reality *sui generis*. For Simmel, "Society merely is the name for a number of individuals, connected by interaction. . . . Society certainly is not a 'substance,' nothing concrete, but an *event*: it is the function of receiving and affecting the fate and development of one individual by the other."[10] Simmel did not believe that either "society" or the "individual" could be self-constituting. Although "society" is a structure that "transcends the individual," it is not abstract. "Society is the universal which, at the same time, is concretely alive."[11] What Simmel means to convey by this statement is that society is nothing but *lived experience*. Of course, humans can replicate lived experience mechanically (as in a bureaucracy); nevertheless, according to Simmel, it would be incorrect for the sociologist to assume that social forces are external to, or necessarily constraining for, the individuals who must reproduce "society" in every living moment.

According to Simmel, then, a fundamental step in the analysis of social reality is the abstract attempt to describe how pure sociation serves to shape and constrain human experience. For instance, according to the first—and most important—of the sociological apriorities mentioned earlier, it is impossible to be a member of a social unit without at the same time being an entity that is something other than a constituent part of this unit. Individuals always distinguish between a personal sense of self and a social self. If an individual is a member of a religious sect, for instance, that individual's consciousness will obviously be shaped and constrained by virtue of this membership. On the other hand, in order to be affected by group membership, individuals must see themselves as something other than merely an efflorescence of group life.

Simmel thus believed that, among other things, social life *mandates* a dialectical relationship between the individual and society. If self-consciousness ceased to exist, symbolic interaction would disappear and human experience would be shaped solely by the genetically predetermined responses that the organism would give to stimuli in the natural world. On the other hand, if individuals were not, in part, the carriers of a cultural and social order that existed before they were born—and will continue to exist after they die—their lives could have no personal meaning for them. As Simmel points out, we live and die in terms of what can be made intersubjectively meaningful. We answer the question "What kind of person am I?" by viewing ourselves—at least in part—in terms of others' responses to us, including people who died before we were born. Different people select different audiences, but the principle of dependence on collectively sanctioned meaning remains the same.

Simmel insisted that the dialectic between the individual and society grounds both the understanding of social life and individual participation in it. The former orientation might be described as "theoretical" and the latter as "practical"; as far as the logic of understanding is concerned, however, Simmel does not distinguish between the two. Simmel believed that the hermeneutical interest of the sociologist is logically the same as that of the subject under investigation, but he also maintained that this hermeneutical interest is absolutely foundational if society is to be made "possible."

Simmel suggested that, at a less abstract level than the social apriorities, "forms" of sociation—the frameworks that structure interaction—also constrain and give shape to the experiences of social individuals. Although they are generated by the social apriorities, particular forms are not logically necessary for *all* kinds of social life. As part of his study on the significance of numbers, Simmel analyzed the differences between sociation in a *dyad* (comprising two people) and a *triad* (comprising three people). To engage in such an analysis, of course, it is necessary to ignore the personalities of the people participating in these groups, as well as the content of all kinds of exchanges. Simmel pointed out that, regardless of *who* is participating in a two-person or three-person group, and regardless of what is under discussion, there are types of sociation that are unique to dyads and different types of sociation that can be found only in triads. Dyads and triads are two different social forms through which interaction is structured. Triads offer individuals chances for alliances that are not found in dyads. Similarly, in a triad, an individual is always playing to two different audiences, not just one. This fact makes interaction more complex.

Another example of a form of sociation is the *historically variable* ways in which the relationship between the sexes is experienced and construed. Although the "biological" or "instinctual" needs of men and women do not fall within the domain of sociology, regardless of content (that is, regardless of the specific personalities of men and women), interaction among men and women is likely to be crucially important in establishing culturally variable modes of reality construction.

In the typical patriarchal society, for instance, the relationship between men and women is likely to be based on reciprocal orientations of dominance and submission. This form of sociation or framework for organizing interaction is fundamental to human life and tends to govern relations between the sexes. In a patriarchal society, these relations might be perceived as "intimate" and "spontaneous." Nevertheless, although they are viewed as permitting the expression of unique subjectivity, such relations are in fact structured by superordinate-subordinate expectations that both parties understand and that contain the degree of intimacy that can be attained by heterosexual lovers. Thus the objective form (of dominance and submission) contains the way in which what is thought of as personal subjectivity can be expressed. At the same time, the superordinate-subordinate form is maintained by the subjective impulses of individuals.

Simmel was particularly interested in analyzing those social forms that were characteristic of the experience of modernity. Fashion is a good example of a form of mediation that is both increasingly emphasized and widely diffused today. The modern city is a "breeding ground for fashion" because it intensifies a multiplicity of social relations, increases the rate of social mobility, and permits individuals from lower strata to become conscious of the styles and fashions of upper classes. Fashion thus is a product of equalization as well as of social differentiation. Lower-class individuals increasingly believe that it is possible to take on some of the traits and attributes of those whom they acknowledge to be more worthy of social attention. At the same time, fashion could have no meaning were it not for the fact that individuals have been separated from those forms of rigid and ascribed mediation into which they traditionally were locked.

Simmel suggests that fashion provides "the best arena for people who lack autonomy and who need support, yet whose self-awareness nevertheless requires that they be recognized as distinct and as particular kinds of beings."[12] Modern individuals tend to be relatively detached from traditional anchors of social support. They also tend to be more self-reflective and self-aware than traditional individuals. Fashion permits the modern individual to participate in a form of social mediation that signals his or her "own" *personal* value to others. Yet, as Simmel points out, the form of mediation represented by fashion must be transitory. When a particular style ceases to express value, that is, when it becomes commonplace, it loses its appeal. Modern life, Simmel suggests, can be an endless round of stylistic revision and invention, driven by the individual's need to differentiate himself or herself from others and to demonstrate, according to a common currency of meaning, his or her own "special uniqueness." Of course, the latter goal is a "fantasy," according to Simmel. Fashion is commercially designed and mass-produced, (more so today, even, than in Simmel's time). As a commodity, fashion contributes to the endless recycling of value in a capitalist economy. It represents a social form of mediation that has value because it supposedly expresses "originality" or "creativity"; thus it dooms the individual to an unending search for the new. Tragicomically, the individual who tries to anchor selfhood through fashion falls victim to the content of unending multiplicity of stylistic forms that do nothing other than provide illusory support for an absent "inner freedom."

In the final analysis, Simmel sees society as *aesthetic form*. "Pure sociation," according to Simmel, is playful; it is social interaction for its own sake. Instrumental action that is oriented toward some goal—defined, say, in terms of some "instinctual" or "material" need—is likely to be social only insofar as such goals are usually attained as a result of collectively articulated action. Communicative interaction that is an end in itself (like that exhibited in the barroom or at the cocktail party) would be seen by Simmel as being of unique interest to sociologists; for it is when individuals are allowed to concentrate on sociality itself that we can learn most about them as social beings.

The Individual in Society

As we have seen, Simmel saw the individual and society as interdependent and inter-penetrative entities. Simmel, more than any other sociologist with the exception of Mead, held that neither the individual nor society could have any kind of existence except in relation to each other. Simmel strongly disagreed with theorists like Marx who argued that human individuals had some kind of nature, essence, or "species-being" that was not in itself the result of communicative interaction. According to Simmel, nascent self-consciousness arises as human impulses are fulfilled and as subjects act on external objects that are separate from self. For instance, Simmel declares that "objective culture" (for example, technology) arises as a result of human need but has the capacity to alter "subjective culture," or the development of the individual. In this manner, human "needs" themselves are altered.

According to Simmel, social divisions are also experienced by humans as part of their "inner" world. Thus divisions within modern society are experienced by individuals as fractures within themselves. This consciousness of fragmentation is quite unknown in traditional societies. Premodern art tends to reflect a sacred "aura," which acknowledges the hold of a holistic and integrated symbolic order on the individual. By way of contrast, aesthetic modernism is forced to come to terms with the feature-less flux of modern existence. Simmel believed that modern art had to try to capture the inner experience of a multifaceted and contradictory social reality so that the modern individual could recognize and hold onto a pattern temporarily imposed on the flux of contemporary sensation and feeling. This belief helps explain why, around 1900, modern art became antirealist and antirepresentational in orientation.

Simmel's treatment of the relationship between the individual and society stresses the *paradoxical* nature of the relationship—that "man is both social link and being for himself, both product of society and life from an autonomous center."[13] "Society" and the "individual" are part of a seamless web of existence, but individuals have to conceptualize themselves as autonomous in certain respects. One reason for this need is that social life must be predicated on our belief that we are, to some extent, self-actualizing—that is, that we have some control over the manner in which our selfhood is authenticated or validated.

In his discussion of the significance of bodily adornment, Simmel gave a good example of the dependence of the self-conscious individual on social relationships with others. Simmel suggests that we wear bodily adornments to please ourselves; clothing and jewelry, for instance, give us the opportunity to tell others something about ourselves. In order to express ourselves by means of the medium of adornment, however, we rely on others to react to what we have prepared for them. Adornments are a recognized medium of self-expression; they permit relationships of reciprocity to emerge among individuals. It is not necessary that we give others the esteem we receive from them, but it is necessary that adornment be mutually recognized as a medium of expression. As a result of this, however, it becomes difficult to separate self and society.

According to Simmel, we cannot express selfhood except through social association. At the same time, society cannot exist except as a medium through which the individual can achieve self-validation.

Unlike Hegel and Marx, Simmel did not view conflict among individuals, or contradiction between the individual and society, as necessarily harmful either to society or for the individual. Competition and conflict among individuals not only help to provide purpose and meaning to life, but can also promote a sense of social unity. For instance, Simmel pointed out that conflict implies mutual understanding of the principles of conflict and, above all, some reciprocity among individuals.

Simmel disagreed with Hegel's and Marx's assertion that a completely harmonious relationship between the individual and society was possible. He believed that tension between the individual and society—as well as conflict and competition among individuals—was unavoidable. Each individual is a partially "autonomous center" and must remain so if the conception of selfhood is to remain meaningful. Simmel believed that a static society of perfectly integrated individuals would be a society made up of individuals who do not know they are alive.

Simmel concluded, therefore, that society's most fundamental problem is "the relation between its forces and forms and the individual's own life." The individual and society are condemned to be interdependent and mutually supportive, but yet to pull in opposite directions when it comes to the unity of the individual versus the cohesiveness of society. In modern societies, this problem is likely to be particularly acute because of structural differentiation and because of the division of labor. As Simmel pointed out, sophisticated individuals are able to play many roles in front of many different audiences. There are advantages to such a strategy: It makes the self flexible, playful, and able to take advantage of a number of social situations. Simmel acknowledged, however, that a fragmentation of the self does not always occur because individuals choose to be sophisticated and flexible; sometimes it occurs because it is institutionally required.

Simmel distinguished between societies that allow individuals to play many parts but leave the onus of choice on the individual in question, and societies in which a particular form of social unity (or social solidarity) requires individuals to fulfill many highly specialized and routinized roles. In the former case, Simmel suggested, a fragmentation of the self can take place without a sense of alienation. In such societies, individuals can be strongly individualized without feeling themselves dehumanized. In the latter case, though, Simmel's analysis of the fragmentation of self is identical to the classic Hegelian and Marxist conception of alienation. Echoing Hegel and Marx, as we have seen, Simmel points out that structural differentiation and a high division of labor guarantee that individuals will experience the conflict between themselves and society as "conflict among [their] component parts."

Simmel acknowledged that the division of labor in modern societies is very pronounced, and he also conceded that the major way in which society *imposes* a fragmentation of the self is through the structural differentiation of occupational roles. Simmel did concede that the rise of the money economy and the spread of commodity relations exacerbate the fragmentation of the self. At the same time, however, he believed that the modern money economy provided liberating opportunities for the "practical man." Most notably, Simmel argued that the money economy is a form of social organization that is highly abstract and fluid; it is capable of integrating diverse contents, including individuals, in a way that would not necessarily impinge on their efforts at self-cultivation in the same way as would other modes of social organization—such as religion. Although money is a measure of value, it does not itself advocate particular values. Thus the money economy frees individuals from constraints imposed by more concrete and substantive modes of integration and, consequently, enhances the potential for the synthesis and development of individual abilities and interests. Moreover, money rapidly increases the "velocity" of social exchange because people do not have to haggle or debate about how much of one product should be exchanged for another. It also makes people more interested in, and attuned to, social exchange for its own sake. Once this occurs, money would have greater significance than ever because actors would increasingly depend on it as the most important medium of personal expression and social interaction. As a consequence, modern individuals, Simmel believed, would become increasingly calculating, cynical, anomic, atomized, detached, and fragmented through their involvement in a multiplicity of interactional situations.

Thus Simmel's interest in the effect of the money economy on individuals was not "economic" in nature. Rather, Simmel was interested in how money affected the "inner world" of individuals. Money possesses no value in itself (although what it can buy is valuable); its function is to relate "everything to everything." As the opportunities for exchange relations among individuals are increasingly generalized—that is, as the social group is enlarged and differentiated—the sense of individuality is more sharply focused. The modern individual internalizes those abstract forms constitutive of modernity, of which exchange value is the best example, and hence experiences not substantive feelings or emotions that are held in common with other individuals but the endless flux of life.

As we have seen, Simmel believed that temporary order and unity can be brought to personal experience only through works of art. The conflict between the individual and society can be resolved (temporarily) only through *aesthetic* expression:

> The individual strives to be an organic totality, a unity with its own centre from whence all the elements of his being and his action derive a coherent and consistent meaning. . . . The totality of the whole—although it gains practical reality only in certain actions of the individual and perhaps even only within the individual—stands in eternal conflict with the totality of the individual. The aesthetic expression of this struggle is particularly impressive because the charm of beauty is always embedded in a whole, no matter whether it has immediate distinctiveness or a distinctiveness that is supplemented by fantasy as in the case of a fragment. The essential meaning of art lies in its being able to form an autonomous totality, a self-sufficient microcosm out of a fortuitous fragment of reality that is tied with a thousand threads to this reality. The typical conflict between the individual and supraindividual existence can be interpreted as the irreconcilable striving of both elements to attain an aesthetically satisfying expression.[14]

Generally, however, Simmel believed that as both the individual and society are striving toward unities of self-expression that are logically incompatible, their relationship ultimately is tragic in nature. Simmel did not ascribe a "mind" to society, but he did accept that, for modern societies, a movement toward enhanced social unity would be a movement away from personal freedom, at least for some people. As

Durkheim pointed out, in societies with a high division of labor, *social* unity is generally enhanced through the specialization of function and through the expectation that special skills and talents be organized in the interests of the social whole, not in the interests of self-expression. Simmel argued, however, that this generalized expectation is likely to run counter to individuals' interest in maintaining some control over their "own" individuality and in the subjective cultivation and application of skills and talents. Thus, with respect to the fate of the modern individual, Simmel's analysis does not differ greatly from that of most of his fellow sociologists.

Simmel also saw an ultimately tragic relationship between individuals as creative agents and the cultural objectifications these individuals help produce. For Simmel, it is "utterly impossible" for the individual to resolve the crisis of modern culture. This "crisis" is felt personally by the modern individual, as well as experienced collectively: It is "deeply familiar and intelligible to us. For in each of us, it is consciously or not, the crisis of our own soul."[15]

In "The Conflict in Modern Culture," Simmel described how cultural and aesthetic objectifications can outlive their human creators. Before long, these objectifications come to impede the fluidity and creative energy of a generation whose members must learn to transcend them before they can become fully creative and fully human. Individuals are faced with a never-ending struggle to replace dead reifications with modes of expression that have—for a transitory period—the function of expressing impulsive and creative energies. According to Simmel, it is the fate of all such modes of expression to ossify and to impede progress before finally being superseded. As Simmel noted, in modern society

> we are confronted by countless objectifications of the mind: works of art, social forms, institutions, knowledge. They are like kingdoms administered according to their own laws, but they demand that we should make them the content and norm of our own individual lives, even though we do not really know what to do with them, indeed often feel them to be a burden and an impediment.[16]

Methodology

For Simmel, the science of sociology is the study of the various forms of sociation acknowledged and acted on by individuals in order to create meaning and order from the flux of life. Sociology studies the forms that people enact—generally in an unconscious fashion—as they "form groups and are determined by their group existence because of interaction."[17] According to Simmel, sociology does not have a unique *topic* of inquiry; it studies the same aspects of social life as political science, history, and several other disciplines. What distinguishes sociology from other academic disciplines is its method of inquiry. As we have seen, Simmel did not believe that either "society" or the elements of society—that is, groups and individuals—existed as autonomous elements in their own right. Simmel viewed the totality of life as relational—as the product of relations among constituent parts. The domain of study for sociology is interaction. What defines sociology, *per se*, is the study of "the form and forms of sociation."

Simmel believed that sociology should not merely examine the more obvious forms of interaction like those imposed by large organizations or by class membership;

it should also analyze microsociological forms of association like friendship, love, and interpersonal conflict. Simmel was the first major sociologist to recognize that the methods of sociology could be applied to the study of small groups and to the analysis of forms of interaction among a few individuals.

Besides the highly abstract investigation of social apriorities (which shows how sociality is possible in the first place), Simmel held that both a generalizing sociology and a sociology that studied the specific characteristics of a form of life were viable, valid points of view. Initially, however, Simmel favored a highly abstract and very formal sociology. Later on in his career, he distinguished between "formal" and "general" sociology. He also defined a third methodological approach: "philosophical sociology." We will look at each of these in turn.

Simmel is best known for his conception of *formal sociology*: "the study of forms of sociation." He described this type of sociological inquiry as "pure sociology," which abstracts and studies "the mere elements of sociation." Thus Simmel's conception of *particular* societies was phrased in terms of their formal characteristics of sociation.

Like the study of grammar, the study of the *form* of sociation is quite independent from the description of what is being conveyed as the *content* of a message. For example, we recognize the sentence "Would you like to dance?" as an interrogative because of formal characteristics such as word order, not because of what it asks. Such formal properties place this sentence in a category with all others that have the same formal properties, although clearly the content of such sentences might vary considerably. Simmel argued that the formal and observable aspects of sociation could likewise be studied. The dyad, for example, always consists of two people. The characteristics of these individuals, what they say to one another, and so forth, are all irrelevant to the study of the formal structure of dyadic relations. Members of all dyads, for instance, know that if one of them should withdraw from the relationship, the dyad would cease to exist. Moreover, this knowledge affects the way in which dyadic relations are carried out. Simmel liked to draw an analogy between formal sociology and geometry:

> Geometrical abstraction investigates only the spatial forms of bodies, although empirically, these forms are given merely as the forms of some material content. Similarly, if society is conceived as interaction among individuals, the description of the forms of this interaction is the task of the science of society in its strictest and most essential sense.[18]

Simmel gives many examples of formal sociology. For instance, in his study of the sociology of sex and feminine coquetry, he analyzes coquetry, or flirtation, as a playful form of interaction between potential lovers. According to Simmel, the nature of feminine coquetry is to tease the man, first by attracting and then by rebuffing him. The flirtatious woman enhances her attractiveness both by exhibiting erotic interest and by subtly disavowing such interest. Men in turn play their part by allowing themselves to be drawn into this game. What is of sociological interest here is how coquetry permits eroticism to free itself from the "contents and personal features" of erotic desire. To learn how to flirt, it is only necessary to learn the formal characteristics of a flirtatious association. It is unnecessary (and probably undesirable) for either partner to understand what is in the other person's mind. More to the point, the sociologist can analyze flirtation by studying the formal aspects of coquettish interaction and can safely ignore the content and substance of erotic feeling. In any case, content can, of course, vary a great deal from one society to another.

Simmel thus defines formal sociology as the study of forms of sociation without reference to the contents "through which these forms, nevertheless, come to life." He points out that cross-culturally and historically, the forms of sociation can remain the same while the content of experience is dramatically different.

According to Simmel, the sociologist should study the logic of sociation both in order to understand particular societies and in order to understand society in general. In other words, he believed that sociologists should study both what is particular to certain societies and what is general to all societies. For instance, he examined the significance of numbers for social life because he wanted to investigate how social interaction was affected by the number of participants involved in such interaction. He believed this approach would give the sociologist an understanding of a structural determinant that was constant in its effects.

Simmel's conception of general sociology—which he seems to have developed after realizing that his identification of sociology with formal sociology was too narrow—is not as clear-cut as his definition of formal sociology. *General sociology* focuses on the *unity* of various institutions (organizations of sociation). Here Simmel seems to be moving tentatively toward functionalism. As he puts it: "The facts of politics, religion, economics, law, culture styles, language, and innumerable others can be analyzed by asking how they may be understood, not as individual achievements or in their objective significance, but as products and developments of society."[19]

Simmel's conception of general sociology is not very precise, and it has largely been ignored by contemporary sociologists. It seems that Simmel introduced this category of sociology because he wanted to explain historical change and because he wanted to think of society as a system. This, of course, is beyond the scope of "pure" or formal sociology.

Simmel's belief that *philosophical sociology* was a legitimate part of the sociological discipline stemmed from his understanding of the close relationship between sociology and epistemology. Philosophical sociology analyzes the preconceptions and presuppositions that ground social knowledge. For instance, Simmel points out that different historical epochs are likely to have quite different conceptions or models of the relationship between the individual and society. (As we have seen, these conceptions or models are constitutive of the very nature of social life.) Eighteenth-century intellectuals, for instance, tended to presume that it was both necessary and desirable for the individual to be relatively detached from society. By the end of the nineteenth century, however, as Simmel points out, most educated men not only thought of themselves as "independent" but also wished to distinguish themselves from other individuals. Thus eighteenth-century males learned to think of themselves as autonomous individuals—like other men. In the nineteenth century, men did not merely view themselves as beings who were relatively detached from society, but also saw themselves as qualitatively unique beings.

Taken-for-granted assumptions about the relationship between the individual and society will have a significant impact on the way in which subjects think about and experience themselves. This relationship, however, will also affect the way in which social theorists—themselves the product of a particular society—will conceptualize social reality. As Simmel points out, if assumptions really are taken for granted, they need to become an object of philosophical, rather than empirical, investigation; for "the conditions, fundamental concepts and presuppositions of concrete research . . . cannot be taken care of by research itself since [research] is based on them."[20] Simmel did not believe that philosophical and empirical inquiry were mutually exclusive. According to Simmel, philosophical inquiry can yield empirical knowledge.

Simmel has been criticized by many well-known sociologists (most notably by Durkheim) for being wholly unsystematic in defining and applying sociological methods. Although Simmel distinguished form from content in his own analyses, that distinction is not always easily made in social life. Although the dyad constitutes a form in itself, it can also help constitute the content of a more encompassing form such as bureaucracy. In any case, Simmel's claim that the sociologist could abstract and dissect form from the complexities of human experience is not a particularly novel strategy. All investigators claim to be able to pick out some "structure" or "order" in their subject matter, which is then specified and explained in terms of theory.

One of the consequences of Simmel's interest in exploring the socioepistemological grounds of hermeneutical interpretation was his assertion that sociology must have an interest in social epistemologies as well as in ordinary empirical investigation. This conception of sociological technique is shared by critical theorists but not, of course, by positivists. Simmel's conception of the dialectical relationship between the individual and society is also a valuable part of his conception of sociological method. His view of individuals as striving to recognize themselves in—and yet to overcome— the social forms that define their "humanity" makes Simmelian sociology, to some extent, critical as well as interpretive. As we have seen, however, Simmel believed that the dialectical tension between subjects and their cultural objectifications was universal. Although he thought that the money economy held out the potential for enhanced human freedom, he did not believe that such liberation was inevitable. Thus, he rejected the idea of an emancipatory methodology—that is, reflective movement toward some ideal intellectual and social reality whereby the tension between selfhood and sociality is finally resolved.

Other Major Themes and Foci: The Social Types

One of the most interesting applications of Simmelian theoretical sociology is Simmel's own attempt to show how various types of individualisms are logically dependent on the social apriorities and on social forms.[21] We often believe that certain highly typical character traits are bestowed subjectively or psychologically. Simmel argued, however, that "social types," like the "stranger," the "miser," the "spendthrift," the "dude," and (as we have seen already) the "coquette," are logically predicated on certain forms of sociation. In his development of the social types, Simmel describes how formal and aprioristic properties of social interaction constrain and direct the possibilities of individual development.

For instance, the "stranger" is a common feature of any social environment. Whether in a small village or in a large city (where the stranger is the typical individual), the person who is an outsider, who does not fit in, is a recognizable and not uncommon phenomenon. As Simmel pointed out, if we try to understand how the role of the stranger is in part fashioned by the social apriorities, we can observe the following: If all individuals are both inside and outside society, the stranger is characterized by being physically part of the group but psychically apart. If all individuals are both objects and subjects within a network of communicative interaction, the stranger is seen to share certain human traits with those who observe him. The stranger's distinctive or particularistic characteristics are alien to others, however. As a result, he has an air of mystery; to some extent, it can make the stranger appear to be a dangerous and potentially threatening object. Paradoxically, it is presumed that the stranger's differences derive from his being an individual "of a certain type" (for example, "Mexican," "gringo," "Indian," "mulatto"). Hence his differences are not seen as personal, subjective, or idiosyncratic qualities. In short, the stranger is treated more as object than as subject. In turn, he views the group more objectively than do those who are an organic part of it. (Because of this objectivity, the stranger often serves as confidant to group members.) If all individuals have an impulse to be self-completing or self-fulfilling, the stranger is given a unique and definitive opportunity to attain *almost* complete autonomy. As Simmel noted, although the stranger must be part of a group in order to have the trait of "strangeness," the mind of the stranger can work "according to its own laws."

In short, Simmel suggests that the stranger is understandable in terms of a particular form of sociation with definable characteristics. These characteristics are explainable by means of the social apriorities. The apriorities, of course, could not explain why a particular person achieves geographical mobility, why he travels, why he arrives in a particular town, or why he sits outside a café drinking beer. However, they do constrain the way in which this person is then viewed by others as a certain type of individual. The typecasting, of course, has nothing to do with personal or subjective attributes. The individual in question did not determine to be a stranger, although he can choose to enter those situations wherein strangeness will determine him.

It has been suggested that Simmel based his understanding of the role of the stranger on his own position in academia. If this is true, he might have selected his social type quite deliberately. To some extent, the sociologist is always the stranger—always the outsider, never an organic part of human society.

Simmel pointed out that there are some intriguing parallels between the role of the stranger and the role of the poor person. The poor, too, are outsiders in that they are treated as *objects* of obligation but are not permitted to negotiate the terms of their social entitlement. In other words, to be poor does not so much mean to have little money as to be compelled to enter into a certain kind of relationship with others, and to become a certain kind of object for others. For instance, public assistance "makes the poor person into an object of the activity of the group." As Simmel notes, like the stranger, the poor person

> also finds himself *confronted* by the group. But this "being confronted" implies a specific *relationship* which draws the stranger into group life as an element of it. Thus the poor person stands undoubtedly outside the group, inasmuch as he is a mere object of the actions of the collectivity; but being outside, in this case, is only, to put it briefly, a particular form of being inside.[22]

Apart from the stranger, Simmel also discusses the "miser" and the "spendthrift" as social types. These types are produced by the same form of sociation: that represented by money. According to Simmel, although the miser and the spendthrift would appear to be the polar opposites of each other, they both rely on money as a "cultural world form" that makes possible the acquisition of goods and services through the use of highly quantified categories of measurement. Both the miser and the spendthrift treat money as an end in itself. Instead of using what money can buy as the expression of their own subjectivity, they succumb to its objective demands and to the logic of its operation. Both the miser and the spendthrift are immoderate—the one in hoarding, the other in spending. According to Simmel, once money becomes an end in itself, no quantitative limits can be placed on the ability of individuals to objectify their means of self-expression. For all intents and purposes, the stock of money is infinite.

In summary, then, the social apriorities and the culturally imposed social forms provide a framework or context by which the action of different individuals at different times can be understood. What Simmel was able to demonstrate in his analysis of the social types was that types of individualism were not a matter of private or personal choice but are explicable in terms of the "logic" of sociation.

SIGNIFICANCE

Vision of the Future

Although much of his sociology was concerned with topics that have a certain timeless significance, Simmel did write one very important book—*The Philosophy of Money*—that analyzes important trends of Western modernization. Although this book is an analysis of symbolic form, and hence is methodologically distinct from Weber's work, Simmel's conception of the future is remarkably similar to Weber's model of rationalization. Furthermore, *The Philosophy of Money* is heavily indebted to Marx's analysis of capitalism and complements Marx's theory of capitalist development.

Simmel points out that economic exchange is a special form of communicative interaction. If we compare communicative interaction in a feudal and traditional society with exchange in a money economy, some dramatic social differences are evident. According to Simmel, the most significant characteristic of money is its ability to *objectify* human exchange to a historically unprecedented extent. In a traditional society, "wealth" is generally measured in terms of social position. In traditional societies, "social position" is not determined—as it is in capitalist societies—by the position that an individual attains through participating in the universal game of income maximization. In a feudal society, ownership is ascriptive. The possession of estates and the possession of certain titles entail wealth, for they engender ownership and control of land and the labor of serfs. Money, however, cannot have the same significance that it has in a modern society. Money alone cannot make a person "great" and hence *deserving* of wealth.

In traditional societies, social hierarchies are quite antithetical to the institutionalization of the money economy. Simmel agreed with Marx that the use of money as a pervasive means of social exchange compels individuals to ignore each other's personal and subjective qualities and requires them to concentrate on the utility that money represents. In any society, a coin in the hand of a beggar is as good as a coin of the same value in the hand of a priest or a baron. Whatever the coin represents, it is not the personal and subjective qualities of the individual. In traditional societies, social stratification is based on a system of mutual recognition that compels subordinates and superordinates to view each other as qualitatively different kinds of people. A money economy systematically undermines the conception of *natural* social hierarchy based on the personal and God-given attributes of individuals because it requires individuals to orient themselves in terms of pure utility, not through subjective and inalienable qualities.

Simmel pointed out that in traditional societies, relations among individuals are more important than relations among individuals and objects. In traditional society, relations of subordination and superordination are nothing other than relations among subjects. The peculiar thing about modern capitalist societies is that, insofar as money plays a part in organizing a system of economic stratification, relations of subordination and superordination are determined by the relationship of individuals to a wholly impersonal measure of value.

In traditional economies, barter and exchange are closely tied to subjective need. In a capitalist society, however, it is commonplace for individuals to engage in economic transactions that are calculated to turn a profit, not satisfy a subjective need. Simmel agreed with Weber that contemporary Western societies have developed impersonal and highly rational ties among individuals. According to Simmel, however, this process occurs largely as a result of the institutionalization of the money form. For example, a society that makes social organization dependent on kin affiliation cannot hope to claim universality for its principle of organization. Kin organization excludes people by virtue of their relationship to some particular family grouping. The money economy, however, is abstract and formal enough to supersede all cultural differences among peoples of the world. Thus Simmel believed that the modern, rationalizing "spirit" of capitalism was nothing other than the supersession of the money economy over other, more traditional modes of communicative interaction.

As we have seen, what distinguishes Simmel's analysis of the spread of the money economy from Marx's or Weber's is that Simmel suggests that the development of the money form can in fact serve human as well as economic ends. Simmel points out that the institutionalization of an objective measure of value for the assessment of personal worth permits individuals to calculate and to manipulate the effects of their symbolic self-representations on others. For instance, individuals who live in societies where garments are treated as commodities can use clothes to differentiate themselves from other individuals—provided they have some disposable income. Just as the development of the money form enables individuals to control "outer nature" by imposing a universal and instrumentally rational mode of orientation, so the money form permits them to control "inner nature" by using instrumental and technical reason to calculate the effects of their actions on others.

Another example of the dramatic effects of the spread of the money form is the way we now take it for granted that we can travel to far-off places and deal with foreigners in terms of cash transactions that are as understandable to others as they are to us. This not only extends the geographical range of our activities, it also enables us to calculate with precision the effect that we are likely to have on those who might not even speak the same language as we do. What is crucial here is that we are no longer dependent on what appear to be the particularistic whims or the alien assessments of others. In the past, it was possible for travelers to visit different countries and to have no idea about whether they were pleasing or insulting the people they met by performing certain actions. With the spread of the money form, we can bend exchanges with others to our own purposes. We would find it difficult to exercise this kind of control over our friends back home.

Simmel thus suggests that the spread of the money form gives individuals a freedom of sorts by permitting them to exercise the kind of *individualized* control over "impression management" that was not possible in traditional societies. In modern societies, ascribed identities have been discarded. Even strangers become familiar and knowable entities insofar as they are willing to use a common but impersonal medium of exchange. This state of affairs, however, does not bring the problem of personal identity to an end. To the contrary, in modern societies, personal identity becomes problematic even for the most ordinary of people. Impression management—or the purely technical and instrumental control over how we are seen by others—is crucial for the modern individual precisely because traditional and taken-for-granted modes of identity construction have been progressively undermined by the process of modernization itself.

Simmel concludes, therefore, that the spread of the money form in Western societies—and its increasing significance in all areas of social life—will have both positive and negative consequences. Simmel agreed with Marx and Weber that the spread of the money form is associated with the fragmentation of the self; but, as we have seen, he also believed that in some respects the money form enhances personal freedom.

Whereas Weber was primarily interested in the historical roots of rationalization itself, Simmel analyzed the long-term consequences of the growth of the money economy as the primary indicator of the spread of instrumentalism. The general expansion of the money form is linked to the development of both scientific-technological and methodical life-style rationalism. Simmel is remarkably accurate in his predictions about the effects of the spread of the money form on selfhood and personal identity. Simmel saw modern individuals as shrewd manipulators who would calculate and engineer the effects of their impressions on others. Money, of course, is a useful instrument and medium by which to achieve this end.

Superficially, it appears that Simmel's conception of the fate of the modern individual is more optimistic than Marx's. Nevertheless, whereas Simmel suggests that what Marx described as the "alienation of self" provides the individual with a form of creativity that is novel and infinite in its possibilities, his view of the individual's fate is more gloomy than Marx's. Whereas Marx believed in the existence of a postrevolutionary society in which personal identity would be determined in terms of human need, Simmel did not believe that the problems of human existence could be resolved by *social* means. Similarly, although he agreed with Marx about the artificiality of forms of sociation based on the money economy, Simmel did not conclude that such artificiality could, or should, disappear. According to Simmel, humans will always inevitably be caught within the web of some artifice that they have spun for themselves.

Contemporary Relevance

Since Simmel's death, few if any sociologists have described themselves as "Simmelian." Simmel's sociology was too diffuse and too little known for this to happen. Nevertheless, Simmel has been influential both in Europe and in the United States.

Simmel had a strong influence on Georg Lukács (1885–1971), one of the most important Marxist theorists of the twentieth century. As a young man, Lukács studied under both Simmel and Weber, and acknowledged that both helped shape his later work. Lukács's major work, *History and Class Consciousness* (1923), in part a study of alienation and reification in the modern world, draws upon Simmelian analyses of the effects of cultural objectification. Another student of Simmel's, Ernst Bloch (1875–1977), like Lukács a Marxist theorist, also was influenced by his former teacher, although Simmel's effect on Bloch was not quite as salutary. Later in his life, Bloch described Simmel as "wholly empty and aimless . . . a collector of standpoints which he assembles all around truth without ever wanting or being able to possess it." According to Bloch, Simmel could have achieved much if he had been born with "a hard core."[23]

American academics were introduced to Simmel's work in the 1890s, when Albion W. Small (1854–1926) translated fourteen of Simmel's essays for the *American Journal of Sociology*. In the 1920s, Simmel was mentioned in some prominent introductory texts. After this time, however, his work seems to have gone into almost a complete eclipse in the United States until the publication of Kurt H. Wolff's (b. 1912) translation of some of his work in 1950. Since that date, Simmel's reputation in the United States has grown slowly. At the end of the 1970s, after the translation of *The Philosophy of Money* and *The Problems of the Philosophy of History*, interest in Simmel seemed to grow rapidly.

Before his death, Simmel wrote in his diary: "I know that I shall die without intellectual heirs—and that this is as it should be. My legacy will be, as it were in cash distributed to many heirs, each transforming his part into use conformed to *his* nature: a use which will reveal no longer its indebtedness to this heritage."[24]

To a large extent, Simmel's view of what he would leave behind has proved to be correct. Many sociologists have taken ideas and insights from his work; but to date, no one has tried to apply Simmelian ideas in an organized manner. Simmel deliberately avoided presenting his ideas in a systematic fashion. He wanted his readers to make a synthesizing attempt for themselves. He also claimed that his method of analysis could not be taught, an argument that did not win him any disciples.

Both in Europe and in the United States, Simmel's work has been influential in at least three major areas of research: (1) formal sociology and the sociology of small groups; (2) urban sociology; and, more recently, (3) the sociology of identity construction and studies dealing with the relationship between the individual and society.

Simmel's conception of sociology as the investigation of a geometry of social life has encouraged some sociologists to develop formal or mathematical modes of theory construction that try to remain faithful to Simmel's belief that sociology should investigate the foundations of interpretive knowledge. In Europe, Leopold von Wiese became the leader of a group of sociologists who tried to develop formal models of social processes. Unlike Simmel, Wiese was a strict positivist who believed that sociology should study the abstract nature and effects of social relations. Wiese's interest in the study of social relations, however, was derived from his reading of Simmelian "pure sociology." In the United States, Simmel's theoretical sociology has been used by sociologists who have specialized in the experimental studies of small groups. Simmel's work on the significance of numbers on the members of groups and his work on conflict and cooperation within small groups have proved to be of particular importance in this area.

Simmel has also had a strong influence on the work of sociologists of the Chicago School, particularly on the work of the urban sociologist Robert Park (1864–1944). Park was a student of Simmel's in Berlin during 1899–1900. Simmel's essays on the city and on the culture of the metropolis were highly regarded by him. Together with Ernest W. Burgess (1886–1966), Park was instrumental in introducing many American students to Simmel's work. Both Park and Burgess accepted Simmel's argument that what was unique to sociology was not its study of social phenomena but its study of the effects of social interaction. This assumption has been shared by all members of the Chicago School.

The interest of sociologists in what might be called Simmelian themes is certainly growing, even if it is not always acknowledged. In the 1950s and 1960s, the work of the exchange theorists George Homans (1910–1989) and Peter Blau (b. 1918) took the model of impersonal *exchange* as the very basis of social life. Blau, for instance, has shown how the logic of an impersonal system of exchange rationality has permeated many domains of communicative interaction in modern societies—including the domain of the love relationship.[25] Simmel would have seen the spread of the model of exchange rationality into previously private areas of life (as studied by Blau) as quite consistent with the thesis presented in *The Philosophy of Money*.

Like Blau's sociology, the work of one of the best known postwar microsociologists, Erving Goffman (1922–1982), dealt mainly with the various ways in which modern individuals calculate the effects of their behaviors and performances on one another.[26] In his theoretical work, Goffman tended to reduce communicative interaction to technical and instrumental calculation. This restrictiveness did not prevent his work from being an insightful description of how activity becomes meaningful to the modern individual. Perhaps more than any other contemporary sociologist, Goffman captured the ways in which modern individuals are "free" to ground what might be called identity work in the rational calculation of subjective profit and loss. Goffman asked: What if it were true that impression management were everything when it came to the construction of an identity? The descriptions of the amoral, but shrewd, individuals that result from the asking of this question are both amusing and insightful. Goffman did not attempt a macrosociological explanation of the social conditions that produced such individuals, but his assumptions about the relationship between the individual and society were wholly Simmelian in nature.

A book that takes seriously the idea that human sociality is in its purest form when human individuals are at play rather than at work is *The Nude Beach* by Jack Douglas and Paul Rasmussen.[27] Douglas and Rasmussen, who manage to combine both Freudian and Simmelian themes in their work, argue that the *foundation* of social life can best be investigated when human nature is investigated in a "human social condition" that is undistorted by the authoritative impact of cultural objectifications designed to thwart play and creativity. They argue that sociologists have taken the myth of rational man too seriously. What is most fully human, they believe, is more likely to be observed when humans are at play than when they are trying to be rational or instrumental.

Another work in sociological theory that, unlike *The Nude Beach,* makes its indebtedness to Simmel explicit is *Escape Attempts,* by the British sociologists Stanley Cohen and Laurie Taylor.[28] Cohen and Taylor describe Simmel as the "most neglected 'founding father' of sociology"; and they deal with perhaps the most significant Simmelian theme of all—the irresolvable tension between the individual and society. *Escape Attempts* describes the modern individual's tragic and absurd search for one's "true" self. According to Simmel, the object of such a search will always prove elusive. In *Escape Attempts,* Cohen and Taylor document the nightmare that many contemporary individuals find themselves living as they experience the contradiction between the public expectation that they be self-contained and the sense of personal failure that results from the inability to construct a self that proves to be invulnerable to the demands of social life.

NOTES

1. *Grunfragen der Soziologie* (Berlin: Göscher, 1917) (my translation).
2. See Lewis A. Coser (Ed.), *Georg Simmel,* pp. 37–39, for the full text of Professor Dietrich Schaefer's report.
3. Leopold von Wiese, "Simmel's formal method," in Coser (Ed.), *Georg Simmel,* pp. 55–56.
4. The full title is *Soziologie: Untersuchungen über die Formen der Vergellschaftung* (Sociology: Investigations of forms of sociation) (Leipzig: Duncker and Humboldt, 1908).
5. See Kurt Gassen & Michael Landmann (Eds.), *Buch des Dankes an Georg Simmel: Briefe, Erinnerungen, Bibliographie* (Munich: Duncker and Humboldt, 1958).
6. Nicholas J. Spykman, *The social theory of Georg Simmel,* p. xxiv.
7. Deena & Michael Weinstein, "Introduction," in Georg Simmel, *Schopenhauer and Nietzsche,* pp. xxvii–xxviii.
8. See ibid., pp. xliv–xlv.
9. Quoted in Kurt H. Wolff (Ed.), *Georg Simmel, 1858–1918: A collection of essays,* p. 347.
10. *The sociology of Georg Simmel,* pp. 10–11.
11. *The philosophy of money,* p. 101.

12. See "Die Mode," in Georg Simmel, *Philosophische Kultur: Gesammelte Essays* (Leipzig: Kröner, 1911), pp. 44–45.
13. *Soziologie,* p. 40, quoted in Coser (Ed.), *Georg Simmel,* p. 11.
14. *The philosophy of money,* pp. 494–495.
15. *Georg Simmel: Sociologist and European,* p. 266.
16. Ibid., p. 254.
17. *The sociology of Georg Simmel,* p. 11.
18. Ibid., pp. 21–22.
19. Ibid., p. 18.
20. Ibid., p. 23.
21. The term "social types" was coined by Don Levine. See *Georg Simmel: On individuality and social forms,* p. lxiv.
22. Ibid., p. 170.
23. Ernst Bloch, *Geist der Utopie* (Munich, 1918), pp. 246–247, quoted in David Frisby, *Georg Simmel,* p. 146.
24. From "Nachgelassenes Tagebuch," *Logos,* 7 (1919), p. 121, quoted in Coser (Ed.), *Georg Simmel,* p. 24.
25. See Peter Blau, *Exchange and power in social life* (New York: Wiley, 1964).
26. See Erving Goffman, *The presentation of self in everyday life* (New York: Doubleday, 1959);

and *Gender advertisements* (New York: Harper & Row, 1976).

27. Jack Douglas & Paul K. Rasmussen, *The nude beach* (Beverly Hills, CA: Sage, 1977).

28. Stanley Cohen & Laurie Taylor, *Escape attempts: The theory and practice of resistance in everyday life* (London: Routledge, 1992).

GLOSSARY

A priori: Function or category of cognition that precedes, and is the basis for, experience.

Categories of mediation: Social-cultural patterns of meaning through which individuals interpret experience.

Content: Simmel's term for the nonorganizational elements of interaction as viewed by the investigator.

Cultural modernism: An idealist and aesthetic response to modernization, that is, to the social divisions, rationalized social forms, and instrumental, disenchanted orientations institutionalized by modern societies.

Culture: For Simmel, the synthesis of objective and subjective culture. Objective culture: the ideas, feelings, and so on of individuals that have been embodied in an intersubjectively understandable form, such as language or art. Subjective culture: the cultivation of the individual through interaction with objects external to the self—for example, reading a book or writing a paper.

Epistemology: A theory of the process by which people can possess knowledge.

Form: Simmel's term for the epistemologically given framework that imposes coherence on the innumerable and various stimuli that constitute experience.

Formal sociology: One of three types of Simmelian sociology. Focuses on "pure" and fundamental forms of *sociation.*

General sociology: One of three types of Simmelian sociology. Focuses on the impact of the social environment on the individual.

Historical realism: View that written history is a re-creation of facts and events of a given period.

Historicism: The doctrine that states that societies and cultures can be understood only as historically unique entities.

Historiography: Principles or methodology of historical study.

Impression management: Erving Goffman's term for the way in which individuals—using technical reason—present desired images of themselves to others.

Methodical life-style rationalism: The organization of an individual's life so that it is routinized and orderly.

Money form: The formal characteristics of relations among people who interact by means of the symbolic medium of money. The money form enhances individualization, subjective control, and personal indifference.

Neo-Kantian: A follower of the philosopher Immanuel Kant. At least three schools of neo-Kantianism were in existence in Germany at the end of the nineteenth century.

Objectification: Something that is treated as an object by human subjects.

Philosophical sociology: One of three types of Simmelian sociology. Focuses on the construction and impact of social epistemology.

Social types: Types of individualism brought into being by *forms* and by *sociological apriorities.*

Sociation: Simmel's term for social interaction in its broadest usage.

Sociological apriorities: The functions or categories of understanding that arise as a result of (1) the innate objective and subjective capacities of mind; and (2) the human capacity for *sociation.* The sociological apriorities are the basis for social experience.

Symbolic form: The formal characteristics of relations among people who use various kinds of symbolic media as the basis for communicative interaction.

ANNOTATED BIBLIOGRAPHY

Primary Sources

Conflict and the web of group affiliations (Kurt H. Wolff & Reinhard Bendix, Trans.; foreword by Everett C. Hughes). New York: Free Press, 1964 [1908, 1922] (paper).

A translation of two of Simmel's essays, the titles of which are the title of this book.

The conflict in modern culture and other essays (K. Peter Etzkorn, Trans.). New York: Teachers College Press, 1968.

A collection of essays by Simmel, including several essays on aesthetics.

Essays on interpretation in social science (Guy Oakes, Trans. & Ed.; introductory essays by Oakes). Totowa, NJ: Rowman & Littlefield, 1980 [1904, 1916, 1917–1918, 1918].

Four methodological essays that deal with interpretive theory and with the problem of understanding history. This book contains a lengthy and useful introduction by Oakes.

Essays on religion (Monograph Series, Society for the Scientific Study of Religion, No. 10) (Neider, Ludwig, & Horst J. Helle, Trans. & Eds.). New Haven: Yale University Press, 1997.

These essays on religion were originally published between 1898 and 1918. This is the first time they have been published in English.

Georg Simmel: On individuality and social forms (Donald N. Levine, Ed.; introduction by Levine). Chicago: University of Chicago Press, 1971 (paper).

A collection of shorter essays by Simmel, dealing with many different subjects. This anthology includes Simmel's famous essays on social types and the article "How Is Society Possible?"

Georg Simmel: On women, sexuality, and love (Guy Oakes, Trans.; introduction by Oakes). New Haven, CT: Yale University Press, 1984.

Essays by Simmel on women, feminism, culture, sex, and love.

Georg Simmel: Sociologist and European (P. A. Lawrence, Ed.; introduction by Lawrence). New York: Harper & Row, 1976.

An anthology of readings from Simmel, with some new translations of his work. This book contains the only translations of some papers by Simmel on culture and an essay on the "idea of Europe."

The philosophy of money (Tom Bottomore & David Frisby, Trans.). London: Routledge & Kegan Paul, 1978 [1900].

A brilliant analysis of the sociological effects of the institutionalization of the money economy. Probably Simmel's most important book, it was not translated in its entirety until 1978.

The problems of the philosophy of history (Guy Oakes, Trans. & Ed.; introduction by Oakes). New York: Free Press, 1977 [1892].

Simmel's analysis of the epistemological foundations of our understanding of human history. His "refutation of historical realism" was highly praised by Max Weber.

Schopenhauer and Nietzsche (Helmut Loiskandl, Trans.; Deena & Michael Weinstein, Eds.; introduction by the Weinsteins). Amherst: University of Massachusetts Press, 1986 [1907].

This is the first translation of this work in English. The forty-page essay by Deena and Michael Weinstein is an excellent introduction to the development of Simmel's philosophy.

Simmel on culture: Selected writings (Featherstone, Mike, Ed.). London: Sage, 1997 (paper).

Deals with Simmel's work on "culture." Topics covered include "female culture," the crisis of culture, the sociology of the meal, spatial and urban culture, fashion and adornment, money, prostitution, religion, and spiritualism.

The sociology of Georg Simmel (Kurt H. Wolff, Trans. & Ed.; introduction by Wolff). New York: Free Press, 1950.

For many years, this was the standard anthology of Simmel's essays, most of which come from Simmel's *Soziologie*.

Sociology of religion (Curt Rosenthal, Trans.). New York: Philosophical Library, 1959 [1906].

Simmel's analysis of the meaning of religion, written largely from a philosophical point of view.

Secondary Sources

Axelrod, Charles David. *Studies in intellectual breakthrough: Freud, Simmel, Buber.* Amherst: University of Massachusetts Press, 1979.

Contains a discussion of Simmel as an innovator.

Coser, Lewis A. (Ed.). *Georg Simmel.* Englewood Cliffs, NJ: Prentice-Hall, 1965.

A collection of essays about Simmel and his work by his contemporaries and by twentieth-century sociologists.

Frisby, David. *Georg Simmel.* New York: Tavistock, 1984 (paper).

This is a short study of Simmel written as part of the Key Sociologists series. The best introduction to Simmel available in English.

Frisby, David. *Fragments of modernity: Theories of modernity in the work of Simmel, Kracauer, and Benjamin.* Cambridge, MA: MIT Press, 1986 (paper).

Frisby has suggested that Simmel was "the first theorist of modernity," that is, the first theorist to be interested in analyzing how modernity is experienced. This work shows the centrality of Simmelian theory for an understanding of the present.

Frisby, David. *Simmel and since: Essays on Simmel's social theory.* London: Routledge, 1992 (paper).

A collection of essays written by the foremost English-speaking commentator on Simmel over the last decade.

Frisby, David. *Sociological impressionism: A reassessment of Georg Simmel's social theory.* London: Heinemann, 1981 (paper).

A now established commentary and discussion of Simmel's contribution to social theory.

Jaworski, Gary D. *Georg Simmel and the American prospect.* Albany: State University of New York Press, 1997 (paper).

This book examines how Simmelian ideas have been received in the United States. Jaworski examines Simmel's influence on the Chicago School, functionalists such as Talcott Parsons, interactionists such as Erving Goffman, and postmodernists such as Deena and Michael Weinstein.

Kaern, Michael, Bernard S. Phillips, & Robert S. Cohen, (Eds.). *Georg Simmel and contemporary sociology.* Dordrecht: Kluwer Academic Publishers, 1990. Volume 119 of the Boston Studies in the Philosophy of Science.

This collection of articles adds to Simmel's reputation as a serious sociologist and philosopher.

Sellerberg, Ann-Mari. *A blend of contradictions: Georg Simmel in theory and practice.* Somerset, New Jersey: Transaction Publishers, 1994.

Sellerberg shows how Simmel employed a dialectical method to discuss, among other things, the significance of motherhood, consumption, fashion, vacations, and interaction in geriatric hospitals.

Spykman, Nicholas J. *The social theory of Georg Simmel.* New York: Atherton Press, 1965 [1925] (paper).

A discussion of Simmel's methodology, formal sociology, and metaphysics. Paraphrases much of Simmel's work.

Weingartner, Rudolph H. *Experience and culture: The philosophy of Georg Simmel.* Middletown, CT: Wesleyan University Press, 1962.

Weingartner argues that Simmel's *Kulturphilosophie* (philosophy of culture) and *Lebensphilosophie* (philosophy of experience) are mutually supportive. Written from a philosophical point of view.

Wolff, Kurt H. (Ed.). *Georg Simmel, 1858–1918: A collection of essays, with translations and a bibliography.* Columbus: Ohio State University Press, 1959.

A collection of essays on Simmel's contribution to sociology.

In what follows I adopt the standpoint, therefore, that an aggressive inclination is an original, self-contained instinctual disposition in man, and I return to my view that it constitutes the greatest obstacle for civilization. At one point in the course of this study I was led to the idea that civilization was a special process that mankind undergoes, and I am still beholden to that idea. I can now add that civilization is a process in the service of Eros, whose purpose it is to combine single human individuals, and after them families, then races, peoples and nations, into one great unity: the unity of mankind. Why this has to happen we know not; yet the work of Eros is precisely this. These collections of men are to be libidinally bound to one another. Necessity alone, the advantages of work in common, will not hold them together. But man's natural aggressive instinct, the hostility of each against all and of all against each other, opposes this program of civilization. This aggressive instinct is the derivative and the main representative of the death instinct which we have found alongside of Eros and which shares world-dominion with it. And now, I think, the meaning of the evolution of civilization is no longer obscure to us. It is the representation between Eros and Death, between the instinct of life and the instinct of destruction, as it works itself out in the human species. This struggle is of what all life essentially consists, and the evolution of civilization may therefore be simply described as the struggle for life of the human species. It is this battle of the giants that our nursemaids try to soothe with their lullaby about Heaven.

—Sigmund Freud, *Gesammelte Werke* (Leipzig, Vienna, Zürich: Psychoanalytischer Verlag, 1925)

10

Sigmund Freud

(1856–1939)

BACKGROUND

Life

Sigmund Freud was born on May 6, 1856, in the small Moravian town of Freiberg—at the time, part of the sprawling Austro-Hungarian Empire. His father, Jacob, was a wool merchant who was unable to provide his family with more than the bare necessities for a respectable middle-class existence. There is some uncertainty about whether Freud's mother, Amalia, was her husband's second or third wife. In any case, when she gave birth to Sigmund—her first child—at the age of twenty-one, Amalia's husband was already past forty—a grandfather who, by a previous marriage, had produced a child who fathered a son the year before Freud was born.

In middle age, Freud recalled that as a child he had never doubted that he was his mother's favorite. Amalia frequently told her eldest son that she anticipated that he would achieve much in his life. Freud's early relationship with his father, however, was far from tranquil. Often there were angry scenes. Once, Jacob accused Sigmund of trying to come between himself and his wife; on another occasion, Jacob was disgusted to find that his seven- or eight-year-old son had deliberately urinated on his parents' bed. His father's judgment on him—"That boy will never amount to anything"[1]—left a deep impression on the mind of the young Freud.

In 1859, Jacob moved his family to Vienna in order to escape the effects of an economic recession in Freiberg. At seventeen, Freud entered the University of Vienna as a medical student. Throughout his life, however, Freud was more interested in scientific research than in medical practice; therefore, in 1876, he was delighted to accept a position as a research scholar at the famous Brücke Institute of Physiology. There Freud worked as a neurologist, spending much of the next six years investigating the nervous systems of marine organisms and the anatomy of the human brain.

After he left the Brücke Institute, Freud conducted research into cocaine and made some extravagant claims about its potential benefits. He gave cocaine to many of his friends, took it himself, and sent some of the drug to his fiancée, Martha Bernays, "to make her strong and give her cheeks a red color."[2] However, Freud did help to alert the medical profession to cocaine's use as a local anesthetic in eye operations.

Freud realized that he would not be able to marry Martha unless he could earn the kind of income generated by a medical practice. Consequently, he belatedly took his final medical exams in 1881 and reluctantly left the Brücke Institute to enter the General Hospital of Vienna. Here he worked in the Psychiatric Clinic and in the Department of Nervous Diseases. After an engagement that lasted six years, Freud set up his medical practice, specializing in neurology.

From 1891 to 1938, Freud lived and worked at the same address in Vienna. Although, judging from his letters, Freud appears to have been deeply in love with Martha when he was courting her, for most of their life together he took her very much for granted. Certainly Freud's sexual interest in his wife faded after the first few years of marriage. Martha nevertheless thought of Freud as a good father to his six children and considered him a dutiful husband. Freud's written instructions to his fiancée specifying that he expected her to give up her own family for him appear extraordinarily patriarchal by today's standards. Martha, however, had anticipated such an order and quietly complied with it.

After his marriage, Freud probably had a long-standing affair with his sister-in-law, Minna Bernays, who lived with the Freuds in Vienna. Freud used to spend much of his vacation time traveling with Minna, while Martha remained at home. Freud's published analysis of his own dream fragments in *The Interpretation of Dreams* (1900) offers tantalizing hints of a sexual relationship with his wife's sister.

In the 1890s, Freud began to develop the ideas that would make him famous. Beginning in 1902, a little group of followers met at Freud's home every Wednesday evening to discuss some of the unfolding principles of the new discipline that Freud had begun to formulate. Gradually, this new discipline came to be labeled *psychoanalysis*, and in 1908, the old Wednesday Society became the Vienna Psychoanalytical Society. People came from all over Europe and from the United States to attend sessions of the society.

It would be difficult to overemphasize the importance and authority of Freud at this society's early meetings. In these early years, an adherence to psychoanalytic ideas was inseparable from personal loyalty to Freud himself. One reason for this was the strength of his personality; another was that Freud had developed the basic ideas of psychoanalysis almost entirely by himself. Starting in 1911, however, with the defection of Alfred Adler (1870–1937) from what had become the psychoanalytic movement, many of Freud's earliest collaborators parted company from him. This number included the Swiss psychiatrist Carl Jung (1875–1961), whom Freud had made his heir-designate by insisting that Jung be appointed the first president of the International Psychoanalytical Association in 1910. The defectors' camp claimed that Adler, Jung, and others had been forced out by Freud's authoritarianism and inflexibility; those who remained faithful to Freud argued that those who left had chosen to flee from the truths that Freud had discovered and that they had found too hard to bear.

After World War I, Freud formed an inner circle of disciples from those of his followers whom he most trusted: Karl Abrahams, Max Eitingon, Otto Rank, and Hans Sachs from Vienna; Sándor Ferenczi from Budapest; and Ernest Jones from London. These six men made up an association that was later referred to as "the Committee." To symbolize the presumption of fidelity that bound these men to the founder of psychoanalysis, Freud presented all the members of this inner circle with heavy Greek intaglio rings, similar to the one that he always wore himself.

As a student, Freud dreamed of the day when he would be important enough for a bust of him to be erected outside the University of Vienna (a dream that became a reality toward the end of his life). He lived to see his theories have an enormous impact on the modern world; and, during the last two decades of his life, he became a very famous old man. In his later years, however, Freud became pessimistic about people's ability to accept his discoveries. He believed that society's resistance toward his ideas would lead merely to a greater unwillingness to acknowledge the unpleasant truths he had uncovered. In addition, Freud was deeply wounded by the many defections from the psychoanalytic movement by colleagues who wanted to soften the iconoclastic impact of his discoveries.

In 1923, Freud learned that he had cancer of the jaw. For the last sixteen years of his life, he lived with constant pain and suffered the effects of thirty-three operations. Nevertheless, he continued to write and to see his patients until the very last week of his life. When he was eighty-two, the Nazis annexed Austria and took over the administration of Vienna. The Gestapo ransacked Freud's apartments and placed Freud under constant surveillance. For a short time, the fascist *Anschluss* succeeded in silencing the man the novelist Thomas Mann described as "the great destroyer of illusions." Thanks to the efforts of influential friends, Freud and the members of his immediate family were permitted to leave Vienna for England in the summer of 1938. Freud died in London on September 23, 1939, a few days after the start of World War II.

For most of his life, Freud was deeply misanthropic, finding it increasingly difficult to conceal his contempt for the "wolf-pack" of humanity. He acknowledged that ordinary individuals could not cope with life without pathetically attaching themselves to discredited and infantile beliefs like Christianity. Like many other theorists, Freud found ideas more interesting and more companionable than people. He did not think much of his species. Writing to a friend in 1918, he commented:

> I do not break my head very much about good or evil, but I have found little that is "good" about human beings on the whole. In my experience most of them are trash, no matter whether they publicly subscribe to this or that ethical doctrine or to none at all.

That is something that you cannot say aloud, or perhaps even think, though your experiences of life can hardly have been different from mine. If we are to talk of ethics, I subscribe to a high ideal from which most of the human beings I have come across depart most lamentably.[3]

To comprehend the development of Freud's ideas, it is necessary to have some understanding of the private struggles and conflicts of the founder of the psychoanalytic movement. The evolution of psychoanalytic ideas was closely associated with Freud's unfolding view of his role as an intellectual and as a social leader. Freud was always sensitive to the charge that he had developed his ideas from the analysis of his own inner consciousness. As with Max Weber, however, the connections between the author's ideas and his inner life are hard to miss. Freud, for example, discovered the existence of the Oedipus complex by analyzing himself and by examining his early relationship with his father; similarly, the emphasis that Freud increasingly placed on the role of a "death instinct" in human affairs paralleled tragic events in his own life: the impact of World War I on his immediate family, the death of a loved daughter and grandson, and his own incurable cancer. The description in *Totem and Taboo* (1913) of the patriarchal leader of the horde who is killed and devoured by his followers bears a striking resemblance to Freud's image of himself as the founder of a new science who is himself set on and dismembered by envious and disloyal disciples. Finally, at the end of his life, in *Moses and Monotheism* (1939), Freud identified himself with a man who had had a messianic destiny but was fated never to reach the promised land.

Any connection that might or might not exist between a person's inner struggles and the development of his or her ideas neither confirms nor undermines the validity of those ideas. Yet, to a very large extent, many of the problems with which Freud grappled are universal. Freud gained insight into the inner workings of the human mind by looking into himself and by refusing to compromise his beliefs for his own— or anyone else's—sake. It is difficult not to see psychoanalytic theory as the personal testament of someone who believed that it was his fate to institutionalize the discipline that would provide the looking glass by which the modern world would come to know itself.

Social Environment

In the nineteenth century, enlightened people believed in science as the cure for most of the world's ills. Freud always insisted that his theories had been scientifically validated by clinical observation, and he stated categorically that psychoanalysis stood or fell as a natural science—that is, as a body of knowledge that could be tested in terms of the positivistic method. Like Comte, Freud believed that the "positive" age of science had displaced the reign of superstition and theology. When Freud was trained as a research scientist, positivism had led to dramatic advances in the physical and biological sciences. In Germany, science was held in the highest esteem, and the discoveries of German scientists were seen as the noblest outgrowths of Teutonic culture. Goethe's essay on nature (which Freud learned as a schoolboy) is a good example of the kind of sentiments that were taken for granted at that time. The essay romanticizes science by portraying the natural world as a bountiful mother who extends only to the most privileged and the most worthy the opportunity to explore her secrets. As an adult, Freud recalled that Goethe's essay had had a great influence on him.

It is not surprising, therefore, that, during the first part of his life, Freud thought of himself more as a product of German culture than as a Jew. As a young man, he was proud to live in the imperial city of Vienna, the capital of Austria-Hungary and, after Berlin, the largest German-speaking city in Europe. Vienna had a mixed population of people drawn from all parts of the empire, including a great number of Jews. The Austro-Hungarian Empire, however, held together by the aging Hapsburg Emperor Franz Joseph, was a decaying entity during this period; it did not survive the defeat inflicted on Germany and Austria-Hungary during World War I.

Although the Vienna in which Freud lived and worked as a young scientist was outwardly tolerant of Jews, the Jewish population had little to do with government. With the election to burgomaster (mayor) of Karl Lueger in 1897, anti-Semitism became widespread. The young Adolf Hitler, who was living in Vienna during this period, counted Lueger as one of his early heroes. Hitler, in fact, was typical of thousands of uprooted, disenchanted, and semieducated people who frequented the city's many coffeehouses and cheap hostels.

By the turn of the century, the leader of Vienna's pan-Germany party was wearing a hanged Jew as a watch-chain ornament; and the official newspaper of the Christian Social Society, the *Illustrierte Wiener Volkszeitung*, was proudly advertising itself as "the organ of anti-Semitism." As he became aware of the growth of anti-Semitism and the end of the more attractive aspects of the empire—like the demise of the idea of a universal culture of enlightenment—Freud stopped thinking of himself as German. As he grew older, he increasingly became aware of his marginality and of his position as a permanent outsider. Toward the end of his life, Freud claimed that psychoanalytic ideas would have met with far less resistance and with less outright hostility if he had been a Christian.

Characteristically, Freud had deeply ambivalent feelings about Vienna. He claimed to hate the city, but he spent most of his life there. Many professional and middle-class Jews had similar feelings about Vienna. On the one hand, as one of the dying capitals of Europe, the city had a *fin de siècle* atmosphere of despair and decadence. On the other hand, with its heterogeneous population of displaced people from all over central Europe, Vienna was comparatively receptive to new ideas.

Thus Vienna was a city of contrasts; it was also the city that fostered many of the most important developments in twentieth-century art, philosophy, and science. After Freud was forced out of Vienna as a very tired and very old man, he wrote from London that his feeling of triumph at being free was tinged with sadness, for, as he put it, "we loved the prison from which we have been released."[4]

Intellectual Roots

As a young scientist, Freud received a rigorous training in the philosophical principles of the Helmholtzian school of scientific research. Hermann von Helmholtz (1821–1894) was a highly authoritative psychologist who influenced the course of

German science in the late nineteenth century by arguing that living bodies must be understood in terms of their underlying chemical and physical properties. Helmholtz believed that it was unscientific for the biological sciences to try to explain living phenomena by reference to the apparent intentions and purposes of living organisms. In short, biological research should exemplify the virtues of positivism and reductionism. It was this school of thought that was enforced in the Brücke Institute of Physiology.

The influence of Helmholtzian principles on Freud was so great that he could accept only the validity of scientific explanation that at least allowed for the existence of mechanistic relationships among variables. Although he always upheld determinism, Freud came to reject the Helmholtzian argument that a reductionist approach to human behavior was best. Ultimately, Freud abandoned his early interest in neurology and physiology and concentrated on the way in which mental disturbances could be treated and banished *by ideas*. He never denied, however, that it might eventually be possible to treat such disturbances by using drugs to induce physical and chemical changes in the body in order to alleviate some neurotic and psychotic symptoms.

When Freud received his training as a doctor of medicine, the disciplines of psychiatry and experimental psychology, as we know them today, did not exist. In the 1880s, the medical profession possessed little knowledge that could be used to help patients who were suffering from what today would be classified as mental illnesses. The psychiatrists of Freud's day were unable to comprehend either the meaning or the causes of neurotic and psychotic symptoms in patients. For the most part, they were content to classify such symptoms and to note down facts that seemed to be important—for example: "the patient does not keep himself clean," "the patient talks nonsense," "the patient is confused." It was generally assumed that any mental disturbance was rooted in the patient's physiological makeup and was caused by some kind of defect in the nervous system. These beliefs, of course, were consistent with Helmholtzian principles of scientific research and diagnosis; but they could not adequately explain cases of mental disturbance. By the end of the nineteenth century, therefore, the medical profession had made little progress in locating causes for psychic disorder.

The young Freud was trained by his professors to recognize hysteria—a common ailment of the time—as a problem that afflicted only women. As the word "hysteria" comes from the Greek word meaning "womb," it was considered self-evident that a hysterical condition would be observed only in female patients. Many of Freud's senior colleagues believed that hysteria could be alleviated by surgically removing a woman's clitoris; others held that the cause of hysteria was a wandering womb and that the unruly organ could be driven back into place by the odor of a chemical called valerian. When Freud read a paper entitled "On Male Hysteria" to some of his professors in 1886, his ideas were ridiculed. This was the first, but not the last, time that Freud had a serious disagreement with his professional peers.

Freud wrote his paper on hysteria in males as a result of what he had learned from a visit to France. In 1885, Freud traveled to Paris to study with Jean Martin Charcot (1825–1893) as part of his neurological training. He was astounded to find that Charcot (one of Europe's leading specialists in nervous diseases) could produce, through hypnosis, those symptoms of mental disturbance in patients that had always been assumed to be solely organic in origin. Unlike most of his colleagues, Charcot was able to make some progress in understanding such symptoms. He demonstrated that it was possible to cause hysterical symptoms by placing certain ideas in the minds of patients under hypnosis. This indicated to Freud that, whatever the unspecified organic or physiological basis of a mental disturbance might be, the symptoms of mental disturbance could be treated—and perhaps removed—by ideas alone. More than anything else, Freud's exposure to Charcot's treatment of hysterics drew him away from neurology and pushed him toward psychology as a means of understanding the disturbed patient.

Freud was greatly impressed by Charcot's ability to make subjects obey posthypnotic suggestions. Charcot, for example, would hypnotize a subject and then order that person to open an umbrella at a certain time and in a certain place later in the day. The individual in question would comply with the order but would not understand why he had acted in such a fashion. Instead, the subject would make a feeble rationalization—saying, for instance, that he had opened the umbrella to see if the lining were torn. What caught Freud's attention was that the subjects in Charcot's experiments were able to operate on two levels. On one level, the hypnotist could speak in a normal fashion to a subject who was not under hypnosis and could ask that person to explain the reason for his behavior. On another level, it was possible to implant ideas *or to recapture memories* from individuals who were under hypnosis, even when such individuals were not *consciously* participating in the investigator's experiment.

While studying in Paris, Freud was strongly influenced by Charcot's views on the sexual etiology of the neuroses. Charcot believed that behind a hysterical condition was always *la chose genitale*—a sexual matter (a discovery, incidentally, that greatly embarrassed him). Freud considered this highly significant because it forged a link between *psyche* (mind) and *soma* (body). Human sexuality has both mental and physiological components; an individual, for instance, can be either psychologically impotent (that is, mentally incapable of performing sexually), or physiologically impotent or sterile (for example, incapable of ejaculation or ovulation). Although, as a Helmholtzian, Freud was basically interested in physical and chemical variables, Charcot had demonstrated to him the importance of mental phenomena or ideas. By locating the source of hysterical symptoms in *la chose genitale*, Freud realized that it was possible to acknowledge the role that *ideas* played in the development of neurotic states without losing touch with what he believed were underlying physical and chemical changes in the body. Freud never stopped assuming that there were important links between an individual's mind and body. His later work was concerned almost exclusively with the importance of mind; nevertheless, Freud always assumed that there were powerful instinctual forces behind most mental activity and that such forces were rooted in the human organism.

The other individual who influenced Freud greatly in his early years was Josef Breuer (1842–1925). Breuer was a Viennese physician whom Freud met at the Brücke Institute. From 1882 to 1892, Breuer treated what has become a famous case of hysteria—that of the woman referred to as "Anna O." One day, Breuer discovered that one of Anna's hysterical symptoms completely disappeared after she described the conditions under which it had first appeared. Breuer treated Anna by hypnotizing her and by asking her to tell him what was disturbing her. He discovered that Anna's symptoms appeared to be related to feelings that Anna had had about her father and that she had "repressed"—that is, forced out of consciousness. Breuer's cathartic method of treating Anna, which came to be known as "the talking cure," was helpful in relieving Anna of her symptoms.

Although Charcot was famous throughout Europe, and although Breuer was a well-known and highly respected figure in Vienna, Freud seems to have been the only person to see a connection between their approaches toward hysteria. Surprisingly enough, even after Freud told Charcot about Breuer's treatment of Anna O, Charcot was not particularly interested in "the talking cure."

In 1892, Freud and Breuer published a book called *Studies in Hysteria.* This work consisted of some theoretical interpretations of hysteria and of a number of case histories, including a report of the case of Anna O. The book was badly received by the medical establishment and largely ignored by psychiatrists. Throughout the 1890s, Freud became increasingly convinced that sexual factors played the major role in the development of neurosis. Breuer conceded that Anna O's hysteria had been caused by repressed sexual feelings, but he could not accept the idea that sexual factors were behind all forms of hysteria and anxiety. Freud accused Breuer of cowardice in the face of what he saw to be undeniable truth, and the relationship between the two men came to a sudden end.

As he began to develop his psychoanalytic theories about human behavior, Freud came to use the term "libido" to describe what he believed was the vital impulse of mental energy. Sexual desire is the major component of the libidinal drive, which, however, includes all life-preserving impulses. Libidinal energy becomes emotionally charged for the individual when a particular object or activity is *cathected*—that is, defined as an appropriate outlet for the discharge of libidinal energy. For example, if an individual's lover dies, that individual might learn to cathect another person as a suitable object of erotic attention. In this manner, libidinal energy can be transferred from one object (or the memory of that object) to another.

Freud used an energy-flow model borrowed from the physical sciences to suggest that libidinal energy (for example, what the individual might experience as sexual tension) is discharged, stored, and channeled or directed along predetermined routes. Freud argued that the individual might wish to enlarge sexual desire (or perhaps to increase the desire for food and drink) so that the release of tension would be the more enjoyable. Thus the individual might focus on external stimuli as the means to a more pleasurable discharge of sexual energy. Freud referred to the individual's tendency to maximize such pleasure as the *pleasure principle.*

As we have seen, sexual desire for Freud was located at the frontier between mind and body. By 1895, there was no longer any doubt in his mind that hysteria and anxiety were caused by the inability of the organism to discharge the tensions that resulted from a surplus of sexual energy. The mechanism of anxiety-neurosis, for instance, was described by Freud as the deflection by the mind of somatic sexual excitation and the subsequent "abnormal use" of such excitation. From this point on, Freud began to concentrate his efforts on a study of the way in which the symbolic resources of the mind coped with the bioorganic demands and impulses of the human organism.

IDEAS

Society

As he grew older, Freud became increasingly interested in cultural and historical problems. He had no theory of society as such. It would be more accurate to say that he theorized about the behavior of individuals within the group or within society. (In fact, in his opinion, sociology was nothing more than "applied psychology.")

Freud believed that *instincts*—which represent bodily demands on the mind—were the fundamental cause of much of human behavior. He also believed that basic instinctual drives (like the drive to reduce a buildup of sexual tension) were powerful forces that could reveal themselves in many different ways. Freud conceded that the ideal society might force individuals to subordinate instinctual drives to analysis and thoughtful reflection. He concluded, however, that such a society could never come into existence because behavior that is emotionally appealing and that panders to the individual's need for cathexis is always more subjectively desirable than activity founded on a disinterested search for truth. Freud argued that social activity is based largely on the ability of the group to repress and channel instinctual needs—in other words, on the ability of the group to block and redirect each individual's libidinal energy. Thus civilization is possible because the force of instinctual motivations is redirected, not abolished.

In *Totem and Taboo*, Freud used anthropological data to speculate about the way in which human society originally developed. He argued that the earliest type of society came into being when human beings left a state of "heedless sexual and primitive egoistic motives" to form the "primal horde"—a simple community dominated by a patriarch with exclusive sexual privileges. An act of revolt, triggered by sexual jealousy, led to the murder of this original patriarchal figure by the younger males of the horde. Freud suggested that the memory of this primal revolt was retained in a repressed form by succeeding generations of savages and that many of the sacrificial feasts involving totemic objects that were noted by early anthropologists were symbolic reenactments of this primal revolt. Freud argued that the group created a taboo against both marriage and homicide within the group in order to avoid the need for further revolt. As norms were institutionalized in this fashion, the horde was transformed gradually into a more civilized type of society.

Civilized society manipulates subjects both by frustrating individuals and by offering them opportunities for socially acceptable forms of cathectic release. Antisocial and highly individualistic forms of sexual behavior are generally thwarted by taboos. Freud believed that, for the sake of social order, the norms against homicide and incest must be enforced. Early sexual impulses must be controlled. Perversion and general promiscuity must be discouraged. Nevertheless, the individual willingly participates in social life and commonly fears the consequences of other people's impulses and desires. Furthermore, individuals are often afraid of and even disgusted by their own instinctual impulses and desires. Freud argued, therefore, that anxiety and guilt could play an instrumental role in shaping society's hold on the individual. He suggested that the relationship between powerful leaders, who enforce norms, and less powerful followers, who obey such norms, reminds the individual of the relationship between parent and child. Thus society often encourages the individual to regress—that is, to return to an earlier state—in this case to one of infantile dependence on a parent figure. In this way a powerful leader—like Hitler or Mussolini, for instance—can be cathected as an object in which libidinal energy can be invested.

According to Freud, the study of religion helped to illustrate the way in which social forces could channel or manipulate human behavior. In *The Future of an Illusion* (1927), he argued that religion was a form of infantile regression—that is, that it permitted and encouraged the individual to return to a childlike state. Freud maintained that religion was based on memories of childhood fears and weaknesses and that the recollection of childhood was the memory of a condition of dependence. According to Freud, the state of such dependence is often felt to be a familiar and comfortable condition for the individual and can remind the adult of earlier, successful cathexes. Reason—the dispelling of illusion—on the other hand, does not encourage cathexis; on the contrary, it discourages orientations that have an obvious emotional charge.

Freud pointed out that the cathexis of God unites a group of believers and permits individuals to direct emotionally charged energy toward socially acceptable activity. Religion dams and diverts libidinal energy by providing people with the opportunity to sublimate mental energy. According to Freud, *sublimation* occurs when the individual is able to transform basic instinctual drives into emotional needs that can be met symbolically. For example, the nun who is celibate and "wedded to Christ" is in many ways the equivalent of the neurotic who deflects sexual excitation and puts it to an "abnormal" use. An important difference between the two, however, is that society looks more kindly on the nun.

Religion can also function to sublimate aggressive orientations. Freud believed that aggressive feelings against others commonly arise when individuals believe that they are prevented from satisfying certain needs or desires. Religion can sublimate aggressive feelings by transforming them into a symbolic renunciation of the self. For instance, Freud believed that the Christian commandment, "Thou shalt love thy neighbor as thyself," was clearly impracticable as stated. As an ideal, this commandment encourages the individual to *identify* with other people; herein lies its social significance. The internalization—or introjection—of norms and values, which leads to the development of a conscience, makes it possible for us to understand how others feel and what others think about a particular situation. Guilt arises when individuals, for whatever reason, have (normal) murderous or destructive feelings about their neighbors. Conscience puts individuals in the place of the people they torment, and thus aggressive desire creates a feeling of unease and discontent that is experienced as guilt. According to Freud, the price of progress in civilization must be paid for by the forfeiture of direct libidinal fulfillment through a heightening of the sense of guilt.

As we have seen, Freud believed that society *both* represses the desires that derive from instinctual drives *and* provides substitute gratifications for these desires. The individual is manipulated by ensuring that the means of cathexis are controlled socially. By its ever-increasing tendency to repress the individual and to heighten the sense of guilt, society generates discontent as it propels the individual to seek such substitute forms of gratification as religion, drug taking, or socially acceptable but cramped forms of eroticism.

The Individual in Society

According to Freud, the needs of the individual and those of society are always in conflict. This conflict, however, is experienced by individuals as the conflict between the force of instinctual drives and the demands that individuals make of themselves as social beings.

Before it learns to recognize its mother as an external object, the very young infant, to use Freud's term, is *polymorphously perverse.* Immediately after birth, the baby does not organize or restrict its discharge of libidinal energy. With the possible exception of the nipple, the infant in the first few weeks of life has not yet learned to cathect any particular object. The newborn baby neither knows of nor respects restrictions on its activities; it might experience frustration, but it knows neither fear nor guilt.

Freud claimed that the first organ to emerge as an "erotogenic zone"—an area of the body from which pleasure can be derived—is the mouth. In the first few months of life, the ability to suck and to take in nourishment through the mouth leads to a release of tension generated by the drive to reduce unpleasant sensations of hunger. As the baby matures, it learns to cathect the mother's breast (or the feeding bottle) as an object of emotional and erotic gratification. Freud believed that the mother's nipple is an object that is invested with erotic significance because it is an instrument of pleasure. Thus sucking comes to be recognized as an erotic activity.

The second erotogenic zone that is recognized by the growing infant is the area of the anus. Children learn to associate pleasure with the evacuation of the bowels, but they are also rewarded by the approval they receive from those who reward persistence and timeliness.

The third erotogenic zone recognized by the maturing child is the genital area itself. The child learns to handle and to stimulate the genitals as a source of pleasure, although such activity generally is restricted by adult guardians. From about the age of five until adolescence, there exists a period of latent sexuality in which no further significant sexual maturation occurs.

Freud pointed out that the fact that the child's first intimate contact is with its mother has great significance. As the child matures, it becomes jealous and resentful of the father, whom it perceives to be more powerful than itself and whom it sees as a rival for the mother's attention and love. Consequently, the child fears the father and learns to conceal its attachment to the mother. The desire that the four- or five-year-old child has for the mother, and the jealousy and aggression that the child feels for the father, were described by Freud as the "Oedipus complex." Oedipus was a mythical figure who slew his father and married his mother, and the story describing these events has been handed down from generation to generation for more than two thousand years. Freud believed that the story had such a great hold because it described what he believed was the primal and formative conflict in the life of every individual.

During that period of early life in which it experiences the Oedipal crisis, the child makes a difficult compromise between its own need for emotional gratification and what it perceives to be the demands and expectations of others. Freud believed that the male child fears that the father wishes to castrate him in retaliation for the son's desire for the mother's attention and love. Of course, the young boy cannot express this fear in words; but the fear makes itself known as a feeling of anxiety about the possible consequences of his desire for the mother. Freud believed that, around the age of five or six, the boy deals with his ambivalent feeling of awe, fear, and hostility toward his father in a highly creative fashion: He identifies with the father-figure and takes him as a role model. By identifying with a feared object, the young boy learns to cope with his secret terror of being punished and engulfed by the father.

The young girl does not typically resolve the Oedipal crisis by identifying with the father. According to Freud, the girl learns at an early age that she is without something that a boy possesses. The secretive and misleading way in which members of the adult world refer to the penis draws the girl's attention to its significance. Freud argued that the sexually mature female learns to transfer her wish for the penis to a desire for the father. Whereas the boy learns to challenge, yet respect, the father's authority, the young girl develops her femininity as she learns to please the father through a display of what are considered to be cute, alluring, and flirtatious acts. Freud believed that the achievement of a mature femininity was a far more difficult task than the achievement of a mature masculine identity. He suggested that many women never recover from their early feelings of inadequacy and, even in adult life, are prone to feelings of jealousy and insecurity.

Freud acknowledged that feminine and masculine traits developed from the interaction between the effects of anatomy and instinctual drives on the one hand, and the demands of culture and society on the other; he also conceded that objects of erotic attachment cathected after the latency period could, in part, be culturally or symbolically defined. However, he did not believe that either men or women could escape the effects of their own particular resolution of the Oedipal crisis. Similarly, Freud did not believe that individuals could escape the effects of their differing anatomies and of the differing physiological processes within their bodies.

The Ego and the Id (1923) was the first major work in which Freud introduced new theoretical ideas and concepts. In this book, he attempted to describe the basic structure of human personality in terms of three agencies or processes—*id, ego,* and *superego.* (A literal translation of Freud's German provides us with the terms "it," "I," and "upper-I.") Freud also attempted to specify more precisely than he had before the way in which personality is the product of somatic and unconscious impulses, conscious thought and calculation, and the introjected demands of culture and society.

In a postscript to his autobiography, written in 1935, Freud explained how he came to the conclusion that larger, cultural processes were a reflection of psychic conflict:

> My interest after making a lifelong *detour* through the natural sciences, medicine and psychotherapy, returned to the cultural problems which had fascinated me long before, when

I was a youth scarcely old enough for thinking. At the very climax of my psycho-analytical work, in 1912, I had already attempted in *Totem and Taboo* to make use of the newly discovered findings of analysis in order to investigate the origins of religion and morality. . . . I perceived ever more clearly that the events of human history, the interaction between human nature, cultural development and the precipitates of primaeval experiences (the most prominent example of which is religion) are no more than a reflection of the dynamic conflicts between the ego, the id, and the super-ego. That which psychoanalysis studies in the individual are the very same processes repeated upon a wider stage.5

Although the workings of the id (*it*) are buried within the unconscious, the individual experiences the effects of the id as impulsive desire. The id, itself, results from instinctual drives and impulses located within the body that cater to the needs of the organism. It does not acknowledge the existence of logic, morality, or good sense; and it is not checked or changed by the passage of time. The organization of experience through time is a rational process, and the id does not recognize any form of rationality. It is possible for the individual to repress an awareness of the id's demands. The id, however, will then continue to have a great impact on the unconscious part of the mind—that is, on that part of the mind that might affect individuals' behavior but of which they are not aware.

The ego (*I*) is that agency of the personality system that engages in "reality testing"—the agency that permits the individual to calculate and to test the effects of certain actions on others. One of the most significant characteristics of the ego agency is that it is capable of defending itself against what are perceived to be threats to its sense of autonomy. The ego, therefore, does not merely engage in reality testing, but also tries to maximize individuals' chances of *control* over themselves and others. Such control, however, is not moralistic but technical; the ego is concerned not with ends but with means. The ego, for instance, would not view criminal activity as wrong—it would merely ask the question: What are the chances of getting away with such an activity, and is the risk justified in terms of the likelihood of the perceived reward?

The ego defends itself by applying genuinely useful technical knowledge (for example, knowledge about how to lie successfully), but it can also defend itself by repressing all memory of what is seen as threatening information. This selective and unconscious mode of forgetting illustrates Freud's belief that the ego has both a conscious and an unconscious component. Another example of a *defense mechanism* is the attempt often made by the ego to project onto other people precisely those weaknesses and perceived deficiencies that subjects most fear in themselves. Similarly, another defense mechanism, *reaction formation*, is the tendency that subjects show toward denying the validity or significance of that which they are denied (for example, fame or power). Defense mechanisms, therefore, permit the individual to maintain a positive sense of self by permitting the ego to view itself as being in control and as being an instrumentally effective entity.

The third and final agency is the superego (*upper-I*). Whereas the ego is self-centered, the superego is concerned with ethical and moral principles that are binding on all individuals. The superego originates as a result of the resolution to the Oedipal crisis, when for the first time the person begins to introject the expectations of others into the conception of self. Although the ego is concerned about how it is viewed by others and how it is forced to view itself, it does not accept principles that restrict its activities unless it perceives them to be expediently related to self-interest. The superego, however, is capable of producing *guilt*—the feeling that results when individuals acknowledge that they have failed to meet social or generalized expectations. The force of the superego, therefore, is the force of conscience; and it can act punitively upon the individual. As this punitive action occurs, the superego denies the id the pleasure that can result from unbridled passion and the rewards that can result from selfish manipulation and from the glorification of self. Like the ego, the superego has both conscious and unconscious components.

Id, ego, and superego often inhibit each other's effects on the person; but they are also capable of mutual assistance and compromise. For example, cultural and expressive activity (like artistic expression) is often a sublimation of the effects of instinctual drives. A romantic—or even a religious—poem can have an obviously erotic quality. Nevertheless, as Freud pointed out, this does not necessarily prevent such a poem from expressing what are taken to be cultural and ethical ideals.

Methodology

As we have seen, Freud was trained as a reductionist and a positivist. He would have preferred to explain the symptoms of mental disturbance in terms of underlying changes in physical and chemical variables. Furthermore, he would have preferred to explain various mental conditions by pointing to the physiological, biochemical, or electrical causes that had determined such conditions. One indication of Freud's greatness, however, was his ability to drop the ideal of reductionism as soon as he realized that local diagnosis and the study of electrical reactions in the body were leading nowhere. Freud never gave up the attempt to try to explain psychological phenomena deterministically. As a theorist trying to understand human behavior, however, he understood that he had to take into consideration human purpose, intention, and conflict. As a compromise between his wish to develop a deterministic model and his understanding of the need to consider human purpose, Freud constructed an energy-flow model of mental energy. According to this model, mental forces can "assist each other," "inhibit one another," "combine with one another," or "enter into compromises with one another." In other words, Freud explained mental forces as if they were physical or electrical forces and as if they were determined by causal factors. Freud's structural model of id, ego, and superego was an attempt to describe and classify the different types of agencies that controlled the way in which mental energy was used.

Although he never denied the ultimate desirability of positivistic explanations, Freud came to emphasize the validity and necessity of interpretive or hermeneutic explanation. He accepted that there were almost certainly underlying physical and chemical variables that caused neurotic symptoms, and his energy-flow model was an attempt to describe the consequences of the still-unknown changes in such underlying variables. He acknowledged, however, that the psychiatrist had to interpret the relationship between the mechanisms that generate neurotic disturbance and the meaning of the patient's symptoms. The meaning of such symptoms, Freud realized, could not be deduced from the postulated underlying mechanisms. Therefore, the psychoanalyst has to engage in a hermeneutic discourse with the patient and has to construct a dialogue with analysands that enables them to understand the true meaning of disturbed or bizarre forms of behavior. Analysts can assist in a process of self-discovery, but they cannot one-sidedly inform analysands of the causes of their behavior. Freud called this new form of treatment "psychoanalysis."

Freud argued that the unconscious part of the mind contained repressed feelings and memories, embodying drives and impulses that could not be expressed in words. Freud once declared evocatively that hysterics were really suffering from reminiscences. What he meant by this was that the patients he studied had repressed (usually sexual) impulses that had generally arisen from traumatic experiences. Breuer's "talking cure" permitted the hysteric to discharge the impulses associated with the trauma. Freud declared that an impulse might give rise to an idea or to a picture that could be trapped within the unconscious by the inability of the hysteric to acknowledge the existence or presence of such a picture. Thus, according to Freud, hysterics could rid themselves of the disturbing consequences of a picture by "turning it into words." The hermeneutic dialogue between analyst and analysand, therefore, is an investigation in depth that has as its goal the ability of the analysand to state what previously had been inexpressible.

In *The Psychopathology of Everyday Life* (1904), Freud analyzed the way in which the errors that humans make (for example, slips of the tongue) illustrate the impact of the unconscious on behavior. Freud argued that many slips of the tongue are meaningful once it is realized that such errors are *compromises* between what the individual is consciously trying to say and what the unconscious mind wills or would like to will. An interpretive or hermeneutic understanding of such slips is made possible by an analysis of the relationship between the error that a subject makes and the unconscious will of such a subject. Such an interpretation could be tested by asking the subject to bring into consciousness what previously had been only unconsciously willed.

The Interpretation of Dreams (1900) nicely illustrates Freud's interest in depth hermeneutics and his interpretive methodology. In this book, Freud, using his own dreams as data, revealed the way in which the analysis of such data had helped him achieve a better understanding of the workings of his own unconscious mind. Freud argued that neurotic symptoms and dreams have at least two things in common: The meaning of both can be interpreted, and both result from the mind's ability to repress and censor impulses and ideas. The true meaning of a dream, however, is not to be found in its manifest content (the story of what happened in the dream) but in the latent content of the dream—which has to be interpreted.

Freud was the first person to argue (correctly, as it turned out) that dreams are the guardians of sleep and not its disturbers. Dreams, in other words, make deep sleep possible; they do not interfere with it. As the mind relaxes during sleep, the agencies that resist the impact of unconscious impulses and ideas during an individual's waking hours are partially relaxed. The dream does not repress such impulses and ideas but uses the manifest substance of the dream to disguise and distort them. Most people are familiar with the way in which the mind can disguise and distort the true meaning of troublesome *external* stimuli. For example, a noisy alarm clock can become a ringing telephone in a dream, and it is possible to sleep through the alarm by searching in one's dream for the hidden telephone. The mind disguises and distorts the true meaning of *internal* stimuli—unconscious impulses and ideas—in the same fashion. If the sleeper could understand the latent content of a dream, "the veil of disguise" erected by the mind to conceal the nature of unconscious wishes and the true meaning of repressed ideas would be swept away.

According to Freud, it is possible to understand the latent content of a dream once certain psychical or mental processes are comprehended. The most important of these processes are condensation and displacement. An understanding of condensation and displacement in a subject's dreams puts the analyst on what Freud called "the royal road to a knowledge of the unconscious."

Condensation refers to the ability of the mind to make one event or object in a dream stand for many things simultaneously. For instance, an individual might dream that a younger brother is sitting on his shoulders. This image could represent two connected, yet unconscious, feelings: that the younger brother's presence is burdensome and that he wishes to raise himself above his elder siblings. The first meaning of the image is linked, of course, to the idea of "riding" someone or of being "on someone's back." In waking life, the elder brother might know that he disliked the presence of the younger brother but might not know why. In such an instance, the elder sibling would have repressed the idea that the younger brother wanted to succeed or to advance himself at the other's expense. Again, the elder brother might do this if he feared secretly that the younger brother was in fact likely to be more successful than he.

Displacement refers to the way in which one event or object in a dream can stand for something with which it is not obviously connected. It is commonplace to dream about something that in itself seems trivial but that arouses great feelings of anxiety. The most successful examples of displacement occur when the significance of an object appears to be great, and yet the reason for this remains obscure. According to the same principle, a secret agent sending to a confederate a message she knew would be intercepted should try to make the most mundane part of the message appear the most significant and the most significant part of the message appear the most mundane.

In order for an interpretation of buried meaning to be considered valid, Freud believed that the following conditions must be met. First, an interpretation of a dream must connect the various interpretations of the meanings of dream fragments to the interpretation of the dream as a whole. Explanation, in other words, must be holistic. Similarly, the psychoanalyst must try to interpret isolated symptoms of psychic disturbance in such a way that these various interpretations are consistent with the analyst's explanation of the analysand's illness taken as a whole. Second, the interpretation of a dream should help a subject understand and recognize the latent content of a dream. The interpretation of dreams—and the interpretation of the meanings of symptoms of mental distress—should help individuals discover that which previously lay undiscovered. The ability of the psychoanalyst to free the patient from impulses and images that previously acted to destroy mental well-being has led some commentators to point out that psychoanalysis incorporates some methodological principles of critical theory as well as those of positivism and hermeneutic inquiry. In fact, psychoanalysis is one of the few methods of inquiry that actively incorporates critical self-reflection into its methodology.[6] Unlike Marx, however, Freud applied his emancipatory interest in language to the individual, rather than to the collectivity.

Freud instructed his patients: "Look into the depths, learn first to know yourself! Then you will understand why you were bound to fall ill; and perhaps, you will avoid falling ill in the future."[7]

In his later years, Freud moved a long way from the positivism of his youth. When he first began to develop psychoanalytic theory, Freud argued dogmatically that the reality of a sexual etiology for hysteria and the existence of the Oedipus complex had been proved clinically—that is, scientifically. In the early part of his career, he was not prepared to settle for anything less than positivistically verifiable discoveries. At the end of his life, however, Freud was more interested in trying to show the way in which psychoanalytic theory could broaden human understanding and open new possibilities of self-understanding. At various points in his career, Freud was both a hard-nosed positivist and someone who engaged in the most imaginative type of speculation. His most important methodological contributions, however, are undoubtedly his writings on depth hermeneutics. These describe the way in which an investigator can pick a way through distorted, yet meaningful, forms of communication to find the hidden message buried therein.

Other Major Themes and Foci

Psychoanalysis as Therapy

Psychoanalytic theory has been used to account for the most diverse forms of cultural and historical phenomena. Yet in the United States it is often thought of merely as a treatment for neurotics.

The practice of psychoanalysis as a means of therapy grew out of Breuer's "talking cure." Throughout most of his professional life, Freud met with five to nine patients, four to six times a week. The analysand would lie on the famous couch in Freud's consulting room and talk about whatever came to mind. Whole volumes have been written about psychoanalytic technique, but the basic principles of psychoanalytic therapy can be explained quite simply.

The analysis of a patient begins with the analysand talking about any feelings or experiences that he or she feels to be significant. The analyst, meanwhile, searches for associations among the patient's ideas and for patterns in response to the analyst's questions. The analyst is particularly sensitive to the way in which the patient will resist certain suggestions because the mind's attempt to censor certain ideas is a possible indication of the way in which the unconscious operates.

Freud often spoke of psychoanalytic treatment as a "reeducation in overcoming internal resistance." The patient's unwillingness to acknowledge the force of deeply buried impulses or strongly repressed ideas was, Freud believed, at the heart of most forms of neurosis. Freud did not believe that the analyst had *carte blanche* to tell analysands what their problems were; he believed that the patient "knew" everything but lacked conscious awareness. The analyst's role, therefore, is to be a neutral and nonthreatening figure who gently probes the patient's mind and asks relevant questions. Ideally, the analyst replaces some crucial figure in the analysand's past, and the patient re-creates the blocked emotions built up at an earlier stage as earlier feelings are transferred to the relationship with the analyst.

According to Freud, the analyst must be prepared for a "perpetual struggle" with the patient. It is a "triumph" if the analyst can prompt the analysand to dispose of something "through the work of remembering" that the patient previously wished to discharge in repetitive, mechanical forms of behavior. Psychoanalytic therapy is really linguistic therapy that investigates how the patient's communicative efforts block the transparent expression of feelings, emotions, and thoughts. An analyst currently practicing in New York describes his work in the following terms: "[I] point out to the patient how he keeps himself from thinking certain things and feeling certain things, so that he becomes self-conscious and the evasion doesn't work so automatically. That's all. That's the analyst's scalpel."[8]

Freud was interested in the study and treatment of mental disturbance not so much because he wanted to cure patients, but largely because he believed that the examination of neurosis (like the analysis of dreams) was a means to critical self-understanding. As a result of this belief, he put aside a half-hour each day to analyze himself. Freud anticipated the ability of modern-day psychiatry to manipulate behavior by the use of chemical agents, but he believed that once this ability was achieved, psychiatrists would lose the opportunity to learn from their patients. Furthermore, patients would lose their ability to learn about themselves.

Overall, Freud was pessimistic about the ability of psychoanalysis to help many people. First of all, analysis is costly and time-consuming and, on occasions, almost interminable. Freud himself analyzed several of his patients over periods of many years. Second, Freud believed that psychoanalysis could be used as effective therapy only with people who were at least *capable* of clear linguistic communication. Therefore, psychoanalysis is not at all useful in treating seriously disturbed psychotics who have lost all contact with the outside world. Third, Freud did not believe that psychoanalysis could help people who were "worthless." By this—rather peculiar—claim, Freud meant that analysis could help only those people who accepted the ethical standards of psychoanalysis. These ethical standards include a commitment to truth, no matter how harsh it might be; a deep desire for self-knowledge; and a respect for the goals of critical inquiry. Finally, Freud admitted that even a successful analysis often achieved no more for the patient than the transformation of "hysterical misery" into "common unhappiness."

The Death Instinct and Social Survival

Freud's book *Beyond the Pleasure Principle* (1920) generated more controversy than did anything else he wrote. In this work, Freud put forward the idea of a death instinct quite speculatively; but later he came to accept, without reservations, the "demonic presence" of such an instinct. For the first twenty years of psychoanalytic practice, Freud had been content to describe the impulses arising from instinctual drives as primarily erotic in nature and as life-preserving in function. Moreover, in his early psychoanalytical work, he had argued that the human organism was dominated by the pleasure principle—the desire to release and discharge tensions built up by instinctual forces.

The behavior of traumatized soldiers who returned from the front during World War I, however, presented Freud with a new challenge to his ideas. What he found particularly difficult to understand was the way in which these soldiers constantly relived in their dreams the original events that had traumatized them. In order to explain this unpleasant repetition of events, Freud hypothesized about the existence of a "repetition compulsion principle." Later he came to believe that repetition compulsion was an important instinctual drive in the life of every individual, and that if the urge to repeat was linked to destructive or painful activity (as it often is), the individual would move inexorably toward death. As further evidence for this drift toward self-annihilation, Freud pointed out that living or organic matter is constantly moving toward an inorganic and less organized state. Plants, for example, are constantly breaking down into their constituent parts. Freud hypothesized that the death instinct was an urge inherent in organic life to restore an earlier state of things. The connection Freud posited between repetition compulsion and the death instinct, however, is unclearly formulated.

Together with the development of his views about the death instinct, Freud began to pay more attention to the role of aggression and submission in human affairs. He believed that a crucial link between the human being and other forms of life could be located in the primary drive of the human organism toward its own destruction. For example, many people are afraid of heights even when there is no real danger of falling. One explanation might be that the individual is responding to a deeply buried impulse within the organism to destroy itself by jumping. Thus fear, in this instance, would be a rational, life-preserving response to an inner danger.

As Freud began to conclude that "the aim of all life is death," he came to see cruelty and sadism not as primary instinctual drives but as a *reversal* of the primary instinctual drive that generated the individual's desire to be subjugated and destroyed. Sadism, therefore, is derived from more fundamental masochistic urgings—that is, from the individual's drive toward self-annihilation. According to Freud, there is a conflict within every individual between the life-preserving force of libidinal energy and the life-destroying force of such masochistic urges. Aggression that is turned outward (of which sadism is an example) is often a *compromise* impulse for these two instinctual drives.

Freud named what he believed were these two fundamental and opposing forces in the mind: the life instinct (*eros*) and the death instinct (*thanatos*). He believed that the victories of *eros* were always temporary. For each individual, and also—and ultimately—for the human species as a whole, *thanatos* prevails.

SIGNIFICANCE

Vision of the Future

All of Freud's work cautions the would-be reformer to take a highly critical view of the possibility of progressive social change and of a significant improvement in the human condition. His often-quoted declarations that "anatomy is destiny" and that "where id was so shall ego be" illustrate Freud's belief in the overriding importance of the needs and impulses of the organism. Freud agreed that individuals, acting in concert, could sublimate the effects of such needs and impulses; it is possible, for instance, for individuals to invest mental energy in a great leader or in an ideal like a

Holy Crusade. As we have seen, however, the power and authority of a great leader are derived, at least in part, from the unconscious impulses and infantile tendencies of his or her followers. Similarly, the moral zeal that fires the indignation of crusaders is often merely an attempt to deflect anxiety and to project feared and despised attributes onto an out-group.

Freud's model of the human condition did not specify any great change through time. The rise of civilization exacerbates the sense of guilt, but it does not permit the individual to escape the constant demands of the organism and the laws that govern the natural rhythm of all living things. Freud conceded that the historian could locate periods in which humankind's mental energy is sublimated and concentrated to an extraordinary extent, and that such periods were likely to be periods of great cultural creativity. The Renaissance, for instance, is an example of a sudden and comparatively rapid concentration of sublimated energy. Similarly, great wars of conquest often require large masses of humanity to focus their energies on highly specific and demanding tasks that are only very indirectly linked to personal goals. To wage war successfully, a society must be able to concentrate and channel the mental energy and aggressive impulses of individuals. Freud suggested that there might be cycles throughout human history that correspond with the rise and fall of a society's or a civilization's ability to concentrate and direct mental energy. The buildup or concentration of neurotic energy, for instance, heightens the desire for tension release. Societies are capable of achieving a great deal by providing socially acceptable means for the release of such tension. Such release, however, especially if it is rapid and intensely meaningful for the individual, leads inevitably to temporary exhaustion and quiescence.

Freud was highly skeptical about the claims of socialism and communism. He questioned what the Bolsheviks in Russia would do when they had liquidated their bourgeoisie. In general, like Pareto (see Chapter 11), Freud reacted strongly against the Enlightenment faith in reason. According to Freud, a social program like socialism that promises a fairer share of material goods and services, that organizes a more effective exploitation of natural resources, and that creates a greater amount of leisure time does not change the impact that destructive and other instinctual urges have on the life of the collectivity. In the 1930s, Wilhelm Reich (1897–1957), a Marxist and one of Freud's followers, claimed that the death instinct was a product of the capitalist system. Freud declared this to be "nonsensical" and repudiated all efforts to tie the existence of instinctual drives to particular social or political systems.

Probably the most successful attempt to link Freudian ideas with the possibility of progressive social change was made by Herbert Marcuse (1898–1979). Marcuse accepted Freud's argument that repression is inherent in any form of civilization, but he distinguished between socially necessary repression and "surplus repression." Marcuse argued that capitalist society originally repressed and redirected libidinal energy to a historically abnormal degree in order to create the conditions for rapid economic growth. Such conditions include the individual's willingness to defer gratification, to deny sensuality, and to prefer work over pleasure. The Protestant work ethic, Marcuse argued, might have been necessary for nineteenth-century societies. Modern, or advanced capitalist, societies, however, do not have to check the drive for pleasurable gratification as much as did early capitalist societies. Such societies are capable of satisfying the material needs of citizens without imposing intense forms of repression on private individuals. Thus Marcuse defined "surplus repression" as the difference between socially necessary repression (that is, the repression necessary for a particular form of production) and the extreme form of control that is found in unnecessarily repressive societies. Marcuse found that modern, technologically advanced societies are unnecessarily repressive, and argued that such societies should be attacked and criticized not for their authoritarian hold on the individual, but for institutionalizing excessive forms of *surplus* repression.

Marcuse conceded that socialist societies like the Soviet Union and China were no less repressive than the United States. He pointed out, however, that socialist revolutions have occurred only in those societies that are in urgent need of modernization or of rapid economic growth, and thereby in need of the degree of repression that inevitably accompanies such sudden change.

Marcuse's early optimism about the possibility of a hedonistic society and the chances of a societally approved "polymorphous sexuality" was dampened by what he saw as the retrogressive and reactionary response to the events of the 1960s. In the 1966 preface to *Eros and Civilization* (originally published in 1955), Marcuse admitted that his earlier claim that the repressive nature of U.S. society was only a temporary phase was probably misguided. He argued that it was still possible for society to activate repressed organic and biological needs and to make the human body an instrument of pleasure rather than of labor. He conceded, however, that he saw few signs that these things would occur in the immediate future. In the final analysis, therefore, Marcuse's position does not depart significantly from that of Freud.

Contemporary Relevance

The influence of psychoanalytic ideas on twentieth-century thought has been enormous. Every year, dozens of new books on Freud appear. As one Soviet academician has commented ruefully of psychoanalytical theory, "In the history of bourgeois social philosophy it would probably be difficult to find a more popular theory, a theory which exerted a more powerful influence on all spheres of intellectual life in capitalist society."[9] Freud's ideas, however, have not been universally accepted. Many scientists and philosophers have denounced his ideas bitterly, calling Freud everything from a fake and a charlatan to a false prophet. Nevertheless, for better or for worse, Freudian ideas have changed forever the way in which humankind views itself. Terms like "repression," "unconscious motivation," "defense mechanism," "resistance," "reaction formation," "projection," "sublimation," and the so-called Freudian slip have entered ordinary language—even if such terms are often used inexactly. Above all, psychoanalytic theory has radically changed people's conception of the possible meanings of behavior. After Freud, it is no longer possible to take the meaning of an action at face value. We are compelled to acknowledge that individuals are capable of the most complex and devious forms of self-deception and that the mind is able to disguise the most base impulses as the noblest and the purest of motives. Most terrifying of all—and most damaging to human self-esteem—is Freud's insistence that individuals always view each other and their situations in terms of felt infantile needs and conflicts.

Nothing we do or think is ever purely "rational" or "irrational"; it is always a mixture of the two, created by a compromise solution between our reason and our infantile, nonrational needs.

Freud himself believed that his achievements were "less the result of intellect than of character."[10] Some of his critics have suggested that Freud was a cult leader who founded a new religion based on a faulty and unscientific methodology. There is at least a grain of truth to the claim that Freud was the leader of a religion. When he was once asked why Adler and Jung had left the psychoanalytic movement, Freud replied with disarming candor, "Because they, too, wanted to be Popes."[11] Freud was certainly the founding father and leading light of an important social *and* intellectual movement. His dogmatism and authoritarianism were probably necessary in the early days of the movement in order to unify and organize disciples. There can be no doubt, however, that psychoanalytic ideas can survive without the patronage of any one charismatic figure.

The number of articles and books that have been written about psychoanalysis during the twentieth century is astonishing. The *Index of Psychoanalytic Writings* lists well over one hundred thousand such books and articles in more than thirty languages; and the number of artists, poets, novelists, and dramatists who have incorporated psychoanalytic ideas in their work is beyond count. It is important to emphasize that the influence of Freud's ideas has reached out beyond the confines of scientific inquiry. It has been claimed, for instance, that Freudianism has had a great impact on the school of surrealism in painting. The Spanish painter Salvador Dalí reported that his understanding of Freud's work on the role of the unconscious affected his work in a number of ways. Similarly, Freud's view of language strongly influenced the writer James Joyce.

Since the 1920s, books on baby care have showed the clear imprint of Freudian ideas. The most famous of these—Dr. Benjamin Spock's *Baby and Child Care*—appeared in 1945 and has been described as having (or, depending on one's point of view, accused of having) a profound effect on the character of several generations of Americans. Dr. Spock advises an antidisciplinarian approach to baby's upbringing, and suggests that the parents' attempts to regulate junior's bowel movements should be deferred. Books like *Baby and Child Care* illustrate the way in which Freud's ideas have been diffused into the general culture.

Today, psychoanalytic therapy is not nearly as important or as influential in the United States as it once was. Psychoanalysis developed outside the American university system. As universities increasingly came to monopolize intellectual life, psychoanalysis suffered a commensurate decline in influence. During the 1940s and the 1950s, psychoanalysis was a significant intellectual force within American psychiatry, but its position of authority has now been displaced—largely as a result of the dubious claims of positivistically inclined chemotherapists, who insist that they can successfully "treat," that is, mask or subdue, many forms of mental distress. Today the vast majority of American psychiatrists do not practice psychoanalysis at all, and teaching hospitals are much more likely to emphasize biochemistry, neurology, and behavior modification rather than psychoanalysis. None of this would have surprised Freud, who never believed that psychoanalysis could be a general, or even typical, form of treatment for psychiatric patients. Undoubtedly, many of the claims made for psychoanalysis in the 1940s and the 1950s were inflated and unrealistic—they certainly were inconsistent with the position taken by Freud.

In the last fifty years, psychoanalytic theory has profoundly influenced the direction and the substance of theory and research in the social sciences. Freud's argument that conceptions of the body are used by culture has had a significant impact on those theorists who believe that individuals' understanding or conception of "natural," unyielding biological reality is instrumental in their search for identity. Some theorists have argued that Freud overemphasized the importance of instinctual drives and impulses, but even they concede that he was brilliant in describing the way in which the symbolic understanding of self is restricted and defined in terms of *beliefs* about the significance of such drives and impulses. What has proved to have a firm and lasting value for social psychology has been Freud's insistence that the discovery of one's body is an important part of finding one's identity. Furthermore, psychologists and sociologists have been greatly influenced by Freud's technique of trying to understand human identity by examining the processes by which individuals *become* what they are.

Freud's views on women—particularly his claim that, because of penis envy, women are prone to jealousy and insecurity—have been given short shrift by most, though not all, feminists. In *Psychoanalysis and Femininism*, for instance, Juliet Mitchell rejects the argument that gender differences are innate, but concedes that Freud accurately described the way in which women (and men) are forced to come to terms with themselves. In other words, Mitchell believes that Freud was writing about the way in which culture is handed down and not so much about the biological facts of life. Freud himself admitted that the sexual life of women was "a dark continent" and pointed out that, although the nature of the mature woman was undoubtedly strongly influenced by sexual function, a multitude of factors influenced the development of the adult personality.

Neo-Freudians like Erich Fromm (1900–1980), Karen Horney (1885–1952), and Harry Stack Sullivan (1892–1949) have developed Freudian ideas by examining how the adult personality is influenced by environmental factors. This more overtly sociological approach downplays the significance of the id in the personality system and concentrates on the role of the ego. For this reason, Horney and Sullivan in particular are often described as "ego psychologists" (as opposed to Freud, who was an id psychologist). The American school of ego psychologists tends to minimize the significance of libidinal energy; among other things, it examines the way in which identity is created and sustained, the mechanisms of defense employed by the ego, and the cultural and interactional causes of neurotic behavior. The ego psychologists, therefore, tend to neglect the role of the unconscious mind in the life of the individual and prefer to concentrate on the conscious and *apparently* autonomous subject.

Two neo-Freudians have been particularly influential for sociologists—Fromm and Erik Erikson (1902–1994). Fromm explored the moral implications of psychoanalytic ideas by attempting to describe the way in which humans can maximize the chances of a "sane society." Fromm also investigated what he believed to be some of the social causes of human destructiveness and hatred. Erikson has written at length about "prospective aspects of the life cycle," and he has influenced a further line of researchers who have examined the stages or "passages" through which all individuals pass. Erikson has also written "psychohistories" that combine biography with psychoanalysis.[12]

Structural functionalism, the theoretical paradigm that dominated American sociology in the 1950s and 1960s, largely accepted Freud's view of the functions of the family. Talcott Parsons (1902–1979), who was most responsible for the implementation of this paradigm, drew on Freudian ideas in describing the way in which children introject or internalize the norms and values of the wider culture. Parsons tended to ignore Freud's claim that society could never exercise the control that it would like to exercise over the individual because the power of social forces was always less potent than the hidden and devious force of the unconscious mind. Nevertheless, in his general theory of action, Parsons argued that the sociologist must try to understand exchanges between the organism and the personality system, as well as exchanges among the cultural, social, and personality systems.

Perhaps the most significant impact of psychoanalysis on sociological theory is its effect on members of the Frankfurt School of social research. Starting in the 1920s, members of this school tried to apply both Marxist and psychoanalytic ideas in an attempt to understand why capitalist societies had survived the breakup of the old order in Europe after World War I. The most influential scholars of the Frankfurt School were Theodor Adorno (1903–1969) and Max Horkheimer (1895–1973). Both men rejected ego psychology and argued that the idea of the strong, autonomous ego was a dangerous bourgeois (that is, capitalist) myth. Adorno pointed out that not only the individual but also the "category of individuality" is a product of society. Furthermore, he argued that society should be viewed not as an objective and stable entity but as a dynamic and fluid process that is located *within* the individual. Thus members of the Frankfurt School acknowledged the force of Freud's argument that the conflict between the individual and society is experienced by subjects as an internal conflict. As a result of their theoretical work, Adorno and Horkheimer probably contributed more to an understanding of the processes of alienation in modern society than had any other social theorist since Marx.

Reich, who was tangentially associated with the Frankfurt school, was probably the most radical of Freud's followers. His work during the 1920s and 1930s on character and the mass psychology of fascism is particularly important. Reich argued that social orders create the character formations that they need in order to perpetuate themselves. Authoritarian social orders create the submissive, neurotic, and guilt-ridden individuals they need largely by repressing genital sexuality among the individuals under their control. For instance, Reich pointed out that the open display of pornography often masquerades as a form of sexual "liberation." In reality, pornography necessarily entails repression and authoritarianism. Reich attempted to organize a social movement in the United States based on the principle that to define freedom one must first define sexual health. The movement was not a success, and Reich died in obscurity.

It would be incorrect to assume that psychoanalytic ideas have been played out by previous generations and that such ideas are no longer as important and as influential to social theorists as they were three or four decades ago. Since the end of the 1960s, for example, psychoanalytic ideas have become a very important part of French intellectual life, largely as a result of the work of Jacques Lacan (1901–1981) at *L'Ecole Freu-*

dienne de Paris. Lacan condemned American ego psychology for being anti-Freudian and for perpetuating the myth that self-improvement is possible without radical social reform. Like Freud, Lacan strongly disapproved of the way in which psychoanalysis in the United States has been incorporated into medical practice. A medical model locates problems—and the solutions to such problems—within the individual, not within society. In any case, as Lacan pointed out, the purpose of psychoanalytic theory is not merely to treat the "maladjusted" individual but also to make individuals more aware of the contradictions and tensions that inevitably beset consciousness. Lacan saw psychoanalysis as a form of "self-discovery" that needed no therapeutic justification. According to Lacan, a psychoanalysis is fundamentally emancipatory, and is always critical of social institutions.[13]

Lacan's rereading of Freud, together with the critique of ideology offered by the French Marxist Louis Althusser (1918–1990), has provided the inspiration for the contemporary school of French semiologists and "deconstructionists." Roland Barthes (1915–1980), for instance, turned both to Freud and to Marx to analyze how subjects are constituted in contemporary societies by the language codes that give them positionality.[14] Barthes tried to develop a "political theory of the production of language": For him, human subjectivity and self-knowledge are predicated on language; psychoanalysis is indispensable for revealing how social positions and identifications are produced by "family life." Although he accepted the Marxist model of class domination in capitalist society, Barthes criticized contemporary Marxists for failing to understand how such domination is grounded by control of the meaning of signs and identifications. Both Lacan and Barthes believed that Freud's major contribution was to hermeneutics and critical theory, not to positivism.

In the United States, Christopher Lasch (1939–1994) applied Freudian theory in his best-selling critique of U.S. society, *The Culture of Narcissism.*[15] This book discusses the interrelationship between U.S. culture and the modern construction of the self. Lasch points out that the type of neurosis that Freud saw in bourgeois Vienna seventy or eighty years ago is relatively uncommon in contemporary societies. The typical kind of illness with which most analysts come into contact today is "narcissistic neurosis," a type of neurosis exhibited by individuals who fail to cathect external objects and compensate by reinvesting libidinal energy in their own egos. The narcissistic self feels empty and is detached from the world, but needs superficial stimulation and attention from others in order to achieve any sense of gratification whatsoever. Lasch points out that, although cultural systems are always changing, it is nevertheless "possible to see types of neuroses and psychoses as in some sense the characteristic expression of a given culture."[16]

Lasch's book on the tragedy of the self in contemporary America, the work of the ego psychologists, the research of the Frankfurt School, and the interpretations of the new French school all attempt to synthesize conventional sociological theorizing with psychoanalytic theory. For the most part, psychoanalysis in the United States is more of a waning tradition than a subversive or critical school of thought. However, the resurgence of interest in psychoanalytic ideas in Europe, particularly the rediscovery of psychoanalytic theory in France, could well be replicated in the United States—the society in which psychoanalysis first began to take root.

NOTES

1. Ernest Jones, *The life and work of Sigmund Freud*, p. 45.
2. Ibid., p. 92.
3. Letter to Oskar Pfister, dated October 9, 1918.
4. Letter from Freud, dated June 6, 1938.
5. Postscript to "An autobiographical study," *The standard edition of the complete psychological works*, Vol. 20, p. 72.
6. See Jürgen Habermas, *Knowledge and human interests* (Boston: Beacon Press, 1971), pp. 214–245.
7. "A difficulty in the path of psychoanalysis," *Standard edition*, Vol. 17, p. 143.
8. Janet Malcom, *Psychoanalysis: The impossible profession*, p. 73.
9. V. I. Dobrenkov, *Neo-Freudians in search of "truth"* (Moscow: Progress Publishers, 1976), p. 11.
10. *Letters of Sigmund Freud*, p. 402.
11. Quoted in Ludwig Binswanger, *Sigmund Freud* (New York: Grune & Stratton, 1957), p. 9.
12. See Erik H. Erikson, *Young man Luther: A study in psychoanalysis and history* (New York: W. W. Norton, 1962), and *Identity and the life cycle* (New York: W. W. Norton, 1980).
13. See Jacques Lacan, *Écrits: A selection* (New York: W. W. Norton, 1977), and *The four fundamental concepts of psycho-analysis* (New York: W. W. Norton, 1981).
14. See Roland Barthes, *S/Z* (London: Jonathan Cape, 1974).
15. Christopher Lasch, *The culture of narcissism: American life in an age of diminishing expectations* (New York: Warner Books, 1979).
16. Ibid., p. 76.

GLOSSARY

Analysand A person who is undergoing *psychoanalysis*.

Cathexis The investment of mental or *libidinal* energy in some external object or in some activity.

Condensation The ability of the mind, especially in a dream, to make an event or an object stand for more than one thing.

Death instinct The impulse that drives the individual toward self-annihilation.

Defense mechanism A technique used by the *ego* that enables the individual to avoid criticism and embarrassment and to maintain poise or a favorable self-image.

Depth hermeneutics An interpretation of the meaning of human behavior and ideas that involves an analysis of the workings of the *unconscious* mind.

Determinism Metaphysical position that relates every event to preexisting events and that denies the possibility of human choice and free will.

Displacement The shifting of meaning, especially in a dream, that enables an event or an object to have a meaning that is unknown to a subject.

Ego That agency of the personality system that protects the individual's autonomy and is in direct touch with external reality.

Ego psychology Freudian psychology that concentrates on the study of the *ego*.

Eros The life instinct. The instinctual drive toward erotic and life-preserving behavior.

Erotogenic zone An area of the body from which pleasure can be derived.

Hysteria A nervous disorder characterized by disorganized thought and a loss of control over self.

Id That agency of the personality system that comprises *unconscious* impulses and instinctual drives.

Instinct An unlearned and innate tendency to engage in certain kinds of behavior under certain conditions—for example, the tendency to search for nourishment when the stomach is empty.

Introjection The use of social norms and values in the conception of self.

Latent content The true meaning of a dream.

Libido The energy that is created by the life instinct. Mental energy that is directed toward the fulfillment of erotic and life-preserving impulses.

Manifest content The story of what happens in a dream.

Narcissistic neurosis The withdrawal of *libidinal* attachments to the outside world and the reinvestment of emotion in the *ego* itself.

Neo-Freudian Someone who accepts the major principles of *psychoanalytic* theory but who has revised some of Freud's ideas.

Neurology The scientific study of nervous systems.

Neurosis A functional (that is, nonorganic) disorder of the nervous system resulting in behavior that tends to be disorganized, repetitive, and apparently meaningless.

Oedipus complex The complex of attitudes and feelings that a child has at about the age of four or five that involves love for one parent and hatred or fear of the other.

Penis envy A girl's envy of the male for possessing an organ that she lacks.

Physiology The scientific study of the structure of, and processes within, the body.

Pleasure principle The tendency that individuals show toward maximizing pleasure.

Polymorphous perversity A type of sexual orientation that is not focused solely, or even primarily, on genital sexuality. Typically found in very young infants and in very experienced adults.

Primal horde The earliest type of community, dominated by a patriarch with exclusive sexual privileges.

Projection A type of *defense mechanism* by which the individual unwittingly attributes his or her own undesirable attributes or fears to other people.

Psychoanalysis The theory of the structure and development of personality developed by Freud. Also, the technique of psychotherapy that Freud pioneered.

Rationalization A type of *defense mechanism* by which the individual finds a justifiable excuse for doing something of which the *superego* might disapprove, or for doing something as a result of *unconscious* impulses.

Reaction formation A type of *defense mechanism* by which the individual denies the existence of a desire that cannot be implemented.

Reductionism The belief that phenomena should be described and explained in terms of more elementary units of analysis.

Regression The reverting of the *libido* to a channel of expression that belongs to an earlier stage of the individual's development.

Repetition compulsion The tendency of an *instinct* to repeat over and over again the same kind of behavior.

Repression The ability to force an idea out of consciousness.

Semiology The science of the life of signs in society.

Sublimation The ability to transform basic instinctual drives into emotional needs that can be met symbolically.

Superego That agency of the personality system that functions as a kind of conscience and that can cause feelings of guilt and anxiety within the individual.

Surplus repression The difference between socially necessary *repression* and the *repression* peculiar to unnecessarily repressive societies.

Thanatos The force of the *death instinct*.

Transference The development of an emotional attitude toward the *psychoanalyst* as the psychoanalyst replaces some crucial figure in the *analysand*'s past experience.

The unconscious Those mental processes of which the individual is unaware.

ANNOTATED BIBLIOGRAPHY

Primary Sources

Beyond the pleasure principle (James Strachey, Trans. & Ed.). New York: Norton, 1961 [1920] (paper).

A very controversial monograph in which Freud lays out his ideas about the existence of the death instinct and about repetition compulsion. A profoundly pessimistic book.

Civilization and its discontents (James Strachey, Trans. & Ed.). New York: Norton, 1962 [1930] (paper).

One of Freud's last books and one in which Freud defines what he sees to be the relationship between individuals and the civilization to which they belong. Of particular interest to historians and sociologists.

The ego and the id (Joan Riviere, Trans.; James Strachey, Ed.). New York: Norton, 1960 [1923] (paper).

Contains a discussion of consciousness and the unconscious. Includes a description of the id, ego, and superego.

Freud on women: A reader (Elizabeth Young-Bruehl, Ed.). New York: Norton, 1990 (paper).

A collection of Freud's writings on women.

The Freud reader (Peter Gay, Ed.). New York: W. W. Norton, 1995 (paper).

Contains selections from all of Freud's major writings. Each section is prefaced by a short introduction by Gay. The best anthology for the serious student of Freud.

The future of an illusion (James Strachey, Trans. & Ed.). New York: Norton, 1961 [1927] (paper).

The "illusion" discussed here is religion. Freud discusses the functions and the future of religious modes of experience.

A general introduction to psycho-analysis (Joan Riviere, Trans.). New York: Washington Square Press, 1965 [1920] (paper).

This book contains twenty-eight lectures written by Freud for the lay person describing the central principles of psychoanalytic theory. A good introduction to his ideas.

The interpretation of dreams (James Strachey, Trans. & Ed.). New York: Science Editions, 1961 [1900] (paper).

The author considered that this book contained the most valuable of all the discoveries that he had made in his life.

Jokes and their relation to the unconscious (James Strachey, Trans. & Ed.). New York: Norton, 1960 [1905] (paper).

In this fascinating book, Freud deals with the psychology and significance of wit and humor, as illustrated by the jokes that are passed on from one person to another.

The letters of Sigmund Freud (Tania Stern & James Stern, Trans.; Ernest L. Freud, Ed.). New York: Basic Books, 1960.

A collection of some of Freud's letters.

Moses and monotheism (Katherine Jones, Trans.). New York: Vintage Books, 1939.

Freud was working on this book during the last two or three years of his life. This highly speculative book applies psychoanalytic ideas to the figure of Moses.

An outline of psycho-analysis (James Strachey, Trans.). New York: Norton, 1949 [1939] (paper).

Freud was working on this when he died. A useful and general description of the general principles of psychoanalysis.

The psychopathology of everyday life (Alan Tyson, Trans.; James Strachey, Ed.). New York: Norton, 1965 [1904] (paper).

Very enjoyable reading. Contains Freud's interpretation of the meaning of "selective forgetting," slips of the tongue, errors, superstition, and so on.

The question of lay analysis (Nancy Proctor-Gregg, Trans.; James Strachey, Ed.). New York: Norton, 1950 [1926] (paper).

Freud wrote this book to deal with the controversy over whether or not psychoanalysts must also be medical doctors. His answer was no, and he cautions against identifying psychoanalysis too closely with the practice of medicine.

The standard edition of the complete psychological works of Sigmund Freud (Trans. under the general editorship of James Strachey in collaboration with Anna Freud, assisted by Alix Strachey and Alan Tyson; 24 vols.). London: Hogarth Press, 1953–1974.

Invaluable collection of all of Freud's work, and especially useful for tracking down some of Freud's less well known writings.

Three essays on the theory of sexuality (James Strachey, Trans.). New York: Avon Books, 1962 [1905] (paper).

One of Freud's most important works. It contains his early statements on infantile sexuality and his interpretation of sexual aberrations.

Totem and taboo (James Strachey, Trans.). New York: Norton, 1950 [1913] (paper).

A speculative view of the way in which the "primal horde" emerged. Also, a discussion of "some points of agreement between the mental lives of savages and neurotics."

Secondary Sources

Anzieu, Didier. *Freud's self-analysis* (Peter Graham, Trans.). Madison, CT: International Universities Press, 1986 [1959].

Anzieu points out that "Freud lived in an atmosphere of permanent self-analysis." This massive study (618 pages) tries to document Freud's lifelong attempt to understand the unconscious forces that drove him.

Bettelheim, Bruno. *Freud and man's soul.* New York: Alfred A. Knopf, 1983.

Bettelheim makes a strong argument in favor of Freud's contribution to the humanities. Psychoanalysis, he says, is not a positivistic science, but strives to document individuals' tragic search for a "deeper understanding" of themselves.

Bocock, Robert. *Sigmund Freud.* New York: Tavistock, 1983 (paper).

A straightforward account of Freud's ideas, with major emphasis given to Freud's contribution to social theory. A good starting place for the sociology student with an interest in Freud.

Brown, J.A.C. *Freud and the post-Freudians.* London: Penguin Books, 1971 (paper).

As the title suggests, this book is about the way in which post- and neo-Freudians, like Horney, Fromm, and Sullivan, have developed and revised psychoanalytic ideas. The theories of Adler and Jung are also discussed briefly.

Elliott, Anthony. *Social theory and psychoanalysis in transition: Self and society from Freud to Kristeva.* Oxford: Blackwell, 1992.

An analysis of contemporary contributions to social and psychoanalytic theory. The book discusses Adorno, Marcuse, Habermas, and Lacan, among other theorists.

Eysenck, Hans, & Glenn Wilson. *The experimental studies of Freudian theories.* New York: Barnes & Noble, 1974.

Edited by two experimental psychologists hostile to psychoanalysis, this book argues that there is little evidence for the truth of psychoanalytic theory.

Ferris, Paul. *Dr. Freud: A life.* Washington, DC: Counterpoint, 1999 (paper).

A critical biography of Freud and his contemporaries. If Jones wrote the "official" biography, Ferris has produced one that is much more critical and "gossipy."

Forrester, John. *Dispatches from the Freud wars: Psychoanalysis and its passions.* Cambridge, MA: Harvard University Press, 1997 (paper).

Very readable essays about Freud's cultural legacy and about the applicability of his ideas today. Respectful, but also critical.

Fromm, Erich. *Greatness and limitation of Freud's thought.* New York: Mentor Books, 1981 (paper).

Fromm's last book. An excellent discussion by a neo-Freudian of what is lasting and what is limiting in Freud's legacy. Fromm argues that Freud's view of women was particularly unsatisfactory.

Gabriel, Yiannis. *Freud and society.* London: Routledge & Kegan Paul, 1983.

Gabriel argues that the central insight of psychoanalysis is its analysis of the relationship between the individual and society—its understanding that the individual is a constituent part of the social but that "society" also confronts the individual as an alien and punitive force. This book contains a good critique of those among Freud's followers who have tried to gloss over the inevitable tension between the individual and society.

Gay, Peter. *Freud: A life for our times.* New York: Norton, 1988.

A recent biography of Freud that testifies to the continuing interest in his life and career. Readable and illustrated.

Hall, Calvin S. *A primer of Freudian psychology* (rev. ed.). New York: New American Library, 1979 (paper).

A concise account of most of the basic principles of Freudian psychology. Has been reprinted several times over three decades.

Jones, Ernest. *The life and work of Sigmund Freud* (Edited and abridged by Lionel Trilling & Steven Marcus). London: Penguin Books, 1977 (paper).

An abridged version of the "official" biography of Freud, written by a member of "the Committee." Jones has been criticized for being too protective of Freud. Nonetheless, this book is required reading for anyone seriously interested in Freud.

Kline, P. *Fact and fancy in psychoanalytic theory.* London: Methuen, 1972.

In contrast to Eysenck and Wilson, this book argues that psychoanalytic theory has been experimentally verified.

Malcolm, Janet. *In the Freud archives.* New York: Random, 1985 (paper).

The Freudian establishment was rocked in the 1980s by the claims of an "outsider," Jeffrey Masson, who had been given access to the jealously guarded Freud archives. Masson maintained that Freud had dishonestly suppressed some of his earlier clinical findings. Although Masson's case is not very convincing, the reaction of leading psychoanalytical authorities to Masson's act of "disloyalty" perpetrated against those who had trusted him makes for fascinating reading.

Malcolm, Janet. *Psychoanalysis: The impossible profession.* New York: Vantage Press, 1982 (paper).

In part, a profile of "Aaron Green," a psychoanalyst who works in New York. Also, a discussion of the professional practice of psychoanalysis. Malcolm is critical, but fair. This is a good introduction to the application of Freudian analysis. Highly readable and strongly recommended. Malcolm's ability to convey to the reader a sense of the power and depth of psychoanalysis is impressive.

Marcuse, Herbert. *Eros and civilization* (rev. ed.). Boston: Beacon Press, 1966 (paper).

A book that applies psychoanalytic ideas to criticize contemporary forms of repression. Marcuse's work was often cited by the student radicals of the 1960s.

Mitchell, Juliet. *Psychoanalysis and feminism.* New York: Vintage Books, 1975 (paper).

Written by a feminist, this book, dealing with Freud's psychology of women, is intelligent, moderate, and imaginative.

Neu, Jerome (Ed.). *The Cambridge companion to Freud.* Cambridge: Cambridge University Press, 1991 (paper).

A good collection of essays showing how Freud changed the way we think.

Rieff, Philip. *Freud: The mind of the moralist* (3rd ed.). Chicago: University of Chicago Press, 1979 (paper).

This book has become a classical statement on the importance of Freud's work. A discussion of the moral and cultural achievements of psychoanalytic theory.

Roazen, Paul. *Freud and his followers.* New York: New American Library, 1976 (paper).

A very useful account of the psychoanalytical movement. As comprehensive in form, as scholarly, and as well researched as Jones's biography of Freud.

Slipp, Samuel. *The Freudian mystique: Freud, women, and feminism.* New York: New York University Press, 1995 (paper).

Samuel Slipp. a New York psychiatrist and psychoanalyst, asks how Freud could be so wrong about women. Unsurprisingly, part of the answer is that Freud's own mother apparently emotionally abandoned him at an early age, leading Freud to have both "preoedipal" and "postoedipal" conflicts that he was unable to resolve. All this evidently affected Freud's relations with, and attitudes toward, women.

Stafford-Clark, David. *What Freud really said.* New York: Schocken Books, 1976 (paper).

Written by a British psychiatrist, this book gives a straightforward and sympathetic account of some of Freud's most important ideas. The chapter on Freud's general theory of the neuroses is particularly valuable.

S*o years, centuries, go by; people, governments, manners and systems of living pass away; and all along new theologies, new systems of metaphysics, keep replacing the old, and each new one is reputed more "true" or much "better" than its predecessors. And in certain cases they may really be better, if by "better" we mean more helpful to society; but more "true," no, if by the term we mean accord with experimental reality. One faith cannot be more scientific than another; and experimental reality is equally overreached by polytheism, Islamism, and Christianity (whether Catholic, Protestant, Liberal, modernist, or of any other variety); by the innumerable metaphysical sects, including the Kantian, the Hegelian, the Bergsonian, and not excluding the positivistic sects of Comte, Spencer, and other eminent writers too numerous to mention; by the faiths of solidaristes, humanitarians, anticlericals, and worshippers of Progress; and by as many other faiths as have existed, exist or will ever exist. Equally remote from the field of experience are Jupiter Optimus Maximum and the Jehovah of the Bible; the God of the Christians and Mohammedans, and the goddess of Truth, Justice, Humanity, Majority; the god People and the god Progress, and as many other gods as people in such infinite numbers, the pantheons of theologians, metaphysicists, positivists and humanitarians. That does not mean that belief in some of them or even in all of them may not have been beneficial in its time, or may not still be. As to that, nothing can be said a priori—experience alone can decide.*

—Vilfredo Pareto, *Compendium of General Sociology*

11

Vilfredo Pareto

(1848–1923)

BACKGROUND

Life

Vilfredo Pareto was born in Paris on July 15, 1848. His mother was French; his father, the Marchese di Pareto, was an Italian nobleman. The Marchese was compelled to live in exile because of his support for Giuseppe Mazzini (1805–1872), the radical leader of the movement for an independent and united Italian republic. Mazzini was an idealistic humanitarian whose followers believed in a modern Italian republic based on Enlightenment ideals. Pareto's family had been active in Italian politics since Napoleon Bonaparte ennobled Vilfredo's grandfather for supporting him in northern Italy. After Italy became one nation in 1861, Pareto's uncle became president of the Italian Senate.

Sometime in the 1850s, Pareto's father was able to return to Italy. At the age of sixteen, Vilfredo entered the Polytechnic Institute in Turin, where he received a degree in mathematics and physics and was admitted to the School of Engineering in 1867. In 1870, Pareto accepted a position in Rome as consulting engineer to a railroad company. As the company did not follow what he considered to be good business practices, Pareto found his work frustrating and unrewarding. In 1875, he moved to Florence to become director of the Italian Society of Iron Works. In 1881, Pareto ran for the Italian Parliament as a supporter of *laissez-faire* economics and free trade. His defeat in this election put an end to his brief political career.

Following this setback, Pareto retreated to his villa in Fiesole. He was thoroughly disenchanted with the populist policies of the Italian government and with Italy itself. He considered Italian society to be without honor: "To live in this country," he wrote at the time, "one must be either a thief or a friend of thieves."[1] At Fiesole, he began a close study of economics and wrote several articles criticizing the protectionist economic policies of the government.

At this stage of his life, Pareto embraced classical liberal doctrines. He was an active member of the Adam Smith Society in Florence and became an ardent supporter of entrepreneurial, free-market capitalism. As a businessman, Pareto had made several trips to England and Scotland, and he very much admired the way the British government had given a free hand to the business and commercial classes in those countries. In Italy, on the other hand, government regulation, business inefficiency, and corruption were widespread. Many government officials were paid to protect the interests of business operations that could not have survived in a free and competitive market system.

After publishing several articles in the prestigious *Journal des Économistes*, Pareto was offered the chair of political economy at the University of Lausanne in Switzerland in 1893. His main interests continued to be economics and political economy, but he inaugurated a course in sociology. At Lausanne, Pareto published the *Cours d'économie politique* (Lectures on Political Economy, 1896) and *Les systèmes socialistes* (The Socialist System, 1901). As Lausanne was part of French-speaking Switzerland, these books were written in French, not Italian.

As an economist, Pareto is best known for his work on equilibrium models of supply and demand and for his income distribution curve. Pareto has been described as "the father of mathematical economics." Certainly he believed that economics should be a pure science; it should analyze the instrumental rationality of an economic system of production and exchange. Pareto was well aware that different systems of production and distribution (for example, socialist as opposed to capitalist) would work against some individuals and for others. Economics, however, could say nothing about the *ethical* significance of this fact.

In 1898, Pareto inherited a large fortune from his uncle. He wanted to resign his position at Lausanne, but the vice-chancellor persuaded him to stay. His teaching load was cut to one hour a week during the term. In 1909, he retired to Villa Angora at Céligny on the shores of Lake Geneva, where he lived with his mistress, Jane Régis, and as many as thirty Angora cats. Pareto's first wife had absconded with his cook (who, to make matters worse, was an ardent socialist); and, because Italian law forbade divorce, Pareto was unable to marry Mme. Régis until shortly before his death. Pareto enjoyed the sensual pleasures of life. He was no sexual puritan, his villa was richly furnished, and he laid down one of the best wine cellars in Switzerland. Although he stressed the functional importance of religion and authority in his sociological writings, in his private life Pareto lived as he pleased. He was more than willing to reject social mores, and he strongly condemned the policies of the Italian government.

After 1909, Pareto concentrated on sociology. In 1916, he published the *Trattato di sociologia generale* (Treatise on General Sociology), his major contribution to sociological theory. In his last years, Pareto was a lonely and isolated figure, described by some as "the hermit of Céligny." He had relatively little contact with fellow intellectuals and was quite ignorant of contemporaries like Freud and Weber. Toward the end of his life, Pareto tempered the liberal social philosophy that he had embraced in his youth. As he grew older, he became more authoritarian and arrogant. He could not identify with ordinary working people and had little sympathy for those who claimed to represent them. Most characteristic of his later years was the contempt he showed for woolly-minded social reformers who talked about "humanitarianism" but ended up doing more harm than good.

In 1922, the Italian Fascist leader Benito Mussolini came to power. Mussolini praised Pareto's work highly and claimed to have been greatly influenced by him. Pareto did not criticize the Fascists' brutal seizure of power, nor did he oppose the violence directed against those who opposed Mussolini. He was inclined to describe both fascists and socialists as "fools." However, he noted that

> whereas in 1920–21 "freedom" forbade Fascist resistance to Red tyranny, now Fascist tyranny is expected to allow the factious opposition of the Reds. . . . The Fascist regime is not good merely because it is dictatorial—it could be extremely bad with the wrong dictator—but because the results up to now have been good, as has been proved by the improvement in the present state of the country by comparison with conditions during the 1919–20 period of the Red tyranny. What will the future bring? Only events can give a definite answer, but we cannot exclude the likelihood of being able to make a favorable forecast if present trends continue.[2]

Mussolini tried to have Pareto made an Italian senator. In March 1923, a royal proclamation was signed that authorized him to hold this honorific position. By this time, however, Pareto was ill and not eager to leave the Villa Angora. In the last year of his life, he appealed to the Fascist regime to govern according to the "sentiments" prevailing in the population; to moderate the use of force, if possible; to acknowledge that socialists had rights as citizens; and to recognize that class conflict was likely to be an unavoidable feature of modern societies.

Pareto did not live long enough to see the long-term effects of Fascist rule. He died on August 19, 1923, two years before Mussolini finally outlawed all political opposition. Two days after his death, the journalist Vincenzo Fani described Pareto as "the Karl Marx of fascism." The following month, another journalist, Alberto di Stefani, declared that Pareto had "theoretically prepared the ground for the coming of fascism."[3] The Fascists were willing to use Pareto when it suited them, and in the years following his death Pareto's reputation was seriously marred by the association between his name and the political order that Mussolini created. This association, however—though not entirely an artifice of propaganda—resulted largely from the Fascists' desire to claim Pareto as one of their own.

Social Environment

In the year of Pareto's birth, Italy, like Germany, was a patchwork of many states. The most important were the Kingdom of Piedmont in the north, the Papal States in central

Italy, and the Kingdom of the Two Sicilies in the south. Nearly all of the rest of Italy was ruled or controlled by the Austrian Hapsburgs.

In 1848, revolts were organized against Austrian rule in many different parts of Italy. In the north—especially in Piedmont—there was a strong nationalist movement. The nationalists, however, were split into two factions. One group, led by Mazzini, favored an Italian republic; the other, led by the monarchist Count Camillo di Cavour—prime minister to the king of Piedmont, Victor Emmanuel II—wanted Italy to be united under Piedmont.

Toward the end of the 1850s, Cavour agreed to cede territory to Louis Napoleon, emperor of France, if the latter would help Piedmont drive the Austrians from Italy. With help from French forces, Victor Emmanuel annexed Hapsburg territory in northern Italy.

The Kingdom of the Two Sicilies, comprising all of Sicily and the southern half of Italy, was ruled by a member of the French Bourbon family, Francis II. In 1860, the Italian patriot and adventurer Giuseppe Garibaldi (1807–1882) set out with a thousand volunteers to liberate the island of Sicily from foreign domination. Within three months, Garibaldi and his so-called Red Shirts had conquered Sicily and taken Naples. At first, Garibaldi wanted to set up an Italian republic under Mazzini, but ultimately he agreed to surrender the territory he had won to Victor Emmanuel, who assumed the title King of Italy on March 17, 1861.

The main barrier to full national unification was Pope Pius IX, who continued to rule Rome and the Papal States. Rome was protected by French troops, but these troops were withdrawn in 1870 to help protect Paris from the Prussians. As a result, Rome was occupied by Cavour's forces and became the capital of Italy. In 1871, the Italian Parliament enacted the Law of Papal Guarantees, permitting the pope to continue to use the title of a reigning sovereign. Pope Pius imprisoned himself in the Vatican to protest the loss of his temporal domains. This practice was continued by all popes until 1922, when a Fascist insurrection enabled Pius XI to conclude that it was now possible for the Catholic Church to come to terms with the rulers of Italy.

Mazzini had believed that Italy's problems would be solved through unification. Before 1861, he had declared that "nations are the individuals of humanity" (a view Pareto was later to deride with characteristic venom). Mazzini believed that after unification Italians would no longer find it necessary to be quarrelsome and mean-spirited; they would be united in a common cause. His dream of a modern, liberal Italian republic, however, was unrealized. After 1861, Italy was ruled mainly by the bourgeoisie who came from the commercial and the industrial cities of the north. Southern Italy, ruled by landowners who resisted all attempts at social reform, was largely ignored. The south was populated by illiterate and superstitious peasants, controlled by the church.

The Italian governing classes were notoriously corrupt. It was generally taken for granted that elections were fixed and that government officials expected their clients to pay for services rendered. Less than 10 percent of the population were enfranchised; nevertheless, there was great support in Italy for socialist and populist candidates who were willing to promise all things to all men. In 1876, populist candidates won a majority of seats in the Italian Parliament. Nothing seemed to change, however.

The governing class ruled in an autocratic fashion. During the 1890s, for instance, there were a number of political scandals involving charges of bribery and corruption, which resulted in little besides finger-pointing. One hundred years later, as far as Italian politics is concerned, it seems that nothing has changed.

The Italian governing classes suffered a great deal from invidious comparisons drawn between their country and Britain, France, and Germany. Economic growth in Italy was far slower than in these other European nations, and feelings of inferiority prompted the Italian government to try to set up colonies in North Africa that would bear comparison with those of the British and French. These attempts at empire build-ing ended ingloriously when an army of 25,000 Italian troops was massacred in 1896 by a large force of "primitive" Ethiopians armed mainly with spears and bows and ar-rows. Although Italy sided with Britain and France against Germany and Austria dur-ing World War I, in which more than 600,000 Italians lost their lives, Italy gained very little from this conflict. Britain and France were charged with not yielding an adequate share of booty, and Italy failed to obtain the ports on the Adriatic that it had wanted.

After World War I, Italy was saddled with high unemployment and a high rate of in-flation. A rapid polarization between rightists and leftists took place. The Socialist Party moved to the left and voted to affiliate with the Moscow-led Third International. After the war, the socialists enjoyed a great deal of support and, despite vitriolic op-position from the church and from rightists, managed to win about one-third of the votes cast in the election of 1919. In 1920, many factories in Turin and Milan were taken over by workers, and in the south "Red Leagues" were organized to try to break the power of the owners of the large agricultural estates.

During this period, Mussolini came to the fore as the leader of the rightists. He had begun his political career as a socialist and, before the war, had been the editor of *L'A-vanti,* the leading socialist daily. Mussolini broke with the socialists when he enthusi-astically supported Italy's involvement in World War I. After the war, it was difficult to determine his political allegiance. In 1919, his organization, the *Fascio Italiani di Com-battimento,* favored universal suffrage, abolition of the Italian Senate, the establish-ment of an eight-hour day, a heavy capital levy and inheritance tax, the confiscation of war profits, and acceptance of the League of Nations. The Fascist movement, however, was a paramilitary and not a parliamentary organization. Fascist *squadristi* were orga-nized to "impose discipline" and "maintain order." Before long, they were leading at-tacks on dissident "Red" organizations.

The Fascists moved to the extreme right after they failed to win any seats in the Chamber of Deputies in the election of 1919. The party developed a political program that was procapitalist and openly hostile to socialism. In the election of 1921, the Fas-cists were able to win thirty-five seats.

Sensing that he would meet with little opposition from dominant groups, Mus-solini made preparations to seize control of the state. Part of his strategy was to use the Fascist *squadristi* to foment disorder. In many parts of the country, leftist local gov-ernments were overthrown. At the same time, the Fascists played on people's fears that the Italian ruling class was losing control and that public safety could no longer be guaranteed. When a general strike was threatened for July 31, 1922, Mussolini gave his party the official title "Party of Order."

In October, the National Fascist Congress officially came to terms with the northern industrialists, the southern landowners, and the army. On October 28, 1922, an army of 50,000 Fascist militia completed the symbolic March on Rome that was supposed to bring an end to the chaos and anarchy of the previous three years. Mussolini's participation in this pseudomilitary "march" was as fraudulent as anything else that he did. He arrived in Rome in a sleeping car; when awakened, he was invited to form a government by King Victor Emmanuel III.

The following year, the Fascists murdered the socialist deputy Giacomo Matteotti, who had been one of the few people in Italy courageous enough to oppose Mussolini. Prominent communists like Antonio Gramsci (1891–1937) were jailed. In the elections of 1923, the Fascists used intimidation, fraud, and violence to help a Fascist slate win 65 percent of the votes cast. The Vatican newspaper praised Mussolini for his "resoluteness" in saving the nation, and Pareto himself admitted that Mussolini had proven himself to be a "politician of the first rank."

Shortly after Mussolini came to power, Pareto tried to explain the reasons for his success. Although he conceded that there were "black sheep" among the Fascists, Pareto argued that Mussolini had succeeded because he had taken advantage of the failure of the postwar Italian government to protect people and property. Mussolini had used "private initiative" to "make good this lack of protection." The Fascists, Pareto declared, "were directed skillfully and firmly by their leaders . . . towards a lofty goal of great importance." He noted, furthermore, that Mussolini's success was an application of principles "already studied in the *Trattato*."[4]

In the long term, Mussolini achieved little. His policies were erratic and inconsistent. (Contrary to popular myth, he was not able to make the trains run on time.) Government and business continued to be inefficient. Mussolini began his rule by favoring and encouraging private enterprise in every possible way, but before long, he was setting up "corporations" run by businessmen, Fascist party leaders, and compliant unionists. Mussolini displaced private enterprise with *state-run* capitalism, a move that Pareto did not foresee and would not have approved.

In the 1930s, Hitler displaced Mussolini as the most prominent dictator in Europe. In the 1920s, however, Mussolini was admired by many people despite the fact that, as he was proud to note, "the Fascist movement has no theory." Mussolini believed that it was unnecessary to justify the policies of the state; for him, the acid test of truth was the effective use of force. As Pareto himself noted, Mussolini's success was made possible in part by the inability and unwillingness of more established ruling groups to oppose him. In Italy (and later in Germany), the dominant classes suffered a momentary loss of confidence. Under attack by their own proletariat, they resented the fact that their position compared unfavorably with that of the ruling classes in the more successful capitalist societies—Britain and the United States.

In both Italy and Germany, the middle classes had never achieved a secure hold on political power. After the Great War, they had nothing to offer except nineteenth-century liberal ideas. In the economically and politically chaotic central Europe of the postwar years, however, liberal ideas did not enable the dominant classes to find their way forward. In the 1920s and 1930s, the middle classes in Italy and Germany were in deep economic and political trouble; they understood that they had nothing new to offer; and they concluded that a Mussolini or a Hitler was preferable to a Lenin.

Intellectual Roots

At the end of the nineteenth century, Italy, like Germany, was one of the youngest nation-states in Europe. Italy, however, was far less homogeneous than Germany; although Enlightenment ideas had affected the northern cities, they were of no significance in the predominantly rural south. The Reformation had bypassed Italy, and the country had no experience with parliamentary democracy. Although Mazzini had received a great deal of support in the 1850s and 1860s, the failure of his vision of a new Italy to materialize had soured the attitude of the middle classes toward liberal-democratic ideals.

Although Pareto had initially supported Mazzini and his idea of bourgeois republicanism, like many other Italians he soon became disenchanted with the emancipatory theme of Mazzini's political program. He could see for himself that the social and political philosophies of the American federalists, the French *philosophes*, and the German idealists did not seem to apply to Italy. Yet Pareto was always a firm believer in classical (or bourgeois) economic theory. He believed that the economic relations of a market economy were integral to any rational society.

The roots of Pareto's social and political theory can be traced back to the Italian theorist Niccolò Machiavelli (1469–1527). Machiavelli's most famous work is *The Prince*, written in 1513 for the ruler of Florence. Although he was born in the fifteenth century, Machiavelli's political philosophy is modern rather than medieval. At the same time, however, it was obviously unaffected by the Enlightenment.

Machiavelli had concluded that it is the duty of subjects to be religious and the responsibility of rulers to be intelligent. Ordinary people have nonrational beliefs that do not bear critical examination. It would be cruel and unreasonable to expect members of the common herd to think clearly. Princes, rather than expecting their subjects to do without their mindless superstitions, should be willing to use fraud and deception to rule. After all, if political subjects prefer superstition to rational calculation, then a sovereign would be failing in his duty if he declined to take this into consideration. As Machiavelli pointed out, if a ruler makes impossible demands of his subjects, or if he has unreasonable expectations about how they might be ruled, the results will be to *everyone's* disadvantage.

The primary duty of the prince is to establish political authority and to make it impregnable. Machiavelli believed that the art of government is largely *technical*; thus the study of the effective means of securing authority is the study of the techniques of artful government. Scholars who wish to aid their rulers should provide them with technical knowledge, not moral argumentation. Moreover, if rulers are to achieve technical control over their subjects, they must rise above the petty ambitions and confused beliefs of common people. Machiavelli pointed out that, although they like to imagine they are virtuous, in reality people are selfish, greedy, unreasonable, and unprincipled—as every historian knows well. Thus the prince who is foolish enough to believe that his subjects would be bound by moral reasoning would be incapable of ruling effectively. In any case, given that the purpose of government is to protect and maintain respect for authority, it is beside the point for a ruler to be concerned about whether or not his subjects see him as honest.

Machiavelli was the first modern political theorist to point out that, if the ends of government can be taken for granted, political theory requires instrumental knowledge. He emphasized the difference between moral argumentation (the discussion of ends or goals) and technical understanding (the determination of the appropriate means to attain set ends). Having made this distinction, Machiavelli insisted that the practice of governing is a technique, not a moral obligation.

Machiavelli's reasoning was impeccable—as long as it can be taken for granted that the ends of government are beyond dispute. This assumption was probably justified in the sixteenth century, when the most that ordinary people could expect was the rule of a strong prince who took the art of governing seriously. Such an assumption, however, is hardly justified in the post-Enlightenment era. Machiavelli's identification of theory with technical knowledge is wholly consistent with the aims of positivism, but it is quite antithetical to critical theory's assumption that the ends of action must be shown to be reasonable. Nevertheless, Machiavelli's sophistication is extraordinary for a man of his time: What he curtly dismissed was the medieval conception of political authority. He argued that political rule in the modern world was an art that could be mastered *intellectually*; it was not merely the prerogative of those who were born great and had merely to express this greatness by a show of pomp and ceremony.

It was Machiavelli's ardent hope that Italy would be united under a prince who would make it a great power in Europe. This was not to be. Machiavellian principles of government were used most effectively by non-Italian sovereigns like the English Tudors. In the 350 years that elapsed between the death of Machiavelli and the birth of Pareto, Italy lost ground continuously to Britain, France, and Germany. Because the impact of Enlightenment ideals had been so slight, the influence of Machiavelli in twentieth-century Italy was still strong. Pareto's tolerance for Fascism, for instance, is understandable largely in terms of his lack of sympathy for Enlightenment ideals— that is, because of his rejection of the doctrine that reflective self-enlightenment was, or could be, the dominating force in the life of individuals. Machiavelli, Pareto, and Mussolini would all have argued that there is an intractable and unchanging nonrational core to human nature. The impact of Machiavelli on Pareto, however, cannot be explained in terms of the latter's cynicism. Pareto would have been less hardheaded if he had believed that a liberal, enlightened Italian republic was a real possibility during his lifetime. The power of the church was too strong, the peasantry too ignorant, the masses too uneducated, and the bourgeoisie too disorganized and too unsure of itself for such a republic to be created.

Although he had no faith in socialism, Pareto admired Marx in some respects. He thought that Marx was a poor economist but a good sociologist. He liked Marx's analysis of class conflict and his conception of history as a continuous struggle for domination among competing groups. Overall, however, Pareto viewed Marxism as a religion for the masses, not as a science. Pareto was much more sympathetic toward Spencer, and he makes reference to some of the English theoretician's ideas in the *Cours d'économie politique*. However, Pareto believed that Spencer—and Comte—were insufficiently positivistic: Neither of them could do without "metaphysical accessories," and neither could resist making "theological" value judgments.

Among his contemporaries, Pareto acknowledged the influence of Georges Sorel (1847–1922) and Gaetano Mosca (1858–1941). Sorel was a syndicalist who advocated working-class control of economic institutions. He agreed with Marx that the proletariat was the hammer of the future; unlike Marx, however, Sorel was an antirationalist. He admired both Lenin and Mussolini (who used Sorelian theory in setting up his corporations), and he believed that the proletariat could organize effectively only when they were bound by some guiding *myth* necessary for revolutionary struggle. Sorel believed that if the working classes did not have a distorted and idealized conception of themselves and of what they could achieve, they would never leave the bars and the gambling halls.

Pareto made a close study of Sorel's *Reflections on Violence* (1906). He agreed with Sorel that it is a mistake to try to explain human activity in terms of the intellectualizations subjects like to use about themselves. Both Sorel and Pareto believed that human behavior is governed, above all, by nonrational impulse. Intellectualizations result when we try to disguise the nonrational roots of our behavior by claiming that, all along, we were guided by good sense.

Mosca's influence on Pareto is difficult to assess. It is known that Pareto read Mosca's *Theory of Government and Parliamentary Government* (1883), in which Mosca suggested that an organized ruling class will always be able to dominate a subordinate majority. Mosca and Pareto both agree that rulers impose their will on the governed through manipulation. Mosca was the first of the two to discuss the "circulation of governing elites," a concept that was to become central in Pareto's work, but Pareto never really gave Mosca credit for this. (In fact, Pareto never acknowledged that he had learned anything very important from his contemporaries.) When Pareto turned to sociology, Mosca accused him of plagiarizing his work. Pareto indignantly rejected the charge, and he never made reference to his younger colleague again. There is no mention of Mosca in the 2,033-page *Trattato*.

IDEAS

Society

Pareto believed that society was a system in equilibrium. He treated individuals as the parts of this system, and he assumed that such individuals are affected by certain forces, the most important of which he described as "sentiments." It is worth noting at the outset that, although Pareto's conception of a "system in equilibrium" sounds precise and highly scientific, his description of this system is often imprecise and unclear. Pareto's discussion of the "social system" is designed to show how "nonlogical" (nonrational) forces or sentiments act to maintain observable uniformities in history. For instance, a society cannot adapt to an external (natural) environment without taking these sentiments into consideration. Similarly, political theories will be nonsensical and impracticable if ideologues ignore the sentiments. Thus, in order to understand Pareto's conception of society, we shall have to look closely at the nature and effects of the sentiments. First, however, it is necessary to comprehend the distinction Pareto made between *nonlogical,* or nonrational behavior, and *logical,* or rational, behavior.

Pareto's theory of social action takes up where economics leaves off. Pareto believed that economists study logical (rational) action. He defined such action as the use of *effective* means to achieve *known* goals. He turned to sociology because he wanted to analyze nonlogical (nonrational) action. All action that fails to be logical was deemed by Pareto to be *non*logical to some degree. The following example should illustrate what Pareto meant by logical action. (Unfortunately, his definition of nonlogical action is not so clear-cut.)

Economists assume that in general people try to "maximize the utility" of their individual acts—for example, to buy a commodity at the cheapest price possible. If we examined the behavior of consumers buying oranges, we would take the following for granted: (1) Customers will prefer to possess more rather than fewer oranges; (2) customers will prefer to pay less, rather than more, for a given number of oranges. Given these assumptions, we can decide whether a particular individual is behaving rationally or not. If store A sells oranges at six for $1 and store B sells identical oranges at seven for $1, we would conclude that consumers were not behaving rationally if they chose to shop at store A.

According to Pareto, concrete logical (rational) action should use the "logicoexperimental" scientific method. This requires individuals to test the truth content of any claims they make about the world and to make only logical (deductive) links between assertions. Positivism is *abstractly* logical. The fixed end of positivism is pure technical-cognitive control, in itself. Hence positivism never views knowledge as an end in itself; it treats theory as if it is to be evaluated in terms of its ability to provide effective means for controlling environments.

The only other orientation that is abstractly logical in Paretian terms (as the foregoing example illustrates) is economic activity. The ends of economic activity are beyond dispute: Economically rational individuals use observation and calculation to achieve the goal of maximizing their utility. It is important to remember that Pareto's model of logical action applies to the individual act and assumes that the ends of action—goals and values—are fixed and do not themselves have to be evaluated. Thus logical consumers do not question or evaluate the goal of maximizing the utility of their individual behavior. Further, positivism is not expected to answer the question, Why should technical knowledge be a goal for human actors? Concrete logical action—utilizing means effectively to achieve a specific goal—can take place only when the goal of action has been set. It is not possible to evaluate specific goals *logically,* except as means to other ends. For instance, if you want to leave someone a message, it would be logical, or rational, to find something with which to write (for example, a pencil) and something on which to write (for example, a piece of paper). In this instance, pencils are useful and effective in achieving a desired end. We would say that someone who was looking for a pencil when she wanted to leave a message was acting logically.

Pareto believed that, whereas economics is restricted to dealing with types of logical behavior only, sociology tries to grasp the totality of all the logical and nonlogical forces that affect human activity. Sociology searches for uniformities in patterns of nonlogical action, just as economics searches for lawlike regularities in the action of many individuals who pursue chains of logical action simultaneously. Because social action is motivated by rhythmically fluctuating sentiments, it is not consistent in orientation. Economics studies constancy in behavior; sociology explains why nonlogical patterns of action change over time.

One possible confusion should be cleared up at this point. Pareto once noted that governments cannot afford to act in a logical manner. Although it might want to use the logicoexperimental methodology to learn how best to *manipulate* subjects, a governing class must implement policy that is designed to appeal to *nonrational impulses and beliefs*, not to the individual's capacity for logical thinking. People respond to nonlogical values more readily than they respond to the need for logical calculation. Furthermore, as Pareto points out, the application of individualized self-interest often brings individuals into conflict. Society must be based, at least in part, on *non*logical action that has the function of sustaining social order. *Social utility*, therefore, is that which permits the institutions of a society to function effectively but which achieves this goal by encouraging nonlogical action in individuals.

Pareto's definition of nonlogical action is notoriously unclear, but he seems to posit two major kinds of nonlogical action: (1) "impulses" that result from a commitment to goals and values that appear to be "good" values but whose utility can be disputed; and (2) action that employs means that are not effectively connected to the stated ends of action. For instance, actors would be behaving nonlogically if they believed that action a would bring about goal g_1, whereas it really brought about goal g_2. In this instance, we would say that the manifest function of a was g_1, but that the latent function was g_2.

According to Pareto, moralists or humanitarians who believe that humans are good and who act on this basis are acting nonlogically. The belief that humans are essentially good cannot hope to receive scientific justification; it is a simple impulse that cannot be proved or verified. Similarly, the ruler who tries to reduce social and economic inequality because he wants his subjects to be happy is acting nonlogically. There is no reason to believe that such action would be effective, given the desired end; and in any case, there is nothing logical about wanting people to be happy.

As we have seen, economists can safely assume that the fixed ends that individuals pursue are determined by individuals' interest in maximizing their utility. It is, therefore, quite easy for them to draw up anticipatory models of logical economic action that assume that individuals will act rationally in their own self-interests. As a sociologist, Pareto asked: If we can see uniformities of behavior in history that make no logical sense, can we explain these regularities in terms of underlying needs or instincts? For Pareto, such underlying needs or instincts are the fixed ends that individuals pursue unknowingly when they engage in nonlogical action.

In the *Trattato*, Pareto describes the biologically inherited characteristics of individuals that drive them to act in a nonlogical manner as "sentiments." Sentiments cannot be observed, and they change slowly over time, if at all. Pareto claimed, however, that it is possible to observe the effects of sentiments. These effects are psychic states, described as unchanging "residues" in social action. According to Pareto, human actors must adapt to the presence of these nonlogical points of orientation. *Residues* represent the underlying psychological substratum of social action; they are not figments of the sociologist's imagination but "facts" that can be documented. In the *Trattato*, Pareto tries to show how society is a system that remains in equilibrium by means of nonrational forces. Residues are basic to this equilibrium, for, as noted earlier, the preferred goal states of this system are defined largely in terms of the underlying sentiments.

Although there are unchanging residues to much of human action, there are also derivations that differ greatly from one type of society to another. *Derivations* are those "nonlogicoexperimental theories" that people use to explain what they think they are doing when they are engaged in nonlogical uniformities of behavior that are explicable in terms of residues. Derivations are appeals and assertions that permit individuals to move toward the preferred goal states that arise because of the residues. Although derivations make action appear to be logical, they do not permit such individuals to understand the real purpose of their action. Derivations, therefore, have much in common with Marx's "ideology" and with Freud's "rationalizations."

Pareto lists six classes of residues and four classes of derivations. We shall discuss these briefly.

Residues

Class 1: Instinct for Combinations   A Class 1 residue is "an inclination to combine . . . things." It explains human intellectual curiosity and the ability to synthesize information. For instance, legends and myths are built up by this residue "and then explained by derivations." Class 1 residues are found in inventors, speculators, and politicians.

Class 2: Group Persistence (Persistence of Aggregates)   Class 2 residues explain the inertia associated with group membership. After a group has been constituted, this instinct "prevents the things so combined from being disjoined." It explains the persistence of kin groups, ethnic groups, and socioeconomic classes. There is a natural tension, or antithesis, between Class 2 and Class 1 residues. Class 2 residues are found in churchmen, family men, and "good subordinates."

Class 3: Need of Expressing Sentiments by External Acts   Class 3 residues are manifested in ceremonies, religious ecstasies, and festivals.

Class 4: Residues Connected with Sociality   "This Class is made up of residues connected with life in society." Class 4 residues explain the persistence of fashion, feelings of pity and cruelty, and acts of self-sacrifice.

Class 5: Integrity of Individuals and Their Appurtenances   Class 5 residues are "the complement" of Class 4 residues. They involve the "defense of integrity and development of personality." This class is manifested in "sentiments of resistance to alterations in the social equilibrium" and in such acts as vengeance. The sentiments to which Class 5 residues correspond are "sentiments of *interest*." They refer to individual acts based on *self*-interest. Class 5 residues are the only ones for which humans have tried to specify a *logical* derivation: economic theory.

Pareto assumed that the nuclei of instincts that fix the ends of economic activity can be made part of a *logical* schema of action. In other words, the ends of a means-ends chain of action that involves pure economic activity are, somehow, "logical" ends. Although this assumption appears to be inconsistent with his assertions that the ends of human action cannot be justified logically, Pareto is in fact being quite consistent. The ends of pure economic action are always means to other ends. Although wealth can be the end of action, money cannot, for it is always the means to some other end.

Class 6: The Sex Residue   Class 6 residues are responsible for "mental states" having to do with sexual activity.

Derivations

Class 1: Assertion   Assertion as a Class 1 derivation is in accord with sentiments. This class of derivation is used with Class 1 residues. For instance, a scientist might see herself as working long hours because she has "a thirst for knowledge." She might describe herself as a thoroughly logical person who is dedicated to "truth." Pareto, however, would have claimed that such a person is embodying the nonlogical "instinct for combinations."

Class 2: Authority   Authoritative relations in this class are in concord with sentiments. This class of derivation is used with Class 2 residues. For instance, residents of ethnic ghettoes might claim that they prefer to stay in their neighborhoods so that they can be with their own people and attend their own churches. They might point out that this is "logical" because, by living in the same neighborhood, they do not have to cross town to get what they want. Pareto, however, would have insisted that their desire to place themselves under the authority of their own communal mores was a derivation from the residue of group persistence.

Class 3: Accords with Sentiments or Principles   Class 3 derivations can be used with different kinds of residues.

Class 4: Verbal Proofs   Class 4 derivations are effective through sheer force of rhetoric.

Pareto's classification of residues is an attempt to classify the psychological substratum of human nature. (Pareto believed that this was a first step to sociological theorizing.) Class 1 and Class 2 residues are by far the most important. As we shall see, they play a crucial role in explaining the circulation of elites in society. Unfortunately, Pareto treats his list of residues and derivations as definitive. Each residue is subdivided into subcategories, so that every social role can be explained as an expression of some combination of these subcategories. Many of Pareto's categories appear quite arbitrary and are not readily understandable. For example, the distinction between Class 3 and Class 4 residues is not clear. Similarly, Class 3 seems to be a catchall class.

Pareto's examples of derivations that are the expression of underlying residues are not always clear-cut either. For instance, Pareto states that it is "readily understandable" that the "ideal of justice" is a combination of Class 2 and Class 5 residues. What he means is that the idea of justice makes an appeal to a combination of two types of residues: the desire to see a persistence in the abstract structure of a group (Class 2 residues) and the desire to resist alterations in the social equilibrium (Class 5 residues).

Implicit in Pareto's view of society is an interesting theory of social change. (We shall mention it briefly here and look at it more closely in the section on the circulation of elites.) According to Pareto, social equilibrium is maintained by the dead weight of the sentiments. From one society to another, and from one era to another, derivations can change a great deal. What is most significant about social change, however, is how little human action itself changes. Throughout history, observable residues have anchored the ends of action in preferred goal states. Pareto refers to social change, therefore, as "undulatory." Different residues might be accentuated in different time periods. Over time, however, there is oscillation around the perpetual manifestation of all the sentiments. For example, if Class 1 residues begin to prevail, there will be a movement back toward their antithesis: Class 2 residues. Thus, according to Pareto, the Protestant Reformation was the result of Class 2 "German force and devoutness" against Class 1 Catholic "intelligence, cunning and rationality." Yet, Pareto claimed that the key to Protestant success in the sixteenth and seventeenth centuries was the German willingness to use force. Hence he makes it plain that political leaders who wish to be effective must use sentiments and be prepared to use force.

The undulatory movement of history is concretely observable in the conflict and struggle between different groups, classes, and parties. Pareto points out that all human societies are socially heterogeneous. In other words, within every type of society there are *individuals* with different interests and abilities, and different *classes* or *groups* of individuals with different characteristics. The essential division among human groupings is that between the governing and the governed. The rulers of a society govern effectively when they successfully use the sentiments of their followers. Governing classes tend to exclude outsiders from their ranks, but in so doing, they exclude those who are resourceful and intelligent. Thus they encourage the formation of oppositional groupings with leaders astute enough to mobilize the population against them.

Hence it is the heterogeneity of society that makes for competition among groups and for change in the content of the derivations. As far as Pareto was concerned, however, the Enlightenment idea of social *progress* is totally without scientific foundation. Pareto believed that "history is a graveyard of aristocracies" who ultimately fell from power because they lacked the intelligence, the cunning, and the will to use sentiments to guarantee their hegemony. Conflict between a governing class and a governed class is a battle over who can use the sentiments most effectively and thus exercise most social control. For instance, Pareto suggests that the "class struggle" to which Marxists refer is a competition between the bourgeoisie and the *leaders* of the proletariat. Pareto predicts that working-class leaders can win if they can use their "propaganda" "to awaken or intensify [appropriate] residues in the proletariat." According to Pareto, the greatest mistake that the bourgeoisie can make is to pander to democratic ideals and to lose confidence in their ability to rule.[5]

The Individual in Society

As we have seen, Pareto grounds his sociology in assumptions about an unchanging psychological substratum. Thus he believed that human nature is relatively immune to the effects of social and historical change. He would have violently disagreed with the idea that forms of selfhood emerge from a social interactional process. Pareto believed that individuals are individuated (formed) *prior* to their participation in society. Accordingly, he would have rejected Hegel's and Mead's view that selfhood is a reflective process within a system of social mediation. Pareto insisted that individuals are born with certain talents and inclinations. Although differences among individuals are accentuated by the participation of individuals in society, they do not result from conditions of social life that such social individuals create for themselves. According to Pareto, the human animal should see society as a means of serving the goal of self-interest. Social relations do not express our common "humanity." Such a belief is merely a derivation.

Pareto believed that tension between the centrifugal force of individuals and the centripetal pull of society was inevitable. His model of social equilibrium posits an uneasy oscillation of individuals around the overlapping—and sometimes antithetical—poles of human sentiments. This oscillation is occasionally violent: Social equilibrium is not static but reasserts itself in a process of dynamic change. Nevertheless, according to Pareto, the analysis of history reveals no significant change in the way in which this equilibrium is maintained. In other words, the sentiments do not change. Leaders are born and die; the content of nonrational belief is transformed. What changes, however, is not as significant as that which remains the same. Pareto's view of history is remarkable: "The centuries roll by, human nature remains the same."

In the first two decades of the twentieth century, Freud and Pareto were among the leading proponents of theories that rejected the idea that humans were rational creatures. Freud reached this conclusion after reflecting on the significance and power of the unconscious mind. Pareto's antirationalism, however, stems more from his extreme positivism. As we have seen, Pareto made a strict demarcation between the logical and nonlogical activity of the individual. According to his definition of logicality, human individuals seldom act in a rational manner. Rather, individuals live and die by reference to values and principles—that is, in terms of derivations. As Pareto points out, there is nothing logical about this.

Pareto believed that logical action has to be instrumental—concerned with the effective use of means in the service of goals that cannot themselves be questioned. As we have seen, such action takes place when the positive evaluation of some ends for which humans are striving can be taken for granted. In the short term, however, the individual can act "rationally," if the ends of action are fixed by some higher authority. For instance, the architects who designed the gas ovens for the Nazi death camp at Auschwitz, which killed 10,000 people a day, were acting "logically." Once the problem of body disposal was explained to them, they solved it expeditiously.

With his strict demarcation between logical and nonlogical spheres of activity, Pareto creates human beings who cannot rationally choose morality. If people choose to be rational in their dealings with others, they are forced to be Machiavellian. As we have seen, Pareto believed that the human condition can be studied scientifically. According to Pareto, however, logicoexperimental inquiry will yield technical knowledge about the ways in which people can be manipulated as social objects. Such knowledge, of course, is likely to be very useful, but it cannot resolve moral issues. We can choose whether to manipulate or not to manipulate; but this is not a *moral* choice, for manipulation in and of itself can serve both "good" and "bad" ends.

Pareto's amoral manipulator is, perhaps, a recognizable being. It is not, however, a being that critical theorists like Hegel and Marx would have recognized as fully human. Nevertheless, there is nothing in Pareto's sociology to suggest that the individual he portrays would suffer from a sense of alienation. According to Pareto, the modern individual has no choice but to acknowledge the incommensurability of moral and rational behavior (i.e., the incommensurability of an "ethic of responsibility" and an "ethic of success"). Consequently, Pareto believed that the self-consciously virtuous person is a fool. Humans should take no pride in the fact that they consider themselves moral. Such belief indicates that individuals are defective as rational beings.

Pareto's belief in a permanent and unchanging psychological substratum condemns individuals to experience part of themselves as part of an environment to which they must learn to adapt. Unlike Freud, Pareto did not believe that individuals have the capacity to liberate themselves from the forces that control them by reflecting on these forces and by learning how to comprehend them as mere distorted forms of subjectivity. As long as we make it an object for thought, Pareto believed that human nature must be fully objective and external to us. To wish that human nature were different is like wishing that our bodily organs had been designed differently.

Ultimately, Pareto was forced to acknowledge that the fate of the modern individual is to experience a total paralysis of will. The logicoexperimental method generates reliable knowledge, but such knowledge has a limited value. The knowledge that individuals gain from the study of society might enable subjects to understand more clearly the forces that determine their behavior. It does not permit them to change either themselves or society, however, because these forces are wholly impersonal, natural forces to which we must learn to adapt. Unlike Freud, who saw unconscious impulses and rational self-reflection as opposing but dueling forces, Pareto did not believe that humans could learn about themselves by using the power of reason to displace the force of sentiment. Science cannot help investigators determine how their actions can be made meaningful. The logicoexperimental method can tell us how to exercise control over given environments, but it can tell us nothing about the purpose of human life.

It follows from Pareto's conception of the intelligent individual that one part of us must observe the world dispassionately while another decides how to act. When material and emotional needs of the body have been met, there can be no good reason for action of one kind as opposed to another. It is the fate of humans as *cognitive* beings to learn that choice cannot be meaningful. Pareto treated all human endeavor as equally valid and as equally indefensible from a moral standpoint: He believed that actions could be more or less effective but not more or less moral.

Pareto's personal solution was to withdraw from the world. Toward the end of his life, he wrote, "With all my strength I seek to be immune from hatred and from love; I have renounced all propaganda activities to defend or to attack any cause whatever and to seek to affect events: I observe them and that is all."[6]

Methodology

Pareto was trained as an engineer. He studied thermodynamics for many years, and the impact of the engineering and natural sciences on his work is evident. For Pareto, a scientific sociology should use the same methods for testing theory as the engineering and natural sciences do. His logicoexperimental method of inquiry is nothing but deductive-nomological explanation. According to Pareto, the sociologist tries to develop laws about the world that describe observable uniformities and regularities in human behavior. Pareto recognized that such laws would always be provisional, for they are built up from empirical generalizations and established inductively. For Pareto, science

> selects particular truths by direct observation, co-ordinates them, and from those that present a common character, formulates partial theorems from which it deduces other more general theorems: thus gradually progressing towards the general principles which underlie the universality of things.[7]

Pareto was an extreme empiricist, insisting that the first principles of any scientific theory (its initial assumptions) must be based on factual observation. For instance, although he found the labor theory of value to be interesting in some respects, Pareto rejected it because such a "premise" was "not a concrete, real fact." He believed that it was possible to engage in theory construction by starting with observations about simple facts and then using theorems to synthesize knowledge about such facts—that is, to show how they are related. Needless to say, Pareto was unable to base the premises on which his sociology was founded in "concrete, real facts" without making certain assumptions about the meaning of these facts as determined by theory. As we have seen, Pareto posited the existence of unobservable sentiments in order to describe the invisible points of orientation toward which nonlogical action was oriented.

Obviously, Pareto was not able to test his sociohistorical theories in a setting where variables were strictly controlled. In the *Trattato*, he searches for those underlying principles that would explain uniformities and regularities of social action across the sweep of history. Pareto's method of "testing" the accuracy of his classification of the residues, for instance, was to dip into the past to demonstrate how patterns of nonlogical action can be explained in terms of the underlying sentiments or, more accurately, in terms of residues: the theoretical conceptualization of the sentiments.

Pareto understood that a nomothetic science must develop theory that is highly abstract. He pointed out that the most successful sciences, like physics, have theories that are so abstract that they are expressed mathematically. For Pareto, this was the ideal for which all investigators should strive. It is, therefore, rather surprising that Pareto's sociology is not particularly abstract but relatively concrete. For instance, Pareto uses ordinary language to list the classes of residues that are so central to his sociology. A residue is an abstract categorization—an analytic category describing uniformities that the scientist can observe in human affairs. Thus sentiments are much more concrete than residues. Nevertheless, the level of abstraction in Paretian theory is far lower, for instance, than that in Marxian or Simmelian theory.

To some extent, Pareto's scientific methodology is extremely antiquated. Rather than seeking abstractions, Pareto ponderously classifies the all-important residues. His method of theory construction is almost pre-Newtonian. As Franz Borkenau has noted, Pareto tries to explain observable social and psychological phenomena in terms of their "metaphysical doubles": residues. Borkenau points out that this approach is like chemists explaining "burning through the phlogiston, light through the light-stuff, heat through heat-molecules and so on."[8]

The basic identification that Pareto made between the methods of the social and engineering sciences make sense when Paretian assumptions about society are taken into consideration. As we have seen, Pareto believed that the human freedom to participate in the social construction of reality was extremely limited. Individuals do construct ideologies, religions, and other fanciful belief systems; and these constructions can be taken very seriously. Pareto believed, however, that such constructs were merely derivations from the underlying sentiments. Thus, although they construct *symbolic* interpretations of the world, which are taken as real, individuals have little free choice in determining the underlying structure of meaning. Human behavior is determined by forces whose effects can be studied; as we have seen, however, these forces will always be external to us in the sense that they are innate and unalterable by human reflection, understanding, or will.

When Pareto looked at human belief, he did not consider how this subjective element might influence and shape social action. For Pareto, ideas were always *dependent*, never *independent* variables. Pareto treated human consciousness as the datum that functioned merely to reveal the presence and nature of the underlying residues. Unlike Durkheim, Pareto did not believe that social facts were the product of social relations. Thus he did not believe that sociology could be used to transform the means by which social integration was achieved. It was Pareto's opinion that the less the masses knew about sociology, the better it was for social cohesion. If ordinary people possessed sociological insight, they would become cynical and more resistant to the efforts of rulers to maximize social utility by appeals to the sentiments.

Pareto did not believe that sociology should try to give monocausal explanations of social phenomena. He believed that the elements of a social system are interdependent: The relationship among all these elements depends on the relationship of each element to the whole. As one would expect, Pareto treats residues and derivations as the most important forces in the social system. Confusingly, he treats "interests"—that is, economic interests—as a third and separate element, even though such interests are logical derivations. The fourth and fifth elements of the social system are "social heterogeneity" (individual and group differences in society) and "class circulation" (the degree of social mobility in society).

Pareto is extremely vague about how the elements of a social system maintain social equilibrium, but his model crudely suggests that balance occurs when opposing forces have exhausted themselves and have reached a state of compromise. (This conception of equilibrium is drawn from engineering.) Pareto suggested that "social utility" requires the correct balance between logical and nonlogical action within society. An example of logical action would be the behavior of a conglomerate of actors all trying to maximize their own utility. There has to be some balance between the manifestation of economic interests and nonlogical action in society, however. No social system could survive if people were entirely logical or exclusively nonlogical.

In the *Trattato*, Pareto concentrates on how residues and derivations function and how the correct mixture of such residues and derivations contributes to social utility. As we know, although the sentiments are rooted in human nature (and are thus constants in history), residues can fluctuate in intensity from one generation to another. In trying to explain these fluctuations, Pareto employs what is essentially a functionalist mode of explanation. The fourth and fifth elements of his conception of the social system ("social heterogeneity" and "class circulation") are used to explain how the intensity of residues can fluctuate. Pareto suggests that certain individuals and certain groups in society are the carriers of specific residues. For instance, a specific individual might be extremely intelligent and imaginative: He is marked by Class 1 residues. If this individual plays an important role in society, it will be because more Class 1 residues are needed for the proper mix of residues and, hence, for the maintenance of social order. If intelligent and imaginative individuals cannot rise to the top of the social hierarchy, adjustments will have to be made in the degree of class circulation permitted in society.

As we have seen, Pareto made a strict demarcation between the domain of *facts* and the domain of *values*. (This did not, of course, prevent him from allowing his own values to influence his interpretation of the facts.) According to Pareto, human subjects are objects moving within a system that is dispassionately observed by the investigator. Just as a moving physical body has preferred goal states (for example, "rest" if it is falling), so, apparently, do humans. Social order cannot be sustained unless the existence of these nonlogical goal states is taken into consideration. Pareto believed that human actors have very limited opportunities to be "logical." He did not believe there is anything characteristically human about scientific analysis.

Other Major Themes and Foci: The Circulation of Elites

Pareto's treatment of "class circulation" or of the circulation of elites is often cited and is generally considered the most interesting part of his sociology. Pareto believed that individuals are born with quite different abilities and acquire quite different skills and aptitudes. He suggests that it is possible to give a numerical score to an individual that would "stand as a sign of his capacity." A man who has made his millions would be a "10"; a man who has made hundreds of thousands would be a "6." To a woman "who has managed to infatuate a man of power and play a part in the man's career" Pareto suggests that a score of 8, 9, or 10 would be appropriate (depending on the woman's ability to manipulate the man). To "a strumpet who merely satisfies the senses of a man and exerts no influence on public affairs," Pareto suggests a score of 0.9

As far as classes and groupings are concerned, Pareto describes two main strata in any population: the elite and the nonelite. The elite are subdivided into the governing elite and the nongoverning elite. A politician would be a member of the governing elite, a rock star a member of the nongoverning elite. According to Pareto, the governing elite (comprising the people who really matter) "is always in a state of slow and continuous transformation." Those who rule are always in a precarious position, for history teaches us that "class circulation" is a never-ending process.

Toward the end of the *Trattato*, Pareto presents his theory of revolutions and his explanation for the occasional occurrence of sudden change within a society. It is worth quoting at length:

> Revolutions come about through accumulations in the higher strata of society—either because of a slowing-down in class circulation, or from other causes—of decadent elements no longer possessing the residues suitable for keeping them in power, and shrinking from the use of force; while meantime in the lower strata of society elements of superior quality are coming to the fore, possessing residues suitable for exercising the functions of government and willing enough to use force.[10]

The governing elite need the correct mixture of Class 1 and Class 2 residues to stay in power. For instance, Class 2 residues (residues of group persistence) are important for the creation of *collective* actors—classes that contain individuals who act in the interests of the group. Once the members of a ruling class have achieved a position of strength and authority, they tend to lose the sense of cohesiveness they possessed at an earlier time. Meanwhile, Class 2 residues are "reinforced by tides upswelling from the lower stratum." Pareto argued that this is precisely what happened during the Puritan revolution in England, when "religious tides originating in the lower classes" rose to engulf "the skeptical higher classes." Religion, in other words, has the function of maintaining a sense of collective identity and makes possible the "persistence of aggregates."

For Pareto, a ruling class is "decadent" when it cannot—or will not—hold onto power. At the turn of the century, the English aristocracy yielded political power to the bourgeoisie. According to Pareto, this surrender proved the decadence of the English aristocracy, not because this class could no longer hope to maintain its hegemony, but because it was willing to give up without a fight.

The governing elite is always faced with a dilemma. If Class 1 residues (expressing the instinct for combinations) are lacking among members of the governing elite, leaders from the lower orders with the right attributes (cunning, imagination, and low guile) will move to displace them. One way to safeguard against such displacement is to co-opt intelligent members of the nonelite—as, for instance, the Rockefellers co-opted Dr. Henry Kissinger by sponsoring his upward social mobility. The danger with this strategy is that the more heterogeneous the governing elite becomes, the more likely it is that members of the elite will lose their sense of group identity. This loss of cohesion will give members of the lower stratum with appropriate Class 2 residues an opportunity to rise, as described earlier. However, Pareto suggests that for "social equilibrium," there should be a predominance of Class 1 residues in the elite and a predominance of Class 2 residues among members of the nonelite. The ruling class needs individuals with intelligence more than it needs individuals who will promote group solidarity.

Pareto points out that "to ask whether or not force ought to be used in a society, whether the use of force is or is not beneficial, is to ask a question that has no meaning."[11] The effective use of force is a means to some end. It is not possible to know whether the use of force is justified without knowing whether it is effective. Pareto believed that the use of force is normal and unavoidable in political life. Organized aggression is simply a means by which necessary adjustments are made by agents seeking to redress a lack of equilibrium resulting from the incorrect mix of residues within society. Thus opportunities for ambitious individuals occur when the social system is out of balance. If a ruling class is unwilling to use organized violence and terror, it is not fit to rule; thus it will be replaced. There is nothing either good or bad about this; according to Pareto, it is merely a "datum of fact."

Pareto believed that a dominant class that takes humanitarian values seriously is thus a doomed class. Pareto points out that revolutions tend to occur more as the result of a governing elite's inability and lack of will to move aggressively against its enemies than as the result of a popular uprising expressing the will of the people. Rapid social change, therefore, is the response to a sudden power vacuum. Pareto concedes that the governing class can defend itself through the use of "craft," "fraud," and "deceit," as well as through the use of organized violence. In this case, power is exercised by "foxes" rather than "lions." *Lions* are members of the governing elites who are marked by Class 2 residues: They rule by force and they value courage and moral fervor. *Foxes*, on the other hand, specialize in Class 1 residues: They rule by guile and deception. Pareto suggests that, in the modern world, governing elites tend to be made up of foxes rather than lions. This pattern leaves the ruling class vulnerable to lions from the lower stratum—vulnerable to the effective use of force exercised from below. In Pareto's opinion, the lower orders were, fortunately, too stupid to realize this.

In the *Trattato*, Pareto goes to extraordinary lengths to excoriate liberals, humanists, do-gooders, and sentimentalists of all description "whose spinal columns have utterly rotted from the bane of humanitarianism." At one point, Pareto gleefully describes the hypothetical actions of a "subject class" who rise against a governing elite that practices "humanitarianism" and preaches the "advent of a reign of reason." Pareto comments that if members of the subject class were to "kill large numbers" of such a governing elite, "they [would be] performing a useful public service, something like ridding the country of a baneful animal pest."[12] Not surprisingly, Pareto refuses to bow to the orthodox view, held by most of his fellow intellectuals, that the leaders of the French Revolution inflicted unnecessary suffering. Pareto congratulates the Jacobins for killing so many: "The use of force was one of the chief merits of the French Revolution, not a fault."

There is a great deal of good sense in much of what Pareto has to say. He discusses candidly what many intellectuals refuse to contemplate: that force—or the threat of force—has always been an integral part of government and that there can be no "freedom of ideas" in society until the really important questions (Who rules? Who dominates?) have already been settled. Both Pareto and Weber were defenders of governments that, they pointed out, opposed "terrorism" in the streets in order to protect their own monopoly on organized violence.

Behind the rhetoric of hard science, however, Pareto is asserting what is quite plain and straightforward, but rather more questionable: Members of the lower stratum can behave in an effective manner only when, in using their inferior and brutish talents, they rise up and give a sharp and painful lesson to their betters for failing to repress them sufficiently.

SIGNIFICANCE

Vision of the Future

Pareto believed that the elements constituting social phenomena moved in rhythmical, periodic undulations. As we have seen, he had no faith in social and political "progress," if by this term we mean a slow but perceptible movement toward some ideal future in which "justice" and "freedom" will prevail. Pareto acknowledged that the ideas of "progress," "freedom," and "equality" were used effectively at the end of the eighteenth century, when Class 1 residues were strongly emphasized by an emerging entrepreneurial class: the bourgeoisie. He suggested that it would be a mistake, however, to see the pretentious ideology of republicans and liberal democrats as anything other than an appropriate way to muster human resources in the interests of the governing elite. Pareto pointed out that democrats, republicans, and socialists do not really believe in freedom or equality and have no intention of sharing power with the suffering masses.

Pareto warns us that "it is because social movement takes an undulatory form that it is difficult to predict, from the evidence of the past, the future direction of this movement."[13] The ideal of bourgeois democracy, with its fake claims to "liberty," has made very effective appeals to human sentiments in the past two hundred years. As noted earlier, Pareto sees liberal democracies as the province of the foxes rather than the lions. Foxes use Class 1 residues and welcome "new combinations." Thus they are not afraid of the idea of change or of progress. They rule by deception and welcome the opportunity to manipulate the masses with buzz words like "democracy," "liberty," and "equality." However, we should not assume that the trend that is apparent over the last two hundred years will somehow be extended indefinitely. On the contrary, if we anticipate change, we should expect a movement away from rule by guile back to rule by force.

Pareto conceded that a trend toward democracy could be observed in many Western societies in the nineteenth century. He argued that democracy is strictly correlated "with the increased use of that instrument of governing which involves resort to artifice and to the [political] 'machine,' as against the instrument of force."[14] It was Pareto's opinion that in Western pluralistic democracies like the United States, the ruling class consolidates its hold on power by institutionalizing a "demagogic plutocracy." He meant that the administration in power looks after the interests of the moneyed classes but maintains its hold on the lower stratum by manipulating sentiments rather than by breaking heads. Pareto would have seen presidential elections in the United States as a series of carefully planned festivals and carnivals that titillate the feeble-minded by permitting them to celebrate "democracy" and "the people's choice." Of course, those who exercise real power in any society are not selected by the will of the people. In a constitutional republic, like the United States, ruling-class delegates—and the specific policies that they adopt—are selected by members of the governing elite. The purpose of elections is to permit the lower orders to express mindless, braying support for members of a self-perpetuating governing elite.

Pareto, therefore, would analyze U.S. politics in the following way: Given that the clever plutocrats in the United States maintain their hegemony largely by relying on the use of Class 1 residues, which of these derivations is the most effective for them? This, of course, is a *technical* problem. Assertions or derivations that are *best* are those that are most effective in allowing the plutocrats to maintain their dominant role. Among members of the governing elite, a great deal of maneuvering and back-stab-bing goes on as cliques and parties strive for dominance. As these elite organizations squabble among themselves, they might even appeal to the sentiments of the people in order to gain a momentary advantage over their adversaries. According to Pareto, this is the absolute limit to which "democratic" rule can be taken:

> A political system in which "the people" expresses its "will"—given but not granted that it has one—without cliques, intrigues, "combines," "gangs," exists only as a pious wish of theorists. It is not to be observed in reality, either in the past or in the present, either in our Western countries or in any others.[15]

Pareto believed, therefore, that the rise of liberal democracies over the last two hundred years is the result of a temporary coincidence of interest between foxes and plutocrats. (This overlap is perhaps most obvious in the United States.) Pareto pointed out that the foxes would rule as long as Western economies were founded on entre-preneurship and speculation. If the capitalist economy were to stagnate, and if future economic growth were not anticipated, the ruling classes would prefer strength and courage (in order to hold on to what they have) to imagination, craft, and guile. The lat-ter qualities are most useful for the art of demagoguery and for creative entrepre-neurship—the extraction of profit through deceit.

Pareto concluded that the claims of the Marxists that mature capitalism will yield to democratic socialism were absurd. For one thing, "democratic socialism" cannot ex-ist. For another, if mature capitalism means economic stagnation, indebtedness, and a decline in the rate of profit, then a decadent elite, forced to acknowledge that its tal-ents for manipulation, intrigue, and general corruption no longer suffice to guaran-tee its hegemony, will yield power to lions who will rule by force and by strict moral fervor. According to Pareto, this latter group will be "made up of soldiers [and] police of one sort or another." Pareto believed, therefore, that the alternative to rule by cor-rupt and fraudulent politicians is rule by a fascist, or neofascist, paramilitary junta. The signal that will tell these strong men when to move will be the breakdown of public or-der and the collapse of central authority.

Pareto thus agreed with Marx that steady economic growth (and the avoidance of massive levels of debt) was the key to the survival of Western bourgeois democracies. Unlike Marx, however, Pareto believed that a governing elite that used mainly Class 1 residues would be replaced by an elite that would return to Class 2 residues. Pareto's vision of the future was realized in Italy in 1922 and in Germany in 1933, when failing "democratic" regimes were replaced by more authoritarian rule.

Pareto would have suggested that if Americans wish to look into their future they should look back to the pre–World War II fascist regimes in Italy and Germany—or to the dictatorships that the U.S. State Department has supported around the world. He would certainly have claimed that the only role the left is likely to play in the future is to signal that it is time for the governing elite to replace artifice with the effective use of organized violence.

Contemporary Relevance

Pareto was introduced to the U.S. public by the translation of the *Trattato* as *The Mind and Society* in 1935. During the 1930s, Pareto was popular among many American intellectuals, especially at Harvard. The entomologist Morton Wheeler (1865–1937) recommended Pareto's work to the physiologist Lawrence J. Henderson (1878–1942), who in turn introduced Talcott Parsons, George Homans, and Robert K. Merton to Pareto's grand system. Parsons was so impressed by Pareto that he included him in his influential book *The Structure of Social Action* (1937) as one of the four leading contributors to theories of social action. Parsons conveniently represses mention of the fact that, for Pareto, the sentiments were *hereditary*; he also downplays the subsidiary role given to values in Pareto's work. The Pareto who was introduced to tens of thousands of students in the pages of *The Structure of Social Action* (which was still being used as a basic text in the 1960s) is not the Pareto of the *Trattato*, but—so Parsons would have us believe—a scholar whose work anticipates Parsons's own "voluntaristic" theory of action. Nevertheless, Parsons was instrumental in making Pareto a "major sociological theorist."

Pareto's ideas were cited by the research sociologists who took part in the well-known Hawthorne Studies under Elton Mayo (1880–1949) in the early 1930s. These researchers discovered that the rate at which factory workers labored—and the attitudes that these men held toward management and toward their fellow workers—could not be easily manipulated as if such workers were governed by simple models of economic utility. Sometimes individuals in an industrial plant act nonlogically: They do not simply try to minimize their efforts and maximize their income. The researchers found that laborers will work harder for no logical (that is, purely economic) reason; at other times, they expend effort in the pursuit of goals (like worker solidarity) that have no obvious instrumental significance. The Hawthorne Studies showed that the actions of workers in an industrial plant cannot be treated simply in terms of logical means-ends schema.[16] Similarly, conflict between management and labor could not be explained merely in terms of conflict caused by different economic interests. The research team involved in these studies of industrial management found that Pareto's residues helped them to explain some nonlogical action and conflict that could not be understood in terms of models of economic utility.

In more recent times, Pareto's work has influenced theories of elite domination (although most contemporary theorists tend to reject Pareto's conception of "social heterogeneity" as being partially explicable in terms of hereditary characteristics). For instance, C. Wright Mills's (1916–1962) book *The Power Elite* (1956) describes what Mills believed to be the dominant governing elites in the United States.[17] Although Mills never claimed that he was influenced much by Pareto, he shared his view of the importance of "myth-making" as a means by which dominant elites in U.S. society maintain their hegemony over their fellow citizens.

George C. Homans and Charles P. Curtis, who published a book on Pareto in 1934, praised him for applying to sociology "the method which has been found successful in the maturer [positivistic] sciences."[18] Many social scientists have found Pareto's extreme positivism attractive—ironically, especially with regard to its value implications. As we have seen, Pareto insisted that sociology can tell us nothing about the appropriateness of ends of action. According to Pareto, concepts like "freedom," "democracy," and "human dignity" have no place in any analysis that claims to be scientific or objective. Today there are still a few social scientists—like the followers of the psychologist B. F. Skinner (1904–1990)—who argue that disciplines like sociology and psychology cannot hope to become fully scientific until they purge themselves of the compulsion to take such concepts seriously. In *Beyond Freedom and Dignity* (1971), Skinner embarked on the peculiar project of tracing out the ethical implications of the decision to deny the validity of making ethical decisions.[19]

The strict demarcation between the domain of logic and experimental science on one hand, and the domain of values and morality on the other, has had a significant effect on contemporary society. With the decline of what Pareto would see as *traditional* nonlogical orientations, like custom and religion, the authority of science has gained ground significantly. If positive science cannot tell us how to live, however, then logical individuals are forced to acknowledge that all personally meaningful choices are nonrational. As noted earlier, it has been claimed that Pareto "theoretically prepared the coming of fascism." If this charge is true, then Pareto's contribution, more than anything else, was to trace out the implications of the strict segregation of logic and facts on the one hand and human values on the other. Fascist intellectuals pointed out that fascism could do without theory because, as all value claims are illogical, all claims are equally valid or equally invalid—it amounts to the same thing. Therefore, there need be no moral restraints on action.

Pareto cannot be held responsible for the actions taken by Mussolini and Hitler in the 1930s. In fact, he would have disapproved of them, arguing that their one-sided reliance on Class 2 residues made for social orders that would move rapidly out of equilibrium. Nevertheless, there is nothing in Pareto's sociology that would have led him to condemn Mussolini and Hitler for doing anything other than not consolidating their hold on power effectively enough.

For Pareto, if logical behavior was always instrumental—always a means for the achievement of an end that could not be assessed rationally—then the exercise of reason itself must be instrumentalism for the sake of instrumentalism. The effect of this on Pareto's sociology is plain. Despite all claims to the contrary, Pareto's sociology begs to be put to work as an ideological support for authoritarian political systems.

Pareto took it for granted that contemporary societies, with their property relations and their unequal share of natural and social resources, must be defended, *because they exist.* Contemporary governing elites are logical by definition because they are successful. According to Pareto, visions of radically new ways of living allow people to believe what they want to believe—or to believe what it is necessary for them to believe—but such dream states are not empirical realities. The effects of such dreams and delusions on the activity of concrete actors can be studied, but one would no more accept such fantasies than one would accept the existence of witches and dragons.

As Pareto liked to point out, contemporary society is a "datum of fact." He believed we have no choice but to assume that what is measured by positivistic theory is the sum total of what exists, and to act as if what exists is the sum total of what is possible for us. This belief, however, is nonlogical by Pareto's own definition, for support of the *status quo* clearly is not in the interests of each individual. If all actors chose to act logically in their own self-interests, they could not at the same time limit their vision of social order to that which merely exists. Either a radically new form of social organization would have to come into existence, or a war of all against all would result. Pareto was unable to contemplate the possibility of radical change in social and political organization. He would have conceded that the alternative to political rule that uses nonlogical action is, indeed, a war of all against all. According to Pareto, society has nothing to gain by opposing ignorance, superstition, folly, and nonrational behavior of all descriptions. The oddest feature of Pareto's sociology, therefore, is that if his ideas are true—and if they are believed—the effects will be wholly negative both from a technical *and* from a humanitarian point of view. If they are not true or if they are not believed, his life's work was an exercise in futility. Pareto was the antirationalist *par excellence*.

NOTES

1. George Bousquet, *Pareto, le savant et l'homme* (Lausanne, Switzerland: Payot, 1960), quoted in Peter Roche de Coppens, *Ideal man in classical sociology*, p. 85.

2. *Gerarchia*, July 1923, quoted in *The other Pareto*, p. 269.

3. Ibid., p. 285.

4. *La natione*, March 25, 1923, quoted in *The other Pareto*, p. 262.

5. *The mind and society: A treatise on general sociology*, para. 1045, Vol. 1, p. 623.

6. *Lettere a Maffeo Pantaleoni*, Vol. 1 (Rome: Gabriele de Rosa, *Edizioni de Storia e di Letteratura*, 1962), p. 54, quoted in de Coppens, *Ideal man*, p. 102.

7. From a lecture given to the Accademia Dei Georgofili, June 29, 1872, quoted in *The other Pareto*, p. 8.

8. Franz Borkenau, *Pareto*, pp. 74–75.

9. *The mind and society*, para. 2027, Vol. 2, p. 1422.

10. Ibid., para. 2057, Vol. 2, p. 1431.

11. Ibid., para. 2174, Vol. 2, p. 1512.

12. Ibid., para. 2191, Vol. 2, p. 1532.

13. From *Les systèmes socialistes*, quoted in *Vilfredo Pareto: Sociological writings*, p. 129.

14. *The mind and society*, para. 2259, Vol. 2, pp. 1589–1590.

15. Ibid.

16. See F. J. Roethlisberger & W. J. Dickson, *Management and the worker* (Cambridge, MA: Harvard University Press, 1939).

17. See C. Wright Mills, *The power elite* (New York: Oxford University Press, 1956).

18. George C. Homans & Charles P. Curtis, *An introduction to Pareto: His sociology*, p. 15.

19. See B. F. Skinner, *Beyond freedom and dignity* (New York: Alfred A. Knopf, 1971).

GLOSSARY

Class circulation: The rotation of dominant classes or elites.

Class 1 residues: The "instinct" of curiosity that drives individuals to synthesize information.

Class 2 residues: The "instinct" that compels individuals toward group membership.

Demagogic plutocracy: Rule by politicians who govern in the interests of financiers and speculators and who maintain their grip on power through deception and guile.

Derivations: *Nonlogical* explanations that differ greatly from one society to another. They permit people to believe what they want to believe, regardless of the truth.

Fascism: Political system based on extreme authoritarianism, nationalism, and anticommunism.

Foxes: Members of the governing elite who rule by fraud, deception, and guile.

Functionalism: Type of explanation often found in sociology and anthropology, which tries to explain the persistence of acts or institutions within society by showing how they contribute to a particular social order.

Inductive method: Method that assumes that scientific truth is the result of the observation of, and generalization from, a large number of empirical observations.

Labor theory of value: A theoretical treatment of "value" that treats the amount of value a commodity has as equivalent to the average amount of labor time necessary for its production.

Latent functions: The unintended and unplanned functions that an act or institution might have in society.

Lions: Members of the governing elite, or would-be members of the governing elite, who rule by force.

Logical action: Action that employs effective means to attain stated goals. Instrumental action.

Manifest functions: The intended and planned functions of acts and institutions.

Nonlogical action: Action that employs ineffective means to attain stated goals, and that is impulsive and irrational.

Plutocracy: A wealthy class that controls a government.

Residues: The conceptualization of human *sentiments* as psychic states.

Sentiments: The unchanging points of orientation toward which *nonlogical action* is oriented.

Theorem: A proposition that is demonstrably true, or assumed to be so.

Theories of utility: Theories that analyze the logic of instrumental action—that is, action that seeks the most effective means of achieving set goals.

Voluntaristic theories of action: Theories that see actors as goal-directed and as consciously using norms in order to achieve such goals. Emphasis is placed on the values that guide action.

ANNOTATED BIBLIOGRAPHY

Primary Sources

Compendium of general sociology (abridged in Italian with approval of the author; Elizabeth Abbott, Ed.). Minneapolis: University of Minnesota Press, 1980.

This is an abridged version of the *Trattato*, originally prepared in Italian by Giulio Farina. The text largely preserves the original Bongiorno-Livingston translation (*The Mind and Society*).

Manual of political economy (Ann S. Schwier & Alfred N. Page, Eds.; Ann S. Schwier, Trans.). New York: Augustus M. Kelley, 1971 [1909].

Pareto's political economy. Contains a discussion of the relationship between economics and sociology.

The mind and society: A treatise on general sociology (2 vols.; Arthur Livingston, Ed.; Andrew Bongiorno & Arthur Livingston, Trans.). New York: Dover, 1963 [1916].

Translation of the *Trattato di sociologia generale*. Pareto dictated this work to a secretary from about 1907 to 1912.

The other Pareto (Bucolo Placido, Ed. & Trans.). New York: St. Martin's Press, 1980.

Selections from Pareto's writings, lectures, and letters, with commentary by Placido.

Pareto. (Julien Freund & Simona Draghici, Trans.). Washington, DC: Plutarch Press, 1986 (paper).

Translation of Pareto's "Theory of Equilibrium."

The rise and fall of the elites (introduction by Hans L. Zetterburg). New York: Arno Press, 1979 [1901].

First published as an article entitled "Un applicazione di teorie sociologiche." This is Pareto's first sociological work and is a good introduction to his theory of the circulation of elites.

The ruling class in Italy before 1900. New York: H. Fertig, 1974 [1893].

First published in English in the *Political Science Quarterly* (1893: 677–721), entitled "The Parliamentary Regime in Italy." Pareto discusses political life in Italy at the end of the nineteenth century.

The transformation of democracy (Charles Powers, Ed.; R. Girola, Trans.). New Brunswick, NJ: Transaction Books, 1984 [1921].

A case study of how power erodes when a state becomes too decentralized. Pareto believed that all political systems oscillate between too much centralization and too little.

Vilfredo Pareto: Sociological writings (S. E. Finer, Ed.; Dereck Mirfin, Trans.). New York: Frederick A. Praeger, 1966.

This book is especially valuable because it includes translations from *Les systèmes socialistes* and the *Cours d'économie politique*, as well as from other works not otherwise translated into English.

Secondary Sources

Aron, Raymond. *Main currents in sociological thought* (Vol. 2; R. Howard & H. Weaver, Trans.). New York: Anchor Books, 1965 (paper).

Part of this introductory work deals with Pareto. Aron's discussion of Pareto's "system" is very good.

Bellamy, Richard. *Modern Italian social theory: Ideology and politics from Pareto to the present.* Stanford, CA: Stanford University Press, 1987.

Contains a chapter on Pareto. It is most useful in providing information about the historical and cultural context in which Pareto worked.

Borkenau, Franz. *Pareto.* New York: Wiley, 1936.

A well-written introduction to Pareto.

Burnham, James. *The Machiavellians: Defenders of freedom.* Freeport, NY: Books for Libraries Press, 1943.

Burnham discusses Pareto and Mosca, among others, as theorists in the tradition of Machiavelli.

de Coppens, Peter Roche. *Ideal man in classical sociology: The views of Comte, Durkheim, Pareto, and Weber.* State College: Pennsylvania State University Press, 1976.

One chapter contains a discussion of Pareto. Very readable, strongly recommended.

Gregor, A. James. *Italian Fascism and developmental dictatorship.* Princeton, NJ: Princeton University Press, 1979 (paper).

Gregor analyzes the rise of Fascism in Italy after the First World War. This book contains useful information about the social and political background of Pareto's country, as well as a short discussion of Pareto and his contemporaries.

Henderson, Lawrence J. *Pareto's general sociology: A physiologist's interpretation.* New York: Russell and Russell, 1935.

Written by the man who introduced the Harvard sociologists George C. Homans and Talcott Parsons to Pareto. Henderson finds Pareto to be a "genius" of the first rank.

Homans, George C., & Charles P. Curtis. *An introduction to Pareto: His sociology.* New York: Alfred A. Knopf, 1934.

An introduction to Pareto written by a well-known American sociologist who has consistently argued that sociology should be a positivistic science.

Meisel, J. H. *The myth of the ruling class: Gaetano Mosca and the elite.* Ann Arbor: University of Michigan Press, 1962.

Discussion of Mosca's theory of elite domination.

Meisel, J. H. (Ed.). *Pareto and Mosca.* Englewood Cliffs, NJ: Prentice-Hall, 1965.

A collection of essays discussing Pareto's and Mosca's theories of the elites.

Parsons, Talcott. *The structure of social action* (Vol. 1). New York: Free Press, 1968 [1937] (paper).

One section of this book deals with what Parsons believes is Pareto's contribution to a general theory of social action. This work was instrumental in introducing Pareto to American sociologists.

Powers, Charles H. *Vilfredo Pareto.* Beverly Hills, CA: Sage, 1987 (paper).

Powers is sympathetic toward Pareto. This is a short but useful review of Pareto's work. The author concludes that Pareto was a major social theorist who "was able to see beyond ephemeral events and actually identify major dynamics giving rise to social change."

Samuels, Warren J. *Pareto on policy.* New York: Elsevier, 1974.

An interpretation and discussion of the *Trattato.*

Tarascio, Vincent J. *Pareto's methodological approach to economics: A study in the history of some scientific aspects of scientific thought.* Chapel Hill: University of North Carolina Press, 1968.

An analysis of the Paretian methodology, with special attention to the way it was developed from economic theory.

But the function of dress as an evidence of ability to pay does not end with simply showing that the wearer consumes valuable goods in excess of what is required for physical comfort. Simple conspicuous waste of goods is effective and gratifying as far as it goes; it is good prima facie evidence of pecuniary success, and consequently prima facie evidence of social worth. But dress has subtler and more far-reaching possibilities than this crude, first-hand evidence of wasteful consumption only. If, in addition to showing that the wearer can afford to consume freely and uneconomically, it can also be shown in the same stroke that he or she is not under the necessity of earning a livelihood, the evidence of social worth is enhanced in a very considerable degree. Our dress, therefore, in order to serve its purpose effectually, should not only be expensive, but it should also make plain to all observers that the wearer is not engaged in any kind of productive labour. In the evolutionary process by which our system of dress has been elaborated into its present admirably perfect adaptation to its purpose, this subsidiary line of evidence has received due attention. A detailed examination of what passes in popular apprehension for elegant apparel will show that it is contrived at every point to convey the impression that the wearer does not habitually put forth any useful effort. It goes without saying that no apparel can be considered elegant, or even decent, if it shows the effect of manual labour on the part of the wearer, in the way of soil or wear. The pleasing effect of neat and spotless garments is chiefly, if not altogether, due to their carrying the suggestion of leisure-exemption from personal contact with industrial processes of any kind. Much of the charm that invests the patent-leather shoe, the stainless linen, the lustrous cylindrical hat, and the walking-stick, which so greatly enhance the native dignity of a gentleman, comes of their pointedly suggesting that the wearer cannot when so attired bear a hand in any employment that is directly and immediately of any human use. Elegant dress serves its purpose of elegance not only in that it is expensive, but also because it is the insignia of leisure. It not only shows that the wearer is able to consume a relatively large value, but it argues at the same time that he consumes without producing.

—Thorstein Veblen, *The Theory of the Leisure Class*

12

Thorstein Bunde Veblen

(1857–1929)

Life

Many details of Thorstein Veblen's early life remain in question. Veblen himself left no written record of his early years, and he requested of those he knew best that no biography be written after his death. Joseph Dorfman ignored Veblen's request (publishing a volume-length biography of Veblen in 1934),[1] but he tended to take anecdotes told by Veblen and treat them uncritically as factual evidence of the events of the social theorist's early years. As Rick Tilman has made clear,[2] Veblen liked to tell exaggerated stories about himself and his rural Minnesota upbringing. Therefore, much of what Dorfman reports is unreliable. For instance, Veblen told tales about how he grew up in a totally isolated, conservative Protestant, Norwegian-speaking community and encountered non-Norwegians and English-speakers only later in life. In actuality, the community he grew up in had both Norwegian immigrants and English-speaking individuals of British descent (one of whom Veblen's sister married), as well as a sizable Roman Catholic minority.

  Despite these uncertainties, we know that Veblen really was born in a log cabin on July 30, 1857, on a small farm in Cato Township on the western Wisconsin frontier. He

351

was the sixth of what was to be a family of twelve children born to a Norwegian immigrant couple. Kari Bunde and her husband, Thomas Anderson Veblen, named their fourth son Thorstein Bunde. Thomas's father had been an independent farmer in Norway who, like many others, had been deprived of his farm through shady legal maneuvers. Thomas thus grew up and first went to work as a poor tenant farmer. Because money was short, his education in Lutheran parochial schools ended when he was fourteen. During the 1847 depression, Thomas and his young wife, together with thousands of other Norwegians, left their native land to settle in the United States. Thomas's life in Wisconsin and, later, in Rice County, Minnesota (where Thorstein grew up), was thus one of pioneer self-sufficient farming. It was a life of log cabins, calfskin coats, homemade clothing, hard work, and simple entertainment. Thomas, however, differed from his fellow farmers by having less attachment to traditional farming techniques and by being ready to implement agricultural innovations. After some early difficulties and relocations, his farm prospered. Not only was Thomas able to send his children to the local school, but he also hired private tutors in Norwegian literature and grammar to instruct them in their cultural heritage.

Although he was the favorite of his mother, Thorstein was perceived to be a strange child, both by his own family and by the small community in which he grew up. As a youth in Minnesota, he was prone to fist fights; he tended to bully boys, tease girls, and humiliate adults with a relentless and piercing sarcasm. He was highly accomplished at practical jokes and at giving individuals uncomplimentary, though often highly appropriate, nicknames.

Even though he was considered odd, lazy (he preferred reading to farm work), and perhaps even antisocial, Veblen was also recognized in his home community as intellectually brilliant. Quickly mastering Norwegian grammar and etymology, young Thorstein was considered the final arbiter of the pronunciation disputes that often occurred between settlers who had come from different parts of Norway. At his Lutheran confirmation, Thorstein outdueled the church examiner on obscure points of church history and theology.

Yet even Thorstein's intellectual skills put him at odds with his fellow Minnesota Norwegians. For instance, although many of his neighbors had served in the Union Army during the Civil War, the youthful Veblen would delight in constructing elaborate pro-Confederacy arguments. Similarly, in a community where a number of individuals had died in encounters with Indians, Thorstein did not hesitate to express and argue the Indians' point of view in various land disputes.

Had Thorstein been the son of another individual, he might have remained a thorn in the side of a small parochial community. For a son of Thomas Veblen who showed intellectual abilities, however, this was not to be the case. One day, when he was seventeen years old, Thorstein Veblen was called into the house by Thomas and informed that he would find his clothing packed in a suitcase in the family carriage and that he was to leave for college at once.

Thorstein followed his brother Andrew to Carleton College. Carleton had been established in Minnesota by New England Congregational ministers in order to "civilize" the West. Its faculty included a large number of clergymen; its curricula stressed classics, religion, and moral philosophy and virtually ignored the physical sciences. All in all, the atmosphere and philosophy at Carleton were thoroughly conservative. Its faculty stressed the cultivation of aristocratic values of taste and leisure and the beliefs that private property was ordained by God and that workers' strikes violated the natural order of things.

Veblen fit into Carleton's highly conservative social climate no better than he had fit into his home community. Teachers tended to see him as odd, and other students saw him as overly intellectual and aloof. These ill feelings were mutual, as Veblen doubted the competency of his teachers and saw his fellow students as intellectually dull. Veblen also continued to develop his sarcastic sense of humor, which would later characterize his style of writing. At one point, he cornered a very religious student and lectured him for a period of hours on the need to develop a club for the promotion of suicide. Veblen also presented his required public addresses on such topics as "A Plea for Cannibalism," "The Science of Laughter," and "The Face of a Worn-Out Politician." In order to avoid detection as to whether or not he attended mandatory church services, Veblen declared himself to be a Moravian and traveled some miles every Sunday to a small German community where he taught himself the language and discussed liberal philosophies and politics.

The only Carleton faculty member who recognized Veblen's great abilities and encouraged him was the economist John Bates Clark. After five years at Carleton, Veblen informed Clark that he intended to take both his junior- and his senior-year exams together. Ignoring Clark's advice about the difficulty of such an undertaking, Veblen passed both sets of exams and, in 1881, went to Baltimore to begin graduate work at Johns Hopkins University. After a year of study and following monetary difficulties, Veblen left Johns Hopkins for Yale. At Yale, Veblen impressed the university's president, Noah Porter, and developed a close friendship with the sociologist William Graham Sumner (1840–1910). The raggedly dressed Veblen and the properly attired Sumner could often be seen in discussion together during long walks across Yale's campus.

Veblen received a Ph.D. in philosophy from Yale in 1884. Although he possessed letters of recommendation from Porter and Sumner, and held what was then still a relatively rare degree in U.S. academia, Veblen was unable to find a university teaching position. At that time, professorships in philosophy usually went to retired ministers. Unemployed, Veblen returned to his family's farm in Minnesota, where members of the community viewed him as a failure.

At home in Minnesota, Veblen claimed, to the skeptical ears of his family, that he often felt too ill to engage in farm work. Instead, he spent his days reading. In 1886, to the disapproval of her family, Veblen became engaged to Ellen Rolfe, whom he had met at Carleton (where she was the niece of the college's president). A daughter from a wealthy midwestern family, she had recently had a nervous breakdown after a short period of employment as a high school teacher. In 1888, the two were married and moved to one of her family's farms in Stacyville, Iowa. There they spent a relatively happy three years—studying Greek and Latin together and reading and discussing books like Edward Bellamy's (1850–1898) utopian socialist novel *Looking Backward.* Although they were well supported by money from Ellen Rolfe's family, Veblen still continually applied for academic teaching positions. After seven years of failed attempts, he decided to change disciplines. In 1891, he left Stacyville for Cornell in order to study economics.

When Veblen arrived at Cornell in the winter of 1891, he walked into the office of Professor of Economics A. Lawrence Laughlin, stated his name, and announced his intention of studying economics. After a brief discussion, Laughlin was sufficiently impressed with Veblen to secure him a special academic fellowship. When Laughlin was appointed head professor of economics at the new University of Chicago the following year, he took Veblen with him as a junior faculty member. Thus Veblen finally acquired a university teaching position.

At Chicago, Veblen became managing editor of the *Journal of Political Economy*, and he wrote and published his first and most famous book, *The Theory of the Leisure Class* (1899). His ironic writing style brought the book quick notoriety, but also led numerous early readers and reviewers to misinterpret the work as mainly a satire on the social activities of the wealthy. (Indeed, one commentator has written of Veblen, "It would be hard to find a writer who indulged himself more in wit, irony, paradox, dialectical rhetoric and convoluted language.")[3] Despite his stylistic peculiarities, the book was recognized as a significant social-scientific work by University of Wisconsin sociologist Edward A. Ross (1866–1951), who suggested to fellow sociologist Lester Ward (1841–1913) that Ward review it for the *American Journal of Sociology* (*AJS*). Ward's extremely positive review alerted sociologists to the significance of Veblen's work and opened up *AJS* to him as a vehicle for publishing a number of his articles. Although none of his later books achieved the notoriety of his first, Veblen was a prolific writer, who published ten more books and many articles in scholarly journals.

Despite the significant number and quality of his publications, Veblen did not get along well with university administration at Chicago and elsewhere. He later moved to Stanford University (1906), the University of Missouri (1911), and the New School for Social Research (1919). Veblen also worked during World War I for the Department of Agriculture and shortly thereafter served as an editor for the current affairs magazine *The Dial*. Veblen's troubles with university administrations probably had multiple origins; they stemmed from Veblen's self-presentation, the condition of his living quarters, his classroom presentations, and his unconcealed extramarital relationships.

Veblen was one of those rare individuals who had a complete dislike of pretentious attire and luxurious living environments. He preferred to wear work shoes ordered from mail order catalogs, and he attached his watch to his vest with a cast-off ribbon and a big safety pin. If Veblen did not dress like the proper turn-of-the-century professor, his housing differed even further from the norm of acceptability. While in California, he lived for a time in a shack of his own construction; in Missouri he lived for a period in another faculty member's basement, climbing in and out of his residence through a window.

Veblen's classroom activity also was unorthodox. Although his lectures were well-thought-out, were highly organized, and synthesized findings from a number of fields, he tended to present them in a barely audible monotone. A number of Veblen's other behaviors that, described by themselves, sound bizarre, were in fact consistent with well-thought-out opinions on higher education (which Veblen expressed in *The Higher Learning in America* [1918]). Veblen was known to make statements discouraging casual students from taking his classes by demanding to know if they had met a series of unusual prerequisites and then just shaking his head when they said they had not. This was consistent with Veblen's belief that students should not just take courses but should be concerned with learning and be self-motivated in their attempts. Veblen was also known to take roll—as required by administration rules—and then to shuffle the cards containing the names of those present with the cards of those who were not. This action was consistent with Veblen's rejection of administrative interference in the classroom and with his dislike of being an agent of coercion for university administration. Finally, Veblen was known to have discouraged students from taking exams that he scheduled and to have given whole classes a middle grade (the equivalent of the modern grade of C). This was consistent with Veblen's belief that scholarship in higher education was best accomplished on a noncompetitive basis. Indeed, when a student came to Veblen in need of a higher grade to graduate, Veblen was willing to raise it as high as necessary.

If Veblen's household, clothing, and classroom activities got him in trouble with university officials, his unhidden extramarital relationships were what most likely cost him his job at the University of Chicago. In the hypocritically puritanical atmosphere of turn-of-the-century U.S. academia, sexual affairs were generally frowned on, but also generally ignored when done "with discretion." Veblen's personal disinclination toward hypocrisy and clandestine intrigue probably cost him dearly. His position in the academic community was additionally injured when, after a number of separations and reconciliations, he and Ellen were divorced in 1911. In 1914, Veblen married Anne Bradley, a divorcée with two daughters. For reasons unknown to us, she was committed to a mental asylum five years later. For all intents and purposes, that event ended the couple's life together.

Throughout his life, Veblen saw himself as an outsider, really neither a part of the Norwegian community in which he was born, nor a part of the larger U.S. society in which he spent his adult years. He compared himself with the secularized European Jew, whom Veblen saw as fully at home neither in his culture nor in the larger society. Nonetheless, Veblen believed it was precisely his partial distance from modern U.S. society that allowed him to see various aspects of social life of which others were not aware.

Veblen died on August 3, 1929. Consistent with his lifelong dislike of ritual, he left a note requesting that his body be cremated as quickly and inexpensively as possible and that his ashes be thrown in the sea without any ceremony. He further requested that no tombstone or monument to him be constructed and that no obituary or biography of him be written.

Social Environment

Veblen's social analysis is animated by a distinction between what he saw as two fundamental classes of individuals—those whom he termed the "predatory class," who survive by manipulations, schemes, military force, and economic speculations, and those whom he termed the "industrious class," who produce the wealth (the useful goods) within society. There were numerous elements in Veblen's social environment that contributed to the creation, development, and application of this predatory/industrious distinction. These included general attitudes in his community of origin, the post–Civil War development of U.S. business, the rise of antibusiness social movements, the development of the American university, and the rise of militant imperialistic nationalism.

Many of the rural Minnesota and Wisconsin Norwegian immigrants had lost their family farms in Norway through fraud and economic manipulations. In the United States, a good number had further been taken advantage of by bankers and land speculators. Unsurprisingly, an attitude of distrust for businessmen, bankers, and speculators was widely shared in the community of Veblen's youth. Generally, these farmers equated moral uprightness with working with one's hands and living off one's own physical labor. This emphasis on self-sufficient labor contrasted sharply with the well-publicized life-styles of the robber barons (the wealthy business speculators) who had been amassing great wealth in the period of industrial expansion that followed the Civil War. Veblen grew up in a United States marked by large trusts, "holding companies," the monopolistic domination of many industries, the rise of large investment houses, the centralization of financial control, the building of large estates, the ostentatious flaunting of wealth, and the development of manipulative mass advertising and professional business managers. In general, it was a society where great wealth was being amassed not by workers, inventors, or engineers, but by speculators, middlemen, brokers, and others who were not actually engaged in the production of useful goods.

One result of such concentrations of wealth was the rise of both respectable, church-oriented liberal reform movements and more radical movements representing those who felt that they had been exploited by the new economic powers. Veblen's youth took place during a period in which midwestern agrarian populism, trade union labor movements, and socialist movements all grew in strength. Many of these movements—particularly those concerned with organizing labor—were met with widely publicized violent police actions that were ordered by business-dominated local and state governments, as well as by the actions of business-employed "goon squads."

The post–Civil War period of Veblen's youth was also the period of the development of the modern American university. As Veblen himself pointed out in his writings on higher education, at this time the American university became increasingly centralized under the control of a powerful administrator appointed by a business-dominated governing board. Because of this business influence, Veblen saw the American universities turning away from the traditional commitment to free inquiry and moving toward a business-management model of expansion, vocational training, quantification, mass production, and an authoritarian destruction of the intellectual independence of the university faculty member.

Finally, Veblen's social analysis not only is marked by social influences originating in his home community and nation, but also reveals a concern with a changing international climate. Veblen, who read a number of languages and who made numerous trips to Europe, was aware of the rising nationalism, patriotism, and imperialistic inclinations that eventually led to World War I. Veblen viewed militaristic adventurism as tied to the predatory mentality that attempts to accumulate wealth without labor and that is injurious to the well-being of society as a whole. Although concern with military conflict and the patriotic exploitation of the industrious majority of society can be seen in his earliest book (*The Theory of the Leisure Class*), it became much more manifest and central to the social analysis involved in Veblen's later major works (*Imperial Germany and the Industrial Revolution* [1915] and *An Inquiry into the Nature of Peace* [1917]).

Intellectual Roots

It is hard to be sure who influenced Veblen. Veblen was not given to autobiographical accounts of the origins of his thoughts; he used citations sparingly; he referred to intellectual disagreements much more often than to intellectual indebtedness; and he did not use others' ideas and concepts without reshaping them to fit his own overall system of thought and the explanatory purpose at hand. Tracing Veblen's intellectual roots is difficult also because Veblen often fused together ideas of individuals from widely different fields and of scholars whose theories are often thought to be in opposition to one another. Thus, within the complex of Veblen's thought, one finds the influence of the philosophers Immanuel Kant (1724–1804), Charles Peirce (1839–1914), John Dewey (1859–1952), and William James (1842–1910); the economists Gustav von Schmoller (1838–1917) and Werner Sombart (1863–1941); the biologists Charles Darwin (1809–1882), Peter Kropotkin (1842–1921), and Jacques Loeb (1859–1924); the anthropologists Lewis Henry Morgan (1818–1881) and E. B. Tylor (1832–1917); the sociologists Auguste Comte, Herbert Spencer, and William Graham Sumner; and the novelist Edward Bellamy. Veblen's work also was influenced by the thought of Karl Marx.

Kant's philosophy was not taught at Carleton during Veblen's stay there; Veblen encountered Kant's writings at that time in the private library of a German immigrant named Pentz. Veblen was most attracted to Kant's conception of knowledge and Kant's concern with the study of peace. Veblen accepted the German philosopher's contention that knowledge of the external world is not directly perceived, but is filtered and shaped by the categories of the mind. Whereas Kant insisted that these categories were *a priori* givens, much of Veblen's work was an attempt to establish the historical and evolutionary socioeconomic activities that influenced the development of mental categories. Additionally, Veblen was influenced by Kant's concern with "peace" as a scholarly problem. Veblen openly borrowed his title *An Inquiry into the Nature of Peace and the Terms of Its Perpetuation* from Kant, and prefaced the book by comparing his work with that of the German philosopher 122 years earlier. Veblen combined his Kantian concerns with a selective influence of the American pragmatic philosophers Peirce, Dewey, and James. Of the three, Peirce, with whom Veblen studied while at Johns Hopkins, had the greatest influence on Veblen's thought. Of particular importance to his theorizing were Peirce's notions that human thought is directed by "guiding principles" of inference and that knowledge is gained through a process involving "musement." Veblen built on Peirce's notion of "guiding principles" to develop his own belief that humans interpret the world according to certain biographically and historically shaped "habits of the mind." Veblen used the notion of musement as the foundation of his own concept of "idle curiosity." According to Veblen, it is idle curiosity that has led to the great scientific breakthroughs that have made modern industrial society possible. In his book on higher education,[4] Veblen defends idle curiosity's place in the university and opposes a mentality that would subordinate research to immediate "practical" ends. (See the section "Methodology.")

Veblen's emphasis on historical analysis in the understanding of social actions is a rejection of atemporal conceptions of human nature in mainstream American economics. In this, Veblen was influenced by the German historical school of economic thought of von Schmoller and Sombart. Essentially, this school emphasized the priority of studying the historical development of economic institutions and motivations over developing abstract mathematical models that assume a constancy in social-institutional and human social-psychological makeup.

The emphasis on historical causality in Veblen's work also involves a view of modern science that Veblen saw exemplified in and diffused by the writings of Charles Darwin. For Veblen, Darwin's *Origin of Species* (1859) showed the world to be the result of a series of environmentally influenced causal changes without internal purpose, destiny, or origins. Although he found Darwin's work highly significant for the logic of modern social science, Veblen did not become a "social Darwinist." Perhaps because of the influence of Peter Kropotkin's *Mutual Aid* (1902), Veblen stressed the role of cooperation over competition and conflict in the long-run achievements of a society. His emphasis on cooperation reveals the influence on Veblen's thought of a third biologist, Jacques Loeb (1859–1924). Loeb, a colleague of Veblen's at Stanford, developed a theory of underlying instinctual inclinations that Veblen modified to account for what he believed was the human propensity to be cooperative, creative, and productive.

Overall, Veblen viewed historical causation as involving an evolutionary development of society. Veblen's earliest acceptance of a social evolutionary position was inspired by reading the writings of Spencer in Pentz's library. Even in later years, when his own social and political positions were in large part in direct opposition to those of the English sociologist, Veblen went out of his way to acknowledge his debt to Spencer. Along with Spencer's ideas, Veblen's evolutionary approach appears to have incorporated elements from the writings of the U.S. anthropologist Morgan and the French sociologist Comte. Veblen uses Morgan's terms—"savagery," "barbarianism," and "civilization"—to denote the three basic forms or types of society. Despite some differences in use and social classification, Veblen, like Morgan, uses "savagery" to denote the most simple and peaceful form of society, "barbarianism" to denote a warlike conquest-oriented society, and "civilization" to denote a society that is more peaceful and more economically developed than the barbarian form.

Paralleling social evolutionary change, Veblen saw an evolutionary development in terms of how individuals conceptualize external reality. Despite differences in terminology, Veblen's views on the development of the mind reveal a marked resemblance to those previously developed by Comte. Comte's three basic stages of mental development are the "theological," the "metaphysical," and the "positive" (or the "scientific"); Veblen's are the "animistic," the "pragmatic," and the "matter-of-fact." Both the *theological* and the *animistic* stages involve a view of the world where the mind interprets external activity as necessarily perpetuated by spirits (gods, demons, or ghosts) with humanlike motivations, desires, and feelings. Both the *metaphysical* and the *pragmatic* stages involve a conception of external reality in terms of its possessing internal, necessary, and teleological (goal-oriented) activity. And both the *positivistic* and *matter-of-fact* stages entail the use of an empirical conception of causation in the external world.

In accounting for the development and change of human mental abilities in the course of social evolution, Veblen appears indebted, among others, to the sociologist Sumner and the anthropologist Tylor. From Sumner, Veblen borrowed a conception of habits that are based on material activity. Veblen asserted that in the long run, as general patterns of work activities change, so should mental habits of thought. Veblen, however, used Tylor's notion of "survivals" to account for those cases in which older habits persisted despite changes in the overall patterns of social activity. From Tylor, Veblen also seems to have developed a conception of social evolutionary change as involving a "cultural" change that should be seen as independent from any underlying bioorganic evolution. Thus, unlike the Lamarckian Spencer, Veblen held that social patterns and habits could change drastically while biological makeup remained relatively constant.

Finally, in attempting to account for the intellectual roots underlying Veblen's persistent critique of capitalist economic and social forms and the socialistic elements that run through some of his works, one can point to the writings of Bellamy and Marx. Bellamy was an American writer whose utopian socialistic novel *Looking Backward* was widely read and discussed. After reading this work, Veblen's first wife questioned her upper-middle-class Republican background and became an advocate of socialism. Its long-run influence on Veblen is unclear. Also difficult to assess is the influence of the writings of Karl Marx on Veblen. Where Veblen explicitly addressed Marx's writings, he is critical of Hegelian and utilitarian elements that he saw underlying Marx's thought. On the other hand, Veblen's materialism, his belief in a two-class system, his critique of the wastefulness of capitalist production, and his view of long-run internal problems generated by capitalism were most likely strongly influenced by the work of the German scholar and revolutionary.

IDEAS

Society

Veblen's definition of a society is ultimately grounded in a materialistic focus on labor activity. According to Veblen, any particular type of productive labor that characterizes a group of people will produce a repeated occurrence of particular activities by the members of that group. Such repetitious activity will, in turn, produce typical ways of thinking and feeling about oneself, other people, and the world in general. Thus any persistent labor activity will result in characteristic habitual ways of thinking and feeling—what Veblen termed "habits of the mind." Veblen's reference to cognitive and emotive forms as "habit" was meant to convey three basic ideas:

1. They occur without rational reflection (they are assumed and not questioned in the course of such reflection).
2. They appear to be in congruity with, and, in fact, form the basis of, commonsense understanding among the people in question.
3. They are resistant to change and tend to persist for a time even after the material conditions (forms of labor activity) that gave rise to them have disappeared.

Veblen believed that habits of the mind are not mentally stored in a random or haphazard way but, rather, in consistency with the overall adaptive nature of human mental abilities; furthermore, they are organized around a people's particular, usual, and typical activities. They thus come to support, cognitively and emotionally, typical ways of behaving and oppose violations of the usual. In other words, a people's habits of the mind form the basis of cultural norms. Thus culturally normative views of what is acceptable and unacceptable are grounded in mental habits that have emerged from repetitive productive activity. Once cultural norms emerge, they both form the basic common stock of knowledge of a people and are strengthened as they are passed down to later generations through socialization. Rather than appearing as materially based products to the people who conform to them, cultural norms seem to be the ultimate criteria of right and wrong. Thus what begin as usual forms of activity become culturally mandatory:

> Under the discipline of habituation this logic and apparatus of ways and means falls into conventional lines, acquires the consistency of custom and prescription, and so takes on

an institutional character and force. The accustomed ways of doing and thinking not only become a habitual matter of course, easy and obvious, but they come likewise to be sanctioned by social convention, and so become right and proper and give rise to principles of conduct. By use and wont they are incorporated in the current scheme of common sense. As elements of the approved scheme of conduct and pursuit these conventional ways and means take their place as proximate ends of endeavor. Whence, in the further course of unremitting habituation, as the attention is habitually focused on these proximate ends, they occupy the interest to such an extent as commonly to throw their own ulterior purpose into the background and often let it be lost sight of; as may happen, for instance, in the acquisition and use of money. It follows that in much of human conduct these proximate ends alone are present in consciousness as the object of interest and the goal of endeavour, and certain conventionally accepted ways and means come to be set up as definitive principles of what is right and good; while the ulterior purpose of it all is only called to mind occasionally, if at all, as an afterthought, by an effort of reflection.[5]

Veblen termed a mutually supportive complex of cultural norms formed around a perceived significant and related set of activities an *institution*. He thought of a society as that which emerged from the sum total of institutions of a particular people. Thus, for Veblen, a *society* is ultimately *grounded in material activity*, although it is more directly a *product of institutions based on cultural norms*, which can vary (at least to a degree), despite a constancy of a material set of circumstances. Nonetheless, Veblen held that the material basis of a society is such that given a major change in the makeup of productive activity one should expect a major change in the institutions of a society.

Veblen thus presented an evolutionary conception of society that is based on changes in material forms of production. As the material conditions of life change, society develops through three basic stages—*savagery*, *barbarianism*, and *civilization*. Each of these stages is divided into earlier (formative) and later (more developed) periods. Within each stage (or period), Veblen posited that there will be a fundamental distinction between two classes of persons, which he termed, respectively, the industrious class and the predatory class. Although the particular form that these classes will take will vary in terms of the stage of a society's social evolutionary development, Veblen drew a consistent distinction between these two classes of people. The *industrious class* includes that portion of a population that engages in productive activity. Such activity includes manual craft labor, machine-aided labor, engineering work, and the technical organization of labor. The industrious class creates the actual wealth of a society, and its actions serve as the impetus for further social evolutionary change. The *predatory class*, on the other hand, is the class of individuals that disdains and avoids actual productive labor and survives by a predatory exploitation of the wealth produced by members of the industrious class. Veblen viewed the predatory class as an essentially cultural, political, and economical conservative force in society, which inhibited or restrained evolutionary progress. The industrious class usually forms the bulk of society's population, whereas the predatory class forms a numerically smaller, privileged upper class.

Veblen conceptualized *savage* society as originally involving small independent and self-sufficient hunting and gathering communities. Over time, a limited degree of domestication of plants and animals developed. Savage society was essentially a peaceable, relatively isolated, stable society. Within savage society, there was little specialization or division of labor; general knowledge of how to produce the necessities of life was shared by all. What division of labor there was occurred between men and women. According to Veblen, men were the hunters, whereas women engaged in the gathering of roots and herbs. Later in this stage of development, women worked at planting crops and tending to animals. Labor in savage society was cooperative; in the absence of private property, there was no bartering of goods, hiring of others, or accumulating of wealth. Instead, assistance between individuals was reciprocal. Religion within savage society tended to be animistic; deities were conceived of as nurturing female "mother" gods.

Savage society is thus, at first, a society that lacks strong distinction between predatory and industrious classes. Over time, however, Veblen asserted, such a distinction began to emerge. The adult males, whose hunting activities actually contributed relatively little to the wealth of the society, began to assert a claim to the right of special privileges at the expense of children and females. It was thus women, whose gathering, planting, and herding actually maintained the well-being of the society, who came to be the first industrious class. This earliest division into predatory and industrious classes began to mark the passage of savage society and the rise of the "barbarian" societal form.

Veblen's formulation of *barbarian* society involved both the agricultural slave societies of the ancient Middle East and Asia and the feudal societies that developed in Europe and Asia. The former belong to an earlier period of barbarianism; the latter represent its most developed form. Veblen saw barbarianism as differing from savagery through a systematic and expanded cultivation of land and an increase in the herding of animals. The resultant increase in food production allowed an increase in specialization and the division of labor, with some individuals engaged in nonagricultural craft production. Accordingly, there arose a surplus of wealth beyond that which was necessary for the bare survival of the society. Thus occurred the possibility of the rise of private property and the accumulation of wealth by a predatory class. Under barbarianism this predatory class is formed by either a single military-priestly group or by separate, though mutually supportive, military and priestly groups. Marked by such a predatory class, barbarian society becomes an extremely hierarchical, conservative, war-oriented, religious-dominated society. Forms of thought and styles of dress, architecture, art, and the like indicate a strong militaristic influence. Religion stresses a supernatural hierarchy dominated by an aggressive, powerful male god or gods and represented by a secretive, dogmatic, and authoritarian priesthood. Meanwhile, the bulk of the population, which is predominantly engaged in agricultural production, maintains itself at a subsistence level.

Veblen's final stage of *civilization* (which he more frequently referred to as "modern civilization" or "modern society") began in the West in the nineteenth century with the industrial revolution. It emerged out of an increase in handicraft production late in the barbarian (feudal) period. The handicraft era involved the improvement of roads and communications, the growth of the population, the development of a mechanical technology, and an increase in the concentration of ownership. The modern civilization (or society) to which this period gave rise is characterized by rational, instrumental, nonsupernatural, matter-of-fact forms of thought and activity. It manifests highly developed machine-factory technology, a well-developed division of labor, increased coordination of the various spheres of life, mass production, and an increased interchangeability of parts.

In terms of modern society, Veblen equated the predatory class with the *business class*. This includes all those persons who make their livelihood through financial deals, speculation, dominating markets, middleman positions, and all other forms of competitive capitalist profit making. Veblen argued that the business class is a predatory class because its members do not produce anything of benefit to the well-being of society as a whole, but merely attempt, through competitive manipulations, to acquire as much personal wealth as possible. He asserted that the actual wealth in modern society is created by the workers, engineers, and technicians who form the society's industrious class. The workers actually produce the wealth of modern society; the engineers and technicians supply the necessary coordination and improvement of productive techniques. On the other hand, Veblen maintained that the predatory business class adds nothing to production. Veblen viewed the capitalist class as the *beneficiary*, not the giver, of work. Instead, in attempting to gain personal profit, it attempts to manipulate markets. This results in an underutilization of machinery and the unemployment of workers, which actually interfere with a smoothly coordinated running of an advanced industrial society.

The Individual in Society

Veblen came to economics after having read widely in sociology, anthropology, and psychology and after having received a doctorate in philosophy. In the light of his prior reading and philosophical training, he found unacceptable the simplistic hedonistic psychology that was taken for granted by mainstream American economic thought. Veblen asserted that a society could not persist if the average person was predominantly characterized by a self-centered, asocial, acquisitive nature. He believed that such characteristics were to be found only in the numerically small, conservative, antiprogressive, and nonproductive predatory class. In contrast to dominant economic opinion, Veblen developed an image of the typical individual as characterized by underlying socially oriented inclinations. He termed such inclinations or propensities "instincts."

In his use of the term "instinct," Veblen *did not* mean simple, noncognitive, immediate stimulus reactions, which he termed "tropisms." "Instinct," instead, was used to refer to a particular species' innate proclivity to act toward some particular adaptive state or goal. According to Veblen, each instinct is characterized by a particular purpose, end, or endeavor that contributes to individual and species survival. In humans, rather than acting in an automatic, mechanistic manner, instincts are accompanied by the conscious pursuit of objectives. They serve as the underlying impulse to achieve particular ends. Veblen argued that any actual empirical human activity will be mediated or guided by cultural and institutional norms and by the knowledge and intelligence of the individual. Thus instincts are not immediately translatable into particular actions in a deterministic fashion but, instead, are carried out in terms of reflection in the context of culturally acquired norms and socially evolved habits of the mind. Veblen believed that the more evolutionarily advanced a society is, the greater the degree of mediation between instinct and activity, and the greater the number of various ways in which an instinctual goal could be accomplished:

As the expression is here understood, all instinctive action is intelligent in some degree;
though the degree in which intelligence is engaged may vary widely from one instinctive
disposition to another, and it may even fall into an extremely automatic shape in the case
of some of the simpler instincts, whose functional content is of a patently physiological
character. Such approach to automatism is even more evident in some of the lower animals, where, as for instance in the case of some insects, the response to the appropriate
stimuli is so far uniform and mechanically determinant as to leave it doubtful whether the
behaviour of the animal might not best be construed as tropismatic action simply. Such
tropismatic directness of instinctive response is less characteristic of man even in the case
of the simpler instinctive proclivities; and the indirection which so characterizes instinctive action in general, and the higher instincts of man in particular, and which marks off
the instinctive dispositions from the tropisms, is the indirection of intelligence. It enters
more largely in the discharge of some proclivities than of others; but all instinctive action
is intelligent in some degree.[6]

Although Veblen was openly hostile to Hegel's philosophy, his emphasis on increased mental meditation does parallel Hegel's position of social development yielding an increase in reflection and self-conscious action. For Veblen, as for Hegel and
Marx, such an increase in self-conscious reflection allowed the formation of a critical
theoretical perspective toward one's own society and the ability to perceive wasteful
and historically passing modes of activity, the understanding of which previously had
been obscured.

Yet Veblen also admitted the possibility that although an individual might be conscious of immediate goals, he or she might be unaware of the underlying instinctual inclinations that the immediate activities fulfill. In other words, one might have in mind
certain reasons for which one is going about a particular activity, but still be relatively
ignorant about the underlying instinctual drive that promotes that particular kind of
activity and determines the activity's long-run adaptive value. Moreover, any concrete action is likely to have been influenced by a multiplicity of underlying instincts.
These may interact or influence one another in a number of different ways: instincts
can combine, overlap, reinforce, or neutralize one another's influence.

Veblen held that, despite some degree of racial and intraracial variation, human
beings, overall, tended to share a relatively similar set of underlying instinctual inclinations. These were ultimately hereditary in nature and developed through biological
evolution in the longest and earliest state of society—that of savagery. The three most
important (that is, adaptive) instincts that Veblen ascribed to humanity he termed the
instinct of workmanship, the *instinct of parenting* (or the "parental bent"), and the *instinct
of idle curiosity*.

After making reference to the great significance of the instinct of workmanship in
socioeconomic evolution in *The Theory of the Leisure Class*, Veblen spent a number of
years developing a book that would further explain and elaborate on that instinct. *The
Instinct of Workmanship* was published in 1914. Veblen presented the instinct of *workmanship* as the most important instinct for collective well-being. As opposed to other,
more focused instincts, that of workmanship is the most general. It is essentially an
underlying creative impulse—a drive to manipulate the world creatively with productive labor. Veblen maintained that its supreme importance lies in the fact that it is the
instinct that facilitates the achievement of all the other adaptive instinctual drives. Its
ends or goals are thus the survival of the human species. The instinct of workmanship

serves as a general drive for the achievement of goals that maintain life and permit social advance. For Veblen, as in the critical theories of Marx and Hegel, labor serves both
adaptation and the self-creation of categories of thought through which the world is
understood, reflected on, and eventually changed.

The only other instinct whose importance for society is close to that of workmanship is that of *parenting*, or what Veblen more usually termed the *parental bent*. Although the protection of children would come under this drive, Veblen in fact saw it as
a more inclusive force in society. Veblen held that the parental bent was the underlying drive that led to a concern with the well-being of others and an identification with
and concern for the community in which one exists. It underlies altruistic and self-
sacrificing behavior when the individual acts to preserve or advance the existence of
the social group, even at the possible expense of his or her own well-being. (It is precisely Veblen's writings on the parental bent that put him in opposition to the positivistic hedonistic psychologies then—and now—current in American economic
thought.) This instinct was extremely important to Veblen in his studies of war and
peace. Veblen argued that feelings of patriotic identification with a nation-state and
patriotically inspired action involve a predatory class-based manipulation of the
parental bent's drive to sacrifice for the community.

The third major instinct about which Veblen wrote was the instinct of *idle curiosity*. He referred to it as a persistent human instinct that leads to the development of systematic knowledge. In essence, idle curiosity involves an insatiable desire for
knowledge apart from any ulterior end and independent of any pragmatic or utilitarian motive. This human drive for knowledge leads to a constant disturbance of the habitual body of knowledge in any society. Thus, though "idle" (nonutilitarian) in origin,
the instinct leads to an advance in knowledge, which provides the basis for technological improvement that ultimately underlies social evolutionary development. In
The Higher Learning in America, Veblen defended the independence of university faculty members from immediate applied or vocational endeavors forced on them by
university administration. He did so by arguing that, by following the instinct of idle
curiosity, the scholar will produce more of benefit for society in the long run than by
any other approach. Again, as with Hegel and Marx, true knowledge arises from an internal drive, and the passion for knowledge is undermined when it is made subservient
to external instrumental logic.

Thus Veblen rejected the principle that humans are basically asocial or self-centered beings. In the course of biological evolution, in the long stage of savagery, humans
developed basic instinctual drives to create, to identify with and to benefit others, and
to accumulate knowledge that provides for technological and social advance. Veblen
maintained that these instincts, mediated by cultural norms and conscious intelligence, provide the foundation for both social organization and social evolution.

Methodology

Veblen's explanations of social phenomena were always evolutionary in nature. He wrote
a number of essays (incorporated in *The Place of Science in Modern Civilization* [1919])
stating that social science must necessarily use an evolutionary form of explanation.
Throughout his work, Veblen would begin his accounts of particular social forms and activities by ascribing them to a particular period in either the "savage," the "barbarian,"

or the "civilized" form of society and relating them to other activities, practices, and "habits of the mind" within that period. Thus, for example, in *The Theory of the Leisure Class*, the full development of a "leisure class"—with its emphasis on honor, etiquette, and military prowess, and its complete disdain for manual and useful labor—is presented as a natural development of the later barbarian (that is, feudal) stage of society.

Veblen's use of evolutionary explanation incorporated Tylor's notion of survivals. *Survivals*, as developed by Tylor and used by Veblen, are those social forms, activities, and ways of thinking that belong to an earlier period of evolutionary development, but which persist beyond the evolutionary conditions that give rise to them. Veblen assumed that, despite their causal significance for people's actions, survivals removed from the forms of material activity that gave rise to them can persist for a limited period of time and thus are destined to disappear. Veblen believed that one of the more significant survivals in modern society is that of the competitive capitalist businessman. Veblen asserted that this personality type was a product of an earlier period of Western civilization (the eighteenth-century industrial revolution) that persisted despite the evolutionary development of an advanced industrial society with which this personality type was incompatible. Accordingly, Veblen argued, the days of the capitalist were numbered; he insisted that the modern businessman type would be replaced by economic coordinators of a new kind.

Veblen argued that typologizing social phenomena in terms of the evolutionary periods in which they developed and were most manifest was necessary but not sufficient for complete social scientific explanation. Rather, Veblen insisted that such explanation must also be "genetic" in nature. By *genetic*, Veblen was emphasizing an approach in which one focuses on the evolutionary sequence (or genesis) of phenomena that led to the phenomenon one wishes to explain. Thus, for example, Veblen accounted for modern scientific thought not simply as an attribute of modern society, but as the outcome of a complex series of evolutionary developments in the industrial revolution, which in turn produced a form of matter-of-fact knowledge from which modern science arose.

Veblen held that, in order to meet the canons of modern science, these genetic evolutionary explanations had to be *materialistic* in form. Veblen argued that he was not a "metaphysical" or "dogmatic materialist" who believed that reality was ultimately reducible to the movement of atoms and molecules. Rather, he claimed to be a "methodological materialist," who saw material assumptions as useful for the development of valid scientific explanations. To return to the example just given, Veblen developed an explanation of the social origins of modern science essentially by the discovery of a series of "genetic" occurrences that were ultimately grounded in change in the material conditions of life—the movement from agricultural to handicraft to industrial productive activities. It is in terms of habits of the mind produced by industrial activity that Veblen accounted for the decline of the dominance of prescientific knowledge and the rise of modern science.

Another good example of Veblen's use of materialistic explanation is his account of the rise of "primitive violence" out of an earlier, more peaceful society due to industrial changes yielding an increase in the number of material goods:

> The substantial difference between the peaceable and the predatory phase of culture, therefore, is a spiritual difference, not a mechanical one. The change in spiritual attitude is the outgrowth of a change in the material facts of the life of the group, and it comes on

gradually as the material circumstances favourable to a predatory attitude supervene. The inferior limit of the predatory culture is an industrial limit. Predation cannot become the habitual, conversational resource of any group or any class until industrial methods have been developed to such a degree of efficiency as to leave a margin worth fighting for, above the subsistence of those engaged in getting a living. The transition from peace to predation therefore depends on the growth of technical knowledge and the use of tools. A predatory culture is similarly impracticable in early times, until weapons have been developed to such a point as to make man a formidable animal.[7]

Veblen termed his overall methodological approach "materialistic continuous causation." It was *materialist* in the sense that social explanation was based on changes in productive activity, *continuous* in the sense of looking at the development of the social phenomenon in question without reference to its ultimate origin or destiny, and *causative* in the sense of seeing social phenomena as arising from earlier phenomena and giving rise to later ones.

Despite his dedication to a materialistic form of explanation, Veblen opposed a simple mechanistic materialism that ignored humans' subjective feelings, thoughts, wishes, and beliefs. He argued that in social scientific inquiry, it was absolutely necessary to focus on both the content and changes in popular feeling and thought. For example, in *The Nature of Peace*, Veblen not only looked at the genetic evolution of material conditions that gave rise to modern warfare, but also analyzed the various meanings that *patriotism* had for individuals in modern society. Veblen asserted that it was only by analyzing the relationship between material causes and subjective states concerning warfare that social science might help discover what were the necessary and sufficient conditions for a peaceful world order.

In the development of his analysis of both material causes and subjective states, Veblen used an approach similar to Weber's ideal-type analysis. (Indeed, Veblen even used the term "institutional ideal" in *The Higher Learning in America,* when he developed a statement of the characteristics that were typical or essential to the makeup of a modern university.) Aware that he could not focus on every particular case in social scientific analysis, Veblen attempted to formulate a conception of the social phenomenon at hand in terms of its most necessary and typical features and its most complete evolutionary development. In the course of analysis, he could then focus on how the social phenomenon under investigation developed in particular concrete situations, what caused it to tend to vary from the ideal type, and what future occurrences the particular phenomenon itself tended to cause. For example, in *Imperial Germany and the Industrial Revolution* and *The Nature of Peace*, Veblen developed the ideal type of the "dynastic state." In doing so, he portrayed the dynastic state's most usual institutional and social-psychological features (traditional hierarchical organization and a willing identification and subservience of underlying populations), its manifestation in two historical cases (Germany and Japan), and what he believed to be a causal outcome of its existence (a militant aggressive nationalism resulting in war).

Again like Weber, Veblen stressed the use of historical comparisons. A good example can be found in *Imperial Germany and the Industrial Revolution*. In an attempt to explain why the industrial revolution resulted in the rise of a dynastic state in Germany, Veblen compared the historical development of Great Britain and Germany before, during, and after the industrial revolution. His comparisons focused both on material causes and subjective social-psychological states, and on the different international contexts of the two societies. He then referred to differences in history and context to explain why one society developed differently from the other.

Throughout his work, Veblen used cultural anthropological and archaeological data together with historical comparisons. His anthropological references were often presented as illustrations of particular types of social activity at particular stages of social development. They were used by Veblen to infer the makeup of a society in periods prior to its written history. Thus, in *The Theory of the Leisure Class* and elsewhere, anthropological evidence was used to support the contention that peaceful savage societies preceded barbaric and feudal societies. Veblen used archaeological data in a similar manner. He most frequently referred to Scandinavian and Baltic archaeological evidence, in which he was a self-trained expert.

Thus, overall, Veblen used historical comparisons, ideal types, and archaeological and anthropological data to develop *evolutionary, genetic, materialistic,* and *causal* explanations. Veblen's methodology endeavored to account for why and how particular social forms arose and for their significance both in terms of the types of personalities that developed in the particular social form and in terms of probable future social occurrences. Although Veblen's overall approach is positivistic in its emphasis on materialistic causality, it is also hermeneutical and historical in orientation.

Other Major Themes and Foci

Veblen was a prolific writer whose intellectual concerns cut across the social sciences and touched on many topics. Three of his concerns, which are of particular interest to the student of sociology, involve Veblen's focus on the symbolic representation of social class, the social position of women, and modernization theory.

The Symbolic Representation of Social Class

In order publicly to demonstrate, maintain, and receive the advantages of upper-(predatory) class status, members of that class have throughout history developed ways of symbolically communicating their superior social position to one another and to the rest of society. Veblen's unique contribution to social science was his critical analysis of the means by which status is symbolically formulated and communicated in society. This analysis formed the central theme of *The Theory of the Leisure Class,* in which Veblen developed four of his most important concepts: *conspicuous leisure, conspicuous consumption, conspicuous waste,* and the *leisure class.*

For Veblen, as mentioned earlier, upper-class status involved a predatory disinclination and disdain for industrious, productive, or socially beneficial labor. Leisure (the pursuit of nonproductive activities) thus comes to signify a degree of higher-class status. In order to convey upper-class status, however, one would need certain mechanisms or techniques that would communicate to others that one spends one's time in the pursuit of nonproductive leisure activities. Over time, these mechanisms or techniques of "conspicuous leisure" come to signify status and to represent the canons of upper-class taste or style. An example of conspicuous leisure includes the growth of extremely long fingernails by members of the traditional Chinese upper class, symbolically communicating that the growers do not participate in any physical labor that would break such nails. Another example would be the elaborate hair styles and frilly silk clothing of the eighteenth-century French aristocracy. Again, such styles, which would be incompatible with any rigorous form of labor, thus signify their wearers' removal from hard work. Other mechanisms of conspicuous leisure would include the demonstration of a knowledge of complex rules of etiquette, useless ancient languages, the proper rules of polo, and the like. All of these would reveal that the individual has invested a large portion of his or her time in the "leisurely" mastering of productively useless activities and thus has a claim to a degree of higher-class status.

Another mechanism or technique for symbolically communicating upper-class status, rather than being based on the conspicuous waste (that is, nonproductive use) of time, would be the public (or conspicuous) waste of wealth. Veblen termed this second mechanism "conspicuous consumption." He argued that, as the upper predatory class has been throughout history a consuming class, the wasteful consumption of wealth (that is, consumable goods) comes to be a symbol of high status. Thus the public display and consumption of expensive items become a sign of the possession of high status. Examples of conspicuous consumption would involve the erection of a mansion larger than anyone would need for comfortable housing, the wearing of current (high-priced) fashions, and the owning of exotic and expensive pets.

Veblen maintained that conspicuous leisure and conspicuous consumption are related to each other; the knowledge of how to consume conspicuously often depends on the use of conspicuous leisure. For example, the conspicuous consumption of the latest fashions involves conspicuous leisure (the spending of time) in order to know what the latest fashions are, when they change, and what they will become. In fact, Veblen asserted that conspicuous leisure and conspicuous consumption are two forms of the same social phenomenon, "conspicuous waste," for both involve the socially nonproductive waste of time and effort. Veblen believed that whether conspicuous leisure or conspicuous consumption would predominate in any particular society would depend on that society's level of social evolutionary development. In simpler and smaller societies that lack great amounts of excess (wastable) wealth and in which everyone knows the activities (at least by reputation) of almost everyone else, conspicuous leisure would predominate. On the other hand, in more advanced, larger societies, where both the amount of wealth and social anonymity have increased, conspicuous consumption would be the main means of demonstrating status:

> From the foregoing survey of the growth of conspicuous leisure and consumption, it appears that the utility of both alike for the purposes of reputability lies in the element of waste that is common to both. In the one case it is a waste of time and effort, in the other it is a waste of goods. Both are methods of demonstrating the possession of wealth, and the two are conventionally accepted as equivalents. The choice between them is a question of advertising expediency simply, except so far as it may be affected by other standards of propriety, springing from a different source. On grounds of expediency the preference may be given to the one or the other at different stages of the economic development. The question is, which of the two methods will most effectively reach the persons whose convictions it is desired to affect. Usage has answered this question in different ways under different circumstances.
>
> So long as the community or social group is small enough and compact enough to be effectually reached by common notoriety alone—that is to say, so long as the human environment to which the individual is required to adapt himself in respect of reputability is comprised within his sphere of personal acquaintance and neighbourhood gossip—so long

the one method is about as effective as the other. Each will therefore serve about equally well during the earlier stages of social growth. But when the differentiation has gone farther and it becomes necessary to reach a wider human environment, consumption begins to hold over leisure as an ordinary means of decency. This is especially true during the later, peaceable economic stage. The means of communication and the mobility of the population now expose the individual to the observation of many persons who have no other means of judging of his reputability than the display of goods (and perhaps of breeding) which he is able to make while he is under their direct observation.[8]

Veblen concluded that much of what is widely considered to be style or fashion in society is, in fact, the attempt by those of lower status to copy the consumption patterns of higher-status individuals in order to increase their own social status. Such emulation continues the domination by the upper predatory classes. Veblen held that only when the waste of the predatory classes was seen critically in terms of its actual antisocial nature (as opposed to being perceived as prestigious) could social exploitation be terminated.

The Social Position of Women

Veblen asserted that, in the course of social evolution, the first systematic form of exploitation and domination was the domination of women by men. He argued that, in the transitional period from savage society to barbarianism, women formed the first industrious class, which was exploited by a predatory class composed of adult males. Women did most of the gathering, herding, planting, harvesting, child-raising, and domestic chores necessary to the well-being of society, whereas men engaged in hunting (and later in warfare), which added relatively less to collective well-being. Simultaneously, the men claimed the right to social and ritualistic prerogatives that were denied to women.

Veblen argued that in the course of social evolutionary change, the form of the exploitation of women changed from the direct exploitation of women as an industrious class to exploitation through what Veblen termed "vicarious conspicuous waste" (with subforms of "vicarious conspicuous leisure" and "vicarious conspicuous consumption"). *Vicarious conspicuous waste* involves the removal of women from types of productive labor in order to enhance the status of men.

According to Veblen, as social wealth increased over time, the men at the very highest level began using others—especially their wives and daughters—in order to display vicarious conspicuous waste. Vicarious conspicuous waste is conspicuous leisure or conspicuous consumption done by one person that benefits the status of another. Thus a higher-class male removes his wife and daughters from productive labor and adorns them with expensive garments in order to demonstrate that he is a high-status, powerful person. An extreme version of vicarious conspicuous waste, in the barbarian period, was the binding of the feet of female members of the Chinese aristocracy. Veblen asserted that this practice was used originally to demonstrate that a male was of such high status that he could support a wife who was physically incapable of productive labor.

Over time, the practice of vicarious conspicuous waste was imitated by other men to enhance their status. Thus the removal of women from productive labor became a sign of male status throughout the society. Attached to the spread of this practice was a change in the ideal of feminine beauty. For status enhancement, males fostered a conception of womanly beauty that was characterized by a frail, pale appearance, symbolizing a person incapable of hard work. Women's styles of clothing demonstrated that they did not engage in labor, emphasized designs that constrained movement, and used fabrics that were impractical for work. Of course, not all males were wealthy enough to support women who were completely removed from labor. Rather than remove women from all labor, males, when economically capable, endeavored to remove women from all *publicly visible labor:*

> The basis of the award of social rank and popular respect is the success, or more precisely the efficiency, of the social unit, as evidenced by its visible success. When efficiency eventuates in possessions, in pecuniary strength, as it eminently does in the social system of our time, the basis of the award of social consideration becomes the visible pecuniary strength of the social unit. The immediate and obvious index of pecuniary strength is the visible ability to spend, to consume unproductively; and men early learned to put in evidence their ability to spend by displaying costly goods that afford no return to their owner, either in comfort or in gain. Almost as early did a differentiation set in, whereby it became the function of woman, in a peculiar degree, to exhibit the pecuniary strength of her social unit by means of a conspicuously unproductive consumption of valuable goods.[9]

Thus began a pattern of job discrimination against women and the perpetuation of myths denying that women have the capacity to undertake work outside the home.

Veblen concluded that, in the course of social evolution, the domination of women moved from a period in which they did most of the productive labor to one in which they were removed from many areas of employment and denied the basic human drive of creative labor (what Veblen termed the "instinct of workmanship"). Veblen believed that, in the future, women's movements would emphasize a striving for the right to equal employment and would attempt to end a form of exploitive domination that began to develop in a much earlier evolutionary period. He believed that the drive of creative labor and self-completion through such labor was such that, despite a historic pattern of discrimination, women would persevere and eventually achieve success.

Modernization Theory

Throughout Veblen's later writings on politics, economics, and society runs a series of arguments on a topic that today would be termed *modernization theory*. Veblen was extremely concerned with the conditions under which a society develops from a backward position to become an advanced society in comparison with other contemporaneous societies. Of particular interest is an argument that Veblen developed in *Imperial Germany and the Industrial Revolution,* and that, at one point, he termed the "advantage of backwardness." In this book, Veblen maintained that those societies that are most industrially advanced in the present will not be so in the future, whereas those that are less developed in the present have the potential to be the most advanced in the future. Although Veblen developed these ideas in the course of a historical comparison of Germany and Great Britain, he presented them as general principles, which he believed would be valid in other cases.

Veblen appears to have held the position that the diffusion of technological and scientific knowledge from one society to another is a natural occurrence, which will happen whether or not a society's political leaders prefer it. He emphasized that technological and scientific phenomena could diffuse across societies independently of cultural phenomena. Thus, for example, he pointed out how British machine technology was incorporated in German society, whereas British liberal democratic conceptions were not. Veblen wrote:

> This modern state of the industrial arts that so has led to the rehabilitation of a dynastic state in Germany on a scale exceeding what had been practicable in earlier times—this technological advance was not made in Germany but was borrowed, directly or at the second remove, from the English-speaking peoples; primarily, and in the last resort almost wholly, from England. What has been insisted on above is that British use and wont in other than the technological respect was not taken over by the German community at the same time. The result being that Germany offers what is by contrast with England an anomaly, in that it shows the working of the modern state of the industrial arts as worked out by the English, but without the characteristic range of institutions and convictions that have grown up among English-speaking peoples concomitantly with the growth of this modern state of the industrial arts.[10]

According to Veblen, this process resulted in Germany having an advanced technological economic system combined with a backward and dynastic government—a condition conducive to military aggression.

The significance of such technological diffusion is that any industrial advantage that one society might have over another is temporary. Moreover, Veblen argued, the less industrially developed society will not only catch up to the more advanced society, but is likely to surpass it—as Germany, for instance, caught up to and surpassed Great Britain in the late nineteenth century.

Veblen maintained that the society that first develops a particular technology will do so in a relatively haphazard manner, without knowing the long-run outcome or economic implications of the new technology. By the time this technology has been fully implemented, a great deal of capital will have been invested in machinery, plants, and the training of personnel. Unfortunately, by the time full implementation occurs, much of the machinery and technology will already be outmoded in terms of the most recent scientific and engineering discoveries. Thus the first society to use a new technology will do so in less than the most efficient possible manner.

When a society that is less developed borrows this new technology, it will have an advantage over the first society (the "advantage of backwardness"). Specifically, the planners in this second society will be able to observe the experience of the first society and thus will develop the new technology in a more systematic and efficient manner. Moreover, they will incorporate the most advanced technology available, producing a more advanced industrial system, superior to that of the first society (which by then will have become somewhat scientifically outmoded). The society that first industrialized with the new technology will thus find itself at a disadvantage. It will have a less advanced and less systematic and efficient industrial system than the second society, but it will have committed enough capital to the present industrial system so as to make a more efficient reindustrialization impractical.

SIGNIFICANCE

Vision of the Future

In focusing on Veblen's ideas about the future, one must separate his views of immediate trends versus long-run probabilities. The former tend to be quite pessimistic in tone; the latter reflect an underlying evolutionary optimism.

According to Veblen, two of the immediate trends involved the likelihood of another worldwide war (after World War I) and an imminent economic collapse. Indeed Veblen, in the late 1910s and early 1920s, seemed to see both the Great Depression and World War II on the horizon. He believed that national patriotic inclination, combined with the business-predatory desire for competitive advantage and the territorial ambition of the two major dynastic states (Germany and Japan), would lead to a worldwide military conflict. Veblen also held that the current business system of competitive capitalism was a survival from eighteenth-century entrepreneurialism. He believed that the increasing separation of financial (business) and technical skills would result in a near-total failure of the business controllers to understand the delicate balance of what had become an advanced industrial socioeconomic system. The end result of this failure would be competitive business manipulations that would produce an unprecedented economic collapse. Thus Veblen, to a great extent, predicted the depression that would follow his death by only a few months.

Veblen's long-run predictions are most forcefully expressed in a series of essays written in 1919 and later published under the title *The Engineers and the Price System* (1921). Building on, but disagreeing with, both Spencerian and Marxist positions, Veblen argued that a "new order" would eventually develop that would go beyond the "contract" form of society (envisioned by Spencer as the most advanced) and would be ushered in by a relatively peaceful "technocratic" revolt (as opposed to a Marxist violent workers' revolution).

Veblen argued that, once initiated, the mechanization of society and the increase in technological knowledge would continue to advance at an accelerating rate. This continued advance would yield an increase in industrial specialization, which in turn would result in business controllers having little knowledge of the day-to-day organization and technology involved in production. Increasingly, businessmen would have to leave actual productive and technological decisions to specially trained engineers, who in turn would rise higher and become more numerous in productive industrial establishments. A state of affairs would then be reached where the controllers of the industrious sphere would have little knowledge or understanding of its functioning. Thus, in order to increase profits, businessmen would not emphasize increased production technologies (which they would hardly understand) but would turn instead to such "wasteful" business practices (or manipulations) as cornering markets, reducing supplies, driving competitors out of business through financial deals, pushing through protective tariffs, gaining governmental supports, and the like.

Veblen declared that, despite the increasing wastefulness of business management and the capitalist competitive system, both would continue to persist for some time. The reasons for this persistence are threefold: (1) the continued use of mass advertising and control of the political sphere by the business interests; (2) the popular habits of mind in the United States, where business is seen as good and the business management of affairs as natural; and (3) the general docility of the engineers and technicians employed by the business class. Yet, according to Veblen, business domination would be terminated in the long run. The mechanism of this termination would not be a widespread bloody revolution but, rather, a takeover of the control of industry by the technical experts who will overcome their docility, organize, and assert themselves.

Veblen did acknowledge that, at first, engineers and technical specialists willingly would be paid employees who would accept the control of industry by business. Indeed, as members of U.S. society, they would accept a business ethos and would view control by businessmen as natural and normal. Over time, however, their view would change. Veblen believed that these technical experts would become aware of the wastefulness of business competitive manipulations and would come to understand the long-run detrimental effects that business control of industry has on industrial productivity and, consequently, on the well-being of society as a whole. In opposition to business's waste of a society's industrial capacity, resources, and labor, the technical experts—exhibiting a strong instinct of workmanship—would organize themselves and make known the antisocial wastefulness of competitive business control of industry. This knowledge would lead to a change in the popular acceptance of business industrial control. Eventually, by means of a strike of the technical experts who actually organize and run industry, business control and competitive capitalism would be brought to an end, to be replaced by a socioeconomic order coordinated by these technical experts—Veblen's "new order."

Veblen's writings about the social organization of this new order are sketchy. He insisted that once the technical specialists take over coordination of industry (and society), production would rise immediately (anywhere from 300 percent to 1,200 percent), thereby raising the general standard of living. Society would be coordinated by a national or "central directorate." Veblen envisioned this as a relatively small body composed of resource engineers, transportation engineers, and distributive engineers who would specialize in the respective areas of resource development and use, transportation of raw materials and finished products, and distribution of the industrial output to the population. This central directorate would seek advice from a group of consulting economists and local directorates in making decisions. Thus essentially Veblen's conception of the future involves a socialization or nationalization of industrial means of production and the termination of corporate and absentee ownership of property (but not the end of private ownership of homes and personal items and not the end of a well-developed division of labor). Veblen argued that such a form of socialization would produce full employment, full use of industrial technology, and continued industrial expansion—thereby raising the general population's standard of living.

Veblen did not predict clearly when the new order would come about. He even warned his readers to beware of arguments of "historical inevitability." He did, however, conclude the final essay in *The Engineers and the Price System* with a cryptic passage in which he assures those businessmen who control industrial production that, in terms of the coming new order, they have nothing to worry about "just yet."

Contemporary Relevance

In his widely read book on the development of sociology, Don Martindale notes similarities between the theorizing of Thorstein Veblen and that of Max Weber. Martindale raises the question, Why has Veblen's influence on later American sociology been so slight when compared with that of a sociologist such as Weber? Martindale's own answer to this question involves Veblen's interdisciplinary training and interdisciplinary approach to his subject matter. According to Martindale, Veblen has "tended to be classified as an economist by the sociologists and as a sociologist by the economists,"[11] and thus no discipline has claimed him as one of their own. Although Martindale is correct that there are some parallels of approach between Weber and Veblen (e.g., Weber twice cites Veblen approvingly in *The Protestant Ethic and the Spirit of Capitalism*,[12] and Veblen develops his own notion of ideal types), other classical theorists, whose work is not easily located in a single discipline (e.g., Pareto in economics and sociology, Mead in philosophy and social psychology, and of course Marx), have not been viewed as underappreciated because of their multidisciplinary orientations. If we accept Martindale's contention that Veblen's theorizing has not been fully appreciated and explored by later generations of social scientists, we must then look at other explanations to account for this lack. Numerous explanations have been offered in the literature; foremost among these is what we can call the "ideological" explanation.

To put it as straightforwardly as possible, the ideological explanation asserts that Veblen's work has been rejected or ignored because his critical theoretical approach to competitive capitalism in general, and American business interests in particular, is and has been incompatible with a supposedly "value neutral" positivistic academic social science that has generally subordinated itself to dominant political and economic interests. A number of writers, like Douglas Dowd, have presented this explanation in the past. Dowd asserted that Veblen was not given full attention due to "the critical attitude taken by Veblen toward the basic institutions of American society."[13] More recently, Rick Tilman has attempted to document precisely the ideological response to Veblen by American social scientists.[14] It is Tilman's contention that much of the literature on Veblen tells us considerably more about the ideological biases of the literature's authors than it does about the structure and implications of Veblen's theory. Veblen's earliest critics, some of whose pronouncements continue to be echoed, were prominent "neoclassical" economists such as John Cummings (1868–1936) at the University of Chicago and Irving Fisher (1867–1947) at Yale. They approached Veblen assuming that individuals by nature are hedonistic beings who act to maximize their individual economic advantage. Such an approach, of course, is at odds with Veblen's understanding of human motivation and Veblen's criticisms of modern capitalist competitive institutions. In other words, such critics *a priori* assumed the necessity of the very institutional activities Veblen chose to critique, and thus they found Veblen's theorizing unacceptable. Later generations of economists have echoed these views, seeing consumption (conspicuous or otherwise) as the driving force of the economy and viewing what Veblen would see as a predatory business class exploiting an industrious class as nothing more than the proper functioning of business activity.

The ideological rejection of Veblen by mainstream sociologists developed after World War II. Tilman sees the ideological attack on Veblen as a multifaceted one that sought to define him as a nonsociologist satirist whose ideas were incompatible with empirical sociology. The sociologists who rejected his work found no place for Veblen's iconoclastic radical critique of American institutions—a critique viewed by them as threatening to their own values, incompatible with rigorous social-scientific methods, and certainly not useful (and probably harmful) in gaining funding for their institutions and their own research.[15] The explicit rejection of Veblen, Tilman asserts, was most developed by a number of sociologists who were either employed or trained at Harvard and Columbia universities. Two significant figures were Talcott Parsons (1902–1979) and David Riesman (b. 1909).

Parsons's ideological attacks on Veblen are highly significant because of the pre-eminent place that Parsons held in American sociology from the 1940s through the 1960s. Tilman maintains that Parsons ideologically rejected any theories that posited a self-interested elite. Thus Parsons followed his rejection of Veblen's ideas with a rejection of the work of C. Wright Mills (discussed later in this section) using very similar language. Tilman also accuses Parsons of a general "pro-European bias" that in the case of Veblen has Parsons asserting that anything of value said by Veblen was said earlier and better by Max Weber.

Tilman sees the most "dangerous" of the ideological attacks on Veblen coming from the pen of David Riesman in a book on Veblen that was originally published in 1953 and has been reprinted since.[16] Riesman's work is viewed as dangerous because, despite disclaimers, it attempts to discredit Veblen's critique of American social institutions not by presenting a careful logical and empirical examination of Veblen's ideas, but by unfairly explaining them as the product of a strange individual and merely the outcome of Veblen's peculiar family, personality, background, and environment.[17]

From the preceding discussion, it might be concluded that the weight of ideological opposition has left Veblen's work without any significant later influence. Such a conclusion would be quite wrong. Despite ideologically based attempts to dismiss his work, his influence has been significant in a number of disciplines including economics, anthropology, social history, and, of course, sociology.

Although rejected by the neoclassical economists in the United States, Veblen's work had an immediate impact on a number of continental European economists like Sombart, who themselves were rejecting the hedonistic psychological assumptions of the neoclassicists in favor of a view of human psychology as a product of cultural and historical forces. Ultimately, Veblen came to be viewed as the founder of a separate school of economics in the United States known as "institutional economics." Institutionalists, such as Veblen's student Wesley Mitchell (1874–1948), differed from mainstream economists by emphasizing a distinction between industry and business. Industry is viewed as the production of useful wealth, whereas business is viewed as the accumulation of profit. Because profit can be amassed without the production of goods, institutionalists view it as a mistake to equate business success with industrial success. Such an approach leads to the exploration by economists of more sociological questions concerning the impact of the organization of business in society on a society's industrial well-being. A number of institutionalists had a direct impact on American economic policy during the New Deal administration of Franklin Roosevelt, and they continue to exist as a school that raises questions concerning the assumptions and conclusions of mainstream American economics.

If Veblen's rejection of a simplistic hedonistic psychology puts him at odds with most American economists, it anticipated, paralleled, and influenced changes taking place in American anthropological thought. Christopher Shannon has recently argued that Veblen's *The Theory of the Leisure Class* began a "reorientation" of American critical social analysis. According to Shannon, prior to that work, American intellectuals considered their contemporary social life as if it were constituted by relatively independent and disconnected "separate spheres." Critiques would be written of aspects of family life, work, leisure activities, religion, manners, and so on without an attempt to apprehend their connections. Veblen's new critique though saw wide-ranging features of American life as reflecting a cultural whole, whose contours were causally linked to underlying economic and social class realities of domination, production, and consumption. Shannon writes, "The historical significance of Veblen's book lies not in its supposed cultural approach to economics but in its economic approach to culture."[18] As early twentieth-century American anthropology shifted from an instinctual orientation to the cultural orientation of Franz Boas (1858–1942) and his students at Columbia University, Veblen's cultural-economic analyses became significant to some, but not all, leading American anthropologists.

Two of Boas's students, Ruth Benedict (1889–1948) and Melville Herskovits (1859–1963), were in harmony with a holistic cultural orientation. But, whereas Benedict would come to develop a position of extreme cultural relativism that was incompatible with Veblen's materialism and class-based critique,[19] Herskovits would incorporate both of Veblen's concepts of "conspicuous consumption" and "leisure class" into presentations in his highly influential text book.[20] Later in the century, a competing school of cultural anthropology developed by Leslie White (1900–1975) at the University of Michigan would, like Veblen, make materialist, evolutionary, and causal assumptions.[21] Two of White's students developed what they called "the law of evolutionary potential."[22] As Dutch sociologist W. F. Wertheim has pointed out, this "law" involved a virtual reiteration of Veblen's "advantage of backwardness."[23] Veblen's renamed "law" would be used to explain why a relatively "backward" society in one historical period would become a more "advanced" society in a later historical period, only to fall later into relative backwardness again.

From the perspective of the field of academic history, Veblen's work became increasingly important as some influential mid-twentieth-century historians rejected the traditional focus of viewing history as an outcome of the actions of monarchs, generals, and other "great men," and turned instead to the writing of a "social history" that reflected the lives, conditions, beliefs, and actions of large population segments.

One of the most influential figures in the rise of social history in the United States has been the Harvard historian Barrington Moore. Moore's most important work, *Social Origins of Dictatorship and Democracy*,[24] explicitly builds on a comparative methodological approach developed by Veblen and on arguments presented in Veblen's *Imperial Germany and the Industrial Revolution*. Like Veblen, Moore is concerned with the diffusion of industrial technology from one society to another and with the implications for a society when a high level of technology is combined with preindustrial attitudes, traditions, and power structures. Moore's work looks at the comparative sociohistorical development of England, France, the United States, China, Japan, and India in a study of how the modern world emerged.

Veblen was trained in philosophy and economics and has influenced the fields of economics, anthropology, and social history. Nevertheless, from the time of Ward's early review of *The Theory of the Leisure Class*, his thought has been of significance to the discipline of sociology. His work was frequently cited by his contemporary sociologists in America, including William Graham Sumner, Lester Ward, Edward Ross, and Franklin Giddings (1855–1931), especially in terms of the social psychology of class. European sociologists of his time, such as Max Weber in Germany, Ludwig Gumplowicz (1838–1909) in Austria, and Maurice Halbwachs (1877–1945) in France, also re-

ferred to his writings. In the years between his time and our own, Veblen has influenced the sociological study of social stratification in America, as well as such varied
sociological thinkers as Robert Merton (b. 1910), the members of the Frankfurt School,
and C. Wright Mills (1916–1962).

European studies of social stratification have generally been developed in a dialogue with the writings of Marx. This was true of the stratification writings of Max
Weber in Germany, Vilfredo Pareto and Gaetano Mosca (1858–1941) in Italy, and
Emile Durkheim in France. This dialogue has resulted (despite arguments and disagreements) in a European focus on stratification in terms of more or less discrete
economically based classes. On the other hand, American stratification studies,
since the early twentieth century, have stressed comparisons of perceived status as
the basis of hierarchical social distinctions. This is not to say that Europeans have ignored status or that Americans have ignored economic differences, but that there has
been a difference in the general development and emphasis in their respective stratification studies. Though he was perhaps not as significant for U.S. thinkers as Marx
was for Europeans, both early and later American thought bears the imprint of Veblen's pioneering studies of status comparisons and symbolic representations. Veblen's influence, combined with American positivistic statistical expertise, has
helped lead to a unique American emphasis on socioeconomic status, prestige, and
life-style in stratification studies. This observation is especially true because later
mainstream American sociologists have generally tended to emphasize Veblen's social-psychological concepts (for example, conspicuous consumption, leisure, and
waste) over his materialism, and have virtually ignored his predatory-industrial
class distinction.

Later sociological theorists have had different reactions toward Veblen and have
used his ideas in a variety of ways. Rather than follow his mentor, Parsons, in an outright dismissal of Veblen's ideas, Robert Merton, for instance, simply ignored both the
critical and the holistic thrust of Veblen's work. Merton redefined some of Veblen's
concepts in terms of his own "middle-range" and "functionalist" approach that left the
status quo unquestioned and unchallenged. Merton wrote, for example:

> The Veblenian paradox is that people buy expensive goods not so much because they are
> superior but because they are expensive. For it is the latent equation ("costliness = mark
> of higher social status") which he singles out in his functional analysis, rather than the
> manifest equation ("costliness = excellence of the goods").[25]

A very differently oriented group of theorists, the German émigré critical theorists
of the Frankfurt School, varied widely in their respective assessments of Veblen's
work. Theodor Adorno (1903–1969) dismissed Veblen on the dual grounds that his
thought was grounded in an American pragmatic philosophical tradition that Adorno
rejected and that Veblen followed a methodology of "Darwinian empiricism"[26] that
Adorno also found wanting. On the other hand, Herbert Marcuse (1898–1979) found
Veblen's analysis both innovative and suggestive. Marcuse viewed Veblen as one of the
first to understand the emergence of a "new rationality" based on machine technology
that influenced all aspects of modern thought and action.[27] Although not explicitly referring to Veblen, in its own way Marcuse's One-Dimensional Man[28] continues the analysis of a link between conspicuous consumption, social-psychological self-conception,
and class domination.

If the émigré critical theorists of the Frankfurt School had a mixed reaction to Veblen, the most prominent home-grown sociological critical thinker in the United States was unreserved in his admiration for Veblen and willingly credited Veblen as the wellspring for much of his own thought. According to C. Wright Mills, Veblen was "the best social scientist America has produced."[29] Mills presents "Thorstein Veblen's brilliant and ironic insight"[30] as a mark of what Mills called "the sociological imagination"—an imagination he saw lacking in contemporary functionalist theorizing and positivistic "abstracted empiricism" that dominated American sociology in the 1950s. Mills's two major studies—*White Collar: The American Middle Classes* and *The Power Elite*—both develop themes that run through Veblen and frequently make references to Veblen's work.

In *White Collar*, Mills uses Veblen's ideas to explain how a new middle class that uses leisure to obtain an appearance of social status has emerged in the United States. Mills wrote:

> The leisure of many middle-class people is entirely taken up by attempts to gratify status claims. Just as work is made empty by the process of alienation, so leisure is made hollow by status snobbery and emulative consumption.[31]

In that work, Mills also builds on Veblen's understanding of how large corporations curtail competition[32] and how salesmanship and the creation of demand have to an extent undermined competition based upon product quality.

Mills's *The Power Elite* is even more directly based on Veblen's concepts and ideas. Mills presents his discussion of a dominant sociopolitical elite not as a refutation of Veblen's predatory business upper class, but as an updating of it that depends on Veblen's earlier ideas. Mills writes of Veblen:

> What he wrote remains strong with the truth, even though the facts do not cover the scenes and characters that have emerged in our own time. It remains strong because we could not see the newer features of our own time had he not written what and as he did.[33]

For Mills, the major change between his time and Veblen's was the rise of a mass media and the creation of media-produced celebrities as part of a dominant national sociopolitical elite. Building on Veblen, Mills stresses the role of leisure activity as serving a coordinating and unifying function that allows a modern elite to maintain its dominance.

Mills's theoretical analyses of mid-century American social life were popular both with the general reading public and within a generation of graduate sociology students who, in the late 1960s and 1970s, saw Mills's approach as better-suited than the dominant functionalist approach of Parsons and Merton in accounting for both the continued inequalities of American society and the horrors of the Vietnam War. Thus through his influence on Mills, Veblen affected many of those who now hold American university positions. But Veblen's work also still directly influences theorists more than a century after *Theory of the Leisure Class* was published. Such influence can be seen in the works of the French theorist Jean Baudrillard and in a number of contemporary—mostly American—social economists.

According to Douglas Kellner:

> Baudrillard's argument is that the "conspicuous consumption" and display of commodities analyzed by Veblen in his *The Theory of the Leisure Class* has been extended to everyone

in consumer society. Conspicuous consumption for Veblen is linked to expenditure, display and the establishing of style, taste and the social power of wealth. Whereas such display is confined to the upper classes in Veblen's book, Baudrillard sees the entire society as organized around consumption and display of commodities through which individuals gain prestige, identity and standing.[34]

In his *For a Critique of the Political Economy of the Sign*,[35] Baudrillard integrates Veblen's concepts of conspicuous waste, conspicuous leisure, conspicuous consumption, vicarious conspicuous waste, vicarious conspicuous leisure, and vicarious conspicuous consumption into his own theory. Baudrillard asserts:

> Veblen shows that even if the primary function of the subservient classes is working and producing, they simultaneously have the function (and when they are kept unemployed, it is their only function) of displaying the *standing* of the Master.[36]

According to Baudrillard, Veblen demonstrates that the "significance of objects" is to be found in their role in designating "the being and rank of their possessor" and that consumption and the use of leisure time should not be understood predominantly in terms of pleasure, but as socially determined activities tied to the differential ranking and classification of members of society. Baudrillard insists that "all of Veblen's work illustrates how the production of social classification . . . is the fundamental law that arranges and subordinates all . . . other logics, whether conscious, rational, ideological, moral, etc."[37]

Some of the American social economists who follow Veblen take exception with "postmodernists" whom they see as rejecting Veblen's key distinction between "useful" objects and those that are valued only for the status acquired through their conspicuous consumption.[38] Although varied in outlook, the recent works of Doug Brown, William Dugger, Gladys Parker Foster, William Hildred, Ann May, Phillip Anthony O'Hara, Paulette Olson, Janice Peterson, Yngre Ramsted, Linda Robertson, and Jacqueline and Ronald Stanfield all focus on applying Veblenian theoretical ideas to a world with an increasingly integrated global economy.[39] Just as Veblen wrote during an era of the post–Civil War consolidation of a national American economy and the rise of a national upper predatory class, these theorists see themselves as writing during an era of both the rise of a global economy and the emergence of a global upper predatory class. Paralleling Mills, they see themselves not as displacing Veblen's ideas, but as updating them in order to understand the social and economic implications of a new situation (i.e., economic globalization). A sophisticated example of such work is Paulette Olson's "My Dam is Bigger than Yours: Emulation in Global Capitalism."[40]

Olson's explicit goal is "to reconceptualize Veblen's nineteenth century analysis of consumption in the historical context of global capitalism."[41] To do so, she focuses not just on the personal use of fashion to indicate high status, but on the waste of public assets by elites to enhance their perceived status. She thus distinguishes between the "micro-emulation" of newly rich leaders of developing countries in "wasteful expenditures on western-style luxury and leisure goods"[42] and "macro-emulation" involving the expenditure of public funds that enhances the status of leaders while simultaneously undermining the well-being of common individuals. Olson takes into account the complicity, encouragement, and sponsorship of Western nations in such wastefulness through the policies of such agencies as the International Monetary Fund. She also discusses the tens of thousands of persons displaced by dam projects in India, China, and elsewhere, as well as the long-term ecological damage that results from wasteful status-enhancing projects undertaken by elites.

One recent work of note that develops and applies Veblen's ideas is an article in *The New Yorker* magazine by Adam Gopnik, who states that, "The man who discovered conspicuous consumption is back in style."[43] Without focusing on the details and complexities of Veblen's theory, Gopnik cogently points to Veblen's continued significance, writing that:

> Where an economist might attempt to explain how one exporting country can make money by selling its coffee beans cheaper than the next, Veblen attempts to explain why, when you offer two identical cappuccinos for sale on opposite sides of the same street, one for six dollars and the other for two, you will see people knock each other down as they flock to pay six.[44]

NOTES

1. Joseph Dorfman, *Thorstein Veblen and his America*.
2. Rick Tilman, *Thorstein Veblen and his critics, 1819–1963: Conservative, liberal, and radical perspectives*.
3. Ibid., p. 11.
4. *The higher learning in America: A memorandum on the conduct of universities by businessmen*.
5. *The instinct of workmanship and the state of the industrial arts*, pp. 7–8.
6. Ibid., p. 31.
7. *The theory of the leisure class*, pp. 15–16.
8. Ibid., pp. 66–67.
9. "The economic theory of women's dress," in *Essays in our changing order*, p. 68.
10. *Imperial Germany and the industrial revolution*, p. 85.
11. Don Martindale, *The nature and types of sociological theory*, 2nd ed. (Prospect Heights, IL: Waveland Press, 1981).
12. Max Weber, *The Protestant ethic and the spirit of capitalism* (New York: Scribner's, 1958), pp. 258, 275.
13. Douglas F. Dowd, *Thorstein Veblen*, p. xi.
14. Tilman, *Thorstein Veblen and his critics*.
15. Ibid., pp. 163–164.
16. David Reisman, *Thorstein Veblen: A critical interpretation*.
17. Tilman, *Thornstein Veblen and his critics*, p. 168.
18. Cristopher Shannon, *Conspicuous criticism, the individual, and culture in American social thought from Veblen to Mills*, p. xiii.
19. See for example her *Patterns of culture* (Boston: Houghton Mifflin, 1959 [1934]).
20. Melville J. Herskovits, *Man and his works: The science of cultural anthropology* (New York: Alfred A. Knopf, 1952).
21. Leslie White, *The evolution of culture* (New York: McGraw–Hill, 1959).
22. Marshall Sahlins & Ellman R. Service, *Evolution and culture* (Ann Arbor: University of Michigan, 1960).
23. W. F. Wertheim, *Evolution and revolution* (Harmondsworth, England: Penguin, 1974).
24. Barrington Moore, *Social origins of dictatorship and democracy* (Boston: Beacon Press, 1967).
25. Quoted in Tilman, *Thorstein Veblen and his critics*, p. 176.
26. Ibid., p. 191.
27. Herbert Marcuse, "Some social implications of modern technology," in Andrew Arato & Eike Gebhardt, *The essential Frankfurt School reader* (New York: Continuum, 1985), p. 142.
28. Herbert Marcuse, *One-dimensional man* (Boston: Beacon Press, 1964).
29. C. Wright Mills, *Images of man: The classical tradition in sociological thinking* (New York: George Braziller, 1960), p. 13.

30. C. Wright Mills, *The sociological imagination* (New York: Oxford University Press, 1959), p. 6.
31. C. Wright Mills, *White collar: The American middle classes* (New York: Oxford University Press, 1956), p. 256.
32. Ibid., p. 35.
33. C. Wright Mills, *The power elite* (New York: Oxford University Press, 1956), p. 58n.
34. Douglas Kellner, *Jean Baudrillard: From Marxism to postmodernism* (Stanford, CA: Stanford University Press, 1989), p. 21.
35. Jean Baudrillard, *For a critique of the political economy of the sign* (St. Louis: Telos Press, 1981).

36. Ibid., p. 31.
37. Ibid., p. 76.
38. See Yngre Ramsted, "Veblen's propensity for emulation: is it passe," in Doug Brown (Ed.), *Thorstein Veblen in the twenty-first century*, pp. 3–27.
39. See Brown, ibid.
40. Olson, pp. 189–207, in Brown, ibid.
41. Ibid., p. 189.
42. Ibid., p. 183.
43. Adam Gopnik, "Display Cases," pp. 176-184, in *The New Yorker*, April 26 & May 3, 1999, p. 176.
44. Ibid.

GLOSSARY

Advantage of backwardness: The potential of a less industrially developed society to advance beyond the leading industrial societies.

Animistic stage: For Veblen, the simplest mental stage. Corresponds to the *savage* stage of social organization and involves ascribing the causes of events to humanlike spirits. (Compare with Comte's "theological stage.")

Barbarianism: In Veblen's usage, middle stage in the social organization characterized by hierarchical religious and political structures, leisure-class activities, warfare, and a high degree of exploitation.

Business class: The form that the *predatory class* takes in a modern capitalist society. Characterized by economic manipulations, exploitation of others, and wasteful interference with the well-being of society.

Central directorate: The national controlling body of engineers (or technical specialists) central to Veblen's conception of a *new order*.

Conspicuous consumption: Form of *conspicuous waste* that involves the publicly visible nonproductive use of wealth in order to gain social status.

Conspicuous leisure: Form of *conspicuous waste* that involves the publicly visible nonproductive use of time in order to gain social status.

Conspicuous waste: The publicly visible nonproductive use of time and wealth in order to gain social status.

Continuous causation: Process whereby (or form of explanation wherein) reality is the product of a never-ending series of causal changes without goal or end state.

Division of labor: Occupational separation of tasks in a group or society.

Domination: The exploitation of *surplus wealth* produced by a group or person, and the ascription of inferior social status to that group or person.

Dynastic state: A hierarchical, centralized, war-oriented society characterized by feudallike states of authority and submission.

Genetic explanation: Statement of the cause of a phenomenon in terms of the prior sequences of events leading to it.

Habit: Nonreflective form of thought and action that is developed out of prior repetitious forms of productive activity and that is characteristic of persons and groups.

Habits of the mind: Nonreflective ways of thinking and feeling that are the product of productive activities and that shape cultural norms.

Handicraft production: Prefactory system characterized by the decentralized creation of products by skilled craftspersons organized into guilds and ranked by skill and seniority.

Hedonism: A position that explains human behavior in terms of self-centered goals of increases in pleasure or rewards and decreases of pain, punishment, or costs.

Ideal type: Methodological approach developed by the German historian Dilthey and modified for sociological use by Max Weber. Involves the development of the usual, typical, or most complete features of a phenomenon in order to facilitate comparison and analysis.

Idle curiosity: Universal instinct or drive to accumulate knowledge and explain phenomena independent of utilitarian or pragmatic ends. Necessary for social evolutionary progress.

Industrious class: Composed of the majority of the population; produces the wealth of society. Exploited by the *predatory class*.

Instinct: As used by Veblen, a biologically based, species-specific drive toward certain ends or goals, which is mediated by consciousness and cultural norms in humans.

Instinct of parenting: Universal human instinct or drive. Involves actions aimed at well-being of the group, society, or others.

Instinct of workmanship: Most basic human drive. Involves a drive to create and produce.

Institution: As used by Veblen, a complex of habit-based cultural norms around a perceived centrally important collective activity.

Materialism: As used by Veblen, methodological position by which phenomena are traced back to causal impetus in forms of productive labor activity.

Matter-of-fact stage: For Veblen, the highest stage of mental development. Corresponds to the *modern society* stage of social organization and involves an empirical observational approach to the causal explanation of events. (Compare with Comte's *positive stage*.)

Metaphysical stage: Auguste Comte's middle stage of society, characterized by explanations of natural events in terms of internal, essential, or underlying nature. (Compare with Veblen's *pragmatic stage*.)

Modern society: In Veblen's usage, a machine-based society characterized by high technology, specialization, matter-of-fact thinking, and business-class waste.

New order: Veblen's perceived future industrial society, which will lack a *business class* and be controlled by technical experts.

Positive stage: Auguste Comte's most advanced stage of society, characterized by empirical observation-based ways of thinking. (Compare with Veblen's *Matter-of-fact stage*.)

Positivism: Type of inquiry based on methodology of the natural sciences that is produced by technical-cognitive interest and that seeks to predict and control. (See Chapter 2.)

Pragmatic stage: For Veblen, the middle stage of mental development. Corresponds to the barbarian stage of social organization and involves ascribing the causes of events to internal, underlying essences or nature. (Compare with Comte's "metaphysical stage.")

Predatory class: Numerically small upper social class that exists by exploitation of the *industrious class*.

Savagery: In Veblen's usage, the simplest stage of social organization characterized by small, peaceful, cooperative communities lacking private property, specialization, or developed *division of labor*.

Surplus wealth: Goods in addition to those that maintain the minimum *survival* level of existence.

Survival: As used by Veblen (after Tylor), an element of an earlier stage of social evolution that persists after that stage's termination.

Technocratic society (technocracy): A society characterized by the dominance or control of a technically trained and competent elite.

Teleological: The process of purposive actions toward internal goals or end states.

Tropism: A hereditary, small, specific, and immediate response or reaction to a specified stimulus or stimuli.

Vicarious conspicuous consumption: The publicly visible nonproductive use of wealth by one person that leads to a gain in social status by another person. Form of *vicarious conspicuous waste*.

Vicarious conspicuous leisure: The publicly visible nonproductive use of time by one person that leads to a gain in social status by another person. Form of *vicarious conspicuous waste*.

Vicarious conspicuous waste: The publicly visible nonproductive use of time and wealth by one person that leads to a gain in social status by another person.

ANNOTATED BIBLIOGRAPHY

Primary Sources

Absentee ownership and business enterprise in recent times: The case of America. Boston: Beacon Press, 1967 [1923] (paper).

Analysis of the socioeconomic organization of modern U.S. capitalism. Emphasis is on the separation of technological knowledge and financial control and the increasing concentration of ownership of the means of production in the business class.

The engineers and the price system. New York: B. W. Huebsch, 1921.

A straightforward series of essays in which Veblen presents his ideas about a future new order controlled by engineers and technicians.

Essays in our changing order (Leon Ardzrooni, Ed.). New York: Augustus M. Kelley, 1964 [1934].

A diverse set of writings put together after Veblen's death. Includes essays that answer criticism, speculate on the future of economic theory, comment on the relationship of Christian ethics and competitive capitalism, and argue the role of Jewish marginality in the rise of modern science.

The higher learning in America: A memorandum on the conduct of universities by businessmen. New York: Augustus M. Kelley, 1965 [1918].

Sharply written analysis and criticism of changes in the U.S. university system. Focuses on the rise of business-dominated governing boards, centralized administrations, powerful university presidents, and vocational training. Contains one of Veblen's clearest discussions of "idle curiosity."

Imperial Germany and the industrial revolution. Ann Arbor: University of Michigan, 1966 [1915] (paper).

Comparative analysis of the development of modern Germany and Great Britain. Includes a discussion and definition of the concept of a "dynastic state."

An inquiry into the nature of peace and the terms of its perpetuation. New York: Augustus M. Kelley, 1964 [1917].

Veblen's study of the social conditions underlying war and peace. Includes analysis of the meanings and manipulations of "patriotism" and speculation on future possibilities for a peaceful world order.

The instinct of workmanship and the state of the industrial arts. New York: Norton, 1964 [1914].

Required reading for the serious Veblen student. Includes clear and detailed discussion of social evolutionary stages, social change, and the nature and significance of "instincts."

The place of science in modern civilization. New York: B. W. Huebsch, 1919.

A very important series of essays. Focus is on the evolutionary development of modern science, the nature of modern evolutionism, the future of socialism, and the ideas of Karl Marx and his followers.

The portable Veblen (Marx Lerner, Ed.). New York: Viking Press, 1984 (paper).

An excellent book with which to begin one's reading of Veblen. Contains excerpts from Veblen's major writings, organized by topic.

Theory of business enterprise. New York: Augustus M. Kelley, 1964 [1904].

Detailed institutional and social-psychological inquiry into the nature and actions of the modern business class. Veblen presents that class as conservative, wasteful, and predatory.

The theory of the leisure class. New York: Penguin, 1979 [1899] (paper).

Veblen's first and perhaps finest volume. Concepts developed include "conspicuous waste," "conspicuous consumption," "conspicuous leisure," "leisure class," "predatory class," and "industrial class." Also includes discussion of fashion, gambling, religious ritual, and the domination of women.

The vested interests and the common man. New York: Augustus M. Kelley, 1964 [1919].

These collected essays include discussion of the relationship of the development of knowledge and the rise of machine production to the role of "vested interests" in the promotion of war and the retardation of progressive social change.

Secondary Sources

Blaug, Mark (Ed.). *Thorstein Veblen, 1857–1929.* London: Edward Elgar, 1992.

A collection of twenty-one articles written in the 1970s and 1980s covering a wide variety of topics.

Brown, Doug (Ed.). *Thorstein Veblen in the twenty-first century: A commemoration of "The theory of the leisure class" (1899–1999).* Cheltenham, England: Edward Elgar, 1998.

An important book whose twelve articles focus on the application of Veblen's ideas to a world characterized by a global economy and an emerging global upper class. William M. Dugger's "Thorstein Veblen and the Upper Class" points to the unique features of Veblen's definition of that class, and Paulette Olson's article extends Veblen's ideas to distinguish between "micro-" and "macroemulation."

Dente, Leonard A. *Veblen's theory of social change.* New York: Arno Press, 1977.

Originally a doctoral dissertation, this book contains a detailed analysis of both the elements and the processes of social change contained in Veblen's work. Includes comparisons of Veblen with the economic thoughts of von Neumann, Schumpeter, and Marx.

Diggins, John P. *The bard of savagery: Thorstein Veblen and modern social theory.* New York: Seabury Press, 1978.

A scholarly volume that focuses on Veblen's life, work, and significance. Interesting comparisons of Veblen with Marx and Weber.

Dorfman, Joseph. *Thorstein Veblen and his America.* New York: Viking Press, 1934.

Despite a rambling style and some minor errors, this is still the most comprehensive analysis of the life, times, and works of Veblen. Definitely worth looking at.

Dowd, Douglas F. *Thorstein Veblen.* New York: Washington Square Press, 1966.

A readable introductory work on Veblen. Although written by an economist, the book's concerns are of a broad scope, and numerous themes of interest to the student of sociology are examined.

Heilbroner, Robert L. *The worldly philosophers: The lives, times, and ideas of the great economic thinkers* (4th ed.). New York: Simon & Schuster, 1972 (paper).

The chapter on Veblen in this book, by one of the leading historians of economic thought, places Veblen in the context of other great socioeconomic thinkers. Heilbroner's clear and concise style is always a pleasure to read.

Qualey, Carlton C. (Ed.). *Thorstein Veblen: The Carleton College Veblen seminar essays.* New York: Columbia University Press, 1968.

Four short essays focusing on, respectively, Veblen's view of capitalism, American business during Veblen's life, Veblen's "theology," and Veblen's intellectual roots. Also includes a personal recollection of Veblen by a former Veblen student and colleague.

Riesman, David. *Thorstein Veblen: A critical interpretation.* New York: Seabury Press, n.d. [1953] (paper).

An interesting psychological interpretation of Veblen's life and its relationship to his scholarly activity, although one might want to question some of Riesman's inferences and conclusions. Rick Tilman has recently attacked this book, arguing that Riesman attempts to reject Veblen's social criticisms not by an analysis of his ideas, but by suggesting that Veblen's ideas should be dismissed as a product of a flawed personality.

Seckler, David. *Thorstein Veblen and the institutionalists: A study in the social philosophy of economics.* Boulder: Colorado Associated University Press, 1975.

Seckler views Veblen as having developed a theoretical outlook that attempts an uneasy synthesis between a "behavioristic" and a "humanistic" outlook. Chapter 2 is a biographical sketch of Veblen; Chapter 3 presents a small sampling of Veblen's writings; and Chapter 4 is a good short analysis of Veblen's social theory.

Shannon, Cristopher. *Conspicuous criticism: Tradition, the individual, and culture in American social thought from Veblen to Mills.* Baltimore: Johns Hopkins University Press, 1996.

Shannon maintains that Veblen's *The Theory of the Leisure Class* began a reorientation of American social thought. This "reorientation" focused on culture as a whole and displaced an older tradition that looked at social life in terms of distinct spheres (e.g., family, work, sports, leisure, and so on). Central to

Veblen's overall new view was an economic interpretation of culture.

Tilman, Rick. *The intellectual legacy of Thorstein Veblen: Unresolved issues.* Westport, Conn: Greenwood Press, 1996.

Tilman focuses on a variety of Veblen topics, including the relationship of Veblen's ideas to those of Charles Darwin, Veblen's relationship to American pragmatic philosophy, and the influence of Veblen's work on the policies of the Roosevelt administration's New Deal.

Tilman, Rick. *Thorstein Veblen and his critics, 1891–1963: Conservative, liberal, and radical perspectives.* Princeton, NJ: Princeton University Press, 1991.

Tilman reviews various assessments of Veblen's work by economists, sociologists, and other social scientists, grouping their authors along ideological lines—conservative, liberal, and radical. His basic theme is that most works on Veblen tell us more about the ideological blinders of their authors than they do about Veblen's theorizing. Sociologists will be especially interested in Chapter 8 (on the sociological criticisms of Veblen coming out of Harvard and Columbia universities) and Chapter 9 (on the critical reaction of the Frankfurt School to Veblen).

There is here, however, a distinction that is of considerable importance. In the physical world we regard ourselves as standing in some degree outside the forces at work, and thus avoid the difficulty of harmonizing the feeling of human initiative with the recognition of series which are necessarily determined. In society we are the forces that are being investigated, and if we advance beyond the mere description of the phenomena of the social world to the attempt at reform, we seem to involve the possibility of changing what at the same time we assume to be necessarily fixed. The question, stated more generally is: What is the function of reflective consciousness in its attempt to direct conduct? The common answer is that we carry in thought the world as it should be, and fashion our conduct to bring this about. As we have already seen if this implies a "vision given in the mount" which represents in detail what is to be, we are utterly incapable of conceiving it. And every attempt to direct conduct by a fixed idea of the world of the future must be, not only a failure, but also pernicious. A conception of a different world comes to us always as the result of some specific problem which involves readjustment of the world as it is, not to meet a detailed ideal of a perfect universe, but to obviate the present difficulty; and the test of the effort lies in the possibility of this readjustment fitting into the world as it is. Reflective consciousness does not then carry us on to the world that is to be, but puts our own thought and endeavor into the very process of evolution, and evolution within consciousness that has become reflective has the advantage over other evolution in that the form does not tend to perpetuate himself as he is, but identifies himself with the process of development. Our reflective consciousness as applied to conduct is, therefore, an identification of our effort with the problem that presents itself, and the developmental process by which it is overcome, and reaches its highest expression in the scientific statement of the problem, and the recognition and use of scientific method and control.

—George Herbert Mead,
"The Working Hypothesis
in Social Reform"

13

George Herbert Mead

(1863–1931)

Life

In most cases, the writers of classical sociological theory can be characterized as outsiders. They tended to be marginal to their own societies and viewed themselves as separate from the average individual. From such a perspective, the social world appears different than it does to the unthinking conformist. Rules of behavior appear clearer and more recognizable; the contours of manners and etiquette are not simply assumed but take on the arbitrariness of custom, convention, and class prerogative. In their own ways, Marx, Pareto, Simmel, Veblen, Durkheim, Weber, and Comte were all such outsiders. Marx was the exile in Paris and London; Simmel, the secularized Jew blocked from university advancement; Pareto, the aristocratic recluse; Veblen, the foreigner in his own land; Durkheim, the provincial rabbi's son in Paris; Weber, the nationalist whose political ambitions were thwarted; and Comte, the disavowed high priest of the "religion of humanity."

If marginality is the rule for great social theorists, George Herbert Mead was the exception. His family of origin, education, professional appointments, marriage, and life-style all reflected a respectable conformity; his thought incorporated an adherence to turn-of-the-century American midwestern values of democracy, self-discipline, social reform, and scientific optimism.

Mead was born in South Hadley, Massachusetts, on February 27, 1863. His father, Hiram Mead, was a local Congregational minister; his mother, the former Elizabeth Storrs Billings, was well-read and cultured and had descended from a prominent New England family. George's one sibling, his sister Alice, was four years older than he. When George was seven, the family moved to Oberlin, Ohio. His father had accepted a chair in homiletics (the writing and presentation of sermons) at the recently opened Oberlin Theological Seminary.

The Meads were a close family with a comfortable standard of living. Their spacious house at 137 Elm Street still stands. (It was later converted into a rooming house for language students and is now an apartment building for Oberlin students.) The most exciting event of George's youth occurred in 1876, when Elizabeth took her two children to the Centennial Exposition in Philadelphia. The massive exhibits of new industrial technology were a thrilling experience to a boy of thirteen, curious about how the objects of the world worked.

In 1879, an intellectually advanced sixteen-year-old George entered Oberlin College. The school had been founded in 1833 on a major path of the Underground Railway, which had helped escaped slaves to make their way to Canada. Its founder, John Jay Shepard, had been a well-known Congregationalist reformer. In 1835, Oberlin was one of the first colleges in the country to admit blacks, and in 1841, it became the first coeducational institution to grant a bachelor's degree to women. Yet, despite such advances, the overall pedagogical, social, and religious atmosphere of the school was extremely conservative. Writing about Oberlin of that period, the historian Robert M. Crunden states:

> Most of the students came from farming or clerical families, and more Oberlin students chose the ministry as a possible career than did students elsewhere. Some classes were so Republican that not a single student would admit to voting for the Democrats. In the overwhelmingly religious atmosphere, strict rules regulated sexual contacts and no one could dance or gamble. Even the library was open to men and women only at alternate times. Evangelism was as much a part of life as were regular meals. With little effort a student could spend the greater part of his time out of class in some sort of religious service. As one visitor reported: "Why, if anyone walking along the sidewalks of Oberlin catches his foot and stumbles, nine chances out of ten, he stumbles into a prayer meeting." Such an environment easily led to smug bigotry. The students suspected the poor and the immigrant of excessive alcoholic consumption and inadequate moral fiber, and they frequently confused patriotism with their own variety of Protestantism.[1]

The curriculum at Oberlin consisted primarily of courses in classics, rhetoric, literature, moral philosophy, and mathematics. Introductory courses in botany and chemistry formed the extent to which education could be had in science. The classroom environment itself was one of dogmatic lectures; questions and remarks from students were discouraged.

Mead, in later years, came to reject much of what was emphasized at Oberlin. After struggling with a loss of religious faith, he turned toward a social reformist concern with making life better in this world. He rejected the narrow elitist view of patriotism in favor of a broad encompassing view of democracy and a concern with the well-being and rights of immigrants. He took part in experimental schools that emphasized discussion and hands-on learning. And he totally rejected the denigration of science and scientific education, writing extensively on both the philosophy of science and how science can best be taught in schools and universities.

In 1881, Hiram Mead unexpectedly died. George, who was still in college, waited on tables to help make ends meet. Nonetheless, severe cuts in the family finances were necessary, and Elizabeth and her children were forced to move from their large house to a number of rented rooms. Elizabeth Mead, however, proved to be a woman who flourished in adversity. She taught at Oberlin College from 1881 to 1883 and served as president of Mount Holyoke College from 1890 to 1900. In 1890, she was presented with an honorary A.M. degree from Oberlin, and in 1900, Smith College granted her an honorary L.H.D. degree.

Choosing a career was difficult for Mead. He felt drawn toward a field in which he could serve humanity, but his increasing religious doubts made the ministry or church-sponsored welfare activities unacceptable. He considered careers in politics and newspaper work, but upon graduation from Oberlin in 1883, financially pressed, he took a position as a schoolteacher. He was assigned a class whose rowdy students had caused a number of previous teachers to resign. Mead, who always had a serious orientation and dedication to education, threw the unruly boys out of school and proceeded to teach the remaining pupils. When the school board told him it was his job to teach *all* the students, Mead resigned after only six months. For the next three years, he worked alternately as a railroad surveyor and a tutor. In the springs and summers, he worked on the Wisconsin Central Railroad, laying the first line from Minneapolis to Moose Jaw, Canada. His precision and hard work led to his appointment as engineer in charge. In the winter, he worked as a private tutor and read a wide range of literature, philosophy, and science.

While he was still at Oberlin, Mead became close friends with a classmate, Henry Castle, who came from a wealthy landowning family in Hawaii. Inseparable during their college days, Castle and Mead endlessly discussed literature, poetry, and other contemporary writings, and together worked out their rejection of religious dogma in favor of empirical science. One summer, they even launched an ill-fated effort together as door-to-door book salesmen. Tired of surveying and uncertain about his future, Mead took Castle's advice and left the railroad to join his friend in graduate study at Harvard.

While at Harvard, Mead continued to work part-time as he diligently applied himself to philosophy and psychology. The teacher who most influenced him was the philosopher Josiah Royce (1855–1916). Royce's overall thought reflected a strong Hegelian influence, which would also be true of Mead's writings. Mead also studied Greek, Latin, German, and French. After sharing an apartment with Castle during his first school year, Mead faced financial uncertainty as summer approached. Fortunately, Mead's demeanor and the quality of his final exam so impressed the philosopher and psychologist William James (1842–1910) that James came to Mead's room on the day after the final to offer him a position as tutor to his children as the family vacationed in New Hampshire for the summer.

That summer for Mead was both educational and highly enjoyable. Between tutoring sessions, Mead found time to study works of Kant, Hegel, and Arthur Schopenhauer (1788–1860), as well as those of two then influential British philosophers—the utilitarian Henry Sedgwick (1838–1900) and the Hegelian Thomas Hill Green (1836–1882). Mead also spent long hours of conversation with James. Unfortunately, no record exists of what they talked about together.

In 1888, Mead won a scholarship to study philosophy and psychology in Germany. He was joined in his trip through Europe by both Henry Castle and Castle's sister Helen. The importance of the trip to Mead's later work and activities involved not just the lectures he attended, but also his observation of what he viewed as the successful implementation of governmentally sponsored social reforms. Mead, who would remain a lifelong member of the Republican Party (albeit its progressive wing), nonetheless was influenced by the ability of the government to improve the lot of the average individual. Dmitri N. Shalin has written:

> The extent of government involvement in the issues of social security, the popularity of the Social Democratic party, and particularly the respect socialism commanded in academic circles . . . impressed Mead, who found the situation in Germany to be in sharp contrast to the one back home, where the idea of state involvement in labor-management relations was still suspect and the term "socialism" had a somewhat odious connotation.[2]

According to Shalin, Mead's letters sent back from Germany were "brimming with enthusiasm for social reforms" and explored the question of how to institute such reforms in the United States.

In the course of their travels, Henry Castle met Frieda Steckner in Leipzig, and the two were soon married. The couple returned to the United States while both Mead and Helen Castle remained in Europe. When news came in 1891 that Frieda had died suddenly, Helen was deeply shaken. Mead's only child, Henry Mead, later wrote of the period that "Helen Castle was none too strong, and she as well as others said that George Mead saved her life or reason at that time."[3] George and Helen Castle were married in October 1891.

Directly after their marriage, the Meads returned to the United States. George had been appointed a philosophy instructor at the University of Michigan. There, Mead began a long and fruitful friendship and intellectual relationship with the philosopher John Dewey (1859–1952). Dewey presented to Mead a role model for a career that combined academic scholarship with working for social and educational reforms. At Michigan, Mead also became friends with the sociologist Charles H. Cooley (1864–1929). Cooley's emphasis on the need to study the socialization of children in order to understand adult social relationships would later be reflected in Mead's own writings.

In 1893, when Dewey was asked to organize and chair the department of philosophy at the new University of Chicago, he invited Mead to join the department's faculty. Mead remained at Chicago for the rest of his life and, in his last years, became head of the department.

Mead's contact with, and influence on, sociological thinking were continued and enhanced when he moved to Chicago, where the first (and, for many years, the foremost) center of graduate education in sociology was being developed under the direction of Albion Small (1854–1926). During Mead's years at Chicago, such eminent teachers as W. I. Thomas (1863–1947), Robert Ezra Park (1864–1944), Ernest Burgess (1886–1966), and others trained hundreds of the first generation of sociologists in the United States. Many of those students learned firsthand from Mead.

Mead's major influence came through his graduate social psychology course, which he initiated in 1900 and taught regularly for the rest of his life. In that course, Mead developed and presented his basic ideas about mind, self, socialization, and society. An impressive and powerful speaker, Mead presented clear, organized, stimulating lectures without benefit of notes. Some of his students were so impressed with Mead's lectures in that course that they hired stenographers to record and transcribe them verbatim. The edited outcome of those recordings, *Mind, Self, and Society*, was published in 1934 (three years after Mead's death) and has remained a standard sociological text.

At Chicago, Mead also formed a friendship and working relationship with Jane Addams (1860–1935). Addams was simultaneously an innovative sociological thinker, the most important founder of professional social work training and practice in the United States, a world-renowned social activist (as in her opposition to U.S. entry into World War I), and both an advocate and practitioner of social reform. The depth of their mutual influence and mutual support of reform-oriented projects has only begun to be explored. They regularly dined together (often with W. I. Thomas); she stayed at Helen Mead's parents' house when visiting Hawaii; they exchanged and developed ideas together (especially on the nature of democracy); he praised a number of her books in reviews he wrote; and they served together on numerous boards involved in reform projects. Mead, always an advocate of women's rights, publicly marched with her in a demonstration for women's suffrage in the streets of Chicago.

In his own lifetime, Mead was best known for his reform activities, his social psychology course, and his many articles on social and educational questions of the day. Concerning Mead's scholarly writings, John Dewey wrote that Mead was highly modest about the depth and profound originality of his own thought. Mead presented his ideas as modifications of earlier scholars' work and underplayed his own revolutionary contributions. Although he wrote numerous papers and articles for academic journals, Mead never produced a written work that would demonstrate the great extent to which his thought formed an innovative, systematic whole. To a degree, this lack was remedied by the publication of some of Mead's lectures, other presentations, and articles after his death on April 26, 1931. Together with *Mind, Self, and Society*, these publications included: *The Philosophy of the Present* (1932), *Movements of Thought in the Nineteenth Century* (1936), *The Philosophy of the Act* (1938), and *Selected Writings* (1964).

Social Environment

In his book *Ministers of Reform: The Progressives' Achievement in American Civilization, 1889–1920*,[4] the historian Robert M. Crunden views Mead as reflecting a somewhat typical religious, class, political, educational, and regional background of a progressive-era reformer. According to Crunden, the reformers of the progressive era tended to be the offspring of conservative Protestant families (often ministers' children) who had lost the strict faith of their parents, but who had accepted a role for themselves in improving the lot of others. This improvement was to be accomplished not by saving souls, but by advocating an enlightened set of private and governmental policies that would aid the mass of the population. Typically Republicans, they kept the party affiliation they were born into, and they had a strong identification with Abraham Lincoln, who had been idolized by their parents (who themselves had often been northern antislavery advocates and activists). It was through peaceful reform and the creation of a reform-oriented ("progressive") wing of the Republican Party, as well as through privately funded activities, that they optimistically assumed they could make the world a better place. Having a faith in science, reason, and their own abilities, they rejected any and all revolutionary politics in favor of cumulative progressive reforms. In this sense, their concern was with helping the masses as opposed to giving them political control. Immigrants were not looked at as providing a base for what is now called "cultural diversity," but as subjects to be "Americanized" and helped to fit into the goals, actions, and demeanor of middle America. These progressive reformers had great faith in the role of education to transform individuals, and many reformers therefore engaged in educational experimentation and suggesting educational reforms. They were themselves the first generation of Americans who had the wealth, inclination, and opportunity to seek graduate education.

Of course, if Mead is in some ways typical of the progressives in his thoughts and actions, he was also an intellectual of the first rate who developed his own justifications for reform actions, developed his own ideas of how to achieve social reforms scientifically, and integrated his reform notions into a set of philosophical conceptions significant to the later development of sociology.

Mead accepted middle-American values of volunteerism, self-discipline, practical action (as opposed to abstract speculation for its own sake), and an optimistic attitude toward social progress. He viewed these values as integrated into the development of American democracy. For Mead, democracy was not just a political system, but an overall emergent pattern of self-identity and social interaction. He viewed the development and expansion of American representational democracy as a fundamental social advance, but as one that had not yet been completed. For Mead, democracy entailed a society in which all individuals were united in the active pursuit of personal goals while simultaneously working together to produce a greater collective good. Mead viewed the expansion of voting rights since the revolution of 1776 as a movement toward such unity. However, he also believed that, when the ideals of democracy were fully realized, it would entail much more than the right to vote. For Mead, a fully realized democracy would involve a development of both increased individualism and enhanced self-discipline in all members of society.

In Mead's philosophy, voluntarism and self-discipline were viewed as connected to democracy. Mead saw voluntarism as an ability of persons to clarify their own goals while understanding their place in society—an ability to *choose* their own actions while engaged in a process of cooperation with others. Although democratic cooperation thus incorporates a sense of individual abilities and goals, it also requires self-discipline. Mead believed that in a democracy, social control arises from the mass of the population itself (as opposed to being coerced by an upper estate or caste). Mead asserted that external coercive and punitive control were antithetical to the fulfillment of the democratic ideals of a self-governing populace.

For Mead, democracy also implied an atmosphere conducive to the increase of scientific knowledge. In an era of technological development and industrial expansion, few restrictions were placed on the advancement of science in the United States during the late nineteenth century. Although Mead's understanding of science was considerably deeper and more sophisticated than that of most individuals, his faith in science matched that of the ordinary citizen. Mead saw the positivistic scientific method of hypothesis construction and testing as the only way of understanding the problems of modern life and of offering viable solutions to them.

Mead viewed the past development of democracy as arising from a natural (although not inevitable) process of social evolutionary emergence. But he believed the future development of democracy could best be achieved through scientifically based reform projects. An heir to the social gospel movement of midwestern Protestantism that undertook social reform in the name of religion, Mead was one of the progressive-era intellectuals who most linked the academic pursuit of knowledge with a call for a scientific justification for social reform to achieve what he viewed as a more developed democracy. This linkage is illustrated by his essays "The Working Hypothesis in Social Reform" (1899),[5] "The Philosophical Basis of Ethics" (1908),[6] "The Psychology of Punitive Justice" (1917–1918),[7] and "Philanthropy from the Point of View of Ethics" (1930).[8] The time span of these illustrative articles (from 1899 to 1930) reveals the extent to which his image of democracy, science, and social reform animated much of his thought throughout the whole of his career.

The environment of the University of Chicago encouraged a focus on questions of social problems and reforms. The philosophy department under John Dewey's direction viewed philosophy as intimately linked with practical problems, and social reform activities were viewed as a direct extension of a faculty member's academic work. The sociology department to which Mead had increasing ties through students and colleagues engaged itself in a series of studies documenting Chicago's social problems and their possible causes. And the university's ties to Jane Addams and her reform projects put Mead in touch with one of the most energetic and influential reform activists of the day. Combined with his own inclination toward social reform, this environment inspired Mead to a degree of involvement with reform projects that, considering his academic duties and scholarly achievements, is nothing short of astounding.

Hans Joas,[9] Dmitri N. Shalin,[10] and, especially, Mary Jo Deegan[11] have undertaken to document the large number of reform activities that Mead undertook in areas of education, women's rights, improving the lives of workers, improving the lives of immigrants, political reform, prison reform, the treatment of juvenile offenders, and race relations. Specific activities included serving on boards of directors of settlement houses, serving as an arbitrator in labor-management disputes, teaching in experimental schools, serving on fact-finding commissions on the causes of labor strikes, involving himself in women's rights activities, and writing and speaking to a variety of groups and organizations. Unlike many other "progressives," who showed great concern for European immigrants but had relatively no involvement in dealing with the plight of racial minorities, Mead showed a concern with the African

American population on the South Side of Chicago and formed a relationship with the pan-African nationalist Harry Dean (1864–1935), whose autobiography he helped get into print.[12]

Although Mead recognized the myriad number of problems facing America and the need to reform that society so that its democracy could evolve, giving everyone the ability to participate fully in the opportunities of the society, his work is nonetheless optimistic in its expectations. Reason and science are viewed as providing a foundation for reform and continued improvement. Even the barbarities of World War I did not dampen this optimistic outlook. Mead disagreed with his close friend Jane Addams in her opposition to the entry of the United States into World War I. An admirer of President Woodrow Wilson, Mead justified entry on the grounds that an allied victory would enhance the goals of democracy. Similarly, rather than concentrating on the outcome of that war in terms of the horrors it produced and the displaced persons whose lives had been shattered, Mead, according to Mary Jo Deegan,

> viewed the outcome of World War I positively. He saw government organizations that were adopted during wartime as a basis for a more socialist, and just, society. Optimistically, he saw World War I as the generator of international rights and organization, pointing to a more sane and secure future.[13]

Reflecting a progressive-era optimism, Mead could see a war, of unprecedented proportions, leading toward the goal of a harmonious and peaceful democratic world order. Indeed, the optimism of his era, which Mead openly expressed, often appears naive to contemporary scholars who otherwise find Mead's ideas well reasoned and acceptable. Repeated wars, economic difficulties, and social discord have made us much more pessimistic (or at least skeptical) than would have seemed reasonable to the professor at Chicago. Yet, it was perhaps the very optimism that we today find untenable that helped motivate both Mead's scholarly and social-reform activities and helped him produce the contributions to sociological knowledge that we still find significant.

Intellectual Roots

Mead maintained that history was not a series of events, but a process of reflection and interaction among individuals from which there continually emerge new forms of thought, action, and social organization. Although the past is essential for the emergence of a future, Mead argued that the emergent future is something qualitatively different from the past, not a simple continuation and elaboration of it. Mead's own intellectual system can be viewed as such an emergence.

Although *Movements of Thought in the Nineteenth Century* shows that Mead was profoundly knowledgeable about developments in philosophy, social thought, psychology, and physical science in the preceding century, and although he used ideas of earlier scholars, Mead's own systematic understanding of society is clearly different from anything that preceded it. It is distinguishable in terms of the force with which it links the development of mind, self, and society within a coherent process of emergence and adaptation. Yet despite his uniqueness, Mead's intellectual roots are clearly anchored in the ideas of a number of earlier thinkers, most significantly Hegel and Charles Darwin (1809–1882). Mitchell Aboulafia has correctly asserted that "Mead's indebtedness to German idealism, specifically Hegel, has not been addressed in the depth it merits,"[14] while Hans Joas argued that, for Mead, "the key figure for a new beginning in philosophy was Darwin."[15]

Mead's emphasis on processes of emergence is most indebted to Hegel. Hegel rejected a division of reality into *a priori* (or fixed) categories and insisted that the reality one encounters is in a continual process of transformation, with new forms transcending and emerging from old. Hegel explained the process of transcendence in terms of a dialectical process of change. In abstract terms, the Hegelian dialectic can be viewed as a triadic model, wherein the oppositional forces inherent in the present interrelate and result in a new form of existence. For Hegel, it is the dialectical process that allows the future to emerge from and yet transcend the present state of affairs. It is the development and working out of the opposed forces of the dialectic that allow novelty to emerge and meaningful change to take place. Furthermore, it is in the course of this working out that self-realization and consciousness of self arise. Mead told his students:

> Hegel took the identity revealed in the subject-object relationship and sought to show that this identity persists in all the different forms of thought. This always brings him back to a contradiction. But what he shows is that this contradiction, instead of leading to a simple destruction of thought itself, leads to a higher level on which the opposing phases are overcome. That is, in the total process he discovers what he calls a "thesis," an "antithesis," and a "synthesis."[16]

Joas has pointed out that "to Mead, Hegel's dialectical method was a discovery the significance of which Hegel himself did not fully understand."[17] The use of dialectical reasoning ran through Mead's arguments about the nature of reality and served as the foundation of his ideas about consciousness, meaning, self, group, and scientific methodology. All of these develop and change in the course of dialectical processes of opposition and emergence. For instance, Mead presented the total self as an emergence from an internal interaction between a knowing, unsocialized self (which he termed the "I") and a known, socialized self (which he termed the "me"). These two selves exist only in relationship to each other. It is through their juxtaposition and interrelationship that the complete self emerges, on the basis of which the individual can act in society and take part in the dialectical process of the production of society. (Society, as we shall see, emerges for Mead from a dialectical relationship of self and other in a process of symbolic communication and mutual role-taking.)

Like Hegel, Mead both viewed the historical emergence of social reality as always containing an element of novelty and unpredictability, and believed that social change embodied a long-run directionality toward a unified "self-realized" society. Whereas Hegel emphasized the quasi-mystical presence of an "Absolute Spirit" that overcomes its own alienation to form a self-realized unity, Mead was concerned with the emergence of a "universal society." At the end of the lectures from which *Mind, Self, and Society* were transcribed, Mead described such a society in which all social potential would be fully realized in a world unity. Although much of his discussion of a universal society is vague, Mead did assert that every individual would relate cooperatively to every other individual and thus would form a collective whole wherein the human so-cial spirit could be realized.[18]

Mead's debt to Hegel involves more than a reliance on Hegel's mode of rea-soning. In *Movements of Thought in the Nineteenth Century*, Mead asserted that Hegel "cogently insisted" that human control over the environment was a social rather than an individual accomplishment. Following Hegel, Mead argued that humans gain selfhood only within the context of an ongoing social group and that the individual does so through an identification with the group. Like Hegel, Mead believed that in-dividuals must be fully social if they are to be fully human. Human development is fulfilled only "in so far as the human form is recognized as an organic part of the so-cial whole."[19]

Armed with the Hegelian emphasis on the emergence of individuality only within and through the social group, Mead attempted to supplant the dominant neo-Kantian social psychologies of his day. Immanuel Kant (1724–1804) had maintained that per-ception and understanding take place only through the mediation of fixed categories of the mind. In the late nineteenth century, there were two schools of thought in so-cial psychology that were essentially neo-Kantian in their acceptance of such fixed or *a priori* mental categories. These were the gestalt psychology of Wolfgang Köhler (1887–1967), Kurt Koffka (1886–1941), and Max Wertheimer (1880–1943), and the school of experimental psychology of Wilhelm Wundt (1832–1920).

Although Mead cited Wundt's work on the role of gestures in communication and the development of the mind, and although he read and noted the observations and arguments about perception made by the gestaltists, Mead rejected both schools of thought as a foundation for a fully developed analysis of social behavior. He saw both schools as mistakenly assuming that the mind was relatively fixed in structure. Furthermore, both schools tended to assume the existence of the self as an innate property of an individual, rather than viewing it as developing through an emergent process in the course of social conduct. Mead's emphasis on the emergent nature of the self led him to a focus on socialization that was not to be found in the work of Wundt or the gestaltists.

The influence of Hegel on Mead's thought is matched only by that of Darwin. Whereas some might see the philosophical speculation of Hegel and the detailed analysis and measured biological theorizing of Darwin as representing antithetical forms of thoughts, Mead found a fundamental harmony in their ideas. Hegel empha-sized that reality was in a constant process of evolutionary emergence; Darwin de-scribed life as a process that gives rise to varying structural forms. Structure in Darwin's thought was the expression of a process of emergence and adaptive change. As with Hegel, Mead saw Darwin as incorporating an element of indeterminism and novelty in the course of evolutionary emergence. For Mead, Darwin's emphasis on random variations and selection in terms of environmental conditions showed a flex-ibility to life. Life could develop in unforeseen structures and adaptive outcomes. In-deed, Mead's dialectic of self parallels Darwin's model of natural selection in the sense that the random variations of action presented by the *I* are judged and selected by the *me* (which incorporates social environmental experience), thus producing novel forms of adaptive behavior.

Mead's concern with adaptation was not just a passing interest but a central concern, which demonstrates his debt to Darwinian thought. For Mead, mind, self, reason, and society were all adaptive mechanisms that allowed for the continuance of life. In a thorough reading of Mead's works, one gets the image of a constant adaptation and adjustment of the social individual to the societal environment.

Mead believed that Darwin's emphasis on adaptation demonstrated that in scientific thinking there was no necessary contradiction between causal and teleological reasoning. Although forms of existence are shaped to a great extent by the exigencies of the environment, they change in a direction of adaptation to environmental circumstances. Mead argued that, with the rise of human reflective consciousness, teleological components of change increase in significance. This increase occurs because social individuals do not directly respond to environmental stimuli but are able to select, reflect on, and respond to stimuli in terms of goal-oriented activity.

In his *Expression of the Emotions in Man and Animals*, Darwin attempted to account for the role of gestures in the course of biological evolution. Mead viewed that work as fundamental in laying the foundations for his own analysis of the central role that gestures and symbols play in the development of mind, self, and society. Mead maintained that in social interaction the simple (nonsignificant) gestures discussed by Darwin are accompanied by significant gestures or symbols. Whereas nonsignificant gestures serve as stimuli to the other with whom one is interacting, significant symbols serve as stimuli to *both* self and other. In doing so, significant symbols permit subjects to reflect on and thus to shape their own actions. Thus the growling of dogs, though a useful adaptive warning system, does not provide the means for self and social development that the use of a human language does.

Hegel and Darwin can be viewed as the paramount influences on Mead's systemic social formulations, but a number of other thinkers were also influential. Among them one can include the French philosopher Jean-Jacques Rousseau (1712–1778), the British economist Adam Smith (1723–1790), a number of American philosophers collectively known as the "pragmatists," the French philosopher Henri Bergson (1859–1941), the theoretical physicist Albert Einstein (1879–1955), and the sociologists Charles Cooley and Jane Addams.

For Mead, Rousseau had demonstrated the possibility of a rational democratic order based on mutual acknowledgment of rights and a shared social identification. Central to Rousseau's political ideas is a distinction between a "particular will" and a "general will." The *particular will* involves those actions whereby individuals act toward their own particular self-interest. The *general will* involves an orientation toward an identification with the good of the collective whole. Rousseau envisioned the possibility of a state in which individuals collectively determined the general will. Such a state would be a rational republic based on a natural feeling for community and society.

In Mead's thought, Rousseau's general will appears in a somewhat transformed state as Mead's concept of the "generalized other." The *generalized other* involves the socialized aspect of the self's (the *me*'s) orientation toward the shared collective meanings and rules in a group, community, or society. Mead did not conceive of the generalized other as biogenetic, but as an orientation that develops in the course of socialization. For Mead, children develop through a series of stages. In this process, they go from being able to orient themselves to only particular others, to a relatively small generalized other, to a generalized other oriented toward a whole community or society. Ultimately Mead envisioned a "generalized other" that would encompass a cooperative, unified orientation toward the whole of humanity. Such a state of affairs would involve the realization of Mead's "universal society."

One of the main socializing forces that Mead saw as contributing to the historical expansion of the "generalized other" and the rise of modern societies was that of economic exchange. Mead believed that the writings of Adam Smith showed that society was a system of production and exchange, and that economic activity was not a static amassing of wealth. Mead's presentation of exchange as a predominantly positive force (for self and social development) reflects the influence of Smith. With his own emphasis on emergence, Mead does not condemn the *laissez-faire* capitalist notions of Smith, but rather sees them as providing a foundation for later modification and reform that would create a more equitable, just, and democratic society. Similarly, while simultaneously rejecting the extreme individualism and hedonism of Smith's works, Mead appreciates him as the founder of social psychology for his concern with how individuals work collectively to come to decisions involving coordinated activity that allows for greater societal adaptation.

Mead's interest in emergence and adaptation was further supported by his understanding and interpretation of the pragmatic philosophy of Charles Peirce (1839–1914), William James, and John Dewey. Mead agreed with the pragmatists' position that ideas were grounded in day-to-day experience. Following the pragmatists, Mead asserted that the "meaning" an object had for an individual depended on the individual's purposes at hand and the environmental context in which the individual found him- or herself. Thus *meaning* is not an abstract underlying essence, but an adaptive mechanism that permits manipulation of objects to attain one's goals. In that meanings arise and are shaped by experience, they also undergo emergent development in the course of social activity.

The emphasis on the notion of goal-oriented action in pragmatic philosophy sharply distinguished Mead from the psychological behaviorists of his day (and ours). For Mead, human action depended on a reflective self that could imagine future alternatives and plan action on the basis of an evaluated choice among alternatives. From the pragmatist James, Mead borrowed the notions that the total self is a process involving the knowing (the *I*) and the known (the *me*) selves and that the outcome of an act depends on the two aspects reflecting on one another and producing a possible novel course of action. Echoing Dewey, Mead asserted that much human action is not based on a simple stimulus-response mechanism but involves a reflective mediation between stimulus and action. In other words, for Mead, human behavioral activity is not automatically triggered by some stimulus in the environment; rather, stimuli are perceived and reflected on before external behavior occurs. Such reflection allows one to escape the simple environmental determinism that the behaviorists postulated and to account for adaptive goal-oriented activities.

Mead saw Albert Einstein's work in physics as significant for his own work because it also viewed science as nondeterministic. For Mead, Einstein's theory of relativity showed that science must take into account a multiplicity of perspectives simultaneously. As one changes one's perspective, the observed relationships between objects change. Mead reasoned that a view of science that included a relativity of perspectives was incompatible with any dogmatic statement of absolute determinism. What appears simply determined from one perspective might not appear so determined from another, equally valid, perspective. Furthermore, how an actor understands and acts toward reality depends on the perspectives the actor learns and develops. Mead insisted that Einstein implied a world in which reality can be conceptualized anew. Mead's social analysis thus escapes the reliance on a strict determinist view of earlier sociological positivists like Comte and Durkheim whose thought is implicitly modeled on a pre-Einsteinian Newtonian physics that allowed room neither for indeterminancy, nor for a multiplicity of perspectives in ascertaining the nature of reality.

Mead was highly sympathetic to the writings of the French philosopher Henri Bergson, who attempted to give a philosophical interpretation and elaboration on the significance of Einstein's ideas. Bergson (a schoolmate of Durkheim) emphasized that, despite the necessity for humans to hold things constant in their perceptions, reality was in fact in a constant state of unforeseen evolutionary emergence, without end. Bergson also emphasized the relativity of time from the point of view of an individual human actor. External time measured by the ticking of a clock, which breaks reality up into discontinuous units, is not the time through which we experience reality and plan our own actions. Rather, for Bergson, humans also have an internal sense of time (or duration) relative to their own actions and psychological states. It is from the perspective of internal time that we can speak of time "flying by" or moving very slowly. Mead accepted Bergson's distinction of external and internal time; he maintained that human acts are measured in duration and that the passing of internal time is based on the development and changes of our actions in relationship to our social environment.

If Mead has had his greatest influence among sociologists, his own thought was influenced by two sociologists of his day. While at the University of Michigan, Mead came into contact with Charles H. Cooley. Cooley, then himself a young instructor in sociology, was unique among his generation of American sociologists in that he was sympathetic toward much of Hegel's thought. In his conception of the "looking-glass self," Cooley emphasized how much our self-conceptions emerge from reflection on our reactions to how we perceive others perceiving us. Cooley saw the self as emerging through social activity. In order to grasp the origins of this self, Cooley spent much of his life in the analysis of the processes of socialization by which the self develops. Although Mead, while taking a course from Wilhelm Dilthey (1833–1911) in Germany, had given some earlier thought to the study of the moral development of children, it was Cooley who most likely influenced Mead's attempts to analyze the social processes by which the self comes into existence and develops a socially cooperative orientation. Mead acknowledged his intellectual debt to Cooley in his 1929 essay "Cooley's Contribution to American Thought."[20] In that essay, however, Mead was critical of what he believed was Cooley's failure to account adequately for human behavior because of an overemphasis on subjective emotional states. Finally, as noted earlier, much of Mead's thought and action was animated by his conception of an emergent democracy. Through a long period in which they exchanged ideas, Mead came to incorporate many of Jane Addams's views in his image of American democracy and its potentiality to de-velop into a more inclusive and just social order.

IDEAS

Society

For Mead, human society was fundamentally a process of adaptation to the environ-ment. It involves a division of labor and the cooperative organization of acting indi-viduals into groups and institutions. In that society allows for the ongoing development of the individual self, it must exist prior to the particular individual. Yet, although society forms the context in which the self develops, society's own exis-tence is dependent on acting individuals to create social groups and structures. The relationship between the individual and society is thus one of mutuality and dialec-tical interdependence. *Individuals emerge from society, and society emerges from indi-viduals' actions.* For Mead, a society was dependent on humans interacting and taking the roles of one another. In the course of such action and mutual role-taking, the so-cial reality of group structure emerges, which then serves as the context for further role-taking and group development. Dependent on role-taking, the dialectical emer-gence of society also depends on the ability of humans to understand one another and to demonstrate their understanding of one another. Communication thus allows so-ciety to exist and to develop.

Mead defined the social in terms of a "process of readjustment" and "mutual ad-justment."[21] Because such adjustments in humans are based on learning and the use of language, human society is much more flexible and capable of rapid adaptive change than are the societies of social insects, such as bees and ants. This flexibility is seen as a great adaptive advance, which separates humans from infrahuman species. Unlike genetically determined insect societies, human societies are founded on a flexible process of shared communications through which collective actions can be planned and adjusted. Their greater malleability has allowed human societies to flourish while dealing with a wide array of environmentally problematic circumstances. Variable in size, group structure, actions, and degree of division of labor, human societies have al-lowed continuity of action from one generation to the next and have developed radi-cally new forms of behavior to meet new internal and external challenges.

In "National-Mindedness and International-Mindedness" (1929),[22] Mead re-ferred to society as an adaptive mechanism in that it produces unity out of diversity. Arising from the combined but different actions of specialized individuals, coopera-tion in a social whole admits the possibility of achievements that otherwise would be impossible. In this essay, Mead argued that there were two underlying sources of so-cial solidarity and social organization: "self-conscious diversity" and "identity of com-mon inputs." The former referred to unity arising from a reflective understanding of one's part in achieving a greater good via cooperation; the latter involved the forma-tion of group structures out of a common feeling of hostility and opposition to others.

Mead was aware that throughout history the latter form of social solidarity was significant in the development of new social organizational forms. For instance, Mead referred to the way social unity that was based on hostility toward other groups led to an advance toward a "wider social organization"—the emergence of tribal from clan-based social organization. Yet despite assertions that groups are most easily formed in opposition to one another, Mead ardently believed in the possibility of social solidarity organized purely around perceived roles and mutually beneficial efforts—that is, in the possibility of a future peaceful world order. In either case, for Mead, a society involved a division of labor in common efforts. At one point, he defined a society as "a systematic order of individuals in which each has a more or less differentiated activity."[23] Once in existence, organized groups provide the basis of more persistent coordinated activities, which cope with major problems of internal or external adaptation. Mead occasionally referred to such persistent coordinated group activity as "institutions."

Although Mead believed that society and social organization depended on the existence of reflective individuals with minds and selves, he also believed that mind and self develop only in the context of society. In order to escape the chicken-and-egg problem of origins, Mead hypothesized that humans lived in social groups before they evolved into their present biological form. Sociality precedes the species; it is through social relationships that mind and self first appeared. Individuals are born and grow up in social circumstances. They are members of society from birth; but in their childhood years, individuals develop an adult mind and self capable of maintaining society. Yet despite the fundamental priority Mead gave society over the individual, society still emerges from individual behavior, and "the social act" is the basic unit of societal existence.

For Mead, social reality appears to be dependent on individuals behaving with conscious attention to other individuals in a situation requiring some degree of cooperative effort. In other words, at the basis of an ongoing society is "the social act." In "Social Consciousness and the Consciousness of Meaning" (1910), Mead defined a social act as "one in which one individual serves in his action as a stimulus to a response from another individual."[24]

In the social act, individuals adapt their behaviors to the actions of each other. Such mutual adjustment is at the basis of the cooperative behavior that underlies group and institutional structures. Mead was insistent that human group activity is not some automatic display of preplanned or preprogrammed behaviors. Social group cooperation, which underlies society's existence, requires continual assessment by actors of the situation and the behaviors of others and the readjustment of their actions to others' situations and actions. "Social conduct must be continually readjusted after it has already commenced, because the individuals to whose conduct our own answers, are themselves constantly varying their conduct as our responses become evident."[25] The social act is thus one in which the actions of self and other, which have been instigated by one another, produce the relationship of cooperation underlying society's existence.

For individuals to engage in a social act, they must be able to project themselves mentally into a position in which they can imagine how others will react to their behavior. Mead terms this process of imagination "taking the role of the other." To take the role of the other allows the individual to assess possible reactions of others to various behaviors and to choose his or her behavior in terms of the most desired reactions. Mutual role-taking thus allows coordination of behavior.

Whereas in a two-person interaction actors might take the role of the particular other person with whom they are engaged in interaction, in a larger group actors must focus on, and imagine, the general reaction of the group as a whole. Imagining the reactions of a group, community, or larger society in assessing one's prospective social acts, Mead terms "taking the role of a generalized other." In "The Objective Reality of Perspectives" (1925), Mead wrote that "it is only in so far as the individual acts not only in his own perspective but also in the perspective of others, especially in the common perspective of a group, that a society arises."[26] In that same essay, Mead asserted that it is only through taking the role of the generalized other that individuals can cooperatively produce and manipulate the physical objects necessary to continued societal existence. Taking the role of the other allows for the continued existence of society, because it allows individuals to experience and evaluate themselves indirectly as objects of their own actions. Mead told his students that a person "becomes an object to himself only by taking the attitudes of other individuals toward himself."[27]

Mead believed that most social control—and the most effective social control—arose from role-taking. In an important passage in *Mind, Self, and Society*, Mead maintained that social control tends to operate most usefully and effectively through "self-criticism." By imagining the reactions of others and not acting in ways likely to produce adverse reactions that would interrupt cooperative group endeavors, individuals keep their own behavior in line. Taking the role of the other, however, is essentially a social behavior. Hence, Mead wrote, "Self-criticism is essentially social criticism, and behavior controlled by self-criticism is essentially behavior controlled socially."[28] Mead thus saw social control as not necessarily either repressive or destructive of human individuality and reason.

Whereas role-taking is fundamental to the social act, to social cooperation, and to social control, meaningful communication underlies role-taking. Communication, in turn, allows individuals to indicate ideas, reflections, plans, and reactions and thus enables them to estimate others' reactions to one's own possible behaviors. It is thus language and language-based communication that allow human society to exist. Although language and meanings are learned and developed through social interaction, it is social acts based on linguistic communication that make society itself possible.

Although society exists through communication, society is, in fact, an emerging structure of groups and institutions. Cooperative social interaction involving mutual adjustments make society a constantly changing phenomenon. As we have seen, Mead believed that society was in a state of "continual emergence." Mead believed the direction of overall development was toward increasing societal size, complexity, and harmonious cooperation. Furthermore, once emergent change has occurred in a society, it is not possible for the society to revert, or to degenerate, to an earlier level of social existence. Mead argued that social change is tied to a change and an expansion in individuals' self-consciousness. With social development, the generalized other toward which individuals orient their actions expands to encompass a larger community. Once this expansion in self-consciousness has taken place, Mead believed it would be perpetuated. Thus social development, once accomplished, cannot be turned back. Like Durkheim, Mead was critical of those who believed it possible to resurrect archaic social forms. With developments in social consciousness, a society's future will not look like its past.

Overall, Mead believed that societal development and the development of the individual occurred together. Rather than larger societies crushing individuality, Mead believed that individuality was least developed in small simple societies. As society expands in size and scope, individuals draw on more and more others whose role they can take. With the expansion of role-taking, actors can imagine and plan more varied and unique actions; thus individuality increases. Without paradox, Mead argued that individualism is tied, not opposed, to increased social size, cooperation, and even (self-disciplined) social control.

In terms of social development, Mead viewed the family as the most fundamental social group, in two senses. It was fundamental *structurally* as the smallest group capable of maintenance and continuation of the species. *Developmentally*, it was the fundamental group out of which larger forms of social organization developed. Mead asserted in *Mind, Self, and Society* that all "larger units or forms of human social organization such as the clan or the state are ultimately based upon, and . . . are developments from or extensions of, the family."[29] Whereas the clan and the tribe developed directly out of a family organization, Mead argued that the modern national state arose historically from tribal organization and thus forms an indirect development out of the family.

Not only is societal development associated with growth, but it also leads to functional differentiation. Mead maintained that with social change comes an increase in specialization, functionally different tasks, and the degree of functional integration and mutual dependence of a society's members. In terms of change, differentiation, and the development of a societal generalized other, the two most important social forces have been those of economics and religion. According to Mead, economic exchange has been historically conducive to societal development by bringing different peoples together in cooperative and mutually beneficial efforts. Although economic exchange has been characterized to some extent by exploitation and one-sided advantage, Mead held that overall it yielded larger amounts of interaction. It made individuals take the roles of others and orient their actions toward others to whom they would otherwise have been strangers.

Paralleling the influence of economic exchange in societal development was the influence of religious belief. Mead maintained that religion, over time, developed universal concepts of unity. It was conducive to getting people to orient their action toward a wider array of others. Secularized conceptions of religious universalism, for Mead, had developed into notions of universal brotherhood and democratic rights. Mead believed in the possibility that universalism might become more than a social idea. Indeed, he believed that a universal society, which would incorporate all of humanity in self-realized unity, mutual concern, and peace, could one day emerge as a reality.

The Individual in Society

Mead maintained that human society was a society of "selves." To be constituted by having a *self* makes humans and human societies distinct from other creatures and the biologically fixed societies to which they might belong. To have a self implies that the individual is neither purely an object pushed around by natural forces, nor a totally free subject capable of choosing his or her actions in a context-free vacuum. Rather, for Mead, to have a self implied that individuals are *both* subject and object of their own acts; on the basis of desired goals, they imagine, plan, and choose the acts that they take. Individuals are objects of their own acts in that they reflect on, and respond to, what they have done. Thus to have a self implies a degree of self-awareness or self-consciousness, an ability both to act and to step back mentally and observe one's actions as objects to which one can respond. To be an object of one's own self involves taking the role of the other through which one can perceive, evaluate, and respond to one's own behavior. It further implies that individuals do not act in a meaningless succession of individual behaviors but, instead, reflect on their acts and modify and coordinate their social actions in the pursuance of conscious goals. Mead pointed out to his students that an individual becomes the subject of his own action "only in so far as he first becomes an object of himself," which is accomplished by "taking the attitudes of other individuals toward himself" in the course of joint behavior.[30] In "The Social Self" (1913), Mead argued that the self as a subject is impossible without the self as an object; in "A Behavioristic Account of the Significant Symbol" (1922), he maintained that the self as a subject arises only when the "individual becomes a social object in experience to himself."[31]

The self can be both the subject and the object of its behavior because it is not a fixed mechanism of some kind. Rather, for Mead, the self was emphatically presented as a *process* of noting, imagining, planning, reflecting, and judging. As we have seen, Mead divided the overall self-process into two phases (sometimes inappropriately referred to as the "parts of the self"): those of the *I* and the *me*.

As a process, the self comes into existence when action is necessitated. That is, self arises when a flow of events is interrupted and decisions and actions must be made. Such interruptions of events are a natural part of social existence; thus society demands the constant arising of selves and the working out of coordinated actions. Mead presented the *I* as that aspect of the self which is involved in the development or "reconstruction" of activity in order to resolve the conflict produced in oneself by the interruption of events. The *I* is the creative or imaginative phase of the self, which creates and suggests new lines of action. It arises in the immediacy of the present and offers proposals that will allow subjects to adapt their behavior to new circumstances—for example, to changes in the behavior of others with whom one is engaged in interaction. As the imaginative phase of the self, the *I* involves the possibility of novelty, uncertainty, and self-surprise: "It is the self of unnecessitated choice, of undreamt hypothesis, of inventions that change the whole force of nature."[32] Besides being the imaginative aspect of the self, the *I* is also the self's knowing and conscious aspect. It is the *I* that is conscious and aware of a break or conflict that needs to be resolved by the development of new action. As the knowing, conscious aspect of the self, the *I* exists only in the present, reflecting phase of the self. It reflects but is not known or reflected on.

The known or reflected-on aspect of the self process is the *me*. The *me* is the aspect of the self of which the *I* is aware. It is a person's conception and understanding of who that person is. The *me* contains subjects' past learning; their knowledge of different roles, situations, and individuals; their awareness of social values; and their understanding of the social implications of various types of acts. Whereas the *I* is the conscious and reflecting aspect of the self, the *me* is the aspect of self-identity that subjects are conscious of and reflect on. And whereas the *I* manifests an imaginative novelty and even an impulsive orientation toward new and previously unforeseen lines of action, the *me* provides the self with a consistency of structure by reference to social rules and values. Mead noted that, to an extent, the *me* can be conceptualized as the judgmental aspect of the self engaged in the self-censorship of one's actions. The *me* contains knowledge of situations where conformity to rules is demanded, as well as knowledge of situations where less conformity is required and in which one might open up and act more freely on the imaginative impulses and ideas of the *I*.

For Mead, a self was essential for day-to-day activity. In the course of our social actions, we are constantly encountering situations in which we must note what is going on, figure out what we want to do, judge and select plans of action that will get the response from others we desire, and act on those plans. Humans were not passive responders to society but beings who chose and reevaluated their own lines of action in the context of social situations. The very fact that we must act in society forces us to choose, reflect on, and reevaluate our actions in reference to ourselves, our goals, and the behavior of others. Whereas society for Mead had certain contours and patterns, it was also seen as a process of mutual adjustment and adaptation—a fabric continually woven by action arising from the reflecting *I* and the judgmental *me*. As actions and situations change, the knowledge of how one has acted and how others have responded is incorporated into the *me*, thus expanding one's self-knowledge and one's knowledge of others and society.

Normally, Mead maintained that the *I* and *me* exist as alternating phases of the overall self-process. In what Mead termed an "internal conversation," there is a movement back and forth between the novel proposals of the *I* and the judgmental reactions of the *me* until a line of action is formulated and emerges in external behavior. The alternation of *I* and *me* is the *typical* mode of the self-process, but there is also an *atypical* mode in which the *I* and *me* phases occur simultaneously or "fuse." In such cases as an immediate team effort to save someone from drowning or in religious experiences or patriotic fervors, the *I* and *me* disappear as distinct phases. The fusion of the two, said Mead, produces "the peculiar sense of exaltation which belongs to the religious and patriotic attitudes in which the reaction one calls out in others is the response which one is making in oneself."[33] Such an attitude of oneness and unity with all those around oneself—a collective sense of shared being—is akin to what Durkheim called "collective effervescense."

For Mead, the self is a process of adaptation and interaction that appears differently in changing circumstances. We appear one way to someone we know at work and another way to someone with whom we play baseball. As Mead put it: "We divide ourselves up in all sorts of different selves with reference to our acquaintances. We discuss politics with one and religion with another. There are all sorts of different selves answering to all sorts of different social relations."[34] Mead maintained that the existence of a plurality of selves was a necessary condition of modern life, not a pathological trait. The only time such a plurality of selves becomes pathological is under a condition of "dissociation," where one self in one situation forgets and is unaware of the person's other selves. Such a case of "multiple personalities" Mead ascribes to an unusually extreme emotional disturbance. Normal individuals, on the other hand, vary their self-presentations while retaining a total overall view of who they are and how they act.

The self both depends on and permits the human ability to think or reflect. Indeed, Mead at times referred to the self as a "reflexive self." Thinking or reflection, for Mead, begins and ends in social action. That is, thought arises from a need to act in a social circumstance and ends with an overt action in relationship to social others. When action is blocked, thought involving an "internal conversation" between the *I* and the *me* commences. Whereas some psychological writers have argued that frustration produces aggression, Mead maintained that frustrated action produces conscious thinking. In his early essay "Suggestions toward a Theory of the Philosophical Disciplines," Mead wrote:

> The assumption made here is that all analytical thought commences with the presence of problems and the conflict between different lines of activity. The further assumption is that it continues always to be an expression of such conflict and the solution of the problems involved; that all reflective thought arises out of real problems present in immediate experience, and is occupied entirely with the solution of these problems or their attempted solution; that this solution finally is found in the possibility of continuing the activity, that has been stopped, along new or old lines, when such reflective thought ceases in the nature of the case.[35]

In terms of human action, thought and reflection play a mediating function between a social stimulus and a behavioral reaction. Rather than external stimuli leading to an automatic response, humans stop and reflect on the significance of the stimuli. Such a temporary delay gives individuals time to take the role of the other. It lets them formulate possible actions and evaluate these actions in terms of others' responses and of their utility in achieving goals. Thought thus permits the simultaneous pursuit of personal goals and social cooperation. It lets humans orient their actions toward a desired future, rather than merely being determined by stimuli in the present. Because of his belief in such abilities, Mead, unlike Freud, posited no underlying antagonism between the development of one's own individuality and goals and the existence of social roles and other social actors. Indeed, one can best achieve one's own ends by being adept at taking the role of the other and imagining forms of action that will aid the other as the other aids you.

Mead's conception of reflective thought is apparent in his discussion of intelligence in *Mind, Self, and Society*. He defined *intelligence* in terms of a delayed reaction to an event that allows one to solve present problems by choosing behaviors in terms of their future consequences. Human intelligence thus depends both on knowledge and memory and on foresight. It involves delaying, selecting, and organizing a response in terms of socially cooperative and purposive behavior.

In the course of thought, the individual must deal with the objects of the environment. Indeed, thought begins with reference to environmental objects that have inhibited one's behavior and terminates with a plan of action about how to handle or manipulate objects. Simply defined, an object in Mead's writings appears to be anything tangible or intangible that one can indicate to oneself and act toward. Thus an object can be a physical thing (for example, a book), an individual (John Smith), a social role (a teacher), an idea (freedom of speech), or oneself. As we have seen in the discussion of the self, for Mead, subjects make themselves an object of attention and act toward themselves from the role of the other. The ability to view objects and situations from different perspectives is itself, for Mead, an essential ingredient of thought and reflection. The more perspectives one can take, the more capable one is of formulating actions to accomplish one's purposes.

If objects are to be handled, they must be both perceived and understood. In *The Philosophy of the Present*, Mead maintained that perception of objects takes place in terms of one's past knowledge and one's purposes at hand. In other words, one does not perceive the world in the same manner in which photography processes images. Rather, one pays attention to things in terms of past learning. For instance, a craftsman will "see" a piece of furniture in a different way than will someone not trained in woodworking; a painter will "see" a work of art in terms of technique not seen by the nonartist who is ignorant of such techniques. Similarly, perception will vary with one's purposes at hand—that is, what one wants to do. One will perceive a wooden plank differently depending on whether one is intending to build a boat, to construct a piece of furniture, or to use it as a weapon of defense. Whereas in the first case, one might note whether it is cracked or not, in the second one will focus on grains and knots, and in the third on how it might be held.

Just as perception varies with past knowledge and purposes at hand, so does how one understands an object—its meaning. Mead noted that earlier philosophers had done their best to obscure the concept of *meaning* by discussing the term in metaphysically obscure language or ascribing it to underlying essences that are not easily discovered. For Mead, the meaning of an object was clearly and simply its prospective use. For instance, based on past learning and usual purposes at hand, the meaning of a chair is generally something to sit down on. On the other hand, for a lion tamer, the meaning of a chair in some circumstances is that it is an object that enables him to keep a lion at bay.

Following Mead's logic, the perception and meaning of objects in one's environment are crucial in influencing one's reflections and the development of one's actions. What one perceives and what one understands objects to mean will influence how one reflects on and plans to achieve one's goals by means of social action. Of course, for the same person in different circumstances, both meaning and perception are variable. One must keep in mind that meaning and perception are not fixed in external nature, but exist in terms of a relationship between persons and their social contexts. Perceptions and meanings are not static but change with an individual's social learning and the context of an individual's reflective thought.

Mead termed the whole process of perception of meaning, reflection, and self-indication (taking oneself as an object) as *mind*. The processes of *mind* and *self* are thus mutually dependent and exist through each other. One can have a self only to the extent that one is "minded"; one can engage in reflection only to the extent that one has a social self oriented toward achieving some goals. Although both mind and self exist only in the relationship to one another, they both, like society, depend on the use of language and on what Mead terms "significant symbols." Indeed, processes of self, mind, and human social relations as a whole exist only because the use of significant symbols makes them possible.

Mead viewed human language as being composed of significant symbols: the building blocks of language and the foundation of self, mind, and reflection. The use of such symbols distinguished humans and human societies from those of other animals. As we have seen, although both humans and animals use a form of gestures called *nonsignificant gestures*, only humans use the more developed form of *significant symbols*. Thus to understand what Mead meant by "significant symbols," we must first understand what he meant by "gesture" and "nonsignificant gesture."

In "The Genesis of the Self and Social Control" (1924–1925), Mead defined a gesture as "that part of the act or attitude of one individual engaged in a social act which serves as the stimulus to another individual to carry out his part of the whole act."[36] In other words, a gesture is any vocalized sound or body movement that one creature uses to instigate or stimulate the action of another creature such that an act involving the mutual influence of both parties occurs. The cry of a kitten instigating its feeding by its mother; the baring of the teeth of one dog, which is followed by the growls of another; and the spoken request to borrow a quarter, followed by the giving of the coin, are all examples of gestures and responses. Yet, although all three are gestures, Mead would term those in the first two examples *nonsignificant gestures* but describe the last example as involving the use of *significant symbols*.

A nonsignificant gesture is a mechanism of adjustment of one organism to another that occurs without reflection, deliberation, or conscious intention. Rather, nonsignificant gestures produce immediate, biologically based, habitual, or reflex reactions on the part of an organism in response to a sound or movement made by another organism. Thus the baring of teeth of one dog is followed by the growling of another without the first dog having intended to produce, or imagined producing, the response by the second. Further, a nonsignificant gesture involves neither reflection nor response by the organism that has made the gesture. The first dog, for example, does not reflect on the significance of having bared its teeth, nor does it decide not to do the same in the future; rather, it responds only to the gestures of the other animal (that is, it reacts to the growling of the second dog by growling itself). Whereas humans use nonsignificant gestures in habitual, unthinking behavior and in such trained immediate responses as the feint and parry of a fencing match, human self and social action depend on the use of significant symbols.

Mead defined the significant symbol as a gesture, sign, or word "which is addressed to the self when it is addressed to another."[37] That is, a significant symbol involves communication wherein the individual takes the role of another and is able to reflect back on the significance and outcome of his or her own action. According to Mead, "It is through the ability to be the other at the same time that he is himself that the symbol becomes significant."[38] Behind the display of a significant symbol is an idea or meaning that is shared and mutually understood by self and other. (Thus, if I say "sit in the chair," the sounds of "sit in the chair" mean roughly the same to the other as to myself.) Significant symbols involve the mutual sharing of the meaning of objects and therefore the ability to adjust and coordinate joint actions and jointly to manipulate objects to achieve actors' goals. By the use of significant symbols, humans' abilities to shape the world, develop new technologies, and modify the environment are developed. Thus the use of significant symbols is an important evolutionary advance in allowing humans to cope with their environment. It provides a flexibility in mutually adjusting actions that is not found in other species.

Significant symbols are at the root of spoken language. Indeed, *language* in Mead's writings appears as a structured arrangement of vocalized significant symbols. Vocalization was highly important for Mead. Vocal gestures are heard by their maker at the same time that they are heard by others. They thus allow one to respond and reflect on one's own remarks simultaneously with, and while noting, the response of the other.

As significant symbols, the meanings of words in language are arbitrary. Unlike nonlanguage vocal gestures (such as the howling of a wolf or the cries of a baby chimpanzee), the words of a language are not genetically fixed in meaning. The vocalization of the term "chair," for instance, is a conventional symbol for something to sit in, and another mutually understood sound would be equally useful. The advantage of the arbitrariness of significant symbols is that terms can be created (or modified) to deal with and allow action using new objects. Thus the invention of words such as "television," "computer," and "spaceship" has allowed the development of new social actions and accomplishments.

For Mead, it was the use of significant symbols that makes *mind* possible. Mental reflection depends on learning and using shared symbols. *Self* also arises from interaction using significant symbols. It is while communicating with others that we develop a self-identity and that the processes of self and role-taking take place. Indeed, for Mead, consciousness, ideas, and actions are planned, undertaken, and conceptualized using significant symbols. Significant symbols allow humans to orient themselves toward a future. They permit us to imagine objects that are not physically present and plan actions toward them. Significant symbols allow the mediation of thought and planning between stimulus and response. They thus permit reflection on, and choice from, a number of alternatives and make human choice a possibility. With significant symbols, people thus escape the strict determinism of present stimuli and are capable of choosing actions aimed at the collective achievement of human purposes and goals.

Methodology

Although Mead's assertions about the composition of the individual and society have generally been viewed as representing an interpretive perspective, his methodological beliefs contained a number of traditionally positivistic assumptions. Most notable among these were Mead's belief in a unity of method among the physical sciences, the social sciences, and even some of the humanities (for example, philosophy and literary studies) and his emphasis on a scientific method grounded in hypothesis-testing procedures. On the other hand, it would be a mistake to view Mead as definitely within the positivistic camp. Although Mead accepted some positivistic ideas, he also held some decidedly humanistic opinions on how to study social reality. These included a focus on facts and concepts as social constructions that can be recast as one's conceptualization of social reality changes. Mead also explicitly used both dialectic and teleological reasoning along with the mechanical and causal reasoning used by positivistic thinkers. Finally, Mead saw the focus of social study as centering on the unit of social act, and taking into account the nondeterministic aspect of the act and the role of subjective reflection and choice.

Mead's strongest statements about the unity of scientific method appeared in his 1906 essay "The Teaching of Science in College." In that paper he wrote:

> The method of study of the languages, history, literature and the so-called social sciences has become to a large degree that of the natural sciences. There is certainly no fundamental

distinction between the researches of the historian, the philologist, the social statistician and those of the biologist, the geologist or even the physicist and chemist, in point of method.[39]

Mead further asserted in that essay that science could be seen as forming "a single body of knowledge" composed of different but mutually determined parts. Fundamental to this postulated unity of method was a problem-solving conception of science that tests hypotheses.

The French philosopher René Descartes (1596–1650) had emphasized an epistemological approach of total doubt—an approach that made all aspects of reality problematic and simultaneously open to reasoned investigation. Mead agreed with Descartes in his bold expansion of rational thinking to the study of all existing phenomena, but he took exception to the idea that one can make any sense of the world by making everything problematic at the same time. In *The Philosophy of the Present*, Mead insisted that scientific research must be focused on a particular problem in which the researcher's assumptions about other aspects of reality are, for the time being, unquestioned. Only by such a process of focused attention on the problematic did Mead believe that scientific advance would be possible. Mead wrote in his essay "Scientific Method and the Individual Thinker" (1917)[40] that something becomes problematic and the focus of scientific analysis when it appears to be inconsistent with the researcher's assumptions about how reality works, when it conflicts with one's assumed ideas and meanings. In the lectures from which *Movements of Thought in the Nineteenth Century* was transcribed, Mead maintained that

> the scientific problem is one that arises out of the exceptional event, something that is contrary to laws as they have been accepted, so that attention is directed toward observation and toward a statement of the so-called "fact" in terms of the problem that arises.[41]

In other words, Mead saw a (dialectical) process where one's actions and observation of reality based on assumed theories and ideas result in an encounter with exceptional events or objects that one cannot explain. Some (but not all) of the facts thus contradict one's theories of reality and force one's attention on the conflict (or contradiction) between the exception and the scientific rule. For Mead, this conflict can be resolved only by scientific research that transcends the present conflict by producing a new explanation that encompasses both the old theory and the problematic elements that did not fit into it.

Although Mead's conception of the scientific problem might sound complex, it is easily understood if one applies it to a concrete case. For example, physicists once assumed that accelerated subatomic particles would react to magnetic fields in a particular manner. Although most observations (by means of photographic plates) corroborated such a theory, a few exceptional cases did not; thus there was a contradiction or conflict between the ideas physicists held and some of the observations they had made on the basis of those ideas. The problematic element of the conflict involved the observed behavior of a small percentage of subatomic particles. The conflict arising from the problematic element instigated research. The conflict was resolved by formulating the conclusions of the research in terms of a new theory, which postulated both matter and antimatter and which encompassed the old theory of subatomic matter as well as explaining the exceptional cases in terms of the behavior of antimatter.

In *The Philosophy of the Act* (1938), Mead asserted that after the presence of a problem has been noted and clarified, the scientist proceeds to formulate hypotheses. Mead, who thought of the problematic as some occurrence that inhibited thought or action, defined the hypothesis as "some possible representation, restatement, or reconstruction of the situation, in which the [problematic] data or facts will no longer inhibit action, thought, or feeling."[42] A hypothesis, in other words, reshapes one's understanding of reality so that the formerly problematic elements are no longer a block to the investigator's theoretical ideas or to actions grounded in such ideas.

Hypotheses are subjected to two types of tests: mental testing and observational (or experimental) testing. Mental testing is essentially a thinking through of one's hypothesis in terms of its logic and its application to various types of situations or events. In doing so, one will find that one's original hypothesis is a "working" or "tentative" hypothesis—that is, a hypothesis that one reworks to improve its logic and scope of explanation. Upon satisfying themselves that the logic and scope (that is, the utility) of the hypothesis overcome the inhibiting problematic contradiction that has instigated research, scientists initiate an observational (or experimental) testing. Such testing involves either finding or constructing actual situations where it can be shown that the hypothesis can overcome the original problematic contradiction. Simply put, observational or experimental testing of a hypothesis involves a behavioral situation in which what was previously problematic and nonproblematic can be predicted. Mead wrote that the test of a hypothesis "lies in its functioning."[43] Given two hypotheses with the same explanatory scope, Mead suggested that scientists should choose the more simple one.

Mead insisted that hypothesis testing was not to be an accumulation, inventory, or categorization of "facts"; nor was it to be the construction of some grand conceptual system. Instead, scientific research should give people some idea of the outcome of particular types of action in specified types of situations. Mead's view of science is ultimately instrumental: "It [science] undertakes to tell us what we may expect to happen when we act in such or such a fashion."[44] Mead's emphasis on the goal of science as prediction does not, however, make him a strict determinist. Mead believed that, although much of the future is determined by the past, novelty and emergence occur throughout all levels of reality. Thus although the method of science necessarily involves the construction of predictive hypotheses, science must accept a degree of indeterminacy and accept that *all* of its hypotheses, no matter how well tested and how accurate in prediction, are, to some extent, provisional "working hypotheses." Mead wrote that

> science does not assume that it has secured an accurate picture of the universe into which every new discovery must fit if it is to be recognized as true. It is eagerly at work reconstructing itself not simply in details but as fundamentally as possible. The doctrines of science, its findings up to date, are essentially working hypotheses, which are not only subject to change but in which change is expected.[45]

Mead's position that all scientific conclusions are tentative led him to assert that scientific reasoning and methodology are incompatible with all forms of dogma. The scientific attitude, though rigorous in its demand for logic and detailed observation, is one of tolerance. Tolerance is absolutely necessary because the emergence of new actions and objects and the corresponding development of new problematic elements in life result in the need for science to be open to new ideas. Truth, for Mead, was not absolute but was relative to human goals and present circumstance. Thus as circumstances change and new realities emerge, scientific truths also develop and change.

Mead believed that the conclusions of science could be presented in terms of both causal and teleological (or functional) logics. Mead saw no contradiction between these two logical forms. A causal logic presents conclusions about phenomena in terms of the sequence of events that led to them; a teleological (or functional) approach presents conclusions of the outcomes of events for the entity involved in terms of their impact on survival and adaptation. Unlike some positivist thinkers, Mead would not banish teleological reasoning from the realm of scientific methodology. For Mead, goals existed in reality and were thus to be openly allowed in scientific formulations. Indeed, goal-oriented thinking was central to human action and social reality.

Whereas the foregoing discussion of methods refers to scientific thinking in general, Mead was also concerned with the development of methodological approaches as they specifically apply to the study of individuals and how they interact to form societies. Most important for Mead was the specification of the primary unit of analysis suitable in social research. For Mead, that unit was the total social act. He thus rejected a stimulus-response approach that ignored the internal subjective component of social acts. Mead wrote:

> The social act is not explained by building it up out of stimulus plus response; it must be taken as a dynamic whole—as something going on—no part of which can be considered or understood by itself—a complex organic process implied by each individual stimulus and response involved in it.[46]

Mead insisted that any societal analysis must include both the subjective and external aspects of the act, its environmental situation, and the objects and other actors involved. He believed that to do otherwise would be to distort the reality that the social scientist is to study and thereby undermine any potential value of one's research conclusions.

Other Major Themes and Foci: Socialization

Unlike both Freud and Durkheim, whose dualistic views of human nature maintained that a persistent part of one's mental makeup and orientation toward others was bioorganic in nature, Mead asserted that the self emerged and developed only through social interaction. For Mead, our actions are never biologically produced, but rather, are produced by beings whose biological processes provide merely a capacity for the development of mind and self via the social process of interaction. In other words, the human brain, nervous system, and vocal mechanisms provide mechanisms for the processing, storage, and communication of significant symbols (the foundation of self and reflection), but such symbols themselves are not biological in nature. They are instead arbitrary products of society, and they are learned only through social interaction. Mead pointed out to his students that the nature of the self

> is different from that of the physiological organism proper. The self is something which has a development; it is not initially there, at birth, but arises in the process of social ex-

perience and activity, that is, develops in the given individual as a result of his relations to that process as a whole and to other individuals within that process.[47]

The earliest behaviors of the infant arise from physical needs and discomfort and from a quasi-instinctual reaction arising in response to stimuli produced by the movements and sounds of others. Mead, however, focused most on self-development in terms of the time periods directly following these earliest behaviors. He termed these periods the "play" and "game" stages. In *play* the child takes the role of a single other person. According to Mead, to play involves playing at a role. Acting in play means learning to plan one's responses in relationship to one other person and noting the responses of the other; it involves learning to develop the reflection or internal conversation of the *I* and *me* so that the child masters the self-process in formulating his or her actions in relationship to another. Play, then, is the beginning of developing goals, imagining prospective actions, judging and selecting one's lines of action, and acting in a socially cooperative manner. Through play, children learn to reflect on who they are and to choose behaviors to meet their own ends. Thus the child produces the self-awareness and self-discipline necessary for further social interaction and self-development. The accomplishment of such learning in the play stage allows the child to progress to the next stage of development—the *game* stage.

The child engaged in play can take the role of a number of others only in sequence. That is, in the play stage, the child is incapable of taking the role of a number of others simultaneously and thus is incapable of being involved in any collective activity. In the game stage, on the other hand, the child develops the ability to take the roles of a number of others at the same time and to engage in activity that involves group participation. A baseball game is an example of such an activity.

In a baseball game, the child, playing a particular position, must be able to orient and produce actions in coordination with a number of others simultaneously. For example, a child playing a ground ball at shortstop must, at the same time, be aware of, and act in coordination with, the actions of the batter, base runners, and other infielders. Thus game activity yields a fuller development of the self, where a child's activity can be planned, judged, selected, and coordinated with the activities of a whole group. The child develops the ability to take the role not just of a single other, but of a generalized other. Once children have mastered the ability to organize their self-activity in relationship to a small group (such as a baseball game's participants), they are able to take part in more complex social activities.

The game stage involves the first development of taking the role of a generalized other. Throughout later interaction and learning, the number of generalized others the child learns to take into account expands. Thus fully socialized adults are capable of orienting actions toward various groups, the community that they live in, the society they are a part of, and perhaps humanity as a whole.

Of course, the number of generalized others, and the particular others to whom individuals learn to orient their actions, are, themselves, products of interaction and thus vary for different individuals. Similarly, in that passage through the play and game stages is social and depends on interaction (as opposed to being biologically determined), the time span of self-development is variable among different individuals.

Though temporally variable, however, these stages of social development are necessary to produce an adult with a normal mind and self.

SIGNIFICANCE

Vision of the Future

Mead's discussions of the future can be categorized in terms of four different ideas: the future as ideation in the present, the future as indeterminate emergence, the future as controlled (or reformed) capitalism, and the future as the "self-realization" of humanity in terms of a "universal society."

For Mead, action depends on the development of goals and plans of actions based on those goals. It further depends on reflection on those goals and plans of actions in terms of individuals' knowledge about the past. In order to judge imagined and prospective goal-oriented actions, however, one needs to project oneself into the future. That is, in order to decide which actions to take, one must imagine the outcomes of various possible actions and choose the plan of action with the most desirable results. Therefore, Mead asserted that we act in the present, with knowledge of the past, but in reference to some future goals. In this sense, the future exists as something imagined in the present—a human mental construct. In his essay "The Nature of the Past" (1929),[48] Mead referred to the future as having a "hypothetical character." For Mead, the later "presents" that our actions produce and in which we must act are never identical to the hypothetical futures that we have imagined. That is, we act on assumptions about what following situations will be like, but they never develop exactly as we imagined them. As things fail to develop as projected, humans are forced to reconstruct their futures constantly—to reconceptualize their understandings of what will come to pass so that they can formulate new plans of action. Thus in a sense, for Mead, only the present has any semblance of a concrete reality; both past and future are only and always ideas in the present that make action possible.

Mead did *not* believe that the development of social institutions, of particular societies, or of humanity as a whole could be understood as totally determined developments arising from past events and moving to absolutely predictable end states. In *The Philosophy of the Act*, he asserted that "we cannot find the meaning of the world or of our societies and their institutions in a process we can trace in the past leading us to a goal we can descry in the future."[49] Conceptions of *inevitable* teleological development were believed by Mead to be inconsistent with modern scientific conceptions of evolutionary emergence, as exemplified in the writings of Darwin and Einstein. They were viewed by him instead as leftovers of the medieval theological thinking that served as the basis for such religious works as John Milton's *Paradise Lost*.

Mead believed that whereas sociologists like Spencer garbed their inevitable evolutionary notions in the language of contemporary science, they were in fact basing their declarations on unfounded and archaic teleological assumptions. Mead's rejection of Marxist ideas in *Movements of Thought in the Nineteenth Century* was, to a considerable extent, grounded in his belief that Marx espoused a view of an inevitable series of economically determined stages leading to a preordained, fully determined societal end state. It is such reasoning that led Mead to dismiss the "Marxian doctrine" as "essentially a religion."

Rather than a linear development out of the present, the future, for Mead, would contain novel emergences arising from the collective actions of individuals in society. Accordingly, the future is not totally predictable. In "A Pragmatic Theory of Truth" (1929), Mead wrote: "The future is really future, it is not merely what we do not see, and no acuity of prophetic vision could bring the morrow in its essential character to our experience. Every morrow emerges."[50] Because of its emergent indeterminate elements, one can only be "partially certain" about what the future will contain. But then, partial certainty for Mead did not mean total ignorance; nor did the assertion of limited knowledge lead Mead to embrace a resigned fatalism. On the contrary, he saw human action as fundamental in shaping the contours of the future, and he optimistically viewed the possibility of possible social reforms and even the rise of what he termed a "universal society."

Mead believed that the development of human adaptive reason and cooperation allowed great scope in the possibility of rationally shaping the environmental contexts and structure of human social organization. In humans, the ability to shape and control has reached a qualitatively new level. Mead held that science in general, and social science in particular, would serve as the foundation on which meaningful social reforms could be constructed. Rather than viewing science as a mere tool to achieve preordained and traditional ends, he believed that scientific research would allow the undertaking of what might have been previously seen as unrealistic or impossible goals. Accordingly, Mead focused his attention not on creating a blueprint of what society was eventually going to be like, but on working out the logic by which science could be used to create reforms that would actually bring about a more just and humane society.

Concern with science as the foundation of social reforms runs throughout Mead's writings and forms the explicit focus of three of his essays: "The Working Hypothesis in Social Reform" (1899), "The Philosophical Basis of Ethics" (1908), and "Scientific Method and the Moral Sciences" (1923).[51] In the first of these essays, Mead maintained that, although the perfect forecast of the future is impossible, scientific reasoning can be used to set up reforms as working hypotheses. As action results in problems and new knowledge is gained, reforms can be modified to achieve desired social goals. Mead asserted that although one cannot simply legislate moral behavior, one can use science to structure the environments in which reforms can come to take place.

In the second essay, Mead elaborated on the theme of the first. Reforms, he insists, should be thought of in terms of aiding the emergence of new environmental conditions that would be conducive to the development of new social structures. Rather than merely reiterating the moral virtues of previous eras and calling for useless reactionary measures to cope with social problems, Mead insists that new solutions must be developed to deal with new emergent circumstances. He wrote: "We can look forward to the time when investigation may enable us to approach understanding the prostitute and her trade and change the social conditions which made her possible instead of scourging an abstract sin."[52] Although old-fashioned punishment accomplishes little, Mead maintained that changing circumstances would produce individuals oriented toward positive social actions.

In the third essay, Mead contrasted the procedures used in medical science to prevent disease and those methods used by society to prevent crime. He noted that traditional punishments serve only as a "palliative" and do not prevent crime the way vaccination prevents disease. Mead argued that society should turn away from the social practice of handling social problems using a quasi-religious approach of punishing violators as if they were sinners. He argued that social progress could be made by following the approach that led to modern medical progress—that is, by dropping cultish superstition in favor of scientific research aimed at changing the environment. Mead maintained that for democracy to work, there was a need to create scientifically based reforms that would produce a population that was voluntarily cooperative, as opposed to one manipulated by worn-out and ineffectual moral platitudes, superstitious fears, and coercion.

While rejecting notions of inevitable social developments and insisting that the ability to predict future social states will always be limited, Mead was faced with an existing capitalist society that was being challenged by a variety of socialist theories and movements. He was confronted with the question of whether he viewed the further development of democracy in capitalist or socialist terms. As we have seen already, Mead in his early trip to Germany was impressed with social reforms and found much of the program of the Social Democratic Party to his liking. Correspondingly, Mead rejected an Adam Smith view of economic *laissez-faire* and believed that in a complex industrial society, governmental regulation of business was necessary for both justice and social order. At the same time, Mead explicitly rejected plans for a complete socialist reconstruction of society and the abolishment of private control of the means of production as advocated in the works of both Marx and Veblen. In an article on Veblen, Mead viewed advocates of total socialist societies as presenting an unrealizable utopian dream that distracted from the possibility of actual social reform.

Mead sought an alternative to both capitalism as it existed and socialism as advocates of revolutionary change conceived of it. As Dmitri Shalin pointed out, Mead used the logic of the Hegelian dialectic to suggest a reformist alternative to both capitalism and socialism.[53] For Mead, socialism was not to be conceived of as a new thesis replacing capitalism (as in Marxist thought), but rather was to be viewed as the antithesis of capitalism. In other words, socialism represents not a replacement for capitalism, but instead an opposing (or contradictory) element that arises inside of capitalist society itself and that brings about a change from a *laissez-faire* capitalist society to some new form of society. That new form is conceptualized by Mead in total harmony with the general aims of intellectual progressive reformers like himself, and might best be termed "regulated" or "controlled" capitalism. In other words, the solution to the question of capitalism versus socialism would be a new synthesis in which private property would continue to exist, but it would be subject to a myriad number of governmental regulations that would inhibit the oppression of the nonowners and provide opportunity to all members of society.

Such a reformed capitalist democracy would, in Mead's terms, provide the basis for further social development and the possible achievement of what Mead called the "universal society." Precisely what such universality would entail Mead does not say. Using Hegelian language, he did discuss the "universal society" as involving the "self-realization" of humanity. This phrase appears to imply the termination of wars and violent hostilities and an ability of individuals to relate and orient their actions toward the totality of humanity, to which they would feel a constant and meaningful bond. It would be an attitude of universal "neighborliness," implying a concern with alleviating the distress that any group or individual in the world might have. The universal society was to be one of unlimited growth and peaceful emergence of new social forms, and thus it was not conceptualized by Mead as a static end stage in human development.

Contemporary Relevance

Today, numerous aspects of Mead's work are better known than they were during his lifetime. Partly because of Mead's posthumous publications, and partly because many sociologists have chosen to present him as their intellectual ancestor, Mead is now generally acknowledged to be a significant figure in the social sciences and the humanities. Mead is often cited by sociologists and others interested in a variety of social issues; he receives positive attention in most American introductory sociology textbooks; he is considered influential in the historical development of "sub-areas" of sociology (e.g., the sociology of deviance, social psychology, the sociology of education, and socialization studies); and he even has a website exclusively devoted to his work.[54] Yet, despite such widespread recognition, there is considerable disagreement about how his influence should be interpreted and assessed. Ironically, Mead, who rejected all neo-Kantian approaches that interpreted reality in terms of supposedly fixed categories of understanding, has himself been categorized one way or another by those who followed him. An intellectual who transcended narrow disciplinary boundaries in terms of the subjects he focused on, the students he taught, and the publications in which he published his ideas, Mead has been variously labeled and categorized as a typical progressive reformer, a symbolic interactionist, a social behaviorist, a social psychologist, a Chicago School sociologist, a social scientist, a humanist, and a pragmatist. Some of these labels and categories, of course, are incompatible with others, and Mead's widespread influence reflects the breadth and scope of his thought went well beyond the boundaries of any of them.

Mead was trained in philosophy and is often grouped with American "pragmatists" (e.g., his teacher Josiah Royce, his early employer William James, and his colleague John Dewey). But he believed that important philosophical concepts (e.g., "meaning," "reason," "consciousness," and "conscience") could be adequately conceptualized only in terms of the social contexts in which they emerge. His citations to philosophers were matched by those to nonphilosophers. He published more in other types of publications (e.g., sociology journals, psychology journals, newspapers, and magazines) than he did in philosophy journals. Among his closest friends were noted sociologists (e.g., Charles Cooley, W. I. Thomas, and Jane Addams). And, although Mead has influenced numerous later philosophers, he is cited more often today by sociologists than by those in any other field. As to Mead being a "pragmatist," whereas the label is convenient in pointing to affinities with Dewey, James, Royce, and Charles S. Pierce, Mead had a greater "social orientation" than others so labeled. Thus grouping him with them is misleading. It is true that Mead borrowed the "I/me" distinction from James. But the self as object, what James called the "me", was modified by Mead to incorporate judgments derived from social experience. Accordingly, for Mead, self-reflection and self-judgment incorporate, and become to a great extent inseparable from, social reflection and societal judgment. It is precisely this "socializing" of the "me" that had made Mead's thought—much more so than that of James—relevant to the theoretical ideas and research questions of later generations of sociologists. For instance, sociologists concerned with questions involving both "primary socialization" (such as how children incorporate social influence into their judgments as they develop) and "social control" (such as how collective judgments of "generalized others" direct individual choices) have built whole careers by developing Mead's insights.

Mead's acceptance of the importance of studying such "judgments" and "choices" raises questions about whether Mead should be categorized as a "humanist," as some commentators suggest, or as a social and behavioral "scientist." Certainly, those who accept a narrow positivistic, exclusively quantitative, and strictly deterministic conception of what constitutes "science" would have difficulty with Mead's focus on "choice" and "judgments." (They would also have trouble with Mead's acceptance of teleological reasoning and the unpredictable "imaginative" aspect of the "I.") On the other hand, as we have seen, Mead had his own conception of science as a unifying hypothesis-testing approach common to many fields. In Mead's conception, the knowledge that one actually does make choices means that such choices must be viewed as real by those doing scientific investigation. Such knowledge takes precedence over a non-scientific unprovable metaphysical position of absolute determinism that would demand *a priori* that any awareness of choice must be dismissed as an illusion. Much of Mead's later significance arises from his provision of a model for investigating choices—whether one is looking at the differences between childhood and adult choices, "normative" and "deviant" choices, or democratic and authoritarian choices.[55]

Just as Mead refused to draw a sharp division between what traditionally had been viewed as areas subject to scientific investigation and those beyond its grasp, he also rejected a sharp distinction between the role of the scholarly oriented academician and that of the social reformer. Social-scientific questions, according to Mead, arise when a researcher seeks solutions to problematic situations that occur in the course of ongoing social life. Part of the testing of any solution is its application to resolving those problematic elements. Mead thus saw social reform as linked to social investigation. His courses helped many of his University of Chicago graduate sociology students systematically develop their community-oriented applied sociological research agenda. But Mead's own reform activities and his emphasis on creating socially applicable knowledge must not blind us to his concerns with broader societal and theoretical questions. Mead, in other words, was not a "Chicago School sociologist" exclusively focused on gangs, drugs, street crime, prostitution, and related urban problems.[56] His linkages to a Rousseauean tradition of broadly exploring the nature of a just democratic order have, for example, made Mead's work relevant to a number of later thinkers, including some post–Cold War European intellectuals trying to conceptualize a "democratic" unification of Europe. In terms of more abstract theoretical questions, devoid of any immediate reform applications, one can point to Mead's late-in-life pioneering analysis of "time," as seen in such works as his *The Philosophy of the Present.* In this work, Mead attempted to develop an understanding of "past," "present," and "future," that was built on, but distinct from, earlier formulations by Bergson and others. The contemporary relevance of Mead's pioneering explorations can be seen, for example, in the focus on "time" as the central topic of the meetings of the British Sociological Association in 2000. Session topics on "theories of time," "time as a social construction," and "public time and private time" echo Mead's interests.

Mead's influence thus clearly goes beyond the area of social psychology. Moreover, his work is not limited to a single orientation—whether that orientation might be called "social behaviorism" or "symbolic interactionism." Charles Morris was not content merely to put Mead into two categories when he wrote in 1934: "Philosophically, Mead was a pragmatist; scientifically, he was a social psychologist."[57] Morris additionally called Mead a "social behaviorist" and entitled a book of Mead's transcribed lecture notes as *Mind, Self, and Society from the Standpoint of a Social Behaviorist.* Morris coined the term to present Mead as a social psychologist who was distinguishable both from nonbehaviorists, such as the "gestaltist" Wolfgang Köhler (who did not focus on explaining external "objective" behavior), and from more simple behaviorists, such as John Watson (who, primarily on epistemological grounds, refused to hypothesize any internal mental states or processes). Morris's term has to a considerable extent declined in usage, but another term, "symbolic interactionism," coined a few years later by Mead's student, Herbert Blumer, and then later applied to Mead's own work, not only is in current use, but represents an orientation in contemporary sociology with its own journal and adherents.

Blumer's definitions of "mind," "self," "I," "me," "generalized other," and "object" are very close to those of Mead and were often presented with direct citations of Mead's writings and transcribed lectures. Blumer's methodological assertions, however, are quite alien to Mead's and appear closer to the direct observation approaches taught at the University of Chicago in Blumer's student days. Unlike Mead, for whom scientific analysis was based on hypothesis testing, the Chicago School stressed a holistic descriptive approach, which involved detailed noting of people's lives and activities without proceeding from any definite problem or hypothesis.[55] Although he was true to Mead's ideas about self and society, Blumer developed a neo-Chicagoan methodological emphasis on participant observation and a major concern with the creation of "sensitizing" (that is, interpretive) research. Nowhere did Blumer acknowledge that a methodological approach that focuses on sensitized understanding is quite different from the hypothesis-testing development of cumulative knowledge advocated by Mead.[58]

Although Blumerian symbolic interactionism has been the most flourishing school of symbolic interactionism, there has been a small school of symbolic interactionist thought known as the Iowa School. This school developed around the writings and research of Manford Kuhn.[59] Ironically, although the Iowa School has been true to the positivistic methodological approach of hypothesis testing advocated by Mead, it has highly distorted some of Mead's more humanistic ideas about self and society. Most important, the Iowa School has tended to ignore the *I* and has focused on the socialized *me.* As a result, Iowa School symbolic interactionism has portrayed a very deterministic view of the individual and society. The emphasis in Mead on human choice and nondeterminism is missing. Thus, though true to Mead methodologically, the Iowa School's symbolic interactionism general view of individuals' social actions cannot really be said to be Meadian at all.

Perhaps a sign of intellectual greatness is for one's work to transcend easy categorization while simultaneously inspiring those who proceed from a variety of perspectives. If so, Mead certainly achieved such greatness.

NOTES

1. Robert M. Crunden, *Ministers of reform: The progressives' achievement in American civilization, 1889–1920*, p. 7.
2. Dmitri N. Shalin, "G. H. Mead, socialism, and the progressive agenda," in Mitchell Aboulafia (Ed.), *Philosophy, social theory, and the thought of George Herbert Mead*, p. 29.
3. "Biographical Note," *Philosophy of the act*, p. xxix.
4. Crunden, *Ministers of reform*, ch. 1.
5. "The working hypothesis in social reform," *American Journal of Sociology*, 5 (1899): 361–371.
6. "The philosophical basis of ethics," *International Journal of Ethics*, 18 (1908): 311–323.
7. "The psychology of punitive justice," *American Journal of Sociology*, 23 (1917–1918): 577–602.
8. "Philanthropy from the point of view of ethics," in Ellsworth Faris et al. (Eds.), *Intelligent Philanthropy* (Chicago: University of Chicago Press, 1930), pp. 133–148.
9. Hans Joas, *George H. Mead: A contemporary reexamination of his thought*.
10. Shalin, "G. H. Mead, socialism, and the progressive agenda."
11. Mary Jo Deegan, *Jane Addams and the men of the Chicago School, 1892–1918*.
12. Harry Dean, *Umbala: The adventures of a Negro sea-captain in Africa and on the seven seas in his attempts to found an Ethiopian empire* (London: Pluto Press, 1989 [1929]).
13. Deegan, *Jane Addams*, p. 111.
14. "Introduction," in Aboulafia (Ed.), *Philosophy, social theory, and the thought of George Herbert Mead*, p. xiv.
15. Hans Joas, "Mead's position in intellectual history and his early philosophical writings," in Aboulafia (Ed.), *Philosophy, social theory, and the thought of George Herbert Mead*, p. 76.
16. *Movements of thought in the nineteenth century*, p. 168.
17. Joas, *G. H. Mead: A contemporary reexamination of his thought*, p. 60.
18. See Andrew J. Reck, "Introduction," in George Herbert Mead, *Selected writings*, p. xix.
19. *Movements of thought in the nineteenth century*, p. 168.
20. "Cooley's contribution to American thought," *American Journal of Sociology*, 35 (1929): 692–706.
21. *The philosophy of the present*, p. 47.
22. "National-mindedness and international-mindedness," *International Journal of Ethics*, 39 (1929): 385–407.
23. Ibid., pp. 86–87.
24. Reprinted in *Selected writings*, p. 123.
25. Reprinted in ibid., p. 131.
26. Reprinted in *The philosophy of the present*, p. 165.
27. *Mind, self, and society*, p. 138.
28. Ibid., p. 255.
29. Ibid., p. 229.
30. Ibid., p. 177.
31. Reprinted in *Selected writings*, p. 243.
32. Ibid., p. 54.
33. *Mind, self, and society*, p. 273.
34. Ibid., p. 142.
35. Reprinted in *Selected writings*, p. 7.
36. Ibid., p. 286.
37. Ibid., p. 264.
38. Ibid., p. 244.
39. Ibid., p. 61.
40. "Scientific method and the individual thinker," in John Dewey et al., *Creative intelligence: Essays in pragmatic attitude* (New York: Henry Holt & Co., 1917), pp. 176–227.
41. *Movements of thought in the nineteenth century*, p. 281.
42. *The Philosophy of the act*, p. 82.
43. *The Philosophy of the present*, p. 23.

44. Reprinted in *Selected writings*, p. 210.

45. *The Philosophy of the act*, p. 39.

46. *Mind, self, and society*, p. 7.

47. Ibid., p. 133.

48. "The nature of the past," in John Coss (Ed.), *Essays in honor of John Dewey* (New York: Henry Holt & Co., 1929), pp. 235–242.

49. *The Philosophy of the act*, p. 487.

50. Reprinted in *Selected writings*, p. 355.

51. "Scientific method and the moral sciences," *International Journal of Ethics, 33* (1923): 229–247.

52. Ibid., p. 92.

53. Shalin, "G. H. Mead, socialism, and the progressive agenda," pp. 30–31.

54. See the Guide to Classical Theory on the World Wide Web near the end of this book.

55. See the discussion in Joas, *G. H. Mead: A Contemporary reexamination of his thought.*

56. For a brief discussion of the Chicago School studies, see Milton Gordon, *Social class in America* (New York: McGraw-Hill, 1963), pp. 21–52.

57. Charles W. Morris, "Introduction," *Mind, Self, and Society,* p. ix

58. See Herbert Blumer, *Symbolic interactionism: Perspective and Method.*

59. See the discussion in Bernard Meltzer, John Petras, & Larry Reynolds, "Varieties of Symbolic Interactionism," in Jerome Manis & Bernard Meltzer, Eds., *Symbolic interactionism*, 4th ed. (Boston: Allyn and Bacon, 1978), pp. 41–58.

GLOSSARY

Determinism The metaphysical position that relates every event to preexisting events and denies the possibility of human choice and free will.

Dialectic The process of development of internal conflict leading to the emergence of a new level or more advanced form of reality. (See Chapter 6 on Hegel.)

Dissociation The pathological state wherein the acting *self* is unaware of his or her own other actions in different situations.

Dualism The position that human nature is composed of two basic irreducible parts, elements, or components.

Duration The translation of the French *duré*. Refers to the subjective sense of time based on experience, as opposed to the external time measured by the ticking of a clock.

Fusion The state or situation in which the *I* and *me* phases of the *self* occur simultaneously. Involves feelings of oneness in religious or quasi-religious emotions.

Game stage Period of self-development that follows the *play stage*. Involves the development of the ability to *take the role of the generalized other* and to take part in group activity.

Generalized other The overall attitude and general reactions of a group, community, or society.

General will In Rousseau's thought, an orientation toward the general good, as opposed to particular self-interest. (Compare with Mead's *generalized other.*)

Gestalt psychology The psychological orientation that stresses the study of perception in terms of mental categories interpreted in the context of a total environment (as opposed to perceiving discrete stimuli).

Gesture Vocalized sound or body movement that one creature uses to instigate or stimulate the actions of another creature such that an act involving the mutual influence of both parties occurs.

Homiletics The study of the art of religious preaching.

I Creative and imaginative phase of the *self*, which notes present circumstances and environmental contexts and suggests possibly novel and surprising new actions. The self as "knower."

Looking-glass self Cooley's notion that an individual's self-conception arises from a perception and interpretation of the reactions of others and an emotional feeling about that reaction.

Me The judgmental and "known" aspect or phase of the *self*.

Meaning For Mead, a process of internal reflection using *significant symbols*.

Nonsignificant gestures The reflex, habitual, or spontaneous gestures that are not meaningful and are not responded to by the individual producing the gesture.

Object For Mead, anything tangible or nontangible that can be pointed or acted toward.

Particular will In Rousseau's thought, an orientation toward action based on one's own perceived self-interest as opposed to the general good. (Compare with *general will*.)

Play stage The period of self-development in which individuals learn to take into account the role of a single other at a time.

Pragmatism American school of philosophy including John Dewey, Charles Peirce, and William James. Emphasis is on action as the outcome of thought.

Role-taking See *Taking the role of the other*.

Self In Mead's usage, a process that arises when action is blocked and that involves *taking the role of the other*, imagining, planning, and selecting action. The self allows the individual to be both subject and object of his or her own actions. Two aspects or alternating phases of self are the *I* and *me*.

Significant symbol A gesture produced by an individual who *takes the role of another* and is able to reflect on the significance and outcome of having made this gesture.

Social act One in which individual behavior serves as a stimulus for the response of another.

Symbolic interactionism The sociological orientation developed by Herbert Blumer, which uses some of the ideas of Mead.

Taking the role of the other The ability to project oneself mentally into a position where one can imagine how another or others will react to one's behavior. The other can be either a particular or a *generalized other*.

Teleological reasoning Thought and explanation in terms of goals, purposes, or end states.

Universal society Mead's conception of a possible future society encompassing all of humanity in peaceful self-realization.

ANNOTATED BIBLIOGRAPHY

Primary Sources

George Herbert Mead: Essays on his social philosophy (John Petras, Ed.). New York: Columbia University, 1968.

Included in this collection of essays are a number of Mead's lesser known educational writings.

George Herbert Mead on social psychology (Anselm Strauss, Ed.). Chicago: University of Chicago Press, 1964 (paper).

A good cross section of Mead's ideas, selected mostly from other published volumes of Mead's thought. Contains the only recently published presentation of "Cooley's Contribution to American Social Thought."

The individual and the social self: Unpublished works of George Herbert Mead (David L. Miller, Ed.). Chicago: University of Chicago Press, 1982.

This book is composed mostly of notes taken in Mead's social psychology course in 1914 and 1927 and an essay entitled "Consciousness, Mind, the Self, and Scientific Objects." This volume is particularly interesting because it allows one to see the development of some of Mead's central concepts over a period of years. It also includes significant discussions of Mead's rejection of dualistic theories of human nature.

Mind, self, and society from the standpoint of a social behaviorist. (Charles Morris, Ed.). Chicago: University of Chicago Press, 1962 [1934].

Usually referred to simply as *Mind, Self, and Society*, this is the most widely read and cited volume of Mead's "writings." The work was not written by Mead, however, but was put together mostly from notes taken in the 1914 and 1927 social psychology courses taught by Mead. Both the title and some of the editing reflect Morris's categorization of Mead as a "social behaviorist." This book is best read with a knowledge of Mead's concepts as he himself intended them to be put into print. (See his *Selected Writings*, below.)

Movements of thought in the nineteenth century (Merritt Moore, Ed.). Chicago: University of Chicago, 1972 [1936] (paper).

Taken from lectures for undergraduate students, this book encompasses Mead's analysis of nineteenth-century thought terminating in the development of Mead's own ideas. Analysis includes, among other chapters, chapters on Kant, Hegel, utilitarianism, Marx, and pragmatism. An appendix contains some of Mead's views on Comte and Bergson.

The philosophy of the act (Charles Morris, Ed.). Chicago: University of Chicago, 1972 [1938] (paper).

This lengthy volume (695 pages) is composed of some long and some fragmentary papers, in varying stages of completion, left by Mead at the time of his death. In it one finds elaborations of Mead's notions of the social act, perception, objects, and mind (among other concerns).

The philosophy of the present (Arthur Murphy, Ed.). Chicago: University of Chicago, 1980 [1932].

Mead was working on this book at the time of his death. Only two of its nine chapters are in the finished form intended by Mead for publication in the volume. Emphasis is on the self, objects, and action in the defined present.

Selected writings (Andrew J. Reck, Ed.). Indianapolis: Bobbs-Merrill, 1964 (paper).

Reck has gathered into this volume virtually all of Mead's essays (with the exception of Mead's essay on Cooley) with which most sociologists would be concerned. Includes writings on social reform, science, perception, methodology, social objects, meaning, the self, significant symbols, and social control, among others.

Secondary Sources

Aboulafia, Mitchell. *The mediating self: Mead, Sartre, and self-determination.* New Haven, CT: Yale University Press, 1986.

Aboulafia writes that "the contemporary challenge as I see it, is to reconcile the apparent truths of modern psychology and sociology—which entail, by and large, deterministic assumptions and conclusions—with the experience of individual autonomy and self-determination." To meet this challenge, he explores the works of Mead and Sartre. The first part of the book contrasts the ideas of these two scholars; the second attempts a synthesis of their thought.

Aboulafia, Mitchell (Ed.). *Philosophy, social theory, and the thought of George Herbert Mead.* Albany: State University of New York Press, 1991.

A very good collection of articles presenting the latest scholarship on the relationship of Mead's life and thought. Especially worthwhile are Dmitri N. Shalin's "G. H. Mead, Socialism, and the Progressive Agenda," Hans Joas's "Mead's Position in Intellectual History," Gary A. Cook's "The Development of G. H. Mead's Social Psychology," and Jürgen Habermas's "The Paradigm Shift in Mead." This work contains an extensive bibliography.

Baldwin, John D. *George Herbert Mead: A unifying theory for sociology.* Beverly Hills, CA: Sage, 1986.

Mead's work is presented as a systematic theory capable of guiding contemporary sociology by integrating micro- and macroperspectives, the analysis of mental and physical events, and the pursuit of academic and more practical concerns. No attempt is made to critique or update Mead's ideas. Includes a good discussion of Mead's rejection of dualistic theories of human nature.

Blumer, Herbert. *Symbolic interactionism: Perspective and method.* Englewood Cliffs, NJ: Prentice-Hall, 1969.

This highly readable collection of essays presents Blumer's sociological orientation as a development of the ideas formulated by Mead. Of special importance is the essay "Sociological Implications of the Thought of George Herbert Mead" (originally published in the *American Journal of Sociology*).

Cronk, George. *The philosophical anthropology of George Herbert Mead.* New York: Peter Lang, 1987.

This short (158-page) book presents a clear summary and sympathetic critique of Mead's central ideas and assumptions. A good place to begin one's reading about Mead.

Crunden, Robert M. *Ministers of reform: The progressives' achievement in American civilization, 1889–1920.* New York: Basic Books, 1982.

This highly readable book by a noted historian places Mead in the context of progressive-era reformers.

Deegan, Mary Jo. *Jane Addams and the men of the Chicago School, 1892–1918.* New Brunswick, NJ: Transaction Books, 1988.

Deegan's fascinating book not only examines Jane Addams's life and her underappreciated significance for American sociology, but also presents a detailed treatment of Mead's social-reform beliefs and activities.

Ferguson, Kathy E. *Self, society, and womankind.* Westport, CT: Greenwood Press, 1980.

A unique attempt to ground a feminist analysis of society in some of the ideas developed by Mead.

Goff, Tom W. *Marx and Mead: Contributions to a sociology of knowledge.* London: Routledge & Kegan Paul, 1980.

Goff's ambitious program is to create a synthesis of Marx and Mead to serve as a foundation for the development of a contemporary sociology of knowledge. Goff focuses on the question, How can valid knowledge exist if knowledge itself is relative to particular social forms?

Hamilton, Peter, (Ed.). *George Herbert Mead, Critical assessment.* London, Routledge, 1992.

An important four-volume collection of articles reflecting widely varied reactions toward Mead's work. One volume is dedicated to

"Mead and Social Behaviorism" and another to "Mead and Symbolic Interactionism."

Hanson, Karen. *The self imagined: Philosophical reflections on the social character of psyche.* New York: Routledge & Kegan Paul, 1986.

Hanson, a contemporary philosopher, attempts to build on some of Mead's ideas in a study of the relationship between "imagination" and "self." Her review of Mead's ideas is accurate and her comments on the strengths and some of the weaknesses of Mead's thought (juxtaposed in part to those of the French philosopher Jean-Paul Sartre) are worth investigating for their sociological relevance.

Joas, Hans. *G. H. Mead: A contemporary reexamination of his thought* (Raymond Meyer, Trans.). Cambridge, MA: MIT Press, 1985.

Written by a German professor of philosophy and translated into English, this volume assumes that the reader is familiar with the basics of Mead's thought and has some knowledge of nineteenth-century German philosophy. Both its presentations of the intellectual context of Mead's views and the development of Mead's thought are unsurpassed.

Kang, G. H. *Mead's concept of rationality: A study of the use of symbols and other implements.* The Hague: Mouton, 1976.

Despite a title which some students might find intimidating, this work offers a good, clear account of Mead's ideas. The author's view that Mead's central problem was accounting for the existence of human rationality has considerable merit.

Lewis, J. David, & Smith, Richmond L. *American sociology and pragmatism: Mead, Chicago sociology, and symbolic interaction.* Chicago: University of Chicago Press, 1980.

A well-researched work on Mead and his significance for American sociology.

Miller, David L. *George Herbert Mead: Self, language, and the world.* Chicago: University of Chicago Press, 1980 [1973] (paper).

Although some students might find the philosophical terminology of this book a bit difficult, it is probably the best overall analysis of Mead's thought in print. Each of the fifteen chapters of this work focuses on a particular aspect of Mead's theorizing (for example, gesture, perceptions, self, ethical ideas); yet the book as a whole presents an integrated focus on Mead's total work.

Rosenthal, Sandra B., & Bourgeois, Patrick L. *Mead and Merleau-Ponty: Toward a common vision.* Albany: State University of New York Press, 1991.

This work finds common themes in the work of Mead and that of the phenomenological philosophy of Maurice Merleau-Ponty.

Fortunately, the world has not been designed with a view to such instincts that only good-natured herd animals could find their narrow happiness in it: to demand that all should become "human beings," herd animals, blue-eyed, benevolent, "beautiful souls"—or, as Herbert Spencer would have it, altruistic—would deprive existence of its great character, and would castrate men and reduce them to the level of dessicated Chinese stagnation.—And this has been attempted!—Precisely this has been called morality.

In this sense, Zarathustra calls the good, now "the last men," now the "beginning of the end": above all, he considers them the most harmful type of man because they prevail at the expense of truth and at the expense of the future.

"The good are unable to create; they are always the beginning of the end; they crucify him who writes new values on new tablets; they sacrifice the future to themselves—they sacrifice all man's future."

"The good have always been the beginning of the end."

"And whatever harm those do who slander the world, the harm done by the good is the most harmful harm."

—Friedrich Wilhelm Nietzsche,
"Why I Am a Destiny,"
Ecce Homo

14

Friedrich Wilhelm Nietzsche

(1844–1900)

Life

It is hard not to view Friedrich Wilhelm Nietzsche as a tragic figure. Virtually ignored during his own lifetime, the man who believed he was a "destiny" and a shatterer of the "false idols" had to rely on his own meager resources to get his books published. Nietzsche's final decade was spent in a vegetative state after he suffered the effects of an irreversible nervous collapse at the age of forty-five. Shortly before his death, though, Nietzsche achieved enough fame to make it worthwhile for his sister, Elisabeth, to dress him up on special occasions and exhibit him to visitors. Indeed, Nietzsche's collapse into madness in 1889 almost exactly paralleled his sudden rise to fame, which began when Georg Brandes gave the first public lectures on the philosopher in Copenhagen in 1888.

But if Nietzsche's life was tragic, it was also absurd. In his writings, the philosopher idolized the "hard," uncompromising warrior who had created himself through an act of self-conquest. Yet, Nietzsche himself was a chubby, emotive, socially challenged hypochondriac who endlessly complained about numerous ailments, including vomiting, nausea, nervous irritation, exhaustion, insomnia, stomach ailments, hoarseness, chest pains, gastric catarrh, sinusitis, dizziness, diphtheria, dysentery, myopia, sensitivity to light, shingles, rheumatism, septic inflammations, and persistent migraine headaches. Drafted by the Prussian army in 1867, Nietzsche posed proudly, in full-dress uniform, sword in hand. Yet a few months later, he virtually impaled himself on his horse's pommel, after his thickly pebbled spectacles failed to ascertain the position of his mount. Because of this unfortunate injury, the twenty-four-year-old Friedrich was forced to abandon his short-lived military career and return to his bookish pursuits.

In his philosophical works, Nietzsche stressed the overriding importance of physical well-being, the ability to withstand hardship, vigor, and the readiness to live dangerously. As he famously stated, "That which does not kill me makes me stronger."[1] Given his own poor health, however, Nietzsche's observation that "everything ugly weakens and depresses man" and "reminds him of decay, danger, impotence"[2] seems poignant, not to mention ironic. Associating physical feebleness with degeneracy, Nietzsche wrote: "The sick man is a parasite of society. In certain cases it is indecent to go on living. To continue to vegetate in a state of cowardly dependence upon doctors and special treatments, once the meaning of life, the right to life, has been lost, ought to be regarded with the greatest contempt by society."[3]

Nietzsche's father—the third in a line of Protestant pastors—died when his eldest son was only four years old. Raised by his mother, his sister, his grandmother, two maiden aunts, and an elderly maid, Nietzsche came to assume what can only be described as a misogynist outlook on life. To quote the words he put into the mouth of his mythical hero, Zarathustra: "Men should be brought up to be warriors; women to be the recreation of warriors. . . . Man's happiness is to say: I will. Woman's happiness is to say: he wills."[4] Yet, other than Elisabeth—who ultimately betrayed him—Nietzsche failed to develop a satisfactory, let alone a commanding, relationship with any woman. He apparently contracted syphilis after one night in a Leipzig brothel to which, against his will, he had been taken by a cabdriver. Under the circumstances, it was, perhaps, fortunate that all his marriage proposals were rejected. Nietzsche's only strong erotic attachments were to Cosima von Bülow—Richard Wagner's mistress—and to Lou Salomé—an extraordinary Russian woman who was twenty-one when Nietzsche first met her, and who published her first (autobiographical) novel when she was only twenty-three. For a time, Nietzsche shared Salomé platonically with the Jewish psychologist Paul Rée. Lou's relationship with the two men has been preserved in a photograph that shows her being pulled in a donkey cart by Nietzsche and Rée, who are both being whipped.[5] Nietzsche's dalliance with Lou—which she, not he, terminated—led to an hysterical outburst from Elisabeth and to yet another emotional breakdown in her brother.

Profoundly mistrustful of modern German nationalism (what he called *Vaterländerei*), and the "coarseness" and "beery materialism" of the German people, Nietzsche renounced his Prussian nationality, pretended his ancestors were Polish aristocrats named Niëzky, and spent much of his adult life successfully avoiding his country of birth. Aspiring to be a "good European," Nietzsche was opposed to nationalism in general and to *German* nationalism in particular. In contrast to Hegel, he regarded the modern nation-state as "the coldest of all cold monsters." "It tells cold lies, too, and a lie creeps out of its mouth when it says, 'I, the state, am the people.' "[6]

After Nietzsche's terminal collapse, Elisabeth began to collect her brother's writings in an archive that she moved to Villa Silberblick, her home in Weimar. In 1895, Elisabeth persuaded her mother to surrender the rights to Nietzsche's literary estate. By this time, Nietzsche's books were beginning to generate significant royalties, which Elisabeth happily milked for nearly forty years. Reinventing herself as her brother's heir and executrix, Elisabeth changed some of Nietzsche's letters, removing comments critical of anti-Semitism, Richard Wagner, the Germans, Jesus, and Christianity.[7]

Toward the end of her life, Elisabeth cultivated a relationship with Benito Mussolini, whom she described as "the genius who rediscovered the values of Nietzsche's spirit."[8] She also lived long enough to see Adolf Hitler become *Führer* and visit her in Weimar. Like Hitler, Elisabeth seems to have grasped little or nothing of her brother's philosophy, but, with her connivance, the Nazi state turned Nietzsche into an early supporter of the Third Reich: a philosopher who had anticipated the fascist "will to power" over the lesser nations and peoples of Europe. Adding to all the confusion, Elisabeth published as completed volumes selections from Nietzsche's notebooks that her brother never intended to be presented as finished works,[9] and she insisted on writing the "official" biography of Nietzsche (for which she expected to receive the Nobel Prize in Literature). Elisabeth received a state funeral in 1935, at which Hitler described her late brother as a great "German genius."

Nietzsche, however, would have loathed Schicklgruber (a.k.a. Hitler), together with everything the little corporal from Austria-Hungary represented. He certainly despised his sister's husband, Bernhard Förster, a swaggering anti-Semite who married Elisabeth in 1885 and took her to "Neuva Germania," an anti-Semitic colony he had founded in Paraguay.[10] Before moving to South America, Förster organized a petition to be presented to the German chancellor, Otto von Bismarck, calling for Jews to be barred from the stock exchange, the universities, and the profession of journalism. When Bismarck rejected the petition's demands, Förster abandoned the fatherland in disgust and spent the rest of his life trying to swindle the German settlers who had believed his stories about the wonderful opportunities that awaited them in the South American jungle. After his misdeeds were exposed, Förster poisoned himself in 1889. But, not at all distracted by this sad turn of events, Elisabeth defended her late husband's life's work by stressing that "anti-Semitism has above all a positive aspect: the urge to deepen and ennoble . . . true German characteristics."[11]

Nietzsche had refused to attend his sister's wedding, and he agreed to meet Förster once only. Unlike his sister (whom he once described as a "vengeful anti-Semitic goose"), Nietzsche was virulently "anti-anti-Semitic," as he put it—not so much because he wanted to defend German Jews, but because he could see, only too clearly, that the anti-Semites were idiots. As he wrote to a friend in 1887: "I have no respect left for present-day Germany, even though, hedgehog fashion, the country is bristling with arms. It represents the most stupid, the most depraved, the most mendacious form of 'the German spirit,' that ever was."[12] In the *Twilight of the Idols* (1888), Nietzsche asked: "The Germans—they were once called a people of thinkers: do they really think at all at present? . . . 'Deutschland, Deutschland über alles.'[13] I fear this was the death-blow to German philosophy."[14] During his final collapse, Nietzsche sent a brief note to his friend Franz Overbeck, raving: "I am having all anti-Semites shot—Dionysus."[15]

Although Nietzsche's life ended sadly, it had begun promisingly. As a boy of fourteen, he won a place at Schulpforta, the most famous boarding school in Germany that offered students a classical education. Educational standards were particularly high, and some boys were not given a certificate of graduation until they were in their twenty-third year. Nietzsche, however, attained his leaving certificate at the age of nineteen and became a student at the University of Bonn. There, he studied philology (the study of the history and development of language) with Albrecht Ritschl (1822–1889), one of the most influential professors in the German university system. When Ritschl left Bonn for the University of Leipzig in 1865, Nietzsche went with him.

In 1869, Ritschl recommended Nietzsche for the Chair of Classical Philology at the University of Basel in Switzerland. According to Ritschl, Nietzsche was "the first from whom I have ever accepted any contribution at all while he was still a student."[16] Nietzsche had not yet completed his dissertation. Nevertheless, the reports written about him were so glowing that, at the age of twenty-four, he was able to attain a coveted associate professorship at one of the oldest universities in Europe. But, in order to accept the post, Nietzsche first had to renounce his German nationality and assume Swiss citizenship. Although he expeditiously completed the first part of this procedure, Nietzsche never got around to registering his new nationality. Because of this, he was legally stateless for most of his life.

Poor health compelled Nietzsche to resign his professorship in 1879. For the next decade, he wandered around Italy, France, and Switzerland, migrating north in summer and south in winter, relying on a pension awarded by Basel, which was just sufficient to cover his needs. From 1875 to 1878, Nietzsche lived with Elisabeth, who, during this period, tended to his ailments and served as his housekeeper; for most of his adult life, however, he lived a solitary existence.

After his final breakdown in Turin, Italy, in 1889, Nietzsche was taken back to Basel by Overbeck. In order to get him to leave his boardinghouse, Overbeck had to tell the sadly deluded Nietzsche that receptions and special events honoring him awaited him in Switzerland. On the journey there, Nietzsche wanted to address the crowd and embrace everyone at each stop. Fortunately, however, he was persuaded that he had become too famous to let his presence be known. On his arrival at the psychiatric clinic in Basel, Nietzsche was diagnosed as suffering from "mental degeneration." A doctor signed a brief note that read: "Claims he is a famous man and asks for women all the time."

The exact causes of Nietzsche's breakdown are still mysterious, because the suddenness of his final collapse is not consistent with the syphilis from which he allegedly suffered. At least two of Nietzsche's contemporaries—Overbeck and Peter Gast—suspected that their friend's madness was simulated, although this seems unlikely. A more probable explanation is that Nietzsche was a victim of syphilitic paresis, which often causes euphoria and delusions of grandeur such as those exhibited in *Ecce Homo* (1888), his final work. Another possibility is that Nietzsche inadvertently poisoned himself with "medicines" containing heavy metal compounds that he took in an abortive attempt to control his numerous ailments.[17] Nietzsche could have been schizophrenic. There is a disturbing autobiographical fragment that he wrote in 1868 or

1869 that hints of hallucinations: "What I am afraid of is not the terrible shape behind my chair but its voice; also not the words but the horribly unarticulated and inhuman tone of that shape. Yes, if only it spoke as human beings do."[18]

Nietzsche died at the threshold of the twentieth century: on 25 August 1900. Elisabeth arranged for a full Christian burial, and her brother was buried in a coffin decorated with a large silver cross.

Social Environment

As a young man, Nietzsche grew up in a state shaped by what came to be known as the *Nachmärz* ("after-March"): the intellectual and political crackdown that followed the failed worker uprising in Berlin in March 1848. After the Prussian army had "restored order," King Friedrich Wilhelm IV (Nietzsche's namesake) imposed a new and far more restrictive constitution on his subjects. This set the pattern for the system of political domination institutionalized by Bismarck. Bismarck granted economic domination to the rising bourgeoisie, but he kept political power in the hands of the Junkers, the monarchy, and the Prussian civil service (see Chapter 8).

The *Nachmärz* limited civil rights and attempted to enforce cultural and political orthodoxy. It led to a purge of the German university system and to the kind of political trial to which Marx and his followers were subjected in Cologne. After 1848, any philosopher who was reckless (or stupid) enough to tackle issues that might be construed as having some connection with German reality stood in danger of being stripped of his post, and it was largely because of this that Nietzsche began his academic career as a philologist rather than as a philosopher—a decision he was later to regret. Because of the *Nachmärz*:

> German philosophy split into two: into an academic philosophy to which no one any longer paid attention and whose reputation sank to an unprecedented low for Germany, and a freelance philosophy existing outside and independently of the university whose practitioners were able to discuss those questions, alone of interest to the nonacademic public, which the academic philosopher was inhibited from approaching.[19]

In 1864, Nietzsche hoped that Prussian expansionism and the creation of the North German Confederation would lead to a united German Parliament, but he quickly became disillusioned. In 1867, Nietzsche was briefly drafted into a Prussian artillery regiment, in which, as we have seen, he did not distinguish himself and from which he was quickly discharged as medically unfit. When war broke out between France and Prussia, Nietzsche was living in Switzerland. But he volunteered to serve as a medical orderly, and, during the autumn of 1870, he spent several weeks helping to care for injured soldiers. Before long, however, Nietzsche contracted diphtheria and dysentery and was again discharged from his duties. By this time, however, he had lost all interest in the war effort, going so far as to declare that "I consider the Prussia of today to be one of the powers most dangerous of all to culture."[20] As he wrote to a friend at the time, "See if you cannot escape from that fatal, anticultural Prussia, where the slaves and the priests sprout like mushrooms and will soon darken all Germany for us with their vapours."[21] Nietzsche's view of the "enemy" was somewhat unorthodox: France, not Germany, he wrote, was "the seat of the most spiritual and sophisticated culture in Europe and the foremost school of taste."[22]

Nietzsche complained that Bismarck had placed the power interests of the German Reich above the cultivation of the "German Spirit." For Nietzsche, the "monstrosity of imperial power" created by the "Iron Chancellor" had contributed nothing to German culture. Instead, as Nietzsche observed, it was designed largely to impress Bismarck's "sickly" and "mediocre" followers. Nietzsche treated the modernization of Germany with disdain. As far as he was concerned, capitalism, bureaucratization, and democratization were all *antihuman*. Of particular concern to Nietzsche was the fact that, once the state becomes a centralized, bureaucratized, and impersonal instrument of domination, the idea of power as something for which the exceptional *individual* can compete is largely eliminated.

As a boy, Nietzsche had lived in a walled Thuringian town (Naumberg) that was still medieval in architecture and habit. At dusk, the citizens were called to their rest by a watchman, and the gates of the town were closed for the night. During the course of his lifetime, Nietzsche saw old Germany destroyed by the modernizers, but—unlike his sister—he did not live long enough to see what modern Germany would become. He recognized, however, that turn-of-the-century Germany was at an historical crossroads, for, as he put it, the Germans "belong to the day before yesterday and the day after tomorrow—*as yet they have no today.*"[23]

Intellectual Roots

Given the iconoclasm of Nietzsche's mature philosophy and his sweeping rejection of the philosophy of his day, we might anticipate some difficulty in locating any individual or school capable of directing his thought. However, four significant influences can be identified. In descending order of importance they are: (1) ancient Greek philosophy; (2) the philosopher Arthur Schopenhauer (1788–1860); (3) the composer Richard Wagner (1813–1883); and (4) the naturalist Charles Darwin (1809–1882). Only the first of these sources, however, can be said to have had a lasting and profound impact on Nietzsche. As one biographer observed, in Nietzsche's hands "classical studies" came to life. When Nietzsche discussed the ancient world, it was "as if he spoke from his own knowledge of things quite self-evident and still completely valid."[24]

Nietzsche's classical apprenticeship led him to believe that the ancients had created the right conditions for rearing exceptional individuals, "higher" than those who had come before or after. Yet Nietzsche did not place Greek accomplishments on some linear model of development. He believed, instead, that the truth the Greeks had discovered was *suprahistorical*: Their culture, in other words, was an achievement that would eternally endure: a cycle of being forgotten and then rediscovered.

The influence of Greek thought on Nietzsche is most obvious in his first published book, *The Birth of Tragedy* (1872), the unconventionality of which ended his hopes for an academic career. The work was highly speculative (and not properly footnoted). Moreover, awkwardly tacked on to a discussion of Greek tragedy was an essay that rather embarrassingly extolled Nietzsche's friend Richard Wagner as the living embodiment of a genius who had synthesized what Nietzsche identified as "Apollonian" and "Dionysian" forces.

For Nietzsche, the "Apollonian" represents "the urge to perfect self-sufficiency." Apollonianism thus creates "the typical 'individual' " and leads to "all that simplifies, distinguishes, makes strong, clear, unambiguous, typical." In short, it means "freedom under the law."[25] By contrast, the "Dionysian" expresses "an urge to unity, a reaching out beyond personality, the everyday, society, reality, across the abyss of transitoriness." It involves "an ecstatic affirmation of the total character of life as that which remains the same, just as powerful, just as blissful, through all change; the great pantheistic sharing of joy and sorrow that sanctifies and calls good even the most terrible and questionable qualities of life."[26]

According to Nietzsche, the Apollonian and the Dionysian represent two violently opposed forces. While the Apollonian attempts to impose some order on the chaos of existence, the Dionysian dialectically attempts to transgress and to subvert established boundaries. In *The Birth of Tragedy*, Nietzsche did not elevate one god at the expense of the other; but, as Walter Kaufmann has pointed out, "if he favors one of the two . . . it is Apollo. His thesis is that it took both to make possible the birth of tragedy, and he emphasizes the Dionysian only because he feels that the Apollonian genius of the Greeks cannot be fully understood apart from it."[27]

Nietzsche, however, was no rationalist; he did not place science or cognition above aesthetic expression. Rejecting the idea that reason could penetrate and correct what nature had left flawed, Nietzsche argued that Greek accomplishment was most accurately represented not by Socrates and his followers but by the pre-Socratics of the sixth century B.C. Nietzsche felt that Socrates' pernicious influence was largely responsible for the mythical—or, more exactly, rational—reconstruction of Greek civilization that later became such a centerpiece of Enlightenment ideology. He claimed that the problem with *philosophes* such as Jean-Jacques Rousseau (1712–1778) and Voltaire (1694–1778) was that they had failed to recognize that the pre-Christian world was dominated not so much by the rational political forms that Plato had identified but by earlier pagan cults emphasizing "sexuality, the lust to rule, pleasure in appearance and deception, great and joyful gratitude for life and its typical states."[28] Unlike the eighteenth-century rationalists, Nietzsche argued that the establishment of law, order, morality, and individuality had been a precarious achievement in the ancient world that was always in danger of being swept away by Dionysian orgies of cruelty and excess.

It is easy to be confused by what Nietzsche means by the "Dionysian," because, in his later works, he uses the term to express a *combination* of the Apollonian and Dionysian tendencies that he first identified in *The Birth of Tragedy*. Here, once again, Kaufmann comes to our aid. As he explains: "The 'Dionysus' in the Dionysus versus Apollo of Nietzsche's first book and the '*Dionysus versus the Crucified*' [i.e., Christ] in the last line of Nietzsche's last book [*Ecce Homo*] do not mean the same thing. The later Dionysus is the synthesis of the two forces represented by Dionysus and Apollo in *The Birth of Tragedy*."[29]

For Nietzsche, while the Apollonian creates form, the Dionysian is that out of which such form is made. In both his early and later work, Nietzsche saw the Dionysian as representing a "will to life," with all of its attendant sufferings, mysteries, cruelties, and joys. Art takes the raw flux of being and materializes or formalizes it—as dramatical tragedy, for instance, or as musical composition. *But it follows from this that even tragedy must be life-affirming.* Contrasting the pinched Christian renunciation of life with the joyous pagan affirmation of existence, Nietzsche hence describes what he believed was the most fundamental divide in human civilization: that between the rejection of what life affords as opposed to the enjoyment of whatever it brings:

> Dionysus versus the "Crucified." . . . One will see that the problem is that of the meaning of suffering: whether a Christian meaning or a tragic meaning. In the former case, it [i.e., suffering] is supposed to be the path to a holy existence; in the latter case, being is counted as *holy enough* to justify even a monstrous amount of suffering. The tragic man affirms even the harshest suffering: he is sufficiently strong, rich, and capable of deifying to do so. The Christian denies even the happiest lot on earth: he is sufficiently weak, poor, disinherited to suffer from life in whatever form he meets it. The god on the cross is a curse on life, a signpost to seek redemption from life; Dionysus cut to pieces is a *promise* of life: it will be eternally reborn and return again from destruction.[30]

In 1865, as a student in Leipzig, Nietzsche came across a copy of Arthur Schopenhauer's *The World as Will and Representation,* first published in 1819. The book profoundly affected him. As Nietzsche later recounted, it seemed to parallel, and to go beyond, what he was already beginning to think.

Schopenhauer began his philosophical career as a colleague of Hegel at the University of Berlin. In what turned out to be a failed attempt to poach Hegel's students, he even scheduled his lectures at the same hour as those of his rival. Yet Hegel's position as the "official philosopher" of the progressive Prussian state put him on a pedestal from which he could not easily be dislodged, and, conceding defeat, the independently wealthy Schopenhauer withdrew into private life. For nearly thirty years, Schopenhauer was virtually ignored, but, after the *Nachmärz,* he finally came into his own, able, at last, to address "a German audience eager to listen to 'philosophy,' to which academic philosophy, however, no longer dared to say anything."[31] Hegel's optimistic ideas had struck a chord with the hopes and aspirations of the relatively idealist, relatively enlightened, emerging bourgeois class. But, after the 1860s, Schopenhauer's philosophy resonated with the increasingly frustrated middle classes and with intellectuals such as Stefan George and Rainer Marie Rilke, who sought aesthetic release and escape from the vulgarities of Bismarck's materialist Reich. Moreover, the image of Schopenhauer as a solitary knight-errant of truth appealed to men such as Nietzsche and Wagner, who also liked to portray themselves as lonely visionaries. In fact, Schopenhauer's image as an outsider probably had a much greater impact on them than did his actual philosophy.[32]

Following Immanuel Kant (1724–1804), Schopenhauer distinguished between the world of appearance (phenomenal reality) and the world of "things-in-themselves" (noumenal reality), or reality as it exists in its own right, before it is reconstituted by human thought. Like Kant, Schopenhauer believed that thought could not penetrate the real world behind appearances, but, unlike Kant, he was ready and willing to speculate about ultimate reality. According to Schopenhauer, the real world is dominated by a blind, nonrational, striving cosmic will that is best revealed in nature: in the struggle of animals to survive, to kill, and to reproduce themselves. Rejecting the idea that human and nonhuman animals occupy radically distinct planes of existence, Schopenhauer equated this will with the noumenal form of the body, and he defined the body as the phenomenal form of the will. He thus detached thought from the rational, ideal, and intangible and made it, instead, part of *bodily* output and expression.

Unlike Nietzsche (and unlike the ancients), Schopenhauer was deeply pessimistic about what might be called the "meaning of life." It did, of course, follow from his philosophical premises that humans cannot hope to master either themselves or their environment intellectually. Moreover, the "will," in Schopenhauer's terms, must be seen as primordially evil; it is oblivious to our "higher," more cultivated and civilized aspirations, and it inevitably places us in situations where our drives clash with those of others whom we are, as a result, condemned to fear, propitiate, or destroy.

What Schopenhauer and Nietzsche had in common was a belief that life is dominated by instinct and impulse, not by thought or conscience. Consciousness, in this sense, is a thin crust that floats on an ocean of feeling, instinct, and emotion. Both Schopenhauer and Nietzsche recognized that the world has no intrinsic ethical significance, and they both accepted that the mind must be used in the service of life, power, and the will to live. For Nietzsche, the alternative would be to have the mind turn *against life itself*—creating, as a result, the kind of person who is consumed by resentment, guilt, self-loathing, and "bad conscience" (fear of one's nature, together with the need to punish oneself because of the belief that one's impulses are cruel, evil, ugly, or sinful).

What Nietzsche ultimately rejected in Schopenhauer was his pessimism: his belief that life was a vale of tears from which art provided but a temporary respite from the torturous and impetuous will. Unlike Nietzsche, Schopenhauer was deeply involved in developing a *philosophy* of ethics. Seeing only too clearly that individuals could never reconcile their moral ideals with the world as it is, Schopenhauer concluded that this world was a sewer. In opposition to this, Nietzsche accepted life on its own terms—with its great horrors and with its beauty. As far as he was concerned, the strong or exceptional individual did not despair, and he did not flee.

Nietzsche first met Wagner in Leipzig in November 1868, and, during the period he taught at Basel, he visited him often at Tribschen, the composer's isolated villa near Lake Lucerne. For about four or five years thereafter, Nietzsche and Wagner happily cooperated in the nurturance of a mutual admiration society. Nietzsche also seems to have been infatuated with Cosima von Bülow, Franz Liszt's illegitimate daughter and the mother of Wagner's children. Wagner had taken Cosima from the conductor Hans von Bülow, whom, meantime, he busied with the task of producing his operas in Munich. Nietzsche and Wagner, though, were an oddly unsuited couple. Apart from a joint interest in Schopenhauer, they had little in common, save confidence in their own respective greatness. Wagner was an anti-Semite, a Francophobe, and what the British call a "champagne socialist." His flowery declarations that the masses could be redeemed through Great Art (chiefly his own, of course) were not at all in accord with Nietzsche's way of thinking. Freud, though, could have made something of the fact that Wagner had been born in the same year as Nietzsche's father, and bore an uncanny resemblance to him.

There can be no doubt about Wagner's genius as a composer. Self-consciously incorporating themes from German Romanticism, Schopenhauerian renunciation, and international socialism, Wagner's "musical dramas" often have a profound emotional impact on audiences. They are certainly innovative and controversial. *Tristan und*

Isolde has Isolde sing in the final scene an aria that depicts, in the most sublime fashion imaginable, sexual ecstasy and death, expressed together, in one surging, overwhelming sensation. Some might consider this a strange association—but not, of course, Schopenhauer (who, deeply affected by Hinduism, saw in art a striving for self-oblivion), nor Freud, who, later, explored what he believed was the subconscious intersection between erotic desire and the "death wish."

Wagner might have been an extraordinarily gifted artist, but he was a repulsive human being. A calculating self-promoter who took whatever he wanted from whoever was ready to supply it, he made a virtue out of his and Cosima's hatred of the Jews. Wagner claimed that the Germans "are by nature the flower of humankind: to fulfill their great destiny they have only to restore their sullied racial purity." By contrast, he asserted, "the Jewish race is the born enemy of pure humanity and everything that is noble in it."[33] At Tribschen, Wagner liked to dress in the style of a seventeenth-century Flemish painter, appearing before his visitors in black satin breeches, silk stockings, a tam-o'-shanter, and a monumental cravat tastefully arranged in a Lord Fauntleroy bow. His villa was turned into a museum to Germany's greatest genius (himself), replete with numerous photographs and busts of the great man. Before the *Nachmärz*, Wagner had been involved in liberal politics, but it cannot be said that his political intelligence matched his musical sagacity, for, as a self-declared republican and socialist, his greatest hope had been to see Germany headed by a Saxon king. After he was forced into exile in 1849, Wagner's outlook on life became increasingly Schopenhauerian, and he subsequently lost all interest in politics.

In 1872, Wagner laid the foundation stone for the opera house in Bayreuth that was to be built in his honor and that, ever since, apart from the war years, has presented an annual festival of his musical dramas. After his friendship with Wagner had begun to cool, Nietzsche took his sister to Bayreuth to attend the first complete performance of *The Ring* in 1876. Elisabeth had the time of her life and adored absolutely everything, but Nietzsche reacted quite differently. As he later complained, the common "riffraff" and the "fat matrons from Marienbad" who patronized the festival were vulgar, jingoistic, anti-Semitic, and bourgeois to the core. It was only too apparent that these fans had traveled to Bavaria not to celebrate Great Art but to participate in a low kind of *Oktoberfest*. Still, as long as the philistines were well connected or wealthy, both the Master and Cosima fawned on them. Nietzsche was beside himself:

> Wherever was I? There was nothing I recognized: I scarcely recognized Wagner. In vain did I leaf through my memories. Tribschen—a distant isle of the blessed: not a trace of any similarity. . . . *What had happened?* Wagner had been translated into German! The Wagnerians had become master over Wagner.—*German* art. The *German* master. *German* beer. . . . Poor Wagner! Where had he landed!—If he had at least entered into swine. But to descend among Germans![34]

The final influence on Nietzsche was that exercised by Darwin, who revolutionized European thought in the final third of the nineteenth century. In *Human, All Too Human* (1878), and *The Joyful Wisdom* (1882), Nietzsche turned away from metaphysics and from his earlier infatuation with Schopenhauer and Wagner and showed a greater appreciation of the scientific quest. As we have seen, Nietzsche was no *social* evolutionist, but, in accepting rather too uncritically the Victorian reading of Darwin, he initially believed that the Englishman had shown how the "survival of the fittest" might help produce an ascending individual. Later, however, Nietzsche recognized that what "preserves the individual," or what turns out an *average* representative of the species adapted to the environment of its near ancestors, "might at the same time arrest and halt [this individual's] evolution."[35] Moreover, he belatedly saw that adaptive traits that evolve by natural selection are unlikely to play much of a role in the formation of the extraordinary individual. Nietzsche accordingly concluded that there was nothing in evolutionary theory that he could use in his philosophy. He also recognized that Darwinism did not address the conditions for the emergence of the *Übermensch* (overman): the individual who had mastered or overcome chiefly *himself.*

IDEAS

Society

Nietzsche did not have *any* theory of "society" as such. Like Freud, he was more interested in psychological than in sociological forces. Although he certainly focused on culture (what he called "the cultural complex"), Nietzsche had no interest in "social structure." In fact, the only "social structure" he ever recognized (and so defined) was the *body.* The reader, then, might wonder why Nietzsche is included in a book on classical sociological theory. One answer is that Nietzsche did offer extraordinary insights into what he called the history or "genealogy" of morality. Another is that Nietzsche had a great deal to say about the microdynamics of social power and domination—a topic of growing concern today. Finally, Nietzsche helped modern intellectuals grasp that knowledge is not beyond or outside power. For Nietzsche, knowledge is a cloak much favored by power.

Nietzsche's views present a serious challenge to classical sociology. For example, his emphasis on the heterogeneity of personality types led Nietzsche to stress that social relations are structured not by shared values but by clashing wills that strive to exhaust themselves within dynamic, shifting force fields. Nietzsche believed that moral claims (i.e., demands that you *should* be like me, or that you *must* obey me) often are weapons wielded by weak and inadequate people. If so, it would be a mistake to assume that such claims are ever even intended to construct a reasoned and universal consensus within a societal community. Nietzsche unsurprisingly dismissed the modern prejudice that a "healthy" or "rational" society can be established on the basis of a reasoned or self-reflective consensus that expresses a Rousseauian "general will." According to Nietzsche, morality more likely feeds on hatred and resentment and requires those whom it organizes to nurture and sustain a "hostile, external world."

Nietzsche's greatest challenge to classical sociology, however, resides in his claim that "there are no moral phenomena at all, but only a moral interpretation of phenomena."[36] To put this somewhat differently; according to Nietzsche, *there is no morality, there are only moralities.* In his own words:

> There are moralities which are meant to justify their creator before others. Other moralities are meant to calm him and lead him to be satisfied with himself. With yet others [those that generate bad conscience] he wants to crucify himself and humiliate himself.

With others he wants to wreak revenge, with others conceal himself, with others transfigure himself and place himself way up, at a distance. This morality is used by its creator to forget, that one to have others forget him or something about him. Some moralists want to vent their power and creative whims on humanity; some others, perhaps including Kant, suggest with their morality: "What deserves respect in me is that I can obey—and you *ought* not to be different from me."[37]

In sum, Nietzsche appears to have challenged the project of "classical" sociology from its very inception. As we have seen, such sociology largely was founded on both the premise and the expectation that social bases for moral order could be located. Nietzsche, though, recognized that modernity was creating human beings without deep foundations, without public convictions, and without lasting commitments. He consequently concluded that the modern age would be unlikely to foundationalize anew what it had already succeeded in bursting asunder.

As a short introduction to some of Nietzsche's more sociological observations, let us recount an incident that happened in a class taught by one of the authors several years ago. The students in this particular seminar were not very lively, and they showed little interest in participating in discussions. So, in order to spare himself the ordeal of endlessly talking to himself, the instructor asked each student to take turns introducing various topics. Unfortunately, most of the presentations were—to say the least of it—unimpressive. Many students seemed to have read nothing; others appeared resentful that they were expected to say something (anything) that might contribute to the life of the class.

One afternoon, while most students dozed quietly, a young woman was laboring over a few obvious points, when, with the intent of speeding things up, the instructor aimed a few queries at her. Her eyes filled with tears, but the probing did seem to have a positive effect, as the focus and tempo of her presentation picked up considerably. But the instructor then made the fatal error of barking out one question too many, and, gathering up her notes, the young woman fled sobbing from the room. Her sudden exit left behind a shocked, animated, excited, bonded, and unusually focused group. After the right pause, a male student, who had barely participated all term, summed up what everyone was feeling—and, to his credit, he got it exactly right. In fact, it was the most effective thing the instructor ever saw him do. "Well," he said to his teacher, "I hope you are proud of yourself."

The red-faced instructor now had to avoid the hostile, reproachful, and self-righteous little faces that suddenly couldn't get enough of him. No longer did everyone seek to avoid *his* glance; the tables had been turned. Everyone knew what the students were thinking: Not only is this guy not much of a teacher, he is also a rude, uncaring, and cruel person. No one likes him—not even his colleagues, and probably not even the members of his own family. No wonder we are not getting much out of this course; no wonder he assigns such boring and pointless readings. *He* thought we were not very bright (and, for a time, we feared he might be right), but we *now* know how well founded our resentments were from the very beginning. *We* were never the problem; *he* was always the problem.

Everything the instructor now had to say was scrutinized carefully. In a sense, this was good, but he soon discovered that his utterances were greeted with widespread suspicion, not to mention derision. As he became increasingly more hesitant, ingratiating, and unsure of himself, the atmosphere in the room only worsened, and he barely made it to the break. Fortunately, the young woman he had brutalized was still on the premises, and, luckily for him, she forgave him his trespasses. At the same time, though, she gave the screw a few more turns by explaining through tear-sodden tissues that she had stayed up all night to work on her presentation. Later, the instructor learned that, because she had had a series of relationships with "abusive boyfriends," she had been in therapy for several months. Apparently, all the students knew about this, so they were, as a result, *particularly* indignant about the way she had been treated. It seemed to the poor professor that nothing could get him out of the hole he had dug for himself. Under the circumstances, the least he could do was raise everyone's grade by at least one letter and hope against hope that this would somehow make up for his bad behavior. Even so, he did not make "Teacher of the Year."

What would Nietzsche have made of the above? Apart from savoring every moment, he would have recognized the following:

1. The presence of *bad conscience,* each student's initial feeling of hatred for himself or herself, caused, in this instance, by their professor reflecting back to them a picture of themselves as weak, powerless, compromised, and inadequate. It is, of course, understandable that students might see a strong (good?) teacher as evil. Yet, perhaps, it is difficult for them to admit *why* they feel this way. One of Nietzsche's epigrams might help: " 'I don't like him.'—Why?—'I am not equal to him.'—Has any human being ever answered that way?"[38]

2. A serendipitous event (the crying jag), which led to the aforementioned revolt. This rebellion relieved the students from doing what Nietzsche would have suggested they should have done, namely to use their discomfort and suffering as a spur to improving themselves. Instead, in what Nietzsche calls "the inversion of the value-positing eye," they turned their aggressive instincts outward—toward the instructor. (Evidently, they liked being hard on *him* a lot better than being hard on themselves.)

3. The constructive use of resentment (what Nietzsche called *ressentiment*) to project hostility and anger outward. As a result, the group in question created a reactive and defensive sense of moral solidarity based on new, shared values.

4. The externalization of guilt as a power ploy, as revenge, and as a method of social control designed to catch the professor in its web.

5. A decadent leader (the instructor), who—let us be hard on *him*—was too weak, too craven, and too unsure of himself to repulse slavishly moral behavior, and who thereby demonstrated that he was not fit to master himself, let alone rule others.

6. In sum (see points 1–5 above): *the triumph of "herd" or "slave" over "master" morality.*

In the preface to *On the Genealogy of Morals* (1887), Nietzsche attempts to put the emergence of "slave morality" in an historical context. Making good use of his training in philology, Nietzsche points out that the distinction between "good" and "evil" originally referred to a social distinction between humans who were "high-born" and "noble," on the one hand, as opposed to those who were "low-born" and "plebeian," on the other. As he observes: "The judgment 'good' did *not* originate with those to whom 'goodness' was shown! Rather, it was 'the good' themselves, that is to say, the noble, powerful, high-stationed and high-minded, who felt and established themselves and their actions as good."[39] We can still locate these original meanings of the terms "good" and "bad" in ancient languages. For instance, the Greek words "*esthlos* and *agathos* had connotations of nobility and bravery, while their antonyms, *kakos* and *deilos*, suggested plebeian cowardice."[40]

Nietzsche observed that, in ancient Greek society, the "good," or noble, type of man *determines* values; he does not need permission from others in order to exist. He thus "honors himself as one who is powerful, also as one who has power over himself, who knows how to speak and be silent, who delights in being severe and hard with himself and respects all severity and hardness."[41] The noble type of man accordingly creates "master morality," which, according to Nietzsche, is nothing but a "lust to rule" that "must be present in the general economy of life (and be further enhanced if life is to be further enhanced)."[42] Noble individuals cultivate a "physical-spiritual discipline" that makes them strong. They feel only "contempt for the cowardly, the anxious, the petty, those intent on narrow utility; also for the suspicious with their unfree glances; those who humble themselves, the doglike people who allow themselves to be maltreated, the begging flatterers, above all the liars."[43] The noble type of person "desires his enemy for himself, as his mark of distinction." Accordingly, "he can endure no other enemy than one in whom there is nothing to despise and *very much to honor.*"[44] "Masters," of course, will always inspire fear in "slaves," because, by its very nature, "slave morality" is a "morality of utility" reactively concerned with the powerful. Because "the man of *ressentiment*" must adapt to the will of others, he "is neither upright nor naïve nor honest and straightforward with himself." According to Nietzsche, "His soul *squints.* . . . He understands how to keep silent, how not to forget, how to wait, how to be provisionally self-deprecating and humble."[45]

For Nietzsche, "Every enhancement of the type 'man' has so far been the work of an aristocratic society [i.e., a society that produces a noble type of man]—and it will be so again and again—a society that believes in the long ladder of an order of rank and differences in value between man and man, and that needs slavery in some sense or another."[46] Nietzsche cautions us that we "should not yield to humanitarian illusions about the origins of an aristocratic society" but "admit to ourselves . . . how every higher culture on earth has so far *begun.*"[47] "In the beginning, the noble caste was always the barbarian caste. . . . They were more *whole* human beings (which also means, at every level, 'more whole beasts')."[48] Like Pareto, Nietzsche believed that this noble caste must retain complete confidence in its right to dominate. Once doubt or guilt creeps in, leaders become decadent and are easily corrupted.

Trying to explain how the meanings of "good" and "evil," and "good" and "bad" were inverted in the Christian era, Nietzsche developed an allegory of eagles and lambs. The eagles (brave, daring, and strong) prey on the lambs (weak and helpless). From the lambs' perspective, "these birds of prey are evil," and, as they say to one another, "Whoever is least like a bird of prey, but rather its opposite, a lamb," is he not "good?"[49] Yet the eagles do not dislike "these good little lambs." Indeed, *they* observe to one another (a little ironically, perhaps), "We love them; nothing is more tasty than a tender lamb."[50] Because the eagles are raptors, what they see as "good" is accomplished by means of predation; it is not, of course, described from the vantage point of prey. And there—at least as far as the nonhuman animal world is concerned—the story is likely to end. What would happen, though, if, by some miracle, the lambs persuaded the eagles to look at the world from the lambs' point of view? The "cruel" eagles would then have to acknowledge that their hunting forays were "evil" and "bad," not "good" at all.

We can see that in the example above, the terms "good" and "evil," and "good" and "bad" do not have fixed meanings. What eagles mean by "good" hunting is not what lambs mean by "good" (lamblike) values (e.g., meekness, softness, gentleness). A modern analytic philosopher might suggest that the eagles and lambs are playing different "language games." Perhaps, then, it was a mistake to encourage them to start trying to speak to each other in the first place! But suppose these troublesome animals now begin a loud argument about what the word "good" *really* means. How would we settle such a dispute? Could predators and prey both refer to a supralinguistic rule book that could resolve such differences? Or—given that they now have invented language—would the quarrelsome little creatures have to "fight" things out? (How do lambs "fight" anyway? Stomp feathers?)

In a famous exchange with Alice Liddell (*Alice in Wonderland*), Humpty Dumpty offered one particular solution to the problem sketched above:

> "When I use a word," Humpty Dumpty said in rather a scornful tone, "it means just what I choose it to mean—neither more nor less."
> "The question is," said Alice, "whether you *can* make words mean different things."
> "The question is," said Humpty Dumpty, "which is to be master—that's all."[51]

To return to our allegory, if lambs manage to become masters over eagles, something pretty strange is going on—but not, as Nietzsche would comment, anything stranger than what is likely to occur when slaves begin to rule masters. In *On the Genealogy of Morals*, Nietzsche contends that if what once was "evil" or powerful has now become "bad," this must be because slave morality has managed to "win the fight" over master morality. But, to restate the central question, how is this possible? Nietzsche's explanation was as follows:

> The slave revolt in morality begins when *ressentiment* itself becomes creative and gives birth to values . . . [and] an imaginary revenge. While every noble morality develops from a triumphant affirmation of itself, slave morality from the outset says No to what is "outside" . . . , and *this* No is its creative deed. This inversion of the value-positing eye—this need to direct one's view outward instead of back to oneself—is of the essence of *ressentiment:* in order to exist, slave morality always first needs a hostile external world; it needs, physiologically speaking, external stimuli in order to act at all—its action is fundamentally reaction.[52]

According to Nietzsche, the *Christian* association of the "good" with those who suffer (e.g., the slaves) was *the* historic event that enabled the values of master morality to be inverted. For Nietzsche, the victory of slave morality is symbolized by the "gruesome" Christian invention of god on the cross: "Never again and nowhere has there been an equal boldness in inversion, anything as horrible, questioning, and questionable, as this formula: it promised a revaluation of all the values of antiquity."[53] Nietzsche hence claimed that the great genius of Christianity is, first, the revaluation of the meaning of suffering and, second, the perverse insistence that *whatever* you do to us, *however much* you make us suffer, *we* are stronger, and *we* will win in the end.

Christianity, of course, purports to be a religion of universal love, but Nietzsche thus insists that it actually is driven by bad conscience and by *ressentiment*. Behind all the talk about love, salvation, and redemption, Christianity fosters "*hatred* of injustice," "*hatred* of godlessness"—the hopeless yearning of the defeated and downtrodden for "an act of the most *spiritual revenge*." In short, the religion promotes:

1. The idea of perpetual suffering, which, rather than being confronted, is made into something "holy."
2. The desire for revenge against the (pagan) "evil" ones who believe they have the right to affirm themselves, regardless of the consequences for others.
3. The use of a drug or palliative (i.e., religion) in order to get through life (or, rather, to *avoid* life). Such "nay-saying" requires the Christian to be slavishly moral, that is, to be a "herd-animal."

Nietzsche was hard on the Christians:

> They are miserable, no doubt of it, all those mutterers and nook counterfeiters, although they crouch warmly together—but they tell me their misery is a sign of being chosen by God; one beats the dogs one likes best; perhaps this misery is also a preparation, a testing, a schooling, perhaps it is even more—something that will one day be made good and recompensed with interest, with huge payments of gold, no! of happiness. This they call "bliss."[54]

Still, Nietzsche recognized that "men of *ressentiment*" (such as those who have been Christianized) are "bound to become eventually *cleverer* than any noble race."[55] How, after all, can the "noble" or "strong" type of person defeat a confederacy of "naysayers" who have made patient martyrdom and lowing indignation their most precious attributes? How can the (pagan) warrior "fight" the dull and insistent values of the herd? Perhaps, then, it is not so hard to grasp how the weak learn to overcome the strong. Let's face facts: It is difficult to be an individual. But how easy it is to be bovine! How good it feels; how *right*! Let us moo the anthem of the cud-chewers: *Moralität ist Herden-Instinkt im Einzelem* (Morality is the herd instinct in the individual).

Contrasting the "unbroken strength of will and lust for power" of the ancients with the slave morality of "sickly" and "mediocre" modern Europeans, Nietzsche despaired of the present. As far as he was concerned, "the *democratic* movement" was—like the socialist movement—the "secular" "heir of the Christian movement."[56] For Nietzsche, "parliamentary government and the press . . . are the means by which the herd animal becomes master."[57] And, by the same token, democracy teaches that "at bottom we are one and all self-seeking cattle and mob."[58] Like socialism and Christianity, democracy thrives on *ressentiment* and disguises a passion for revenge.

In addition to master and slave morality, Nietzsche identifies a third source of values that intersects with these first two wellsprings: that of religious renunciation and ascetic self-denial. Here, though, it should be emphasized that Nietzsche is talking about the actions of *leaders*, not followers. Religious ascetes, such as Jesus, appear to love their suffering, but, according to Nietzsche, they are primarily interested in self-mastery as the royal road to mastery of others. (We can note here that, although Nietzsche did not think much of Christians, he showed a certain admiration for Christ.)

Nietzsche argued that ascetic individuals are powerful because they manage to overcome what is base or slavish in *themselves*. Because they enjoy punishing themselves, such ascetes fall far short of what Nietzsche saw as the human ideal, but, by the same token, they are not slaves either, because they have mastered their own weaknesses. Individuals capable of ascetic self-renunciation are able to make something positive out of bad conscience and suffering, and we can see, in this regard, why "asceticism and puritanism" tend to be favored by those who *aspire* to be leaders. As Nietzsche points out, these qualities "are almost indispensable means for educating and ennobling a race that wishes to become master over its origins among the rabble and that works its way up toward future rule."[59] Still,

> in this psychical cruelty there resides a madness of the will which is absolutely unexampled: the *will* of man to find himself guilty and reprehensible to a degree that can never be atoned for . . . ; his *will* to infect and poison the fundamental ground of things with the problem of punishment and guilt . . . ; his *will* to erect an ideal—that of the 'holy God'—and in the face of it to feel the palpable certainty of his own absolute unworthiness. Oh this insane, pathetic beast—man! What ideas he has, what unnaturalness, what paroxysms of nonsense, what *bestiality of thought* erupts as soon as he is prevented just a little from being a *beast in deed*.[60]

The Individual in Society

Nietzsche equated the spread of egalitarianism, utilitarianism, the market society, and the rise of formal democracy with the *loss* of individuality—a condition, he believed, few of us were capable of achieving, even under the best of circumstances. "Classical" sociology tended to equate modernity with the emergence of relatively autonomous and self-interested individuals. By contrast, Nietzsche argued that the modern age had developed an "ethic of utility" that was destroying the "sovereign" individual. Like Marx, he recognized that the frenetic pace of capitalist commodity culture reduced the human to the status of a herd instrument: "One is now ashamed of repose: even long reflection almost causes remorse of conscience. Thinking is done with a stop-watch, as dining is done with the eyes fixed on the financial newspaper; we live like men who are continually 'afraid of letting opportunities slip.' 'Better do anything whatever, than nothing'—this principle also is a noose with which all culture and all higher taste may be strangled."[61]

As noted earlier, Nietzsche believed that democracy and socialism could strive only for a lowest common cultural denominator. These political systems, moreover, devalue, displace, and sideline the few people who are genuinely fit to rule. This is a position with which Weber had a certain amount of sympathy, for, as he later emphasized, the "inescapable" mechanism of administration in the modern nation-state is bureaucracy, and bureaucracy's main characteristic is its hatred of anything personal. Formal administration hence subjugates precisely those individuals who, under different circumstances, might be capable of something other than "herd morality." Using Bismarck's Germany as his guide, Nietzsche recognized how banal modern "politics" was becoming. Anticipating the kind of transition suggested by the shift from Lincoln or FDR to William Jefferson Clinton, Nietzsche foresaw a descending line of continuous degeneration.

As might be expected, Nietzsche's view of the ascendant, complacent, and self-satisfied nineteenth-century English neoliberals was not at all in accord with the ideological presuppositions of his day. Identifying the English (not the French) with the introduction of modern ideas and with "an over-all depression of the European spirit,"[62] Nietzsche described intellectuals such as John Stuart Mill and Herbert Spencer as ponderous mediocrities with the outlook and aspirations of "shopkeepers." In Nietzsche's terms, such men do not want

> to know or even sense that 'the general welfare' is no ideal, no goal, no remotely intelligible concept, but only an emetic—that what is fair for one *cannot* by any means for that reason alone also be fair for others; that the demand of one morality for all is detrimental for the higher men. . . . They are a modest and thoroughly mediocre type of man, these utilitarian Englishmen, and . . . insofar as they are boring one cannot think highly enough of their utility.[63]

Rejecting the Anglo-American belief that it was possible to locate one set of rules that would be right or "good" for all individuals, Nietzsche "viewed the genuine 'self' to be a nonsocial, irreducible, individual particularity [that was] contradictory to the 'herd'-like 'ego' (i.e., the social self)."[64] In contrast to Hegel, Comte, Mead, and Durkheim—but not, perhaps, entirely in opposition to Simmel and Freud—Nietzsche hence believed that the strong, healthy, "whole" individual could become what it was only by *distancing* itself from the moral sentiments of surrounding collectivities. In Nietzsche's terms, the sheep bleat "morality" to all who will listen, but the "overmen," understandably, "shudder slightly" at every association with these herd-animals. As *Übermenschen*, they are, of course, *beyond* the kind of morality that is the invention of creatures such as they. According to Nietzsche, they have a natural right to lead because they, alone, can create the values to which—if we could—we *should* aspire. In this context, some of Nietzsche's more puzzling epigrams begin to make some sense: " 'Pity for all' would be hardness and tyranny toward *you*, my dear neighbor!—"; "The great epochs of our time come when we gain the courage to rechristen our evil as what is best in us."[65]

In Francis Ford Coppola's great masterpiece *Apocalypse Now* (based on Joseph Conrad's *Heart of Darkness*), Captain Willard is sent upriver to "terminate" the command of Colonel Kurtz, a rogue special forces operative who no longer is following orders. Kurtz turns out to be a highly intelligent and compassionate man, who, nonetheless, was willing to commit terrible deeds for the "good" of his country. When Willard finally locates Kurtz—who is now living amongst savages who worship him—he discovers that the colonel has suffered a complete paralysis of the will.

While Willard musters up courage to strike a fatal blow against Kurtz (a blow he knows will also be aimed against what is best in him), Kurtz describes an incident he experienced early in the war. As part of a "heart-and-minds" propaganda offensive, his unit went into a Vietnamese village to give some preventive shots to children. Shortly thereafter, the enemy neatly hacked off every little arm that had been inoculated. As Kurtz emphasizes, the men who did this were not monsters; indeed, they had children of their own just like those they had mutilated. The "absolute purity" of this act forces Kurtz to confront his own weakness. The event is pivotal for him, for he is forced to concede that the cosseted American troops will never defeat men capable of mastering themselves so completely.

Apocalypse Now is not, of course, strictly *about* Vietnam—any more than *Moby Dick* is strictly about whaling.[66] Rather, Coppola seeks to depict the "interior" space of the two protagonists: Willard and Kurtz. In Nietzschean terms, Kurtz is an exceptional individual. What makes him appear "insane" to his superiors in the corps is his uncompromising honesty: his refusal to deny that he has sacrificed his integrity in the service of an organization that is decadent to its very core—made up of mediocrities, incapable, even, of despising what they have become. The American state (that "cold liar," that "coldest of all cold monsters") had the material resources to start a murderous war at practically no cost to itself. But it could not find strong individuals capable of finishing what the impersonal machine had begun. Unlike the American forces, the Vietnamese had an undifferentiated, personal involvement in what, to them, was a war of national defense. They also had an unyielding belief in their absolute *right* to prevail, at whatever cost—particularly to themselves.

Nietzsche would have liked the allegory of *Apocalypse Now*: A decadent organization that needs and rewards mediocrities will fear, subjugate, and seek to destroy any individual that struggles to rise above it. Even so, the noble type of person is worth more than the most advanced technology. What makes the individual sovereign is the purity of its will, which, inevitably, will be seen as "evil" from the vantage point of the herd. Kurtz's puzzling indifference to his protagonist's mission reflects his choice that the instrument of his death should be an expression of the forces he had previously let destroy him as a complete human being. Even in defeat, Kurtz "would rather will *nothingness* than *not* will" at all.[67] Kurtz, then, is great because he will not spare himself, and he cannot pretend to be other than what he is: the rejected tool of a dehumanized and insane system. We can say of a man like him: "The attraction of knowledge would be small if one did not have to overcome so much shame on the way."[68]

Nietzsche is often portrayed as a philosopher who downplayed the importance of conscience and of cognitive self-reflection. But, like Freud, he was chiefly opposed to the idea that the drives of the body and of the will could be separated from the workings of the mind or intellect. Nietzsche certainly disapproved of the elevation of "spirit" or soul at the *expense* of the body. He believed there is more "common sense" in our bodies than in our best wisdom. According to Nietzsche, the mind-body dualism that Christianity had taken to extremes was responsible for many of the ailments from which modern, civilized humans suffered. As he explained, all drives

> that do not discharge themselves outwardly *turn inward*—this is what I call the *internalization* of man: thus it was that man first developed his "soul." . . . Those fearful bulwarks with which the political organization protected itself against the old instincts of freedom . . . [turned] those instincts of wild, free, prowling man . . . backward *against man himself.* Hostility, cruelty, joy in persecuting, in attacking, in change, in destruction—all this turned against the possessors of such instincts: *that* is the origin of the "bad conscience." . . . Thus began the gravest and uncanniest illness, from which humanity has not yet recovered, man's suffering *of man, of himself*—the result of a forcible sundering from his animal past, as it were a leap and plunge into new surroundings and conditions of existence.[69]

Nietzsche emphasized that brutality and sadism were the outcome of slave morality and of bad conscience, *not* of master morality. As we have seen, the "overman" is the most likely to be "a beast in deed." Nonetheless, because he is chiefly concerned with mastering *himself*, the "overman" is not primarily concerned with brutality toward others. By contrast, lesser or flawed individuals who are slavishly moral or tormented by bad conscience are most likely to turn their aggressive impulses against themselves. Finally, sadists who take pleasure in inflicting pain on others typically are seeking a temporary form of relief from what Nietzsche called "man's" internalized "suffering of man." This third group comprises the lowest type of humans—those incapable of being hard on *themselves*.

Methodology

On the first page of his study of Nietzsche's life and work, R. J. Hollingdale suggests that Nietzsche's "distinctive contribution to European thought was to recognize and face the consequences of a radical change in Western man's apprehension of and attitude towards 'truth.' "[70] Nietzsche did not espouse solipsism or relativism. But he did teach that all knowledge was perspectival, that is, historically and culturally situated. Moreover, Nietzsche argued that "the *more* affects we allow to speak about one thing, the *more* eyes, different eyes, we can use to observe one thing, the more complete will our 'concept' of this thing, our 'objectivity' be."[71]

Unlike a modern rationalist, Nietzsche did not treat the Kantian domains of "cognition," "morality," and "art" as autonomous life spheres—with "cognition," of course, placed at the top of the pile. Yet Nietzsche also acknowledged that these life spheres of cognition, morality, and art should not be conflated. Art, for instance, expresses a truth of its own, governed by its own set of rules: "For a philosopher to say, 'the good and the beautiful are one,' is infamy; if he goes on to add, 'also the true,' one ought to thrash him. Truth is ugly. We possess *art* lest we perish of the truth."[72]

Nietzsche believed that those humans who insisted most strenuously that they were "realists" were the least likely to recognize how reality was humanly, not objectively, constructed.[73] As we have seen, Nietzsche did not believe that the world we experience is a product of the conscious intellect; in his terms, "the greater part of our intellectual activity goes on unconsciously and unfelt by us."[74] Unsurprisingly, Nietzsche emphatically rejected the familiar dualism of appearance versus reality, together with the conventional idea that thought can pierce the "surface" of the world to reach the "essence" beneath.

Nietzsche, then, cannot easily be categorized. In sum, he was *anti*systemic; he believed that all systems—including all systems of knowledge—are based on foundations that cannot be questioned. He was certainly not a positivist (he despised those such as the "pedantic Englishman" Spencer "whose main task" had been "to arrange a variety of material, distribute it in drawers, and systematize it generally");[75] he did not believe in *Vernunft*, or Hegelian-Marxist critical theory, and he was not interested in surface hermeneutics. The only person to whom he can satisfactorily be compared (and whom he profoundly influenced) was Freud.

As might be expected, Nietzsche was quick to explode positivism's claims about its own detachment from human purpose and interest. As he points out in *The Joyful Wisdom*, modern science did not emerge in a cultural vacuum. Rather, it was developed

(1) because "it was hoped that God's goodness and wisdom would be best understood therewith" (Newton); (2) "because the absolute utility of knowledge was believed in, and especially the most intimate connection of morality, knowledge and happiness" (Voltaire); and (3) "because it was thought that in science there was something unselfish, harmless, self-sufficing, lovable, and truly innocent to be had, in which the evil human impulses did not participate" (Spinoza).[76] Today, though, the age of innocence is over: (1) Science no longer is seen as a form of worship; (2) only ignoramuses could still believe that scientific knowledge makes you a happier person; and (3) post-Auschwitz, post-Hiroshima, and post-Chernobyl, who, among us, could argue that technical-cognitive instrumentalism is "innocent" or "harmless"?

Nietzsche respected the accomplishments of modern science. At the same time, he strongly believed that, although the modern individual *describes* more meticulously than ever, we "explain just as little as our predecessors."[77] As he perceptively asked, "How can explanation ever be possible when first we make everything a *conception*, our conception! It is sufficient to regard science as the exactest humanizing of things that is possible."[78] "Materialistic natural-scientists," of course, believe that their "insignificant, four-cornered human reason" has its equivalent and measure in a "world of truth." Yet, as Nietzsche acerbically commented:

> What? do we actually wish to have existence debased in that fashion to a ready-reckoner exercise and calculation for stay-at-home mathematicians? We should not, above all, seek to divest existence of its *ambiguous* character: good taste forbids it, gentlemen, the taste of reverence for everything that goes beyond your horizon! That a world-interpretation is alone right by which *you* maintain your position, by which investigation and work can go on scientifically in *your* sense . . . is a piece of grossness and naïvety. . . . Would the reverse not be quite probable, that the most superficial and external characters of existence—its most apparent quality, its outside, its embodiment—should let themselves be apprehended first? perhaps alone allow themselves to be apprehended? A "scientific" interpretation of the world as you understand it might consequently still be one of the *stupidest*, that is to say, the most destitute of significance, of all possible world-interpretations.[79]

Not content with popping positivism's balloon, Nietzsche worried about the long-term effects of placing "materialistic natural science" at the core of human existence. He suggested that the triumph of the modern scientific world view represented not something positive but an *abyss*—an abyss of meaning. Science, of course, is not itself directly responsible for this, because, throughout human history, "science" (i.e., rational inquiry) has taken many forms. Nonetheless, the outlook of highly routinized, highly systematized *modern* science does reflect and exacerbate what Weber called the "disenchantment" of the world. Nietzsche recognized that modern science gave "modest and worthy laborers" many "little nooks" and crannies within which they could busy themselves. Yet, in anticipating the emptiness of most "scientific research," together with the careerism, militarization, and bureaucratization of "big science," Nietzsche also foresaw that modern science would become a "*hiding place* for every type of discontent, disbelief, gnawing worm . . . [and] bad conscience—it is the unrest of the *lack* of ideals, the suffering from the *lack* of any great love, the discontent in the face of involuntary contentment."[80]

In an argument that profoundly affected Weber, Nietzsche concluded that modern science was the great destroyer of ideals, of values, and of purpose. It promotes nihilism, which Nietzsche defined as a condition where "the highest values devaluate themselves."[81] In short, the rise of modern science does not signify progress or something positive but hints at the ultimate "destruction, ruin and overthrow" of "man" himself. Admittedly, modern, positivistic, experimental science is associated with the rise of purposive instrumentality. But, as Nietzsche asked: What *ends* are served by modern science? Once culture has been thoroughly disenchanted, can we still get back "home"?

> We have left the land and have gone aboard ship! We have broken down the bridge behind us,—nay, more, the land behind us! Well, little ship look out! Besides thee is the ocean. . . . Times will come when thou wilt feel that it is infinite. . . . Alas, if homesickness for the land should attack thee, as if there had been *freedom* there,—and there is no more "land" any longer![82]

SIGNIFICANCE

Vision of the Future

Nietzsche grasped that *modernity* itself was the source of nihilism, and he can, in this regard, be placed in the same exalted company as Marx. In *The Communist Manifesto*, Marx and Engels claimed that to be modern is to be part of a universe where "all fixed, fast-frozen relations . . . are swept away, all new-formed ones become antiquated before they can ossify. All that is solid melts into air, all that is holy is profaned."[83] For Marx, *capital* was the great destroyer of all fixed and traditional values. Nietzsche, by contrast, identified the " 'death' of the Christian God" as "the cardinal event of modern history."[84] Yet he also recognized that humanity had not yet grasped the full significance of this event.

According to Nietzsche, "God is dead" not because he has "died" in a literal sense *but because modernity has undermined the cultural bases that previously made belief in God meaningful*. Nietzsche expressed this idea in the famous parable of the "madman in the market-place." (Note that the "insane" man, once again, is the only one who has grasped the truth.)

> Have you heard of the madman who on a bright morning lighted a lantern and ran to the market-place calling out unceasingly: "I seek God! I seek God!"—As there were many people standing about who did not believe in God, he caused a great deal of amusement. Why! is he lost? said one. Has he strayed away like a child? said another. Or does he keep himself hidden? Is he afraid of us? Has he taken a sea-voyage? Has he emigrated?—the people cried out laughingly, all in a hubbub. The insane man jumped into their midst and transfixed them with his glances. "Where is God gone?" he called out. "I mean to tell you! *We have killed him,*—you and I! We are all his murderers! But how have we done it? How were we able to drink up the sea? Who gave us the sponge to wipe away the whole horizon? What did we do when we loosened this earth from its sun? Whither does it now move? Whither do we move? Away from all suns? Do we now dash on unceasingly? Backwards, sideways, forwards, in all directions? Is there still an above and below? Do we not stray, as through infinite nothingness? Does not empty space breathe upon us? Has it now become colder? Does not night come on continually, darker and darker? Shall we not have to light lanterns

in the morning? Do we not hear the noise of the grave-diggers who are burying God? Do we not smell the divine putrefaction?—for even Gods putrify! God is dead! God remains dead! And we have killed him! How shall we console ourselves, the most murderous of murderers? . . . Shall we not ourselves have to become Gods, merely to seem worthy of it? There never was a greater event,—and on account of it, all who are born after us belong to a higher history than any history hitherto!"—Here the madman was silent and looked again at his hearers; they also were silent and looked at him with surprise. At last he threw his lantern on the ground, so that it broke in pieces and was extinguished. "I come too early," he then said, "I am not yet at the right time. This prodigious event is still on its way, and is travelling—it has not yet reached men's ears. Lightning and thunder need time, the light of the stars needs time, deeds need time, even after they are done, to be seen and heard. This deed is as yet further from them than the furthest star,—*and yet they have done it!*"[85]

The parable above illustrates Nietzsche's belief that a time was coming when subjects would be stripped of those reference points that previously had enabled them to recognize moral finitude: moral horizons. As a result, "man" no longer would be able to conceive "a whole in order *to be able to believe in his own value.*"[86] Nietzsche foresaw that contemporary (postmodern?) "man" would, "at bottom," "lose" the faith in his own value because he would see that "no infinitely valuable whole works through him."[87]

Nietzsche recognized that traditional society had given "man" a "natural" social hierarchy and a taken-for-granted sense of a social whole that was underpinned and legitimated by fixed ideas of God. As we have seen, modern intellectuals such as Durkheim tried to re-create an holistic sense of the social whole *artificially.* (And it can be said of Durkheim that, for him, "society" was little other than a functional substitute for the old—now deceased—Judaic God.)

From our vantage point, though, the writings of modern intellectuals look like a desperate rear-guard action. As Nietzsche anticipated, declining confidence that moral criteria can ever be foundationalized leaves us not with a sense of humanity but with a mosaic of shattered, residual expressions and power plays—"a monster of energy, without beginning, without end . . . , enclosed by 'nothingness' as by a boundary . . . set in a definite space as a definite force, and not a space that might be 'empty' here or there, but rather as force throughout, as a play of forces and waves of forces."[88]

Nietzsche once commented that "he who no longer finds what is great in God, will find it nowhere. He must either deny it or create it."[89] Encapsulated in this remark is Nietzsche's ambivalence about the coming nihilistic age. After all, do we really want to live in a world of infinite horizons where "God is dead" and "everything is permitted?" Yet Nietzsche recognized that such nihilism would permit the individual to create *new* values and *new* forms of life. Like Simmel, he anticipated "an essentially supra-national and nomadic type of man" who might escape the life-deadening influence of the herd. Such an individual would possess, "physiologically speaking, a maximum of the art and power of adaptation as its typical distinction."[90] Still, the "nomadic" type of individual would not, in Nietzsche's terms, be *"material for a society"*[91]—at least, not the kind of "society" that Durkheim and his followers would have recognized.

Nietzsche's hope was that the outmoded values that had taken us into the modern world both could and would be *revalued.* But he knew that the storm was coming and that, for modern Europeans, "nihilism stands at the door." Nietzsche believed he was the prophet of such nihilism and that he was recounting "the history of the next two centuries." As he wrote during his terminal crisis: "I know my fate. . . . My truth is *terrible*. . . . One day my name will be associated with the memory of something tremendous—a crisis without equal on earth, the most profound collision of conscience, a decision that was conjured up *against* everything that had been believed, demanded, hallowed so far. I am no man, I am dynamite."[92]

Contemporary Relevance

In a recent article on "Nietzsche's Antisociology," Robert J. Antonio writes that

> in contrast to Marx, who has finally been included among the founders of "sociological theory," Nietzsche is glaringly absent from sociological discourse. In the United States, he is left out entirely, and elsewhere he is seldom discussed. While many nonsociologists . . . and relatively minor thinkers . . . have often received close sociological attention, Nietzsche is usually ignored even in detailed analyses of the social theorists (e.g., Weber, Simmel, Scheler) he influenced. This is still the case today, in spite of the major resurgence of interdisciplinary interest in his social theory.[93]

Antonio identifies this and other social theory texts as ignoring Nietzsche completely (a defect we hope we have now corrected), but, in a sense, it is easy to see why such neglect occurred. The answer can be found in the title to Antonio's own article: It is that Nietzsche developed "*anti*sociology," not sociology. Given this, it is perhaps surprising that, in 1995, the lead article in *The American Journal of Sociology* was Antonio's lengthy discussion of Nietzsche's importance *for* sociology and a critique of his "absence *from* sociology."[94] Is this not a trifle contradictory? Antonio, though, wishes to emphasize that contemporary American sociology is still shaped by the intellectual orientations that were prominent during its "Golden era"—the bygone era of 1946–1968. His argument is that now "is an appropriate time for sociology to entertain a wider range of social theories, including the new visions of radical democracy. Inclusion of Nietzsche among the founders would enhance the discipline's historical sense as it rethinks its foundations and practices."[95]

Antonio acknowledges that the recent turn to Nietzsche might reflect more of a "crisis" than a solution for social theory in that it possibly indicates that intellectuals now concede that contemporary culture is "too fragmented to provide resources for voicing and reconciling societal contradiction."[96] Here we have the nub of the matter. In order to make his article palatable to a leading sociological journal, Antonio understandably emphasized how Nietzsche might help *revitalize* sociology. Perhaps, though, the modern project of sociology is beyond all such resuscitation. Just as Marxism's fate is to some extent associated with the viability of generalized beliefs about the feasibility and desirability of socialism, so, too, in a larger sense, the fate of sociology always was hostage to the idea of "society" as something grounded in a unified, *self-reflective*, and potentially self-constituting moral order. As we have seen, it is precisely this image of society that is now in decline. Can sociology's modern, liberal, humanistic pretensions be reconciled, in any case, with a cultural complex that is nihilistic to its very core; that "elects" its "conservative" leaders with the same images used to sell Pepsi; that turns the pornographer Larry Flynt into a lifelong defender of liberty; that reduces "national political culture" to the spectacle of the week?

Instead of trying to argue that Nietzsche can save an exhausted sociology, it might be better to acknowledge that he tried to throttle this discipline in its cradle. Nietzsche regarded sociology as little other than a banal attempt to measure the "dead" social residues of the modern era, and he despised "founding fathers" such as Comte and Spencer. Furthermore, Nietzsche, as we have seen, was chiefly concerned with the fate of the (exceptional) individual, not in studying how doomed (and—from his perspective—worthless) modern democracies might be made to work. His curt dismissal of modernity's achievements (including sociological insight!) makes it all but impossible to pretend that his outlook can be merged with that of "classical" sociology. In short, the crisis with which sociology is now confronted was largely anticipated by Nietzsche, who, during the course of his lifetime, exhibited no interest in trying to "solve" it.

If we want to trace Nietzsche's influence on intellectuals in this century, we must follow a line that increasingly diverges from the concerns of "classical" sociology. Such a path takes us from Weber, to Freud, to the early poststructuralists of the 1930s, to more recent poststructuralists such as Michel Foucault (1926–1984). Finally, it leads us to those who proclaim and even celebrate postmodernism. Let us begin with Max Weber.

Weber is often quoted as saying that he turned to sociology because he wanted to see how much he could bear. But this remark derives from Nietzsche, who once wrote that "the strength of a spirit should be measured according to how much of the 'truth' one could still barely endure."[97] Because Weber was very much a part of the German intellectual establishment, he found it difficult—one might say inexpedient—to emphazise how much he had been influenced by the bad boy of Western philosophy. Nonetheless, Weber admitted that "the honesty of a contemporary scholar . . . can be measured by the position he takes vis-à-vis Nietzsche and Marx. . . . The intellectual world in which we live is a world which to a large extent bears the imprint of Marx and Nietzsche."[98] Marianne Schnitger Weber once claimed that her husband had grasped that both Marx and Nietzsche "tried to destroy the valuations stemming from the diverse and contradictory mixture of 'Christian civilization.' "[99] Yet it would be more accurate to say that Weber saw that, rather than trying *themselves* to "destroy" such "valuations," Marx and Nietzsche had both perceived that the modern world was quite capable of accomplishing this task all by itself, without any assistance from outside. Marx and Nietzsche both anticipated the fateful decline of the once ascendant bourgeois-Christian world, and in this context, it might be said of Weber that what is best in his sociology is his measured response to what he saw as most percipient in Marx's and Nietzsche's views of the modern era.

In the well-known lecture "Science as a Vocation," Weber grapples with Nietzsche's observation that science is nihilistic. Modern science, Weber concedes, *disenchants*—it disabuses us of what previously we took for granted (think of Darwinism as an example). Yet, while it undermines overarching normative culture, such science cannot replace what it destroys, for it is unable to tell us *how* to live, or *what particular* values to follow. In the historical or cultural sciences, this leads to a peculiar paradox. Unless they can speak to us on a human level, history and sociology will cease to exist as interpretive or critical modes of inquiry. Yet, as disinterested modes of inquiry, these disciplines inexorably weaken belief in what is seen as most sacred and meaningful to humans. But how might the critical scholar resolve this essential contradiction?

Weber's "solution" was to suggest that "plain intellectual integrity" in the historical and cultural sciences can help "find and obey . . . the demon who holds the fibers of [our] life."[100] In this fashion, the project of disinterested, rational inquiry can be reconciled with what is meaningful to the individual subject. Such a "solution," though, was suggested first by Nietzsche, who argued that the human value of rational human inquiry was anticipated by the ancients, who were the first to ask: "Why am I alive? what lesson have I to learn from life? how have I become what I am, and why do I suffer in this existence."[101] Yet, for both Nietzsche and Weber the "vocation" of the scholar is to be *unsparing* of himself—hence honest and truthful. But, at the end of the day, what "returns" to the truth-seeker, what "at last . . . comes home" to him, according to Nietzsche, is nothing but the discovery of his "own Self."[102]

The influence of Nietzsche on Freud was profound. In fact, according to Freud, it was so profound that he deliberately avoided reading Nietzsche until he was confident he could express what he wanted to say in his own words. Even so, it is often difficult to distinguish between the two men's writings. The following quotations (all from Nietzsche) help make the point:

> If one has character one also has one's typical experience, which occurs repeatedly.[103]

> [Dreaming] continually mistakes things on the basis of the most superficial similarities; but it was the same arbitrariness and confusion with which the tribes composed their mythologies. . . . All of us are like the savages when we dream.[104]

> Consciousness is the last and latest development of the organic, and consequently also the most unfinished and least powerful of these developments.[105]

> However far a man may go in self-knowledge, nothing . . . can be more incomplete than his image of the totality of *drives* which constitute his being.[106]

Like Freud, Nietzsche argued that what makes us laugh is the innocuousness of what normally is recognized as dangerous or repressive; similarly, like Freud, Nietzsche posited what he called a "will to nothingness" in the individual. Nietzsche was the first to talk about how, "under the pressure of Christian value judgments . . . the sex drive sublimated itself into love."[107] Before Freud, Nietzsche explored "the dangerous thrills of cruelty turned *against oneself.*" With Freud, Nietzsche believed that "those of [man's] abilities which are awesome and considered inhuman are perhaps the fertile soil out of which alone all humanity . . . can grow."[108]

Nietzsche was, by far, the most important influence on Foucault, who, at the time of his death was perhaps the most influential intellectual alive. Foucault developed his "genealogies," such as *Discipline and Punish* and the three-volume *History of Sexuality*, directly from Nietzsche—"under the sun of the great Nietzschean quest," as he put it. *Discipline and Punish* treats the second essay of Nietzsche's *On the Genealogy of Morals* largely as an introductory statement to an argument it then proceeds to develop. Some commentators have suggested that Foucault's first book, *Madness and Civilization*, was "to the culture of the classical age [i.e., the period of the Enlightenment] . . . what Nietzsche's *Birth of Tragedy* was to ancient Greek culture: it casts light on the Dionysian element repressed under the Apollonian order" that had provided such an essential undergirding for the modern period.[109]

Following Nietzsche, Foucault treated knowledge as an "invention" "behind which lies something completely different from itself: a play of instincts, impulses, desires, fear, a will to appropriate."[110] Knowledge is produced as a result of these elements battling one another; hence it is not something settled but an event. Knowledge is enslaved to the instincts that produced it, and, if it convincingly presents itself as the truth, this is only because it has succeeded in fabricating to its own advantage a distinction between "appearance" on the one hand and "reality" on the other.[111]

Following Nietzsche, Foucault was centrally interested in the question of how knowledge serves to cloak the workings of power. Unlike most Marxists, Foucault was less interested in "conventional" politics than in how power can operate in a world increasingly devoid of structural reference and of foundations. As Foucault once explained: "The role of political power" is best seen as an attempt "perpetually to re-inscribe [force] through a form of unspoken warfare; to re-inscribe it in social institutions, in economic inequalities, in language, in the bodies themselves of each and everyone of us."[112] If you want to grasp how Marx envisioned power, watch the movie *Germinal*, based on Émile Zola's novel. But if you want to see what Foucault (and Nietzsche) thought of power, look at the movie *One Flew Over the Cuckoo's Nest*, from the novel by Ken Kesey.

Nietzsche was a major influence on the man who has been described as the "father of post-structuralism," George Bataille (1897–1962). He helped shape the arguments of "existential" philosophers such as Martin Heidegger (1889–1976), Jean-Paul Sarte (1905–1980), Karl Theodor Jaspers (1883–1969), and Maurice Merleau-Ponty (1908–1961). Nietzsche also made a strong impact on the work of the dramatist Johan August Strindberg (1849–1912) and of the novelist Albert Camus (1913–1960), and his presence is dominant in the theories of Gilles Deleuze (1925–1995) and in the writings of Jacques Derrida (who once described Nietzsche as the "patron of deconstruction"). Nietzsche is also an important presence in the works of theorists of postmodernity such as Jean-François Lyotard, Arthur Kroker, and David Cook.[113] Perhaps surprisingly, Nietzsche was well respected by the critical theorists Theodor Adorno (1903–1969), Max Horkheimer (1895–1973), and Herbert Marcuse (1898–1979). All of these neo-Marxist members of the Frankfurt School particularly enjoyed Nietzsche's evisceration of modern, bourgeois pretensions.

Postscript: Nietzsche and the New "Knowledges"— The End of Sociology?

Nietzsche's growing importance today merits special attention. It can be explained, first, in terms of the support his writings gave to many of the claims of poststructuralism and, second, by reference to Nietzsche's anticipation of postmodernism. Let us define our terms: Poststructuralism acknowledges that it is impossible for intellectuals to grasp the foundation of social order. The reason for this is easy to explain: Such a foundation no longer exists. Postmodernism, by contrast, has no sense of history and, consequently, has no sense of what has been lost. Best described as nihilism with a happy face, it *celebrates* the pulverization of all fixed identities, all established values, and all certainties. It is what is left once the traditional and modern values that once possessed transcendent or generalizable authority have all been trashed.

For modern, classical sociologists such as Durkheim, sociology was a self-reflective project that was both scientific and value-orienting. Durkheim and his followers believed that the discipline they helped found was both the expression *and* the self-understanding of modernity. Sociology, in other words, could foundationalize itself. In Mead's terms, it could sweep *itself* into the field of knowledge. As a result, the new discipline would weld Hegel's project of collective self-reflective discovery onto Comte's model of a capstone "queen science." Today, though, the dream is dead. Knowledge is far less likely than before to be regarded as transcendent or as inclusive in scope. For contemporary postmodernist intellectuals, just as there is no morality but only moralities, so, too, apparently, there is no knowledge but only "knowledges."[114]

Poststructuralism helped intellectuals recognize that their earlier support for the moral integrity of what used to be known as the societal community represented chiefly a will to power on the part of a now outmoded cultural elite. Old-fashioned (i.e., modern), liberal, establishment intellectuals, such as Kant, Mead, or Talcott Parsons, claimed to speak for everyone. But—as Nietzsche, himself, would have been the first to point out—these tightly knit intellectuals always insisted that the key to the "good society" was the elimination of resistance to the institutional complexes on which *they* happened to rely. Today, the kind of intellectual establishment that once gave birth to Durkheim, Mead, and even Weber has not only lost confidence in itself but has also—and perhaps consequently—disintegrated. No longer is it out of place to criticize *this* text, for instance, as a mausoleum for dead, white, "Eurocentric" males who seem to have invented "classical sociology" largely to show that they—and they alone—had the right to represent others to themselves. Intellectuals today no longer speak with one voice—"a voice of reason," a voice capable of explaining how something called "society" should behave as a whole. Instead, the discourse of contemporary intellectuals gives rise to a cacophony of voices, each striving to make itself heard above the general din.

Nietzsche had no great affection for the old, modern, liberal Academy (and would, in any case, have been unable to function within it). But he would have been even more scathing about the new "postmodern" university. If the old (i.e., modern) liberals used knowledge as a "humanistic" weapon of inclusion (claiming, in effect, that all properly educated people ought to think like them and ought to obey like them), the new "postmodern" intellectuals are not at all interested in "Humanity," nor do they want to develop and shape matters of "public" (i.e., *universal*) concern. Instead, many of them seek to twist and to shape knowledge to show how much the factionalized groups they represent have suffered. As a result, *ressentiment* is splintered, highly competitive—and more significant than ever. On the surface, the Academy is now a caring, liberal, humane place, obsessed with the hatred of injustice(s), the hatred of hatred(s), and so on. Nietzsche, though, would have pried loose the lid of congratulatory self-righteousness:

Here the worms of vengefulness and rancor swarm . . . ; here the web of the most malicious of all conspiracies is being spun constantly—the conspiracy of the suffering against the well-constituted and victorious. . . . And what mendaciousness is employed to disguise that this hatred is hatred! What a display of grand words and postures, what an art of "honest" calumny! These failures: what noble eloquence flows from their lips! How much sugary, slimy, humble submissiveness swims in their eyes! What do they really want? At least to *represent* justice, love, wisdom, superiority—that is the ambition of the "lowest," the sick. And how skillful such an ambition makes them! They monopolize virtue, these weak, hopelessly sick people, there is no doubt of it: "we alone are the good and just," they say, "we alone are *homines bonae voluntatis* [men of good will]." [But] how ready they themselves are at bottom to *make* one pay; how they crave to be *hangmen.*[115]

Nietzsche would say that the present "culture wars" in the United States are degenerative and reflective of a nation in decline. This is *not* because "traditional" (i.e., modern) values are being jettisoned. Such values, Nietzsche would have insisted, deserve to be trashed, and their fate, in any case, was sealed long ago. No—it is because, in the American "culture wars," the "center" of intellectual, social, cultural, and political life increasingly is occupied by squabbling intellectuals, each striving to represent, among other things, "women," "Afro-Americans," "Chicanos," "Chicanas," "gays," "lesbians," and the like, each desperate to show that *it* owns the group victimized most thoroughly. From Nietzsche's perspective, it would be hard to imagine a more decadent state of affairs. No longer do we see a battle waged by those who scoff at the idea they must attain permission from others in order to exist. No more can we enjoy Grand Emancipatory Narratives such as Marxism that once glimpsed a representation of Humanity in one glorious, intellectual symphony.

Contemporary political culture is driven by a "play of forces" (i.e., a fight to the finish) among tattered social remnants fit only to sharpen *ressentiment* as they cultivate—and profit from—the familiar passion for revenge. Should we be surprised? Maybe the principle that Nietzsche unearthed is timeless: Those that *can* prevail will prevail; the rest must strive to turn others' consciousness into something willing to be parasitized.

Nihilism has made it all but impossible to believe in a "public good." But nihilism has not detracted from the eternal struggle for power and for social domination.

NOTES

1. *Twilight of the idols*, p. 2.
2. Ibid., p. 76.
3. Ibid., p. 88.
4. *Thus spake Zarathustra*, pp. 64, 65.
5. Lou Andreas-Salomé (as she later was known) joined Sigmund Freud's psychoanalytic circle in 1911. Freud thought highly of her as a brilliant woman.
6. *Thus spake Zarathustra*, p. 45.
7. Walter Kaufmann, *Nietzsche*, p. 443.

8. Quoted in Ben MacIntyre, *Forgotten fatherland*, p. 177.
9. See, for instance, *The will to power*, which offers a selection from Nietzsche's notebooks of the years 1883 to 1888. The 1930 edition of this work was edited by the Nazi philosopher Alfred Bäumler, who called it Nietzsche's "crowning achievement."
10. For a fascinating account of the remnants of this forgotten colony and for a description

of Paraguay as a refuge for Nazis such as Joseph Mengele, see MacIntyre, *Forgotten fatherland*.

11. Elisabeth Förster-Nietzsche, *Dr Bernhard Förster's Kolonie Neu-Germania in Paraguay* (Berlin, 1891), p. 45; quoted in MacIntyre, *Forgotten fatherland*, p. 133.

12. Nietzsche to Reinhardt von Seydlitz, February 24, 1882; quoted in J. P Stern, *Nietzsche*, pp. 36–37.

13. "Germany, Germany, above all else"—a line from the jingoistic German national anthem.

14. *Twilight of the idols*, p. 51.

15. *Selected letters of Friedrich Nietzsche*, p. 346.

16. *The portable Nietzsche*, p. 7.

17. This possibility was suggested to me by Professor Richard Howey, a Nietzsche scholar, who has examined the sparse medical records in the Nietzsche Archives in Weimar.

18. *Werke in drei bänden*, Vol. 3, 1868–1869; quoted in *Selected letters of Friedrich Nietzsche*, p. 45.

19. Bernd Magnus & Kathleen M. Higgins, *The Cambridge companion to Nietzsche*, p. 74.

20. Nietzsche to Erwin Rohde, November 23, 1870; quoted in Ronald Hayman, *Nietzsche*, p. 131.

21. *Selected letters of Friedrich Nietzsche*, p. 71.

22. *Beyond good and evil*, p. 192.

23. Ibid., p. 174.

24. Carl Albrecht Bernoulli, *Franz Overbeck and Friedrich Nietzsche: Eine freundshaft*, Vol. 1 (Jena: 1908), p. 67; quoted in R. J. Hollingdale, *Nietzsche*, p. 48.

25. *The will to power*, §1050.

26. Ibid.

27. Kaufmann, *Nietzsche*, p. 128.

28. *The will to power*, §1047.

29. Kaufmann, *Nietzsche*, p. 129.

30. *The will to power*, §1052.

31. Magnus & Higgins, *The Cambridge companion to Nietzsche*, p. 74.

32. See, for instance, Nietzsche's essay "Schopenhauer as educator," in *Unmodern Observations*.

33. Quoted in Kaufmann, *Nietzsche*, p. 40.

34. *Ecce homo*, pp. 284–285.

35. *The will to power*, §647.

36. "Epigrams and interludes," §108, in *Beyond good and evil*.

37. *Beyond good and evil*, pp. 99–100.

38. "Epigrams and interludes," §185, in *Beyond good and evil*.

39. *On the genealogy of morals*, pp. 25–26.

40. Hayman, *Nietzsche*, p. 306.

41. *Beyond good and evil*, p. 205.

42. Ibid., p. 31.

43. Ibid., pp. 204–205.

44. *On the genealogy of morals*, p. 39.

45. Ibid., p. 38.

46. *Beyond good and evil*, p. 201.

47. Ibid.

48. Ibid., p. 202.

49. *On the genealogy of morals*, pp. 44–45.

50. Ibid., 45.

51. Lewis Carroll, *Alice's Adventures in Wonderland* and *Through the looking-glass* (New York: Liverwright, 1932), p. 247.

52. *On the genealogy of morals*, pp. 36–37.

53. *Beyond good and evil*, p. 60.

54. *On the genealogy of morals*, p. 47.

55. Ibid., pp. 36–37.

56. *Beyond good and evil*, pp. 115–116.

57. *The will to power*, §753.

58. Ibid., §752.

59. *Beyond good and evil*, p. 73.

60. *On the genealogy of morals*, p. 93.

61. *The will to power*, §329.

62. *Beyond good and evil*, p. 191.

63. Ibid., p. 157.

64. Robert J. Antonio, "Nietzsche's Antisociology," p. 7.

65. "Epigrams and interludes," §§ 82, 116, in *Beyond good and evil*.

66. Coppola put it best: " 'Apocalypse Now'," he once explained, "is not about Vietnam; it is Vietnam."

67. *On the genealogy of morals*, p. 163.

68. "Epigrams and interludes," §65, in *Beyond good and evil*.

69. Ibid., pp. 84–85.

70. Hollingdale, *Nietzsche*, p. 1.

71. *On the genealogy of morals*, p. 119.

72. *The will to power*, §822.

73. *The joyful wisdom*, part II, §57.

74. Ibid., part III, §333.

75. Ibid., part V, §348.

76. Ibid., part I, §37.

77. Ibid., part III, §112.

78. Ibid.

79. Ibid., part V, §373.

80. *On the genealogy of morals*, p. 147.

81. *The will to power*, §2.

82. *The joyful wisdom*, III, §124.

83. Karl Marx and Friedrich Engels, *The communist manifesto* (New York: Washington Square Press, 1964), p. 63.

84. Stern, *Nietzsche*, p. 92.

85. *The joyful wisdom*, part III, §125.

86. *The will to power*, §12A.

87. Ibid.

88. Ibid., §1067.

89. "Notes from the time of transvaluation," *Gesammelte werke* (Munich: Musarion-Ausgabe, 1922–1929), Vol. 16, p. 80; quoted in Erich Heller, *The importance of Nietzsche*, p. 11.

90. *Beyond good and evil*, p. 176.

91. *The joyful wisdom*, part V, §356.

92. *Ecce homo*, p. 326.

93. Antonio, "Nietzsche's Antisociology," p. 4.

94. Ibid., p. 32; emphasis added.

95. Ibid., p. 35.

96. Ibid., p. 34.

97. *Beyond good and evil*, p. 49.

98. Quoted in Antonio, "Nietzsche's Antisociology," p. 3.

99. Marianne Weber, *Max Weber: A biography*, trans. Harry Zohn (New York: John Wiley, 1975), p. 319.

100. "Science as vocation," in Hans H. Gerth and C. Wright Mills (Eds.), *From Max Weber* (New York: Oxford University Press: 1974), p. 156.

101. "Schopenhauer as educator," §IV, in *Thoughts out of season*, p. 145.

102. *Thus spake Zarathustra*, p. 155.

103. "Epigrams and interludes," §70, in *Beyond good and evil*.

104. *Human, all too human*, §12.

105. *The joyful wisdom*, §11.

106. *Daybreak: Thoughts on moral prejudices*, §119.

107. *Beyond good and evil*, p. 102.

108. Quoted in Kaufmann, *Nietzsche*, p. 217.

109. J. G. Merquior, *Foucault* (London: Fontana, 1985), p. 25.

110. From lectures given by Foucault; quoted in James Miller, *The passion of Michel Foucault* (New York: Doubleday, 1993), p. 214.

111. Ibid.

112. Michel Foucault, *Power/knowledge: Selected interviews and other writings, 1972–1977*, ed. Colin Gordon (New York: Pantheon, 1980), p. 90.

113. See Jean-François Lyotard, *The postmodern condition* (Minneapolis: University of Minnesota Press, 1984 [1979]); and Arthur Kroker and David Cook, *The postmodern scene: Excremental culture and hyper-aesthetics* (New York: St. Martin's Press, 1986).

114. See Steven Seidman, *Contested knowledge: Social theory in the postmodern era* (Oxford: Blackwell, 1994).

115. *On the genealogy of morals*, pp. 122–123.

GLOSSARY

Apollonianism: The critical-rational; i.e., a rational, objective, harmonious, balanced, and measured orientation (so-called after the god Apollo).

Ascete: One who practices *asceticism*.

Asceticism: A life-style based on self-discipline and self-denial.

Bad conscience: Fear of one's own "sinful" nature, leading to hatred of one's self and the desire for self-punishment.

Big science: Large-scale science, organized by major educational, economic, or political entities.

The crucified: Christ.

Dionysian: The creative-passionate; i.e., a sensuous, frenzied, orgiastic, unbounded, and non-rational orientation (so-called after the god Dionysus).

Dionysus: See *Dionysian*.

Evil: For Nietzsche, activity that is not bound by *herd morality*.

Genealogy of morality: Historical reconstruction of the emergence of moral tendencies in human civilization.

Herd morality: Similar to Pareto's "Class 2 residues." The instinct that supposedly binds us together and makes us fear what would happen if we left the herd.

Master (or noble) morality: The morality of those who do not shrink from *evil*.

Nihilism: The devaluation of all high values, including the belief in absolute principles, absolute moral rules, absolute aesthetic standards, and the like.

Overman: See *Übermensch*.

Philology: The study of the history of language and literature, together with the analysis of meaning and syntax.

Postmodernism: A cultural complex that celebrates rootlessness, timelessness, contingency, chance, and flexibility.

Postmodernity: The period after modernity—sometimes regarded as the period after 1968.

Poststructuralism: An intellectual movement that began in the 1930s and attained maturity in the 1960s. An attack on modern ways of thinking rather than a critique of existing political or social orders. The rejection of the idea that human intellect can self-reflectively discern the foundations for such order.

Reich: The German nation (no more than an idea before 1871).

Ressentiment: French for "resentment." Meant to convey the idea of injured merit.

Slave morality: The morality of the herd. A value system designed to constrain, weaken, and homogenize the individual.

Übermensch (plural **Übermenschen**) Extraordinary, sovereign individual who has mastered all the impulses that would otherwise make one weak.

Vernunft: Critical, self-reflective understanding. (See Chapter 6.)

The will: Blind, largely unconscious, nonrational, nonintellectual drive that represents barely understood life energies.

ANNOTATED BIBLIOGRAPHY

Primary Sources

Beyond good and evil: Prelude to a philosophy of the future (Walter Kaufmann, Trans.). New York: Vintage Books, 1966 [1866] (paper).

Nietzsche describes this work as "a critique of modernity." It is concerned with the "reevaluation of all values" and with a critique of the goals and presuppositions of contemporary philosophy. It also examines the "natural history of morals." Together with *On the Genealogy of Morals*, this work has proven to have the most influence on social theory.

The birth of tragedy (Walter Kaufmann, Trans.). New York, Vintage, 1967 [1872] (paper).

Nietzsche's first book: a critique of contemporary culture, as well a creative new account of the meaning of tragedy for the Greeks. The work was strongly criticized for being too speculative, but it clearly is written by a scholar who knew about as much as anyone alive about ancient Greece. The book changed forever the way in which modern Europeans thought of the ancient, pre-Christian world.

The complete works of Friedrich Nietzsche (18 vols.; Oscar Levy, Trans.). New York: Russell & Russell, 1964 [1909–1911].

Still the standard version of Nietzsche's works in English. However, later translations are often better.

Daybreak: Thoughts on moral prejudices (R. J. Hollingdale, Trans.). New York: Cambridge University Press, 1982 [1881].

An elaboration of Nietzsche's critique of Christianity.

Ecce homo (Walter Kaufmann, Trans. & Ed.). New York: Vintage, 1967 [1888].

Nietzsche's last work. Not published during his lifetime. Reveals Nietzsche's state of mind in October and November 1888. That the author suffered from delusions of grandeur is only too evident from scanning the chapter titles, which include "Why I Am So Wise" and "Why I Write Such Good Books." Nonetheless, the work is interesting because it shows Nietzsche in his last semilucid moments, trying to justify the course of his life's work.

Human, all too human: A book for free spirits (Paul V. Cohn, Trans.). New York: Russell & Russell, 1964 [1878].

Nietzsche's first major work in philosophy, written at the age of thirty-six, in which he develops his views on, among other topics, "perspectivism": the view that all forms of knowledge are contextually bound and represent the point of view of the observer. The publication of this book marked the end of Nietzsche's "early" period (influenced by Schopenhauer and Wagner) and the beginning of his "middle" period.

The joyful wisdom (Thomas Common, Trans.). New York: Russell & Russell, 1964 [1882].

One of Nietzsche's most important books (sometimes translated as *The Gay Science*). It is here that he first announces that God is dead. Much of the book is a discussion of the need to develop *la gaya scienza*: a science that does not take itself too seriously, but is capable of making something joyful, inventive, and life-affirming out of knowledge.

My sister and I (Oscar Levy, Trans.). New York: Amok, 1990 [1951].

Almost certainly a forgery. The book was supposedly dictated by Nietzsche after he had been confined to the lunatic asylum in Jena. Among other things, it contains a lurid "confession" about an incestuous relationship between Nietzsche and his sister Elisabeth. However, the provenance of this manuscript is highly suspicious (for details see Levy's introduction); the writing style does not bear much resemblance to anything Nietzsche is known to have produced; and, in any case, according to Nietzsche's biographer Walter Kaufmann, one David George Plotkin gave him a signed confession in 1965 describing how he had

forged "Nietzsche's final autobiography" for a flat fee paid him by the publisher.

The portable Nietzsche (Walter Kaufmann, Trans. & Ed.). New York: Viking Penguin, 1982 (paper).

The best single resource for a student. The volume contains the complete text of *Thus Spake Zarathustra*, *Twilight of the Idols*, *The Antichrist*, and *Nietzsche contra Wagner*, with additional selections from *Human, All Too Human*; *Beyond Good and Evil*; *On the Genealogy of Morals*; *Ecce Homo*; and other works. Kaufmann's later translations are better and more reliable than most earlier versions.

Selected letters of Friedrich Nietzsche (Christopher Middleton, Trans. & Ed.). Chicago: University of Chicago Press, 1969.

Nietzsche was an extraordinarily prolific letter-writer. This collection reproduces some of his most important communications, which reveal Nietzsche's state of mind and his thinking at various points in his life.

Thoughts out of season (Adrian Collins, Trans.). New York: Russell & Russell, 1964 [1874].

From Nietzsche's "early" period. Contains the essays "Schopenhauer as Educator," "We Classicists," and "The Use and Abuse of History."

Thus spake Zarathustra: A book for all and no one (Marianne Cowan, Trans.). Chicago: Henry Regnery, 1957 [1883–1885] (paper).

A most unorthodox work of philosophy, written in a fictional format. Here, Nietzsche explains the significance of the *Übermensch*, and he also introduces the idea of "will to power." The work was written in four parts over two years. Part Four is often ignored, as it was published separately in a limited edition in 1885. During World War I, the German military authorities recommended that *Zarathustra* and the Gospel of Saint Mark be carried in the knapsack of every German soldier. The decision to pair these two particular works must reveal something about the intellectual capacities of the German high command.

Walter Kaufmann cogently summarizes some of the difficulties associated with *Zarathustra* when he writes in *Nietzsche* that the work "contains most of Nietzsche's ideas in veiled and symbolic form and is hence a good summary for those who know Nietzsche thoroughly, but hard to understand correctly for those who do not" (p. 65).

Twilight of the idols, or, how to philosophise with the hammer (Anthony Ludovici, Trans.; Oscar Levy, Ed.). New York: Russell and Russell, 1964 [1889].

The German title of this book, *Götzendämmerung*, is a pun on the title of Wagner's opera *Götterdämmerung* (Twilight of the Gods). With his hammer, Nietzsche attacks the Germans, Christianity, moralism, and philosophical error. Nietzsche also explains "things I owe to the ancients."

Unmodern observations (William Arrowsmith, Ed.). New Haven: Yale University Press, 1990.

A new translation of "Untimely Observations." Contains important new critical commentary that successfully shows a certain unity in Nietzsche's work. As Arrowsmith emphasizes: "If Nietzsche repeatedly invokes classical antiquity, he does so not in order to advocate return to an idealized past, but rather to reassess that past, to 'judge' it as the first step in surpassing it, and thereby creating a nobler future culture" (p. xi).

The will to power (Walter Kaufmann, Trans.). New York: Random House, 1967 [1883–1888].

Never intended to be a book, this volume was put together from notebooks that Nietzsche left from his "late" period: 1883–1888. Nonetheless contains some of Nietzsche's most influential writing. The discussion by Kaufmann is invaluable.

Secondary Sources

Antonio, Robert J. "Nietzsche's antisociology: Subjectified culture and the end of history." *American Journal of Sociology*, Vol. 101 (July 1995), pp. 1–43.

An excellent discussion of Nietzsche's significance for sociology written by a leading social theorist. Antonio manages to touch on all of the important issues. As discussed earlier, this article both reflects and anticipates the turn to Nietzsche by social theorists.

Bernstein, John Andrew. *Nietzsche's moral philosophy*. London: Associated University Presses, 1987.

A well-written attempt to discuss Nietzsche's diverse writings on the topic of morality. Particulary valuable for the sociology student.

Brandes, Georg. *Friedrich Nietzsche*. New York: Haskell House Publishers, 1972 [1889].

Initially entitled "An Essay on Aristocratic Radicalism" and written by a Shakespeare scholar, this was the first study of any length to be devoted to Nietzsche, and helped make him famous in the 1890s. Brandes concentrates on Nietzsche's stature as "the most interesting writer in German literature at the present time," not on his prowess as a philosopher.

Förster-Nietzsche, Elisabeth. *The life of Nietzsche* (Anthony M. Ludovici, Trans.). New York: Sturgis and Walton, 1912.

An abridged version of Elisabeth's three-volume biography. Heavy on all of the important people that Elisabeth got to know because of her association with Friedrich; light on Nietzsche's philosophy.

Gilman, Sander L., & Parent, David J. *Conversations with Nietzsche: A life in the words of his contemporaries*. New York: Oxford University Press, 1987.

A collection of anecdotes and stories about Nietzsche's life, written by people who knew or met him.

Hayman, Ronald. *Nietzsche: A critical life*. New York: Oxford University Press, 1980.

A comprehensive account of Nietzsche's life that also discusses his ideas in the context of their time.

Heller, Erich. *The importance of Nietzsche: Ten essays*. Chicago: University of Chicago Press, 1988.

Written by a foremost Nietzsche scholar.

Hollingdale, R. J. *Nietzsche*. London: Routledge & Kegan Paul, 1973.

Perhaps the best book on Nietzsche written in English by a philosopher intimately familiar with the details of Nietzsche's life's work.

Kaufmann, Walter. *Nietzsche: Philosopher, psychologist, antiChrist,* 3rd ed. Princeton, NJ: Princeton University Press, 1968 [1950].

The man who rescued Nietzsche from the "Nazi past" to which he had so unfairly been banished. In some ways, this continues to be the definitive study of Nietzsche. Yet, Kaufmann, who died in 1980 and who translated much of Nietzsche's work into English, had a somewhat detached relationship with his subject. In the preface to the first edition of this work, Kaufmann is careful to note that "the decision to write on Nietzsche . . . was not inspired by agreement with him" (p. xvi), and in the preface to the third edition, Kaufmann assures his readers that "I love Nietzsche's books but am no Nietzschean" (p. vii). In the 1968 preface, Kaufmann describes an experience he had as a young man visiting Cambridge University. This is worth telling here, because it does suggest how difficult it was for professional philosophers in the 1940s and 1950s to admit an interest in Nietzsche: "In 1952, when I visited C. D. Broad at Trinity College, Cambridge, he mentioned a man named Salter. I asked whether he was the Salter who had written a book on Nietzsche, to which Broad, one of the most eminent British philosophers of his generation, replied: 'Dear no; he did not deal with crackpot subjects like that; he wrote about psychical research' " (p. v).

Klossowski, Pierre. *Nietzsche and the vicious circle.* (Daniel W. Smith, Trans.). Chicago: University of Chicago Press, 1998 [1969] (paper).

Klossowski argues that Nietzsche's ideas are best understood as a reflection on his own fluctuating physical and mental ailments.

Koelb, Clayton (Ed.). *Nietzsche as postmodernist: Essays pro and con.* Albany: SUNY Press, 1990.

A collection of essays by contemporary philosophers discussing Nietzsche's contribution to deconstruction and postmodernism. Don't miss Robert C. Solomon's article on postmodernism "as an expression of frustration, desperation and resentment" (p. 285).

Love, Nancy S. *Marx, Nietzsche, and modernity.* New York: Columbia University Press, 1986.

A comparison of Marx's and Nietzsche's critiques of modern society, organized around various issues. This book is particularly valuable for sociologists. Love's Nietzschean critique of Marx and Marxist critique of Nietzsche work particularly well. Love says the following about the use of "gender-specific language" in her book (a position that we have elected to follow ourselves): "I find [gender-specific language] offensive, but also recognize that occasionally it is appropriate. This, in my opinion, is such an occasion. . . . Nietzsche was arguably a misogynist. To discuss [his philosophy] in sexually neutral terms might conceal, rather than reveal, sexual biases" (p. x).

MacIntyre, Ben. *Forgotten fatherland: The search for Elisabeth Nietzsche.* New York: Farrar, Straus, Giroux, 1992.

MacIntyre recounts how Elisabeth Förster-Nietzsche "tried to graft" her husband's commitment to "anti-Semitism, vegetarianism, nationalism, Lutheranism . . . on to Nietzsche." "A measure of her success," MacIntyre notes, "is the fact that Nietzsche's name has still not fully shaken off the taint of fascism."

In 1991, MacIntyre visited "Neuva Germania," the anti-Semitic colony Bernhard and Elisabeth Förster founded in Paraguay in the 1880s. He talked with the few surviving grandchildren and great-grandchildren of the founders. Somewhat ironically under the circumstances, these surviving Germans seem to have been enfeebled by inbreeding—largely because they insisted on keeping themselves apart from the "inferior" Paraguayan stock.

Magnus, Bernd, & Kathleen Higgins, (Eds.). *The Cambridge companion to Nietzsche.* Cambridge: Cambridge University Press, 1996 (paper).

An opening essay gives a chronologically organized introduction to, and summary of, Nietzsche's published works. The contributors discuss the relation of Nietzsche's philosophy to a modern and postmodern world.

Schact, Richard (Ed.). *Nietzsche, genealogy, morality: Essays on Nietzsche's genealogy of morals.* Berkeley: University of California Press, 1994.

A series of essays on what was perhaps Nietzsche's most sociological study.

Sedgwick, Peter R. (Ed.). *Nietzsche: A critical reader*. Oxford: Blackwell, 1995.

Sedgwick brings together in one volume discussants of the three principal traditions influenced by Nietzsche: (1) German (the Frankfurt School, Heidegger, and Hans-Georg Gadamer); (2) French (Bataille, Deleuze, Foucault, and Derrida); and (3) Anglo-American (Kaufmann, Arthur Danto, and Hollingdale).

Simmel, Georg. *Schopenhauer and Nietzsche* (Helmut Loiskandl, Trans.; Deena Weinstein & Michael Weinstein, Eds.). Amherst: The University of Massachusetts Press, 1986 [1907].

The first English translation. The work shows how much Simmel was influenced by Schopenhauer and Nietzsche. Simmel indicates in this work that he believes Nietzsche helped define the conditions for "ascending life," and he mistakenly associates this insight with Darwinian theory.

Smith, Gregory Bruce. *Nietzsche, Heidegger, and the transition to postmodernity*. Chicago: University of Chicago Press, 1996 (paper).

A difficult book, but important because it shows how both Nietzsche and Heidegger are the two most important philosophical figures for those attempting to grapple with the possibilities inherent in postmodern culture.

Solomon, Robert C. (Ed.). *Nietzsche: A collection of critical essays*. New York: Anchor, 1973.

Short essays on key aspects of Nietzsche's thought. Probably the best such collection.

Stern, J. P. *Nietzsche*. London: Fontana Press, 1985 (paper).

An excellent, short introduction to Nietzsche. Clearly and cogently written. If you want to know more about Nietzsche's ideas, this is a good place to start.

Warren, Mark. *Nietzsche and political thought*. Cambridge, MA: MIT Press, 1988.

Warren looks at Nietzsche "in light of critical and postmodern political thought" (p. ix). As he explains; "This means that the study is not primarily about Nietzsche's own political theory, but rather about what his philosophy as a whole implies for political thought today" (ibid.). Warren defines the "modern" as that which embodies "rationalist approaches" that have relied on "metaphysical (that is, real but nonempirical) characterizations of human agency," and he defines the "postmodern" as "those approaches that try to do without metaphysical characterizations of human agency—attempts that begin, at least self-consciously, with Nietzsche" (ibid.).

Zeitlin, Irving M. *Nietzsche: A re-examination*. London: Blackwell, 1994 (paper).

Critical study of Nietzsche and his significance, written by a leading sociologist.

15

The Paradoxical Failure of Classical Sociological Theory

A Concluding Essay

CLASSICAL SOCIOLOGICAL THEORY: THE HERITAGE

Several reviewers of previous editions of this book suggested adding a concluding chapter that would assess classical sociological theory, considered as a whole. Their recommendation was that we go beyond a detailed analysis of each particular theorist and evaluate classical theory *as if* it had been a unified project that could be subjected to a single evaluation.

Of course, such an endeavor is fraught with problems. For one thing, the numerous and highly diverse studies discussed in the preceding chapters were written by quite an assortment of people, from different nations, over a period of several decades, based on a variety of concerns, and in the context of quite different research traditions. Neither Marx, nor Comte, nor Durkheim, nor Freud—nor, indeed, *any* of the theorists considered in this text thought that they had produced a piece of "classical theory" that could be combined with pieces produced by other scholars with whom they were likely to have had a number of profound disagreements. Each of the individuals that we have labeled as "classical theorists" was confident that his theoretical formulations could be justified on their own terms, without need of further clarification or discussion. They would not have been happy to see their work clumped together with that of others, to be evaluated as part of some "common project."

Nonetheless, we believe it is possible (though difficult) to treat classical theory as a single entity. As we stressed in Chapter 1, despite national and biographical differences, all of the theorists considered in this book drew from a common Western intellectual heritage. Furthermore, they all responded to issues and problems stemming from *modernity*, which, we have suggested was established in Western Europe and North America between the great French Revolution of 1789 (with its promise of *liberté, egalité,* and *fraternité*) and the Great War (1914–1918).

Of course, we must acknowledge that classical sociological theory had major internal discontinuities and disagreements. As described in Chapter 2, these fissures included differences among positivistic, interpretive, and critical approaches. Yet, over and above such metatheoretical differences, we must also concede that our "classical theorists" would not even have agreed about the value of "sociology." Whereas Comte and Durkheim were enthusiastic supporters of the new "science," Nietzsche rejected what he believed was a stillborn child of a decadent era. Veblen regarded himself as an economist, Mead spent his career in a department of philosophy, Freud founded psychoanalysis, and Nietzsche could not even stomach academia, let alone sociology. Marx viewed "sociology" as a fraudulent academic activity designed to show that the crises and contradictions of capitalism could somehow be "solved" without having to address the structural forces that had created these problems in the first place.

Bearing all of these rather significant differences in mind, we must be careful not to turn this concluding chapter into a "rational reconstruction" of what classical theorists were *really* trying to do, that is, to argue that our classical theorists were anticipating sociology in its current form. This would be the kind of arrant nonsense that leads to the kind of historical retrospective best described as mythical.

If we set to one side difficult cases, such as Marx and Nietzsche (both of whom wanted to bury sociology, not save it), we must conclude that classical sociology was on its own terms largely a failure. In one way only can it be said to have been a success. Because the sociological outlook was itself part of the modern era, modern institutions played a major role in helping to consolidate and legitimate sociological knowledge. Yet, by the same token, the increased pessimism about, and declining confidence in, the modern age that came to a head after 1968 subsequently served to undermine—and, perhaps, to delegitimate—the classical sociological perspective. One justification for including Nietzsche in this text, in this regard, is that (with the possible exception of Marx) he seems to have understood sociology's embeddedness in modernity more clearly than any sociologist.

Of course, even if we have to conclude that classical sociological theory was a failure, it does not follow that works by individual authors are not worth reading. Just as Marx could reject political economy as a failed discipline and still make use of ideas drawn from Adam Smith (1723–1790) and David Ricardo (1772–1823), so, too, contemporary theorists can jettison the presuppositions of classical sociology but still find much to admire in the works of Marx, Weber, or Durkheim. Moreover, it should be stressed that classical sociological theory was not an *unmitigated* failure. Apart from helping to embody and express the increased reflective of the modern era, such theory also gave birth to professional academic sociology, which proved eager to claim classical theory as an inchoate version of itself.

THE CONTEMPORARY APPROPRIATION OF CLASSICAL THEORY

As mentioned earlier, one of the criteria we used to select "classical" theorists was that these particular individuals did indeed influence latter-day sociological research. Given this, it is not surprising that there is broad agreement between us and most other professional sociologists regarding the question of which particular individuals were responsible for "classical statements." But we do not view the heritage of classical theory in quite the same manner as do most practicing sociologists. We prefer to let such theory speak for itself.

Contemporary professional sociologists tend to argue (backward) that classical sociology was successful by virtue of the fact that it laid the foundations for today's prevailingly positivistic sociology. Again, we see the familiar "rational reconstruction." Reduced to its simplest formulation, the argument goes as follows:

1. Contemporary sociology is assumed, *a priori*, to be "good" in and of itself.
2. Such sociology is built (albeit, selectively) on classical sociological theory.
3. Therefore, classical sociological theory, taken as a whole, was successful, because it led to a result known to be "good."

This argument has the following flaws. First, it is assumed that what now exists is "good." Second, those aspects of classical theory that have been ignored, discarded, or even contradicted by more recent research are safely tucked out of sight. Third, we find the Panglossian assumption that we inhabit "the best of all possible worlds." Even if we assume some kind of cause-effect relationship between classical and contemporary sociology, what is not even considered is that a different heritage of classical theory might have yielded a different and perhaps "better" version of contemporary sociology. Finally, the goals that classical sociological theory set for itself are conveniently ignored. This last problem, we believe, is the most serious of all.

In pursuit of rational reconstruction, contemporary sociologists have adopted some very dubious practices. A case in point is the tendency to count citations of classical theorists in introductory sociology text books as a measure of the continuing "significance" of their work. Yet, citations in introductory texts—all of which are written with certain pedagogical, marketing, and ideological criteria in mind—often reflect an after-the-fact attempt to create the kind of intellectual history that can give a discipline legitimacy. They do not, of course, demonstrate why a particular theorist's work still might be relevant today.

Another (more sophisticated) technique used to demonstrate the continuing significance of classical theory has been to examine how particular "classical statements" still inform contemporary sociological research. According to this technique, Mead's concepts of the "I," the "me," the "social object," and "the generalized other" can be judged "significant" because they are still used by the school of interactionists founded by Herbert Blumer. In a similar fashion, Durkheim's work can be judged "significant" for generating ideas leading (via A. R. Radcliffe-Brown [1881–1955]) to later functionalist analysis; Marx's theories can be cited for helping to develop Ralf Dahrendorf's work in social class; and Weber's sociology can be honored for developing the ideal-typical definition of bureaucracy still used by contemporary "organizations" specialists.

What gets ignored in this latter approach is that each of these "borrowings" from the classics has necessitated a distortion or even a negation of the ideas of the classical theorists in question. It would not be too far off the mark, in this regard, to suggest that classical theory has often been judged "successful" owing to its having been successfully misunderstood or stretched in order to meet the needs of latter-day theorists. The best example, in this regard, is the way in which nearly every American introductory text book has turned "conflict theory" into a major theoretical approach and then attributed this approach to Marx. "Conflict theory" in introductory textbooks thus becomes a sanitized Marxism: the kind of Marxism that bravely recognizes that the United States can accept the presence of conflict, not the kind of Marxism that claimed that American "democracy" was fraudulent and dishonest from its very beginnings.

Numerous other examples can be cited of how the statements of classical theorists have been distorted by latter-day sociologists. To return to the examples cited earlier, Blumer's symbolic interactionism misinterprets or completely disregards central epistemological and methodological elements in Mead's social thought. Functionalists have ignored Durkheim's insistence that a functional analysis not linked to an evolutionary theory of change is completely invalid. Dahrendorf's reconceptualization of class in terms of organizational power (which turns Marx's emphasis on relationship to the means of production into a "special case") is a major departure from, and possibly a refutation of, Marxist theory. Weber's ideal-typical description of bureaucracy was developed to answer specific sociohistorical questions; it was never intended to be a rigid, ahistorical model that described the "essence" of formal organization for all epochs and places.

A third—and even more sophisticated—way of judging classical sociology from the vantage point of the present would be to try to discern *general features* of classical theory, taken as a whole, that have been broadly disseminated in contemporary sociology. Among other things, these might include:

1. The rejection of climatological and racial explanations of variations in social organizations.
2. A focus on social structural elements that can be analyzed independently of the psychological makeup of particular individuals.

3. The reliance on a secular approach that does not explain social variation by reference to the will of a deity or other supernatural agencies.

4. A belief in the value of empirical social research.

5. A distinction between the self-declared motivations of actors and the underlying structural constraints that limit or direct social behavior.

Yet, as with the previous two examples, this third technique still embodies a rational reconstruction showing that classical theory is a success story leading to a good result. The criteria that classical theorists themselves thought were important continue to be occluded.

CLASSICAL SOCIOLOGICAL THEORY AND CONTEMPORARY ACADEMIC SOCIOLOGY

The presence of thousands of employed Ph.D. sociologists in hundreds of graduate and undergraduate degree-granting programs across North America alone does not in itself indicate that classical sociological theory achieved what it set out to accomplish. Marx did not suffer poverty in the slums of London, Spencer spend his own inheritance, Comte sacrifice all his energies, nor Durkheim labor obsessively so that hundreds of thousands of first-year students could later appreciate the difference between "status" and "role" or take classes in "the sociology of the family." These men never intended that sociology should become another "social science" offering yet another career path for academic professionals.

Even Durkheim—who, among all the theorists in this book, was the most committed to academic sociology—never believed the institutionalization of sociology was an end in itself. Durkheim wanted to see a professionalized sociology, but he did not want to see it professionalized in its current form. For Durkheim, sociology was not just another academic specialization but the *only* discipline capable of bringing about much-needed social change. Durkheim hoped that sociology's placement in the university would facilitate a specialized division of labor between those who studied how to reform society (sociologists) and those capable of implementing and administering policy. In short, he defended the new discipline on the basis of its ability to bring about large-scale social change. Like Comte, he never thought that sociology could be justified with the claim that knowledge should be developed for its own sake.

During the middle third of the twentieth century, sociology in North America was established more as a professional career track than as an intellectually coherent discipline. First attaining departmental status a century ago in the land-grant universities of the Midwest, sociology's scope on this continent was soon hemmed in by "turf" battles among various university departments. As a result, classical theory's initial attempts to integrate material from many fields were quickly abandoned. The investigation of premodern societies became the bailiwick of anthropology; the analysis of "modes of production" was left to economics (which soon excised the "political" from political economy); research into the history of ideas was left to historians; and the more abstruse issues addressed by Durkheim, Comte, Nietzsche, and Marx became intellectual fodder for the more adventuresome kind of philosopher. In sum, it was the successful institutionalization of sociology in the United States that played the major role in separating the discipline from most of the issues and problems with which the classical theorists had wrestled.

It is, of course, a familiar bromide that increased academic specialization in the twentieth century was a "necessity." Yet it might just as plausibly be argued that such specialization has been even more of a "necessity" for the continued growth of the system of higher education. Whatever the case, it is nonetheless clear that the kind of inclusive, applied discipline that the classical theorists once hoped to greet did not take shape in twentieth-century sociology departments. Comte's "queen science" never established itself within ivy-covered walls. Nor did sociology integrate the other "partial" social sciences, as Durkheim once hoped. Nor, still, has academic sociology become an integrative formal discipline in the way envisioned by Simmel.

Not only has contemporary, mainstream, positivistic sociology settled for a very limited "turf" view of its status (vis-à-vis the other social sciences), but it has also abandoned the hope that it could integrate knowledge in subfields such as criminology, deviance, the sociology of the family, and organizations. Contemporary American sociologists have even reduced the study of "social change" to a subfield best taught in a course with the same tag. By contrast, theorists as varied as Spencer, Pareto, Hegel, Freud, Durkheim, Marx, Comte, and Veblen all believed that social understanding necessitated an integrated field theory. They saw that, without the guidance of theoretically inclusive theory, the results of research would be largely uninterpretable, meaningless, and, hence, useless. But as far as contemporary positivists are concerned, the rewards that derive from limited, technical social knowledge outweigh any defects such knowledge possesses.

At the middle of the twentieth century, the American sociologist Robert K. Merton came up with a widely hailed justification for abandoning any attempt to create a theoretically integrated model of society.[1] In his call for the development of what he called "theories of the middle range," Merton clearly recognized the classical interest in a unified theoretical image of society, but he also argued that such theory was unobtainable. Merton argued that if theoretical goals were limited to the construction of partial theories, such theories would somehow, someday, in some unspecified manner, by some unknown mechanism, be integrated into a general theoretical viewpoint. Regardless of the dubious merits of this argument, it certainly is in conflict with the classical belief that, without a coherent macrotheoretical overview, one ends up largely with useless data points. But Merton's model of sociological theory construction does, of course, fit the needs of specialists institutionally required (1) to teach disconnected course modules, and (2) to locate funds from state and corporate agencies primarily interested in the kind of knowledge that will never grasp, let alone challenge, vested interests.

Contemporary sociology is not, of course, totally devoid of theoretically oriented individuals. But new theorists are increasingly marginalized in a discipline that continues to reward methodological sophistication far more than theoretical insight. Yet such dislocation does not prevent even the most ardent instrumentalists from representing themselves as the intellectual heirs of classical sociological theory. How, though—one might ask—can such narrow-minded instrumentalists claim to be the rightful descendants of classical theorists whilst, at the same time, rejecting nearly everything for which these theorists once stood? To oversimplify somewhat, there are three general rules that make such a feat possible: (1) the rule of selectivity; (2) the rule of decorativeness; and (3) the rule of the subfield contribution.

1. According to the *rule of selectivity*, the classical theorist is treated selectively, and those elements that call for a transcendence of the empirical, or—to put this in a different way—major social reorganization, are not mentioned. For example, Durkheim's insistence on a need for the "corporate" restructuring of society, Marx's view of "contradictions" as something felt *throughout* the individual's social existence, and Mead's linkage of "generalized other" with the emergence of "universal society" are all prevailingly ignored in contemporary research.

2. The *rule of decorativeness* requires that, although classical theory should be cited in the literature review, it can safely be ignored thereafter. What we see here is the invocation of classical theory as a means of ideological justification. The assumption seems to be that when the names of the Great are invoked, research becomes legitimate, and, by this method, an article that is vacuous can be transformed into something of value. (For numerous illustrations, see any mainstream journal of sociology.)

3. The *rule of the subfield contribution* requires contemporary sociologists to turn classical theorists into the founders of discrete, separable, and unintegrated subfields, and not to recognize them as the holistic, integrative, and synthetic thinkers they actually were. Thus Durkheim is presented as one who developed a "sociology of religion," a "sociology of deviance," a "sociology of anomie," a "sociology of education," and so on. Marx (who attained the status of Great Thinker in American sociology only in the 1960s) is introduced as the man responsible for a "theory of alienation," a "theory of class conflict," and a "theory of social revolution." Weber is credited with having thought up a "sociology of organizations," a "sociology of religion," and a "political sociology." Reference is similarly made to Mead's "theory of socialization," "theory of the self," and so on.

If we want to judge whether classical social theory, taken as a whole, was indeed a success, we must extend to classical theorists the courtesy of judging their legacy in terms of the criteria *they* would have chosen. As we have seen, the work of the classical theorists was diverse. Even so, four common (and interrelated) goals in classical theory can be identified:

1. The creation of the kind of society that enabled its members to take control of future development and live a "rational" existence.

2. The belief that (modern) normative culture was subject to global convergence and the subsequent attempt to find the basis for a common humanity.

3. The attempt to bend knowledge to the amelioration of needless human suffering.

4. The production of a just world that would transcend, or go beyond, what is empirically given.

Let us examine each of these goals in more detail.

The Search for Rational Social and Self-Control

To know how to live a rational—and, hence, a "good"—life, was the central goal of much social philosophy from the time of Socrates (470?–399 B.C.) to Immanuel Kant (1724–1804). By expropriating this goal as one of its own, classical sociological theory attempted to complete what had not been fulfilled in the previous twenty-two centuries.

As we have seen, the concept of a "rational" existence did, of course, vary significantly from one theorist to another. Whereas Spencer and Pareto identified "rationality" with cognitive instrumentalism, Hegel and Marx argued that a "rational" society would enable subjects to develop communal arrangements that no longer would set one person against another nor divide individuals against themselves. Still, all of our classical theorists had the following in common. First of all, they contrasted rationality or reason, on the one hand, with traditional religion and established dogma, on the other. Second, they all believed that "rationality" mandated some kind of social reflectivity, which, they claimed, would compensate, and perhaps substitute, for what earlier had been lost with the dissolution of *Gemeinschaft*, a small, intimate, face-to-face community. Let us look at a few examples.

Following Maximilien Robespierre's attempt to create a "religion of reason," Comte tried to create his own (scientific) "religion of humanity." Many later sociologists treated this project as extraneous to Comte's sociology, but Comte, himself, believed it was his crowning achievement. Comte recognized that a "spiritual force" was necessary for social harmony, and he tried to embody this force in a "positive" science. According to Comte, sociology itself represented an "evolutionary" shift in consciousness from superstition and error to reasoned comprehension.

Mead's analysis of the social world *began* with the effort to account for the origins of human reason. For Mead, reason had to arise from—and, therefore, be perfectible in—human sociation: our ability to "take the role of the other." In a somewhat similar fashion, Hegel and Marx saw reason as something that unfolded in history itself and that could not be detached from what we can learn from history. For them, rational existence meant overcoming the societal contradictions that prevented the full application of reason. Marx's early writings located the proletariat as the "universal class" whose interests could be identified with human progress. What made the proletariat unique was that all other classes had a vested interest in maintaining social relations that would retard the human capacity for collective self-transcendence.

Freud, Pareto, Durkheim, and Nietzsche all tried to show that traditional religion was based on the human need for myth, fantasy, or illusion, and they all concentrated on the attempt to try to dispel religious forms of consciousness. In *The Future of an Illusion* (1927), Freud claims that, if we wish to live rationally, we must cast off the "illusions" of religion in favor of a more difficult life based on critical self-insight. Like Marx, Pareto regarded religion as a means by which dominant groups control and manipulate subordinate groups. Durkheim viewed religious "truths" as myths that were essential for more primitive "social types" but unnecessary for the "higher" kind of society containing subjects who had grasped that "God" is the mythologization of society itself. According to Nietzsche, Christianity was a "slave religion" based on *ressentiment* and the spiritual desire for revenge against those most fit to rule.

Weber emphasized that a variety of "rationalities" are possible in society. Nonetheless, he associated Occidental rationalization and the emergence of an increasingly "disenchanted" world view with a Protestant outlook that he foresaw would likely result in an increasingly secularized culture. Like Nietzsche, Weber to some extent lamented the modern disenchantment of the world. At the same time, though, he firmly believed that modern sociology could help modern subjects align themselves with the inexorable processes of increasingly inclusive normative rationalization.

Regardless of whether their theory was prevailingly positivistic, interpretive, or critical, all of the classical theorists believed that the source of reason was to be found in social life itself. Furthermore, they all believed that the location of the source of reason would enable individuals to guide social activity more effectively. Some theorists (e.g., Hegel and Marx) believed that all of humanity was capable of reason; others (e.g., Pareto and Freud) argued that most people were incapable of accepting the truth about the forces that dominated their lives. Nonetheless, like other classical theorists, these four all endeavored to ensure that human sociation would be based more on reason than on myth, dogma, or superstition.

The Attempt to Understand the Basis for a Common, Global Humanity

Before the emergence of modern sociology, religious tradition had tended to place limits on knowledge and posit an insurmountable obstacle to hermeneutic understanding by separating humanity into two opposed camps: "believers" and "nonbelievers." Those in the latter camp were viewed as mired in faithlessness and error and therefore beyond (or not worthy of) comprehension. By contrast, classical sociologists adopted what might be described as a global perspective. Although they were interested in different cultures and in different civilizations, they were even more interested in grasping principles that would explain forces affecting humanity as a whole.

Today, of course, many students are encouraged to believe in "cultural diversity" and are often taught that each culture is uniquely special and valid in its own right (a perspective that most people in most cultures would vehemently reject). By contrast, the classical theorists were not cultural relativists. Rightly or wrongly, they believed either in the innate superiority of modern, Western, rationalized cultural forms or in their inevitable triumph within the world system. At the same time, they did not of course think that such forms were beyond critique. On the contrary: They tended to regard sociology as a means by which such forms could either be perfected or more adequately understood. Because they believed that modernity was creating *one* world, they concluded that the task of the modern intellectual was to show humanity as a whole how to adapt, understand, or appreciate the forces that controlled a common destiny.

It would be instructive to compare classical theorists with the school of "culturally relativistic" anthropology developed by Franz Boas (1858–1942) and refined by his students Margaret Mead (1901–1978), Alfred Kroeber (1876–1960), and Ruth Benedict (1887–1948). This anthropological school of thought—which became quite influential in this country—opposed social evolutionary principles and argued that, although we can understand the diversity of moral standards, we cannot determine which of them are superior. By the same token, these anthropologists also claimed that we cannot say that one society is "better" than another, nor can we say how society might be changed so as to reduce overall human suffering. Classical sociological theory made no such assumptions. Instead, it claimed that interpretive and critical insights were not incompatible with the need to define "better" normative standards (i.e., more inclusive mechanisms of social or moral integration).

As we have seen, nearly all of our classical theorists accepted, to various degrees, the tenets of social evolutionism, and this, of course, also explained why they rejected cultural relativism. According to Comte and Spencer, ideas and values were the by-products of particular stages of social evolution. In a somewhat more sophisticated approach, Durkheim argued that each type of society generated its own forms of understanding that were appropriate to the needs of moral cohesion in that particular context. Nonetheless, Durkheim, like Weber, believed that modern culture was irreversible.

This last point is particularly important. With the single exception of Nietzsche (who was not a sociologist), all of the classical theorists believed there was something cumulative and inexorable about modernity. Even Weber, who rejected social evolutionism, would have regarded with incredulity the (post)modern dogma that there is no good reason to set a Beethoven symphony above Arunta drumming, or to place formal law above *Khadi* justice. Weber would freely have admitted that a preference for Beethoven's string quartets over, say, traditional Chinese folk music reflects a *value* judgment—as does a preference for living in a modern, as opposed to a traditional, society. Nonetheless, he would also have pointed out that, in the modern era, cumulative or irreversible processes of cultural development clearly have been identified and that these have to do with increasing complexity and reflectivity. Weber believed that, because such change was irreversible, its impact on humanity as a whole had to be acknowledged. After all, he would have asked, you might well *prefer* to live in a "traditional" setting as a "traditional" subject, but, if you have been shaped by modernity, do you have such a choice?

Social Prediction as the Means to Ameliorate Human Suffering

Classical sociological theorists strongly advocated *social prediction* largely because they believed it would enable sociologists to manipulate the future so as to reduce needless human suffering. For Comte, sociology as a whole is concerned with prevision; Spencer similarly believed the discipline must go beyond historical analysis to see where we are heading; and Durkheim insisted that sociology must look beyond the horizon of the present "transitional" period to perceive a new type of societal organization. Following Hegel, neither Marx nor Mead attempted to describe the exact contours of historical movement, but Marx did outline the fundamental features of the coming society, and Mead discussed the possibility of a universal society in which each of us can take into account a generalized other that represents the totality of humanity. Weber believed that our ability to predict was somewhat limited. But he nevertheless argued that, if we are to deal with modernity's effects, we have to come to terms with its inexorable tendencies.

Based on their vision of the future, each classical theorist disagreed somewhat how human suffering might be lessened. Pareto (the most pessimistic of classical theorists in terms of ameliorating human suffering) and Spencer (among the most optimistic) both advocated a quietistic, noninterventionist, *laissez-faire* approach. Pareto's noninterventionism arose from his commitment to a model of cyclical change, the underlying logic of which is that all attempts at perfecting life are in the long run doomed to failure. Moreover, Pareto also doubted that the longstanding effects of human "instinct" could ever be overcome. By contrast, Spencer's noninterventionist, *laissez-faire* outlook arose from his social evolutionary belief that society was perfecting itself by slowly eradicating the sources of all ("nonadaptive") evil. According to Spencer, the sociologist's role was to tell people what *not* to do, so as not to interfere with society following its own self-set path toward self-perfection.

But, for most classical theorists, the ability to predict meant that social theory could analyze present suffering and discover what action might be taken toward its reduction or eradication. Suffering was often seen by the early sociologists as arising from an imperfect social structure that, among other things, generated anomie, alienation, exploitation, crime, conspicuous waste, self-destructive behavior, antisocial competition, avarice, egoism, violence, the stifling of creativity, and the division of humanity into antagonistic nations, groups, and classes. The concern with social division was not just a focus of Marx's work but occurred throughout classical theory as a whole, and is addressed in varying ways by Comte, Durkheim, Weber, Veblen, Pareto, and Mead.

In some cases (e.g., in the work of Marx and Spencer, albeit for radically different reasons), the reduction of human suffering was seen as something quite separate from the search for the "right" kind of public policy. Other classical theorists (e.g., Durkheim and Mead) advocated wide-ranging social reforms that would effectively remake society. Still other theorists (e.g., Weber and Freud) believed that any such amelioration would be limited, for a variety of reasons. Yet, notwithstanding the differences sketched above, classical sociological theory, taken as a whole, was centrally concerned with the task of improving the human lot.

Theory and the Search for a Different, More Just Society

As Marx famously said: "Philosophers have only interpreted the word. The point is to change it." Broadly speaking, the classical theorists would not have disagreed with this statement. They believed as a group that empirical analysis should be guided by the search for a better, more just world.

Most classical theorists regarded what was empirically given in the nineteenth century as a passing social order that was both unjust and temporary. This is especially obvious in the works of Comte, Spencer, Durkheim, Marx, and Veblen, all of whom firmly believed that the purpose of classical theory was to force the pace of change, not merely document the transitional. These men did not believe that the development of an all-encompassing theory could safely be postponed until additional data had been gathered. We can note, in this regard, that Durkheim's study of suicide (often hailed as the first "modern" empirical study) was not arbitrarily selected. Rather, Durkheim believed that his research would help facilitate movement from a transitional period to the more just stage he previously had anticipated. Like Marx, Durkheim realized that a "scientific" focus on the world as it is now exists in its present form would serve largely to reinforce and to legitimate existing inequality and injustice. Durkheim believed that "sociological method" must be tailored not just to theory but also to the metatheoretical goals of sociology. Marx, of course, eviscerated those who claimed that they had understood the world once they had measured its properties in their current (and temporary) form. Even the more positivistic classical theorists, such as Spencer, were relatively sensitive in noting that the tools of understanding changed through time and were not themselves impersonal, objective, and unchanging.

Of course, classical theory was also vitally concerned with grounding theory in empirical data. But no classical theorist believed that narrow, disembodied, positivistic studies could accomplish anything worthwhile of their own accord. Most contemporary sociological departments separate the teaching of "theory" from the teaching of "methodology." But most classical theorists would have found this kind of division simply indefensible. As far as they were concerned, methodology is something you do to work with theory. It cannot be taught in advance. You can teach people skills (e.g., how to count, how to turn on a computer), but the application of such skills does not, in itself, automatically lead to an advancement in knowledge. Many contemporary sociologists seem not to have grasped this, but an obsession with "methodology" is a sign of the weakness (or, perhaps, decadence) of a discipline, not an indicator of how "scientific" it is. Ph.D. candidates in chemistry do not take courses in "methodology" before they are allowed to proceed with a dissertation. Biologists who are expanding the scope of Darwinian theory do not spend time publishing articles whose main contribution to the field is to display "objective" methods.

The classical theorists always regarded *theory* as taking precedence in defining the questions that empirical data are to answer. They believed it was *theory* that shows research how to produce not a career track for new specialists but a better and more just social order. Even Pareto, who rejected the idea that intellect could change the world, associated sociology with the attempt to bring about such change.

SOCIOLOGY AND POSTMODERNITY

If classical sociological theory is a "paradoxical failure" (i.e., a failure on its own terms but still a major presence in the university system), we need to ask why this is. Might the answer be that "classical theory," as we have defined it, represented the ideals and the self-understanding of an historical epoch that is slipping away? Perhaps sociology, as Durkheim seemed to comprehend, was a self-understanding of the modern. If so, we should, perhaps, end this chapter by discussing briefly the emergence of "postmodernity" as a real, historical alternative to modern society.

Over the last couple of decades, there has been an increasing debate in sociology about the significance of "postmodernism."[2] Some theorists have argued that the rapid social change that has occurred in advanced capitalist societies since 1945, and that accelerated after the 1960s, has created mostly cultural transformations that seem to take humans beyond a recognizably *modern* stage of development. In fact, some theorists suggest that, if you were born in the West after about 1965, you do not know what it is like to live in an old-fashioned modern society—the world as it used to exist before Elvis, the Beatles, shopping malls, prosthesis bodies (think of Michael Jackson's), and MTV.

Advanced capitalist societies today can no longer be described, primarily, as *industrial* societies. In the United States, for instance, the production of consumers seems at least as important for economic growth as the production of goods and services, and contemporary U.S. presidents see nothing wrong with urging citizens to help *spend* the country out of a recession. In the last decade or so, the leisure and entertainment sectors of the economy, and not the manufacturing sector, have been the most profitable. It has become increasingly difficult for many contemporary theorists to argue that economic growth today is rational or instrumentally adaptive in some sense. Rather, consumerism seems to be an end in itself. Capitalists now develop new and highly profitable markets by selling consumers new needs, new experiences, and new forms of meaning, all of which are defined exclusively by the marketplace.

In the early modern period, it was assumed that economic development would make people wiser, stronger, and more, rather than less, human. Yet, in contemporary capitalist societies, the relationship between economic growth per se and human "progress" no longer seems as obvious as it was a century ago. For one thing, most of the truly impressive products of the industrial era (e.g., the steam engine, the internal combustion engine, the jet engine, the airplane, artificial fabrics, plastics, radio, television, etc.) were invented and merchandised before most people alive today were even born. For another, in the most developed capitalist societies, economic growth now seems to rely on entrepreneurs' ability to sell symbols or culture, and not on their capacity to develop new industrial products or market technological breakthroughs. Perhaps it's not surprising that people today have less faith than they used to in science and technology's ability to create a better world. In a modern society, technology and economic development went hand in hand. In a postmodern society, economic and cultural domains of activity become increasingly difficult to separate—a development that was, to some extent, anticipated by Veblen in his *Theory of the Leisure Class.* The great increase in the number of people in postmodern societies who sell information, knowledge, or credentials to the masses has led some sociologists to talk about the rise of a New Class—a class that specializes in the development and sale of culture.[3] This new class is neither bourgeois nor proletarian in Victorian terms.

Postmodern societies are relatively more dependent on knowledge and information than modern societies, and they are less immediately involved in producing material artifacts. As people become "consumers" rather than "citizens," they also tend to become politically indifferent. To the extent that individuals can access, or enjoy, symbolic meaning only by having it sold to them, postmodern culture becomes increasingly self-absorbed and self-enclosed—claustrophic even.

Ronald Reagan has been described as the first postmodern president because his office was so transparently a victory of style over substance. His 1984 "Morning in America" election campaign dispensed with modern versions of political will formation and wooed voters by selling them feel-good images that they could either like or not like. These images, of course, had no connection with "reality." They might just as well have been McDonald's commercials, which, like political commercials, are not intended to give consumers reliable information about real people. The voters were not supposed to test Reagan's advertisements or subject them to any kind of critical scrutiny. Of course, the kind of messages that sold Reagan to a large portion of the United States can work only when consumers lose the capacity to use criteria or standards that are *extrinsic* to a message to evaluate its meaning—in other words, when they lose the ability to exercise critical judgement.

Successful versions of postmodern symbolism are less representational than modern symbolism and more obviously self-referential or self-contained. Although

U.S. presidential candidates have always used rhetoric and images to get themselves elected, Reagan's handlers took the "selling of the president" to new and unprecedented levels. For instance, they *relied* on surveys to find out what consumers would buy—just as any manufacturer might want to poll its customers to discover what images will encourage them to purchase a certain type of pantyhose. In a postmodern society, the "modern" emphasis on the responsibility of political leaders and on the duties of citizens disappears. Commercial and political activities become almost indistinguishable. Thought is folded into emotion and feeling.

Postmodernism is also linked to the "death of the subject" or to the "end of the individual." Modern versions of individuality emerged with the Reformation and, as we have seen, with the Enlightenment. In a postmodern society, individuality (or the relatively autonomous reproduction of the self) is undermined in at least two ways. First of all, whereas early modern societies required and rewarded self-mastery and self-control, postmodern culture emphasizes and encourages hedonism, self-indulgence, and an obsession with "personal" image or style, as opposed to an "old-fashioned" (modern) reliance on character or vocation. Second, the transcendental, or generalizable, theologies that were so important during the Enlightenment and in the early modern era now seem to have lost their power. The postmodern subject is besieged by an endless jumble of messages, codes, and ideas, most of which are incompatible, inconsistent, and quite infantile. Many people respond to the current cacophony of mostly commercial messages that bombard them daily by abandoning all hope that they ever could attain some kind of rational understanding of the world.

Whatever its merits, or lack of merits, Marxism, for instance (or traditional religion, come to that), did give people some overarching guidelines or standards that enabled them to participate in a common and supposedly *universal* program of human or spiritual development. Postmodern belief systems (such as "New Age" religions) lack a transcendental perspective. The postmodern deity turns out to be consumer friendly, and most people today see nothing wrong with putting together a "personal philosophy" using precisely the same methodology they would adopt to select new clothes or decide on a new hair style. At the end of the twentieth century, humans are much less optimistic about the future and less sure about their grip on the present than they were 150 years ago. They appear to have fewer "inner" resources. The postmodern subject is a feather for each wind that blows.

Unless humans are able to internalize some kind of moral code or learn some kind of generalizable philosophy on which they can rely in diverse circumstances, it is difficult to see how they can be categorized as "individuals" in the modern or Enlightenment sense of the term. Some contemporary postmodernists—Jean Baudrillard, for instance—see the postmodern subject as an empty shell that is incapable of exercising any kind of critical judgement.[4] This picture is quite at odds with the idea of human potential developed by eighteenth-century philosophers like Immanuel Kant or by nineteenth-century theorists like Marx.

Postmodern transformations can usually be understood as an extension of cultural modernism (classically defined by Simmel), not as unique developments in their own right. Perhaps the best way to approach postmodernism is to see it as "the cultural logic of late capitalism," the description favored by the critic Frederic Jameson.[5] In any case, before the meaning of postmodernism can be grasped, modernization and modernism have to be understood in their own right as conditions that postmodernism supposedly has surpassed. For the most part, postmodernism is what happens to modern societies once they reach a certain level of maturity and development. It is a tribute to theorists like Nietzsche, Simmel, Weber, Marx, and Velben that they managed to anticipate many of the cultural trends that are today being labeled postmodern.

CONCLUDING REMARKS

In a "postmodern" era have the goals of classical sociological theory been achieved, even approximately? More than a century after many of the works of classical theory were written, do we indeed have a more just, harmonious, modern social order that contains subjects with an enhanced capacity for critical self-reflection? The answer, of course, is no. Irrationality, violence, alienation, anomie, crime, suicide, superstition, bigotry, and the like continue unabated. Yet, even though classical sociological theory *failed* in these terms, it did help to generate an academic field whose mainstream positivistic practitioners continue to cite their classical "predecessors" in order to legitimate their contemporary endeavors. As a result, sociology students are forced to "learn the classics" (and hence take a course in which books such as this are required).

Perhaps we are in some "transitional period," and sociology will soon turn away from its narrow methodological obsessions and again try to create a theoretically unified project designed to create a better world. Perhaps, too, we can still talk about sociology being in its "infancy." Yet, if the sociology of the last two or three decades is any guide, sociologists are retreating even further from the idea that something called "sociology" could be made into a collective, integrated, scientific endeavor that (one day) will produce inclusive, generalizable knowledge that can be used to optimize the social good. According to postmodernists such as Jean Baudrillard, the "social" ceased to exist around the 1960s.[6] From this perspective, what we now are experiencing is something that perhaps only Nietzsche could have explained. But, as we have seen, Nietzsche developed not sociology but what is best described as an *anti*sociology.

We inhabit a world that still contains all of the recognizable ills of modernity. But does it possess a conscious alternative to itself that can be phrased in the language of classical sociological theory? This, we believe, is the question that must be posed—and answered—before the fate of classical sociology finally can be determined.

NOTES

1. Robert K. Merton, *On sociological theory* (New York: The Free Press, 1967).
2. See Jean-François Lyotard, *The postmodern condition* (Minneapolis: University of Minnesota Press, 1984); Mark Poster (Ed.) *Jean Baudrillard: Selected writings* (Stanford, CA: Stanford University Press, 1998); David

Harvey, *The condition of postmodernity* (Oxford: Basil Blackwell, 1989); Frederic Jameson, *Postmodernism or the cultural logic of late capitalism* (Durham, NC: Duke University Press, 1991); Stephen Best & Douglas Kellner, *Postmodern theory: Critical interrogations* (New York: Guilford Press, 1991); and

Stephen Crook, Jan Pakulski, & Malcolm Waters, *Postmodernization: Change in advanced society* (London: Sage, 1992). Also, see Alex Callinicos, *Against postmodernism: A Marxist critique* (New York: St. Martin's Press, 1989).

3. See Alvin W. Gouldner, *The future of intellectuals and the rise of the New Class* (New York: Oxford University Press, 1979), and Hansfried Kellner & Frank W. Heuberger (Eds.), *Hidden technocrats: The New Class and new capitalism* (New Brunswick, NJ: Transaction Books, 1992).

4. See, for instance, Jean Baudrillard, *In the shadows of the silent majorities* (New York: Semiotext[e], Foreign Accent Press, 1983).

5. Frederic Jameson, "Postmodernism, or the cultural logic of late capitalism," *New Left Review*, 146 (1984), 53–93.

6. See Jean Baudrillard, *In the shadows of the silent majorities*.

GLOSSARY

Critical theory Theory based on the reflective critique of language and oriented toward human emancipation.

Cultural relativism As used by Franz Boas and his students, the assumption that no sociomoral system is superior to any other sociomoral system.

Epistemology A theory of the process by which humans can possess knowledge.

Gemeinschaft Social organization possessing traditional and reciprocal communal obligations and a sense of moral responsibility. Literally "community."

Generalized other As developed by Mead, the overall attitude and general reaction of a group, community, or society.

Ideal type Methodological approach developed by Wilhelm Dilthey. Involves the development of the usual, typical, or most complete features of a phenomenon in order to facilitate comparison. Weber stressed that ideal types were "one-sided" and "partial" descriptions of reality.

Positivism Inquiry based on the methodology of the natural sciences that is produced by a technical instrumental interest.

Rational reconstruction As used in this context, the attempt to rewrite history so as to show that what is good at the present time was always intended in the past.

Theories of the middle range Ideological argument developed by Robert K. Merton, according to which sociology can maintain its legitimacy by linking empirical studies to low-level subfield theories and by, for the foreseeable future, abandoning the development of general holistic theories of society.

Universal society Mead's conception of a possible future society encompassing all of humanity in peaceful self-realization.

Appendix: Classical Theory on the Web

Many classical theory texts can now be found on the World Wide Web, which is also a great source for commentaries and discussion. Any of the major search engines, such as Yahoo, Lycos, Excite, and so on, can be used to find works by, and on, the major classical theorists, but the best search engine we have come across is Webferret, which can be downloaded free from: *http://www.ferretsoft.com/netferret/index.html* Webferret compiles results from a number of other search engines, so the results are usually impressive.

Web material does, of course, vary greatly in quality and usefulness. Some commentaries are unreliable, so beware. Furthermore, many of the posted translations are not the best, or most up-to-date, available. Text put on the web has to be in the public domain (i.e., not copyrighted), so older translations usually appear before more recent ones. As a result, a theorist's later—and, possibly, more important—works often are not included.

You may find the following addresses helpful. They are all English-language sites. Of course, by the time this book goes to press, some of these sites and links will have disappeared. You will also find that the addresses described below inevitably duplicate some sites.

Good hunting! If all else fails, access a search engine and type in a theorist's name.

An excellent place to start is: *http://www.socsci.mcmaster.ca/~econ/ugcm/3ll3/* *authors.html* which provides original texts from over one hundred authors, including

Marx, Durkheim, Pareto, Simmel, Veblen, Bentham, Condorcet, Cooley, Hobbes, Locke, Mill, Montesquieu, Rousseau, and Turgot.

Another address of general interest is: *http://www.selfknowledge.com/index.htm* and the University of Pennsylvania's collection of "on-line books" at: *http://www.cs. cmu.edu/books.html*

A similar site—Columbia University's "Bartleby Project"—(where you can find Mary Wollstonecraft's *Vindication of the Rights of Woman*) is at: *http://www.bartleby.com*

One of the best sites for sociologists is: *http://www.socioweb.com/~markbl/ socioweb* with a link to "sociological theory" at: *http://www.cm-inc.com/~markbl/ socioweb/theory*

The "Giants of Sociology" (including Marx, Durkheim, Comte, Mead, and Blumer) can be accessed at: *http://www.cm-inc.com/~markbl/socioweb/giants*

Notes about, and extracts from, Marx, Weber, Durkheim, and Simmel can be found at: *http://www.spc.uchicago.edu/ssr1/PRELIMS/Theory/*

A very smart sociology student from Canada has created another great site at: *www.geocities.com/CollegePark/Quad/5889/socialth.htm* with links to Marx, Durkheim, Weber, and Rousseau, as well as contemporary theorists (and we love the soundtrack).

Another site of general interest to students of social theory is: *http://www.trinity. edu/~mkearl/theory.html* This "Sociological Tour Through Cyberspace" has numerous theory links.

Several sites feature the works of "Dead Sociologists" (and you usually have to be dead to be "classical"). These include: *http://staff.uwsuper.edu/hps/mball/dead_soc.htm* (with links to Jane Addams and W. E. B. Du Bois); *http://www.runet.edu/~lridener/ DSS/DEADSOC.HTML*; *http://www.pscw.uva.nl/sociosite/TOPICS/Sociologists.html*; and *http://www.cf.ac.uk/socsi/undergrad/introsoc/index.html*

Two anarchist sites that are a little bit different are: *http://dwardmac.pitzer.edu/ Anarchist_Archives/archivehome.html* and *www.nothingness.org*

By contrast, *http://www.libertyjournal.com/viewlinks.cfm* has great links to conservative, libertarian, and right-wing associations, as well as texts from Adam Smith, Edmund Burke, J. S. Mill, Thomas Paine, and Herbert Spencer.

Another "specialist" site is: *http://www.cs.cmu.edu/~mmbt/women/writers.html* which specializes in the contributions of women writers throughout history.

For Marx, the best sites are:

http://csf.colorado.edu/psn/marxist-sociology/marx_text.html; *http://eserver.org/marx/*; and *http://www.anu.edu.au/polsci/marx/marx.html* (listen to the Internationale).

Hegel is represented at: *http://www.hegel.org/links.html*

Some of Durkheim's works can be found at: *http://www.runet.edu/~lridener/ DSS/INDEX.HTML#durkheim* and *http://www.pscw.uva.nl/sociosite/TOPICS/Sociologists. html#durkheim* while more of his writings and a chat room about the greatest French sociologist can be found at: *http://home.freeuk.net/ethos/durkpage.htm*

Max Weber's "home page" is located at: *http://msumusik.mursuky.edu/~felwell/http/ weber/whome.htm* while another useful site for Weber where you can find "Science as a Vocation," "Politics as a Vocation," and "The Protestant Ethic and the Spirit of Capitalism" is: *http://www.asahi-net.or.jp/~hw8m-mrkm/weber/weber_texts.html* Don't miss: *http://www.runet.edu/~lridener/DSS/INDEX.HTML#weber*

"The Simmel Page" comes to us from Switzerland at: *http://socio.ch/sim/work.htm* while "George's [Mead's] Page" can be found at: *http://paradigm.soci.brocku.ca:80/ ~lward/*

Other sites that reproduce extracts from some of Mead's writings include: *http://varenne2.tc.columbia.edu/www/class/bib/medoogerg_bib.html*

A Mead discussion list can be found at: *http://www.cla.sc.edu/PHIL/faculty/burket/ g-h-mead.html*

Pareto's writings on "The Circulation of Elites" from *The Mind and Society* are located at: *http://www.runet.edu/~lridener/courses/CIRCELIT.HTML*

Many links to Spencer can be found at: *http://www.geocities.com/Athens/Delphi/ 6061/h_spence.htm*

Man Versus the State is reproduced at: *http://socserv2.socsci.mcmaster.ca/~econ/ ugcm/3113/spencer/manvssta* while other of Spencer's texts on line can be read at: *http://geocities.com/CapitolHill/6181/spencer.htm*

Both Nietzsche and Freud are well represented on the Web. An introduction to Nietzsche is available at: *http://setis.library.usyd.edu.au/stanford/archives/win1997/entries/ nietzsche/* while "The Friedrich Nietzsche Society" (with links to Nietzsche's works in both English and German) can be found at: *http://www.geocities.com/Athens/Olympus/2147/ comte.html*

The best source for Freud is: *http://plaza.interport.net/nypsan/* which is the web page for the New York Psychoanalytical Institute and Society and has many links to Freud texts and writings on Freud.

The best web page for Comte we have found is: *http://www.hgx-hypersoft.com/ clotilde*

Veblen's legacy is explored at a "Great Norwegians" site: *http://www.mnc.net/norway/ veblen.html* and at: *http://melbecon.unimelb.edu.au/het/veblen/index.htm* which contains Veblen's *Theory of the Leisure Class,* among other writings.

Finally, it is worth pointing out that Allyn and Bacon have an excellent Web page at: *http://www.abacon.com/sociology/soclinks/index.html* with several links to topics in sociological theory.

Another potentially useful address is: *http://www.soc.iastate.edu/dictionary/d.html* which provides a dictionary of Critical Sociology.

NAME INDEX